ESOTERICIS?

MW01194296

Academics tend to look on "esoteric," "occult," or "magical" beliefs
with contempt, but are usually ignorant about the religious and philosophical traditions to which these terms refer, or their relevance to
intellectual history. Wouter J. Hanegraaff tells the neglected story of
how intellectuals since the Renaissance have tried to come to terms
with a cluster of "pagan" ideas from late antiquity that challenged the
foundations of biblical religion and Greek rationality. Expelled from
the academy on the basis of Protestant and Enlightenment polemics,
these traditions have come to be perceived as the Other by which academics define their identity to the present day. Hanegraaff grounds his
discussion in a meticulous study of primary and secondary sources,
taking the reader on an exciting intellectual voyage from the fifteenth
century to the present day, and asking what implications the forgotten
history of exclusion has for established textbook narratives of religion,
philosophy, and science.

WOUTER J. HANEGRAAFF is Professor of History of Hermetic
Philosophy and Related Currents at the University of Amsterdam.
He is the author of *New Age Religion and Western Culture* (1996) and
Lodovico Lazzarelli (1447–1500) (with R. M. Bouthoorn, 2005). He is
editor of the *Dictionary of Gnosis and Western Esotericism* (2005), and
co-editor of six other books including *Hidden Intercourse: Eros and
Sexuality in the History of Western Esotericism* (co-edited with Jeffrey
J. Kripal, 2008).

ESOTERICISM AND THE ACADEMY

Rejected Knowledge in Western Culture

WOUTER J. HANEGRAAFF

CAMBRIDGE
UNIVERSITY PRESS

CAMBRIDGE
UNIVERSITY PRESS

University Printing House, Cambridge CB2 8BS, United Kingdom

Published in the United States of America by Cambridge University Press, New York

Cambridge University Press is part of the University of Cambridge.

It furthers the University's mission by disseminating knowledge in the pursuit of education, learning and research at the highest international levels of excellence.

www.cambridge.org
Information on this title: www.cambridge.org/9781107680975

© Wouter J. Hanegraaff 2012

First published 2012
Reprinted 2012
First paperback edition 2013

A catalogue record for this publication is available from the British Library

Library of Congress Cataloguing in Publication data
Hanegraaff, Wouter J.
Esotericism and the academy : rejected knowledge in western culture / Wouter J. Hanegraaff.
pages. cm.
Includes bibliographical references and index.
ISBN 978-0-521-19621-5 (hardback)
1. Occultism – History.   2. Philosophy, Renaissance.   3. Cabala – History.   4. Cabala and Christianity.   5. Psychology – History.   I. Title.
BF1411.H363   2012
130.9 – dc23   2011045460

ISBN 978-0-521-19621-5 Hardback
ISBN 978-1-107-68097-5 Paperback

Contents

Chapter epigraphs

Acknowledgments

This book is the outcome of more than twenty years of intense involvement in a new field of research that is carried by a large and rapidly growing international community of scholars. The bibliography documents the impact that they have had through their publications; but behind this formal array are memories of innumerable personal encounters, conversations, collaborative enterprises, and friendships. I am deeply grateful to my colleagues from all over the world for how they have enriched my life on both the intellectual and the personal level. If I mention only a few of them here by name, this is because their contributions to this book have been particularly concrete and indispensable.

The Foundation for the Chair of History of Hermetic Philosophy and Related Currents at the University of Amsterdam made it possible for me to take a sabbatical during the academic year 2009–2010, and it is only because of their generosity that I have been able to finish the manuscript at all. This is the right place to express my gratitude to the founder of the Chair, Rosalie Basten, for all the things that she has done, through the years, to enable this field of research to flourish. Next to her, I wish to thank the other members and former members of the Foundation (Willem Koudijs, Frans Tilman, Sijbolt Noorda, Roelof van den Broek, Ernestine van der Wall, Karel van der Toorn, Jan Bremmer, and Pieter van Onzenoort) for their continuing support.

Secondly, I want to thank my colleagues (permanent Staff and Ph.D. candidates) at the Center for History of Hermetic Philosophy and Related Currents: Marco Pasi, Peter J. Forshaw, Egil Asprem, Tessel M. Bauduin, Gemma Kwantes, Joyce Pijnenburg, and Osvald Vasiček. It is a pleasure to work with such a warm and committed group of people, and I am grateful for the many larger and smaller ways in which they have all helped me – perhaps sometimes without realizing it – to bring this project to completion (in the cases of Marco and Peter, I particularly want to mention their reading and commenting upon the final manuscript under heavy time pressure, and their stepping in during my sabbatical). Naturally, my gratitude extends also to the former members of the Center, Jean-Pierre Brach, Olav Hammer, Kocku von Stuckrad, Roelie van Kreijl, and Marieke J. E. van den Doel; and last but not least, I wish to thank all my present and former students, whose enthusiasm and openness of mind have made teaching in Amsterdam a pleasure through the years.

From my wider circle of colleagues, a few must be mentioned here by name: Ruud M. Bouthoorn for his help with some problems of Latin translation; Roelof van den Broek for some crucial feedback on Chapter 1; Dylan Burns for help with some Greek translations and identifying the source of a mysterious set of quotations; Antoine Faivre for reading and commenting upon the manuscript (including the section about himself) and giving me access to his personal records; Hans Thomas Hakl for allowing me to profit from his invaluable library, and sharing the still unpublished English translation of his book on Eranos; Kristine Hannak for providing me with photocopies of a hard-to-find book; John Monfasani for sending me articles and providing feedback on the section about Plethon; Victoria Nelson for her reading of the manuscript and her continuous support and encouragement; Monika Neugebauer-Wölk for exactly the same gifts; Lawrence M. Principe for reading and discussing the first three chapters, and particularly the sections on alchemy; Hereward Tilton for reading and commenting upon the first two chapters; Chiara O. Tommasi Moreschini for sending me photocopies of an extremely rare book; and Jan A. M. Snoek for indispensable information and feedback regarding Freemasonry.

Finally, I want to thank the editorial team of Cambridge University Press – particularly Kate Brett, Anna Lowe, Laura Morris, and Sarah Roberts – not only for their professionalism, but also for having made a new author feel welcome by taking a personal approach and showing genuine interest in his work: an attitude that is unfortunately not universal in the world of academic publishing, and therefore all the more appreciated. Last but not least, I am indebted to Ann Lewis for her thorough and efficient copy-editing and want to thank her for the pleasant collaboration.

Writing a large book feels like building a cathedral. In order to prevent it from collapsing, one needs to give equal attention to the general architectural design and the tiniest details of construction; and next to the hard physical labor of collecting the building materials (books, articles, more books . . .), this requires a state of continuous mental concentration that sometimes borders on meditation. In other words, during most of the time it took me to write this book, I lived the life of a monk. I could not have done it without the company of two little demons, Lilith and Pillows, who came walking over my keyboard or sat purring in front of my screen at the most inconvenient moments. They kept reminding me that life just goes on beyond the enchanted circle of scholarly concentration, and therefore this book that they will never understand, and that leaves them wholly indifferent, is fondly dedicated to them.

Introduction
Hic sunt dracones

Quod tanto impendio absconditur, etiam solummodo demonstrare, destruere est.

Tertullian, *Adversus Valentinianos* III.5

We are vaguely aware of its existence in our culture and our history. But we would not be able to define what it is, and are at a loss about what to call it. It has many names, but none of them seems to have a clear and straightforward meaning, and each carries associations that are somehow questionable or confusing. And yet, all these names – "esotericism," "hermeticism," "the occult," "magic," "mysticism," "superstition," "the irrational," and so on – refer to something that unquestionably seems to exist, in our history and all around us. Bookshops have special sections devoted to it, artists and poets claim to be inspired by it, theologians warn against its dangers. We are bound to come across its representatives or its ideas when we are studying the sources of our cultural past, or just while reading a popular magazine or watching television. And whenever that happens, most of us are at least dimly aware of an emotional response of some kind: discomfort, irritation, amusement, contempt, or perhaps some vague feeling of curiosity, puzzlement, even excitement. What we do *not* do, or only very rarely, is take a persistent look at it and ask ourselves questions about what we see. What is all this, really? Where does it come from? How does it all hang together? What is it doing in our society and our history? And why is it that we tend to smile about it, feel embarrassed, or look the other way?

The generic "we" in the above refers primarily, although not exclusively, to intellectuals and academics like myself. Questions of this kind have occupied me since the day, during my years as an undergraduate student, when I came across a book by a German scholar, Will-Erich Peuckert. It was titled *Pansophie*, and dealt with a range of early modern authors

I had never heard of before: a platonic philosopher (Marsilio Ficino), an author on magic (Cornelius Agrippa), a rebellious physician (Paracelsus), a cobbler given to visions (Jacob Böhme), and many others. I learned about their ideas, which turned out to be complex, unusual, and located in some hard-to-define no-man's-land between philosophy, religion, literature, art, and science. And it became clear that, far from being marginal outsiders, they had been remarkably influential in their own time, and stood at the origin of large and complex intellectual traditions that could be traced through the centuries and even up to our own time. In short, an unknown world opened up for me. Why had I never come across all of this before?

I was intrigued, and wanted to learn more, so I asked my professors for advice. And that is when I began having my first experiences with a phenomenon that has ultimately led me to write this book. My interest in this domain seemed to make my teachers uncomfortable, and to my repeated requests for information and suggestions, they responded by tossing the embarrassing topic on to another colleague as if it were a hot potato. Nobody seemed willing to touch it, and it did not take me very long to decide that if this were the case, then somebody had to do it. This is how I began my explorations of an unknown continent that seldom appeared on the maps of respectable learning, except with a negative travel advice attached to it: *hic sunt dracones*. Few guidebooks were available, and even fewer proved reliable. With only rare exceptions, scholars who had made serious ventures into this unknown territory had stayed in only one of its towns or provinces, refusing to go anywhere else, and many were those who claimed profound knowledge about it without having learned even just one of its languages. Almost nobody had attempted to map the continent as a whole, however provisorily, and the very few who had tried disagreed about its very boundaries.

Over the past twenty years, the situation has begun to improve. At the time when I began exploring it, there was exactly one academic chair devoted to this continent of learning as a whole, and no university program where students could study it as part of a regular curriculum. At the time of writing, there are at least three, all in Europe: still a very modest number, especially if one considers the vastness of the terrain, but an encouraging beginning that promises more to come. Several academic journals and learned societies, countless international conferences, and great numbers of articles and books demonstrate that what used to be, arguably, the single largest stretch of *terra incognita* in modern academic research is now attracting scholars in ever greater numbers. They even seem to have agreed about what to call it: Western esotericism.

In this book I make no attempt to provide a map of the domain, or write its history. Instead, I have set out to write the history of how scholars and intellectuals have *imagined* it, ever since the time that its contours first began to be drawn by those who claimed to know of its existence. It is only through their eyes that we will be introduced to it here, and it will quickly become apparent that many of those who have confidently described its nature – sometimes as a lost paradise, sometimes as a dark realm filled with demons, or a resort of fools – have been projecting their own hopes or fears onto it, or have just been repeating what others said about it. But no matter how extravagant the claims that have been made about this continent, one thing is clear: it has always been considered the domain of *the Other*. It has been imagined as a strange country, whose inhabitants think differently from us and live by different laws: whether one felt that it should be conquered and civilized, avoided and ignored, or emulated as a source of inspiration, it has always presented a challenge to our very identity, for better or worse. We seldom realize it, but in trying to explain who "we" are and what we stand for, we have been at pains to point out that we are not like *them*. In fact, we still do.

How much truth there is to these perceptions of otherness is an open question, which I will not try to answer directly. What must be emphasized, however, is that our perceptions of "esotericism" or "the occult" are inextricably entwined with how we think about ourselves: although we are almost never conscious of the fact, our very identity as intellectuals or academics depends on an implicit rejection of that identity's reverse mirror image. It is for this reason that the field of "Western esotericism" has potentially explosive implications for academic research as a whole. If our inherited assumptions about it prove to be inadequate, because they are reflective of ideological constructs and stereotypes rather than unprejudiced investigation of the historical record, then we will be obliged to reconsider the foundations of our own identity. Our imaginal constructs of esoteric or occult otherness are simultaneously constructs of ourselves, and therefore if "they" turn out to be different, the question is what does this imply about us.

In short: setting out to explore the blank spaces on the maps of learning and confront their dragons is a dangerous business. It will affect us possibly beyond recognition, and should do so: if we return from our expeditions unchanged, this means that the dragons have won. In this book we will be following a range of scholars who made the attempt, with greater or lesser degrees of success. I have written it in the hope that after traveling through six centuries in their company, and returning home to our own time, intellectuals and academics will discover that their familiar world no longer looks quite the same.

CHAPTER I

The history of truth
Recovering ancient wisdom

Down that road, the past did not grow darker with distance, but
brighter; that way lay the morning lands, wise forefathers who knew
what we have forgotten, radiant cities built by arts now lost.

John Crowley, *The Solitudes*, 96

The history of human thought emerged as a topic of intellectual fascination
among Italian humanists in the fifteenth century,[1] and the historiography
of what we now call Western esotericism was born along with it. The
grand Renaissance project of recovering the sources of classical antiquity
and its philosophical traditions forced Christian thinkers to reconsider
basic questions concerning the relation between human rationality and
divine revelation, and stimulated them to trace the historical origins and
chronological development of both. However, at a time when critical neutrality had not yet emerged as a historiographical ideal, any such history
had to be based upon theological and metaphysical premises and assume
the shape of a *history of truth*: it was not expected merely to discuss the
various opinions of earlier thinkers, but rather, to demonstrate the sources
of true knowledge and wisdom, trace the paths they had followed through
time, and make clear how those trajectories harmonized or coincided with
the unquestionable truth of Christian doctrine. This Renaissance project,
generally recognized as central to the history of Renaissance hermeticism

---

[1] See the monumental history of the history of philosophy edited by Giovanni Santinello, *Storia delle
storie generali della filosofia*; vol. 1 translated into English, under the general editorship of C. W. T.
Blackwell, as Bottin *et al.*, *Models of the History of Philosophy*. See there esp. Malusa, "Renaissance
Antecedents," 4, and the bibliography on p. 59. See also, for example, Spini, "Historiography," 92–
93; Copenhaver and Schmitt, *Renaissance Philosophy*, 332. That the history of philosophy originated
in the Italian Renaissance was emphasized as early as 1888 by Ludwig Stein in the first issue of
Archiv für Geschichte der Philosophie, in an article that contained a full transcript of an *Epistola... de
Nobilioribus philosophorum sectis et de eorum inter se differentia* (1458, addressed to Marsilio Ficino),
by Johannes Baptista Buonosegnius, "the first modern historiographer of philosophy" (Stein, "Handschriftenfunde"; cf. Malusa, "Renaissance Antecedents," 8–9; and Braun, *Histoire de l'histoire de la
philosophie*, 54).

and Western esotericism, is usually referred to as *prisca theologia* (ancient theology) or *philosophia perennis* (perennial philosophy).

From contemporary academic perspectives, the very idea of a "history of (metaphysical) truth" might strike us as contradictory and self-defeating: how can truth be absolute and yet subject to historical development, or conversely, how should we imagine a history of something that is immutable and beyond change? But such questions are inspired by a secular development of historical consciousness that was still alien to the Renaissance humanists who will be discussed in this chapter: for them, metaphysical verities grounded in divine revelation were the self-evident foundation for intellectual inquiry, and there was not yet any compelling reason to see them as incompatible with the business of historiography. Although we can now see these Italian intellectuals as having made the first tentative steps in a direction that would eventually lead towards the history of philosophy as an autonomous discipline[2] (while also laying some early foundations for the future development of another one, the comparative study of ancient religions),[3] it is of the utmost importance to emphasize that their essential project was not historiographical in our sense of the word, but doctrinal and theological throughout: in studying the ancient wisdom discourse[4] of the Renaissance, we will be dealing with a species of Christian apologetic theology[5] that derived its vigor and its religious urgency from the intellectual challenge posed by the newly discovered "pagan" literature.

The overall argument of this chapter is that this Renaissance project resulted in the emergence of a powerful grand narrative which seriously challenged traditional perspectives on the relation between philosophy and theology, or rationality and revelation, and remained a highly important factor in Roman Catholic thought until its decline under the influence of the "anti-apologetic" discourse developed by Protestant authors during the seventeenth century (the main topic of Chapter 2). After the victory of anti-apologeticism during the eighteenth century, this grand narrative

---

[2] Malusa, "Renaissance Antecedents," 14–25 (section "'Prisca Theologia' and 'Perennis Philosophia'"). The pioneering importance of Renaissance platonism, and Agostino Steuco in particular, for the historiography of philosophy was highlighted by Otto Willmann as early as 1894 (*Geschichte des Idealismus* III, 126–154).

[3] Kohl, "Geschichte der Religionswissenschaft," 227–229.

[4] In what follows, I will adopt the convention of using the term "discourse" for the entirety of discussions about ancient wisdom, whether by defenders or opponents, and "narrative" for the perspectives of the defenders only. In other words, the narratives of those who wished to defend the ancient wisdom gave rise to a complex apologetic/polemical discourse.

[5] As emphasized by Walker in the opening sentence of his classic study on the *prisca theologia* tradition: "By the term 'Ancient Theology' I mean a certain tradition of Christian apologetic literature which rests on misdated texts" (Walker, *Ancient Theology*, 1).

of "ancient wisdom" survived as a widespread but officially discredited countercurrent at odds with mainstream intellectual thought. It has been accepted or implied, in one version or another, by most of the authors and practitioners studied under the umbrella of Western esotericism, up to the present; but, interestingly, it has also strongly influenced the thinking even of the most important modern scholars who have shaped and developed that field. Were these scholars attracted by the ancient wisdom narrative in spite of its incompatibility with post-Enlightenment intellectual and academic culture or, rather, *because* of it? As the narrative unfolds, we will see that in addressing such questions, we get to the heart of what is at stake in the modern and contemporary study of Western esotericism.

The story that will be told here is one of apologetic and polemical battles and negotiations over the "wisdom of the pagans," and their continuations or reverberations right into the present: a story with winners and losers, but without a final victory in sight. Moreover, it will be argued, not only do we see the complex processes of secularization and modernization reflected in this story at each and every turn, but, far more importantly, the battle between the apologists of "ancient wisdom" and their anti-apologetic enemies has *shaped* and *determined* the emergence of modernity to an extent that has rarely been recognized.

COMPETING MACROHISTORIES

Much has been written about the "ancient theology" or "perennial philosophy" of the Renaissance,[6] but, surprisingly, there have been almost no attempts to be precise about definitions or think systematically about the relation between the two central terms *prisca theologia* (first used by Marsilio Ficino and "launched" into scholarly debate in 1954)[7] and *philosophia*

---

[6] The most important general discussions (in chronological order) are Walker, "*Prisca Theologia* in France"; Wind, *Pagan Mysteries*, chapter 1 ("Poetic Theology"); Schmitt, "Perennial Philosophy"; Facoltà ... Perugia (ed.), *Filosofia e cultura in Umbria* (a conference volume largely devoted to articles on the perennial philosophy, plus a very extensive appendix based upon round-table discussions); Schmitt, "*Prisca Theologia* e *Philosophia Perennis*"; Trinkaus, *In Our Image and Likeness*, vol. ii, chapter 15 ("From *Theologia Poetica* to *Theologia Platonica*"); Walker, *Ancient Theology*; Di Napoli, "Il concetto di 'philosophia perennis'"; Purnell, "Theme of Philosophic Concord"; Malusa, "Renaissance Antecedents"; Muccillo, *Platonismo, Ermetismo e 'Prisca Theologia'*; Allen, *Synoptic Art*, chapters 1–2; Schmidt-Biggemann, *Philosophia perennis*; Vasoli, "Mythos der 'Prisci Theologi'"; Mulsow, "Ambiguities."

[7] D. P. Walker claimed to have "launched" the term in 1954 (*Ancient Theology*, 1 n. 1, referring to his groundbreaking "*Prisca Theologia* in France"), but it appears literally in Marsilio Ficino's writings, for example "De laudibus philosophiae" (*Opera*, 768: "Prisca vera Aegyptiorum et Arabum theologia"); Argumentum to the *Pimander*; or *De Christiana religione* 22 (*Opera*, 25: "Prisca Gentilium Theologia").

perennis (introduced by Agostino Steuco and put on the agenda of Renaissance historiography in 1966).[8] The only notable exception is the historian of Renaissance philosophy Charles B. Schmitt, who in an Italian article of 1970 called attention to the fact that the notion of an "ancient" wisdom is different from that of a "perennial" one, both in its contents and its implications:

> The concept of *prisca theologia* indicates that the true knowledge would be anterior to Greek philosophy and would actually be found, although perhaps in an enigmatic and esoteric form, among the pre-classical sages such as Zoroaster, Mercurius Trismegistus, and Orpheus. Usually it is thought that, directly or indirectly, they had derived their wisdom from Moses, and therefore they assumed a high level of authority within the Jewish–Christian tradition. From this point of view the *sapientia*, having been developed among the *prisci*, or ancient sages, passed on to the Greeks by way of the platonic current, that is to say, from Orpheus to Aglaophemus to Pythagoras and, finally, to Plato.[9]

From such a perspective, the rediscovery and translation not only of the works of Plato, but also of writings attributed to Zoroaster, Hermes and Orpheus in the later fifteenth century, had to be a momentous event resonating with millenarian overtones.[10] For the first time in history, and at a time when the moral degeneration of the Church was becoming more obvious every day, Christians had unexpectedly been granted access to the most ancient and therefore most authoritative sources of true religion and philosophy: surely the hand of Providence was at work here, showing humanity a way towards the needed reformation of Christian faith by means of a return to the very sources of divine revelation.

We will see that Marsilio Ficino (1433–1499), the virtual founder of the Renaissance *prisca theologia* narrative, indeed believed that in translating Hermes, Orpheus, Plato and the later platonists he was acting as God's chosen instrument.[11] However, in a penetrating analysis of his perspective, Michael J. B. Allen has warned against too easy associations between the concept of *prisca theologia* and that of *philosophia perennis*, linked to the name of Agostino Steuco.[12] Charles B. Schmitt, too, had called attention to the differences:

---

[8] The term was introduced in 1540 by Agostino Steuco, *De perenni philosophia*, and put on the agenda of Renaissance scholarship by Charles B. Schmitt in 1966 ("Perennial Philosophy").

[9] Schmitt, "*Prisca Theologia* e *Philosophia Perennis*," 212–213 ("scienza" is translated here as "knowledge").

[10] *Ibid.*, 213.   [11] Allen, *Synoptic Art*, 14, 17–18. Cf. also Malusa, "Renaissance Antecedents," 52.

[12] Allen, *Synoptic Art*, 42.

the *philosophia perennis*...would seem to have larger implications. It likewise makes wisdom originate in a very ancient time, often applying the same genealogy of the transmission of *sapientia* like the *prisca theologia*, but it also puts emphasis on the continuity of valid knowledge through all periods of history. It does not believe that knowledge... has ever been lost for centuries, but believes that it can surely be found in each period, albeit sometimes in attenuated form.[13]

This second perspective strongly emphasizes the unity and universality of wisdom, rather than its decline, and therefore lacks the millenarian implications of Ficino's outlook. It seems significant that Agostino Steuco published his grand synthesis *De perenni philosophia* in 1540, only a few years before the Council of Trent: while the Roman Catholic adherents of *prisca theologia* and the new Protestant theologians both wanted to reform the Church by means of a return to what each of them saw as its origins and foundations, Steuco's grand synthesis did not seek to reform but to *preserve*. It did so by strongly affirming the unity and universality of the one, perennial faith, very much in line with a perspective that had been proclaimed in the strongest possible wordings even by St. Augustine: "The very thing which is now called the Christian religion was with the ancients, and it was with the human race from its beginning to the time when Christ appeared in the flesh: from when on the true religion, which already existed, began to be called the Christian."[14] What we find, therefore, is a strong tension between two opposed tendencies: on the one hand, a historically/chronologically oriented narrative of ancient wisdom which held considerable revolutionary potential, and, on the other, an essentially conservative doctrine which preaches the futility of change and development by emphasizing the trans-historical continuity and universality of absolute truth.

Still, this is not all. If we further unpack the Renaissance discourse on ancient wisdom, we may even distinguish a third, "prophetic" tendency: this one claims that, due to divine inspiration, the ancient philosophers before Christ had been granted prophetic glimpses into the superior religion of Christianity.[15] Such a third option, which might conveniently be referred to as *pia philosophia*,[16] introduces an element of "progress": whereas

---

[13] Schmitt, "*Prisca Theologia* e *Philosophia Perennis*," 213.

[14] Augustine, *Retractationes* I.12.3 (trans. Wind, *Pagan Mysteries*, 21).

[15] With regard to this third option, I am grateful to Jean-Pierre Brach for his fruitful suggestions during a train journey from Strasbourg to Paris in October 2008.

[16] There is an element of convenience in the use of *all* three terminologies. We already saw that the exact term *prisca theologia* is used so rarely in the Renaissance that Walker thought he had invented it (see n. 7). The term *philosophia perennis* was invented by Steuco, but Schmitt expresses surprise at how rarely it is actually used in his *De perenni philosophia* ("Perennial Philosophy," 522); and,

the *prisca theologia* combines a narrative of decline with hopes of imminent revival, and *philosophia perennis* emphasizes continuity, *pia philosophia*
thinks in terms of growth and development, imagining a gradual "education of humanity" to prepare it for the final revelation.

If we wish to do justice to the full complexity of the ancient wisdom
discourse, this third tendency must be clearly recognized. And yet, its actual
relevance to Renaissance culture remains relatively limited. Contrary to the
two other perspectives, it concerned a period that had ended with the birth
of Christ, and therefore had little social or political relevance for the present:
neither revolutionary nor conservative in its implications, it amounted to
little more than a historical opinion concerning a time that now belonged
to the remote past.[17] It could certainly offer some theological support for
antiquarian studies of pre-Christian sources, but lacked political potential
in the tense religious climate of Renaissance society. However – and this
is an important point – adherents of the *prisca theologia* perspective could
and did evoke it rhetorically, to counter criticisms that their narrative of
ancient decline and contemporary recovery left no room for explaining
how the advent of Christianity had been a step forward in the history of
truth.

In sum: the concepts of *prisca theologia* and *philosophia perennis* are
most central to the ancient wisdom discourse of the Renaissance, but,
to avoid simplification, we need to keep the *pia philosophia* option constantly in mind. From a systematic perspective, then, the problem inherent
in this discourse was that it somehow encompassed no fewer than three
mutually exclusive macrohistorical schemes: evolution, degeneration, and

---

ironically, it only became famous after having been divorced from its original meaning, by Leibniz
in 1714 (letter to Remond of August 26, 1714; see Schmitt, "Perennial Philosophy," 506, 532; see
below, page 130), after which it embarked upon a new career in a variety of new contexts, including
neo-scholastic theology and the East/West philosophy of Aldous Huxley (see references in Schmitt,
"Perennial Philosophy," 505–506). Likewise, *pia philosophia* is merely one option among many
similar terms that were used at the time, such as, for example, *prisca sapientia*, *christiana philosophia*,
mosaica philosophia, *caelestis philosophia*, *vetus theologia*, and even *nova theologia* (see Di Napoli,
"Il concetto di 'philosophia perennis'," 266–268).

[17] There are exceptions even to this: the hermetic philosopher Lodovico Lazzarelli (1447–1500) developed a variation on the ancient wisdom narrative that implied progress from the ancient revelation
of wisdom given by Poimandres to Hermes long before the time of Moses, via the incarnation of
Poimandres as Jesus Christ, to the final return of Christ/Poimandres in the person of his spiritual
teacher Giovanni "Mercurio" da Correggio (see Hanegraaff, "Lodovico Lazzarelli and the Hermetic
Christ," 47, 95–96). However, this radical doctrine was intentionally concealed by Lazzarelli, and
can only be reconstructed today by close textual comparison of the various manuscripts. It notably
influenced Cornelius Agrippa, who adopted Lazzarelli's identification of Poimandres with Christ,
but not his adherence to Correggio (Agrippa, *Oratio habita Papiae* [Zambelli ed.], 125; see discussion
in Hanegraaff, "Better than Magic").

continuity.[18] The evolutionary or educational perspective, which appreciated ancient wisdom only as a *praeparatio evangelica*, was most obviously orthodox but implicitly minimized the relevance of studying the newly discovered sources: as a matter of principle, anything of value that they might contain was believed to be expressed more fully and clearly by Christian theology, and anything not included in it had to be pagan error by definition. Starting from a very similar assumption of Christian doctrine as the self-evident truth, the perspective of *philosophia perennis* emphasized its universality, sometimes to the point of embracing a perspective of "everyone is right," but the implication was, again, that study of the new sources could not possibly yield any new insights, but could only provide ever more confirmation of truths already known. If, however, the most ancient authors had been closest to the truth, as suggested by the *prisca theologia* perspective, this implied an exciting promise of new discoveries, and gave vital importance to the study of the ancient writings; but by implication, the chronologically more recent Christian faith risked becoming irrelevant or superfluous at best, and a phenomenon of decline at worst. Critics had therefore good reasons to fear that the new sources might turn out to be a Trojan horse: rather than pointing towards a reform of Christianity, did they not instead contain the seeds of its destruction and its future replacement by a revived universal pagan religion?

That the ancient wisdom narrative is constituted of no fewer than three macrohistorical models, each with their own implications and internal logic, may have been a weakness theoretically, but could be an advantage in practice. The very ambiguity of the narrative gave it a peculiar flexibility: it allowed authors – provided they possessed sufficient erudition and rhetorical skill – to have recourse to different apologetic strategies at different times or to mix elements taken from all three models, and thereby elude their critics almost forever in a never-ending maze of references to unquestionable authorities.

In addition, what made the narrative even harder to pin down was its ambiguous relation to both theology and philosophy. This is already clear, of course, from the very terminologies that were used: the ancient *theologians* had actually been *philosophers*, but the perennial *philosophy* was the basic doctrine of a universal *religion*. Tools sharp enough to really keep the ancient theology apart from philosophy were not developed until the emergence of Protestant anti-apologeticism in the later seventeenth century, as will be seen. Before that period, believers in the ancient wisdom

---

[18] For concepts of macrohistory as applied to Western esotericism, see Trompf, "Macrohistory."

could usually have their platonic cake while eating it too: one could always assume the mantle of a philosopher when attacked by theologians, but appeal to divine revelation when questioned by philosophers. *Sapientia*, wisdom, was the most convenient term for an intellectual ideal that was supposed to include *and* transcend theology as well as philosophy.

From which sources did this ancient wisdom narrative develop, and how did it succeed in becoming the foundational narrative of Western esotericism from the fifteenth century to the present? To find answers to those questions, we have to travel far back into the past – perhaps not to the very sources of wisdom itself, but certainly to those of Western philosophy.

PLATONIC ORIENTALISM

As has been well formulated by Peter Brown, what caught the enthu-siasm of our platonic Renaissance humanists was "not the Plato of the modern classical scholar, but the living Plato of the religious thinkers of Late Antiquity."[19] Specifically, these thinkers belonged to what is known as middle- and neoplatonism, and what characterizes their perspective is that they evidently did not wish to remain on the level of abstract philosophical speculation and the pursuit of rational knowledge for its own sake. Rather, in the late Hellenistic world, platonism was transformed by them into a religious worldview with its own mythologies and ritual practices, focused on the attainment of a salvational gnōsis by which the soul could be lib-erated from its material entanglement and regain its unity with the divine Mind.[20] Allowing for the great differences between various systems, this is what the gnostic, hermetic, and theurgical currents of late antiquity all had in common; and to an extent that has not always been sufficiently recog-nized, this is what platonism came to mean for its Renaissance admirers.[21]

---

[19] Brown, *World of Late Antiquity*, 73.

[20] As formulated by Majercik, with reference to John Dillon's concept of an "Underworld of Platonism" (see text): "This movement away from the school traditions of Platonism towards an unabashed religiosity is the hallmark of these systems" and "knowledge for its own sake passes over to 'gnosis' for the sake of *soteria*, with spiritual enlightenment often coupled with magic and ritual as a means of freeing the soul" (Majercik, "Introduction," 4–5). For typologies and general characterizations of the middle-platonic milieu, see Dillon, *Middle Platonists*, 396; Majercik, "Introduction," 4 (analyzed in detail by Burns, "ἄρρητος λόγος τέλειος," 64–112); and Nock, "Préface," vii. On the hierarchical relation between philosophy and gnōsis in this context, see Fowden, *Egyptian Hermes*, 97–104; and Hanegraaff, "Altered States of Knowledge."

[21] In that context, the so-called "gnostic" currents are a case apart. While modern scholarship sees them as belonging to the same middle-platonist milieu, for Renaissance intellectuals they were still evident heresies unconnected to their understanding of "platonism." A continuity between Platonic Orientalism and the gnostic heresies first came to be suggested by sixteenth-century

These middle- and neoplatonic transformations of philosophy into religion, mythology and ritual have been a source of barely concealed embarrassment for classicists. Thus, in his standard work *The Middle Platonists*, John Dillon discussed them under the telling rubric "Some Loose Ends," and referred to this "murky area" as the "Underworld of Platonism" dominated by "sub-philosophical phenomena":[22] although their existence had to be recognized, the philosophical inferiority of their occult speculations was clearly taken for granted. Likewise, when the great French scholar André-Jean Festugière discussed the same milieu in the introduction to his classic study of late antique hermetism, he saw no reason to conceal his distaste for the superstitious pseudo-philosophies that marked the "decline of rationalism" in the late Hellenistic world.[23] And if modern scholars noted that the Syrian platonist Iamblichus of Chalcis introduced theurgical rites into neoplatonism, they have tended to dismiss this as a "corruption of the tradition" or an "irresoluble enigma," while ignoring the fact that Iamblichus' approach was far more typical of neoplatonism as a cultural phenomenon than the non-ritual philosophy of Plotinus, which remained a relative exception.[24]

To understand the historical origins of the ancient wisdom narrative, we need to overcome such normative biases, which judge religious practices and speculations by the unsuitable yardstick of rational philosophy and anachronistically project modern stereotypes of "the occult" back into the ancient past.[25] At the same time, we must take care not to fall from one error into another, namely that of denying serious philosophical content to these traditions, merely because they are now classified as "religious" or, even worse, "occult": that most of the neoplatonists practiced or at least endorsed theurgy obviously does not disqualify them as philosophers, and

representatives of the anti-magical reaction, as will be seen. The first apology of gnosticism, Abraham von Franckenberg's *Theophrastia Valentiniana*, dates from the seventeenth century (written in 1627, first published in 1703: see Gilly, "Das Bekenntnis zur Gnosis," 416–422), and of course the Nag Hammadi Library crucial to our current understanding of "gnosticism" was still lying undiscovered in an Egyptian cave.

22   Dillon, *Middle Platonists*, 384 (followed by short analyses of Valentinian gnosticism, the hermetic *Poimandres*, and the *Chaldaean Oracles*). Dillon's concept of an "Underworld of Platonism," including even the reference to its "murky quality," was adopted by Majercik, *Chaldean Oracles*, 3–4, whose very first sentence already stresses the "abstruse" character of the *Chaldaean Oracles*.

23   Festugière, *Révélation d'Hermès Trismégiste* I, 1–88.

24   See the pertinent observations in Shaw, "Theurgy," 1, 3. Cf. Celenza, "Late Antiquity and Florentine Platonism," 71–84.

25   Cf. Fowden, *Egyptian Hermes*, 80: "there is little profit, from the historian's point of view, in condemning magic just because it failed to measure up to the sublime conceptions of a Plotinus, or, even more irrelevantly, because it conflicts with the Christian or 'scientific' prejudices of modern scholars." On the development of stereotypes of "the occult," see Chapter 3.

to understand the gnostic, hermetic and related platonic religiosities of this period one certainly needs to take their philosophical underpinnings very seriously.

If Dillon's "Underworld of Platonism" is unsuitable as a label, how should we then refer to the milieus in question? Festugière points us towards a better alternative in one of his introductory chapters, "Les Prophètes de l'Orient," which begins with a characteristic passage by the second-century Pythagorean Numenius of Apamea:

> On this point [i.e. the problem of God], after having cited and taken notice of Plato's testimonies, one should go further back and connect them to the teachings of Pythagoras, calling next upon the peoples of high renown so as to include their initiations, dogmas and cultural foundations, which they accomplish in full accord with Plato, in short, to all on which the Brahmans, the Jews, the *Magi* and the Egyptians were in agreement.[26]

Far from being an isolated instance, this statement was utterly typical of the period: there are innumerable references[27] to the ruling idea that the most ancient "barbarian" peoples possessed a pure and superior science and wisdom, derived not from reason but from direct mystical access to the divine,[28] and that all the important Greek philosophers up to and including Plato had received their "philosophy" from these sources. The modalities of such transmission were not seen as problematic: after all, countless testimonies confirmed that Plato himself and all his notable predecessors had personally traveled to Egypt, Babylon, Persia and even India, where they had studied with the priests and sages.[29] In short, not only was Greek philosophy seen as derived from oriental

---

[26] Numenius, Περί Ταγαθου, Bk. 1, frag. 1 a (des Places ed., 42). Reference in Festugière, *Révélation d'Hermès Trismégiste* 1, 19. On Numenius and "oriental theologies," see Henri-Charles Puech, "Numénius d'Apamée," who also calls attention to the strong *philosophia perennis* aspect in Numenius. More than anything, he was looking for "a philosophy without schools or factions, and, one might add, without history: a wisdom modeled after the transcendent God, which, like him, would remain above time, residing in the peace of an absolute immutability" (*ibid.*, 767).

[27] Festugière, *Révélation d'Hermès Trismégiste* 1, 20, and see the many testimonies discussed in the rest of the chapter.

[28] As formulated by Festugière (*Révélation d'Hermès Trismégiste* 1, 20): "The ruling idea was that the Barbarians possessed purer and more essential notions concerning the Divine, not because they used their reason better than the hellenes but, on the contrary, because, neglecting reason, they had found ways of communicating with God by more secret means." For the larger historical development of this idea, see Dörrie, "Wertung der Barbaren."

[29] The many late antique references are conveniently listed in Hopfner, *Orient und griechische Philosophie*, 1–9; and see the discussion of sources in Dörrie, "Platons Reisen zu fernen Völkern." The very earliest source for Greek "philosophical tourism" in Egypt is Hecataeus of Abdera (fourth century), much of whose work, while no longer extant in the original, survives in the first book of Diodorus Siculus' *Bibliotheca Historica* (1.10–98). On the crucial importance of Hecataeus and Diodorus to the phenomenon of Greek Orientalism, see Droge, *Homer or Moses?*, 5–8.

sources, but the Egyptians in particular could even claim to be the true founders of philosophy as such.[30] In this context, "philosophy" was well understood to be much more than the pursuit of knowledge by unaided human reason: its true concern was divine wisdom and the salvation of the soul.

Platonism understood as ancient "divine wisdom derived from the Orient" is precisely what characterizes the currents and textual traditions under discussion here, and this fact has long been known to specialists. Nevertheless, it is only as recently as 2001 that a contemporary Suhrawardī specialist, John Walbridge, drew the logical conclusion in coining the term "Platonic Orientalism."[31] The perspective in question was grounded in widely shared assumptions, as Walbridge explains:

> By the late Hellenistic period an informed and not overly skeptical Greek would have seen the situation as follows: The ancient Persians had their philosophers, who were known as *Magi.* Zoroaster was a Persian sage who had probably lived some six millennia earlier. Some of his writings still existed, showing that he was a great authority on astrology. He had something to do with the Chaldaeans, for Pythagoras met him or his disciples in Babylonia. Other works of the *Magi* showed that the ancient Persians had mastered the occult sciences.[32]

Very similar assumptions were common about Hermes Trismegistus as the greatest Egyptian wise man, and about the legendary sages of various other ancient nations. The thesis of a continuity between Plato's philosophy and the ancient "barbarian" peoples could even claim some support from Plato himself[33] and from scattered references to a lost work of Aristotle.[34] Further confirmation came from authoritative Greek and Roman historians,

---

[30] Hopfner, *Orient und griechische Philosophie*, 8.

[31] Walbridge, *Wisdom of the Mystic East*, x, 2–3, 8–12. "Platonic Orientalism" is a new coinage, independent of the famous work of Edward Said. For the present discussion it is not necessary to explore the nature of the relation between these two theoretical frameworks.

[32] *Ibid.*, 7. For an exhaustive study of how Zoroaster and the *Magi* were perceived in Greek and Latin literature, see de Jong, *Traditions of the Magi.*

[33] *Alcibiades* I, 122A, where Socrates refers to Zoroaster's *mageia* as "the worship of the gods." While the authenticity of the dialogue is contested today (but defended in the thorough recent discussion by Denyer, "Introduction," 14–26), Plato's authorship was never doubted in antiquity. As pointed out by de Jong, the fragment is quoted in a "surprisingly large number of classical passages" ("Contribution of the Magi," 86, referring to the list of references in de Jong, *Traditions of the Magi*, 213 n. 29). A particularly important reference is Apuleius, *Pro Se De Magia* 25–26 (Hunink ed., 54; cf. de Jong, "Contribution," 85–86).

[34] Judging from two references in Diogenes Laertius and Joannes Philoponus (Fragments 6–7, in: [Aristotle], *Complete Works* II, 2390), Aristotle's "On Philosophy" may have been one of the first attempts at a genealogy of wisdom, transmitted from the Persian *Magi* to Egypt, and from there to the most ancient Greek "theologians," Orpheus, and the fabled "Seven Sages." See discussion in Festugière, *Révélation d'Hermès Trismégiste* I, 22; Droge, *Homer or Moses?*, 14–15; and Bywater, "Aristotle's Dialogue 'On Philosophy'," esp. 68–69.

notably Diodorus Siculus[35] and Plutarch,[36] and from neoplatonic philosophers such as Iamblichus or Proclus.[37] And as will be seen, the Renaissance
intellectuals who rediscovered all these traditions regarded the *Chaldaean
Oracles* and the hermetic writings as first-hand testimonies from Zoroaster
and Hermes Trismegistus respectively. All this makes Platonic Orientalism
a perfectly appropriate label for the late antique milieus and traditions to
which the ancient wisdom discourse of the Renaissance referred.

Against this background, the very emergence of that discourse ceases to
be a surprising phenomenon. Since their sources seemed to be in general
agreement about the oriental origins of platonism, it would have been
peculiarly unplatonic (and, from their perspective, unhistorical) for our
Italian humanists *not* to have believed in the concepts of *prisca theologia* and *philosophia perennis*, or, for that matter, to have denied at least
a potential validity to the ritual practices and "occult" arts which had so
clearly been central to the sublime religion of the ancients. The sources
at their disposal all seemed to concur in suggesting that this – and not
just a rational philosophy grounded in Socratic dialogue – was what platonism was all about. For such a proposition one did not even need to
find direct confirmation in Plato himself.[38] Given the basic assumption
(peculiarly unhistorical to us, but quite natural to them) that all the great
sages represented one and the same, timeless and universal wisdom tradition, it was not just unproblematic but perfectly logical to read Plato's
dialogues through what we now see as middle- and neoplatonic lenses.
Hence Ficino, for example, could claim that in reading the *Enneads* we
are listening to Plato speaking through Plotinus' mouth.[39] The point was
that, even more precisely, both Plotinus *and* Plato were seen not as original
and innovative thinkers, but as mouthpieces of one and the same ancient
and universal fountain of wisdom, whose author was ultimately God
himself.

---

[35] See above, n. 29.   [36] Plutarch, *De Iside et Osiride*, 353–371, esp. 354d–f, 360d.

[37] Iamblichus, *Myst.* 1.1–2. Proclus, *Theol. Plat.* 1.5 mentions only a lineage of Greek authorities
(Orpheus, Aglaophemus, Pythagoras, Philolaus, Plato), but according to his biographer Marinus
of Samaria (*Vita Procli* 26 and 38) he preferred the *Chaldaean Oracles* and Plato's *Timaeus* above all
other writings.

[38] This is not to say that Renaissance Platonists could not find such confirmation if they wished. For
example, the *Phaedrus* was clearly not grounded in Socratic dialogue at all, but presented Socrates
as passing on knowledge received in an inspired state of *mania* or divine frenzy, and it is significant
that Ficino saw it as the "protodialogue" which contained the seeds for all the others (Allen, *Marsilio
Ficino*, 13; Hanegraaff, "Platonic Frenzies").

[39] Ficino, *Exhortatio* to Plotinus' *Enneads*, in: Ficino, *Opera*, 1548. On how the neoplatonic interpretation of Plato began to crumble in the centuries after Ficino, culminating in the eighteenth century,
see Tigerstedt, "Decline and Fall," and Chapter 2.

So far, so good. But how should we explain that such a strong commitment to the religion of ancient pagan nations could be seen, by Renaissance platonists, as not just perfectly compatible with Christian belief, but even as a necessary prerequisite for truly understanding the nature of Christianity? This brings us to a second crucial background to the ancient wisdom discourse.

THE CHRISTIAN APOLOGISTS

Apologeticism – the polemical defense of one's own position as superior to others[40] – was central to the ancient wisdom discourse from its very beginning, and "Tradition" was the symbolic capital[41] over which the various participants were competing. Thus, when Hecataeus of Abdera (fourth cent. BC) described how Orpheus, Homer, Solon, Pythagoras, Plato and many others had acquired their knowledge and wisdom while visiting Egypt,[42] his point was to highlight that country as the original source of higher truth while dismissing Greek culture as derivative and second hand. In sharp contrast, but following the same logic, Diogenes Laertius (third cent. CE) opened his famous book about the lives of the eminent philosophers by refuting the barbarians' claim: those who believe that philosophy originated among the Persians, Egyptians, Babylonians, Assyrians, Indians, Celts, or Gauls "forget that the achievements which they attribute to the barbarians belong to the Greeks, with whom not merely philosophy but the human race itself began."[43] Likewise, historians such as Berossus with his *Babylonian History*, Manetho with his *Egyptian History*, or Philo of Byblus with his *Phoenician History* all sought to present their respective nations as the true origin of the cultural achievements claimed by the Greeks.[44] The unquestioned assumption they all held in common was that antiquity equaled superiority, or, as formulated by Arthur J. Droge in his fundamental study of the Christian apologists,

---

[40] As pointed out by Hammer and von Stuckrad ("Introduction," vii–ix; with special reference to Cancik, "Apologetik/Polemik"), the concepts of apologeticism and polemicism are "inextricably entwined: by defending one's own position, one questions that of others; by denouncing the doctrines and practices of others as false, one asserts one's own claims to orthodoxy and orthopraxy." Hence any instance of apologeticism is inherently polemic, and any polemicism is inherently apologetic.

[41] See, for example, Bourdieu, *Language and Symbolic Power*, 72–76.

[42] Diodorus, *Bibliotheca Historica*, 1.96–98.

[43] Diogenes Laertius, *Lives*, 1.3 (Hicks ed., 4–5). The rest of the Prologue is devoted to a refutation of the barbarians' claims.

[44] Droge, *Homer or Moses?*, 4.

the assertion of modern origin was equivalent to the assertion of historical insignif-
icance. Nothing could be both new *and* true. It was a general conviction of the
age that the oldest was always best, that the present was an age of decadence, a low
point on the universal cycle; that the "ancients" were nearer to the gods and the
beginnings of things and therefore knew much more about them.[45]

For a new religion like Christianity, this was obviously a problem. To
make a convincing claim of superiority towards pagan religion, Christian
authors needed to counter the objection that their faith was merely a
recent invention without historical depth, and hence without the legitimacy
conferred by Tradition. In other words, they were faced with a task that
might seem impossible: that of preaching the "good news" of the gospel
while simultaneously denying its novelty. To meet this challenge and defeat
their opponents, the trump card they played was "Moses."

The first reference to Moses in pagan Greek literature occurs in
Hecataeus, who predictably claims him for Egypt:

A man called Moses, highly esteemed in both practical wisdom and courage, went
out of Egypt into what is now called Judaea. He took possession of the region
and founded cities, among them the one named Jerusalem which is now the most
famous. He also dedicated a temple most honored by them, introduced the ritual
and worship of the deity, and legislated and regulated political affairs.[46]

This account seems to be echoed in a passage attributed to an early Jewish historian, Eupolemus, where we read that Moses was "the first wise
man," who taught the alphabet to the Jews and wrote laws for them.[47]
A more explicit and influential refutation of Hecataeus occurs in a fragment attributed to another Jewish historian, Artapanus,[48] who was also
responding to the hostile picture of Moses in Manetho's *Egyptian History*.
Artapanus is explicit about Moses' Jewish ancestry, identifies him with
the poet Musaeus, and calls him the master of Orpheus.[49] Moses emerges
as the great benefactor of Egyptian civilization: he made many practical inventions, but also invented philosophy, organized religious worship,

---

[45] *Ibid.*, 9; with reference to Armstrong, "Pagan and Christian Traditionalism." Cf. Hanson, "Christian
   Attitude," 188–189. See also, for example, Wilken, *Christians*, 121–125.
[46] Hecataeus, as preserved in Diodorus, *Bibliotheca Historica*, 40.3.3 (trans. according to Droge, *Homer
   or Moses?*, 6).
[47] Eusebius, *Praeparatio Evangelica*, IX.26.1. The reference to Eupolemus occurs in a passage attributed
   by Eusebius to Alexander Polyhistor. On Eupolemus, see detailed discussion in Droge, *Homer or
   Moses?*, 13–19. The case of Pseudo-Eupolemus (see *ibid.*, 19–25), who seems to have made Abraham
   into the father of civilization, is interesting but not immediately relevant for us.
[48] Eusebius, *Praeparatio Evangelica*, IX.27.1–37. See discussion in Mussies, "Interpretatio Judaica";
   Mussies, "Moses"; Droge, *Homer or Moses?*, 25–35; Assmann, *Moses the Egyptian*, 36.
[49] Eusebius, *Praeparatio Evangelica*, IX.27.3–4.

founded cities, and, last but not least, gave the Egyptians their hieroglyphs. Because of his skill in the interpretation (*hermeneia*) of the sacred letters, the priests, judging him "worthy of divine honors," called him Hermes.[50] With this identification, Artapanus (as preserved in the Christian apologetics of Eusebius of Caesarea, on whom more below) had made a particularly smart move in the interest of Jewish anteriority: not only were the Egyptians presented as depending on Moses, but all the achievements claimed for the Egyptian Hermes could now be seen as Moses' achievements![51] Finally, like these predecessors, but independently from them,[52] the great Jewish historian Flavius Josephus likewise sought to demonstrate the superiority of Jewish over Greek culture by claiming chronological primacy for Moses: "our legislator exceeds in antiquity the legislators referred to anywhere else. The Lycurguses, and Solons, and Zoleukos, the legislator of the Locrians, and all those admired by the Greeks seem to have been but 'yesterday or the day before' compared to him . . ."[53]

To convince their contemporaries about the great antiquity of their new religion, the Christian apologists of the second to the fifth century likewise presented Moses as their key witness. The essential logic of their argumentation, which would become basic to the ancient wisdom discourse of the Renaissance, is presented with particular lucidity in an anonymous treatise from the third or early fourth century, titled *Ad Graecos de vera religione* but traditionally known as the *Cohortatio ad Graecos* and attributed, incorrectly,[54] to Justin Martyr (second cent.). The latter, generally considered the most influential of the early Christian apologists, and possibly the

---

[50] *Ibid.*, IX.27.6.

[51] The passage in Eusebius does not explicitly identify Moses as the Egyptian Thoth-Hermes, but all specialists seem to agree about the implication (see, for example, Festugière, *Révélation d'Hermès Trismégiste* 1, 70; Fowden, *Egyptian Hermes*, 23, 27, 36–37; Faivre, *Eternal Hermes*, 76–77; Mussies, "Moses," 804).

[52] Droge, *Homer or Moses?*, 45 with n. 104.

[53] Josephus, *Against Apion* 2.154 (Barclay ed., 254–255; as explained on p. 13 n. 34, the expression "yesterday or the day before" is a reference to Plato, *Laws* 677d, and also appears in *Against Apion* 1.7 and 2.14). For further analysis (including a comparison between Josephus' *Jewish Antiquities*, which presents a picture of cultural decline modeled after Hesiod, and *Against Apion*, which emphasizes progress) see Droge, *Homer or Moses?*, 35–47. In both works Josephus "boasted that the Jews enjoyed a history reaching back five millennia, making them an older people than the Greeks" (*ibid.*, 3).

[54] For the debate on authorship and dating, see the exhaustive study by Riedweg, *Ps.-Justin (Markell von Ankyra?) Ad Graecos de vera religione*, who suggests the fourth-century bishop Marcellus of Ancyra as the most likely author (*ibid.*, vol. 1, 167–182), and notes that the eventual attribution to Justin may have to do with Marcellus' condemnation as a heretic at the Council of Constantinople in 381. Renaissance authors, of course, did attribute it to Justin Martyr (on manuscripts and early editions available to them, see *ibid.*, vol. 1, 183–197). In fact the treatise contains no specific references to contemporary political or ecclesiastic events and its perspective is so thoroughly traditional (*ibid.*, vol. 1, 28) that it can be used here as particularly representative of the basic apologetic narrative.

first one,[55] was born around 100 CE in Syrian Palestine. He began his career
as a religious philosopher typical of the middle-platonic milieus discussed
above, believing at one point that Plato's philosophy would surely lead him
to "gaze upon God."[56] He claims to have been converted to Christianity
due to his meeting with an old man who "corrected" his platonism and
told him about the Hebrew prophets: "blessed men" who had lived "long
before the time of those reputed philosophers," and who "alone knew the
truth and communicated it to men."[57] He set up a philosophical school
in Rome, where he was executed during the reign of Marcus Aurelius,
sometime between 162 and 168. His major works are two Apologies and a
Dialogue with Trypho. Since the differences with Pseudo-Justin's *Ad Graecos*
are inconsequential for our purposes, and the latter is particularly useful
to introduce and summarize the basic apologetic perspective, it will be our
primary textual reference here.

The author addresses his non-Christian contemporaries in moderate
tones, trying to persuade them by reasonable arguments about the inferiority of Greek religion and philosophy. The poets have evidently quite silly
ideas about the origins of the gods (2.1),[58] and the philosophers before Plato
have an even more ridiculous theology (3.1). Plato and Aristotle present a
more serious challenge, but they often contradict one another and even
themselves (5–7); and in any case, the question one should ask is from
whom they had acquired their knowledge, for they cannot have invented it
by themselves (5.1). In other words, even if one wishes to accept Plato's or
Aristotle's views, one still has to search further to find their ancient origins.
These, as it turns out, are the Jewish teachers beginning with Moses:

> they lived long before your teachers, and what they taught was not of their
> own invention. Neither did they contradict or argue with one another. Instead,
> without strife or quarrel, they passed on to us the knowledge they had received
> from God . . . Therefore, as if by one mouth and one tongue, without contradicting

---

[55] The claims traditionally made for Aristides and Quadratus as earlier pioneers of Christian apolo-
geticism are rejected, in favor of Justin, by Parvis, "Justin Martyr and the Apologetic Tradition."
For detailed discussion of Justin's perspective on "ancient wisdom," see Droge, "Justin Martyr," and
Droge, *Homer or Moses?*, 49–72. Generally on Justin, see Parvis and Foster, *Justin Martyr and his
Worlds*; Minns and Parvis, *Justin, Philosopher and Martyr*.

[56] "The perception of incorporeal things quite overwhelmed me and the platonic theory of ideas
added wings to my mind, so that in a short time I imagined myself a wise man. So great was my
folly that I fully expected immediately to gaze upon God, for this is the goal of Plato's philosophy"
(Justin Martyr, *Dialogue with Trypho* chapter 2, trans. [Justin Martyr], *Writings*, 150–151).

[57] Justin Martyr, *Dialogue with Trypho* chapter 7, trans. [Justin Martyr], *Writings*, 159. On the historicity or fictionality of Justin's account, see Droge, "Justin Martyr," 304 and the literature cited
there.

[58] All references are to the edition and translation in Riedweg, *Ps.-Justin*, vol. II, 531–620.

themselves or one another, they have instructed us concerning God, the origin of the world, the creation of man, the immortality of the human soul, the future judgment, and all other things which we should know. Thus, in various places and at different times they have handed down to us the divine doctrine (8.1–2).[59]

To show that Moses was much older than any of the Greek philosophers, *Ad Graecos* invokes a long list of historians, including Flavius Josephus and Diodorus Siculus (9; cf. 12). Nothing taught by Moses and the later Prophets came from their own intellect: their knowledge was based entirely upon a "divine and prophetic" gift bestowed upon them by God (10.2).

Such privileged divine inspiration was not granted to the Greeks. It was only because of their visits to Egypt, where they profited from the Mosaic wisdom, that Orpheus, Homer, Solon, Pythagoras, Plato, and other Greeks "began to circulate doctrines concerning the deities very different from the unfavorable opinions they had previously held" (14.2). As for Plato himself: although it was in Egypt that he must have read the Pentateuch (28.1), the author suggests (and keeps repeating) that if he did not speak more openly about Moses' teaching of the One and Only God, this was only out of fear that what had happened to Socrates might happen to him too (chs. 20.1, 22.1, 27.1). Nevertheless, if one reads the *Timaeus* or the *Republic*, one will find that it contains the same opinion as Moses concerning God (ch. 22.1). In other words, many divine truths are present in Plato's writings, but in a concealed manner; and this partly hidden doctrine is derived from Moses, who in turn had received it directly from God.

Still, this reasoning does not suffice to resolve the fundamental dilemma of a new religion claiming to be ancient. Why would one need Christianity if all its divine truths were already available in the books of Moses? The answer is that Jesus Christ *restored* the ancient religion after it had been abandoned due to the pernicious influence of the demonic entities which the pagans worship as their gods (38.1). As emphasized by the real Justin Martyr, Christianity is not radically new: it is a revival of the ancient religion inspired by the eternal *Logos*:

Christ is the first-born of God, being the *logos* in which the whole race of human beings shares. And those who lived with the *logos* are Christians, even if they were called atheists, such as among the Greeks, Socrates and Heraclitus and those similar to them, and among the barbarians, Abraham and Ananias and Azarias and Misael and Elijah and many others . . . [60]

---

[59] Translation following [Justin Martyr], *Writings*, 383–384.
[60] Justin, *Apology* 1.46.2–3 (trans. Minns and Parvis, *Justin*, 201).

Such a notion of the ancient religion as "unconscious Christianity" could easily be supported with reference to a particularly authoritative model of the Christian mission to the Greeks, St. Paul's Areopagus speech. At their altar devoted to "the Unknown God," the Athenians had been worshiping the Christian God without knowing it, and hence Paul told them that "whom you ignorantly worship, him I declare unto you" (Acts 17:23). Following the same logic, the apologetic argument in the wake of Justin Martyr made it possible for Christian platonists to interpret Plato and all the other authorities of "Platonic Orientalism" as unconscious Christians, who had been inspired by the divine *Logos* without knowing it.[61]

It is important to be precise about the type of macrohistory implied by this perspective. The argumentation follows the essential logic of *philosophia perennis*, but could also easily be interpreted in support of *pia philosophia*, suggesting some kind of progress: the implicit or unconscious Christianity of the good pagans who lived in accordance with the universal *Logos* has now become explicit and conscious, so to speak, in the Christian message. In other words, the true and universal religion has recently found its most perfect expression in the teachings of Christ. It is for this very reason that *Ad Graecos* cannot be properly interpreted as defending a *prisca theologia* in the strict "genetic" sense. It may be true that Christianity restores the "ancient wisdom" of Moses, but the true religion does not depend on that reference, nor is Judaism its most perfect expression. That Moses happens to have been the earliest sage surely gives him greater authority than his pagan competitors; but it is not concluded that earlier always means better, for that would have forced Christians to prefer Moses over Jesus Christ. In short: although radical novelty equals inferiority, it does not necessarily follow that great antiquity equals superiority.

Pagan intellectuals could afford to make an easier and more straightforward argument against novelty. Probably in 175 or 176[62] – that is to say, shortly after Justin's death, and very probably in response to his work[63] – an otherwise unknown platonist philosopher named Celsus wrote the first systematic pagan attack on Christianity.[64] His *Alethes Logos* rested on the

---

[61] For Justin's perspective as a typical example of "orthodox" middle platonism, see Andresen, "Justin und der mittlere Platonismus." As pointed out by the same author, already well before his conversion Justin understood platonism as a religious doctrine, whose goal was to liberate the soul from earthly entanglements and lead it upwards to the divine Being (*ibid.*, 194–195).

[62] See discussion in Droge, *Homer or Moses?*, 74–75.

[63] Andresen, *Logos und Nomos*, 308–400; Nock, review of Andresen, 316–317; Wilken, *Christians*, 101; Droge, *Homer or Moses?*, 76–77.

[64] Generally on Celsus' critique of Christianity, see, for example, Dodds, *Pagan and Christian*, 102–138; Nestle, "Haupteinwände"; Labriolle, *Réaction païenne*, 111–169; Wilken, *Christians*, 94–125.

by now familiar assumption that "there is an ancient doctrine [*archaios logos*] which has existed from the beginning, which has always been maintained by the wisest nations and cities and wise men."[65] But among the many ancient peoples and traditions cited by Celsus (Egyptians, Syrians, Indians, Persians, Odrysians, Samothracians, Eleusinians, Hyperboreans, Galactophagoi, Druids, and Getae), the Jews are conspicuously absent; and likewise, Moses does not figure in his lists of inspired theologians. The reason is simply that, far from being the original source of the ancient religion, Moses with his doctrine of radical or exclusive monotheism had been responsible for its corruption: "the goatherds and shepherds who followed Moses as their leader were deluded by clumsy deceits into thinking that there was only one God, [and] without any rational cause . . . these goatherds and shepherds abandoned the worship of many gods."[66] But while the Jews at least kept following their own native tradition, peculiar and misguided as it might be, Christianity is even worse: "I will ask them where they come from, or who is the author of their traditional laws. Nobody, they will say."[67] Not only did Christianity originate as a rebellion against Jewish tradition,[68] which is already bad enough, but the Christians with their new religion deliberately break with all other traditions as well: they are a people without roots, who "wall themselves off and break away from the rest of mankind."[69]

With Justin Martyr on the one hand, and Celsus on the other, the two opposing perspectives on "ancient wisdom" were clearly defined. In Tatian's *Against the Greeks* (written probably between 176 and 178)[70] we find an argument that is similar to Justin's, but marked by a virulent anti-Greek sentiment. Far from being the original source of higher culture, the Greeks are mere imitators; Christianity is the most recent manifestation of the "wisdom of the barbarians," of which Moses is the earliest representative.[71] In Clement of Alexandria, a generation later, the imitators have become

---

[65] Origen, *Contra Celsum* 1.14 (Chadwick ed., 17).

[66] Origen, *Contra Celsum* 1.23 (Chadwick ed., 22). Cf. 1.24, where Celsus contends that "it makes no difference" whether one calls the supreme God by the name used among the Greeks, or that among the Indians or that among the Egyptians (Chadwick ed., 23: and similar argument in 5.41 [Chadwick ed., 296–297]). For Origen, of course, it did make a difference. As rightly pointed out by Droge (*Homer or Moses?*, 79), it would not be correct to refer to Celsus' perspective simply as "polytheism"; rather, it is an "inclusive" or "qualitative" monotheism as opposed to the "exclusive" or "quantitative" monotheism of Jewish religion.

[67] Origen, *Contra Celsum* 5.33 (Chadwick ed., 289).

[68] Origen, *Contra Celsum* 2.1, 4; 3.5; 5.33, 41; cf. Wilken, *Christians*, 112–117.

[69] Origen, *Contra Celsum* 8.2 (Chadwick ed., 454).

[70] See discussion in Droge, *Homer or Moses?*, 83–84.

[71] Waszink, "Some Observations," 49–52; Droge, *Homer or Moses?*, 82–101.

thieves: the Greeks have "stolen" their philosophy from the wisdom of the
barbarian nations (the Egyptians, Chaldaeans, Druids, Celts, Samanaeans,
Magi, and Indians), who have ultimately derived it from Moses.[72] But similar to Justin Martyr, Clement seems to perceive no sharp conflict between
such a "genetic" approach and a universalist doctrine of *theologia naturalis*
(again based upon the concept of the universal *Logos*) according to which
the pagan philosophers, including the Greeks, can also have discovered
some important truths by their own reason or by divine inspiration.[73] One
example mentioned specifically by Clement (which would later become
important to Ficino as well) was that of the Persians, whose *mageia* had
allowed them to predict the birth of Jesus and who had followed a star to
find their way to Bethlehem.[74] Although Moses is the earliest authority,
the pagans therefore do not entirely depend on his influence to find truth.

The apologetic literature of the second and third centuries culminated
in Origen's treatise *Against Celsus*. Criticizing Celsus' exclusion of Moses
from the list of ancient sages, he refers to Platonic Orientalists such as
Numenius to defend Moses as the earliest "barbarian" authority on which
the Greeks are dependent.[75] It is on this foundation that he proceeds to
a point-by-point refutation of Celsus. But again, like his predecessors,
Origen concedes that the pagans may also have been inspired by God
directly: "God has implanted in the souls of all men the truths which He
taught through the prophets and the Saviour."[76]

If the earlier phase of Christian apologetics was dominated by the positions of which Justin Martyr and Celsus were the pioneers,[77] a second
phase developed in the wake of a new pagan attack on Christianity, by the
neoplatonist Porphyry.[78] Porphyry may have been raised as a Christian, and

---

[72] Clement's "theft of the Greeks" theory occurs throughout the *Stromateis*, except for books III and VII.
See discussion in Munck, *Untersuchungen*, 127–151 ("Diebstahl der Hellenen"); Molland, *Conception
of the Gospel*, 52–67; Droge, *Homer or Moses?*, 142–149.

[73] See, for example, Clement, *Strom.* 1.57.1–58.4; 91–96; and the excellent discussion in Lilla, *Clement of
Alexandria*, 12–28, who discusses in detail how, according to Clement, the *Logos* may be responsible
both for the "dim" knowledge that may be achieved by means of natural reason and for a more
direct gnōsis received by divine inspiration. Next to the "theft theory" (see above, n. 72), Clement
presented a second story of theft inspired by the Enochian literature, claiming that some inferior
powers or angels gave philosophy to men after having stolen it from God, who providentially
allowed this to happen (Lilla, *Clement of Alexandria*, 29). Fascinating though it may be, this theory
is marginal to our present discussion.

[74] Clement, *Strom.* 1.71.4.

[75] Origen, *Contra Celsum* 1.15; see Droge, *Homer or Moses?*, 152–167, esp. 158–159 on the Platonic
Orientalist background, referred to by him as the "left wing" of middle platonism.

[76] Origen, *Contra Celsum* 1.4 (Chadwick ed., 9).

[77] I am following Droge's overall's argument that Celsus reacted to Justin, and the later apologists
(Tatian, Theophilus, Clement, and Origen) reacted to Celsus.

[78] See den Boer, "Pagan Historian"; Labriolle, *Réaction païenne*, 223–296; Wilken, *Christians*, 126–163.

was acquainted with Origen, but around age thirty went to Rome where he became a student of Plotinus. In his *Against the Christians* (written in the last decades of the third century or the first decade of the fourth,[79] and preserved only fragmentarily in quotations from later, mostly Christian authors)[80] we again find the accusation of rootlessness and rebellion against tradition: the Christians do not even "adhere to the god who is honored among the Jews according to their customary rites, but... cut out for themselves a new kind of track in a pathless desert."[81] Unlike Celsus, however, Porphyry attacked Christian claims for the anteriority of Moses from a historian's perspective, with precise philological and chronological arguments.[82] Many Christian authors seem to have responded to Porphyry, but only fragments of their work remain. What we do have is the systematic refutation by Eusebius in his *Praeparatio Evangelica*, written between 314 and 318.

Eusebius offers a systematic history of culture in order to defend a by now familiar thesis: not only is Christianity true and ancient, but it is true *because* it is ancient.[83] But while he repeats many of the arguments of earlier apologists, the scholarly sophistication of Porphyry's polemics forces him to develop an account that is considerably more complex than theirs, and will be summarized here only in its barest outlines.[84] The earliest period of human history, starting with the Fall, was marked by primitive savagery; and from this wholly negative matrix of ignorance emerged the paganism of the Egyptians and Phoenicians, which was adopted by the Greeks and, under the increasing influence of demons, finally led to the pagan superstition that filled the Graeco-Roman world. Next to this demonic development, however, and independent of it, the true religion emerged thanks to God's action through his *Logos*.[85] During the earliest time of savagery and ignorance, a very few men "through incontrovertible reasonings led up their thoughts from visible things to the creator of the whole

---

[79] On the problem of dating, see Droge, *Homer or Moses?*, 179–180, who argues that *Against the Christians* was most probably written briefly before the persecution of the Christians by Diocletian (303–313) and may have served as its ideological justification.

[80] Collected by Adolf von Harnack, in Porphyrius, *"Gegen die Christen."* Porphyry's work was condemned at the Council of Nicaea in 325, and the emperors Theodosius II and Valentinian III ordered it to be burned in 448.

[81] Eusebius, *Praep. Evang.* 1.2.4 (trans. according to Droge, *Homer or Moses?*, 175) = Fragment 1 in Porphyrius, *"Gegen die Christen"* (Harnack ed.), 45.

[82] Den Boer, "Pagan Historian," 199–200, who goes as far as to refer to Porphyry as a precursor of the nineteenth-century higher criticism of the Tübingen school (*ibid.*, 203).

[83] Droge, *Homer or Moses?*, 180.

[84] In what follows, I rely mostly on the analysis in Droge, *Homer or Moses?*, 180–183; and Barnes, *Constantine and Eusebius*, 174–188. See also Hanson, "Christian Attitude," 187–188.

[85] Droge, *Homer or Moses?*, 171.

world and the great maker of the universe; and thanks to the purification of the eyes of the soul, they perceived that he alone was God, the savior of all, and sole giver of good gifts."[86] These were the biblical patriarchs, from Enoch to Moses, who thus established the true religion. By the time of Christ it was still preserved by the Jews, as an alternative to the false religion of paganism, which, however, still dominated the empire. In this situation, the coming of Christ and the diffusion of the gospel accomplished something new and unique: it spelt the death of the demons and thereby brought the end of paganism.[87] Although Eusebius introduces a clear element of progress here, the true religion established as Christianity was itself not new: it embodies the ancient religion of the Hebrews, as it had existed prior even to the establishment of Jewish religion by Moses:

> The Hebrews who were earlier in time than Moses, having never heard of the Mosaic legislation, enjoyed a free and unfettered mode of religion, being regulated by the manner of life which is in accordance with nature, so that they had no need of laws to rule them because of the extreme freedom of their soul from passions, but had received true knowledge of the doctrines concerning God.[88]

Christianity, in other words, is the original and most ancient religion of the Hebrews, in which the freedom of the gospel once again takes precedence over the strictures of Jewish Law. While this does not make Judaism inferior, it does make Christianity superior.

Eusebius was writing in the church library of Caesarea, where he was using a collection that had previously been owned by Origen. Apart from the works of historians, the philosophical core of this library consisted of Plato and a particularly rich assortment of middle- and neoplatonic texts representative of the "oriental" school.[89] Eusebius' knowledge of this tradition was very profound[90] and particularly important for us, for although the religion of the pagans is rejected as demonic, he believes the platonic *philosophy* to be derived from Hebrew sources and to agree in its essence with Christianity. It is from this context that we must understand Eusebius' famous quotation of a statement by Numenius: "What is Plato but Moses speaking Attic Greek?"[91]

The basic lines of argumentation developed by the apologists from Justin to Eusebius were taken up, and thereby received further confirmation, by

---

[86] Eusebius, *Praep. Evang.* II.6.12.   [87] Eusebius, *Praep. Evang.* v.17.6–14, esp. 13–14.
[88] Eusebius, *Praep. Evang.* VII.6.4 (trans. according to Droge, *Homer or Moses?*, 186).
[89] Listed in Mras, *Praeparatio Evangelica*, vol. II, 439–465; Grant, "Porphyry among the Early Christians," 183–184; Droge, *Homer or Moses?*, 191–192; and esp. Carriker, *Library of Eusebius of Caesarea*, 299–311.
[90] Moreau, "Eusebius of Caesarea," 1081.   [91] Eusebius, *Praep. Evang.* XI.10.14.

other and later Christian authorities. Lactantius, for example, still finds it important to point out that the Hebrew prophets predate the Greeks,[92] and Augustine emphasizes that Hermes Trismegistus may have lived "long before the sages or philosophers of Greece, [but] nonetheless after Abraham, Isaac, Jacob, and Joseph, and, indeed, after Moses himself."[93] Plato had visited Egypt, where he studied not only the writings of its native sages but probably the Hebrew scriptures as well.[94] The Platonic Orientalist background still reverberates strongly in the crucial eighth book of *De Civitate Dei*, where Augustine insists that "no one has come closer to us than the platonists,"[95] but adds that the true beliefs shared by Christians and platonists might also be held by wise men or philosophers of other nations, "be they Atlantic Libyans, Egyptians, Indians, Persians, Chaldaeans, Scythians, Gauls or Spaniards."[96] Augustine is pleading his cause with the platonists "because their writings are better known," but he points out that "any other philosophers of any nation" who have thought in the same way concerning God are, to that extent, in agreement with Christianity as well. In other words, Augustine does defend a *philosophia perennis*: it represents the true religion that had already been known to the pagan nations, and which came to be called the Christian religion after the universal *Logos* had been incarnated as Jesus Christ.[97]

We may conclude that, as long as Moses was highlighted as the ultimate source of true religion, the ancient wisdom narrative of the Renaissance could claim very secure patristic authority. Pagan wisdom could be seen as inspired by the *Logos*, or derived from Mosaic origins, and as foreshadowing Christian truth; and platonism in particular (or more precisely, its "orientalist" middle- and neoplatonic orientation) was bound to play a special role as providing the privileged language of mediation by which the gap between philosophical reason and revealed religion could be bridged. And yet, although Platonic Orientalism and Patristic apologetics did indeed provide the ancient wisdom narrative of the Renaissance with its necessary foundations, these are by no means sufficient to explain the emergence of that phenomenon in the fifteenth century, which is characterized by a series of new features.

---

[92] Lactantius, *Div. Inst.* IV.5.8–9.   [93] Augustine, *Civ. Dei* XVIII.39.

[94] *Ibid.*, VIII.4 and 11 (Augustine qualifies his earlier statements to the effect that Plato had heard the prophet Jeremiah and read the prophets while in Egypt, pointing out that they had not yet been translated into Greek, but suggests that he might have been using an interpreter).

[95] *Ibid.*, VIII.5 (and many equivalent statements in the following chapters).   [96] *Ibid.*, VIII.9.

[97] See, again, the passages from Augustine's *Retractationes* I.12.3 and Justin's *Apology* I.46.2–3 quoted above (pp. 9 and 21).

Perhaps most important in that regard is the fact that power relations were now reversed: while Christian authors of the first centuries were apologists for Christianity within a living culture of paganism, it was inevitable that the admirers of Plato in the Italian Renaissance, their strong Christian commitments notwithstanding, became apologists for pagan sources within a living culture of Christianity. Hardly less important is that they were vying over a different kind of symbolic capital, according to the rules determined in each case by the dominant culture: the patristic apologists had needed to prove that their religion could claim the authority of an ancient and venerable Tradition, but the Renaissance humanists needed to demonstrate that the pagan sources could be reconciled with theological orthodoxy.[98] And finally, whereas the presence and wide diffusion of pagan literature was the obvious point of departure for Christian apologists (so that the need for its preservation or destruction might be an object of discussion, not its recovery), Renaissance humanists were dealing with a situation where pagan literature was being newly recovered and brought to light after a long period of near-absence and oblivion. This fact alone was sufficient to give a revolutionary slant to the Renaissance narrative that had been unimaginable in the early centuries: its potential for instigating a *revival* of paganism in one form or another, implicitly or explicitly, within Christianity itself or perhaps even in competition with it. With this possibility, the outlines of Western esotericism begin to emerge.

THE WISE MAN FROM THE EAST: GEORGE GEMISTOS PLETHON

In the last week of November 1437, a delegation under the Byzantine Emperor John VIII Paleologus and the Orthodox Patriarch Joseph II embarked on vessels sent to Constantinople by Pope Eugene IV. They had been invited to participate in a Council in Italy, to discuss a possible reunion of the Eastern and Western churches. On their arrival in Venice they were given a brilliant reception, after which they traveled on to meet the pope in Ferrara, where they arrived on March 4, 1438.[99] Following the official inauguration a month later, the actual proceedings started after a

---

[98] Ultimately, of course, such orthodoxy means alignment with theological tradition, so that "Tradition" could still be seen as the symbolic capital in this case as well. Nevertheless, the official yardstick is now no longer that of "ancient origins" but that of doctrinal correctness.

[99] Generally on the history of this Council, see Gill, *Council of Florence*, and brief summary in Gill, *Personalities*, 1–14. For a short overview of the Council in the wider historical context of relations between Byzantium and Western Christianity, see Angold, "Byzantium and the West." For overviews focused on the protagonist of this section, Gemistos Plethon, see Masai, *Pléthon*, 315–327; Woodhouse, *George Gemistos Plethon*, 119–188.

considerable delay, on October 8; and mainly for financial and security reasons the entire Council was transferred to Florence in January of the following year, where the discussions continued well into the summer.

A notable personality in the emperor's party was a Byzantine philosopher of considerable renown in his own country, George Gemistos (*c.* 1355/1360–1452), who would later call himself Plethon.[100] He was already around eighty years old, and several of the Greek delegation's outstanding intellectuals (Johannes Bessarion, Mark Eugenikos, very probably Isidore of Kiev)[101] had once been his pupils. The impression made by Plethon at the Council, and eventually among the humanist circles of Florence, has since become the stuff of legend:

> When there was a wonderful gathering in the West of wise and eminent men, and a great debate on the matter of the Church's doctrines, how can one describe the admiration they felt for this man's wisdom and virtue and his powers of argument? He shone among them more brightly than the sun. They regarded him as their common teacher, the common benefactor of mankind, the common pride of nature. They called him Plato and Socrates, for he was not inferior to those two in wisdom, as everybody would agree.[102]

Much later, in 1492, Marsilio Ficino would evoke a similar picture in the dedication to Lorenzo de' Medici of his translation of Plotinus' *Enneads*: at the time of the Council, he writes, the young Cosimo de' Medici had often listened to Plethon, who had "spoken of the platonic mysteries like a second Plato."[103] The implication is that during those meetings Plethon had sown the seeds that had blossomed two decades later in the Platonic Academy of Florence. We will return to the veracity of this.

[100] On Plethon, see Schultze, *Georgios Gemistos Plethon*; Masai, *Pléthon*; Woodhouse, *George Gemistos Plethon*; Blum, *Georgios Gemistos Plethon*; Tambrun, *Pléthon*; [no editor], *Sul ritorno di Pletone*. In addition, important chapters are devoted to him by Hankins, *Plato in the Italian Renaissance*, vol. I, 193–217 and his appendix "Pletho's Influence" in vol. II, 436–440; and Stausberg, *Faszination Zarathushtra*, vol. I, 35–82. For a short and up-to-date overview, see Tambrun, "Plethon, Georgius Gemistos"; and for a discussion in relation to "Platonic Orientalism," see Burns, "*Chaldean Oracles.*"

[101] On the case of Isidore, see Hankins, "Cosimo de' Medici," 158, and literature cited in his n. 48.

[102] Hermonymos, "Kyrio Georgio to Gemisto," 807D; trans. according to Woodhouse, *George Gemistos Plethon*, 12.

[103] Ficino, *Opera*, 1537: "Magnus Cosmus . . . philosophum graecum, nomine Gemistum cognomine Plethonem, quasi Platonem alterum de mysteriis Platonicis disputantem frequenter audivit." For an English translation of the full passage, see Hankins, "Cosimo de' Medici," 150–151 (with Latin in Appendix II, *ibid.*, 160–161). As pointed out by Tambrun (*Pléthon*, 28), "Platonic mysteries" was a technical reference to the curriculum of late neoplatonism, which had progressed from the "lesser mysteries" of Aristotle to the "greater mysteries" of Plato, but culminated in the Orphic literature and the *Chaldaean Oracles* (Hoffmann, "Fonction des prologues exégétiques," 212–213). The attraction of Plethon for the Italian humanists in Florence was also confirmed by Scholarios (see Monfasani, *George of Trebizond*, 202).

The journey of this "second Plato" from Byzantium to Florence is of great significance not only historically, but symbolically as well, for in the person of Plethon the humanists made first contact with a living embodiment of Platonic Orientalism who believed that the true wisdom had originated with Zoroaster, the chief of the *Magi*. Of course the Council was not about philosophy but about church doctrine and politics; and that an ancient Persian sage could have something to do with Plato may have been neither apparent nor particularly relevant to the Italian churchmen and politicians. But that a suggestive parallel could be drawn between the visit of the Byzantine delegation to the head of Western Christianity, and the biblical story of the *Magi* who had come from the East to venerate the Christ child – thereby confirming the concordance of their ancient wisdom with the teachings of Christianity – was certainly not lost on them. Hence during the festivities around the feast of St. John at the closing of the Council in 1439, the Greeks were dazzled by a luxurious procession of men dressed up like the *Magi* following the star. This spectacle was staged presumably in honor of their own presence, but carried a subtext of Western superiority that they were unlikely to miss: for all their wisdom, the Eastern sages had been obliged to travel all the way to the West, and having reached their destination they had knelt and paid homage to God's representative on earth.[104]

Twenty years later, in 1459, Cosimo de' Medici commissioned a great fresco by Benozzo Gozzoli called *The Journey of the Magi*, in which the memory of the Council still resonates strongly.[105] As convincingly argued by Brigitte Tambrun with reference to this work of art, Cosimo's well-attested fascination with the biblical *Magi*[106] from the East is inseparable

---

[104] This procession and its significance was first called to the attention of scholars by Tambrun, *Pléthon*, 26. The procession in question, on June 23, 1439, was modeled after similar ones organized annually on the occasion of Epiphany, by a para-liturgical fraternity known as the *Compagnia de' Magi* under the patronage of the Medici (Hatfield, "Compagni de' Magi," esp. 113; Chastel, *Art et humanisme*, 240–248; Buhler, "Marsilio Ficino's *De Stella Magorum*," 350–351). The subtext of Western superiority is not mentioned by Tambrun, but seems obvious given the consistently arrogant attitude of the Latin theologians towards their Byzantine counterparts, for whom the Council became a mostly humiliating experience (see, for example, Woodhouse, *George Gemistos Plethon*, 119–120, 123, 125, 176).

[105] Tambrun, *Pléthon*, 23–33. Possibly the picture of Balthazar is based upon the portrait of Emperor John VIII. It has also been suggested that the picture of Melchior is based upon Patriarch Joseph II, but Tambrun rejects that identification because it does not accord with another known portrait of the patriarch (*ibid.*, 24–25).

[106] See also Cosimo's fresco of the *Magi* in his personal monastic cell at the convent of San Marco (Tambrun, *Pléthon*, 28), Botticelli's portrayal of members of the Medici family as *Magi* in his "Adoration of the Magi" in the Galleria degli Uffizi (Chastel, *Art et humanisme à Florence*, 240–248), and several other paintings and a wall-hanging representing the *Magi* in the Medici Palace (Hatfield, "Compagni de' Magi," 136–137). Cosimo and his brother Piero also appear in Gozzoli's fresco.

from his memory of the Council and from the revival of Plato that took shape under his patronage in Florence. The key factor in that constellation was Plethon. Referring directly to the time of the Council, Ficino later wrote to Cosimo that Plato's spirit, living in his writings, had left Byzantium to fly like a bird (*advolavit*) to Cosimo in Florence;[107] and it was taken for granted that the *Magi* who venerated the Christ child could have been none other than the disciples of Zoroaster. Hence Tambrun's conclusion:

> Plato makes his return because he is the inheritor at the same time of the *Magi* (according to Plethon) and of Hermes (according to the Latin Fathers, notably Augustine and Lactantius) . . . The fresco of Benozzo Gozzoli presents a genealogy of wisdom: the *Magi* – Plato – Christ, doubled by a geographical orientation of temporality: the Orient – Greece – Florence. The procession magnifies the point of culmination while at the same time always recalling and referring to the point of · origin: the oriental *Magi* are the originators of the wisdom of which the Greeks – Pythagoras, Plato, Plotinus, Plethon – are the inheritors, and this wisdom comes to Florence thanks to the Medici who gather it.[108]

Who was this "second Plato" who had come from the East, and made such an impression on his audience at the time of the Council? One of the most notable philosophers of the late Byzantine era, George Gemistos was born in Constantinople and raised in a well-educated Christian family. After studying in Constantinople and Adrianople, he established himself as a teacher of philosophy in his city of birth. Probably toward the end of the first decade of the fifteenth century, Emperor Manuel II Paleologus sent him to Mistra in the southern Peloponnese, a town with a relatively free-spirited atmosphere where the ancient Hellenistic traditions still survived, and which would remain his residence for the rest of his life. Far from being an ivory-tower philosopher, Gemistos seems to have been active in a variety of public functions: in Constantinople he was a member of the Senate, and during his life he held various administrative positions, acted as a judge, and was frequently consulted by the emperors and the despots of the Morea. If not consulted, he offered his advice anyway. Although the Church suspected him of heresy, the imperial family seems to have thought highly of him, and he was richly rewarded for his services.[109] Although he

---

[107] Ficino, Proemium, in Kristeller, *Supplementum Ficinianum* II, 104–105 (and see Kristeller, "Marsilio Ficino as a Beginning Student," 103 with n. 32).

[108] Tambrun, *Pléthon*, 31; and see the entirely analogous argument made by Allen, *Synoptic Art*, 37–40. Tambrun's reference to Augustine as an authority for the revival of Hermes is questionable (for Augustine's actual view of Hermes, see Hanegraaff, "Hermetism"), but this does not affect her argument.

[109] Woodhouse, *George Gemistos Plethon*, chapter VI, esp. 87.

was a layman, his presence in the imperial delegation to the Council of Ferrara and Florence was therefore not surprising.

It might seem strange for a man approaching his eightieth birthday, but the Council was undoubtedly the turning point of his life, as indicated not only by his adoption of a new pen-name "Plethon" (probably with deliberate reference to his status as a "second Plato"),[110] but most significantly by the fact that his major writings were produced during and after the trip to Italy. Although as an opponent of Union he made some active contributions to the official proceedings of the Council,[111] their theological hairsplitting left him rather indifferent; but he immediately felt at home among the Florentine humanists, who eagerly sought his advice about Greek philosophy. Plethon must have been flattered by their attention and admiration, but shocked by their lack of knowledge about Plato and Aristotle. The former had only just begun to be rediscovered, with pioneering but as yet limited translation efforts by Uberto Decembrio, Leonardo Bruni and a few others;[112] and the latter was poorly understood not only by the humanists, but even by the scholastics, who claimed his authority but actually knew him mainly through Latin and Arab sources and read him through the lenses of Averroes – who had not even known Greek.[113] To correct such misunderstandings, Plethon during his sojourn in Florence wrote a short text in Greek, *Wherein Aristotle disagrees with Plato*, usually referred to as *De differentiis*. It purported to demonstrate that Aristotle went wrong whenever he departed from Plato and is considered the opening shot in the famous Plato–Aristotle controversy of the Renaissance, which lasted until the early 1470s.[114]

---

[110] On this pseudonym, see Masai, *Pléthon*, 384–386; Woodhouse, *George Gemistos Plethon*, 186–188. His pupil Michael Apostoles also addressed him as a "second Plato," and Bessarion not only referred to him as "second only to Plato" (Woodhouse, *George Gemistos Plethon*, 186–188), but at one point even as his reincarnation: "Plato's soul . . . has been sent to earth to assume the body of Gemistos and his life" (letter of condolences to Plethon's son, as reproduced in Masai, *Pléthon*, 307; it is amusing to read, on the same page, how much this has shocked modern commentators).

[111] See Laurent, "*Mémoires*"; and discussion in Woodhouse, *George Gemistos Plethon*, 136–147.

[112] See Hankins, *Plato in the Italian Renaissance*, vol. I, Parts I–II.

[113] Woodhouse, *George Gemistos Plethon*, 147–153.

[114] Modern edition in: Lagarde, "Le *De differentiis* de Pléthon"; English translation in Woodhouse, *George Gemistos Plethon*, 192–214; German translation in Blum, *Georgios Gemistos Plethon*, 112–150. Although *De differentiis* was a pioneering attempt (Tambrun, "Marsile Ficin et le 'Commentaire'," 12–13 with n. 13), it may have been too sophisticated for Italian humanists at the time (Monfasani, *George of Trebizond*, 203), and its influence on the eventual development of the Plato–Aristotle debate must not be exaggerated (Tambrun, "Marsile Ficin et le 'Commentaire'," 9). For overviews of the Plato–Aristotle debate against the background of Plethon's text, see Hankins, *Plato in the Italian Renaissance*, vol. I, 193–217; Monfasani, *George of Trebizond*, 201–229; Monfasani, "Marsilio Ficino and the Plato–Aristotle Controversy." See also Monfasani, *George of Trebizond*, 202: Plethon

Much more important, indeed central, to our concerns is Plethon's version of the *Chaldaean Oracles* and his commentaries on them. As we have seen, this collection – famously referred to by Franz Cumont as the "Bible" of the late antique theurgists – is among the most important textual references of "orientalist" middle platonism and had enjoyed an exalted status in the late neoplatonist curriculum.[115] Plethon knew it from the collection preserved by Michael Psellus in the eleventh century, but eliminated six oracles from it and presented the result together with his commentary and a brief "explanation" under a new title: *Magical Sayings of the Magi, Disciples of Zoroaster.*[116] From "Chaldaean" the oracles had therefore become "magical"; and for the first time in history[117] they were attributed to Zoroaster, the chief of the *Magi*.

Whence this attribution, and what is its significance? Most specialists today explain it in terms of a specific chain of transmission from pagan antiquity to Islamic culture, from where it could have reached Plethon, who was raised as a Christian, by means of a Jewish intermediary: a combination which derives much of its fascination from the suggestion that Platonic Orientalism could function as a privileged medium enabling "discursive transfer" across the boundaries of all the three great scriptural traditions.[118] Crucial to this story of transmission[119] is the shadowy figure of a certain

claimed to have written *De differentiis* "without serious intent" during an illness that kept him indoors, "to comfort myself and to please those who are dedicated to Plato."

[115] See above, nn. 22, 37, 103. On the *Chaldaean Oracles* generally, see Majercik, "Introduction"; des Places, *Oracles Chaldaïques*, 7–57; Lewy, *Chaldean Oracles and Theurgy*; Saffrey, "Neoplatoniciens"; Stausberg, *Faszination Zarathushtra*, vol. I, 44–57.

[116] The standard critical edition is Tambrun-Krasker, Μαγικά λογια. Woodhouse, *George Gemistos Plethon*, 48–61, gives an English translation of Plethon's version of the Oracles and his "Brief Explanation," and summarizes the Commentary.

[117] Stausberg, *Faszination Zarathushtra*, vol. I, 61 with n. 162 (correcting Bidez and Cumont, *Mages hellénisés* I, 160–161, with respect to a document printed in their vol. II, 251). On a reference to τὰ τε Ζωροάστρου λόγια by Nicolas of Damascus in the first century (*ibid.*, 81–82) see Dannenfeldt, "Pseudo-Zoroastrian Oracles," 9 n. 16 and Stausberg, *Faszination*, vol. I, 62.

[118] The term "discursive transfer" is derived from von Stuckrad, "Western Esotericism," 84–85. For the notion of transconfessional Jewish/Christian/Muslim milieus in this time and context, see Wasserstrom, "Jewish–Muslim Relations," 71–74; Panaino, "De Zoroastre à Georges Gémiste Pléthon"; and as illustration see the Arab translation of Plethon's writings presented in Nicolet and Tardieu, "Plethon Arabicus."

[119] The importance of Elissaeus was first highlighted by Masai in 1956 (*Pléthon*, 55–60) and adopted by Dannenfeldt ("Pseudo-Zoroastrian Oracles," 12). The connection with Suhrawardī was suggested by Shlomo Pines in an oral response to a paper by Masai at a conference on neoplatonism in 1969 (Masai, "Pléthon," 442–444, and discussion Pines/Masai on 445). The resulting notion of a Suhrawardī–Elissaeus–Plethon transmission was adopted by Corbin in 1971 (*En Islam Iranien* II, 34–35) and explored at greater length by Tardieu in 1986 ("Pléthon lecteur des oracles," 141–148). It has been accepted by the leading contemporary specialist Tambrun (Μαγικά λογια, 41–44; "Marsile Ficin et le 'Commentaire' de Pléthon," 21–22; *Pléthon*, 36–37, 92–94). Some doubts about this line of transmission are expressed by Stausberg, *Faszination Zarathushtra*, vol. I, 37–41.

Elissaeus, a Jewish teacher mentioned in two letters by George Scholarios, who attacked Plethon as a heretic and a pagan inspired by demons:

The climax of his apostasy came later under the influence of a certain Jew with whom he studied, attracted by his skill as an interpreter of Aristotle. This Jew was an adherent of Averroes and other Persian and Arabic interpreters of Aristotle's works, which the Jews had translated into their own language, but he paid little regard to Moses or the beliefs and observances which the Jews received from him. This man also expounded to Gemistos the doctrines of Zoroaster and others. He was ostensibly a Jew but in fact a Hellenist. Gemistos stayed with him for a long time, not only as his pupil but also in his service, living at his expense, for he was one of the most influential men at the court of these barbarians. His name was Elissaeus.[120]

In another letter, Scholarios repeated most of these elements, referring to Elissaeus as a "polytheist" and adding that he met his end in the flames. He writes specifically that Plethon had "no previous knowledge" of Zoroaster before being introduced to the Persian sage by his Jewish master.[121]

Plethon himself never mentions Elissaeus, and his enemy Scholarios remains our only direct source, but the latter's statements make sense if they are placed in context. The "court of the barbarians" (that is to say, the Muslims) in this period could only be Adrianople, which had been captured by the Turks in 1360, and where many Jews enjoyed high office in the Ottoman magistrature and administration. That Elissaeus was an adherent of "Averroes and other Persian and Arabic interpreters of Aristotle's works" identifies him as a philosopher typical of this time and place, who combined the occidental aristotelianism in the tradition of Averroes (imported and translated by Spanish Jews) with its oriental and Avicennian counterpart in the influential "illuminationist" philosophy of Suhrawardī and his *ishrāqī* school.[122] That the latter was wholly grounded in Greek philosophy, and Platonic Orientalism in particular, has been demonstrated exhaustively by John Walbridge.[123] At the very opening of

---

[120] Letter to Princess Theodora Asesina, the wife of the Despot of Mistra, Demetrios Palaiologos. Scholarios, *Oeuvres*, IV, 152–153; trans. according to Woodhouse, *George Gemistos Plethon*, 24.

[121] Letter to the Exarch Joseph, but here written as if addressing Plethon in the second person. Scholarios, *Oeuvres*, IV, 162; trans. according to Woodhouse, *George Gemistos Plethon*, 25.

[122] Tardieu, "Pléthon lecteur des oracles," 144–146; and cf. his quotation from Plethon's response to Scholarios, according to which he has derived Averroes' opinion about the soul from learned Italians and from Jewish teachers. For Suhrawardī and his influence, see, for example, Corbin, "Récit d'initiation"; Nasr, "Shihāb al-Dīn Suhrawardi Maqtūl"; Walbridge, "Suhrawardī and Illuminationism." For the Ishrāqi "subculture" against the background of emigration of Andalusian Jews, see Wasserstrom, "Jewish–Muslim Relations," 71–74.

[123] Walbridge, *Leaven of the Ancients*; Walbridge, *Wisdom of the Mystic East*. On the genealogies of wisdom of Suhrawardī's school, see also Nasr, "Shihāb al-Dīn Suhrawardi Maqtūl," 376.

Suhrawardī's *Philosophy of Illumination* we indeed find a passage so clear that it might almost be called a Platonic Orientalist *credo*:

In all that I have said about the science of lights and that which is and is not based upon it, I have been assisted by those who have traveled the path of God. This science is the very intuition of the inspired and illumined Plato, the guide and master of philosophy, and of those who came before him from the time of Hermes, "the father of philosophers," up to Plato's time, including such mighty pillars of philosophy as Empedocles, Pythagoras, and others. The words of the Ancients are symbolic and not open to refutation. The criticisms made of the literal sense of their words fail to address their real intentions, for a symbol cannot be refuted.[124]

In an analogous passage much further on, Suhrawardī emphasized the limits of peripatetic reason when it comes to understanding the "science of lights," whose nature and reality can ultimately be known only by the direct intuition of "pure souls" during a state of divine ecstasy:

All those possessing insight and detachment bear witness to this. Most of the allusions of the prophets and the great philosophers point to this. Plato, Socrates before him, and those before Socrates – like Hermes, Agathodaemon, and Empedocles – all held this view . . . Whoso questions the truth of this . . . let him engage in mystical disciplines and service to those visionaries, that perchance he will, as one dazzled by the thunderbolt, see the light blazing in the Kingdom of Power and will witness the heavenly essences and lights that Hermes and Plato beheld. He will see the spiritual luminaries, the wellsprings of kingly splendor and wisdom that Zoroaster told of . . . [A]ll the sages of Persia were agreed thereon . . . These are the lights to which Empedocles and others alluded.[125]

If Elissaeus was indeed a Platonic Orientalist and adherent of Suhrawardī's "science of lights" – and all our information seems to support that assumption – this provides us with a background for better understanding how Plethon could have arrived at his ideas about the *Chaldaean Oracles* as the most ancient source of the universal wisdom tradition. With their pervasive symbolism of light and fire as representing the divine, they would be seen as highly representative not only of Suhrawardī's ancient preplatonic "science of lights" but also, more specifically, of the fire cult that had always been associated with Zoroastrian religion.[126] In the Introduction to his *Philosophy of Illumination*, Suhrawardī distinguished explicitly between the true doctrine of light that was taught by the ancient Persian

---

[124] Suhrawardī, *Hikmat al-ishrāq*, Introduction (Arab orig. with English trans. in Suhrawardī, *Philosophy of Illumination*, 2).

[125] *Ibid.*, II.2.165–166 (in: Suhrawardī, *Philosophy of Illumination*, 107–108).

[126] De Jong, *Traditions of the Magi*, 343–350.

philosophers, and the false doctrine of the "infidel *Magi*," or the heresy of Mani.[127] Furthermore, anybody looking at the Greek sources from that perspective – and everything Plethon writes about Zoroaster can ultimately be traced to them[128] – could not fail to notice that the term *magos* had a double meaning there as well: it could mean a "sage" practicing the ancient cult of the true gods[129] or it could have the negative meaning of a sorcerer, a practitioner of *goetia*.[130] Plethon, for his part, now seems to have concluded that whereas Zoroaster and the *Magi* were the depositors of the ancient, true and universal[131] religion of Zoroaster, the "Chaldaeans" represented a later development that had corrupted the truth, leading to the false doctrine of dualism and practices of sorcery. Hence all three oracles that dealt with *goetia* were removed by him from Psellus' collection[132] along with the adjective "Chaldaean," and the remaining series was attributed to Zoroaster and the *Magi*. In this manner, Plethon believed he had restored the most ancient source of the platonic tradition to its original purity.[133]

Back in Mistra, Plethon wrote his major philosophical synthesis, the *Nomoi* (Laws), which seems to have been made known only to the select membership of his intimate circle of pupils. Around 1460–1465, when Plethon's manuscript turned up in the possession of Princess Theodora, his enemy Scholarios (now Patriarch of Constantinople) had most of it burned and ordered the destruction of any surviving copies on pain of excommunication.[134] Scholarios himself, however, preserved those parts he felt he needed to back up his accusations. In the surviving opening chapters of the work, the Platonic Orientalist perspective is developed in some detail, beginning with an introduction to the major ancient "lawgivers and sages" who came after Zoroaster: Eumolpus (founder of the Eleusinian mysteries), Minos (the Cretan lawgiver), Lycurgus (the Spartan lawgiver), Iphitus (the reviver of the Olympic games), and Numa (who had instituted religious laws among the Romans). Plethon continues by stating that the

---

[127] *Ibid.*, Introduction (in: Suhrawardī, *Philosophy of Illumination*, 2).
[128] Woodhouse, *George Gemistos Plethon*, 26, 63.   [129] See again n. 33 (*Alcibiades* 1.122A).
[130] Tambrun-Krasker, Μαγικά λογια, 43–44; Tambrun, "Marsile Ficin et le 'Commentaire'," 21–22.
    And see the extensive discussion of the term *magos* in de Jong, *Traditions of the Magi*, 387–394.
[131] As pointed out by Dannenfeldt, Zoroaster's priority does not mean that the philosophical principles
    of his religion were believed to be invented by him: "they are as old as the universe and were always
    among mankind" ("Pseudo-Zoroastrian Oracles," 10, quoting Plethon, *Nomoi* [Alexandre ed.,
    252]).
[132] It concerns Psellus' oracles 6, 8, and 39 (resp. 150, 206, and 149 in the standard edition of Des
    Places). See discussion in Tambrun-Krasker, Μαγικά λογια, 155–156, who also discusses possible
    reasons for the removal of three more oracles.
[133] Tambrun, "Plethon," 961; Tambrun, *Pléthon*, 94.
[134] On this story, see Woodhouse, *George Gemistos Plethon*, 357–361.

Indian Brahmans and the *Magi* are to be preferred among the barbarians, and the *kourètes* among the Greeks; and he finishes with a further list of authorities, including the priests at the oracle of Dodona, "inspired men" like Polyides, Tiresias, Chiron and the Seven Sages, and finally Pythagoras, Plato and other philosophers belonging to their school, notably "Parmenides, Timaeus, Plutarch, Plotinus, Porphyry, and Iamblichus."[135]

At least three things must be noted about this list. First, Plethon is explicit in presenting his list of "lawgivers and philosophers" as a positive category against its negative counterpart, consisting of "poets and sophists." This latter term turns out to be a code for the founders of revealed religions, and Christians in particular.[136] Second, as the very title of the work suggests as well, the combination of "philosophers and lawgivers" has evident political implications: by preaching a return to the "ancient wisdom" away from the "sophists," Plethon was advocating a reform not only of religion but of the state and its legislation as well.[137] And third, on his list of ancient authorities there are some surprising absentees. Orpheus is not mentioned among the early Greek sages[138] nor is Proclus among the neoplatonists;[139] but most striking is the absence of Hermes and Moses. In trying to explain this omission, we get to the heart of the matter: the relation between paganism and Christianity in Plethon's version of the ancient wisdom narrative.

Plethon's genealogy is a deliberate alternative to the Christian apologetic literature since Justin Martyr, according to which the Greeks were dependent upon Moses.[140] Brigitte Tambrun has made a plausible case that the first chapters of his *Nomoi* are modeled after the Prologue of Justin's *Dialogue with Tryphon*, and that, in writing them, Plethon took inspiration from the satirical writings of Lucian of Samosata, with which he was familiar.[141] With the experience of the Council fresh in his mind,

---

[135] Plethon, *Nomoi* 1.2 (Brague ed., 31–33); and see discussion in Tambrun, *Pléthon*, 85–89.

[136] Webb, "*Nomoi*," 215–216 and n. 16. One negative characteristic of "sophists" is that they are forever in search of the new, whereas Plethon declares that he has invented nothing (*ibid.*, 216). Of course this line of thought is typical of the late antique discourse of ancient wisdom.

[137] Webb, "*Nomoi*," 219.

[138] Orpheus is absent, along with Homer, undoubtedly because Plethon had just emphasized that poets are unreliable as guides to wisdom (*Nomoi* 1.2 [Brague ed., 29]). See Tambrun-Krasker, Μαγικά λογια, 46; Tambrun, "Marsile Ficin et le 'Commentaire'," 23–24; Tambrun, *Pléthon*, 89.

[139] Scholarios had noted this absence, and his explanation is probably close to the truth: "Proclus, whom you have used most of all, you mention not a single time, probably in order not to have to share the glory of your inventions with him" (Letter to the Exarch Joseph, see Tambrun, *Pléthon*, 89). In other words, Plethon was so dependent on Proclus that he preferred not to call attention to his influence.

[140] For a discussion of Plethon's systematic inversion of the perspective of the patristic apologists, see Tambrun, *Pléthon*, 72–80.

[141] Tambrun, *Pléthon*, 60–63.

the supremacy of Greek tradition had to be reaffirmed; but the origins of true philosophy were traced back not to Moses but to a rival legislator, Zoroaster. The polemical intention cannot possibly be overlooked: in clear contradiction of the entire tradition of patristic apologetics, Plethon was trying to replace the religion grounded in Mosaic Law by a different one grounded in Zoroaster's ancient philosophy of fire and light.[142] In doing so, he was essentially adopting Celsus' strategy of excluding Moses from the genealogy of wisdom.[143] That he also ignored Hermes is slightly more puzzling, but may be explained by a combination of factors: a traditional Greek disrespect for the ancient Egyptians,[144] the fact that Hermes was also known as a legislator and might therefore weaken the claim Plethon was making for Zoroaster,[145] and, most importantly, the fact that Hermes could always be presented as having learned his wisdom from the Egyptian Moses, which would weaken the strength of Plethon's argument by reintroducing the patristic alternative through the back door.[146]

Plethon, defending a universal and perennial tradition of ancient wisdom grounded in the religion of Zoroaster and the *Magi*, was breaking so deliberately with the patristic apologetic tradition that the conclusion cannot be avoided: what he had in mind was nothing less than a revival of paganism in deliberate opposition to Christianity. A typical manifestation of Platonic Orientalism, it was to replace the exclusive monotheism linked to the name of Moses by an inclusive or qualitative monotheism along the lines of Celsus and Proclus.[147] If we give credence to the testimony of George of Trebizond, Plethon believed that his philosophy was destined to replace Christianity and Islam as the religion of the future. In George's words:

I myself heard him at Florence . . . asserting that in a few more years the whole world would accept one and the same religion with one mind, one intelligence, one

---

[142] Tambrun-Krasker, Μαγικά λογια, 46; Tambrun, "Marsile Ficin et le 'Commentaire'," 22–23; Tambrun, *Pléthon*, 53–104.

[143] Tambrun, *Pléthon*, 80–81.

[144] As argued by Dannenfeldt, "Pseudo-Zoroastrian Oracles," 10–11, who points to Plethon's dismissal of Menes' legislation as incomplete and inferior, and to his insistence in the *Nomoi* that the Egyptian priests were much later than Zoroaster in discovering doctrines comparable to his.

[145] Tambrun, "Marsile Ficin et le 'Commentaire'," 24, with reference to Cyril of Alexandria's *Against Julian*.

[146] Cf. Tambrun, *Pléthon*, 91.

[147] On the distinction between inclusive and exclusive monotheism, see n. 66: the difference is, of course, that the former has room for a hierarchy of lower deities which do not detract from the ultimate unity of the One. It seems to me that the scholarly discussion about whether Plethon was a polytheist or not (Allen, *Synoptic Art*, 2 n. 3 *contra* Masai, Woodhouse and others, to whom could now be added Tambrun, "Marsile Ficin et le 'Commentaire'," 25; Tambrun, *Pléthon*, 85) can be easily resolved along these lines.

teaching. And when I asked him "Christ's or Muhammad's?," he said, "Neither; but it will not differ much from paganism." I was so shocked by these words that I hated him ever after and feared him like a poisonous viper, and I could no longer bear to see or hear him. I heard, too, from a number of Greeks who escaped here from the Peloponnese that he openly said before he died . . . that not many years after his death Muhammad and Christ would collapse and the true truth would shine through every region of the globe.[148]

Concerning the fact that Plethon was indeed a "neo-pagan" opponent of Christianity (although he obviously had to conceal this, since preaching his views openly would have been a capital offense in Byzantium) there is near-universal agreement among specialists.[149] In view of the overall argument made in this chapter, it is important to emphasize how unique and exceptional this was: the historiographical cliché of a "Pagan Renaissance" is certainly misleading in its suggestion that the platonic and hermetic revival of the later fifteenth century involved a conscious rejection of Christianity on the part of its major representatives.[150] On the contrary, we will see that Renaissance platonism was a deeply Christian phenomenon; and if Plethon was certainly the crucial pioneer of Platonic Orientalism in the fifteenth century, he seems to have remained virtually alone in his radical turn away from Christianity.[151]

Nevertheless, one might say that with Plethon, the pagan cat was out of the bag. His case shows that once the basic textual sources of the platonic tradition became available to a Christian culture where the need for religious reform was widely felt, paganism became a religious option in theory at least. The importance of Plethon does not reside primarily in his immediate influence, which remained quite limited,[152] or even in the

---

[148] George of Trebizond, *Comparatio Platonis et Aristotelis*, fol. v63; trans. Monfasani, "Platonic Paganism," 59–60 (with a few modifications; cf. Monfasani, *George of Trebizond*, 39–40, and discussion there; and Monfasani, Review of Woodhouse, 119, with reference to Woodhouse, *George Gemistos Plethon*, 168).

[149] See, for example, Dannenfeldt, "Pseudo-Zoroastrian Oracles," 10; Woodhouse, *George Gemistos Plethon*, 78; Monfasani, "Platonic Paganism," 52; Stausberg, *Faszination Zarathushtra*, vol. I, 73–82. A notable exception is James Hankins, *Plato in the Italian Renaissance*, vol. I, 197–205; but I would agree with the refutation of his argument by Stausberg, *Faszination Zarathushtra*, vol. I, 81–82.

[150] Monfasani, "Platonic Paganism," 45–46; Godwin, *Pagan Dream*, 1–2; Edelheit, *Ficino, Pico and Savonarola*, 24 with n. 51, 206–207 n. 3 (against Edgar Wind's references to Ficino as a "neo-pagan thinker," in *Pagan Mysteries*, 68).

[151] Monfasani, "Platonic Paganism," esp. 52 and 58.

[152] In recent years, most specialists have emphasized this against earlier generations of scholarship: see Woodhouse, *George Gemistos Plethon*, ix, 156–166; Hankins, *Plato in the Italian Renaissance*, vol. I, 207–208, and esp. "Pletho's Influence" in vol. II, 436–440; Monfasani, "Platonic Paganism"; Tambrun, *Pléthon*, 16. Of particular importance is the simple fact that Plethon does not seem to have known Latin or Italian, and few of his alleged admirers would have been able to converse with him in Greek. Any conversation or teaching therefore had to take place by means of interpreters,

impact of his writings during the later fifteenth century, to which we will return. His true significance lies in the domain of cultural mnemonics,[153] that is to say, in his symbolic status as the "second Plato" from the East whose memory was eminently suited for being romanticized or demonized, depending on one's perspective. The idealizing perspective is evident for example in the passage quoted above from Charitonymos Hermonymos[154] and in the famous image, conjured up by Ficino, of the young Cosimo de' Medici conceiving the idea of a "Platonic Academy" while sitting at Plethon's feet. As recently as 1986, in the opening passages of his monograph, Woodhouse referred to this as the "legend" of Plethon, which still dominated the philosopher's memory among historians of the late Byzantine Empire and the early Renaissance.[155] Among many examples of the romanticized Plethon in modern scholarship, a perfect example is that of Will-Erich Peuckert in his *Pansophie* of 1936:

[the Italian humanists] had heard of Plato as of a land that is magical. The name had fascinated the spirits of the young new age, and created the highest expectations. And now, here is somebody who knows him, who knows everything, and whose age – he is almost ninety years old – glows upon him like ripening wine [*dessen Alter... an ihm erglüht wie greisender Wein*]. After having sown his seed, he returned back to Misithra. But what remained was his idea ... [156]

The negative image of Plethon contributed to his notoriety as well. We already saw that in the frankly paranoid imagination of George of Trebizond, who believed in a full-blown conspiracy of platonists seeking the destruction of Christianity, Plethon was a "poisonous viper" hiding behind the mask of a venerable philosopher.[157] In a very similar vein, Scholarios described Plethon as a man who had been "dominated by Hellenic ideas" since his youth and was reading the Greek poets and philosophers not for the sake of their language but "in order to associate himself with them." As a result, he had come under the influence of demons and had fallen into the same errors as Julian the Apostate. This development had culminated in his apprenticeship with the lapsed Jew Elissaeus. Ever since, he had been trying to conceal his true ideas for opportunistic reasons, but was unable to do so in teaching his pupils.[158]

which seriously modifies the attractive picture of a Plethon freely discoursing about Plato within a circle of admiring pupils.

[153] See discussion of mnemohistory on pp. 375–376.   [154] See above, page 29.
[155] Woodhouse, *George Gemistos Plethon*, ix.   [156] Peuckert, *Pansophie*, 10–11.
[157] On George of Trebizond's megalomania and paranoid extremes, see Hankins, *Plato in the Italian Renaissance*, vol. I, 167–174.
[158] Letter to Princess Theodora Asesina, in Scholarios, *Oeuvres*, IV, 152–153; trans. Woodhouse, *George Gemistos Plethon*, 24.

Next to the idealized picture of the wise philosopher and herald of ancient truth, then, we have its counterpart: the sinister picture of the pagan subversive, a kind of secret agent of demonic forces hiding behind a mask of benevolence. As our story unfolds, we will continue to encounter both images in endless variations.

THE PLATONIC THEOLOGIAN: MARSILIO FICINO

We have seen that according to the traditional "legend of Gemistos Plethon," it was while listening to his lectures during the Council at Florence that the young Cosimo de' Medici conceived the idea of refounding Plato's Academy in his own city. About twenty years later, so the story goes, he met Marsilio Ficino, the son of his personal physician, and realized that this bright young philosopher with his obvious love for Plato could make his dream a reality. He therefore arranged for him to learn Greek, gave him a manuscript of Plato's complete dialogues,[159] and a villa in Careggi that became the center of the new Platonic Academy under Ficino's leadership. This attractive story has been repeated by nearly every scholar who has written on the revival of platonism in Renaissance Florence until 1990,[160] when it was exploded as a typical case of mnemohistorical fiction by the researches of James Hankins.[161]

---

[159] Ms. Florence, Laur. LXXX,9, copied during the time of the Council from Plethon's own original (Gentile, in Gentile *et al.*, *Marsilio Ficino*, 28–31; Gentile, "Note sui manoscritti"; Diller, "Autographs"). See summary discussion in Hankins, "Cosimo de' Medici," 157.

[160] See overview of titles in Hankins, "Cosimo de' Medici," 144 n. 1; and Hankins, "Myth of the Platonic Academy of Florence," 430–433.

[161] Hankins, "Cosimo de' Medici"; "Myth of the Platonic Academy of Florence." Hankins offers a series of arguments. We have no independent evidence that Cosimo actually met Plethon; if he did, there was a serious language barrier between them; the picture of Cosimo as a Platonist is questionable; the idea of the "Platonic Academy" rests on only two passages by Ficino himself; the Academy is never mentioned even in the correspondence between Cosimo and Ficino; and all other fifteenth-/sixteenth-century sources show a near-total absence of any allusions to it. Hankins concludes that Ficino formed the center only of a kind of "informal gymnasium" for his pupils, which, moreover, was not particularly platonic in orientation, did not stand under the patronage of the Medici, and was not located in Careggi ("Myth," 449 and 457–459). Ficino's two references to a platonic "academy" (in a letter to Cosimo of September 1462 and the preface to his Plotinus translation of 1490/1492; Latin original and English trans. in Hankins, "Cosimo de' Medici," 149–151, 159–160) should be understood as metaphorical references to Plato's writings (Hankins, "Cosimo de' Medici," 152–156; "Myth," 433–436). Hankins' two articles came shortly after the publication of Field, *Origins of the Platonic Academy*, but he did not position himself against the latter. In his "Platonic Academy of Florence," published in 2002, Field conceded many of Hankins' points but disagreed with some others, and concluded that even if there was no formal institution under Medici patronage, the term "Platonic Academy" remains appropriate for referring to Ficino's circle (*ibid.*, 376). Hankins responded with a third long article, "Invention of the Platonic Academy," which polemicizes against Field at length, and continues by tracing how

Another, no less attractive, story concerns the arrival in Florence, in 1462, of a manuscript of the *Corpus Hermeticum* attributed to Hermes Trismegistus, which had been brought from Byzantium by a monk, a certain Leonardo da Pistoia. Cosimo ordered Ficino to postpone his work on Plato and translate this document first: Hermes had been arguably the most ancient and therefore most authoritative source from which Plato had derived his wisdom, and Cosimo wanted to have a chance to read him before his death. Ficino duly finished the translation in April 1463, and it was published in 1471 as *Liber de Potestate et Sapientia Dei* or *Pimander* (with reference to C. H. I, the "Poimandres").[162] According to the extremely influential narrative of Frances A. Yates in her *Giordano Bruno and the Hermetic Tradition* (1964), to which we will return at length, this was the beginning of the "Hermetic Tradition" of the Renaissance. Yates was undoubtedly right about the crucial importance of Ficino's *Pimander* for the reception history of hermetism in the Renaissance; but rather than seeing the latter as a quasi-autonomous tradition of hermetic magic, I will suggest it is better understood as merely a dimension – albeit a very important one – of the more general history of Platonic Orientalism in the Renaissance.

Of course the fictionality of the Florentine Academy does not detract from the unquestionable importance of the platonic revival of the second half of the fifteenth century, or from Ficino's centrality to it;[163] and neither do doubts about Frances Yates' narrative diminish Ficino's crucial importance in view of the subsequent fascination with Hermes among Renaissance intellectuals. However, to properly understand and contextualize the vogue of "Plato" and "Hermes," it must be emphasized once more that from the orientalist perspective, neither of the two (not to mention other ancient sages such as Orpheus, Zoroaster or, indeed, Moses) were perceived as autonomous philosophers in their own right, who might possibly

the "myth" has developed historically after having been created by Francesco Verino in 1577 (*ibid.*, 18–35). The bottom line is that Field does not seem to consider the matter as important as Hankins does. In line with my emphasis, throughout this book, on the distinction between mnemohistory and historiography (see below, pp. 375–376), I would agree with Hankins here.

[162] For the basic story, see Kristeller, "Marsilio Ficino e Lodovico Lazzarelli," 223; it was repeated notably in Yates, *Giordano Bruno*, 12–13. Since then it has been retold so often that any attempt at listing the references would be futile. On the details of Ficino's translation and their significance for how he understood the hermetic message, see Hanegraaff, "How hermetic was Renaissance Hermetism?".

[163] The scholarly literature is immense. Here I will mention only Allen, *Platonism of Marsilio Ficino*; Allen, *Synoptic Art*; Allen, "Ficino"; Allen and Rees, *Marsilio Ficino*; Garfagnini, *Marsilio Ficino*; Gentile, Niccoli, and Viti, *Marsilio Ficino*; Hankins, *Plato in the Italian Renaissance*, 265–359; Kristeller, *Philosophy of Marsilio Ficino*; Marcel, *Marsile Ficin*.

have developed original ideas of their own. On the contrary, for a thinker like Ficino their importance resided in their status as inspired mouthpieces of the ancient, timeless and universal wisdom whose ultimate author was God. We will not grasp the nature of the ancient wisdom narrative of the Renaissance unless we clearly understand this point, which so evidently clashes with the most basic and natural assumptions shared by modern historians of philosophy.

In a very similar vein, when Ficino described how the ancient wisdom preserved in Byzantium had traveled to Florence, he was not thinking primarily of Greek manuscripts carried westward by monks and middlemen, or eighty-year-old philosophers crossing the Mediterranean by boat. In his mystical and poetic imagination, such mundane contingencies of history were merely the external manifestation of profound spiritual influences and meaningful synchronicities, all working mysteriously under the guidance of divine providence.[164] From a historian's perspective, however, we must still ask ourselves how his concept of ancient wisdom emerged and developed over time, and what were its main sources of inspiration. If we begin with Plethon, we find that apart from his symbolic significance as the "Wise Man from the East," his writings did exert a limited but specific influence on Ficino's thinking. Ficino owned and annotated at least one of Plethon's own manuscripts, which contained several of his own writings along with fragments from other authors, including Eusebius, Julian and Synesius;[165] and the influence of the *Chaldaean Oracles* and Plethon's commentary can be traced particularly in his *Platonic Theology*.[166] Whether he had any familiarity with Plethon's *Nomoi* remains somewhat unclear.[167]

Ficino's concern with ancient wisdom went through several phases. His youthful enthusiasm for the platonic philosophy, at a time when he did not yet read Greek, was based upon Latin authors such as notably Augustine, Macrobius, Calcidius, and Apuleius, who looked at Plato through

---

[164] See the two letters mentioning the Platonic "Academy" (above, n. 161) with Hankins' commentary ("Cosimo de' Medici," 149–152): they are full of references to synchronistic correspondences between the moments of Ficino singing Orpheus' "Hymn to the Cosmos" and the writing and delivery of Cosimo's letter; minds in higher mental states influencing and "impregnating" others "in some unknown way," both during life and after death; and meaningful patterns of relation between various specific moments in time.

[165] Ms. Florence, Riccardianus graecus 76 (Gentile and Gilly, *Marsilio Ficino*, 90–91; Tambrun, "Marsile Ficin et le 'Commentaire'," 14–15).

[166] Klutstein, "Marsile Ficin et les 'Oracles Chaldaïques'," 331–338; and especially Tambrun, "Marsile Ficin et le 'Commentaire'." A Latin translation of the *Chaldaean Oracles* long attributed to Ficino, *Magica (id est philosophica) dicta magorum ex Zoroastre* (Ms. Florence, Laurent. XXXVI, 35), turns out not to be by him (see Klutstein, "Marsile Ficin," 332, with reference to her *Ficino et la théologie ancienne*).

[167] Tambrun, "Marsile Ficin et le 'Commentaire'," 15.

middle- and neoplatonic lenses and presented him as a religious philosopher. He began to read Plato himself in the early translations by Bruni and probably Decembrio.[168] Already at this early stage, around the mid-1450s, he was full of enthusiasm about the wisdom of the "ancient sages,"[169] and his attraction to pagan thinkers seems to have alarmed some of his mentors. Lorenzo Pisano's dialogues, based upon real discussions that took place in his circle in Florence, describe some dramatic confrontations between elderly conservative clerics and rebellious youths entranced with poetry and paganism, prominent among whom was Ficino. These young men were defending the beauties and virtues of Plato and pagan poetry, but were frequently exhorted to rather follow the "pure and sincere wisdom of the Church Fathers" and turn away from the degenerate pagan philosophy, particularly Plato, "a pagan alien from God and from the gifts of Christ."[170] In a telling dialogue by Antonio degli Agli, the author warns Ficino against the vanity and error of pagan thought, and exhorts him to "Tarry not in turning yourself back to the knowledge of God, and leave Plato and others of his sort behind!"[171] And Bartolomeo Scala was almost certainly thinking of Ficino when, in his *De nobilioribus philosophorum sectis*, he chided platonists and other "fools who philosophize with the pagans."[172]

Having reached a more mature age, Ficino seems to have regretted his youthful extravagances. According to a credible account by Zanobi Acciaiuoli, Ficino had "very often" told him that as a young man he had indeed fallen into "pernicious heresy," but had been saved by the providential intervention of the aged archbishop of Florence, Antoninus, an opponent of humanism who had told him to read Aquinas' *Summa contra Gentiles* as an antidote against his unregulated study of Plato.[173] The most direct evidence for such a turnaround comes from Ficino himself, in a letter to Martinus Uranius:

---

[168] Hankins, *Plato in the Italian Renaissance*, vol. i, 279 (and see his reference to Ficino's no longer extant *Institutiones Platonicae disciplinae*, which seems to have been a digest of Plato's philosophy pieced together from Latin sources).

[169] Ficino, "De laudibus philosophiae" and "De laudibus Medicinae" (*Opera*, 757–760; English trans. in *Letters*, vol. iii, 18–25; see discussion in Hankins, "Development," 460–462); Ficino, "De quattuor sectis philosophorum" (Kristeller, *Supplementum Ficinianum* ii, 7–10); Ficino, "Di Dio et Anima" (*ibid.*, 128–158).

[170] Lorenzo Pisano, *De amore* and *Dialogi quinque*, discussed in Field, *Origins of the Platonic Academy*, 158–174, esp. 165 and 167; cf. Hankins, *Plato in the Italian Renaissance*, vol. i, 276. Field sees Pisano's circle as the "Prototype of the Platonic Academy" (*Origins*, 171).

[171] Antonio degli Agli, *De mystica statera*, Ms. Naples, Bibl. Naz., cod. viii F 9, 33; quoted in Field, *Origins of the Platonic Academy*, 174, who points out that even in this fictional dialogue, Ficino responds by defending his course of studies.

[172] Hankins, "Ficino's 'Spiritual Crisis'," 456 and n. 13.

[173] *Ibid.*, 455, with the Latin passage in n. 6.

I have always been reluctant to publish the literal translations I made in my youth, for my private use, of the *Argonautica* and *Hymns* of Orpheus, Homer and Proclus as well as the *Theology* of Hesiod . . . I did not want readers to think I was trying to bring back the ancient worship of the gods and demons, now for so long rightly condemned . . . Maturer years and more careful judgment, as Plato says, often condemn what frivolous youth either rashly believed, or at least (to be fair) was too ignorant to condemn. For (as Plato also remarks) it is more dangerous to imbibe noxious opinions than the worst poisons.[174]

Testimonies such as this one and the accounts of Pisano's circle hint at yet another important source of Ficino's beliefs about the ancient wisdom. Whereas Plethon had been dismissive of poetry, Ficino undoubtedly saw it as a genuine source of revelation, at least up to a point.[175] He followed Petrarch and Boccaccio in his belief that the *prisci theologi* had often been *prisci poetae* who had spoken about divine things under the guise of mythological fable. Petrarch had been explicit in his conviction that "the first theologians were the poets"[176] and Boccaccio had defended the same concept of "poetic theology," with Orpheus and Moses among its major representatives, in his highly influential *De genealogia deorum*.[177] We will return to the relation between poetic myth and the notion of "hidden wisdom."

Nothing indicates that the young Ficino was very concerned with the question of how to reconcile the primacy of the ancient wisdom with the superiority of Christianity, or with safeguarding the primacy of Moses; and indeed it is doubtful whether the question ever assumed any real importance to him at all. In the introductory *Argumentum* to his *Pimander* (1463), we find a famous genealogy of six *prisci theologi*: Mercurius (Hermes) Trismegistus, Orpheus, Aglaophemus, Pythagoras, Philolaus, and Plato.[178] Except for Hermes, the list was derived from Proclus, but Ficino begins by quoting Augustine's opinion that Trismegistus lived several generations after Moses.[179] This has often been interpreted as a position statement about Moses' anteriority with respect to Hermes,[180] but in fact, it is relativized

---

[174] Ficino, Letter to Martinus Uranius, in: *Opera*, 933; trans. according to Hankins, "Ficino's 'Spiritual Crisis'," 456–457.

[175] See, for example, Allen, *Synoptic Art*, 25; but see how in his letter to Pannonius (see text, below), Ficino sets up Plotinus' philosophy as superior to the "impious" imagery of the poets.

[176] Petrarch, *Epistolae rerum familiarum* x.4, in: *Lettres familières*, vol. III, 280; Petrarch, *Invective contra medicum*, Bk. 3, 71–92, see Latin original and English trans. in Trinkaus, *In Our Image and Likeness*, vol. II, 692 and 864 n. 19, and see Trinkaus' general discussion on pp. 689–697.

[177] Trinkaus, *In Our Image and Likeness*, vol. II, 693–697 (with a series of long quotations and their Latin originals); and cf. the first chapter, "Poetic Theology," in Wind, *Pagan Mysteries*, 17–25.

[178] Ficino, "Argumentum" (*Opera*, 1836).

[179] Proclus, *Theologia Platonica* I.5; Augustine, *De Civitate Dei* 18.39.

[180] Also by the present author: Hanegraaff, "Tradition," 1127.

immediately by Ficino himself: he notes that this is Augustine's opinion ("Hoc autem de illo scribit Augustinus"), and continues by offering the alternative views of Cicero and Lactantius, according to whom there were no fewer than five "Mercuries," the fifth of whom was Trismegistus.[181] Ficino merely mentions these opinions, does not take a position himself, and never returns to the question of historical primacy. Therefore even if he did mean to endorse Augustine's position, one can hardly say that he paid much attention to the matter.[182] In any case, one year later the question was settled once and for all, in favor of neither Hermes nor Moses: in 1464,[183] and henceforth until the end of his life, Ficino decided to give preference to Zoroaster as the very earliest *priscus theologus*. Inspired undoubtedly by Plethon's attribution of the *Chaldaean Oracles*, and by the biblical story of the *Magi* interpreted as Zoroastrians who had worshipped the Christ Child as "the ultimate Zoroastrian,"[184] Ficino now made the Persian sage precede not only Hermes Trismegistus, but Moses as well. In fact, associating Zoroaster with both the Chaldaeans and the Persians (and differing in that regard from Plethon, as we have seen), he suggested that Abraham himself had already taken the Zoroastrian wisdom with him when he set out from the city of Ur of the Chaldaeans in quest of the promised land.[185] Accordingly, in Ficino's *Philebus* commentary (1469) and his *Theologia Platonica* (finished in 1474), Philolaus vanished from the scene and Zoroaster was added as the very first ancient authority in the list, with Hermes second in rank.[186]

That Ficino assigned to Zoroaster the first place in his chain of wisdom is of considerable importance for understanding how the *prisca theologia* could come to be seen, during the Renaissance, as lending support to a revival of magic and occult philosophy. Since the neoplatonic theurgy of the *Chaldaean Oracles* (known as *magica logia* since Plethon) was attributed to Zoroaster, the chief of the *Magi* and the most ancient sage, nothing could

---

[181] The reference is to Cicero, *De natura deorum* III.56; and Lactantius, *Divinae Institutiones* I.6.1–3. Cf. van den Broek, "Hermes Trismegistus I," 476–477.

[182] Nevertheless, Ficino's contemporary Lodovico Lazzarelli did interpret him as adopting Augustine's position, and disagreed with it: quoting Diodorus Siculus as his authority, he argued that Hermes lived a long time before Moses (Lazzarelli, first of his "Three Prefaces," 156–157).

[183] Already in his *Epitomae in Minoem, vel de Lege* (dated to 1464 by Kristeller), Ficino placed Zoroaster as lawgiver before both Hermes Trismegistus and Moses (Stausberg, *Faszination Zarathushtra*, vol. I, 122; *contra* the usual reference to the *Philebus* Commentary of 1469 as the earliest reference, as in, for example, Hankins, "Development of Ficino's 'Ancient Theology'," 461).

[184] Allen, *Synoptic Art*, 37–40.   [185] *Ibid.*, 39.

[186] Ficino, "Commentary . . . on Plato's Philebus" chapters 17, 26, 29 (Allen ed., 180–181, 246–247, 270–273); *Theologia Platonica* 4.2.1; 6.1.7; 10.3.5; 17.1.2; 17.4.4; 17.4.11. On reasons why Ficino did not expand the list to seven, but kept to the number six, see Allen, *Synoptic Art*, 25.

be more logical than seeing the ancient wisdom and *mageia* as equivalent: an association that can be traced through countless later authors, from Pico della Mirandola to Agrippa and many others. The *prisca theologia*, in other words, became indistinguishable from a *prisca magia*. Ficino himself was too cautious to be very explicit about this implication, but it appears to have been expressed without any ambiguity by Giovanni Pico della Mirandola:

That divine philosophy of Pythagoras, which they called Magic, belonged to a great extent to the Mosaic tradition; since Pythagoras had managed to reach the Hebrews and their doctrines in Egypt, and knowledge of many of their sacred mysteries. For even the learning of Plato (as is established) comes quite near to Hebrew truth; hence many called him a genuine Moses, but speaking Greek. Zoroaster, the son of Oromasius, in practicing magic, took that to be nothing else but the cult of God and study of divinity; while engaged in this in Persia he thoroughly investigated every virtue and power of nature, in order to know those sacred and sublime secrets of the divine intellect; which subject many people called theurgy, others Cabala or magic.[187]

We will return to the kabbalah as yet another equivalent of the ancient wisdom, and to Pico's perspective generally. At this point it is important to see how easily the ancient wisdom could be transformed into a *prisca magia* by being attributed to Zoroaster, the chief of the *Magi*, as its most ancient authority.

As Ficino's ideas about the ancient wisdom developed, the degree of importance he attached to pagan sources kept worrying his contemporaries. A particularly clear testimony is a letter he received in 1484 or 1485 from his Hungarian correspondent Johannes Pannonius, who failed to understand how a revival of the non-Christian theology of the ancients could possibly "serve the cause of providence."[188] In his important response to Pannonius, Ficino summarized his mature perspective on how ancient paganism is related to the superior religion of Christianity. His argument relied on three important points: a notion of religious progress by divine education, a notion of concealment and purification, and a distinction between philosophy and religion.[189]

---

[187] Pietro Crinito, *De honesta disciplina*, as printed in Eugenio Garin's edition of Pico, *De Hominis Dignitate*, 79–81. English trans. according to Walker, *Ancient Theology*, 50 (with minor modifications). While this passage is transmitted secondhand, it fits perfectly with the strong defense of good magic in Pico's *Oratio*, where it is discussed at length, and referred to as "the perfect and highest wisdom" and "knowledge of divine things" (Pico, *Oeuvres philosophiques*, 54–61; English trans. in Pico, *On the Dignity of Man*, 26–29).

[188] Pannonius, letter to Ficino, in: Ficino, *Opera*, 871; English trans. in Allen, *Synoptic Art*, 5–6.

[189] For a much longer analysis and interpretation of Ficino's letter to Pannonius, and of his concept of ancient wisdom generally, see the extremely learned and sophisticated discussion in Allen, *Synoptic Art*, chapter 1 ("Golden Wits, Zoroaster and the Revival of Plato"), to which I am much indebted.

As regards the first point, Ficino's perspective amounted to a new formulation of the basic "educational" perspective of the *pia philosophia*, found
in the patristic apologists, Eusebius in particular. He tells Pannonius that
since the ancients lived before the birth of Christ, of course one cannot
expect them to have attained the supreme level of Christian truth. However, they were being guided by God towards the truth that would finally be
revealed in Christianity. In explaining how divine inspiration has worked
in all periods of history and among all peoples, Ficino uses his favorite
metaphors of generation, birth, nurturing, and the gradual growth to
maturity:[190]

Thus it happened that a pious philosophy was born in those days among the
Persians under Zoroaster and among the Egyptians under Mercurius, and that each
was in accord with the other. This pious philosophy was then nurtured among the
Thracians under Orpheus and Aglaophemus. It reached its early manhood among
the Greeks and Italians under Pythagoras. At length it came to maturity in Athens
under the divine Plato.[191]

However, the ancient theologians were accustomed to concealing the divine
mysteries by means of number symbolism and poetic fable. Only in a
much later period, Ficino writes, was the underlying theology unveiled
and laid bare by Plotinus, who, under divine influence, was the first to
really penetrate the secrets of the ancients. But Plotinus himself is difficult, complex and profound, and therefore Ficino himself has now been
"destined by God" to translate his writings and comment upon them.
When that work is finished, we will finally have direct access to the true
ancient philosophy in its purified form: while the poets have been recount-
ing the mysteries of piety "impiously," hiding them under mythological
images of pagan deities, and the peripatetics have been responsible for
the world-wide spread of opinions that "completely destroy all religion,"
Plotinus gives clear and unambiguous expression to true ancient philosophy. In other words: the true wisdom will be definitively divorced from
its association with pagan mythology, and will emerge as obviously superior to the "old wives' tales" of the scholastics. This is how Ficino expects
the recovery of ancient wisdom will lead to a reform of Christianity in
his own day. He points out explicitly that a "mere simple preaching of
faith" will simply not be sufficient. Unless it pleases God to intervene
directly and restore true religion by means of "the revelation of divine
miracles everywhere," the intellectuals whose influence over the Church

[190] On Ficino's preference for such metaphors, cf. Hankins, "Cosimo de' Medici," 151.
[191] Ficino, letter to Pannonius, in: *Opera*, 871–872, and translation in Allen, *Synoptic Art*, 14.

is so pervasive will need to be persuaded by authority and philosophical reasoning.[192]

As pointed out by Michael J. B. Allen, Ficino did not really conceive of his list of the six earliest sages in terms of strict historical genealogy: rather than assuming a transmission based upon direct contact between one sage and the next, he was mainly concerned with a "transmission of vision" to each of the gentile nations,[193] without worrying too much about logistics.[194] This fits very well with James Hankins' thesis that Ficino distinguished between a period of "inspiration" terminating with Plato among the gentiles and the last prophets among the Jews, and a second period of "interpretation" beginning with the birth of Christ.[195] Ficino, I would argue, did not think about the first period in historical terms at all, and this helps explain why the question of Moses' priority with regard to the gentile sages does not seem to have been of any great concern to him.[196] If Moses, the prophets, and the pagan philosophers all had been inspired by God directly, then the question of who had been first or later becomes very much a non-issue. We have seen that it had been a crucial issue for the patristic apologists and their opponents, but although Ficino inherited a body of texts that had been based upon the premise that earlier was necessarily better, that premise was no longer so binding or central for him. In discussions with his critics, the "symbolic capital" at stake was, as has been suggested above, no longer "Tradition" but "orthodoxy."[197] For this reason, if Ficino had responded by arguing that the pagan philosophers were older than Christianity (an argument that, whether accepted or not,

---

[192] *Ibid.*, 14–15. As pointed out by Allen, Ficino's reference to the possibility of direct divine intervention through miracles cannot be divorced from the popular excitement, in this period, about astrological and prophetic speculation concerning the imminent arrival of a "pastor novus," heralded by a grand conjunction of Jupiter and Saturn (*ibid.*, 24).

[193] For Ficino's concern with assigning at least one witness of truth to all the gentile cultures or peoples, see Allen, *Synoptic Art*, 25, 42 with n. 88; Hankins, "Development of Ficino's 'Ancient Theology'," 464.

[194] Allen, *Synoptic Art*, 25, 41. Allen writes that the chain was "a symbolic, not an historically, let alone chronologically, accurate genealogy," and calls it "a gentile equivalent, so to speak, of the apostolic succession." This latter comparison seems somewhat confusing, since the apostolic succession would seem to imply precisely a transmission by direct personal contact. I would suggest that Ficino's own approach was closer to the one highlighted by Henry Corbin with reference to Suhrawardī, i.e. that of the various ancient sages (and their contemporary adherents) as "members of one spiritual family" who are connected simply by virtue of their participation in the same metaphysical worldview (Corbin, *En Islam Iranien*, vol. II, 123; and cf. Walbridge, *Wisdom*, x).

[195] Hankins, *Plato in the Italian Renaissance*, vol. I, 283–284.

[196] Even in his letter on "The Harmony between Moses and Plato" (*Opera*, 866–867; English trans. in *Letters*, vol. VII, 9–12), Ficino merely repeats Numenius' famous statement about Plato being a "Moses speaking attic Greek" (see above, page 26) but makes no attempt to discuss his anteriority with respect to the pagan sages.

[197] See above, page 28.

would have made perfect sense in the early centuries), Pannonius would have been merely puzzled: he simply would not have seen the point. But he might perhaps be impressed if his opponent could demonstrate that the pagan writings prefigured Christian doctrine, if only imperfectly, and could back this up with patristic authority. In thinking about the most ancient period of wisdom, before Plato, the historical and chronological concern with genealogical transmission seems to have receded, in Ficino's mind, in favor of timeless metaphysics: if the divine truth revealed to the ancients had been absolute and immutable, and all of them had been in perfect accord about it, this rendered the "search for origins" a somewhat futile exercise. Even if Zoroaster had been the first, this did not make the rest of the *prisci theologi* "dependent" on him: they really depended on direct inspiration from God himself.

The development of ancient wisdom *after* Plato and the Hebrew prophets was a different matter entirely: about this period Ficino does seem to have thought along historical lines. In terms of Hankins' distinction between a period of "inspiration" followed by one of "interpretation" this is entirely logical. By definition, divine inspiration must be one and unbroken, and wholly reliable; but human interpretations can diverge, and they can be wrong. Hence what one might call the "pre-historical" unity of metaphysical truth gave way to a multiplicity of historical opinions, and it should be possible to trace the emergence of correct and false interpretations. In Ficino's presentation, this takes the shape of a succession of periods of "veiling" and "unveiling."[198] After the initial period of inspiration was over, the Jews and the gentiles both fell into ignorance and superstition; even most of the post-platonic academies falsified the true tradition, which survived only in the schools of Xenocrates and Ammonius Saccas, and (significantly) thanks to sibyls, priests and divinely inspired poets outside the academy.[199]

After the "catastrophic" decline of true wisdom following Plato, it was restored in superior form with the coming of Christ and codified in the theology particularly of St. Paul, St. John the Evangelist, and Dionysius the Areopagite (still considered, of course, as Paul's contemporary mentioned in Acts 17:34). However, due to some unknown "calamity in the Church,"[200]

---

[198] See Hankins, *Plato in the Italian Renaissance*, vol. 1, 284, whose account I am following here.

[199] Allen, *Synoptic Art*, 62. Generally on Ficino's portrayal of six post-Platonic academies (the Greek ones of Xenocrates, Arcesilas, and Carneades; plus the Egyptian school of Ammonius Saccas, the Roman school of Plotinus and the Lycian school of Proclus), see *ibid.*, chapter 2 ("Catastrophe, Plotinus and the Six Academies of the Moon").

[200] Ficino, letter to Pier Leoni (1491), in: *Opera*, 925 (English trans. in Allen, *Synoptic Art*, 68–69). See also Hankins, *Plato in the Italian Renaissance*, vol. 1, 284; and cf. Edelheit, *Ficino, Pico and Savonarola*, 253–256.

the books of Dionysius were "hidden away" and the true wisdom became veiled again, until it was recovered by the *platonici* (that is to say, what we would call the neoplatonists) under the influence of Christian authors:

> For the Platonists used the divine light of the Christians in order to interpret the divine Plato. Both the great Basil and Augustine maintain therefore that the Platonists had appropriated the mysteries of St. John the Evangelist. Beyond a shadow of doubt I myself have found that the principal mysteries in Numenius, Philo, Plotinus, Iamblichus, and Proclus were in fact received from St. John, St. Paul, Hierotheus and Dionysius the Areopagite. For whatever the Platonists have to say about the divine mind, about the angels, and about other theological matters that strikes one as admirable they clearly appropriated from them.[201]

On these foundations the great Church Fathers, Augustine in particular, re-established the ancient religion in its superior Christian form; but in later centuries it had evidently become "veiled" again, as the later platonists themselves went astray[202] and the peripatetic sects gained dominance in Christianity. Thanks to divine providence, however, it is now being brought to light again by the work of Marsilio Ficino.

In sum, then, Ficino presents us with a "history of religion" in which the universal wisdom goes through three successive periods of decline followed by three restorations:

Prisca theologia (Zoroaster–Plato)	Christianity			1st Rescue of Christianity through the platonists	2nd Rescue of Christianity through Ficino
	1st catastrophe: decline of Platonic Academy	2nd catastrophe: unknown "calamity in the Church"		3rd catastrophe: medieval aristotelian-ism	

It is important to emphasize how strongly this perspective differs from Plethon's agenda of restoring Hellenistic paganism as an alternative to Christianity. Ficino was undoubtedly sincere in his conviction that

---

[201] Ficino, *De Christiana religione* 22 (*Opera*, 25; English trans. according to Allen, *Synoptic Art*, 72, and cf. 70). See also discussion in Edelheit, *Ficino, Pico and Savonarola*, 230–235.

[202] See analysis in Allen, *Synoptic Art*, 80–85: prominent among the *platonici* who had used "the divine light of the Christians" to interpret Plato had been Ammonius Saccas (whom Ficino believed to be a Christian), Numenius, Amelius, and Plotinus. But Ficino was aware of the embarrassing fact that Celsus, Porphyry, Proclus, and Julian had all written against Christianity. Clearly, then, something had gone seriously wrong beginning with Plotinus' immediate successor Porphyry (*ibid.*, 84).

Christianity was the supreme manifestation of the ancient wisdom as such, and that any decline of true "platonism" therefore meant quite literally a decline of Christianity itself. In restoring the ancient wisdom one does not set up a pagan alternative; on the contrary, one rescues true Christianity from degeneration and heresy. As formulated by Michael Stausberg:

Ficino's program of a *religio* that transcends (almost!) all single religions should . . . not be confused with pluralism, syncretism, irenicism or ecumenism, for, in *De christiana religione*, Ficino uses a variety of (apologetic) arguments to prove that the true religion is only and exclusively the Christian one![203]

In his manner of reasoning, Ficino was basically following in the footsteps of the early Christian apologists and unassailable authorities like Augustine. But the context in which he was doing so was new and different, because it involved a *revival* of hitherto unknown pagan sources serving an agenda of Christian *reform*. As expressed in a famous letter to Paul of Middelburg, Ficino believed that he was living at the beginning of a "new age": after the long darkness of the Middle Ages, the Golden Age was now returning, with Florence as its center.[204] The recovery of ancient wisdom at this time and place was ordained by divine providence, and he himself was God's chosen instrument.[205]

The reformed Christianity dreamt of by Ficino did not materialize, or at least not in the way that he was hoping for: less than twenty years after his death it would be superseded by a movement of church reform that could not have been more different from his ideals. But with his translations, commentaries and original writings, Ficino did indeed succeed in laying the foundations of a new development in European religion that would prove to be of great historical importance. To call it "Renaissance platonism" is somewhat misleading, insofar as that term suggests platonic "philosophy" according to our modern understanding of the term, and a

---

[203] Stausberg, *Faszination Zarathushtra*, vol. I, 113–114. This conclusion fits with Amos Edelheit's insistence, likewise with primary reference to Ficino's *De christiana religione*, on the notion of a humanistic theology and on Ficino as a Christian theologian generally (*Ficino, Pico and Savonarola*, 2, 32–36 and *passim*; see also Lauster, "Marsilio Ficino as a Christian Thinker"; Euler, "*Pia Philosophia*," 39–97, esp. 80–92).

[204] Ficino, letter to Paul of Middelburg, in: *Opera*, 944 (English trans. in Allen, *Synoptic Art*, 12); cf. Hankins, "Popes and Humanism," 480.

[205] See the very title of Ficino's letter to Pannonius, "That divine providence has ordained that the matters of antiquity will be renewed," and its repeated references to providence: "I have been destined by God to do this work," "[i]n this age it pleases divine providence . . . to confirm religion as a genus," and even in Ficino's horoscope "it is signified that a man will renew the ancient mysteries" (and Ficino is at pains to point out that astrological fate "serves divine providence," not the other way around, and to refute determinism: "our souls are thought to be most free when they accord with the divine will").

central focus on Plato as a philosopher. Rather, Ficino stands at the origin of a non-institutional current of *religious* speculation, the development of which can be traced in European culture through the sixteenth and into the seventeenth century, and where "Plato" stands as a generic label for a much wider complex of practices and speculations largely inherited, as we know today, from the Hellenistic culture of late antiquity. We have been referring to it as Platonic Orientalism. This complex phenomenon now became the conceptual foundation of what has been called, in recent scholarship, the basic "referential corpus"[206] of Western esotericism. In the course of its development from the fifteenth to the seventeenth century, as will be seen, it came to include the various traditions of mystical and occult speculation and practice associated with the names of the "ancient sages," notably Zoroaster, Hermes, Pythagoras, and Plato. But next to these traditional bodies of spiritual, theurgical, magical, arithmological, astrological, and alchemical lore (and their complex combinations), the referential corpus came to include one more traditional current of thought, which has not been discussed so far, but was eminently suited for emphasizing the primacy of Moses among the ancient theologians. This, of course, is the kabbalah.

SECRET MOSES:
GIOVANNI PICO DELLA MIRANDOLA AND CHRISTIAN KABBALAH

In 1486, a young Italian nobleman and intellectual prodigy embarked upon a project so grandiose, or megalomaniacal, that one will search in vain for parallels either before him or since. Giovanni Pico della Mirandola (1463–1494), then twenty-three years old, was planning to invite a large group of intellectuals from all over Europe (he offered to pay their expenses), who would gather in Rome under the leadership of the pope and engage in public debate with Pico himself about a series of no fewer than 900 theses that he had written for the occasion. Public disputes of this kind were not unknown at the time, but the number of theses rarely went beyond twenty or twenty-five, and even debates of a single thesis could last for hours or even days.[207] Pico's project was of an altogether different magnitude:

The following nine hundred dialectical, moral, physical, mathematical, metaphysical, theological, magical, and kabbalistic opinions, including his own and those of the wise Chaldaeans, Arabs, Hebrews, Greeks, Egyptians, and Latins, will be disputed publicly by Giovanni Pico della Mirandola, the Count of Concord . . . The doctrines to be debated are proposed separately by nations and their heresiarchs,

---

[206] Faivre, *Access*, 6; *L'ésotérisme* (3rd edn, 2002), 8.   [207] Farmer, *Syncretism in the West*, 5–6.

but in respect to the parts of philosophy they are intermingled as in a medley, everything mixed together.[208]

Nothing like this had ever been seen before. Pico's project is like the platonic form of all philosophical debates – an imaginary dispute of universal dimensions by which all problems should be resolved once and for all – and, not surprisingly, it never materialized. After initial censorship of thirteen specific theses, Pope Innocent VIII eventually condemned all 900 of them in 1487, with special emphasis on those "renovating the errors of pagan philosophers," those "cherishing the deceits of the Jews," and those devoted to "certain arts, disguising themselves as natural philosophy" (that is to say, magic). It was the first case in history of a printed book universally banned by the Church, and almost all copies were burned.[209]

Pico's project was a supreme (and extreme) example of the ancient wisdom narrative in the Renaissance, as will be seen, but its most innovative feature was the inclusion of a great number of theses concerned with kabbalah, the secret tradition of the Jews. In both categories of the 900 theses (those formulated "according to the opinions of others" and those "according to his [Pico's] own opinion"), they were placed at the very end of the series, as the final culmination of an argument concerned with the most ancient teachers of pagan wisdom and their disciplines. In so doing, Pico became the founder of a new tradition known as Christian kabbalah, which would be taken up by numerous authors after him and developed into one of the most important currents of Western esotericism in the early modern period.[210]

Research of this phenomenon has been flourishing in recent decades,[211] with numerous specialists investigating how Christian intellectuals began studying the sources of kabbalah and other Jewish traditions[212] in an

---

[208] Pico, 900 Theses, First Preface (in: Farmer, *Syncretism in the West*, 210–211).

[209] Farmer, *Syncretism in the West*, x, 16.

[210] On earlier usages of kabbalistic arguments by converted Jews, see Scholem, "Beginnings of the Christian Kabbalah"; McGinn, "Cabalists and Christians." Pico's novelty lies not only in the fact that he was the first Christian of non-Jewish origin who used kabbalah for Christian-apologetic ends, as emphasized by Scholem, but also in the fact that his Christian kabbalah was a specific manifestation of *prisca theologia* (as correctly stated by Mallary Masters, "Renaissance Kabbalah," 140 and *passim*).

[211] The most important general studies and collective volumes, in chronological order, are Blau, *Christian Interpretation of the Cabala*; Scholem, "Beginnings of the Christian Kabbalah" (1954 orig. "Zur Geschichte der Anfänge"; the English translation is based upon the revised and expanded French version, "Considérations sur l'histoire"); Secret, *Kabbalistes Chrétiens*; Secret, *Hermétisme et Kabbale*; Dan, *Christian Kabbalah*; Kilcher, *Sprachtheorie der Kabbala*; Schmidt-Biggemann, *Christliche Kabbala*.

[212] As pointed out by Joseph Dan, numerous Talmudic and midrashic materials were misunderstood as "kabbalah" by its Christian enthusiasts, and, conversely, they were very selective in their usage

attempt to integrate these materials within their own theological and philosophical frameworks. In the wake of this research it is becoming ever more evident that the influence went both ways: the emergence of Christian kabbalah had, in turn, a significant impact on how Jewish kabbalah itself developed during the Renaissance, which makes the phenomenon highly relevant to the study of Jewish culture in early modern Europe.[213] The new wave of scholarly research in these domains has led to a new appreciation of both the significance and the complexity of Jewish–Christian relations in the early modern period, which in turn fits the emerging view of European religion as a highly pluralistic field of competing discourses.[214]

Now if one tries to reach clarity about the relation between Christian kabbalah and the Renaissance discourse of ancient wisdom, one makes an interesting discovery. For obvious reasons of linguistic competence, the bulk of research concerned with Christian kabbalah is written by scholars with a strong background in Jewish studies, who tend to perceive it primarily as a phenomenon of Jewish–Christian interaction. Probably because of this focus, they usually mention the *prisca theologia* only in passing, as a neighboring but presumably somewhat separate phenomenon concerned with pagan rather than Jewish sources. The main exception to this rule is Moshe Idel, to whose work I will return. On the other hand, scholars who write about the *prisca theologia* or *philosophia perennis* of the Renaissance tend to concentrate on the relation between Christianity and pagan sources, and rarely give much attention to Christian kabbalah.[215]

Against the background of my previous discussions, this is clearly unfortunate: Christian kabbalah must be seen as a typical, although specific, manifestation of the ancient wisdom narrative, not as a separate

of actual Jewish kabbalistic sources (Dan, "Kabbalah of Johannes Reuchlin," 62–67; "Christian Kabbalah," esp. 126–129). It is interesting to compare Dan's analysis with Idel's: whereas the former states that the Christian kabbalists minimalized the sefirotic system and mistakenly considered common midrashic methodologies (*gematria, temurah*) as specifically kabbalistic, the latter claims exactly the opposite (Idel, "Reflections on Kabbalah in Spain," 9).

[213] Idel, "Kabbalah, Platonism and *Prisca Theologia*," 208–209 and *passim*; Idel, "Jewish Kabbalah and Platonism"; Idel, "Jewish Thinkers versus Christian Kabbalah," 57–60; Ruderman, *Kabbalah, Magic, and Science*, 139–160 (at the example of Abraham ben Hananiah Yagel).

[214] See, for example, von Stuckrad, "Christian Kabbalah and Anti-Jewish Polemics"; and for the general trend of "European History of Religions," see the new *Journal of Religion in Europe* and Kippenberg, Rüpke, and von Stuckrad, *Europäische Religionsgeschichte*.

[215] The neglect may have resulted simply from the influence of Schmitt and Walker, who put the *prisca theologia* and *philosophia perennis* on the scholarly agenda (see above, nn. 7–8) and whose presentations seem to have been adopted by later scholars as "models" for what the two terms were all about. Schmitt's discussion of Pico is notable for the near-absence of any reference to Jewish kabbalah ("Perennial Philosophy," 511–513, with only a passing mention of "Hebrew mystics"). Walker, on the other hand, calls the absence of kabbalah in his book a "grave omission" resulting only from his personal inability to read Hebrew and Aramaic (*Ancient Theology*, 14).

development.[216] It is crucial to appreciate the subtle point that Pico della Mirandola, Johannes Reuchlin, and those who followed in their wake, were *not* concerned with Jewish esotericism on its own terms, but with the ancient and universal wisdom as they saw it. Simply because this wisdom was true and divine in its very nature and origin, it was "Christian" by definition, regardless of where it was found: hence, the kabbalah was not really the property of the Jews at all, but had merely been preserved by them. It followed that the Jews would surely have to convert to Christianity once the true secret of their own tradition was revealed to them.

This entire line of reasoning was adopted straight from the patristic apologists, *including* – and this is the crucial point – their insistence on Moses as the original and most ancient source of wisdom. The only difference was that whereas the Fathers had been concerned with proving the anteriority of the Mosaic Law with respect to pagan scriptures, Christian kabbalists believed they had made a sensational new discovery: Moses had received from God not only the written Law intended for all, but also a more profound teaching of secret theology reserved for the few:

> Moses on the mountain received from God not only the law, which, as written down in five books, he left to posterity, but also a more secret and true interpretation of the law. But God commanded him to publish the law indeed to the people, yet not to pass on in writing the interpretation of the law, or to make it generally known, but to reveal it himself under a great oath of silence [*magna silentii religione*] to Jesus Nave alone, who in turn should unveil it to the other high priests succeeding him.[217]

To the extent that they were in accord with this original kabbalah, and could be interpreted from that perspective, the philosophies of the pagan nations participated in the true religion. This is why kabbalistic materials play a crucial role not only in Pico's kabbalistic theses, but also in the Hermetic, Zoroastrian/Chaldaean, Magical, and Orphic ones.[218] But whereas the religions of the Persians, Egyptians or Greeks had long been superseded by the advent of Christianity and now survived only through textual remains, the kabbalah survived as a *living* tradition in Pico's own time![219] All that remained, therefore, was to enlighten its adherents about its true meaning: the Jews could now be converted to the Christian message by showing that

---

[216] This point is made only rarely in the secondary literature (see, for example, Mallary Masters, "Renaissance Kabbalah"; Toussaint, "Ficin," 69 with n. 20; Black, *Pico's Heptaplus*, 95–97).

[217] Pico, *Oratio* (*Opera Omnia* 1, 328–329). English trans. (with minor modifications): Miller ed., 29–30. On Jesus Nave, see text (below).

[218] As demonstrated in detail by Wirszubski, *Pico della Mirandola's Encounter*, 185–200.

[219] As emphasized by Idel, "Kabbalah in Italia," 120.

it had been concealed in their own tradition all along. Once they would accept Jesus Christ as the messiah, the way would be clear for all peoples to unite under the banner of the ancient and universal wisdom.

The conversion of the Jews to Christianity was, of course, a topic rife with millenarian implications. As pointed out by Steven Farmer, Pico wanted his great debate to begin on January 6, the feast of Epiphany and "symbolic date of the submission of the pagan *gentes* to Christ in the persons of the *Magi*."[220] Again, therefore, we encounter the basic motif of the "wise men from the east" confronted with the superior religion of Christ. But Pico's ambition went well beyond anything that Ficino had imagined, and had Plethon been alive, he would no doubt have been horrified: as the debate over the 900 theses would reach its culmination (with a victorious Pico, of course) not only would the pagan sages be seen as bowing down symbolically before the truth of the gospel, but the Jews would submit themselves to Christ quite literally, as it dawned on them that Jesus had been the true secret of their own ancient traditions all along.[221] Farmer suggests that although we can obviously never be sure, Pico may have seriously considered the possibility that "his Vatican debate would end with the Four Horsemen of the Apocalypse crashing through the Roman skies."[222]

This, then, was the missionary dream to which Pico devoted himself and which was taken up by Reuchlin and his successors. Clearly the project had very little to do with attitudes of religious tolerance, irenism, or an appreciation of Judaism on its own terms. On the contrary, it was thoroughly apologetic and polemic, *adversus Iudaeos, pro Christianis.*[223] Pico's own statements are clear about this point:

If they agree with us anywhere, we shall order the Hebrews to stand by the ancient traditions of their fathers; if anywhere they disagree, then drawn up in Catholic legions we shall make an attack upon them. In short, whatever we detect foreign to the truth of the Gospels we shall refute to the extent of our power, while whatever

[220] Farmer, *Syncretism in the West*, 4, 43–44.

[221] For how Pico found the name of Jesus in the Hebrew tetragrammaton, see especially his kabbalistic theses "according to his own opinion" 11>6, 11>7, 11>14, 11>15 (Farmer, *Syncretism in the West*, 522–523, 526–527) and useful short discussion in Schmidt-Biggemann, "Einleitung," 18–19. Johannes Reuchlin famously made the final step of claiming that by inserting the letter Shin into the unspeakable tetragrammaton, it could be verbalized as IHSUH, i.e. Jesus: the "wonder-working word" (*De verbo mirifico*, Bk. 3; and see Schmidt-Biggemann, "History and Prehistory of the Cabala of JHSUH").

[222] Farmer, *Syncretism in the West*, 44.

[223] Wirszubski, *Pico della Mirandola's Encounter*, 185; cf. Idel, "Jewish Thinkers versus Christian Kabbalah," 51–52 ("No dialogue with Kabbalah, no change to be expected in Christianity").

we find holy and true we shall bear off from the synagogue, as from a wrongful possessor, to ourselves, the legitimate Israelites.[224]

As already indicated, the only major scholar who has looked systematically at the relation between Christian kabbalah and the ancient wisdom narrative is Moshe Idel. In a long series of publications, but most explicitly in an article published in 2002,[225] he has proposed to distinguish between "unilinear" and "multilinear" perspectives on the origin of religious truth, and this argument is sufficiently relevant for us to briefly discuss it here. In all likelihood it was originally inspired by a passage in a classic article by D. P. Walker, where he distinguished between the "orthodox" (and patristic) idea of a transmission from Moses to the gentiles and the less orthodox alternative of "partial pre-Christian revelations other than that given to the Jews."[226] In Idel's formulation, a unilinear perspective means that there has been one single line of transmission starting with Moses, as opposed to the more radical and controversial multilinear view according to which the truth has been revealed separately to both pagan and monotheistic spiritual leaders.[227]

Idel's uni/multilinear distinction seems to make sense at first sight, but I believe its usefulness evaporates once an attempt is made to apply it. An initial problem is that there is no particular reason why unilinearity would automatically imply a Mosaic origin: it is quite possible to envision a unilinear transmission starting with a pagan sage, such as Zoroaster in the cases of Plethon and Ficino, or Hermes in the case of Lodovico Lazzarelli.[228] Furthermore, Idel claims that the unilinear theory was developed "mostly by Jewish authors" whereas Christians were "fascinated more" by the multilinear view,[229] or in other words: Christians were largely tempted by a "paganizing" perspective whereas the Jews held on more firmly to their

---

[224] Pico, *Heptaplus*, Proem to 3rd exposition (*Opera Omnia* I, 23). Trans. Carmichael, in Miller ed., 106–107.
[225] Idel, "Magical and Neoplatonic Interpretations"; "Kabbalah, Platonism and Prisca Theologia"; "Jewish Kabbalah and Platonism"; "Introduction to the Bison Book Edition," xv; "Jewish Mystical Thought"; "Reflections on Kabbalah in Spain"; "Jewish Thinkers versus Christian Kabbalah"; "Italy in Safed"; *Cabbala in Italia*; "Kabbalah in Italia."
[226] Walker, "*Prisca Theologia* in France," 210.   [227] Idel, "Prisca Theologia," 138–139.
[228] Zoroaster is the original author *if* Ficino is read in a linear fashion; but on the plausibility of a nonlinear reading, see text (above). The case of Lazzarelli proves beyond any doubt that unilinear non-Mosaic perspectives could indeed exist in the Renaissance. His *Crater Hermetis* 3.1–2 (and cf. the first of his "Three Prefaces," as in n. 182, above) could not be more explicit: Lazzarelli quotes Porphyry's statement that "The first of those who began to pass on the tradition were those who drank the clear waves of the Nile," and continues by stating about Hermes that "it was by way of him that wisdom reached the Hebrews. For Moses, who was a Hebrew born in Egypt, transferred it to the Hebrews . . ." (Hanegraaff and Bouthoorn, *Lodovico Lazzarelli*, 171–173).
[229] Idel, "Prisca Theologia," 139, 141.

monotheistic identity. However, although their perspective was supposedly dominated by multilinearity, Idel has to concede that Christians did not actually expound that theory in a very elaborate manner;[230] and I will argue below that whereas Idel interprets Pico della Mirandola as a multilinearist, he was in fact a firm believer in Mosaic origins. As for Ficino, it is only with the greatest trouble that Idel manages to force him into a multilinear mold, more or less.[231] Here the core problem, in my opinion, lies in the unquestioned assumption that *prisca theologia* implies linear genealogies at all. As I argued above, Ficino probably thought of the ancient wisdom up to Plato as "pre-historical" in a quite literal sense. It did not really matter that much to him whether the divine revelation had been received by Persians, Egyptians, Greeks or Jews, for it had always been "Christian" in essence and by definition, for the simple reason that it came from the one true God. What ultimately undermines Idel's theory, then, is its neglect of a third, nonlinear option which emphasizes the wisdom of an era in which time itself had barely begun: a notion that may sound exceedingly strange to the modern historian, but came quite naturally to metaphysicians living in a period when our brand of historical consciousness was still in its infancy.

It has been claimed that Pico's system of extreme syncretism[232] was essentially concerned with placing all philosophies in parallel, while showing no attempt at developing a "developmental history."[233] I believe this is true only up to a point. Pico's major writings in which kabbalah play a role are in fact predicated upon the common patristic thesis that, as formulated in his *Oratio* with direct reference to Eusebius, "all wisdom flowed from the barbarians to the Greeks, and from the Greeks to us,"[234] and the most ancient barbarian source in his opinion was Moses. When Pico begins discussing the various ancient wisdom traditions in his famous *Oratio* written for the opening of the debate, he does indeed begin with Moses and calls him "scarcely inferior to the fountain fullness of holy and

---

[230] *Ibid.*, 145. Cf. the similar criticism in Ruderman, *Kabbalah, Magic, and Science*, 142 with n. 13. In an article on Menasseh ben Israel, Idel interprets him as unilinear, but also quotes his statement that ancient pagan philosophers had discovered the soul's immortality "by means of natural light alone" ("Kabbalah, Platonism and Prisca Theologia," 212): a viewpoint that in his terms would clearly qualify as multilinear.

[231] Idel, "Prisca Theologia," 145–147: he first attributes a multilinear reading of Ficino to Kristeller and a unilinear one to Schmitt, then discusses (and rejects) a third "developmental" reading attributed to Hankins and adds a "double truth" approach as a fourth alternative, only to conclude at the end that "Ficino's real views" must have been unilinear.

[232] On Pico as a syncretistic thinker, see the Introductory Monograph in Farmer, *Syncretism in the West*, 1–179.

[233] Schmidt-Biggemann, "Einleitung," 9.

[234] Pico, *Oratio* (*Opera Omnia* I, 325). English trans. by Charles Glenn Wallis, in: Pico della Mirandola, *On the Dignity of Man* (Miller ed.), 23–24.

inexpressible intelligence."[235] In other words, Moses was just one degree below the divine source itself from whom he received his wisdom. Displaying a more explicit sense of temporality than Ficino, Pico therefore points to Moses as the most ancient theologian.

Having discussed the main pagan (Greek, Chaldaean, Egyptian) traditions, Pico returns to Moses in order to reveal the true secret on which they all depend. From an obscure reference in Ecclesiasticus 46:1 to a certain Jesus son of Nave (see quotation, above), described as "the successor of Moses in prophecies" who was "made great for the saving of the elect in God," Pico concludes that this person must therefore have been the first inheritor of Moses' secret wisdom, the kabbalah, who in turn passed it on to the other high priests. He then continues by stating that the ancient philosophers (Pythagoras, the Egyptian priests, Plato, and also Aristotle) faithfully maintained this custom of secrecy, as did Jesus himself. Although he does not write explicitly that the pagan sages derived their wisdom from the Mosaic tradition (or indicate who among them was the first to do so), this clearly implies that they at least participated in its lineage of succession. The secret interpretation of the Torah was called kabbalah, or *receptio*, meaning that it was passed on not by the written word but orally from man to man. Only after the Babylonian captivity, under Esdras, was it finally written down in seventy volumes, to preserve it from getting lost.

This ancient and secret Mosaic wisdom has now finally reached the Christians, who are capable of perceiving the great truth to which the Jews themselves are blind: that their most ancient and most sacred tradition is in fact Christian! Pico's formulation is famous, and must be quoted here in full:

When I had procured myself these books at no small expense and had read them through with the greatest diligence and unwearied labor, I saw in them (God is my witness) a religion not so much Mosaic as Christian. There is the mystery of the Trinity, there the incarnation of the Word, there the divinity of the Messiah; there I read the same things on original sin, on Christ's atonement for it, on the heavenly Jerusalem, on the fall of demons, on the orders of angels, on purgatory, on the punishments of hell, which we daily read in Paul and Dionysius, in Jerome and Augustine. In those matters that regard philosophy, you may really hear Pythagoras and Plato, whose doctrines are so akin to Christian faith that our Augustine gives great thanks to God that the books of the Platonists came into his hands. In short,

---

[235] Pico, *Oratio* (*Opera Omnia* I, 319). English trans.: Miller ed., 12. In my opinion, Boulnois and Tognon's commentary (Pico, *Oeuvres philosophiques*, 25–27 n. 14) misses the mark in reading the reference to "inferiority" (*paulum deminutum*) as an indication of Moses' limitations rather than of his closeness to the divine source.

there is hardly any dispute between us and the Hebrews on this wherein they cannot be disproved and refuted from the books of the Kabbalists, that there is no corner left in which they can hide.[236]

Everything indicates, then, that Pico indeed believed in a succession of wisdom that began with Moses. From the Hebrews it had somehow "flown" to other "barbarian" peoples and to the Greeks; but details such as whether the latter learned about it only by mediation of Chaldaeans or Egyptians, or directly from the Hebrews, or both, simply do not seem to interest him. His central concern is not with historical genealogies, but with the apologetic notion that Christians can find their basic doctrines back in the most ancient source of secret theology, the kabbalah, and that important traces of it have been preserved by pagan authors as well. Again, this is simply another restatement of the basic patristic perspective, only expanded now to include the new factor of kabbalah; nothing in Pico's statements (or in those attributed to him by Pietro Crinito)[237] requires us to assume a deliberate "multilinear" doctrine of independent pagan revelations, although nothing refutes it either. Such a doctrine is simply not there.

In conclusion, then, the primacy accorded to "Secret Moses" is a constant in Pico's oeuvre, but we do not find any attempt to establish a precise order of succession *after* the initial transmission from God to Moses to Jesus son of Nave and the rest of the priesthood. Pico seems concerned only with the broadest outlines of what we have been calling a Platonic Orientalist perspective, and with emphasizing the centrality of the Hebrews among them.[238] The historiographical question of how, and by what routes, divine wisdom might have been transmitted among those peoples does not seem to interest him; and even the question of possible pagan revelations next to the one given to Moses seems very much a non-issue.[239]

While it was Pico who set the stage for Christian kabbalah as a specific manifestation of the ancient wisdom narrative, later authors in that tradition of course introduced their own variations. For example, in his *De verbo*

---

[236] Pico, *Oratio* (*Opera Omnia* I, 330). English trans.: Miller ed., 32.

[237] See above, page 47 with n. 187. The same passages are quoted by Idel in his argument for a "multilinear" Pico ("Prisca Theologia," 142–143).

[238] This is further confirmed by the ordering of Pico's 900 theses, which are divided into two parts, both running in counter-chronological order culminating in the most ancient sources of wisdom: Pythagoras, the Chaldaeans, Hermes Trismegistus, and the Kabbalists in the first part, and Pythagorean mathematics and numbers, Zoroaster and the Chaldaeans, magic, the Orphic hymns, and again the kabbalah in the second.

[239] For example, at the beginning of the *Heptaplus* he gives the commonplace reference to Moses having been "learned in all the lore of the Egyptians," but ignores the obvious question of whether this implies a dependence of Moses on Egyptian wisdom, or what this implies for the nature or special status of the kabbalah he received on the mountain.

mirifico (1494) Johannes Reuchlin shows a bit more interest in the traditional accounts of ancient Greek philosophers (Thales, Pythagoras, Plato) traveling to the countries of the barbarians. But as with Pico, his point is to emphasize the superiority and primacy of the Mosaic revelation:[240] who could doubt, he writes, that thinkers who had traveled all the way to Egypt driven by their ardent desire for the truth would not have visited Judaea as well, so that "after having tasted from the streams, they might drink from the fountain as well"?[241] But while he is clearly concerned with placing Moses first in a line of temporal succession, he also suggests that because these earliest phases of human history are so close to the divine origin, they somehow partake of eternity as much as of temporality: "The ancient approaches the primordial, the primordial borders on the eternal, and the eternal is close to God, who rules over eternity."[242] In other words, somewhat similar to what we found in Ficino's "period of inspiration," moving backwards to the very divine origin one gradually leaves time and history behind: according to a paradoxical logic reminiscent of Cusanus, if the eternal comes "first" and time comes "second," the search for the ultimate origin can be successful only if it will never end . . .

Interestingly, in his much later *De arte cabalistica* (1517), Reuchlin departed from the Mosaic lineage and traced the origins of kabbalah further back than ever, although remaining within the confines of biblical revelation: it was now Adam himself who had first received some form of kabbalah after the Fall, as an essentially messianic doctrine by which man would be restored to his original state of felicity (the reference being, of course, to Jesus).[243] From there it was handed on from generation to generation, and although it was certainly passed on by Moses, Reuchlin puts remarkably little emphasis on the latter's role.[244] As for his central Greek author, Pythagoras, Reuchlin was quite vague about where, how and from whom he learned his wisdom, except for the insistence that they were all

---

[240] Reuchlin, *De verbo mirifico*, Bk. 2 (Ehlers *et al.* ed., 164–167). Reuchlin continues by discussing the younger origins of the Greeks (*ibid.*, 166–169) and, with even more emphasis, the Egyptians (*ibid.*, 169–173), who are treated quite negatively throughout this work. Among the pagans, Zoroaster is considered the most ancient authority (*ibid.*, 162–163, 174–175). The Brahmans and Druids are even younger than the Greeks (*ibid.*, 176–177). When Reuchlin finally reveals the nature of the "wonder-working word" (the tetragrammaton verbalized so as to produce the name of Jesus), this ultimate kabbalistic secret is set in the sharpest opposition to pagan superstitions and sorceries of all kinds (*ibid.*, 380–381, 386–389).

[241] Reuchlin, *De verbo mirifico*, Bk. 1 (Ehlers *et al.* ed., 104–105).

[242] Reuchlin, *De verbo mirifico*, Bk. 2 (Ehlers *et al.* ed., 162–163).

[243] Reuchlin, *De arte cabalistica*, Bk. 1 (Goodman ed., 72–73).

[244] See Reuchlin's discussion of biblical history from Adam to Moses, *De arte cabalistica*, Bk. 1 (Goodman ed., 73–81).

barbarians: he "got it partly from the Egyptians, partly from the Hebrews and Chaldaeans, partly from the deeply learned Persian Magi,"[245] but in any case not from the Greeks or Romans.[246] In other words, the orientalist perspective remains strongly in evidence; but Christian kabbalah had by now mutated into a *prisca theologia* derived neither from pagan nor from Mosaic wisdom, but from Adam himself.

We do not need to trace these and other mutations in any further detail here, fascinating though they are. Our main point so far has been to establish that Christian kabbalah, although a new phenomenon, emerged as a specific manifestation of the more general Renaissance narrative of ancient wisdom. Once it existed, however, and as Christians began to delve more deeply into Jewish kabbalistic literature, they found that they had entered a strange new world: one based upon exegetical techniques and general modes of thinking that had no parallel in any type of religious speculation familiar to them. As Chaim Wirszubski remarks in his classic study, Pico set out to prove the Christian truth by means of Jewish kabbalah, but "as thesis after thesis yields up its secrets, a remarkable thing emerges: Pico's [kabbalistic theses] evidently outgrew their original purpose."[247] The same can be said about Christian kabbalah as a whole. In the attempt to apply midrashic techniques such as *gematria*, *temurah* and *notarikon*, which had formerly been restricted to Jewish circles, within a broader symbolic framework based upon new concepts such as the ten *sefirot* and the many divine names, unheard-of new possibilities seemed to open up for scriptural exegesis and metaphysical speculation. Not only did the biblical text reveal hidden levels of meaning never suspected before, but the correspondences that could be established with pagan mythology and philosophy seemed simply stupefying. It began to look as if all domains of knowledge were linked together by a web of secret, hidden, invisible connections, and Pico seemed to have discovered the hermeneutical key that could make them visible.[248]

---

[245] Reuchlin, *De arte cabalistica*, Bk. 2 (Goodman ed., 212–213, cf. 128–129).

[246] Reuchlin, *De arte cabalistica*, Bk. 2 (Goodman ed., 128–129).

[247] Wirszubski, *Pico della Mirandola's Encounter*, 186.

[248] Still, how careful one must be in suspecting profound kabbalistic secrets in Pico's riddles might be demonstrated by the example of the first thesis quoted by Wirszubski to illustrate his statement quoted in the text. Seventeenth kabbalistic thesis "according to his own opinion" (Farmer, *Syncretism*, 526–527): "Whoever knows what the purest wine is among the kabbalists, understands why David says *I will be made drunk by the abundance of your dwelling*, and what drunkenness the ancient seer Musaeus says is happiness, and what so many Bacchae mean in Orpheus." The thesis might suggest deep kabbalistic correspondences between David and the ancient Greeks, but the mystery evaporates once it is discovered that everything except the reference to the purest wine is taken simply from a passage in Ficino's commentary on the *Republic* (*Opera*, 1399).

This discovery of hidden, or "occult," correspondences and the means to decipher them is best understood against a background that was already briefly mentioned above, with reference to Petrarch and Boccaccio: the idea that the *prisci theologi* had often been *prisci poetae* who had spoken about divine things under the guise of mythological fable. This assumption made it possible for pagan mythology to play a serious role in Christian theology, since it meant that beneath the external surface of stories about the gods, one could discover their hidden secret: the ancient wisdom concordant with Christian truth.[249] Pico at one time even planned to write a book entitled *Poetica Theologia*:

> It was the opinion of the ancient theologians that divine subjects and the secret Mysteries must not be rashly divulged . . . the Egyptians had sculpted sphinxes in all their temples, for no other reason than to indicate that divine things, even when they are committed to writing, must be covered with enigmatic veils and poetic dissimulation . . . How that was done . . . by Latin and Greek poets we shall explain in the book of our Poetic Theology.[250]

In other words: "ancient wisdom" equaled "hidden wisdom." It may well be argued that the notions of secrecy and concealment are inherent in the very structure of the Renaissance narrative of ancient wisdom,[251] for the simple reason that, in one way or another, its Christian adherents always needed to make the argument that beneath the surface crust of pagan religion there lay a hidden core of Christian truth.

Pico's fascination with secrecy and concealment, however, went far beyond anything found in Ficino, and would become crucial for the subsequent development of the discourse on ancient wisdom. Pico seems to have enjoyed obscurity for its own sake, and reveled in the pleasure of mystifying his audience: for example, writing to a friend about his first essay in the philosophy of myths, he boasts that it is "filled with many mysteries from the secret philosophy of the ancients," and written in such exotic language that it would be "intelligible only to a few."[252] In all his main writings, he kept emphasizing secrecy as a fundamental dimension of

---

[249] The classic discussion of this topic is Trinkaus, *In our Image and Likeness*, vol. II, 689–697.

[250] Pico, *Commento*, Libro Terzo, Cap. XI, Stanza Nona (Garin ed., 581). Note that in the printed edition of 1519 (used by De Angelis in his 1994 edition, see his page 133), the mention of "poetic dissimulation" had vanished and "Poetic Theology" had become "Poetic Philosophy." See also, for example, Pico, *Oratio* (*Opera Omnia* I, 331): "Orpheus covered the mysteries of his doctrines with the wrappings of fables, and disguised them with a poetic garment."

[251] Thus Walker, "*Prisca Theologia* in France": "The whole structure of the *prisca theologia* rests on the belief that ancient theologians wrote with deliberate obscurity, veiling the truth, and, correlatively, that religious texts should be interpreted allegorically."

[252] Pico to Baldus Perusinus, in: Dorez, "Lettres inédites," 357–358.

the ancient wisdom,[253] while cultivating a deliberate practice of speaking in riddles so that his words might be "published and yet not published" (*editos esse et non editos*).[254] Although it could easily be defended with reference to Pythagoreanism and other traditions of Greek antiquity, the concept of ancient wisdom as "hidden wisdom" was raised to a new level of prominence due to Pico's introduction of kabbalah; and the resulting combination was made even more potent by the addition of yet another ingredient pioneered by Pico, that of the symbolism of numbers.[255] The dialectics of concealment and revelation are central to Jewish kabbalah,[256] and were obviously highlighted even more because of Pico's emphasis on its status as the secret revelation to Moses:

> To disclose to the people the more secret mysteries, things hidden under the bark of the law and the rough covering of words, the secrets of the highest divinity, what would that have been other than to give what is holy to dogs and to cast pearls among swine? Consequently it was not human prudence but a divine command to keep these things secret from the people, and to communicate them only to the perfect.[257]

Kabbalistic truth was not kept hidden merely for elitist reasons, but also because its mysteries resisted verbalization: too subtle and refined to be caught in the either/or categories of discursive logic, kabbalistic truth required a paradoxical language in which any statement implied its own denial.[258] Pertaining to levels of reality higher up on the platonic scale of being, and therefore far more abstract than the concrete domain of the senses, supreme metaphysical verities could be approximated by means of complex linguistic and numerical calculations, and intuited by the intellect or the mind, but not grasped or comprehended fully and directly. As formulated by Joseph Dan, the basic perspective implied a "rejection of

---

[253] See for example his *Oratio* (*Opera Omnia* 1, 328–329) or the opening passages in the first Proem of the *Heptaplus* (*ibid.*, 1–5). And see the general discussion in Wind, *Pagan Mysteries*, 8–11, and cf. 17–22. These influential pages remain important for our topic in spite of Wind's gratuitous disdain for Platonic Orientalism (typical of his generation, as we have seen): see, for example, page 10 about Pico's fondness for "Asiatic richness" or page 22 about the Renaissance "recrudescence of that ugly thing which has been called 'late-antique syncretism'."

[254] Referring here to Aristotle in his *Metaphysics*, in: *Oratio* (*Opera Omnia* 1, 329).

[255] On this important current, see Brach, *Simbolismo dei numeri*; "Number Symbolism"; "Mathematical Esotericism."

[256] See, for example, Idel, *Kabbalah*, 253–256; Wolfson, "Beyond the Spoken Word"; Halbertal, *Concealment and Revelation*.

[257] Pico, *Oratio* (*Opera Omnia* 1, 329).

[258] For Jewish kabbalah specifically, this point has been emphasized in particular by Elliott Wolfson: see his *Language, Eros, Being*. As for Reuchlin, one must also take into account the influence of Cusanus on his thinking (cf. Schmidt-Biggemann, "History and Prehistory").

communicative language as an expression of truth, and the claim that in the non-semantic layers of language ancient wisdom is hidden."[259] When Reuchlin defined the kabbalah as "symbolic philosophy,"[260] he meant something very similar; and an understanding of symbols as ambiguous mediators that simultaneously reveal and conceal spiritual realities has been seen as common to both the Jewish kabbalah and its Christian interpretations.[261]

The complex linguistic and scriptural hermeneutics of Jewish and Christian kabbalah have been discussed at great length elsewhere.[262] For our purposes, it is important mainly to emphasize that in the wake of Pico and Reuchlin, not only did kabbalah become an integral part of the Renaissance discourse of ancient wisdom, but this innovation resulted in a very strong emphasis on "esotericism" in the specific sense of a concern with hidden or concealed secrets and the possibility of discovering or revealing them.[263] As has been argued, such concerns were already implied by the very concept that Christian truths lay concealed under the surface of ancient pagan myths and philosophies, but could be uncovered by means of allegorical or symbolical exegesis. This potential now came to full development under the influence of a tradition, the Jewish kabbalah, which had always been esoteric to its very core.[264] It lies entirely in the line of this development that – to give only one famous example – when Heinrich Cornelius Agrippa published his great compendium of ancient wisdom in 1533, he called it *De occulta philosophia*: on hidden philosophy. His well-known dedicatory letter to Johannes Trithemius confirms that he saw his work as an attempt

---

[259] Dan, "Christian Kabbalah," 117 n. 1. Cf. Dan, "In Quest of a Historical Definition of Mysticism," 79: "Mysticism is the negation of the veracity of communicative language, and the belief in a non-communicative truth lying in a symbolical fashion deep within revealed divine language."

[260] Reuchlin, *De arte cabalistica*, Dedication to Pope Leo X (Goodman ed., 38–39). Cf. Scholem, "Stellung der Kabbala," 11, about Reuchlin's understanding of kabbalah as *receptio symbolica*.

[261] For Scholem's perspective, see Biale, *Gershom Scholem*, 89–92; and cf. the comparison between Scholem and Dan in Hanegraaff, "On the Construction," 47–54. Moshe Idel has criticized Scholem for over-emphasizing the importance of symbolic language in kabbalah at the expense of other dimensions, suggesting that he essentially "adopted Reuchlin's vision on the nature of Kabbalah as quintessentially symbolic, but formulated his vision of symbolism under the impact of Goethe and Benjamin" ("Jewish Thinkers versus Christian Kabbalah," 63–65).

[262] See, for example, Scholem, "Name Gottes und die Sprachtheorie"; Kilcher, *Sprachtheorie der Kabbala*; Wolfson, *Language, Eros, Being*; Idel, *Absorbing Perfections*.

[263] This specific understanding of "esotericism" as pertaining to secrecy and concealment is basic to Jewish kabbalah but cannot be simply transposed to "Western esotericism" (see Hanegraaff, "Esotericism").

[264] See, for example, Dan's references to the traditional terms *ba'aley sod* ("esoterics") and *torat ha-sod* ("esoteric lore") for what came to be described as Jewish "mysticism" due to the success of Scholem's great studies ("In Quest," 62 with n. 6; "Christian Kabbalah," 117 n. 1).

to revive the science of the *Magi* and other sages of antiquity,[265] and its third and final book was dominated by kabbalah. One might say, then, that this *summa* perfectly encapsulates all the main developments I have been tracing so far: the ancient wisdom of the pagan sages (seen as including magic and the other so-called "occult sciences"),[266] the kabbalah received by Moses, and the notion of a hidden philosophy grounded in Christian truth.

The increasing emphasis on secrecy and concealment within the ancient wisdom discourse of the Renaissance resulted largely from a confluence of traditional sources and authorities. The main factors mentioned so far have been the basic notion (implicit in the patristic perspective) of Christianity as the hidden core of ancient paganism; the understanding of the *prisci theologi* as *prisci poetae* hiding the truth under the guise of mythological fable; the frequent allusions in "Platonic Orientalist" authors to the need for secrecy, oral transmission from master to disciple, and initiations into mysteries reserved for the few; concepts of symbolism and allegory as alternatives to aristotelian logic and discursive language; the dialectics of concealment and revelation central to Jewish kabbalah; the very nature of the new exegetical techniques as tools for revealing hidden dimensions of the sacred texts; not to mention a personal taste for mystery-mongering in authors such as Pico. To all these factors must be added the very simple but basic one of caution: being perceived as an apologist of paganism, Judaism, or the magical arts could be dangerous. Because of its very nature, one will rarely find references to this factor in official printed sources, but it does turn up in private correspondence. To give one example: in a letter by the German humanist Mutianus Rufus to his close friend Heinrich Urban (1505), one reads these radical statements:

There is one God and one Goddess. But as there are many divinities [*numina*] there are likewise many names [*nomina*]: Jupiter, Sol, Apollo, Moses, Christus, Luna, Ceres, Proserpina, Tellus, Maria. But take care not to say that out loud. Such things must be kept hidden in silence like the mysteries of the Eleusinian goddesses.[267]

---

[265] Agrippa, *Occulta Philosophia*, Dedicatory letter to Trithemius (Perrone Compagni ed., 68), discussing the tragic fact that although magic had once been considered the "height of sublimity" by all the ancient philosophers, sages and priests, it had come to be confused with false beliefs and wicked superstitious practices, until finally it was rejected and condemned by the Fathers and the Catholic Church.

[266] We will return to this notion in Chapter 3.

[267] Letter of Mutianus Rufus to Heinrich Urban (1505), in: Krause (ed.), *Briefwechsel des Mutianus Rufus*, 28.

Reading such a passage, one realizes that the Pandora's box of paganism was now wide open. It is not hard to imagine how orthodox readers would react to seeing Moses, Maria and even Christ presented as *numina* on a par with Jupiter, Apollo, or the goddess of the moon. Mutianus Rufus' evident awareness that such ideas must be kept hidden leads us to the basic question of how the ancient wisdom narrative was related to religious orthodoxy. Initially the answer might seem clear: Gemistos Plethon had been accused of being a pagan subversive, Ficino's love for the ancient sages worried his friends, Pico's theses were condemned by the pope, and Agrippa's writings on magic caused him to be perceived (very unfairly) as a black magician in league with the devil. The list could easily be expanded. Do we then have to conclude that, in spite of its patristic foundations, the ancient wisdom narrative was perceived as heretical and alien to the doctrines of the Church? Before drawing such conclusions, let us consult the librarian of the Vatican.

THE UNIVERSAL CATHOLIC: AGOSTINO STEUCO

Since the last decades of the fifteenth century, starting from Italy but spreading toward other countries such as France and Germany, the ancient wisdom narrative came to dominate the assumptions of what might be called the "esoteric clerisy" of early modern Europe.[268] In the wake of Ficino and Pico, it deeply informed the thinking of greater or lesser authors such as Lodovico Lazzarelli, Symphorien Champier, Jacques Lefèvre d'Etaples, François Foix de Candale, Francesco Giorgio da Veneto, Johannes Reuchlin, Guillaume Postel, Cornelius Agrippa, Francesco Patrizi, Giordano Bruno, Ralph Cudworth, and many others.[269] I have been arguing that this ancient wisdom narrative, grounded in Platonic Orientalism and patristic apologetics, is the conceptual foundation of the initial "referential corpus" of Western esotericism[270] to which later generations have kept referring to the present day. However, although all these influential authors believed

---

[268] The term "clerisy," introduced by Peter Burke in 2000 (*Social History of Knowledge*, 18–31), refers to circles of "knowledge specialists" in various periods and societies.

[269] For introductions to all these authors and their work, see the entries devoted to them in Hanegraaff, *Dictionary*. For a pioneering overview of Platonic Orientalism in the Renaissance, which seems to have been forgotten by later scholars in the wake of Frances Yates, see Dannenfeldt, "Renaissance."

[270] This initial referential corpus was grounded in a platonic paradigm and dominated by a highly erudite Roman Catholic discourse. In its later development, particularly under the influence of Paracelsianism, the corpus was greatly expanded with texts reflective of an alchemical rather than a platonic paradigm, grounded in direct personal experience rather than erudite references to traditional authorities, and hence congenial more to Protestant than to Roman Catholic sensibilities. For this development, see below, pp. 192–195.

profoundly in a primordial tradition of ancient wisdom, it does not seem to have occurred to any of them to publish a book specifically devoted to it. The credits for having made such an attempt must go to Agostino Steuco (1497/1498–1548), who with his *De perenni philosophia* of 1540 published the standard treatment of the subject.[271]

Steuco was a cleric with excellent personal connections to Pope Paul III, and spent his entire life in service to the Church. He was born in Gubbio in 1497 or 1498 and entered the Augustinian convent around the age of fourteen. During his studies at the University of Bologna he showed great proficiency in languages, and in Venice in 1525 he was put in charge of the library of Cardinal Domenico Grimani: one of the most important book collections of his time, including many valuable manuscripts previously owned by Pico della Mirandola. Steuco worked as a prior in Reggio and Gubbio from 1533 on, and in 1538 received the honorable invitation to take charge of the Vatican library: "the most prominent scholarly post open to a humanist."[272] Somehow he managed to combine this with a parallel appointment as Bishop of Chissamo in Crete. Steuco worked for ten years as librarian of the Vatican, and was involved in the Council of Trent from 1546 until his death two years later.

Interestingly, it would seem that, in his youth, Steuco rejected the new platonic and kabbalistic philosophies: among his early writings that have not been preserved, there were titles such as *Liber contra theologiam platonicorum* and *Liber contra cabalistas* or *Contra cabalisticas superstitiones*.[273] In his mature work, however, he developed a concept of *philosophia perennis* that may be characterized as both extreme in its universalism *and* orthodox in its relative distance with respect to kabbalistic and magical-symbolical methods of interpretation.[274] This combination might seem somewhat peculiar at first sight, but is in fact quite logical for a Catholic professional like Steuco in the early decades of the sixteenth century. As already suggested,[275] he was defending a deeply conservative *philosophia perennis* perspective, not the potentially revolutionary doctrine of a revival of the

[271] On Steuco, see (in chronological order) Willmann, *Geschichte des Idealismus* III, 128–132; Ebert, "Augustinus Steuchus"; Freudenberger, *Augustinus Steuchus*; Schmitt, "Perennial Philosophy," 515–524; Di Napoli, "Il concetto di 'Philosophia Perennis'"; Schmitt, "*Prisca Theologia* e *Philosophia Perennis*," 221–224; Crociata, *Umanesimo e theologia*; Malusa, "Renaissance Antecedents," 19–22; Muccillo, *Platonismo, Ermetismo e "Prisca Theologia"*, 1–72; Muccillo, "La 'prisca theologia'"; Stausberg, *Faszination Zarathushtra*, vol. 1, 262–290.

[272] D'Amico, *Renaissance Humanism in Papal Rome*, 35.

[273] Di Napoli, "Il concetto di 'Philosophia Perennis',," 245; and Freudenberger, *Augustinus Steuchus*, 393. On the development of Steuco's view of kabbalah, see *ibid.*, 182, 201–202.

[274] Malusa, "Renaissance Antecedents," 21.   [275] See above, page 9.

prisca theologia;[276] and this might help explain why Ficino and Pico are only seldom mentioned by name, in contrast to numerous references to ancient sources.[277] The essence of his perspective has been well formulated by Maria Muccillo:

> Steuco proposes his "perennial philosophy," deeply permeated by platonism, in 1540, on the eve of the Council of Trent: at a moment when, after the Protestant Reformation, the chance of restoring the unity of the Christian world would seem to be exhausted, and the very ideal – dear to many exponents of the so-called "Catholic Reform" – of a close interpenetration of the Humanist and the Catholic spirit is beginning to decline. In this historical/religious context, Steuco's work comes to assume the significance of a desperate last attempt, effected by the means of historical erudition, of reuniting and reconciling the fragmented Christian world . . . [It] represents perhaps one of the last attempts to utilize the Humanist ideals in the interest of Catholic Reform, before the latter "will yield to the disciplinary and dogmatic force of the Counter-Reformation, which will preserve from Humanism only the splendid but henceforth empty outer form."[278]

We might conclude, then, that if the Renaissance narrative of ancient wisdom was born at a council of union between East and West, its first life cycle ended about a century later under the shadow of another council, which sought to restore and impose unity in the face of institutional fragmentation and doctrinal dissent. From the perspective of conservative intellectuals like Steuco, the crisis of Christianity could not be overcome by a return to the sources of revelation (the Bible and the apostolic community according to Protestants, the *prisca theologia* according to the new platonic theology), as though those sources had ever been lost and the Church had gone astray. On the contrary: the truth had always been available, and always would be, and the Church had been its legitimate representative since the birth of Christ. This is the point that Steuco emphasizes at the very outset of *De perenni philosophia*:

> there must always have been one wisdom, whether handed down by succession or derived by conjecture and assessments, to recall each of them and compare them with the true; [and therefore this work] has the title *Conformationes* or *On the Perennial Philosophy*. For since there is one heavenly religion, consisting in

---

[276] I am referring here to my terminological distinctions in the section "Competing Macrohistories," not necessarily to Steuco's own emic usage of the terms *philosophia perennis* (which he uses rarely) and *prisca theologia* (which is actually more frequent in his work: see Schmitt, "Perennial Philosophy," 520, 522, and see also my n. 16).

[277] Ebert, "Augustinus Steuchus," 97; Schmitt, "Perennial Philosophy," 524; Malusa, "Renaissance Antecedents," 19.

[278] Muccillo, *Platonismo, Ermetismo e "Prisca Theologia"*, 7–8 (the quotation is from D. Cantimori, *Umanesimo e religione*, 155).

excellent piety and doctrine, whoever will may understand that it has been the same ever since the human race began – either nature pointed it out, or revelation came to the rescue – formerly somewhat obscure and confined to a few, afterwards shining forth in all radiance, and blazing in the whole world. Seeing these traces, these remnants of wisdom, we believed they had been as it were the rays of a light greater in the early ages, and later most great; and thus that all things faced towards one truth.[279]

Even in a short fragment like this, we encounter a profound macrohistorical ambiguity which is typical of Steuco's thinking. Have we *progressed* "from less light to more" (from some spiritual elite among the pagans to the religion of Christ, presumably), or has there been a period of temporal *decline* in between the "greater" light of the ancient wisdom and the "most great" light of Christianity? Steuco does not tell us clearly.[280] It does not seem to matter to him whether the true religion was passed on from one generation to the next in a chain of historical succession, or discovered independently by natural reason, or revealed from above. Hence, although he does sketch the broad outlines of a development from Chaldaea and Egypt (with Zoroaster and Hermes as the most ancient sages, but Moses as the oldest *scriptor*)[281] to the Greeks and the Hebrews, his real concern is not with historical questions of primacy, dependence, influence, or "theft" of later thinkers from earlier ones.[282] All that ever matters to him is the basic point that the One Truth has always been available for those who search for it, although never more perfectly than in the Catholic Church.

[279] Steuco, *De perenni philosophia*, Bk. 1.1.

[280] Schmitt ("Perennial Philosophy," 517–518) rightly emphasizes that Steuco thinks in terms of continuity, but might be overstating his case by denying any notion of progress, which would imply that not even Christianity means any advance over the ancient wisdom. Ebert ("Augustinus Steuchus," 355) and Muccillo (*Platonismo, Ermetismo e "Prisca Theologia"*, 18) seem more correct in interpreting Steuco as suggesting a natural process of birth, decline and rebirth: philosophy was born in perfect health, then it gradually declined until the decay of old age, but it attained a hitherto never attained height of sublimity after having been reborn in Christianity. On the details of this development, see Muccillo, *Platonismo*, 17–22.

[281] Steuco, *De perenni philosophia* VII.8 (Stausberg, *Faszination Zarathushtra*, vol. I, 273; Freudenberger, *Augustinus Steuchus*, 122, 203).

[282] That the Chaldaeans (who were closest to the divine wisdom because they lived near the location of the earthly paradise: Muccillo, *Platonismo, Ermetismo e "Prisca Theologia"*, 23) and the Egyptians are presented as more ancient than the Hebrews should certainly not be understood as a polemical position taken against the patristic apologists; rather, Steuco emphasizes their theology of the universal *Logos* to such an extreme extent that questions of historical "genealogy" become largely irrelevant to him. On Zoroaster's role in *De perenni philosophia*, see Stausberg, *Faszination Zarathushtra*, vol. I, 262–290. More generally on the "Chaldaean" theology and the Egyptian and Greek (Orphic and Pythagorean) dimensions, see Muccillo, *Platonismo, Ermetismo e "Prisca Theologia"*, 22–56, 56–72 respectively. Crociata (*Umanesimo et teologia*, 234–239) has counted the references to ancient sages in Steuco's *Opera omnia*: no fewer than 214 for Hermes, 96 for Orpheus, and only 16 for Zoroaster, but Stausberg (*Faszination Zarathushtra*, vol. I, 272–273 n. 69) remarks that Crociata did not count the far more frequent references to *Chaldaei* or *Chaldaeus*.

Perhaps most important of all is to see that Steuco's basic point is not
historical but exegetical: because Roman Catholic doctrine – grounded in
the gospel – is the supreme manifestation of the perennial philosophy, it is
the exclusive model by which everything else must be measured, and the
supreme hermeneutical key that uncovers the true nature of all religion
and philosophy.[283] Steuco is not trying to learn from or about the pagans,
but rather, intends to teach them the true nature of their own philosophy.
As Freudenberger writes, with a nice touch of irony,

> The passages taken from the ancient poets and philosophers he often explains
> quite arbitrarily as confirming his own ideas, and then finds himself overwhelmed
> by the weight of his witnesses... If a passage really refuses to fit into his system,
> he earnestly addresses the author and admonishes him in a fatherly way to come
> to his senses.[284]

It follows that Christians will not discover any new truths in the pagan
sources (and hence need no new exegetical methods, whether kabbalistic
or otherwise), but merely confirmation that the divine *Logos* incarnated as
Jesus Christ has been active among all peoples from the beginning of time.
Once it is understood that whatever is true in pagan doctrine is already
present in Catholicism, but "cleansed of errors and restored to [its] rightful
place,"[285] the supreme spiritual authority of the Church can no longer be
in any doubt.

The solid orthodoxy of this position[286] makes it much easier to understand that (as will be seen in the next chapter) the Protestant anti-
apologetic authors who would attack "Platonic-Hermetic Christianity"
from the seventeenth century on did not see themselves as targeting some

---

[283] See Muccillo, *Platonismo, Ermetismo e "Prisca Theologia"*, 20, on Steuco's understanding of the
gospel as the sole and unique foundation for reconstructing, interpreting, and evaluating the ancient
wisdom. This further confirms my point in n. 282 (also emphasized by Muccillo, *Platonismo*, 71)
that Steuco is not thinking in historical but in theological terms.

[284] Freudenberger, *Augustinus Steuchus*, 122.

[285] Steuco, *De perenni philosophia*, Bk. 1.2. It would be a mistake to think that for Steuco "everyone is
right": Lutheranism he saw as a "plague" that undermined all true religion (Muccillo, *Platonismo,
Ermetismo e "Prisca Theologia"*, 15 n. 26). It is plausible to see in his attitude an echo of the
late antique and patristic abhorrence of novelty and innovation: from a Tridentine perspective,
the Protestants were "dangerous innovators" who broke with Tradition (Delumeau, *Catholicism
between Luther and Voltaire*, 9), quite similar to how the Christians had been perceived by critics
like Celsus or Porphyry.

[286] *De perenni philosophia* was dedicated to Paul III, reprinted three times during the sixteenth century,
and never placed on the Index (Schmitt, "Perennial Philosophy," 516, 525; Freudenberger, *Augustinus
Steuchus*, 123). The most important attacks on Steuco all seem to date from a considerably later
period (seventeenth–eighteenth centuries; *ibid.*, 525–530), when it had become much easier –
particularly for Protestants – to include him in the ranks of paganizing Christians.

paganizing heresy introduced by humanist erudites but, much more importantly, Roman Catholicism as such. While Steuco sought to reveal Roman
Catholic doctrine as the hidden core of paganism,[287] they reversed the
argument entirely, and sought to expose paganism as the hidden core of
Roman Catholicism. From such a perspective, the new platonic and kabbalistic philosophies in the wake of Ficino and Pico were merely an extreme
manifestation of the pagan potential that had been slumbering in Catholicism generally, ever since the times of Justin Martyr and the later patristic
apologists.

THE END OF A CYCLE

Before moving on to the anti-apologetic reaction, it is important to provide a brief evaluation of what the preceding discussion contributes to the
leading problematics of this book as a whole. I have been arguing that
the ancient wisdom narrative of the Renaissance, grounded in Platonic
Orientalism and patristic apologetics, created the conceptual foundation
of the initial "referential corpus" of Western esotericism. This means that
Western esotericism is ultimately grounded in a *historiographical* concept,
rather than in a common philosophical or religious worldview, a specific
approach to knowledge, or a "form of thought." However, because the
Renaissance narrative of ancient wisdom was itself derived from Platonic
Orientalism, the philosophical worldviews and salvational epistemologies
basic to that late antique phenomenon certainly became central to it. This
is why concepts of correspondences, living nature, imagination/mediations
(all typical of the late antique philosophies that flourished in the Platonic
Orientalist context) and perhaps even transmutation (linked more specifically to the somewhat later development of an "alchemical" paradigm,
see Chapter 3) are indeed pervasive throughout the corpus, as has been
famously emphasized by Antoine Faivre.[288] For the same reason, concepts
of "higher knowledge" or gnosis, whose centrality to the late antique currents in question is well known, were likewise bound to become highly
important within the Renaissance narrative of ancient wisdom and its later
developments. And finally, we have seen that the closely related concern
with secrecy and concealment has strong roots in the Platonic Orientalist

---

[287] As clearly shown by the very structure of *De perenni philosophia*, which is ordered not chronologically but doctrinally: the first six books are about theology (Bks. 1–2 on the Trinity; Bks. 3–6 on
the Unity of God), Bk. 7 is about the created world, Bk. 8 on the spiritual world (angels, demons),
Bk. 9 on theological anthropology, and Bk. 10 on ethics and eschatology.

[288] See discussion in Chapter 4, pp. 334–355, esp. 353–355.

matrix as well, but was given a new degree of prominence due to Pico's introduction of kabbalah and its novel exegetical techniques.

That the initial referential corpus of Western esotericism was grounded in a historiographical concept of "ancient wisdom" has far-reaching implications, as will be seen throughout the rest of this book. As I emphasized at the very beginning of this chapter, the discourse developed at a time when historical consciousness as we understand it was still in its infancy, and the enthusiasts of ancient wisdom were arguing on the basis not of critical historiography, but of unquestionable theological and metaphysical assumptions. As a result, what emerged from their studies of ancient wisdom was not a history of human opinions and their development through time, but a *history of truth*.[289] As pointed out at the beginning of this chapter, such a project is by its very nature ambiguous and, indeed, self-defeating. It is easy to conceive of a "history of error" describing the many ways in which human beings have lapsed from true religion into a variety of erroneous doctrines and heresies; but by definition, and in sharp contrast, absolute metaphysical or divine truth cannot possibly change and develop through time while still remaining absolute. In other words: the ancient wisdom narrative of the Renaissance was grounded in what must now be seen as an inherently a-historical approach to historical questions. In the period of the Renaissance this was not a conscious choice – it is only with hindsight that we now see the Italian humanists as early pioneers of the history of human thought; but we will see that since the eighteenth century, it made the narrative of ancient wisdom highly attractive for authors with deliberate *anti*-historical agendas, including not a few influential academics.

We have concentrated on how the discourse of ancient wisdom developed during roughly a century, between the Councils of Ferrara/Florence and of Trent. It was during the later sixteenth century and into the seventeenth, with the development of critical philological methods, that the truth of history began to catch up, slowly but surely, with the history of truth. The story of how this happened has often been told, most famously by Frances A. Yates in her *Giordano Bruno and the Hermetic Tradition*, which emphasizes very strongly how the entire edifice of "the Hermetic Tradition" had rested upon the erroneous dating of ancient texts and therefore had to collapse as a result of source criticism.[290] Yates believed that

---

[289] Cf. Celenza, "Revival of Platonic Philosophy," 72, 74.

[290] Yates, *Giordano Bruno*, esp. chapter 21. The point had already been made by Wind, *Pagan Mysteries*, 22; and an important later discussion is Grafton, "Protestant versus Prophet." By far the most complete discussion of all aspects of the "dating of Hermes Trismegistus," including editions and facsimiles of all the major primary sources, is Mulsow, *Ende des Hermetismus*.

it was Isaac Casaubon who exploded the myth of Hermes Trismegistus by demonstrating, in 1614, that the *Corpus Hermeticum* had not been written in very ancient times but as recently as the first centuries of the Christian era. Today we know that Casaubon's work was, rather, the culmination of a process of historical criticism that had begun already in the 1560s.[291] Eventually, critical philology proved lethal to the intellectual legitimacy not only of "the Hermetic Tradition," but of all varieties of the ancient wisdom narrative: not only the hermetic writings were robbed of their ancient origins and turned out to be from the first centuries CE, but so were the *Chaldaean Oracles*[292] and the *Orphic Hymns*.[293] Furthermore, as the history of philosophy developed into a critical discipline, scholars began to differentiate between Plato's own philosophical ideas and those developed by the various later, middle- and neoplatonic currents, including the idea of an "esoteric Plato" whose doctrines were derived from ancient oriental sources.[294]

Frances Yates was right in emphasizing that philological criticism destroyed the very foundation of the ancient wisdom narrative and rendered it intellectually untenable. However, historians of religion know that, no matter how definitive and irrefutable such scholarly arguments may be, they are seldom sufficient to destroy religious conviction. As remarked by the anthropologist of religion Evans-Pritchard, and confirmed by countless examples world-wide,

outside empirical or scientific behavior, people aim at ensuring that their notions and conduct shall be in accord with sentiments and values, and they do not worry whether their premises are scientifically valid or their inferences entirely logical; and these sentiments and values form a system of thought with a logic of its own.[295]

For the argument developed in this book, this has two consequences. One is that we should not be surprised by the fact that the ancient wisdom narrative survived the era of Casaubon and remains alive and well even up to the

---

[291] The main early critics were Gilbert Genebrard, Matthieu Beroalde, Johannes van der Gorp, Teodoro Angelucci, and Antonio Persio. See Mulsow, *Ende des Hermetismus*, particularly Purnell, "Francesco Patrizi"; Purnell, "Contribution"; Mulsow, "Reaktionärer Hermetismus"; Mulsow, "Epilog." For a summary and overview, cf. Hanegraaff, review of Mulsow. For the case of William Harrison's "Great English Chronology" (written in the 1570s), which belongs in the same series of pre-Casaubon critics but is surprisingly overlooked in the Mulsow volume, see Parry, "Puritanism, Science and Capitalism."

[292] Stausberg, *Faszination Zarathushtra*, vol. 1, 84–86.

[293] Walker, *Ancient Theology*, 22–41; Athanassakis, *Orphic Hymns*, vii–xiii.

[294] Tigerstedt, "Decline and Fall"; and specifically about the "esoteric interpretation," cf. Tigerstedt, *Interpreting Plato*, 63–91.

[295] Evans-Pritchard, *Theories of Primitive Religion*, 97. Cf. Hanegraaff, "How Magic Survived," 372–373, with reference to Luhrmann, *Persuasions*, 321, 353.

present day.[296] It managed to do so, not primarily because adherents found ways of refuting the philological argument (although some did, at least to their own satisfaction),[297] but for the reasons suggested by Evans-Pritchard: the "sentiments and values" associated with a given system of thought are usually given preference over rational considerations, and people tend to favor arguments that support their beliefs.[298] A second consequence is that the philological "destruction" of the ancient wisdom narrative should itself be understood within a wider context as well: it did not stand on its own, but was part of a much wider and more complicated series of religious narratives, which had the common feature that their basic "sentiments and values" demanded a sharp rejection of "paganism" and a criticism of its historical *liaison* with Christianity. We will turn to this in the next chapter.

---

[296] See, for example, Hanegraaff, *New Age Religion*, 302–330; Hammer, *Claiming Knowledge*, 85–200. Among an endless series of relevant titles, particularly influential has been Schuré, *Grands initiés*. Characteristic for its background in nineteenth-century theosophy, it expands the traditional Western genealogy of wisdom so as to move its earliest origins from Egypt to India, resulting in a lineage of Rama, Krishna, Hermes, Moses, Orpheus, Pythagoras, Plato, Jesus. In modern and contemporary versions of the ancient wisdom narrative, the source is frequently moved even further back, to mythical lost continents such as Atlantis, Lemuria, or Mu (Sprague de Camp, *Lost Continents*; Ramaswamy, *Lost Land of Lemuria*). As an extreme consequence of the same logic, a large branch of contemporary esoteric literature assumes that the ancient cultures had derived their wisdom from other planets, notably Sirius or the Pleiades (see, for example, Colavito, *Cult of Alien Gods*).

[297] For the important case of Ralph Cudworth's criticism of Casaubon, see Assmann, "'Hen kai pan'"; Hofmeier, "Cudworth versus Casaubon."

[298] If we replace "sentiments and values" by the equivalent formulation "moods and motivations," there is an interesting parallel in Clifford Geertz's discussion of how a given religion's symbolic system formulates conceptions of a general order of existence and clothes these "with such an aura of factuality" that the moods and motivations in question "seem uniquely realistic" (Geertz, "Religion as a Cultural System," 4 and *passim*). *Pace* the oft-quoted critique of Talil Asad ("Construction of Religion"), which makes some valid points but exaggerates their relevance while distorting Geertz's perspective, and with due attention to the function of ritual, a Geertzian analysis remains extremely fruitful for understanding the specificity of religious as opposed to rational or scientific modes of thinking (Hanegraaff, "Defining Religion in Spite of History"; Schilbrack, "Religion, Models of, and Reality").

CHAPTER 2

The history of error
Exorcizing paganism

Exorciser, c'est produire pour maudire.

Jean Baudrillard[1]

The development of the ancient wisdom narrative during the Renaissance was possible only because platonism had been an integral part of Christian theology since the first centuries. As we have seen, when the complete dialogues of Plato and a range of ancient texts attributed to his supposed predecessors – notably Zoroaster, Hermes, and Orpheus – became available in new Latin translations, the Florentine humanists and those who shared their enthusiasm could appeal to a range of Fathers of the Church in support of their claim that these pagan writers had been inspired prophets of Christian truth. The intellectual plausibility of that argument in a Roman Catholic environment explains why, in spite of its increasing association with such problematic dimensions as magic and Jewish kabbalah, the *philosophia perennis* could be presented as thoroughly orthodox even by a Vatican cleric like Agostino Steuco in the years before the Council of Trent.

But the climate was changing. A complicated series of historical developments, each with its own causes and internal dynamics, had begun to work against the vision of the Florentine humanists and, indeed, against the very notion of a platonic Christianity compatible with pagan wisdom. As formulated by Frances Yates,

as the century moved on into darker years, the orthodox opposition to Renaissance occult philosophy hardened . . . The hopes for unity had not materialised; Reformation and Catholic reaction had increased disunity. The Council of Trent intensified the lines of opposition . . . Gradually it became apparent to the Congregation of the Index that the whole of Renaissance Platonism was dangerous, particularly in its combination of Platonism and Cabala. Thus the movement of suppression gained momentum.[2]

---

[1] Baudrillard, "La part maudite," 9.
[2] Yates, *Occult Philosophy*, 61–62; and cf. Firpo, "Flowering and Withering."

The papacy of Clement VIII (1592–1605) might be seen as a culmination of that development, with the burning of Giordano Bruno in 1600 as an obviously symbolic low point. But political suppression of heretics was only one factor, although an important one; at least as significant was the fact that, particularly during the seventeenth century, the ancient wisdom narrative and its attendant disciplines began to lose intellectual credibility as their underlying assumptions were challenged by new discoveries and theoretical perspectives in the realms of philology, philosophy, and natural science. Each one of these dimensions is of great importance for the study of Western esotericism, or for understanding the complicated "process of destruction" by means of which the great Western tradition of Christian platonism gave way, between the sixteenth and the eighteenth centuries, to worldviews that we recognize as "modern."[3] We will return to them, but in this chapter I will concentrate on another dimension: that of the historiography of ideas and of theological doctrine. The overall argument of this chapter is, in a nutshell, that the field of research nowadays referred to as "Western esotericism" first began to be perceived and conceptualized as a domain in its own right by the so-called "anti-apologetic" authors of the later seventeenth century. This happened, however, as the outcome of a long tradition of anti-platonic[4] and, more generally, anti-pagan polemics which had been provoked by the platonic revival of Florentine humanism and its heirs.

AGAINST THE PAGANS

From the very moment that Platonic Orientalism made its first entrance on the stage of Italian humanism, it was accompanied by its anti-platonic shadow. We have seen how the aristotelian George of Trebizond[5] met Gemistos Plethon during the Council in Florence, and hated him ever after as a "poisonous viper" out to destroy Christianity and replace it with Hellenistic paganism. One of the major humanists of quattrocento Italy, George was also a paranoid fanatic who believed in a conspiracy of platonists preparing the coming of the Antichrist. His *Comparatio philosophorum*

---

[3] Mulsow, *Moderne aus dem Untergrund*, 261; Lehmann-Brauns, *Weisheit*, 1, 15, 27.

[4] As pointed out by Hankins ("Antiplatonism," 36–37), criticisms of Plato in the Renaissance can be reduced to three heads: his teachings were seen as unsystematic and therefore pedagogically useless, as morally deficient, and as inconsistent with Christian truth. The second and particularly the third elements are most important here.

[5] See Monfasani, *George of Trebizond*; Monfasani, *Collectanea Trapezuntiana*; Monfasani, "A Tale of Two Books"; Hankins, *Plato in the Italian Renaissance*, vol. 1, 165–192, 236–245; Matton, "Quelques figures de l'antiplatonisme," 369–387.

Platonis et Aristotelis, finished in 1458,[6] has been described as "one of the most remarkable mixtures of learning and lunacy ever penned."[7] Not only is Plato attacked there as a pitifully poor philosopher, but he is also accused of every possible error, sin, or weakness (including sexual depravity, drunkenness, idolatry, sorcery, and demon-worship) and described as the very fountainhead of all heresies.[8] To make matters even worse, not only had Plato exerted a pernicious influence on Christianity by means of his writings, but in George's apocalyptic imagination he had given birth to a whole series of successors who continued his work. Muhammad was the second Plato, Plethon the third, and George's *Comparatio* culminated in dire warnings against Cardinal Bessarion, the fourth Plato, who wanted to become pope and might very well succeed. For proper perspective, one should realize that George of Trebizond and Bessarion were both Greek converts to Roman Catholicism; but Bessarion was a former pupil of Plethon who remained faithful to his teacher, and came to the Council as a strong proponent of union. Because George saw Greek Christianity as platonic, and Roman Catholicism as aristotelian, the idea of the "fourth Plato" on the throne of St. Peter evoked the specter of a Greek/platonist takeover of the Church of Christ. Even though Trebizond's *Comparatio* circulated only in manuscript, Bessarion responded with his important *In calumniatorem Platonis*, first written in Greek, then translated into Latin, and printed in 1469. Deeply influenced by Plethon's perspective, it defended Plato's thought and argued for its profound compatibility both with Christianity and with Aristotle. It is considered the most important synthesis of Renaissance platonism prior to Ficino's. With this remarkable couple of Catholic converts (one born in Trebizond and the other from a family that came from there) the battle lines were drawn in the sharpest possible manner.

Among the sympathetic early readers of George of Trebizond's *Comparatio* were the famous Florentine prophet Savonarola and his follower Gianfrancesco Pico della Mirandola, Giovanni's nephew. With the two Picos we encounter another striking couple of close antagonists: if Giovanni was undoubtedly one of the most central authors of the ancient wisdom narrative, Gianfrancesco's *Examen vanitatis doctrinae gentium*

---

[6] Published in Venice in 1523 and available in eleven manuscripts (see Monfasani, *Collectanea Trapezuntiana*, 600–602; and see discussion of their limited circulation in Monfasani, "A Tale of Two Books," 3–4).

[7] Hankins, *Plato in the Italian Renaissance*, vol. I, 236.

[8] For good summaries of the *Comparatio*, see Hankins, *Plato in the Italian Renaissance*, 237–241; and especially Matton, "Quelques figures," 370–386.

(1520) was essentially an attempt "to destroy what his uncle had built."[9] This fact is remarkable and confusing, particularly because the relation between Giovanni and Gianfrancesco (who differed only six years in age) appears to have been close and affectionate, and Gianfrancesco always wrote about his uncle with great respect and admiration. Ultimately, however, nobody was more important to him than Savonarola, who decisively influenced his worldview and whom he kept defending even after his excommunication in 1497 and his public execution the following year. Giovanni Pico had died four years earlier, in 1494, to the great distress of his nephew, and for unclear reasons his unpublished manuscripts had fallen into the hands of Savonarola and his Dominican friars at San Marco in Florence. Here Gianfrancesco had unlimited access to them, and in 1496 he published a laudatory biography of his uncle and two volumes of his collected writings: a large although incomplete selection, which has remained the foundation of all later versions of Pico's *Opera Omnia*.

In spite of these great efforts on behalf of Giovanni Pico's legacy, everything that Gianfrancesco published under his own name goes straight against the "pagan learning" that was so essential to his uncle's program.[10] This bizarre combination cries out for explanation. From a provocative discussion by Steven Farmer,[11] there emerges a sinister scenario according to which Giovanni Pico's legacy may deliberately have been doctored and manipulated by his nephew, under the immediate influence of Savonarola and his circle at the San Marco. Farmer argues that Gianfrancesco (in collaboration with his personal physician Giovanni Mainardi, an ardent Savonarolan) tampered with his uncle's legacy to an extreme degree,

9   Schmitt, "Gianfrancesco Pico's Attitude," 312. Pico's *Examen* was written between 1502 and 1514, and published at Mirandola in 1520; it is available in Pico, *Opera Omnia*, vol. II, 710–1264. Generally on Gianfrancesco Pico and his work, see especially Schmitt, *Gianfrancesco Pico della Mirandola*; Schmitt, "Gianfrancesco Pico: Leben und Werk"; Raith, *Die Macht des Bildes* (focused on Pico's criticism of the *imaginatio*). For Gianfrancesco Pico as a historiographer, see Malusa, "Renaissance Antecedents," 38–49. For Pico's criticism of Renaissance magic, see Walker, *Spiritual and Demonic Magic*, 146–151; and for his attitude towards the ancient wisdom, see Walker, *Ancient Theology*, 33–35. On the relation between the two Picos, see Schmitt, "Gianfrancesco Pico's Attitude"; and Farmer, *Syncretism in the West*, 133–179.

10 Gianfrancesco Pico's *De studio divinae et humanae philosophiae* (1496) cautions against the reading of pagan literature, poetry, and learning in general; *De imaginatione seu Phantasia* (1501) criticizes the theory of images and imagination, central to Ficino's understanding of the "faculties of the soul" (see van den Doel, *Ficino en het voorstellingsvermogen*, 31–118); *De rerum praenotione* (1506–1507) discusses and rejects all forms of divination except the true divine prophecy represented by a person like Savonarola (see Walker, *Spiritual and Demonic Magic*, 146–151); and his *Strix* (1523) is an early example of anti-witchcraft literature (see Burke, "Witchcraft and Magic"). On Pico's *Examen vanitatis*, see text.

11 Farmer, *Syncretism in the West*, 133–179. For an important alternative reading, see Copenhaver, "Studied as an Oration."

including deliberate omissions, distortions and outright forgeries, in addition to substantial plagiarism by means of which Giovanni's defense of the gentiles was actually used to attack them in Gianfrancesco's *Examen vanitatis*. If Farmer is right – his argument is persuasive, but he is careful in pointing out the difficulties that still stand in the way of a definitive conclusion – we could be dealing with a shocking case of historical falsification, which had the result of greatly exaggerating Savonarola's impact on the later Giovanni Pico. The strongly worded rejections of *prisca theologia* that are found in his unfinished *Disputationes* against astrology would seem to suggest that in the last years of his life, he came to renounce his pagan errors and was "converted" to evangelical Christianity under Savonarola's influence: a picture wholly in Gianfrancesco's interests, as it allowed him to highlight Savonarola's beneficial influence while at the same time preserving his uncle's posthumous reputation. But the manuscript is no longer available, and those attacks on the *prisci theologi* may also be interpolations by Gianfrancesco,[12] in which case we could be dealing with a blatant attempt at "depaganizing" Giovanni Pico in the interest of posthumously turning him, as strongly as possible, into a Christian evangelical convert.

Be that as it may, the correct Christian perspective on paganism as Gianfrancesco saw it is presented most clearly in his *Examen vanitatis*: a work that deserves special attention here as the earliest example of an "anti-pagan" reaction in the Renaissance historiography of thought, and as the first in a line of publications preparing the way for the anti-apologists of the seventeenth century. Pico's work has mostly been discussed as an example of philosophical skepticism: taking his cue from Sextus Empiricus, he sets out to demonstrate the vanity and uncertainty of all philosophical reasoning and humanistic learning.[13] Like Savonarola, Gianfrancesco points to sacred scripture as the sole, exclusive and absolutely infallible source of true knowledge: the certainty given by absolute faith in the Bible, down to the smallest iota,[14] is thereby placed in sharp opposition to the uncertainty of any conclusions based upon the weak instrument of human reason. Hence

---

[12] Interestingly, Farmer suggests that modern computer techniques may make it possible to identify interpolations on the basis of the stylistic differences between Giovanni's and Gianfrancesco's Latin (*Syncretism in the West*, 172).

[13] The actual distance between ancient skepticism and Pico's perspective has, however, been emphasized in recent scholarship: see, for example, Farmer, *Syncretism in the West*, 156–157; and esp. Cao, *Scepticism and Orthodoxy*.

[14] See the opening sentences of Savonarola's treatise against astrology (*Trattato contra li astrologi* 1.1, in Savonarola, *Scritti filosofici*, vol. 1, 278): "The foundation of Christian religion is the sacred Scripture of the New and Old Testament, which we are obliged to believe to be true down to the smallest iota, and we must approve all that it approves, and disapprove of all that it disapproves of, since it is made by God, who cannot err."

the peculiar combination of skepticism and fideism, very similar to what we will find much later in the work of Cornelius Agrippa.[15] The considerable implications for the history of philosophy as a discipline have been well formulated by Luciano Malusa:

> Gianfrancesco Pico held that the aim of the historical study of philosophy was to demonstrate the conditions of human philosophical thinking when deprived of the light of revelation, or claiming independence from it. This involved going back to the past in order to discover why the errors were made and why the philosophers had become divided.[16]

In other words, the history of philosophy unaided by divine inspiration can only be conceived of as a history of error and division. Further on in his excellent analysis, Malusa emphasizes that for Pico, human philosophy was merely a "humble and totally inadequate preparation" for the study of scripture, and explains why it was precisely this fact that made it into a possible object of historical research. Since the biblical truth is absolute, it is beyond modification or historical change, that is to say, it does not develop through time – and therefore all one might do is illustrate how theologians and Church Fathers have been defending this one and universal divine revelation "against the explicit and implicit attacks of pagan philosophers."[17] In other words, Pico understood that a "history of truth" is self-contradictory. It follows that the proper domain of historiography, in contrast, must consist in describing the development of merely human and hence fallible opinions. From the perspective of absolute biblical truth, any proper history of thought is therefore necessarily a history of error. We will see that this crucial insight became the very foundation from which emerged the history of philosophy as a modern discipline.

In contrast to George of Trebizond, Pico was somewhat softer on Plato than on Aristotle;[18] and this is perhaps not surprising, because it made it easier for him to keep seeing the early Fathers as preservers of biblical revelation in spite of their platonic leanings. Nevertheless, *prisci theologi* such as Zoroaster, Hermes, or Orpheus had been looking for the truth in vain: deprived of revelation, they merely discovered attributes of divinity instead of penetrating its essence.[19] In the ancient world, only the Hebrews had been in possession of divine truth. The history of philosophy as a

---

[15] On the possible influence of Pico's *Examen* on Agrippa, see Nauert, *Agrippa and the Crisis*, 148–152; Schmitt, *Gianfrancesco Pico della Mirandola*, 239–242.

[16] Malusa, "Renaissance Antecedents," 41.

[17] *Ibid.*, 45. As Malusa puts it, in Pico's vision the study of the "true philosophy" of revealed doctrine "was not 'research into' but 'possession of' the truth."

[18] Schmitt, *Gianfrancesco Pico della Mirandola*, 62–63.

[19] For example, G. F. Pico, *Examen veritatis* I.I (*Opera Omnia*, vol. II, 723–724).

pagan tradition independent of Judaism had begun with Pythagoras, and later split up into two directions: the Ionic and the Italic schools. After Socrates, there had been a proliferation of no fewer than nine philosophical sects, all of them opposed by the skeptics, who rightly argued that none of them could claim to possess the truth.[20] All that the philosophers had done was introduce new errors, and create dissent and confusion. In polite but explicit opposition to his uncle's program of reconciliation, Gianfrancesco therefore states that the teachings of the pagan philosophers "must be demolished" and "invalidated."[21] In the last three books of his *Examen vanitatis*, Pico concentrated on criticizing Aristotle's philosophy in particular. After these lengthy polemics, his invitation to simple faith based upon the study of scripture and the sacred theologians came as a natural conclusion.[22]

It is important to realize that even authors who were generally sympathetic to the ancient wisdom might still be cautious about the dangers of magic, paganism, and heresy: as has been clearly pointed out by D. P. Walker, this was particularly true for the reception of the *prisca theologia* in France, with important authors such as Jacques Lefèvre d'Etaples, Symphorien Champier, and a series of others.[23] Moreover, and as one background reason for their attitude of caution, one should never lose sight of the fact that in the wake of the notorious *Malleus Maleficarum* of 1486 (the very year in which Pico planned his great debate), the great witch craze of the early modern period developed in perfect parallel with the ancient wisdom discourse. Given that context, it was inevitable that critics would begin to question whether the "learned magic" of the Florentines was as innocent of demonism as they claimed. The *Malleus* itself came too early to be influenced by Pico's magical theses or Ficino's astral and talismanic magic in his *De vita coelitus comparanda* (1489), but the impact of their work and its reception can be clearly seen in the important witchcraft treatise by the Dutch physician Johann Weyer (or Wier), *De praestigiis daemonum*, written in 1561–1562 and published a year later.

From age fourteen to eighteen, between 1530 and 1534/1535, Weyer was an apprentice to Cornelius Agrippa.[24] These were the final years of Agrippa's life, during which he published his two main works, *De incertitudine* and

[20] *Ibid.*, 1.2 (*Opera Omnia*, vol. II, 735–739).

[21] *Ibid.*, 1.2 and IV.2 (*Opera Omnia*, vol. II, 738 and 1026).

[22] Malusa, "Renaissance Antecedents," 45.

[23] Walker, "*Prisca Theologia* in France," 204 and *passim*; cf. Walker, *Spiritual and Demonic Magic*, 167–170.

[24] For Weyer's life and career, see George Mora's Introduction to the English translation of *De praestigiis daemonum*: Mora *et al.*, *Witches, Devils, and Doctors*, xxvii–xlv. On his main work, see Walker, *Spiritual and Demonic Magic*, 152–156; Baxter, "Johann Weyer's *De Praestigiis Daemonum*."

De occulta philosophia libri tres, so Weyer must have been well aware of how Agrippa combined his adherence to the ancient wisdom and the *artes magicae* with a "skeptical fideism" very similar to Gianfrancesco Pico's. Since Weyer's perspective was influenced both by Agrippa and by the younger Pico,[25] it is important to be precise here about the relation between those two. Agrippa emphasized the "uncertainty and vanity" of all human arts and sciences no less strongly than Gianfrancesco Pico, but did not conclude that this made them false and pernicious: all it implied was that they had their limitations and could not claim the absolute truth that is given only by faith. God's revelation in the Bible, Agrippa points out,

cannot be grasped by any judgment of our senses, by any reasoning of our mind, by any syllogism delivering proof, by any science, by any speculation, by any contemplation, in short, by any human powers, but only by faith in Jesus Christ, poured into our soul by God the Father through the intermediary of the Holy Spirit . . . [T]he intellect . . . must be subjected to faith, and faith must not give way to the intellect, but must firmly place its hope in God. [Therefore] we must not debate over divine matters, but firmly put our faith in them. On the other hand, we are permitted to philosophize, dispute, and formulate deductions by means of our intellect concerning all created things, but we are not to place our faith and hope in them.[26]

Weyer knew that Agrippa's piety was genuine, and later defended his master against accusations of black magic and demon-worship; but he moved much closer to the younger Pico's position in arguing that the magical arts were not only uncertain, but pernicious and dangerous as well. Published in the final year of the Council of Trent, his *De praestigiis daemonum* stands at the beginning of a period in which the witch hunt was gaining momentum on the Continent, while at the same time, as formulated by George Mora, "that natural blending of paganism and Christianity – which had sustained the masses of peasants confronted with all sorts of dangers, real or imaginary – was being destroyed by the actions of the renewed Church."[27]

[25] Schmitt, "Who Read Gianfrancesco Pico della Mirandola?," 116; Pico is referred to explicitly in *De praestigiis daemonum* II.3–4, 16; III.31.

[26] Agrippa, *Opera*, 299 and 553. Translation according to van der Poel, *Cornelius Agrippa*, 57–58 and 103. It should be noted that there is a specific dimension of concealment to Agrippa's statements on "faith": although he would seem to be defending a kind of biblicism similar to Savonarola's and Gianfrancesco Pico's, he was actually referring to a hermetic doctrine of gnosis strongly influenced by Lodovico Lazzarelli (Hanegraaff, "Better than Magic").

[27] Mora, "Introduction," lvi, and following pages. Mora also notes that there were relatively few witch trials in the period between 1520 and 1550, "perhaps under the influence of the sceptical, humanist current" (*ibid.*).

For our specific concerns, Weyer's importance lies in how he transformed the notion of a history of pagan error into one of demonic infiltration: the ancient sages are presented by him not just as philosophers deprived of the light of revelation, but as instruments of the devil and his legions of demons. The story begins with the fallen angels, their success in bringing about the fall of Adam and Eve,[28] and their perverting influence on Noah's son Ham after the Flood. Thus begins a historical lineage of darkness, for Ham's son Misraim, who turns out to be identical with Zoroaster,[29] "first discovered the blasphemous and notorious impiety of Magic."[30] The results were disastrous: even while Noah was still alive, he had to watch helplessly how out of his own bloodline, "dreadful forms of idolatry burst upon the Church of God."[31] The Egyptians, Babylonians and Persians are all descended from Zoroaster,[32] and transmitted the arts of idolatrous magic on to other peoples, so that finally the whole world came to be filled "with the fumes of impiety as though from a furnace or factory of wickedness."[33] Weyer continues by explaining how magic spread from the most ancient cultures to the Greeks, not least because eminent philosophers such as Pythagoras, Democritus and Plato picked it up during their travels:

Upon their return, they extolled the art and preserved it among their secret teachings. In fact, we know that Pythagoras and Plato approached the seers of Egyptian-Memphis in order to get a knowledge of magic and travelled through almost all of Syria, Egypt, Judea, and the schools of the Chaldaeans . . . the Assyrians, the Persians, the Arabs, the Ethiopians, and the Indians . . .[34]

In this narrative, "magic" means idolatry: it consists of invocation and worship of the pagan gods, who are really demons. However, Weyer had not entirely forgotten Agrippa's insistence on differentiating between the sublime religion known as *mageia* among the ancients, and the sacrilegious practices that had come to be confused with it.[35] He grudgingly admits that there must be such a thing as acceptable natural magic, not least because of the gospel account of the *Magi* from the East who followed a star; but in practice, almost invariably one finds it to be hopelessly mixed up and confused with "impious superstition," the "allurements of sorcery and theurgy," and the "impostures of demons."[36] Likewise, the Jewish

---

[28] Weyer, *De praestigiis daemonum* 1.1–3 (Mora ed., 3–11).   [29] *Ibid.* 11.3 (Mora ed., 100).
[30] *Ibid.* 1.4 (Mora ed., 11).   [31] *Ibid.*   [32] *Ibid.* 1.4 and 11.3 (Mora ed., 11, 100).
[33] *Ibid.* 11.3 (Mora ed., 100–106) for the details of transmission to various peoples.
[34] *Ibid.* 11.3 (Mora ed., 103).
[35] Agrippa, *Occulta Philosophia*, Dedicatory letter to Trithemius (Perrone Compagni ed., 68; see Chapter 1, n. 265).
[36] Weyer, *De praestigiis daemonum* 11.3 (Mora ed., 103–104).

kabbalah may originally have been just "the more secret interpretation of divine law," but it has come to be "defiled and corrupted by magic."[37] In any case, the idolatrous practices of magic were continued by platonists like Porphyry, Plotinus, and Proclus; and they became the *fons et origo* of the Christian heresies, beginning with Simon Magus: "From Simon, as though from a seed pod, there sprouted forth in long succession the monstrous Ophites, the shameless Gnostics . . . the impious Valentinians, Cardonians, Marcionists, Montanists, and many other heretics."[38] Borrowing directly from Gianfrancesco Pico's *De rerum praenotione*, Weyer continues the lineage up to the present, with special mention of Julian the Apostate, Roger Bacon, Peter of Abano, Albertus Magnus, Arnaud of Vilanova, *Picatrix* (which he believes to be the name of an author), and Cecco d'Ascoli. Many of them suffered a terrible death, for after the demons have used human beings, they destroy them.

Interestingly, and probably due to the formative influence of Agrippa, Weyer's genealogy of demonic magic is continued into the high Middle Ages but does not include the Florentine platonists or their sympathizers.[39] Moreover, Plato is not given a place of any special prominence. Nevertheless, Weyer's genealogy of demon-worship is a perfect example of Platonic Orientalism turned negative. A lineage is drawn that begins with Zoroaster and the ancient cultures of the Orient, moves on westward to the Greeks, and is adopted from there by the neoplatonists; but far from being a tradition of venerable ancient wisdom, it is a demonic genealogy of darkness. It is this simple fact that makes it possible for Weyer not to finish with the platonists who influenced the Fathers, but to *continue* his story with the gnostic heresies of the first centuries. From this time on, this connection would become increasingly common.

In major anti-witchcraft tracts after Weyer we usually find some references to the origins and subsequent history of magic, but these tend to be sketchy and derivative. The implied historical narrative largely remains similar to Weyer's, with a satanically inspired Zoroaster at the origin and the platonists as primary culprits,[40] but the Florentine humanists and their

---

[37] *Ibid.* 11.3 (Mora ed., 104).   [38] *Ibid.* 11.3 (Mora ed., 106).

[39] Having discussed Weyer's somewhat remarkable inclusion of Albertus Magnus, who is condemned as "a superstitious maker of talismans," D. P. Walker claims that "It is as a follower of Albert that Wier casually condemns Ficino, 'otherwise a most learnèd philosopher'" (*Spiritual and Demonic Magic*, 153). On the contrary, I would suggest that since Weyer was certainly aware of Ficino's discussions of talismans in *De vita coelitus comparanda*, it is remarkable that he does not condemn him, but lets him off the hook so easily.

[40] See for instance De Lancre, *Tableau* VI.2.1 (*Inconstancy*, 417–419), who sees all the great philosophers of antiquity as sorcerers, and repeats the story of Ham's son Misraim being identical with Zoroaster.

sympathizers (Ficino, but more frequently Giovanni Pico and Cornelius Agrippa) now begin to be mentioned as well. Thus Jean Bodin in his chatty and chaotic *De la démonomanie des sorciers* (1580)[41] writes that although the Persian word magic referred simply to philosophy, it was perverted into "diabolic sorcery" under the influence of the devil; and "the first who served Satan to publish this impiety in Persian" was Zoroaster.[42] Socrates admitted himself that he was inspired by a demon,[43] and among later examples of the same lineage are Iamblichus, Proclus, Plotinus, Porphyry, and the emperor Julian. Among contemporaries, Bodin highlights Pico and particularly Agrippa, "the grand doctor of the Diabolical art."[44]

Much more solid and systematic was the discussion in the Jesuit Martin del Rio's *Disquisitionum magicarum libri sex* (1599). Beginning with questions of etymology and definition, he discussed magic as a manifestation of "superstition" in the technical scholastic sense which made it inseparable from idolatry.[45] Del Rio is more respectful than Bodin towards the distinction between natural and demonic magic, describing the latter as a perversion of the legitimate natural knowledge that God had bestowed already on Adam. Quite similar to what we saw in Plethon, he writes that from the Persians emerged a good magic concerned with knowledge of the innermost nature of things, and a bad kind concerned with the worship of false gods and linked to the heresies of Marcion and Mani.[46] There were several Zoroasters, one of whom is supposed to have written the *Chaldaean Oracles*, a book he finds more obscure than useful. With this lineage, del Rio appears to associate a whole series of platonic authors, many of whom (he mentions Proclus, Psellus, and Plethon) defend an acceptable magic concerned with the secrets of nature. He ends with a list of authors who are inspired by the devil or may at least be suspected of heresy to some degree: they include Peter of Abano, Roger Bacon, Ramon Llull, Arnaud of Vilanova, Geber, the author of the *Picatrix*, Cecco d'Ascoli, al-Kindi, Cornelius Agrippa, Paracelsus, George Ripley, Girolamo Cardano, Giovanni Baptista della Porta, Pietro Pomponazzi, Giovanni Pico della Mirandola[47] and, surprisingly, Jean Bodin. Del Rio's discussion, and this list, are

---

[41] Bodin, *Démonomanie*; but see also his *Colloquium Heptaplomeres* VI (Noack ed., 278–284). On Bodin and Renaissance magic, see Walker, *Spiritual and Demonic Magic*, 171–177; Lange, *Untersuchungen*; Mesnard, "Demonomanie."

[42] Bodin, *Démonomanie* II.1 (p. 35).   [43] *Ibid.* I.2 (p. 10).   [44] *Ibid.* II.1 (p. 36).

[45] On the historical development of the terminology of *superstitio*, its origins in the Greek *deisidaimonia*, and its relation to "idolatry," see Chapter 3, pp. 156–164.

[46] Del Rio, *Disquisitionum Magicarum* I.3.

[47] Here del Rio seems to be confused: he attributes *positiones magicas* to "Francesco" Pico della Mirandola (*Disquisitionum Magicarum* I.3). Presumably he intends Giovanni's magical theses.

significant in several respects. They show the Counter-Reformation concern with censorship in full swing, resulting in a whole series of medieval and Renaissance authors now enlisted in the category of demonic magic and therefore eligible for being placed on the Index. But del Rio's perspective is less paranoid than Bodin's and Weyer's, and although his narrative is quite compatible with a Platonic Orientalist framework understood negatively, there is no particular emphasis on the dramatic notion of a platonic or pre-platonic "genealogy of darkness." I would suggest that this reflects the predicament of an erudite Catholic professional in this particular period, who (consciously or not) had to steer some middle course between the association of platonism and its pre-platonic origins with diabolic magic, on the one hand, and the fact that Catholic doctrine would seem to be implicated with very similar origins, on the other. This combination was something of an intellectual time bomb, which came to explode in the seventeenth century, as will be seen.

If del Rio's primary concern was with demonic magic, other Catholics during the last decade of the sixteenth century were beginning to crack down on platonism (and Platonic Orientalism) specifically. Although eventually it would probably have happened anyway, this reaction was provoked specifically by Francesco Patrizi and his *Nova de universis philosophia* of 1591.[48] This grand philosophical synthesis on Platonic Orientalist foundations was dedicated to Pope Gregory XIV, and recommended by its author as an instrument for converting the Protestants and the Muslims by rational, peaceful means. Virulently anti-aristotelian, it was intended as an alternative textbook[49] for the teaching of philosophy: Patrizi went so far as to ask the pope to have it put on the curriculum of every school and university in Christendom, to replace the old scholastic manuals that were based upon what Patrizi denounced as the anti-Christian heresies of Aristotle. Perhaps surprisingly, the initial reaction was more than encouraging: Patrizi was invited to teach philosophy at the University "La Sapienza" in Rome, with strong encouragement by Cardinal Aldobrandini, who himself became Pope Clement VIII on January 30, 1592.[50] It is one of the cruel ironies of history that Giordano Bruno seems to have thought that this development might signal a turning of the tide in his favor as well,[51] whereas of course he was to be executed in Rome under the same pope.

---

[48] On Patrizi and this work, see Schuhmann, "Francesco Patrizi"; Leijenhorst, "Francesco Patrizi's Hermetic Philosophy"; Puliafito, "Searching for a New Physics"; Puliafito, "Hermetische Texte"; Purnell, "Francesco Patrizi"; Mulsow, "'Philosophia Italica'"; Brach, "Patrizi."

[49] Leijenhorst, "Francesco Patrizi's Hermetic Philosophy," 129–130.

[50] Firpo, "Flowering and Withering," 275–276.

[51] See Leijenhorst, "Francesco Patrizi's Hermetic Philosophy," 142 n. 12, with reference to Mercati, *Sommario del Processo*, 56–57.

That Patrizi's work was initially received as being in perfect accord with Christian piety by the highest clerical circles of Rome is remarkable, for in fact Patrizi goes even farther than Ficino in downplaying the importance of the Hebrew patriarchs and prophets in favor of the pagan philosophers.[52] Strangely enough, his lineage of divine wisdom starts like Weyer's genealogy of darkness: with Noah's son Ham, usually considered the originator of idolatry, superstition, and demonic magic. Patrizi's genealogies exist in several variations, but their main elements are that Ham either is identical with Zoroaster or had a son of that name, who was a contemporary of Abraham and was known in Egypt as Osiris. Zoroaster/Osiris' counselor there was Hermes Trismegistus, whose grandson carried the same name, and wrote the *Corpus Hermeticum* in a period slightly *before* Moses: a clear departure, surprisingly again, from the patristic perspective. Orpheus learned the hermetic wisdom when he traveled to Egypt, and took it to Greece, whence it was passed on from Aglaophemus and Pythagoras to Plato and his pupils. The lineage was temporarily interrupted by Aristotle, who had no respect for the ancient wisdom, but was fortunately taken up again by Ammonius Saccas and continued by the other neoplatonists. After another period of decline during the Middle Ages, again caused by the influence of Aristotle, it was revived again by authors such as Ramon Llull, Ficino and his school, but also Paracelsus.

The powerful defenders of scholastic theology were bound to experience Patrizi's *Nova de universis philosophia* as a provocation; and with hindsight, it seems clear that this eventually resulted in a considerable increase of anti-platonic sentiment from the final decade of the sixteenth century on. Already in 1592 Patrizi was forced to defend himself against accusations of heresy, and in spite of his willingness to submit to the Church's authority and amend the text wherever necessary, his book was finally prohibited in 1594. To his terror and deep humiliation, he was severely rebuked for his errors, and ordered to collect all copies of his work and hand them over for destruction.[53] Nevertheless, in spite of this condemnation, the initial welcome accorded to Patrizi shows that even by the early 1590s the debate over platonism was by no means settled among Counter-Reformation theologians, and a *philosophia perennis* along the lines of Agostino Steuco still had considerable credibility. Patrizi was allowed to keep teaching until his death in 1597; and even in Antonio Possevino's *Bibliotheca selecta de ratione studiorum* (1593), a highly influential bibliographic almanac intended for

---

[52] Brach, "Patrizi," 937; Leijenhorst, "Francesco Patrizi's Hermetic Philosophy," 128; Hanegraaff, "Tradition," 1128.

[53] For the details of Patrizi's condemnation, see Firpo, "Flowering and Withering," 275–284.

the instruction of Jesuits, Plato is discussed critically but still in a quite balanced manner.[54]

It was just one year later, however, and three years after Patrizi's *Nova de universis philosophia*, that from the same Counter-Reformation milieu there came a full-scale attack on platonism which is of pivotal importance for our concerns: it belongs in the immediate succession of Gianfrancesco Pico's *Examen vanitatis* as far as the historiography of philosophy is concerned, but also stands at the very beginning of the seventeenth-century debate about the "Platonism of the Fathers." Written by a little known scholar from Gallipoli, Giovanni Battista Crispo, the massive tome was titled *De Platone caute legendo*. It was presented as the first volume of an even larger project titled *De ethnicis philosophis caute legendis*,[55] which was never completed but would have covered virtually all other pagan thinkers connected with the *philosophia perennis*. Arriving in Rome around the same time as Patrizi, in 1591, Crispo's connections in the high circles of Counter-Reformation intellectuals seem to have been so excellent that he could afford to have his book printed without the standard note of ecclesiastical approval, flaunting the names of an impressive array of high ecclesiastical dignitaries and theological authorities instead.[56] Given the general climate of repression and persecution in Italy at the time, this fact alone must have lent an intimidating quality to what turns out to be a thorough indictment of the platonic enemy.

At the beginning of his book, Crispo printed a catalogue of authors who should be "read with caution." They included Zoroaster, Hermes Trismegistus and Orpheus, followed by a long series of pre-socratics, Plato and Aristotle, and a large array of what we would describe as middle- and neoplatonic philosophers. The list was continued with the main medieval Muslim philosophers plus a few from the Greek and Latin domain, with Plethon and Leone Ebreo as the most recent names. Ficino is conspicuously

---

[54] Matton, "Quelques figures," 403–404. Interestingly, Possevino believed that if Plato is close to biblical teachings in some respects, his ultimate source is Pythagoras, who was himself a Jew and learned from Jewish teachers.

[55] On Crispo and his work, see Romano, "Crispo"; Malusa, "Renaissance Antecedents," 46–48 (placing Crispo in the succession of Gianfrancesco Pico as pioneers of the historiography of philosophy); Glawe, *Hellenisierung des Christentums*, 24–26 (discussing Crispo as the earliest Catholic author in the debate on the "Platonism of the Fathers"); Blau, *Christian Interpretation of the Cabala*, 36–37; Rotondò, "Cultura umanistica e difficoltà di censori," 45–50; Matton, "Quelques figures," 405–406; Kraye, "Ficino in the Firing Line," 394–397.

[56] Rotondò, "Cultura umanistica e difficoltà di censori," 46. The list included a whole group of cardinals including Roberto Bellarmino, Francesco de Toledo, Federico Borromeo, and Odoardo Farnese, as well as many other important figures such as Possevino, Bartolomeo de Miranda, Giovanni Pietro di Saragozza, the great scholastic theologian Francisco Suarez, and the author of the famous *Annales ecclesiastici*, Cesarius Baronius.

absent, possibly because Crispo was planning an entire volume entitled *Animadversiones in animarium Platonicum Marsilii Ficini.*[57] In the body of his work, however, he did criticize Ficino, along with Bessarion, the "odious comparisons" of Agostino Steuco, and the "monstrous" phenomenon of kabbalah (the so-called "secretiores theologi," who should better be called "superstitiosiores").[58]

Crispo's attack on platonism is belligerent in the extreme, and permeated by military metaphors.[59] His story begins with Satan, the "ancient serpent" who had fallen from his heavenly seat far before the creation of man. From the very moment that the heavenly truth was "sent down to us from heaven" with the birth of Christ, the devil began to fight against it, using the gentile philosophers ("the patriarchs of the heretics") as his primary tools. At first sight it might look as if the battle was lost by the pagans and their perverse teachings, since the Church of Christ was victorious. However, the Fathers made a fatal mistake: rather than insisting on the exclusive truth of the Christian faith against the absolute evil of pagan religion, they engaged in a practice of "comparative religion."

Thus . . . it often happened that the Fathers allowed religion to be compared with religion, that is to say, the sacred one with the profane. And mortal men (whom they made into gods) were allowed to be compared with the immortal God, angels and holy men with their demons, household gods, and even ghosts, genii and what more impure there is.

Having once entered the "unworthy arena of comparison" (*indignam comparationis arenam*) the Fathers ended up attributing anything genuinely pious or religious to the gods of Greece; and from there, "not daring to refuse to the Egyptians what they allowed the Prophets," they were led to see it as having originated in Egypt. The tragedy, according to Crispo, is that in this manner, the war against paganism became "domestic and hidden" (*domesticum, atque occultum*): even though the "external" battle with the other religions might have been won, the Church now had to fight the enemy within. Having been victorious in their battle against the pagans,

---

[57] According to his contemporary biographer de Angelis, Crispo left manuscripts of the second and third parts, entitled *De ethnicis philosophis*, various "Dissertazioni, Discorsi, e Poesi varie" and, very interestingly, a work called *Animadversiones in animarium Platonicum Marsilii Ficini* (de Angelis, "Vita di Gio. Battista Crispo," 56; Romano, "Crispo," 807).

[58] Crispo, *De Platone caute legendo*, 39–40 (Steuco: "Odiosa Eugebini comparatio"), 41–43 (with the "Bessarionis sententiae impugnatio" on p. 42), 44–49 ("Digressio ad eos, qui secretiores Theologi nuncupari affectant"). On the references to Ficino, see Kraye, "Ficino in the Firing Line," 394–397.

[59] All quotations in the following summary can be found in the Preface "To the Christian Philosopher and Student of True Wisdom" (Crispo, *De Platone caute legendo*, unpaginated).

the Christians had failed to kill the enemy's great commanders – "the Zoroasters, the Mercuries, Socrates, the Platos, Aristotle, the Procluses, the Plotinuses, and enemies of that kind" – but had brought them home as captives instead. Among these "captives of the enemy who were spared" was Plato:

Humanely received by our people, and more kindly than was fitting – for he was a pagan and the most famous standard-bearer of the enemy, fully drenched in vain superstitions, not just of the Greeks but also of foreign peoples – by the sharpness of his mind, his knowledge of the teachings of various peoples, and his famous voyage to Egypt, he made the powers of his mind (which had already been more than excellent) so strong, and so much strengthened his teaching with his inborn eloquence, that whether he discoursed about God and his one or I do not know what trinity, his goodness, his providence, the creation of the world, the celestial minds, demons, or the soul, or finally morals, he was the only one among the Greeks who seemed to have reached the final summit of Greek wisdom.

From here came our first fall into evil. From here, heretics have dared to spread their ambiguous voices among the people. From here all kinds of superstitions, lies and depravities could form an array and begin to infect the Church of God. From here on the heretics have waged a horrific and nefarious war, saturated with all hatred and wickedness, against the walls, the roof, and the holy doorposts of the Church.

So great was Plato's wisdom, and so sweet his eloquence, that he largely succeeded in overcoming his victors: the writings of Clement, Origen, Justin Martyr, Eusebius, Theodoretus, and Augustine all demonstrate how strongly the Fathers of the Church were seduced by the ability of "the prisoner Plato" to "insinuate his very self into the souls of many." Which brings Crispo to his conclusion, printed in capitals, about Plato, "WHOM WE SHOULD BETTER CORRECT WITH CARE, or (as I now hope to do) READ WITH SUFFICIENT CAUTION, rather than keep as a prisoner of war." Through contact with Plato, many people became "deserters and defectors" from the army of Christ. As examples, Crispo mentions various gnostic heresies and platonic philosophies, but he clearly sees Plato as the very source of heresy as such: not only does he mention Arianism and Donatism, but he even lists "the Luthers, Calvins, Melanchthons of our almost fallen age, and six hundred others like them." Everything shameful in their writings and actions can ultimately be traced back to the philosophers in general, and Plato in particular. Clearly Crispo has become so convinced of Plato as the "source of all heresies" that he ends up believing that anything heretical must be platonic by definition.

Even though the bulk of Crispo's work was devoted to systematic rather than historical discussions,[60] his *De Platone caute legendo* plays a role of particular importance in the process by which the notion of a "history of truth," grounded in the *philosophia perennis*, was about to give way to properly historical perspectives during the seventeenth century. Crucial in this respect was the fact that Crispo no longer approached the Fathers as unassailable authorities, but as fallible human beings who had allowed themselves to be influenced by pagan philosophies and whose work therefore needed to be read "with caution," that is to say: critically. In other words, they were turned into objects of historical investigation, whose opinions could be judged and evaluated by criteria external to themselves. Crispo's tragedy is that he does not seem to have realized that, in taking such a perspective, he was pioneering an approach that would become an extremely effective weapon in the fight of the Protestant "heretics" against the Church he was trying to defend. As subsequent developments would demonstrate, this weapon had the peculiar characteristic of not getting blunt but, on the contrary, becoming ever sharper and more deadly the more it was being used.[61] It would end up destroying the grand Renaissance tradition of Christian platonism, but did not stop there: having been turned with great effect against the foundations of Roman Catholic theology in general, and the dogma of the Trinity in particular, it finally became a threat even to the Protestants who were wielding it, and opened up the doors towards secularization and Enlightenment.

AGAINST THE FATHERS

It might be useful to take a step back now to gain perspective. We have seen how, from the very beginning, there were critics who rejected any attempt at accommodation between platonism and Christianity. For them, Plato's doctrines were immoral and incompatible with Christian truth; and if he was perceived as standing in a long tradition of oriental "wisdom," this

---

[60] The organization of *De Platone caute legendo* is based upon a complex tree diagram (printed right before the beginning of the numbered pages) that begins by discussing ideas of the soul before, during, and after embodiment, and continues by splitting up each of these categories into further ones, which are again split up, and so on. Each chapter is devoted to a category, and begins with a short summary of biblical passages that should be read with caution (because if interpreted incorrectly, they might give rise to heretical ideas about the soul), followed by a listing of the most relevant patristic, dogmatic and theological authorities, as well as the specific heresies connected to the opinion in question. In each chapter, Plato is discussed first, in great detail, followed by shorter but substantial sections devoted to the relevant Fathers, theologians, and heretics.

[61] As nicely formulated by Glawe, *Hellenisierung des Christentums*, 38.

merely confirmed that his ideas were grounded not in biblical truth but in ancient pagan error. To the minds of such critics, the fact that Christian platonists – from Ficino to Patrizi – even went as far as defending such things as magic and kabbalah only confirmed their worst suspicions. Clearly the defense of "ancient wisdom" amounted to nothing less than a demonic attempt at undermining and perverting Christianity by reintroducing the gods of the pagans along with the errors of the Jews.

But critics who investigated the Florentine agenda more closely were bound to discover a disconcerting truth: to a surprising extent, those paganizing heretics seemed to have the Fathers of the Church on their side! The so-called "Platonism of the Fathers" (more precisely, as I have argued, the "Platonic Orientalism of the Fathers") was a problem that had been slumbering in Christian theology from its very beginning, almost like a kind of latent disease; but it had now become acute because the newly available sources made direct and precise comparisons between the pagan philosophers and the patristic apologists unavoidable. As demonstrated by the case of Crispo, critics who wished to refute the Florentine agenda were now forced to consider the possibility that the ante-Nicene Fathers themselves had been responsible for inviting the virus of paganism into the body of Christ.

The implications proved far-reaching. At stake was nothing less than the very nature and origin of Christianity, and the "purity" of the Christian message. Did the dogmatic system that had been developed by the Church fairly represent the gospel message and the beliefs of the original apostolic community, or had it allowed itself to get contaminated by alien doctrines derived from the pagan and platonic environment? If one wished to avoid the latter conclusion, worrying as it was, only very few options were available: unless one wished to defend the implausible thesis that no such platonic influence had taken place at all,[62] one necessarily had to concede

---

[62] Examples can be found among conservative Catholics even as late as the eighteenth century: see, for example, Baltus, *Défense des SS. Pères* in 1711 (see Glawe, *Hellenisierung*, 138–144) and the author of the anonymous *Histoire critique de l'éclecticisme* published in 1766 (*ibid.*, 254–358). More sophisticated versions survive even in modern scholarship. For example, Charles Partee (*Calvin and Classical Philosophy*, 115 n. 55) approvingly quotes Etienne Gilson's statement that "For the Fathers of the Church, neither the truth of the faith, nor the dogma defining it, depended in any way on philosophy" and "The formula 'The Platonism of the Fathers' would lead to an absurd interpretation if it were meant to say that the Fathers were Platonists" (*History of Christian Philosophy*, 93). On the contrary, as suggested in the previous chapter, such neat distinctions between philosophy and theology are a modern projection, here used for covert apologetic ends: to keep the Fathers conveniently "clean" of platonic contamination. The same bias is present to a stunning degree even in relatively recent discussions of the "Platonism of the Fathers" by highly qualified scholars such as Meijering ("Zehn Jahre Forschung") and particularly Dörrie ("Was ist 'spätantiker Platonismus'?").

that pagan philosophy could be harmonized with the biblical message at least up to a point, and thereby had to end up endorsing some version of the ancient wisdom narrative. If, on the other hand, any such acceptance of pagan thought was considered taboo, one was forced to conclude that the Fathers had been fallible, or even wrong, and the dogmatic system of the Church had been contaminated with error since the first centuries. It then became necessary to investigate how much of it might still be salvaged, and by which criteria. It is not hard to see that this second possibility carried an enormous polemical potential from Protestant perspectives, since it strongly suggested that Roman Catholicism and its dogmatic tradition as a whole might be exposed as a pagan perversion.

The controversy over the Platonism of the Fathers – often referred to by the famous but problematic catch-phrase of a "Hellenization of Christianity" – is of great complexity, and has played a crucial role in theological and philosophical controversies from the sixteenth through the nineteenth century, focused in particular on Trinitarian theology.[63] Strange though it may seem to us, used as we are to thinking of rational philosophy and science as primary agents of "progress," these debates must be counted among the most important factors in the historical process leading towards "modernization." As pointed out by Martin Mulsow, the anti-platonic critique resulted in the gradual but inexorable "destruction" of a great intellectual tradition that had been integral to Christian culture before the Reformation.[64] The overall effect of the controversy was that of creating a sharp opposition between two logical alternatives: one either

---

[63] The standard treatment remains Glawe, *Hellenisierung*, and cf. the excellent short discussion of the "Hellenization theorem" in Lehmann-Brauns, *Weisheit*, 7–20 (recent studies of the reception of the Fathers during the sixteenth and seventeenth centuries are amazingly silent about the debate concerning their "platonizing" tendencies: see, for example, Quantin, *Catholicisme classique*; Backus, *Reception of the Church Fathers*, vol. II). The term "Hellenization of Christianity" (famous, of course, from its earlier usage by Adolf von Harnack) is extremely problematic, as it reflects the normative theological idea of an originally "pure" apostolic Christianity infected or contaminated "from outside" by Hellenistic paganism, as emphasized by Glawe himself: "The typical characteristic of the concept of the hellenization of Christianity [is its] pernicious influence [*ihre verderbliche Einwirkung*] on the simplicity of the apostolic teaching upon which the Church's credo is based" (*Hellenisierung*, 4–5; and cf. his closing remarks on p. 322, according to which the Hellenistic "form" of Christian dogma can be kept separate from its "content," so that "in their innermost essence, the objective truths of the religion of salvation and those of hellenism were so disharmonious, heterogeneous and without any mutual affinity that a syncretism of their highest values as a permanent product had to be excluded from the outset"). In a famous essay, Jonathan Z. Smith has demonstrated how precisely this non-historical bias, based upon the Protestant anti-Catholic polemics of the early modern period, has survived as a hidden assumption basic to the mainstream of New Testament scholarship and study of ancient religions (Smith, *Drudgery Divine*, esp. 33–34, 42–46).

[64] Mulsow, *Moderne aus dem Untergrund*, 261.

adhered to a narrative of ancient wisdom based upon a synthesis of some kind between Christianity and pagan wisdom, or one separated the true biblical and apostolic message sharply from the error of paganism in all its forms.

These two alternatives cannot be neatly distinguished along confessional demarcation lines, as will be seen, but there is no doubt that Protestants were overwhelmingly dominant in the anti-platonic camp. For our concerns in this chapter, it is of crucial importance to understand that precisely their criticism of patristic platonism is inseparable from the emergence of a new kind of historical consciousness. The basic point was well formulated by Ferdinand Christian Baur already by the mid-nineteenth century:

> If for the Catholic there is no such thing as a historical movement through which the Church has become essentially different from what it was at its origin, if in the entire development of the Church he merely sees its immanent truth coming to ever greater realization and ever more general recognition, from the perspective of the Protestant, in contrast, the Church as it exists in the immediate present is separated from what it originally was by an abyss that is so wide, that between these two points in time there must have been an immeasurable series of changes.[65]

In other words, in sharp contrast to the unbroken continuity of truth proclaimed by Catholic historians from Agostino Steuco to Cesarius Baronius (see below), the Protestant perspective was based upon the conviction that the Church had badly gone astray between the apostolic period and the present time. Precisely how and why the Church had degenerated from its original purity could only be discovered by critical study of the historical sources. As pointed out by Mark Pattison in his monograph about Isaac Casaubon, and highlighted by Jonathan Z. Smith,[66] it is important here to see that the emphasis on scripture was not itself the "moving spring" of the Reformation but, rather, a response to the ever more urgent sense of "decay and degeneracy": just as man had fallen and needed to be restored by divine grace, likewise the Church itself had fallen into corruption in the course of its historical development, and needed to be cured of its affliction. The disease was identified as platonism – shorthand for paganism – and the diagnostic method was that of historical criticism.

The essential logic of this development, but still without the focus on Plato, can be clearly observed already in the great Protestant church history

---

[65] Baur, *Epochen der kirchlichen Geschichtsschreibung*, 40. In the context of Baur's discussion, the two alternatives are represented in exemplary fashion by Baronius' *Annales* on the one hand, and the "Magdeburg Centuries" on the other (see text).

[66] Pattison, *Isaac Casaubon*, 322; Smith, *Drudgery Divine*, 13. On Pattison and his work, see Grafton, *Worlds made by Words*, 216–230.

known as the "Magdeburg Centuries," published in thirteen folio volumes from 1559 to 1574 by Matthias Flacius Illyricus (Matija Vlačić Ilirik) and a whole group of associates working under his direction.[67] It combined an impressive erudition grounded in meticulous research of primary sources with a virulent agenda of anti-Catholic polemics. The overall narrative was based upon an extreme dualism that opposed the pristine purity of the original gospel to the heaps of superstitions adopted by the Roman Church from the pagans and the Jews.[68] The resulting picture was one of ever-increasing darkening and degradation, as elegantly formulated by Pattison:

> In this protestant delineation, the church starts in the apostolic age in perfect purity, and is perverted by a process of slow canker, till it has become changed into its opposite, and is now the church not of Christ, but of anti-Christ, an instrument not for saving men but for destroying them.[69]

Thus the Centuriators describe how, since the first centuries, the true doctrine preached by Christ and the apostles (which, not surprisingly, turns out to be identical with the Lutheran doctrine)[70] had been struggling for survival against the satanic counter-church of Rome and its worldly power, represented by the papacy. Most relevant for our concerns is how ambivalent the "Magdeburg Centuries" nevertheless remained about the role of the early Fathers of the Church. Although these Fathers could not possibly be interpreted as adhering to Lutheran doctrine, they still lived close to the apostolic period and well before Constantine, and the Centuriators did not dare go so far as to classify them among the heretics: instead, they merely reproached early patristic doctrine for having some "weak spots" or blemishes (*naevi*).[71] From this we may conclude two things. First, if even an anti-Catholic polemicist as extreme as Flacius Illyricus still hesitated to attack the ante-Nicene Fathers, this says something about how daring it was for a Counter-Reformation ideologist like Crispo to criticize them only a few decades later. And second, it shows that by the 1560s and 1570s, even the strongest enemies of Roman Catholicism had not yet discovered the real potential of anti-platonism as a weapon against it.

---

[67] Flacius, *Ecclesiastica historia*. See discussion in Baur, *Epochen der kirchlichen Geschichtsschreibung*, 39–71; Polman, "Flacius Illyricus"; Polman, *L'élément historique*, 213–234; Moldaenke, *Schriftverständnis*, 315–366; Scheible, *Entstehung der Magdeburger Zenturien*; Lyon, "Baudouin, Flacius"; Meinhold, *Geschichte der kirchlichen Historiographie*, vol. 1, 268–295; Grafton, *Worlds made by Words*, 102–108.

[68] See overview in Polman, "Flacius Illyricus," 41, 43–44.

[69] Pattison, *Isaac Casaubon*, 322; cf. Moldaenke, *Schriftverständnis*, 317–325.

[70] Baur, *Epochen*, 61; Polman, "Flacius Illyricus," 40 ("The Lutheran interpretation of the Gospels is put in the mouth of the Saviour").

[71] Polman, "Flacius Illyricus," 43; cf. Moldaenke, *Schriftverständnis*, 356–363.

The Roman Catholic response to the "Magdeburg Centuries" came in the form of a no less massive work of history: Cesarius Baronius' *Annales Ecclesiastici* (1588–1607), which in turn caused Isaac Casaubon to write his *De rebus sacris et ecclesiasticis exercitationes* XVI (1614). Casaubon's dating of the *Corpus Hermeticum*, in reaction to Baronius' listing of Hermes Trismegistus as a gentile prophet, has received much attention in the wake of Frances Yates, and rightly so;[72] but for our discussion it is important to emphasize his treatment of the Fathers. Baronius' work (criticism of which had been officially prohibited by the Church!)[73] was utterly typical of the standard Catholic approach: his *Annales* "exhibited the visible unity and impeccable purity of the church founded upon Peter, and handed down inviolate, such at this day as it had ever been."[74] In other words, in spite of an incredibly impressive documentation (the full resources of the Vatican library and other Italian libraries were put at his disposal), Baronius' approach was wholly lacking in any sense of historical criticism, and merely compiled heaps of data without seeking to differentiate pious legend from plausible fact.[75] In sharp contrast, Casaubon asked hard questions of a historical nature, about how Hellenistic culture could have influenced early Christianity, emphasizing in particular the link between the Greek mysteries and patristic views of the sacraments. He concluded that the Fathers had indeed adopted quite a number of terms, rites and ceremonies from the "ancient superstitions," although he added that in doing so, they had turned them into something pious and good. Casaubon's focus here was on the influence of pagan rites rather than of philosophy, but he must be seen as a pioneer in recognizing the importance of analyzing the relation between Hellenistic culture and Christianity.[76]

The first author who fully developed the concept of a "Hellenization of Christianity" was, interestingly, again a Jesuit, although one who had been influenced by Casaubon. With his unfinished *De theologicis dogmatibus* (1644–1650) in five volumes, Denis Pétau (Dionysius Petavius) was the first to treat the development of Christian doctrine systematically from a historical point of view.[77] Like Crispo, he pinpointed platonism as the source

---

[72] Yates, *Giordano Bruno*, 398–403 (cf. Chapter 1, page 74 and n. 290).

[73] Pattison, *Isaac Casaubon*, 196.

[74] Pattison, *Isaac Casaubon*, 325; cf. the chapter on Baronius as a historian in Pullapilly, *Caesar Baronius*, 144–177. Baronius' approach is the ultimate example of the Catholic perspective on church history as summarized by Baur (see quotation in text, above).

[75] Pattison, *Isaac Casaubon*, 323–341; cf. Baur, *Epochen*, 72–84.

[76] Glawe, *Hellenisierung*, 21–24 (esp. 23).

[77] Glawe, *Hellenisierung*, 26–33; Hofmann, *Theologie, Dogma und Dogmenentwicklung*, 194–225.

of all heresies, focusing particularly on those concerning the Trinity. The tragedy of his position is that, to his worry and concern, his work became a source of inspiration for Socinian, Unitarian and other "heretical" authors to attack Catholic dogma. Pétau's actual intention was to emphasize the Council of Nicaea as the foundation of the true doctrine, while criticizing the ante-Nicene Fathers who still tended to be claimed by Protestants; but that strategy was bound to backfire, as Protestants came to apply the anti-platonic critique ever more rigidly to *all* the Fathers, whether before or after Nicaea.[78]

Particularly good examples are several works by the Arminian Jean le Clerc published in the final decades of the seventeenth century, who traced the process of Hellenization back even further.[79] Judaism itself had already been Hellenized by the time of the apostles, with Philo as the clearest example, and platonic elements could be found in the Gospel of John. The allegorical method of scriptural exegesis, which had perverted the literal understanding of the Bible, had been adopted by the Fathers from Jews like Philo, who in turn had been inspired by the Egyptians and the Greeks, who had been accustomed to hiding the secrets of their philosophy under the guise of emblems and fables; and the *disciplina arcana* of the Fathers was likewise an imitation of pagan cultic practices transmitted by way of the Pythagoreans, Platonists, and Epicureans. As a result of such influences from pagan philosophy, the purity and simplicity of the gospel was lost, and heretical sects began to spread.

The works of Pétau and le Clerc are merely two of the more prominent and important examples of a large stream of similar works published during the later seventeenth century. What they all have in common is that they describe the Church, since the early centuries, as having been influenced – that is to say, perverted – by Hellenistic culture and by platonism in particular. The culmination of this genre came in 1700, with a famous treatise entitled *Le platonisme dévoilé*, the first monographic treatment of the concept of Hellenization.[80] It was published anonymously but is now generally attributed to Jacques Souverain, a former Reformed minister who had been removed from his office because of Arminian sympathies, and eventually went to England, where he became an Anglican. Discussing the development of the *Logos* concept in early Christian theology, Souverain argued that the Roman Catholic concept of the Trinity was in fact the

---

[78] See analysis in Glawe, *Hellenisierung*, 31–33; and cf. his discussion of Petrus Daniel Huetius (*ibid.*, 32–36), whose predicament was very similar to Petavius'.

[79] See Glawe, *Hellenisierung*, 47–60.

[80] Glawe, *Hellenisierung*, 115–132, here 131; Matton, "Quelques figures," 409–413.

product of a "gross platonism" introduced by the Fathers of the second and third centuries. Plato himself had come to believe in the existence of one single, supreme divinity; but to avoid problems with the polytheist beliefs of his environment, he had spoken about God's three main characteristics (goodness, wisdom, power) in allegorical terms, as if they were hypostases or gods. Unfortunately, and ironically, many of the early Fathers had taken this allegorical sense literally, resulting in quasi-polytheist understandings of the Trinity as three persons. From this perspective, Souverain denounced them, along with their modern heirs, as covert Gnostics and heretics,[81] and associated them with the kabbalah as well:

> I make no distinction at all between the Jewish *Cabala* & the Valentinian *Pleroma*: these two systems are either equally ridiculous, that is if you take them literally, or they are equally reasonable, that is if you search in them for the hidden sense that rests under the cortex of allegory. For in fact it is the same insistence on allegory that has thrown the Jews as well as the heretics into this cabalistic philosophy that looks so extravagant and bizarre from the outside . . . We may therefore say of the Jews as well as of the Valentinians that under these Theological Fictions they wanted to hide their veritable Doctrine concerning *Cosmogony* and the origin of things.[82]

A quotation like this may serve to teach us caution concerning the complexity of the seventeenth-century debate on the "Platonism of the Fathers." Apparently, criticizing their platonism did not necessarily imply a full-scale rejection of Plato himself; it was possible for a Protestant author to denounce Catholics for misunderstanding allegory and the "hidden sense" of doctrine; and literal-mindedness (usually seen as a Protestant specialty opposed to the Catholic emphasis on allegory) could be construed as the actual cause of heresy!

The complexities of Trinitarian and anti-Trinitarian theology in this seventeenth-century genre of literature do not need to detain us further. For our concerns, most important is the fact that, in the century after Crispo, those who denounced platonism as the essence of pagan error no longer perceived it only as an enemy coming from outside, but had begun to see it as a virus that had infected Christianity from within, starting with the Patristic apologists. The historiographical implications would prove to be far-reaching, not only for the study of philosophy, but also for the study of what we nowadays refer to as Western esotericism.

---

[81] [Souverain], *Platonisme dévoilé*, 83.   [82] *Ibid.*, 87–88.

THE ANTI-APOLOGIST: JACOB THOMASIUS

As we have seen, the concern of the Florentine humanists with ancient wisdom stands at the very origin of the historiography of philosophy as a discipline, and it is now time to pick up that thread again. During the period roughly between the mid-sixteenth and the mid-seventeenth century, the question of the origins of philosophy and its historical development up to the present became an important focus of interest for intellectuals, leading to a copious literature that still remains largely unknown today.[83] It is clear that in most of this material, the general chronological framework remained compatible with Platonic Orientalism. For example, a *Disputatio prima de origine philosophiae* of 1565, published by Jean Riolan, asserted that philosophy was not a human invention but a gift from God, as confirmed by the Indian Brahmins, the Persian *Magi*, the Egyptian priests, the Hebrew prophets, the Gallic Druids, the Orphic poets, the Pythagoreans and all the platonic philosophers.[84] In 1576, Benito Pereira devoted a book to the ancient philosophers, emphasizing that there had been sages among all the "barbarian" peoples, whose philosophy was not only more ancient but also much purer than that of the Greeks.[85] A very similar emphasis on the primacy of the barbarians over the Greeks as the inventors of philosophy can be found in many other historians over the decades to follow,[86] from a Counter-Reformation author like Ludovico Carbonari[87] all the way – surprisingly – to even a Dutch Protestant like Otto van

---

[83] Tolomio, "'Historia Philosophica'." He usefully distinguishes four main categories in the historiography of philosophy during this period, but my concern here is mainly with the continuity of the assumptions basic to the ancient wisdom narrative. For many of the important authors, see also Braun, *Histoire de l'histoire de la philosophie*.

[84] Tolomio, "'Historia Philosophica'," 116–118, here 116.

[85] *Ibid.*, 92–96, here 94 (with reference to Book IV of Pereira, *De communibus omnium rerum naturalium principijs et affectionibus libri quindecim*, Rome 1576).

[86] For example, Guillaume Morel, *Tabula compendiosa de origine, successione, aetate, et doctrina veterum philosophorum* (1580); Johann Friedrich Schröter's "Digressio de praecipuis autoribus et de propagatione Philosophiae" (1585) appended to a larger work on Hippocrates; Caspar Bucher's *Oratio de philosophiae antiquitate* (1603); or Jean Cecile Frey's "Philosophia Druidarum" (orig. 1625). See discussion in Tolomio, "'Historia Philosophica'," 86–87, 96–97, 113–114, 118–120. See also the representatives of polyhistory, notably Peter Lambeck's *Prodromus historiae literariae* of 1629 (Tolomio, "'Historia Philosophica'," 78–80) and Daniel Georg Morhof's *Polyhistor* of 1688–1692 (*ibid.*, 82–85), whose discussions of the ancient wisdom largely followed in the tracks of Patrizi. Thomas Stanley's *History of Philosophy* (1655–1662), with its fourth volume *Of the Chaldaick Philosophers*, is a case apart in that Stanley kept to Diogenes Laertius' framework and his discussion of the oriental philosophies avoided questions of periodization (Malusa, "The First General Histories of Philosophy," 172–203, esp. 179–181, 183).

[87] Bk. I.7 and Bk. III of Carbonari's *Introductionis in universam philosophiam libri quattuor* (1599) contain a history of philosophy clearly influenced by the platonism of Ficino and Steuco (see Tolomio, "'Historia Philosophica'," 99–104).

Heurne (Heurnius).[88] A particularly interesting case from a few decades later is that of Theophilus Gale, whose four-volume *Court of the Gentiles* (1667–1671) combined an ancient wisdom narrative broadly along the lines of Steuco and the Cambridge platonists with an extreme "theft of the Greeks" thesis according to which all true philosophy came exclusively from Hebrew sources, while at the same time denouncing all forms of paganism as perversions springing from original sin.[89] Here we see that, at least by this time, adherence to the Platonic Orientalist perspective did not necessarily imply a positive appreciation of paganism.

It was from the second half of the seventeenth century onwards that German Protestant historians began to mount a systematic attack against these traditional approaches and, in so doing, developed a novel theoretical perspective from which was to emerge the history of philosophy as a modern academic discipline.[90] This development will prove to be crucial for my argument: while the concept of a "history of truth" discussed in the first chapter was ultimately grounded in the apologetic tradition of Roman Catholicism, these Protestant historians reciprocated with a "history of error" based on a radical rejection of that same tradition. Hence their approach has usefully been labeled "anti-apologeticism":[91] a term which emphasizes their ambition of developing a radical alternative to the patristic apologetic tradition, which they held responsible not only for the pernicious "Hellenization of Christianity" since the first centuries, but (eventually) for a parallel degeneration of philosophy into pseudo-philosophy as well. In analyzing the anti-apologetic current, we will find that its main representatives systematized the anti-pagan, anti-platonic and anti-patristic perspectives, sketched in the earlier sections of this chapter, into a logically coherent narrative based upon a peculiar combination of critical historiography and a rigorous insistence on the exclusive truth of Protestantism as opposed to pagan error in all its forms.

The story of anti-apologeticism begins with Jacob Thomasius (1622–1684),[92] father of the more famous Christian Thomasius, and one of the

---

[88] Heurnius, *Barbaricae philosophiae antiquitatum libri duo* (1600). See discussion in Tolomio, "'Historia Philosophica'," 106–113.

[89] See the excellent analysis in Malusa, "The First General Histories of Philosophy," 292–330.

[90] Lehmann-Brauns, *Weisheit*, 1.

[91] The term was introduced by Lehmann-Brauns, *Weisheit*, for example, 7, 16, 23, 26, and *passim*. For the following sections, I wish to acknowledge my profound debt to Lehmann-Brauns' researches. Not only is the anti-apologetic current the crucial link without which it would have remained impossible to understand the eighteenth-century construction of "the occult" as rejected knowledge, but Lehmann-Brauns also provides us with by far the most sophisticated and profound (and often the only) critical discussion of all the major authors.

[92] On Jacob Thomasius and his significance, see the section devoted to him in Micheli, "History of Philosophy in Germany," 409–442; Häfner, "Jacob Thomasius und die Geschichte der Häresien";

teachers of Leibniz. Thomasius senior was born in Leipzig, and spent his life there teaching philosophy and philology at the university and two grammar schools. He built up a strong reputation as a pedagogue, and produced a large oeuvre of learned studies in the domains of philosophy, theology, church history, philology, and literary theory. Undoubtedly his most important and lasting contribution to the history of philosophy was published in 1665 under the title *Schediasma historicum*, and it is on this relatively short but seminal work that I will concentrate.[93] As will be seen, the *Schediasma* was revolutionary in its radical and systematic manner of distinguishing pagan philosophy from biblical religion. Thomasius went much further in this regard than other early historians of philosophy, such as Georg Hornius and Gerhard Johannes Vossius,[94] and his argument was based upon a combination of careful philosophical analysis and historical criticism. He has sometimes been regarded as the founder of the history of philosophy as a discipline, and for good reason; but it is important to understand that his basic source of motivation was not philosophical or historical, but dogmatic. His goal was to "purify" Christian theology from its contamination by pagan error.[95] However, as the theoretical implications of his approach were further developed by his successors, not only did this result in the autonomization of history of philosophy as a discipline (not to mention that of "Western esotericism," as will be seen), but also in profound problems for Christian theology: as pointed out by Sicco Lehmann-Brauns in his indispensable study of the anti-apologetic current, Thomasius' razor-sharp distinction between the philosophy of antiquity and the religion of Christianity may have been drawn with the most pious of intentions, but ended up undermining the very orthodoxy it was supposed to defend.[96]

Thomasius' explorations were guided by a strongly professed "love of historical truth," and a severe rejection of any attempt to manipulate it for the sake of promoting personal interests of whatever kind, including those of historians.[97] The goal should be to discover what the philosophers being

and particularly the brilliant analysis in Lehmann-Brauns, *Weisheit*, 21–111. For the details of Thomasius' academic career, see Micheli, "History," 409–411, and Lehmann-Brauns, *Weisheit*, 24–27; for an overview of his writings, see Micheli, "History," 411–414.

[93] A second edition of the *Schediasma* was published by his son Christian in 1699, under a different title: *Origines historiae philosophicae et ecclesiasticae*.

[94] Lehmann-Brauns, *Weisheit*, 47–48. On Vossius and Hornius as historians of philosophy, see Malusa, "The First General Histories," 222–259.

[95] Lehmann-Brauns, *Weisheit*, 22 and n. 5.

[96] Lehmann-Brauns, *Weisheit*, 17–18, 46, 108, 185–186, 221–222 (cf. above, page 93 with n. 61, on the Platonism of the Fathers as a weapon that gets sharper with use).

[97] Micheli, "History of Philosophy in Germany," 414–415; Häfner, "Jacob Thomasius und die Geschichte der Häresien," 156–157. Obviously Thomasius did not see his own Protestant beliefs as a bias, but simply as the correct perspective on history, the truth of which was confirmed by historical criticism.

studied had really taught, and this made it necessary to clean away the many distortions created by *syncretism*: a term loaded with negative connotations for Protestants, and understood by Thomasius as the phenomenon that a philosopher's original ideas are interpreted in such a way as to make them conform to later agendas that are actually different from his own. A primary example of such syncretism is the "concordist" approach of the ancient wisdom narrative: in a misguided attempt to make pagan philosophy appear compatible with Christianity, it ends up creating a confused mixture of both, which makes pagans look like half-Christians and Christians like half-pagans.[98] Thomasius will have nothing of this: "where history is concerned, I cannot go against my principles by trying to persuade others that what I see to be Ethiopians are actually swans."[99] Pagan philosophy and biblical truth are entirely different animals: blurring the distinction between them results in bad history as well as doctrinal confusion.

As already noted, Thomasius was not just a critical historian of philosophy. First and foremost, he was a pious Lutheran who believed that the biblical revelation was the only reliable source of religious truth and who saw the history of Christianity from the patristic period to the Reformation as a history of error and degeneration, along the general lines of the "Magdeburg Centuries." However, whereas Flacius Illyricus and his collaborators had pointed to the papacy as the diabolical cause of Christian perversion, for Thomasius the ultimate source of heresy was pagan philosophy, and platonism in particular.[100] Having read Crispo and other critics of the Platonism of the Fathers, the patristic apologists were no longer a stumbling block for Thomasius: it was clear to him that by misinterpreting platonic philosophy as compatible with Christian faith they had introduced the virus of Hellenistic paganism.

But what was it, precisely, that made pagan philosophies so utterly alien to biblical revelation? Historically, Thomasius traced all of them to their origin in the dualistic doctrine of Zoroaster and the Persian *Magi*, which in turn had been inspired by the devil:[101] it was from this barbarian source that philosophy had reached Pythagoras, Plato, Aristotle and the other

---

[98] Thomasius, *Schediasma Historicum* § 46 note o; cf. § 42 on Hermes Trismegistus as a "Platonic half-Christian."

[99] Thomasius, *De stoica mundi exustione* § 20 and note p, here quoted according to Micheli, "History of Philosophy in Germany," 416.

[100] Thomasius' view of aristotelianism is more complex and beyond the scope of our discussion. For a detailed analysis, see Lehmann-Brauns, *Weisheit*, 53–70.

[101] Thomasius, *Schediasma* § 37 note s. As pointed out by Micheli, "History of Philosophy in Germany," 422–423, the debate on origins was not a central concern for Thomasius, who was interested in Zoroaster mainly as the source from which Simon Magus developed his heresies.

Greek philosophers.[102] But this dualism, in turn, reflected the "original fallacy" (Πρῶτον ψεῦδος) on which the whole of pagan philosophy was based: its conviction that "it is impossible for anything to be born out of nothing."[103] The true core of all pagan error was, in other words, its rejection of the doctrine of *creatio ex nihilo*, in favor of *the eternity of the world*.[104] Against the biblical distinction between God and the world, or Creator and creation, paganism made the world eternal like God himself. All heretical beliefs were ultimately grounded in this belief: emanationism (souls or intelligences are not newly created by God but pour forth from his eternal essence), dualism (form and matter, or God and matter, are two co-eternal principles), pantheism (the world is God), and materialism (God is the world). In their different ways, all these variations amounted to deification of the creation at the expense of its Creator.[105]

For Thomasius, the temptation of man by this ultimately diabolical doctrine of pagan philosophy was a direct parallel to the temptation of Adam and Eve that had resulted in the Fall, and accordingly, the Christian revelation was presented by him as its radical salvational counterpart.[106] But although the coming of Christ should have spelled the end of paganism, through the devil's machinations its basic philosophical doctrine succeeded in infiltrating Christian theology, particularly in the form of platonism. Any such continuation of pagan philosophy under the guise of Christianity was understood by Thomasius as a case of syncretism, and thus as heresy, whether it occurred in the Fathers and Roman Catholic doctrine or in the various forms of gnosticism and other sectarian movements that had sprouted from the "arch-heretic" Simon Magus.[107] As a result, the *entire* history of the Church prior to the Reformation became synonymous with the history of heresy. As formulated by Lehmann-Brauns,

From this perspective, without the pagan counterpart there would be no history of Christian theology at all, for although its center had manifested itself historically in the (New Testament) Revelation, it [i.e. theology] was not itself subject to historical development, and moreover, was impervious to any philosophical analysis. The history of Christianity, in contrast, was dominated by the contrast between pagan

---

[102] Thomasius, *Schediasma* § 34 and note k.   [103] *Ibid.*, § 19 note c.

[104] Actually the doctrine of *creatio ex nihilo* is not biblical but was first formulated in the second century by Theophilus of Antioch (*Apol. ad Autolycum*, 2.4).

[105] The conceptual logic of monotheism implies that such deification, in turn, is a form of the ultimate sin of idolatry (see Hanegraaff, "Idolatry," 82–83).

[106] Lehmann-Brauns, *Weisheit*, 43 ("Die antike Philosophie galt gleich dem Sündenfall als Verführungsversuch"). In the interest of this sharp pagan–Christian dichotomy, Thomasius ignored ancient Judaism, which was no longer treated as a prefiguration of Christian revelation (*ibid.*, 32).

[107] Thomasius, *Schediasma* § 36.

corruption and pious Christian restitution – a further consequence of the *sola scriptura* doctrine, which could not accept any historical development of biblically legitimated theology.[108]

We find ourselves back, then, with the basic opposition between history and truth. I argued in the first chapter that the Renaissance narrative of Ancient Wisdom was based upon the paradoxical concept of a history of truth. Thomasius' Protestant counter-narrative, in contrast, recognized that ultimate religious truth cannot be subject to change and development without losing its absoluteness, and therefore cannot have a history. It followed that the history of thought could only be a history of error.

Thomasius considered the Reformation as the most thorough attempt at a de-Hellenization of Christianity thus far, but in his own century he was concerned about seeing the pagan heresies of platonism making their comeback even in Protestant contexts. He predicted, quite accurately, that these forms of heterodox spiritualism would spread ever more in the decades to come.[109] The central characteristic of this new development was "enthusiasm" (*Enthusiasmus, Schwärmerei*), that is to say, the extreme emphasis on personal religious or even ecstatic experience at the expense of doctrinal belief.[110] Like all manifestations of heresy, enthusiasm was based upon the core error of the eternity of the world: in this case in the form of the platonic doctrine of emanation and restitution, which held that the soul has its origin in an eternal, divine substance and will return to it again. Emanationism implied that human beings could return to God by attaining direct experiential knowledge of their own divine nature, by means of "ecstatic" states of mind, and this was clearly equivalent to the quintessential gnostic heresy of auto-salvation and deification by means of a salvational gnosis. Hence Thomasius was able to draw a straight line from Simon Magus and the various gnostic sects in the early history of the Church, all the way to the enthusiasm of spiritualist and early pietist currents in his own time. Next to the eternity of the world, the ψευδώνυμος γνῶσις, or "gnosis falsely so called," was highlighted as the second core aspect of pagan heresy in Thomasius' synthesis, and an analysis of the notion of γνῶσις τῶν ὄντων (knowledge of the things that are, that is to say, of the world as an eternal substance) was central to the *Schediasma Historicum*.[111] Furthermore, by associating

---

[108] Lehmann-Brauns, *Weisheit*, 44.   [109] Thomasius, *Schediasma* § 52 note k.
[110] Lehmann-Brauns, *Weisheit*, 71.
[111] Thomasius distinguished between a "gnosis falsely so called" and a true gnosis culminating in *pistis*; and the relation between his understanding of γνῶσις τῶν ὄντων as a philosophical pursuit and the salvational gnosis of gnosticism and hermetism is of greater complexity than can be explained here. For a full analysis, see Lehmann-Brauns, *Weisheit*, 89–99.

it with the vain search for worldly knowledge known as *curiositas*, he was able to suggest a close connection with the pagan "sciences" of magic and astrology (an argument that was, of course, all the easier because he had highlighted Zoroaster, the inventor of magic, as the originator of pagan philosophy).[112]

On the basis of Thomasius' argument, heresy could now be defined as any form of syncretism between Christianity (grounded in the doctrine of *creatio ex nihilo* and strict biblical faith) and pagan philosophy (grounded in the doctrine of the eternity of the world and the pursuit of gnosis). The *Schediasma Historicum* was a technical Latin treatise intended for academics, with a structure (short numbered paragraphs in logical sequence, plus many often lengthy notes incorporated into the text at the end of each paragraph) that made it difficult to read; but its significance was recognized by influential contemporaries such as Leibniz, Bayle, and Thomasius' own son Christian,[113] who all studied it carefully. For our concerns, most important is the fact that it laid the conceptual foundations for the landmark book that gave birth to the study of Western esotericism as a specific domain of research: Ehregott Daniel Colberg's *Platonisch-Hermetisches Christenthum* of 1690–1691.[114]

THE HERESIOLOGIST: EHREGOTT DANIEL COLBERG

Anybody who opens Colberg's book should be prepared to enter a dogmatic battlefield in the company of an author who is shooting to kill. The work consists of an uncompromising and frontal attack against what was known as the "fanatical" or "enthusiastic" theology typical of the milieus of Reformation spiritualism, with strong emphasis on Paracelsianism, Weigelianism, Rosicrucianism, and Christian theosophy in the tradition of Jacob Böhme. Considering Colberg's extreme hostility to these currents and their ideas, and the fact that he studied them not for their own sake but in order to destroy their credibility, what is it that makes him into a pioneering figure in the study of Western esotericism? The answer is that his book was the first one to outline a complete and internally consistent historiographical concept that connected everything nowadays

---

[112] Thomasius, *Schediasma* § 34 note k; cf. § 28 note r.
[113] Micheli, "History of Philosophy in Germany," 439–442.
[114] Hanegraaff, "Birth of Esotericism," 209–212. The first modern scholar of Western esotericism to have called attention to Colberg's importance in this regard seems to have been Antoine Faivre, in an article co-published with Karen-Claire Voss in 1995 ("Western Esotericism and the Science of Religion," 55; and see also Faivre, *Accès*, vol. II, 73–78).

studied under that rubric: not only did Colberg draw lines of continuity from the platonic and hermetic currents of late antiquity through those of the Renaissance and onward to the present day, but he managed to do so on the basis of a clearly formulated theory of how and why they were all hanging together. In short, "Platonic-Hermetic Christianity" emerged from Colberg's book as a specific religious domain with an identity of its own – *not* by virtue of its supposed participation in a timeless realm of metaphysical truth, but on the basis of an analysis of what had been believed and proclaimed by its historical representatives.

In his battle against heterodoxy, Colberg (1659–1698) followed closely in the footsteps of his father, Johannes Colberg, a belligerent Lutheran minister of very strict persuasions whose life and career were dominated by theological conflicts.[115] Father and son both became professors at the University of Greifswald, where Ehregott Daniel wrote his *Platonisch-Hermetisches Christenthum* along with other treatises on the history of heresy[116] and practical theology. Although he received an ordinary professorship in 1691, he left that position three years later, to spend the last years of his rather brief life as a minister in Wismar.

Colberg's *Platonisch-Hermetisches Christenthum* is conceptually grounded in the radical critique of syncretism developed in Thomasius' *Schediasma*, which is extensively quoted; but it is important to see that Colberg does not consider philosophy to be evil in itself. It is only the mingling of philosophy with biblical faith that must be condemned:

The greatest – I would almost say: the only – danger for theology comes from the scandalous *mixing of philosophical teachings and the Word of God*. For although the philosophical arts and sciences are, in and for themselves, a wondrous gift of God from which great profit can be drawn in civil life, and which, if rightly applied, can be of no small use in other respects as well, they create much confusion if they are applied to the divine mysteries of revelation and transcend their natural boundaries of reason.[117]

The basic argument is strikingly similar to what we encountered already in Gianfrancesco Pico della Mirandola's *Examen vanitatis*. With reference to the apostle Paul (Coll. 2:8), Colberg continues by emphasizing that

---

[115] On the lives and careers of father and son, see Lehmann-Brauns, *Weisheit*, 112–114. By far the most complete critical discussion of Colberg and his work is Lehmann-Brauns, *ibid.*, 112–186; but see also the shorter analysis by Schneider, "Das *Platonisch-Hermetische Christenthum.*"

[116] See notably his *Specimen historicum de origine & progressu haeresium & errorum in ecclesia* and his *Sapientia veterum Hebraeorum* (both 1694; for an analysis of the latter, see Micheli, "The History of Philosophy in Germany," 460–473).

[117] Colberg, *Platonisch-Hermetisches Christenthum*, vol. 1, Vorrede (pp. 1–2). Here and in later quotations, all emphases are in the original.

what must be condemned is not philosophy as such, but its improper application to divine matters, which are simply beyond the scope of the weak human intellect. The gospel is a teaching "which has been hidden from the beginning, which is not grasped or understood by the human mind, but has been revealed by the son of God."[118] Now the "mingling of theology and philosophy" can take two forms:

First, if one tries to be smarter than Scripture, that is, if with the help of philosophy one tries to fathom the nature of the revealed mysteries about which God's Word keeps silent. *Second*, if one tries to be smart against Scripture, that is, if one refuses to accept what does not accord with the blind intellect and its invented axioms.[119]

The second type is represented mainly by aristotelian philosophy, leading to the "philosophical fancies and school quarrels" of the medieval scholastics, but Colberg's true concern is with the first type. It was widespread in the early Church, including the work of Fathers such as Origen and Clement of Alexandria, who maintained many of their earlier platonic beliefs after their conversion;[120] it is the core approach of Simon Magus and his many followers, such as the Menandrians, Saturnians, Nicolaites, Gnostics, Marcionites, Carpocratians, Valentinians, and Manichaeans;[121] and it was continued during the Middle Ages in the monasteries and the *Theologia mystica* in the wake of Dionysius the Areopagite and Scotus Eriugena.[122] Much of the papist and scholastic darkness was dispersed thanks to "the faithful effort of the holy Luther" (*des heiligen Lutheri*) but, sadly, Satan continued to spread the bad seeds of syncretism.[123] From his many personal discussions with Weigelians and Böhmians, and from studying their writings, Colberg had discovered that their entire philosophy was still based upon the same pernicious mingling of Christian faith with platonic and hermetic philosophy, and this he now set out to demonstrate.

---

[118] *Ibid.*, Vorrede (p. 4).   [119] *Ibid.*, Vorrede (pp. 5–6).

[120] *Ibid.*, Vorrede (p. 7) and 1.6–8 (pp. 26–37).   [121] *Ibid.*, Vorrede (pp. 7–8) and 1.5 (pp. 19–26).

[122] *Ibid.*, 1.11–16 (pp. 47–88). By including the *Theologia mystica*, Colberg went much further than Thomasius, and it earned him severe criticism by Jacob's son Christian (Lehmann-Brauns, *Weisheit*, 130–131). That both Jacob and Christian Thomasius refused to include the mystical theology under the rubric of pagan heresy is important for evaluating their intellectual positions, as carefully analyzed by Lehmann-Brauns. That Thomasius senior saw Johann Arndt's *Vier Büchern vom wahren Christentum* as exemplifying an acceptable *Theologia mystica*, placing it in a tradition of non-enthusiastic speculative mysticism (*Schediasma* § 54 note i; and Lehmann-Brauns, *Weisheit*, 104–108) is significant and ironic, given the fact that Arndt's theology has recently been analyzed as "spiritualist-hermetic" in a major study by Hermann Geyer, *Verborgene Weisheit*. Exploring the actual relations between Protestant spiritualism, pietism, and the currents denounced as "Platonic-Hermetic" by Colberg would lead us far beyond the present study's limitations, but remains a particularly important desideratum in the study of Western esotericism.

[123] Colberg, *Platonisch-Hermetisches Christenthum*, vol. 1, Vorrede (p. 13).

In tracing heresy back to its historical origins, the primacy of the "barbarians" over the Greeks seems to have become a non-issue for Colberg, for reasons that are not very difficult to guess. Whether the pagan philosophies come from Chaldaea, Egypt, Greece, or anywhere else is simply of no great consequence in his narrative: all that matters is their pernicious influence once they come into contact with Christianity. Colberg belonged to a generation for which the late date of the Hermetica was common knowledge, Zoroaster was simply ignored by him, and he evidently did not believe in the great antiquity of the kabbalah either.[124] Hence his story begins with Pythagoras, whose entire philosophy was focused on the search for deification by means of self-knowledge or gnosis, purification from "the filth of the body," and the "way inward."[125] Plato continued these teachings and made them famous; he developed some kind of Trinitarian theory, which should not be confused with the Christian one, but has been taken up by Weigel, Böhme, and others. From Plato on, the line is continued through the early Fathers, Simon Magus and all later heretics, and the various forms of *Theologia mystica*, as already indicated.

Why did Colberg choose to call the syncretistic tradition "Platonic-Hermetic"? Having traced the "platonic" line from Pythagoras to the present in sections 1–16 of his first chapter, he discussed the hermetic component in the final three sections. Apparently, he needed Hermes Trismegistus as a bridge to connect platonism with the "chymical" *Naturphilosophie* of Paracelsus, Weigel, Böhme, and the Rosicrucians:

Also it should not be forgotten that the desire to investigate the foundation of chymistry [*Chymie*] – which, according to its devotees, provides the right scientific foundation for investigating and understanding divine and natural things – has driven many newcomers to read the writings of Hermes Trismegistus, and, since they found there many platonic *Fundamenta*, to conclude that nobody could find the way back to the original wisdom lost in Adam except by purifying himself from the uncleanliness of the body and being enlightened, partly through Scripture, partly through the Book of Nature, that is, the *Cabala vera*, *Magia*, *Astrologia* and *Pansophia*.[126]

Alchemy and the hermetic books are considered to be among the main reasons for the recent spread of "fanaticism." Colberg refers to the *Corpus Hermeticum* to prove that Hermes Trismegistus teaches a form of platonism, but goes on to emphasize his traditional status as founder of alchemy in order to connect hermetic platonism with the "pansophical" study of

---

[124] Lehmann-Brauns, *Weisheit*, 132.
[125] Colberg, *Platonisch-Hermetisches Christenthum*, vol. 1, 1.2 (pp. 4–7).   [126] *Ibid.*, 1.17 (p. 89).

the Book of Nature. In other words, he takes advantage of the fact that Hermes Trismegistus is seen as the author of (in modern terminology) the "philosophical" as well as the "technical" Hermetica. But Colberg also notes that whatever his modern admirers may believe about Hermes, it is all "a poem without foundations," since the hermetic writings were evidently written after the birth of Christ, as demonstrated by Casaubon and others.[127]

In Colberg's heresiological imagination, the many "sects" of Platonic-Hermetic Christianity were like a filthy breed of vermin (*Geschmeiss*) that had come crawling from the "platonic egg."[128] He kept emphasizing that although its sectarian divisions were many, they all agreed in essence. God is the "spirit of the universe" and manifests himself as a triple power from which emerges a triple world (a spiritual/angelical world, a hidden astral world of power and light, and the external world of the elements). The human soul is a particle of the divine essence that should rest in God; but misusing its freedom and following its own will instead of God's, it turned towards the external world and alienated itself from the divine source. As a result, it became a triple being consisting of soul, spirit, and a "coarse, animal, earthly" body; and this fall into matter is what is meant by sin. To find the way back, man must attain self-knowledge, and the desire for returning to his source must be awakened in him. To attain that goal, he must purify himself from sin by overcoming his bodily passions ("Affekten") and his selfish will. Having thus "killed the old Adam" by relinquishing his own will and his passions, he will have become sinless, and in a passive state of *Gelassenheit* can give himself wholly over to God's will. He will then experience an inner illumination or rebirth, and be reunited with the inner Christ, which is another word for deification (he will be "vergöttert und verchristet"). The body is left behind, and will never rise again.[129]

Colberg put particular emphasis on the enthusiasts' obsession with distinguishing each and every thing into "external" and "internal." While rejecting the "things of this world," they internalize all theological concepts and speak of the inner word of God, the inner Christ, inner faith, inner justification, inner sanctification, inner prayer, inner sacraments, inner eucharist, inner absolution, inner cult, inner calling, inner teaching, inner heaven, and inner hell. Colberg finishes by reducing the Platonic-Hermetic theology to its ultimate core: its belief in the "spiritus universi

[127] *Ibid.*, 1.19 (pp. 98–100).   [128] *Ibid.*, 1.16 (p. 75). Cf. Weyer's "seed pod" (above, page 86).
[129] *Ibid.*, II.2 (pp. 103–107).

or general world spirit" (*Welt-Geist*).[130] Although he does not emphasize the belief in the eternity of the world nearly as systematically as Jacob Thomasius had done, this analysis still reflects the essential thesis of the *Schediasma Historicum*.

Having thus presented his readers with one homogeneous heretical tradition based upon the mingling of platonic philosophy with biblical Christianity, Colberg argued that it presents itself in two forms. The first one focuses on knowledge of one's self (the microcosm) through inner illumination, the other on knowledge of the world (the macrocosm) through reading the Book of Nature. Although this clearly reflects his general distinction of "platonic" and "hermetic," Colberg continues by referring to the two (rather confusingly) as *Cabala* and *Magia*. This peculiar understanding of *Cabala* reflected hardly any real familiarity with Jewish kabbalah, but seems to have been based rather on a quotation (attributed to an *Isagoge* by Paracelsus) that must have impressed Colberg:

> The *Cabala* is the Olympian spirit, or the sacramental body of the inner, spiritual, deified man *in Amadei*: seeing into the heavenly thrones and the truth of God with the bodily eyes of the heart [*des Gemütes*]. From this, the holy *Cabala* gives us to understand that we men can know all things, like the angels and the spirits, insofar as God permits it . . . [131]

Colberg specifies that this does not refer to the "literal and superstitious" kabbalah, which is focused on manipulating letters and words, but to the type known as *Mercava*. He was adopting the distinction from Robert Fludd, and found confirmation of his view of kabbalah as a form of platonism in Abraham Cohen Herrera's "Gates of Heaven," which he knew in the Latin translation of Knorr von Rosenroth's *Kabbala Denudata*.[132] This was a convenient choice, for Herrera himself had interpreted Lurianic kabbalah in strongly neoplatonic terms, and the very title of the (heavily doctored) version printed in Knorr's compendium emphasized its program of demonstrating the harmony between kabbalistic and platonic philosophy.[133] To Colberg's program, with its background in Thomasius' thesis about the "eternity of the world," it was particularly important that,

---

[130] *Ibid.*, II.7 (p. 118).   [131] *Ibid.*, III.3 (pp. 136–137).

[132] "Liber Scha'ar ha-Schamaiim seu Porta Coelorum," in: Knorr von Rosenroth, *Kabbala Denudata*, vol. II.

[133] See discussion in Lehmann-Brauns, *Weisheit*, 171–177. Knorr's was a Latin translation of Isaac Aboab's Hebrew translation of the Spanish original; and Aboab and Knorr had both strongly manipulated and partly paraphrased the latter, resulting in a strongly reduced version that presented kabbalah as a "concise neoplatonic system" (*ibid.*, 172).

from this perspective, the kabbalistic Adam Kadmon could be interpreted as an equivalent of the neoplatonic "first intellect" or of the "world spirit."[134]

Next to *Cabala*, the second form of Platonic-Hermetic Christianity was *Magia*. Colberg mentioned the common distinction between diabolical and natural magic, but emphasized that the Enthusiasts speak, rather, of a "divine supernatural magic."[135] Julius Sperber divided it into three types, Robert Fludd into four; but essentially, *Magia* means "knowledge of divine and natural things from the Book of Nature."[136] Here, of course, Colberg was referring to notions such as the Adamic Ur-language and the doctrine of signatures in the tradition of Paracelsus or Oswald Croll: by learning to read this mysterious script of the "language of nature," one was supposed to gain access to the hidden ideas in the light-world of the *spiritus universi*.

For assessing the impact of Colberg's work, perhaps his own (often rather sloppy) definitions and demarcations are less important than the simple fact that he brought all these loaded terms into close connection with one another under one general rubric and presented them as parts of one unified tradition. Most readers would probably not remember the exact manner in which Colberg defined, or tried to distinguish between, enthusiasm, paganism, mysticism, platonism, hermetism, kabbalah, or magic, but they certainly got the point: that under so many names, one always encountered the same heretical doctrine. In other words, Colberg's *Platonisch-Hermetisches Christenthum* amounted to a compendium of all traditional claims that needed to be rejected by Christians:

And now we should overturn this double foundation of the Neo-Pythagorean and Platonic Theology, and show that the *Cabala* and the divine revelation that springs from it is nothing, that no such Light-World or threefold common World-Spirit is to be found, that the Magical letters of light that are supposed to be present in all created things . . . are Jewish and Pagan fairy-tales . . . [137]

Even though it is clear to see that all these claims are groundless, Colberg continues, it is still necessary to refute them in detail. Partly this is because the enthusiasts are used to hiding their true meaning under "ambiguous and dark manners of expression," probably because they are afraid that otherwise their pagan and even atheist beliefs would be all too obvious.[138] Furthermore, deep down they know that their beliefs have no foundation, and therefore they refuse to give arguments or engage in discussion and

---

[134] See analysis in Lehmann-Brauns, *Weisheit*, 171–177, esp. 173–174.
[135] Colberg, *Platonisch-Hermetisches Christenthum*, vol. I, III.4 (p. 151).
[136] *Ibid.*, III.4 (p. 153).   [137] *Ibid.*, III.6 (p. 174).   [138] *Ibid.*, III.6 (p. 175).

insist instead on blind belief and obedience: "Hence they reject philosophy and dispute, so that their opinions may not be brought to the light and investigated, for they do not hold up."[139] Here it must be noted that, his extreme Protestant dogmatism notwithstanding, Colberg was rejecting the discourse of secrecy and mystery by formulating principles of clear language and open rational discussion that were to become foundational to the Enlightenment agenda and modern critical scholarship.

Thus to bring the doctrines of the Enthusiasts out into the open and make them available for critical discussion, the rest of Colberg's first volume consisted of detailed chapter-by-chapter discussions of the main forms of "enthusiasm," particularly Paracelsianism, Weigelianism, Rosicrucianism, and Böhmian theosophy.[140] The second volume covered the whole terrain once again, this time from a systematic angle. The essential doctrine of "enthusiasm" – immediate inner revelation or illumination – was analyzed in detail in the first chapter, followed by chapters on God, man, means of salvation, Christ, spiritual calling, rebirth, baptism, justification, good works, the eucharist, unification, eschatology, ecclesiology, the ministry, the government, and marriage.

In his attempt to expose the "enthusiasts" of his time as crypto-pagans and place them in a long Platonic-Hermetic tradition, Colberg became the first author to outline a complete and internally consistent historiographical concept that connected everything (obviously, up to the late seventeenth century) nowadays studied under the rubric of "Western esotericism." His extreme hostility notwithstanding, this makes him a crucial pioneer. We will see that in the decades after him, the logic of anti-apologeticism was further developed, in new directions which made it important not just to orthodox Protestants worried about sectarians, but to general historians of philosophy as well, and ultimately to the establishment of the modern academy.

THE PIETIST REACTION

In the wake of Thomasius and Colberg, accusations of "platonism" became an important weapon in the battle of the orthodoxy against "enthusiasm."

---

[139] *Ibid.*, III.6 (p. 178); and cf. the final section of the Preface (Vorrede) to the second volume, where Colberg emphasizes the need to bring order and clarity to the "babel and confusion" created by the enthusiastic theology.

[140] Colberg devotes chapters to several other currents, but in each of these cases he clearly realizes that including them requires special justification: see notably the openings of his chapters on the Quakers (*ibid.*, VII.1 [p. 292]), the Anabaptists (*ibid.*, IX.1 [p. 330]), and the Labadists (*ibid.*, XI.1 [pp. 414–415]).

Moreover, only eight years after *Platonisch-Hermetisches Christenthum*, a minister from Danzig, Friedrich Christoph Bücher, turned the same weapon against pietism in his *Plato Mysticus in Pietista redivivus* (1699).[141] Strongly influenced by Jacob Thomasius, Bücher adopted Colberg's metaphor of platonism as a "poisonous egg" from which magic and sorcery had infected Christianity[142] beginning with Origen and Simon Magus, and continuing since the Florentine Renaissance in authors such as Ficino, Pico, Trithemius, Agrippa, Paracelsus, and "enthusiasm" in all its forms, to which Bücher now added Philipp Jakob Spener's pietism. Its conceptual center was, again, the doctrine of emanation, and Bücher spoke about the whole tradition in drastic terms as "Satan's school of the Platonists and Kabbalists."[143] While connections between heterodox Protestant spiritualism and pietism had often been drawn before, it was Bücher who now provided such associations with a theoretical foundation, by using the logic of anti-apologeticism to describe them both as latter-day manifestations of the grand heretical tradition of platonism. In its pietist manifestation, Bücher argued, ecstatic states (*innerliche Entzückungen*) were now understood as providing immediate divine knowledge, so that all traditional means of salvation (the Bible, the sacraments, divine grace, ecclesiastical institutions) became superfluous. Hence Thomasius' double notion of the eternity of the world and the centrality of "gnosis" remained crucial to how the heretical tradition was construed.

Bücher's attack provoked a variety of responses from pietists, including Spener himself, who claimed that he had never read Plato or the platonists and (with profound irony) expressed his surprise at learning from Bücher "that there was so much good in the writings of the Platonici."[144] If affinities did indeed exist, he suggested that Plato must therefore have been familiar with the Jewish revelation and might even have read the Pentateuch. Elements of pagan philosophy might well have been adopted by the Jewish–Christian wisdom traditions, but rather than seeing this as evidence of syncretistic corruption, Spener saw no reason why the pagans

---

[141] Discussed in detail by Lehmann-Brauns (*Weisheit*, 187–222), who remarks that although the accusation of platonism is the conceptual center of anti-pietist polemics, it has been completely neglected by scholars of pietism (*ibid.*, 193 n. 22).

[142] Bücher, *Plato mysticus*, 9 (here quoted according to Lehmann-Brauns, *Weisheit*, 204). On Bücher's view of platonism as the foundation of a "secret science" of magic and sorcery, see Lehmann-Brauns, *Weisheit*, 202–206.

[143] Bücher, *Plato mysticus*, a3 (Lehmann-Brauns, *Weisheit*, 200).

[144] Spener, "Erste Vorrede!" § 5. Spener backs this up with a detailed account of his personal curriculum at the university; somewhat implausibly, given the length of his own Preface, he also mentions that he has had no time to read Colberg, and does not know whether it might contain statements similar to Bücher's.

might not have been granted "divine ecstasies" (*göttliche Entzückungen*)
similar to those that had inspired the apostle Paul:

> But we cannot do better than judge the art of divine ecstasies . . . from the examples
> [here Spener quotes Acts 10:10, 11:5, 22:17; 2 Cor. 12:2/4, Rev. 1:10, 4:2] which we
> find only in Scripture, from which one could also, for example, grasp the fact that
> it is through such an action of God that He binds man's senses for a while, so that
> they rest a bit from their own actions and stand still, and know of nothing else,
> because in the meantime God is working in their souls, and in his own manner
> gives them to understand, and impresses upon them, what it is that he now wishes
> to reveal to them or to others.[145]

In other words, the "inner knowledge" by means of ecstatic states which had
been denounced as pagan gnosis by Thomasius and Colberg, was accepted
by Spener as a legitimate avenue of revelation; and accordingly, elements
of truth might well be found in the writings of pagan philosophers.

Spener's text appeared as the Preface to Balthasar Köpke's response to
Bücher, published in 1700 as *Sapientia Dei in mysterio crucis Christi abscondita*. In yet another variation on the patristic "theft of the Greeks" motive,
Köpke argued that there was much truth in Greek philosophy, but it had
all been adopted from Judaism:

> Socrates, Zeno, Plato, and Aristotle have written many good things . . . Their lives
> and teachings are similar in many respects to the divine truth and wisdom, and
> a cause for shame for many Christians. In Egypt they have had dealings with the
> Jews, and undoubtedly have seen and read the Holy Scripture . . . But they have
> not admitted it, so that they might reap fame from it and would not be second to
> the Jews; so they have presented it covertly and by other words, and mixed it with
> pagan fables, so that their own people, who disliked the Jews and their doctrine,
> would take no notice, but would accept it all the more eagerly. Thus, in many
> divine things they have nevertheless possessed the truth, in particular the γνῶσον
> Θεῶν, the knowledge of God . . . and have known and taught it quite well, against
> the vulgar polytheistic opinions of the people.[146]

Thus we see that in response to critics such as Thomasius and Colberg,
Köpke's pietist alternative amounted to yet another variation on the ancient
wisdom narrative; and this included a rehabilitation of the early Fathers
of the Church, who had not really been platonists but had merely used
platonic terminology as allegorical confirmation of the revealed truth of
monotheism.[147] As indicated by the very title of his book, which mentioned the "false and pagan philosophy of Plato," Köpke was as hard on

---

[145] Spener, "Erste Vorrede!" § 12.   [146] Köpke, *Sapientia Dei* § 21 (p. 43).
[147] Lehmann-Brauns, *Weisheit*, 243–246.

paganism as his anti-apologetic opponents, describing the Egyptians as drenched in the "most shameful idolatry and blindness," as shown by the fact that they built temples to worship "creatures of the most horrible kind (shocking to human nature)," and as also shown by his treatment of Hermes Trismegistus:

> In the meantime the Egyptian sages still retained much that resembled the truth, but out of hate and envy they did not want to admit that they had received it from Joseph and the descendants of Jacob; instead, they attributed it to another author or original source, whom they called Hermes or Mercurius, about whom all kinds of things can be read in the pagan writers . . . But it should be noted that some scholars attribute the writings that the world has come to know under the name of Hermes Trismegistus not to the ancient Egyptian Mercurius, but to a much younger philosopher, who lived after the birth of Christ, and claim that he was nothing but a *cento*, or (similar to how Luther speaks about the al-Koran of Muhammad) a beggar's mantle patched together from the Christian, Platonic and Egyptian doctrine . . . Therefore the origin of the false mystical stuff actually comes from the envious imitation of the aforementioned people, and from the mingling of divine and worldly wisdom.[148]

Furthermore, Köpke agreed with his anti-apologetic opponents in rejecting the doctrine of the eternity of the world; but unlike them, he argued that the early Greek philosophers had adopted the teaching of *creatio ex nihilo* from the Jews, and the turn towards heresy had occurred only at a later stage. The true doctrine had declined among both the Jews and the pagans, until it was restored by Christ. Simon Magus and the other Gnostic heretics had then tried to reintroduce the pagan error of the eternity of the world:

> The first and worst impostor was Simon Magus with his followers, who has sown weeds among the grain. Outside the churches, the pagan philosophers had reunited against Christianity in their opinion about the eternity of the world, which was also adopted by the platonists who had not converted, and who out of Plato's writings sought to prove the opinion that the matter from which the world is made is uncreated and co-eternal with God, so that in this way they might all the more strongly contradict Christianity and its promise of eternal life.[149]

Thus in Köpke's argument, an acceptable lineage of Jewish wisdom transmitted partly by pagans could be distinguished from a heretical counter-tradition of pure paganism. The crucial point of distinction was, once

---

[148] Köpke, *Sapientia Dei* § 7 1 (pp. 13–14).   [149] Köpke, *Sapientia Dei* § 28 (p. 59).

again, the question of whether the world was created or eternal: all orthodox opinions were seen as following logically from the former alternative,
and all heresies from the latter.

Next to Köpke, Bücher's main pietist opponent was Spener's friend
Johann Wilhelm Zierold, the author of a church history in which the
patristic apologetic tradition and its continuation in the Renaissance *prisca
theologia* attempted one of its last comebacks.[150] The full title is significant:
*Einleitung zur gründlichen Kirchenhistorie, mit der Historia philosophica
verknüpfft, darinnen die Kraft des Creutzes Christi als der einzige Grund des
wahren Christentumb wider die Feinde des Creutzes von Anfang der Welt biß
auf unsere Zeit vorgestellet wird* (Introduction to the thorough History of
the Church, interconnected with the History of Philosophy, in which the
Power of Christ's Cross is presented, against the enemies of the Cross, as
the only foundation of true Christianity from the beginning of the world
to our time). Published in 1700, this title contains the entire program of the
work: it assumes that church history cannot be discussed separately from
the history of philosophy, and argues that the true theology grounded in
the "mystery of the cross" has been available not just since the birth of
Christ, but since the very beginning of the world.

Zierold referred explicitly to the authority of the patristic apologists,
particularly Origen, Clement, and Eusebius.[151] From this perspective, he
tried to turn the tables on Bücher by placing him in the same camp as their
anti-Christian opponents: philosophers like Celsus or Porphyry![152] What
they had in common was their rejection of the humble "piety of the heart"
which, in Zierold's view, had been the true core of the one revealed religion.
Any such piety was grounded in a deeply felt recognition that, due to the
Fall, man had lost his original paradisical state of participation in God's
being and wisdom. Only on the basis of such a profound sense of human
sinfulness – the "mystery of the cross," which had been intuited already
by the most ancient sages – was it possible for man to purify himself and
regain his lost divinity. Zierold sharply opposed this meek and humble
pietism to the arrogance of the philosophers and their worldly belief in
the autonomy of human reason. Man's very capacity of understanding

---

[150] For detailed information on Zierold's life and his controversies with Bücher and others, see the
anonymous entry in the *Große Zedler*: Anon., "Zierold (Johann Wilhelm)." The only detailed
analyses are Longo, "Storia della filosofia tra eclettismo e pietismo," 350–360; Lehmann-Brauns,
Weisheit, 246–265.

[151] Lehmann-Brauns, *Weisheit*, 250. Important recent influences on Zierold were Philippe Duplessis-
Mornay, Hugo Grotius, Pierre-Daniel Huet, G. J. Vossius, Theophilus Gale, Peter Lambeck and
Daniel Georg Morhof (*ibid.*; and cf. above, n. 86).

[152] Lehmann-Brauns, *Weisheit*, 249–250.

had been deeply perverted due to the Fall, resulting in a sharp opposition between those who humbly recognized the unreliability of reason, and those – the philosophers – who kept putting their faith in it.

For Zierold, following here in Patrizi's footsteps, Aristotle was a model example of such impious philosophy; but Plato belonged to the lineage of the ancient wisdom. Due to the Fall, the true piety had already declined in antediluvian times, but it was preserved by Noah. Like many pre-Enlightenment historians, Zierold believed that after the Flood, all the world's peoples and cultures had descended from Noah's sons. For him, this meant that they stood at the origin of – broadly speaking – the Oriental, African, and Mediterranean traditions:

Ancestor →	Peoples/cultures	Most important sage
Shem →	Assyrians, Chaldaeans, Lydians, Syrians, Arabs, Armenians, Indians.	Zoroaster
Ham →	African peoples, incl. Egyptians.	Hermes
Jafeth →	Galatians, Celts, Scythians, Iberians, Cappadocians, Greeks.	Plato

As pointed out by Lehmann-Brauns, this meant that all forms of ancient paganism were included in a Jewish–Christian biblical narrative: Zierold's approach left no room for paganism as a competing counter-tradition, and hence "error" of any kind could only be described in terms of decline or deviation from the one ancient truth.[153] This wisdom tradition was grounded in monotheism and taught that the world had been created by God: polytheism and belief in the eternity of the world were later perversions. The original language of wisdom had been Hebrew, and the decline of true piety went hand in hand with the decline of this perfect language. Zierold was particularly radical in his manner of preserving the centrality of Moses: Moses was the crucial ancient sage indeed, for not only was he the author of the Pentateuch, but (in spite of the division into three post-Noachite streams located in different geographical areas) Zierold suggested that he was probably identical with both Zoroaster *and* Hermes![154] It was not these ancient pagan traditions that were the sources of heresy, but the impious philosophy of Aristotle. As for Plato: he stood in the lineage of Egyptian wisdom mediated by Pythagoras, but had also learned much from the Jews and had read the Pentateuch.[155] All these ancient traditions finally led towards their culmination in the gospel.

---

[153] *Ibid.*, 253.　　[154] *Ibid.*, 254–260.　　[155] *Ibid.*, 260–265.

THE BIRTH OF RELIGIONISM: GOTTFRIED ARNOLD

Köpke and, particularly, Zierold were well-known authors in Germany around 1700 (the *Große Zedler* of 1732–1754 introduces the latter as "a famous Lutheran theologian," and devotes a long and detailed article to him), but while they are important to our story, they are almost completely forgotten today. This cannot be said about the radical pietist Gottfried Arnold, author of the famous *Unparteyische Kirchen- und Ketzer-Historie* published in 1699–1700.[156] There are several reasons to consider this work as the major historiographical counterpart to Colberg's *Platonisch-Hermetisches Christenthum*. Most obviously, the *Impartial History* sought to rehabilitate as "Christian" most of the currents that had been denounced as quasi-pagan heresy by the anti-apologists; but even more important for our concerns, it introduced a novel theoretical perspective that would eventually become of great importance to the modern study of Western esotericism. It will be argued here that, whereas Colberg was the earliest pioneer of "Western esotericism" as a historiographical concept, Arnold is the originator of its "religionist" alternative, to which I will return at length in Chapter 4.

The first thing to notice about Arnold's *Impartial History* is its striking lack of interest in the entire problem of the historical relation between paganism, or pagan philosophy, and Christianity. It is illustrative of this approach that, in his opening pages, all that Arnold has to say about the religious environment in which Christianity was born is how "miserable and depraved" the whole world had been at the moment when the light of the gospel began to shine.[157] The Jewish religion was in a sorry state due to the degeneration of its priests, and among the pagan peoples the situation was even worse: they were living "like dumb cattle" under the domination of a corrupt priesthood and its "self-invented religion," and their quarreling philosophers had absolutely nothing better to offer.[158] Arnold knew the works of Thomasius Sr. and Colberg, and politely referred to them from time to time, but here and elsewhere in his *Impartial History* he systematically refused to be drawn into any historical-critical discussion about whether, or how, pagan philosophy might be related to Christianity in any of its forms, whether "heretical" or "orthodox."[159]

---

[156] The extensive secondary literature on Arnold is documented in Blaufuß and Niewöhner, *Gottfried Arnold*, 415–424 (up to 1993).

[157] Arnold, *Unparteyische Geschichte*, 29 (Bk. 1 § 1.2).   [158] *Ibid.*, 30 (Bk. 1 § 1.6–7).

[159] The very few passing references in Arnold's *Unparteyische Geschichte* to pagan and platonic influences are discussed in Glawe, *Hellenisierung*, 105–107. For some further short discussions, see

To understand the reasons for this attitude, it is crucial to notice that Arnold appears to have *agreed* with the anti-apologists that there could be no concord of any kind between pagan philosophy and Christian faith. Whereas pietists like Köpke and Zierold reacted to Thomasius and Colberg by reviving some form of the patristic apologetic perspective, Arnold's attitude to paganism was perfectly in line with the radical *anti*-apologetic stance taken by other early Fathers of the Church! The classic reference comes from Tertullian's *De praescriptione haereticorum*:

Hence [i.e. from philosophy] spring those "fables and endless genealogies" (1 Tim. 1:4) and "fruitless questions and words" (Tit. 3:9) which "spread like a cancer" (2 Tim. 2:17). Wishing to restrain us from them, the apostle specifically states that we should be on our guard against philosophy and vain deceit, when he writes to the Colossians: "See that no one beguile you through philosophy and vain deceit, after the tradition of men" (Col. 2:8), and contrary to the wisdom of the Holy Ghost. He had been at Athens, and had through his meetings [with its philosophers] come to know that human wisdom which pretends to know the truth but only corrupts it, and is itself divided into its own manifold heresies, by the variety of its mutually repugnant sects. What indeed has Athens to do with Jerusalem, the Academy with the Church, heretics with Christians?[160]

Surprising though it might seem at first sight, Arnold's entire *Impartial History* was grounded in this radical anti-apologetic approach, but the conclusions he drew from it were very different from those of Thomasius Sr. and Colberg. These authors had criticized the pernicious influence of "Athens" (platonic philosophy) on "Jerusalem" (Christian doctrine), and had argued that Christian theology should be purified of pagan and platonic influences so as to get back to the original biblical revelation. But as the later development of anti-apologeticism would demonstrate, the vulnerable point in this argument was that it ultimately undermined Christian theology *as such*: as historians became ever more adept at recognizing traces of pagan philosophy in Christian doctrine, it was beginning to dawn on them how little of it was free from such influence, and how difficult (or rather, impossible) it was to do without it, and build a theological system on the Bible alone. The profound irony was that the logic of anti-apologeticism therefore ended up undermining the orthodoxy that it had set out to defend, while greatly strengthening the pietist argument that the Bible was all about practical piety and not about theological doctrine.

also Arnold, *Erste Liebe*. Arnold's *Historie und Beschreibung der Mystischen Theologie* (1703) can be considered his response to the methodology of the anti-apologetic school (see analysis in Lehmann-Brauns, *Weisheit*, 297–307).
[160] Tertullian, *De praescriptione haereticorum* chapter 7.7–9 (Schleyer ed., 244).

In short: wielding the ever-sharpening weapon of patristic criticism, the orthodox anti-apologists had been busy cutting off the branch on which they were themselves sitting.[161]

Gottfried Arnold seems to have understood this, and his approach to historiography shows how pietists could turn the anti-apologetic argument to their own advantage. Contrary to Köpke and Zierold, Arnold refused to even discuss questions concerning the historical relation between paganism and Christianity because, in his view, *there could be no such relation*. "Athens" and "Jerusalem," or philosophy and faith, are not just incompatible but wholly *incommensurable*: they share no common measure that is applicable to both, and therefore no discussion is even possible.[162] Christian faith is sufficient to itself, and has no need of entering the arena of philosophical dispute. According to Arnold, the tragedy of the orthodox polemicists was that, while claiming to offer a cure for the disease of heresy, they were themselves symptomatic of that disease: as shown by their addiction to doctrinal quarreling, not only had they entered the arena of philosophy, but they had been thoroughly perverted by it. One might say that they had become "Athenians" without realizing it. They believed that the battle between orthodoxy and heresy should take place in the arena of theology, but failed to realize that only "Athens" has such arenas; they wished to purify Christian theology from pagan contamination, but were blind to the fact that their own theology was a product of such contamination. Whereas all the discussions we have been surveying so far had been structured according to the polarity between "biblical faith" and "pagan philosophy," Arnold changed the rules of the game by building his history upon a different polarity: that between "Christian piety" and "doctrinal theology." As a result, paganism ceased being a factor of any importance in his narrative.

The nature of the "paradigm shift" represented by Arnold's *Impartial History* is important but subtle, and can easily be misunderstood. From the above, one might be tempted to conclude that since the patristic apologists

---

[161] See above, page 103, and note 96. Lehmann-Brauns explains how "precarious" the situation of orthodox Protestantism had become on the eve of the Enlightenment: "it rejected Pietist attempts at an intensified piety as an un-biblical paganization of Christianity, and denounced allegory, while at the same time basing itself upon a dogmatism whose biblical legitimacy had long come to be doubted. The rigorous orthodox Biblicist lost philosophical exegesis of Christianity to pagan philosophy and its heretical successors. Living piety had to be conceded to the Pietists, who should be kept distinct from those platonic-philosophical heretics. All that remained was the bible, and what came next was radical biblical criticism."

[162] Van Dongen, *Geen gemene maat*, 173 (summary in English). The concept of incommensurability was introduced into modern philosophy of science by Thomas S. Kuhn and Paul Feyerabend; for discussion, *ibid.*, 27–66.

had so evidently entered the arena of platonic philosophy, Arnold would therefore have to reject them as "Athenians" as well. But this would be missing the whole point about Arnold's oeuvre, which is replete with positive references to all the early Fathers. Rejecting the patristic apologists merely for their involvement with platonism would imply that criteria for distinguishing between true Christianity and heresy could be found on the level of verbal doctrine (whether one calls it philosophical or theological) – but this would be precisely the "Athenian" error that Arnold was criticizing. The only true criterion, for Arnold, is whether an author's works exemplify the spirit of humble faith and practical piety that is the mark of the true Christian. As long as they do, it does not matter whether or not they have been meddling in philosophy, for their heart is in "Jerusalem."

Arnold's point of reference for true Christianity was the original apostolic community, which he painted in highly idyllic terms: its members had been all about pure faith, love, unity, peace, and pious practice. The central core of this true Christianity of humble piety had consisted in direct inner illumination and the experience of spiritual rebirth in Christ through the Holy Spirit.[163] But very soon, this pure spiritual community had fallen into sin: faith degenerated into dogmatism, communal love gave way to self-love, and inner peace and unity were broken by external strife and sectarian disputes. The Inner Church of the spirit degenerated into an ecclesiastical institution focused on power and domination, sadly culminating in the religious politics of Constantine. From then on, the *Verfallsgeschichte* of Christianity[164] had continued with depressing repetitiveness up to the present (discussed by Arnold in seventeen books, one for each century, like Baronius' *Annals* and the "Magdeburg Centuries" before him). Luther's Reformation was no exception to the spectacle of decline, for it had degenerated quite as disastrously as the Roman Catholic Church, leading to the unsavory spectacle, in Arnold's own time, of theologians fighting like cats and dogs over who was "orthodox" and who were the "heretics."

These polemicists did not behave as Christians should, and had clearly forgotten what the gospel was supposed to be all about. If Arnold called his history "impartial," this certainly did not imply an attitude of "disinterested" neutrality on his part, let alone a position of methodological agnosticism as we might understand it today. On the contrary, he clearly took a position:

---

[163] See, for example, Schlögl, "Hermetismus als Sprache der 'unsichtbaren Kirche'," 173–174; Lehmann-Brauns, *Weisheit*, 267–272.

[164] For example, Baur, *Epochen*, 90; Meinhold, *Geschichte der kirchlichen Historiographie*, vol. 1, 430–431; Buchholz, "Historia Contentionis," 171–172; Lehmann-Brauns, *Weisheit*, 288.

so we raise a powerful protest against all those who have a taste for quarreling [*welche lust zu zancken haben*] and who would like to pick a fight about this or that doctrinal point . . . considering that the entire History demonstrates how much malice, error, excess and destruction has come out of such wars about words [*wortkriegen*] . . . the whole world is still filled with entire armies of scholars who busy themselves with such destructive battles and are lying in ambush against one another.[165]

The schoolmen and worldly theologians have obscured the "clear waters" of the Christian faith with their intellectual games and doctrinal quibbling: while the Church of Christ should live in peace and unity, they have turned it into a filthy "cesspool" (*Mist-Pfütze*) of quarreling, slandering, violence, and vain ambition.[166]

Arnold could claim to write from a position "above the parties" because, in his opinion, the distinction between true and false had nothing to do with doctrinal matters at all. As a result, the historian was entirely free to search for "true Christians" regardless of their doctrinal positions, that is to say, among the so-called heretics as well as among the orthodox. In an era dominated by confessional strife, this principle seemed tolerant and non-dogmatic, and it has earned Arnold a positive reputation among early Enlightenment thinkers, beginning with (interestingly) Jacob Thomasius' son Christian.[167] But as already suggested, Arnold's "impartiality" did not imply neutrality, for in fact his church history amounted to a simple reversal: the "orthodox" emerged from his History as the real heretics, and the "heretics" as the true Christians. It is important to understand that this happened not merely because of Arnold's personal biases, but because his claim of impartiality was self-defeating to begin with: in terms of the underlying theory of decline, the orthodoxy that was supposed to be treated "impartially" was already marked as heretical by virtue of being institutional and doctrinal.

Against the depressing spectacle of historical Christianity and its endless doctrinal disputes, Arnold posited a supra-historical principle of immediate religious experience, grounded in Sophianic wisdom:

But what this principal work of wisdom really is, can better be experienced than described, and may be indicated here only insofar as God reveals it in the soul, outside and beyond which it behooves one to be silent . . . As much as one may have spoken about the essence of wisdom, and would wish to speak even more, she still

[165] Arnold, *Unparteyische Geschichte*, Vorrede §§ 13–15.
[166] Arnold, *Historie und Beschreibung*, 15–16 (chapter 1.19).
[167] Lehmann-Brauns, *Weisheit*, 266–268; Pott, "Christian Thomasius und Gottfried Arnold," esp. 252–255.

remains even higher, yes, unspeakable and unfathomable in herself. "Expressing the speech of wisdom (let alone her essence) in words is beyond man's power" as the ur-ancient Hermes already said.[168]

Arnold emphasizes that, like God himself, the true wisdom is a hidden and secret mystery[169] that transcends human reason, and reveals itself only in the intimacy of the humble and pious heart. Because of the focus on wisdom rather than words, the term "theosophia" is more appropriate than "theologia."[170] Obviously, all this was yet another variation on the pervasive theme of "inwardness" which had been criticized by the anti-apologists as a form of gnosis; and as the above quotation demonstrates, Arnold saw no problem in referring even to Hermes (quoting indirectly from Lactantius) in support of what he saw as the core and essence of Christian spirituality.

It is particularly important to understand the implications of Arnold's perspective concerning the logic of historical criticism, and historiography as such. His approach to history rested upon methodological premises that were wholly incompatible with those of the anti-apologists; and from this perspective, the arguments of these *Critici*, as he called them, were misguided and irrelevant. Arnold was convinced that only a historian who had personally experienced "inner illumination" would be able to write an adequate history of Christianity at all, because otherwise he would be missing the all-important criterion for recognizing truth. It was possible to discover documented evidence of instances of inner illumination by studying the historical sources, but the experience itself had a transcendent origin and therefore could not be accounted for by means of historical research. How unimportant historical criticism really is to Arnold, becomes clear for example from the ease with which he dismisses the thrust of Thomasius' *Schediasma*:

But when some author, and also the Leipzig Schediasma, mentions yet another source of this [mystical] theology, namely platonic philosophy, then this question may easily be resolved . . . For the true and essential source of this divine gift remains, like all other good and perfect gifts, none other than God alone, with his holy revealed Word, and never some teaching or doctrine created from the human will, let alone a pagan philosophy.[171]

---

[168] Arnold, *Geheimnis*, 165 (chapter XXIII) and 39 (chapter V). On the importance of Sophia, wisdom, in Christian theosophy, see Faivre, "Sensuous Relation."

[169] Arnold, *Historie und Beschreibung*, 4 (chapter I.6), and for the theme of "inexpressibility," cf. *ibid.*, 83 (chapter V.5) and 89 (chapter V.11). Against this background, Arnold also strongly defended the use of "obscure" or enigmatic language, and a "theologia symbolica" based on images rather than words (*ibid.*, 91–94 [chapter V.14–16]).

[170] Arnold, *Historie und Beschreibung*, 5–6 (chapter I.8).   [171] *Ibid.*, 45 (chapter III.9).

Because it is impossible by definition to denounce the authentic experience of God as the product of external influences, any historical-critical attempt to trace the *Theologia mystica* to philosophical sources, or even discuss their relation, is futile and misguided by definition.[172] This is why, unlike his fellow-pietists Spener, Köpke and Zierold, Arnold almost wholly ignored paganism and platonism even in his discussion of the first centuries of Christianity, and made not the slightest attempt to discuss previous ancient wisdom traditions. His only concern was with "true" Christianity as he saw it, not with Christianity as a historical phenomenon that emerges in close interaction and exchange with its cultural environment. Because the gospel had made paganism obsolete, pagan traditions were irrelevant to the history of churches and heretics. As shown by the reference to Hermes, Arnold did not exclude the possibility that ancient sages might occasionally have said something true; but again, simply because philosophy is pagan and not Christian, it is of no concern to a historian of Christianity.

While all the approaches we have been discussing so far could be seen as rudimentary exercises in the comparative history of religions, Arnold's leading principles were in fact incompatible with historiography proper: they rested on a pure essentialism that ruled out any historical comparison from the outset. His *Impartial History* presents the reader with a remarkably de-contextualized description of the supposedly "real" and "pure" Christian faith and its many degenerations, which never result from pagan influence – or from any other historical influence, for that matter – but are explained exclusively from sinful human tendencies such as pride, egoism, or the pursuit of power.[173]

Arnold's approach to the history of Christianity may be described as a more specific development of the "history of truth" approach. It is grounded in the same paradox as its Renaissance ancestors – it tries to write the history of something that cannot have a history, because it is considered beyond change and development – but is considerably more radical in its insistence on direct "inner" spiritual experience or gnosis as the only reliable means of access to the one universal truth, which is now sharply juxtaposed against any "external" and therefore (from this

---

[172] Lehmann-Brauns, *Weisheit*, 297, 306. On Arnold's response to the approach of the *Critici* in his *Historie und Beschreibung der Mystischen Theologie* (1703), see *ibid.*, 297–307.

[173] Arnold's reputation as a pioneer of modern academic historiography and a predecessor of Enlightenment perspectives (see, for example, Schlögl, "Hermetismus," 165–166, 169–174; Lehmann-Brauns, *Weisheit*, 266–269) is therefore hard to justify: the relatively neglected anti-apologetic tradition culminating in Jacob Brucker has much stronger and more convincing claims in this regard. In contrast, the most representative church histories at least up to the 1970s display a non-historical bias quite similar to Arnold's (see Hanegraaff, "Dreams of Theology," 713–715).

perspective) merely relative or contingent historical developments. We will be referring to this novel approach as "religionism."[174] What makes it different from earlier attempts at writing the "history of truth" is that, emerging at a time when modern historical consciousness is beginning to come into its own, it does present itself as historiography but nevertheless seeks to escape from the "reductionist" implications of historical criticism and comparative research. On the level of doctrines and ideas (whether religious or philosophical), the Renaissance "history of truth" tradition was in the process of losing the battle against the *Critici*, whose arguments were simply superior; but by moving the center of attention from ideas to non-verbal "experience," authors like Arnold could claim that historical criticism itself had its limitations, and that historical-mindedness might make one blind to the true experiential core of faith. This line of argumentation would prove to be compelling to many: we will see that in its more radical later manifestations, the basic religionist logic would finally lead to explicitly anti-historical perspectives that nevertheless present themselves as "history of religion."

ENLIGHTENMENT AND ECLIPSE

At the threshold of the eighteenth century, we have now reached a crucial point in our story. In 1690–1691 Ehregott Daniel Colberg used Jacob Thomasius' anti-apologeticism to write the first historical account of "Western esotericism" (under the label of "Platonic-Hermetic Christianity"), and we have seen that his synthesis was firmly rooted in a tradition of polemics against "Platonic Orientalism" that can be traced back to the fifteenth century. Up to this moment, there had been essentially two positions in the debate: one that defended some sort of accommodation between pagan philosophy and Christian theology (from the patristic apologists to humanists in the tradition of Ficino, Pico, Steuco, or Patrizi, and from there all the way up to pietists like Köpke and Zierold) and another one that rejected any such accommodation and insisted on keeping Christian truth sharply apart from pagan error (beginning with anti-apologetic Fathers like Tertullian, and from Renaissance authors like the younger Pico or Crispo

---

[174] In the modern study of religion, the term "religionism" has come to be used for the methodological counterpart of social-scientific "reductionism." Associated in particular with the so-called "Chicago school" dominated by the legacy of Mircea Eliade, religionism insists that religion is an irreducible phenomenon *sui generis* which cannot be explained in terms external to it, such as, for example, sociology or psychology (for a very readable introduction to the religionism–reductionism debate, see Allen, "Is nothing Sacred?"; for a more theoretical discussion focused on Western esotericism, see Hanegraaff, "Empirical Method"). See further discussion in Chapter 4.

all the way up to Thomasius Sr. and Colberg). The ancient wisdom discourse of the early modern period was constituted by the complex dialectics between these two opposed positions.

But to account for developments from the end of the seventeenth century on, this framework ceases to be sufficient. The "religionist" paradigm pioneered by Arnold escaped from the traditional terms of opposition by declaring paganism irrelevant to the history of Christianity, while at the same time creating a new conceptual foundation (the centrality of inner spiritual experience) for defending the legitimacy of the "heretical" tradition. Moreover, still in the final decades of the seventeenth century, there emerged a second alternative paradigm as well, to which we will now turn. This one proclaimed not just the irrelevance, but the futility and even the foolishness of paganism, denouncing it as superstitious "prejudice" in the name of Reason and finally delegating it to the dustbin of history. This perspective became dominant in the age of the Enlightenment, and would come to exert a powerful influence over how "Western esotericism" has been perceived up to the present day.

From the perspective of my discussion so far, the Enlightenment historiography of "ancient wisdom" may be considered the closing chapter in the history of anti-apologeticism. We have seen that Jacob Thomasius had sought to define the nature of true Christianity as incompatible with anything pagan; but his more famous son Christian used his father's critical tools rather to liberate the history of philosophy from its theological dependencies and turn it into an autonomous discipline.[175] It was not so much that pagan philosophies had to be wholly rejected, but that they must be recognized for what they were: attempts to understand the world by purely human means, without the aid of Revelation. Such an approach has, of course, become constitutive of the history of philosophy as a modern discipline; but necessary and inevitable though this process of academic emancipation may have been, we will see that it came at a price.

Christian Thomasius is traditionally seen as the "Father of the German *Aufklärung*," and not without good reason. Nevertheless, his case shows how reductive such labels can be: his strong Enlightenment commitments did not keep him from receiving a strong influence of pietism and the Christian theosophy of Jacob Böhme and Pierre Poiret, even to the point

---

[175] The literature on the younger Thomasius is extensive. For his role in the history of the history of philosophy, see Longo, "Storia della filosofia tra eclettismo e pietismo," 341–350; for his relation to the anti-apologeticism of his father, the indispensable discussion remains Lehmann-Brauns, *Weisheit*, 308–354.

of having his own experience of "illumination" in 1693, and developing a *Naturphilosophie* explicitly along Platonic-Hermetic lines in his *Versuch von Wesen des Geistes* (1699).[176] As regards the history of philosophy, Thomasius inherited his father's dislike for syncretic mixtures of theology and philosophy; but he went far beyond him in defending the ideal of a practical and useful philosophy wholly free of metaphysics[177] and, indeed, of any non-rational "prejudice" (*Vorurteil*) – a term that was understood by him as strongly overlapping with "superstition" (*Aberglaube*).[178] This program implied the need for a critical revision of the entire history of philosophy as traditionally understood, for as Thomasius put it, "man will never be freed from prejudices, unless with the help of history he understands the origin of prejudices."[179] The method for doing so came to be known as "eclecticism." Using his own faculty of rational judgment, the historian of philosophy should seek to separate the wheat from the chaff, accepting true tenets wherever he might find them while rejecting false ones, instead of dogmatically following the claims of one particular philosophical "sect."[180] Against the notion of *philosophia sectaria*, with its wholesale obedience to the tenets of this or that philosophical school, Thomasius' *philosophia eclectica* exhorted the historian to "think for himself" instead of blindly following some traditional authority.

This method of eclecticism was a clear alternative to sectarian dogmatism, and would become central to the historiography of philosophy as it developed during the eighteenth century; but it may also serve to illustrate how complex the relationship is between the early German Enlightenment and pietism. Although his criterion of selection was very different, Gottfried Arnold's "impartiality" was a reflection of the same eclectic principle: the historian of Christianity should disregard sectarian prejudice, so as to "investigate everything and keep what is good" (1 Thess. 5:21). Far from being a concern of strict Enlightenment ideologues alone, then, the "praise of eclecticism" in fact became a central aspect of popular philosophy during

---

[176] Meumann, "Diskursive Formationen," 78–83 (analyzing the attempts by earlier scholars to "protect" Thomasius' Enlightenment identity by downplaying the embarrassing theosophical/pietist dimensions of his life and work); Kemper, *Gottebenbildlichkeit*, 244–257.

[177] Lehmann-Brauns, *Weisheit*, 312: "For Christian... the history of the mingling of philosophy and theology was the dark background against which the light of his philosophy liberated from metaphysics should shine in all the brilliance of its practical usefulness."

[178] Schneiders, *Aufklärung und Vorurteilskritik*, esp. 92–115 on Thomasius.

[179] Thomasius, *Cautelae* § 53 (p. 94).

[180] On the difference with earlier understandings of eclecticism, see Albrecht, "Thomasius"; Lehmann-Brauns, *Weisheit*, 313–317; Schmidt-Biggemann, *Theodizee und Tatsachen*, 203–222. An extensive reference work for eclecticism in all its historical forms is Albrecht, *Eklektik* (see pp. 398–416 for Christian Thomasius).

the eighteenth century.[181] It is one of the ironies of history that precisely this eclectic method in historical research was praised in a famous passage by Leibniz under a title which, against the background of our previous discussions, could not have been more badly chosen: that of *philosophia perennis*!

The truth is more widely spread than one might think, but very often it is blurred, and very often also enveloped, even enfeebled, mutilated, corrupted, by additions that spoil it or render it less useful. By calling attention to these traces of truth in the ancients (or, to speak more generally, in our predecessors) one would be lifting the gold from out of the mud, the diamond from its mine, and the light from the shadows; and in fact, that would be a kind of perennial philosophy (*perennis quaedam philosophia*).[182]

So great was Leibniz's authority among later generations, and so complete was the eclipse of the ancient wisdom narrative after the period of the Enlightenment, that this evident confusion between *philosophia perennis* and Enlightenment eclecticism would become normative among philosophers for over two and a half centuries, until Charles B. Schmitt revived the memory of the original Renaissance perspective in his seminal article of 1966.[183]

The implications of Enlightenment eclecticism for the history of philosophy are presented with particular clarity in the writings of Christoph August Heumann (1681–1764), "the Thomasius of Göttingen,"[184] who is widely considered the founder of the history of philosophy as a modern

---

[181] Zimmermann, *Weltbild des jungen Goethe*, vol. 1, 19–27.

[182] Leibniz, letter to Remond (August 26, 1714), in: Gerhardt, *Philosophischen Schriften von Gottfried Wilhelm Leibniz*, III, 624–625. Leibniz continues by noting that "the orientals had beautiful and great ideas about the Divinity," the Greeks added reasoning and "a form of science," the Fathers of the Church did away with "what was bad in Greek philosophy," and the scholastics tried to make "what was passable in the philosophy of the pagans" useful for Christianity, which is why Leibniz has often said that some gold can be found even in the "dung" of scholastic barbarianism (*ibid.*, 625).

[183] Schmitt, "Perennial Philosophy." Schmitt was clearly mistaken in seeing the Leibniz quotation as representative of "the tradition of perennial philosophy as envisioned by Steuco" (*ibid.*, 530), as my discussion in Chapter 1 has hopefully demonstrated. Likewise, Rolf Christian Zimmermann's pioneering discussion of *Vernünftige Hermetik* in the period of the Enlightenment (the importance of which is rightly highlighted by Neugebauer-Wölk, "Esoterik im 18. Jahrhundert," 20–22; "Aufklärung – Esoterik – Wissen," 20–21, 26–27) unfortunately uses the Leibniz quotation to suggest that eighteenth-century eclecticism implied an adherence to the *philosophia perennis* (*Weltbild des jungen Goethe*, vol. 1, 19–27, here 21), and even that eclecticism was equivalent to "syncretism" (*ibid.*, 19–20); and similar statements can be found in the earlier work of Antoine Faivre (*L'ésotérisme au XVIIIe siècle*, 62–64; "Children of Hermes," 425). It is certainly true that the eclectic method allowed eighteenth-century thinkers to investigate "Platonic-Hermetic" traditions in search of the truths they might contain (and this is more than sufficient to explain the examples given by Zimmermann); but by no means does this imply that eclecticism is itself a manifestation of perennial philosophy, or that the latter is inherently eclectic. Likewise, we have seen that eclecticism was explicitly set *against* syncretism.

[184] Mühlpfordt, "Ein kryptoradikaler Thomasianer."

discipline.[185] At the age of twenty-five, the academic career of the young Heumann at the University of Jena was cut short because he had rejected a biblical story (that of Lot's wife being turned into a pillar of salt) as incompatible with sound reason. After working for many years as a Gymnasium teacher and administrator, in 1734 he was appointed at the new University of Göttingen, but his historical-critical methods and their implications kept creating controversy, culminating in a conflict with the university that forced him into early retirement. He has left a very large and impressive oeuvre, but most important for our concerns are his *Acta Philosophorum*, history's first periodical devoted to the history of philosophy, that appeared from 1715 to 1727 and was filled mostly by Heumann himself. The second volume contained a long treatise "Von denen Kennzeichen der falschen und unächten Philosophie," in which Heumann discussed six characteristics which allow us to distinguish "false and bogus" from "real" philosophy.

(1) Pseudo-philosophy has a preference for *useless speculation*. Examples are scholastic metaphysics, the Lullian philosophy (which should better be called "Nullian"), Leibniz's *Ars Combinatoria*, and a whole range of divinatory systems: "the *ars onirocritica*, the *ars chiromantica*, the *ars geomantica*, the *ars astrologia*, in one word: all the *artes divinatoriae*, which are nothing else but pagan miscarriages."[186]

(2) Pseudo-philosophy appeals merely to *human authority*. Here, Heumann's target is the *philosophia sectaria*, which from all the philosophers chooses to follow only one, thereby accepting his errors along with his true insights and treating him as if he were a god ("for a man without errors is not a man but a god"), while dismissing all other philosophers as if they were "dumb asses." A true philosopher should not appeal to vain authorities, but to clear evidence [*Beweis-Gründe*];[187] and this allows him to eclectically sift truth from error in any philosophical school.

(3) Even worse is the appeal to *Tradition* instead of reason. Here, Heumann's prime target turns out to be the *prisca theologia*, or more specifically what we have been referring to as "Platonic Orientalism":

> Thus I also consider Plato's philosophy to be false in many respects, because again and again he appeals to the *traditiones veterum*, to which belongs his entire *Daemonologia*, which should not therefore be considered a part of the platonic Wisdom, but of platonic foolishness. For the same reason I must deny the title of true wisdom to the Jewish Cabala... For even though it

---

[185] Braun, *Histoire de l'histoire de la philosophie*, 100–119; Longo, "La teoria della 'historia philosophica'," 437–476; Mühlpfordt, "Ein kryptoradikaler Thomasianer," 306; Lehmann-Brauns, *Weisheit*, 355–399.
[186] Heumann, "Von denen Kennzeichen," 190.   [187] *Ibid.*, 192–193.

might contain some truth or another, we have no way of distinguishing the
true from the false.[188]

(4) Heumann's longest discussion by far is devoted to the fourth characteristic: the syncretism of philosophy with *superstition*, that is to
say, with "irrational religion" [*ein unvernünfftiger Gottesdienst*]. The
true religion of Christianity is perfectly compatible with reason, and
thus with philosophy: "wherever the true divine revelation is, philosophy finds a secure shelter."[189] In contrast, the false religion known as
superstition – Heumann never bothers to define the term, but evidently
considers it equivalent to paganism – fears philosophy as its deadliest
enemy, and cannot possibly live in its vicinity. The two are mutually
exclusive: "Superstition is foolishness, and can tolerate wisdom as little
as darkness tolerates the light." It is born from ignorance, and leads to
"absurd teachings" and "horrible acts."[190] Finally, Heumann addresses
the enemy directly, in its concrete historical manifestation, in a passage
that announces the final expulsion of the "philosophia barbarica" from
the citadel of academic philosophy:

> From what has been said thus far, it clearly follows that the philosophy
> by which the papists were driven into paganism, and which is known as
> *philosophiam barbaricam*, is necessarily a false and fake philosophy. So adieu,
> dear *Philosophia Chaldaeorum, Persarum, Aegyptiorum*, &c, that one usually
> makes such a fuss about, out of blind veneration of Antiquity. [Heumann
> now refers to Michael Maier's and Morhof's references to secret philosophical
> schools in antiquity, and continues:] . . . I am certain that all these *Collegia sac-*
> *erdotum Aegyptiorum, Orphaicorum, Eumolpidarum, Samothracum, Magorum,*
> *Brachmanum, Gymnosophistarum* and *Druidum*, which Morhof sometimes
> calls *occulta*, then again *arcana*, or *secreta* and *secretiora* . . . that all of these
> were schools, not of Wisdom, but of foolishness [*Thorheit*], which attempted
> to bring *superstitio in formam artis* [i.e. to make superstition into an *ars*, or art]
> and sought to draw profit from deceiving the people . . . So nobody should
> hold it against me if I have not the slightest respect for all those *Collegia*
> *philosophica secreta*, but judge that the passing of time has quite rightly made
> a secret of these mysteries, by dumping them into the sea of oblivion; and
> that even if the writings of these *philosophorum barbarorum* were preserved

[188] *Ibid.*, 200–201.
[189] *Ibid.*, 204. Heumann calls reason "God's voice in our mind," but adds that because this inner
Word that is written in our hearts has been darkened by the Fall, the external Word was necessary
in order to achieve a "complete illumination."
[190] *Ibid.*, 206–207.

by posterity, they would deserve to be sent *ad loca secretiora* right away, for superstitious idiocies belong in no better library.[191]

This is a new tone entirely, compared to all the polemics against paganism that we have been investigating so far, and it would become increasingly common as the century progressed. Continuing his discussion of superstition, Heumann makes a sharp distinction between the barbarian nations drenched in superstition, and Greece as the home and origin of true philosophy. In discussing the Greek philosophers, he makes a point of attacking the common reference to them as "wise pagans" or "pagan philosophers." A pagan (*ein Heyde*) is defined as a man who is "wholly drenched in superstition, and who worships gods of gold and wood."[192] But the true philosophers were no idolaters, on the contrary: their religion was a reasonable *theologia naturalis*, and therefore they are best referred to as "naturalists."[193] But after antiquity "it was over again with philosophy," as the "gruesome Papacy" (*das greuliche Pabsttum*) and the monks caused humanity to sink into a new age of barbarian superstition.[194] Only with Erasmus and the Reformation did it become possible for philosophy to revive again.

(5) Heumann's fifth characteristic of pseudo-philosophy is its preference for obscure and enigmatic language and symbolism. Whereas philosophy should bring enlightenment, by the so-called "symbolic philosophy" one is led from darkness to darkness. As examples, Heumann refers to the kabbalah (to which he devotes a special

---

[191] *Ibid.*, 209–211. Cf. Heumann, "Von der Barbarey," where he splits up "religious barbarism" into "pagan barbarism" (consisting in "tasteless ceremonies, veneration of lifeless creatures, and other irrational and godless things"), "mohammedan barbarism," and "papist barbarism." We have been liberated from all this by Luther, the "great *Antibarbarum*" (*ibid.*, 229–230).

[192] Heumann, "Von denen Kennzeichen," 215–216.

[193] *Ibid.*, 217. But note that there are two kinds: "blind pagans" may become naturalists when philosophy opens their eyes and frees them from idolatry, but if Christians become naturalists they fall from light into darkness, imagining against reason that the Christian religion is no better than paganism. Thus the implicit hierarchy is clear: philosophy is higher than paganism, but Christianity is higher than philosophy.

[194] *Ibid.*, 220–221. See also Heumann, "Von dem Namen der Welt-Weißheit," 317–318, on the role played by the Fathers of the Church: "I am convinced, and can prove it with examples, that from among those who went over from the Lutherans to the Papist Church, and did so seriously and without hypocrisy, most were induced to this by industrious reading of the *Patres*. For in this manner they have learned that the errors of the Papists have a much better foundation in the latter's writings than in our doctrines. Therefore it is quite good that most of our learned men, including the clergy, do not know the *Patres* better . . ." And cf. *ibid.*, 318–320, for examples of Heumann's utter lack of respect even for Augustine.

discussion in his next treatise),[195] alchemy, the "hieroglyphian philosophy," Pythagoreanism, and even the Chinese I Ching.[196]

(6) The final characteristic of pseudo-philosophy is its immorality. Here
Heumann makes a point of arguing that the human will is subservient
to the intellect (*das Verstand*): only by training and improving man's
intellect is it possible to bring evil impulses under control. By doing so,
the human will comes to be ruled by the "three fundamental articles"
of all true philosophy: that there is one God, who is the origin of all
beings; that the world stands under God's providential rule; and that
the human soul is immortal.[197] In juxtaposing these principles against
the "fundamental errors" which lead to false philosophy, Heumann
shows himself a faithful heir of Thomasius father and son (who are
quoted continually throughout the treatise): these errors are the belief
that the world is co-eternal with God, that the human soul is material,
and that matter is capable of thinking and acting out of itself.[198]

Having dispensed with pseudo-philosophy, Heumann proceeded to sketch
the history of real philosophy in an essay titled "Von dem Ursprung und
Wachstum der Philosophie." Evidently to find a compromise between his
Protestant and Enlightenment commitments, he distinguished between
two types of wisdom, a "plain and simple" and a "learned and thorough"
one, tracing the former back to Abraham, and the latter to the Greeks.
But in order to show the superiority of both, he had to demarcate them
clearly from their counterparts: foolishness (*Thorheit*) in its "simple" and
its "learned" forms. Foolishness or stupidity (*stultitia*) just being what it
is, he disposed of the former quite quickly; but he needed more space
to demonstrate that the so-called scientific achievements of the ancient
civilizations were "foolishness" in spite of their learned and erudite nature:

> [The pagans] began to study, and their minds that were loaded with evil impulses
> they began to exercise in all kinds of sciences. But because their will was perverted
> in its foundation, this resulted in sciences that were partly vain and useless, partly
> false and unfounded. [They devoted themselves to answering] useless questions
> inspired by mere curiosity, through which they created the illusion of great wisdom.
> Partly they concentrated their curiosity on studying natural causes, partly on the
> arts of divination.[199]

Pagan learning was fed from three sources: practical necessity, curiosity,
and superstition. The first one was quite straightforward (for example,

---

[195] Heumann, "Von denen vier Cabbalistischen Welten."
[196] Heumann, "Von denen Kennzeichen," 227–228.
[197] The last is expanded further in Heumann, "Von dem Ursprung und Wachstum," 251–252.
[198] *Ibid.*, 235–236.   [199] Heumann, "Von dem Ursprung und Wachstum," 268–269.

the Egyptians had to develop geometry in order to contain the flooding of the Nile, the Chaldaeans studied astronomy in view of agriculture), and Heumann treated the second one in a quite neutral manner as well; but having come to the third source, superstition, he again gave free rein to his contempt, mentioning such examples of divination as oniromancy, haruspicy, auguries, and astrology. In spite of the obvious foolishness of such arts, Heumann admits that the sciences were developed in countries like Egypt earlier than in Greece, and even that the Egyptians were the first to philosophize "about physics and other curious sciences"; and he also conceded that the Greeks sent their sons to study in such countries. But nevertheless, Diogenes Laertius was right that only in Greece was philosophy developed into its true form: this was the case for logic, moral philosophy, and even physics, for "from their travels to Egypt and other countries, Thales, Democritus and others brought home so little natural wisdom that they had to start all over again from the beginning, and discover the *principia* themselves."[200] The so-called "barbarian philosophy" does not deserve that name, for its goal is not wisdom but idolatry.[201]

Throughout his treatise, Heumann used metaphors of growth and development to describe how – far from having declined from some original state of perfection – philosophy had progressed through the three stages of early childhood, adolescence, and full maturity:[202]

so we must describe the origins of philosophy by means of stages, as follows. With the ancient Hebrews we find the origin (admittedly not of philosophy, but nevertheless) of plain and simple wisdom. In Chaldaea and Egypt, but particularly in the latter environment, not only the arts, but also studying (but not the *studium philosophicum*) were practiced and cultivated. The Greeks were the first to spread the wings of their understanding [*Verstand*] upwards, and start to philosophize: at first only *particulariter*, but eventually also *systematice*, and finally even *universaliter* and *systematice* at the same time, or in one word, *pansophice*. From the Greeks, philosophy was passed on to the Christians, who, because they also have a perfectly pure religion as well as a divine revelation, could surpass in wisdom even the most learned of the Greek *Philosophos*.[203]

As for the relation between philosophy and Christianity, Heumann ended with a quotation from Arnold Geulinx: "What we understand from Divine Revelation, and would not have understood without it, we afterwards also understand through reason – and even so clearly that we imagine we could have understood this truth through the light of reason alone."[204]

---

[200] *Ibid.*, 287.   [201] *Ibid.*, 289.   [202] Explicitly stated in *ibid.*, 293.   [203] *Ibid.*, 290.
[204] *Ibid.*, 291.

The "Enlightenment paradigm" announced so clearly in Heumann's *Acta Philosophorum* was the beginning of the eclipse of "Western esotericism" in modern intellectual discourse. So far, the "pagan" philosophies associated with Platonic Orientalism had always been considered serious players in the philosophical arena; and this had happened because even their most outspoken opponents could not deny that they were part of the traditional canon of some of the most ancient and venerable philosophical schools or "sects," the platonic one in particular. But the eclectic method changed the rules of the game entirely: it denied any established tradition the right to decide what was and what was not to be considered "philosophy" in the first place, and handed that authority over to the human faculty of rational judgment. Strongly amplified by two centuries of Protestant opposition against the Roman Catholic claim of representing "the" only universal tradition of wisdom, Enlightenment historiography specifically targeted the ancient wisdom narrative and everything that had come to be associated with it, such as the appeal to ancient oriental paganisms and initiatory schools, divinatory systems, demonologies, the kabbalah, the "occult mysteries" claimed by symbolic theology, and the "enthusiastic philosophy" known as theosophy.[205] For an author like Colberg, all this had still been part of the dangerous heretical stream of "Platonic-Hermetic Christianity," but in Heumann's eyes they had lost even the dignity of a serious opponent. He was laughing in their face while waving them goodbye: "adieu, dear *Philosophia Chaldaeorum, Persarum, Aegyptiorum,* &c..."

Thus the foundations were established not only for the disappearance of most references to "Western esotericism" in textbooks of history of philosophy, but also for a new genre of Enlightenment literature intended for "learning and entertainment": that of "histories of stupidity."[206] Christian Thomasius himself published a *Geschichte der Weißheit und Thorheit* (also published in Latin as *Historia sapientiae et stultitiae*) in 1693, but

---

[205] On this last current, see Heumann, "Von dem Ursprung und Wachsthum," 312.

[206] At its ultimate extremity, this perspective could lead philosophers to deny any significance to history as such, as exemplified in the twentieth century by A. J. Ayer's characterization of Bertrand Russell's well-known history of philosophy as "a brief introduction to the history of human stupidity" (Ayer, *Part of my Life*, 183; and see the more general discussion of anti-historical philosophical perspectives in Hankins, "Renaissance Philosophy between God and the Devil," 591ff.). Essentially, we are dealing again with the basic paradox of a "history of truth," but now from a rationalist perspective: as clearly formulated already by Hegel, "The object of philosophy is the unchangeable, eternal truth as it exists in and for itself. History, however, narrates what existed at one time, but then disappeared and was replaced by something else; thus philosophy cannot have a history, and in history philosophy cannot exist" (*Werke*, vol. XIII, 19, as quoted in Freyer, *Geschichte der Geschichte der Philosophie*, 7).

the most famous example is certainly Johann Christoph Adelung's seven-volume *Geschichte der menschlichen Narrheit*, published at the height of the Enlightenment, in 1785–1789. It shows paradigmatically to what an extent "stupidity" as such had now come to be identified with adherence to quite specific beliefs and historical traditions: Adelung's cabinet of fools includes Nicolas Flamel ("an alchemist"), Sebastian Franck ("an enthusiast"), Giordano Bruno ("a bold blasphemer"), Tommaso Campanella ("a philosophical enthusiast"), Guillaume Postel ("a chiliast"), Paracelsus ("a kabbalist and charlatan"), Nostradamus ("a diviner"), Jacques Gaffarel ("a kabbalist and diviner"), John Dee ("a crystal-gazer"), Arthur Dee ("an alchemist"), Michael Sendivogius ("another adept"), Jan Amos Comenius ("an enthusiast"), Johann Konrad Dippel ("an indifferent enthusiast"), Johannes Baptista van Helmont ("a theosophical physician"), Franciscus Mercurius van Helmont ("a pantheist"), Jacob Böhme ("a theosopher"), Friedrich Breckling ("a mystic"), Johann George Gichtel ("a theosopher"), and many others. But even at this time, on the eve of the French Revolution, the legacy of anti-apologeticism had not been forgotten, on the contrary. Adelung identified "stupidity" not just with lack of intelligence or credulity, but more specifically with adherence to the "heretical tradition" as understood by Colberg:

> At bottom, this entire dream is nothing else but the old system of emanation...which [having emerged in Asia and Europe since the earliest times][207] has been continued by the Platonic and Kabbalistic philosophy, and has been warmed up again a hundredfold in recent times. Most completely, however, it rules in Theosophy, particularly since Paracelsus, Val. Weigel, Rob. Fludd and our Jacob Böhme managed to present and spread it in newly embellished forms. The inner light, or as the Quaker and mystic calls it, the Christ in us, is then nothing else but the imagination, which according to such enthusiasts is the true divine soul, whereas reason and understanding are faculties of the earthly soul, which are denied here.[208]

Even here, then, we still encounter the two central characteristics that we have seen so often before: the system of emanation based upon belief in the eternity of the world, and the emphasis on inner illumination.

THE HISTORIAN: JACOB BRUCKER

In 1730, Heumann showed extraordinary generosity by lending extensive manuscripts on the history of philosophy, based on many years of work, to

---

[207] Adelung, *Geschichte der menschlichen Narrheit*, vol. i, 168.   [208] *Ibid.*, 221.

a thirty-four-year-old colleague who was making his living as a pastor in the Evangelical Church, Johann Jacob Brucker. Brucker promised to return the materials within a year's time, and later claimed that he had in fact tried to do so; but he had entrusted the task to a certain Mr. Stübner in Leipzig, who turned out to be unreliable and caused the materials to be lost. Heumann never saw them again.[209] This painful episode seems particularly significant against the background of a remark by a contemporary biographer of Brucker, Paul von Stetten, who found it hard to understand how Brucker could have created his extensive works in the small towns where he was living: "He lacked the advantages of a rich public library . . . and particularly in the beginning, his material circumstances were not at all such that he could have spent much on buying the important works without which he could not do."[210] The real extent to which Brucker's seminal writings on the history of philosophy (the most important of which began to appear one year after he received Heumann's manuscripts) may have relied on the results of Heumann's enormous erudition will never be established, but it is certain that his monumental *Historia critica philosophiae* (1742–1744) represents the full flowering of Heumann's program.

Johann Jacob Brucker was born in Augsburg on January 22, 1696, and studied philosophy and theology in Jena. Reading the accounts of his life, one can only be amazed at his extreme productivity: during his career he published about 20,000 pages on the history of philosophy,[211] and while his writings made him famous, they were all written alongside his very busy work as a pastor in the Evangelical Church, where in some periods of his life he had to give sermons twice or three times a week and teach Latin for eight hours each day, while also visiting the sick, leading funerals, doing administrative work, and looking after his gravely ill wife.[212] According to a contemporary biographer, his herculean labors on the history of philosophy were at least partly therapeutic: in addition to a weak physical constitution, Brucker suffered from heavy attacks of "melancholy," and only by studying very hard could he distract himself from his fears and depressions.[213] The manner of Brucker's death in 1770 could not have been more symbolic for this archetypical *Stubengelehrter* and exemplary representative of the Protestant work-ethic: he fell in his study, having tried to lift a heavy volume from an upper shelf.

---

[209] The episode is described in a biography of Heumann (1768) by Georg Andreas Cassius, quoted and discussed in Longo, "Geistige Anregungen und Quellen," 175–176 with n. 34.
[210] Von Stetten, "Jacob Brucker," 295, quoted in Stammen, "Jacob Brucker," 82.
[211] Braun, *Histoire de l'histoire de la philosophie*, 120.
[212] Behler, "Eine unbeachtete Biographie," 42.   [213] *Ibid.*, 42–43.

Most of those 20,000 pages produced by Brucker during his lifetime belonged to his multi-volume history of philosophy, published in German from 1731 to 1736, and its strongly revised Latin version first published from 1742 to 1744 and again in a further expanded edition from 1766 to 1767.[214] The German version is titled *Kurze Fragen aus der Philosophischen Historie*: it seeks to cover the entire history of thought from before the Flood until the present day, and does so in a question-and-answer format. The title is deceptive, for while the questions may be short enough, the answers are often extremely lengthy; and increasingly from one volume to the next, everything Brucker cannot put in his main chapters he puts in his notes, which are printed in small letters and often turn into minor monographs of their own, with incredibly detailed references and bibliographies. Nothing like this had existed before. In response to the increasing demand for a Latin version accessible to a non-German readership, Brucker decided to rewrite the entire history anew, and in even greater detail – but with fewer footnotes – and the result was his *Historia critica philosophiae*, which is now generally considered *the* monument of the history of philosophy in the eighteenth century.

The importance of this work can hardly be overestimated. It became the indispensable reference for the history of philosophy not only in Germany, but over the whole of Europe, throughout the eighteenth and even far into the nineteenth century. Of particular importance is its relation to two other famous and extremely influential reference works: the so-called *große Zedler*, and Diderot's *Encyclopédie*. Johann Heinrich Zedler's *Grossem vollständigen Universal-Lexicon* appeared in sixty-four volumes and four supplemental volumes from 1732 to 1754 and stands as *the* German lexicographical monument of the Baroque era. As has been shown in detail by Ursula Behler, its many articles in the domain of philosophy, while published anonymously, are in fact mostly paraphrases or literal copies of Brucker's work;[215] in other words, Brucker was the invisible but omnipresent authority on philosophy in this largest and most influential of all German lexicons.

Even more interesting is the case of Diderot's famous *Encyclopédie*, which was first announced around the time the *Zedler* was completed[216] and

---

[214] To make clear how massive these two works really are, *The Kurze Fragen* are printed in a small format in seven volumes: I (1120 pp.), II (1086 pp.), III (1344 pp.), IV (1450 pp.), V (1517 pp.), VI (1326 pp.), VII (1210 pp.); and the first edition of the *Historia* is printed in five large quarto volumes plus a volume of additions and supplements: I (1357 pp.), II (1092 pp.), III (916 pp.), IV (789 pp.), V (939 pp.), VI (1032 pp.).

[215] Behler, "Eine unbeachtete Biographie," 19–30.   [216] *Ibid.*, 26.

appeared between 1751 and 1765. For its many entries on the history of philosophy, Brucker was again *the* decisive source: Diderot in fact plundered the *Historia critica philosophiae* without any scruples, while taking care to turn the heavy and serious prose of the German Protestant minister into elegant French. His editorial work has been described as a "masterwork of adaptation and subtle deception: by a few interventions, Diderot artfully change[d] . . . the serious chapters of the *Historia critica* into a graceful reading full of allusions and *double entendres*, which were excellently suited to the *esprit philosophique*."[217] If we take into account the well-known centrality of the *Encyclopédie* to the French Enlightenment, the centrality of "philosophy" to Diderot's project, and the paradigmatic role of the French *philosophes* in defining internationally what the Enlightenment was supposed to be all about, one understands the conclusion that was drawn by Lucien Braun in his standard work on the history of the history of philosophy:

In the second half of the eighteenth century there appear a whole series of works that are based exclusively on the *Historia critica*; and in that regard, there is nothing in the domain of the history of philosophy that can be compared to this work. It is the monument to which all the Enlightened spirits in Europe referred at the time . . . The eighteenth century is dominated by Brucker: he is the only point of reference here.[218]

What, then, do we find in Brucker's *Magnum Opus*, and what is it that makes him such a crucial author for the history of the study of Western esotericism? Following the basic principle of Enlightenment eclecticism in the tradition of Christian Thomasius and Heumann, Brucker undertook the task of surveying the entire history of human thought with the aim of separating the philosophical "wheat" from the pseudo-philosophical "chaff." Hence he did not at all restrict himself to what had been defined as "real" philosophy by Heumann; rather, *all* forms of pagan philosophy as well as Christian–pagan syncretism were studied and discussed by him in meticulous detail, with the goal of demonstrating in each and every case whether it was based on reason or on superstition. As a result, Brucker's *Kurze Fragen* and *Historia critica* both consist of two interwoven strands, referred to by him as "philosophia eclectica" and "philosophia sectaria": the first one traces the history of philosophy from its earliest beginnings, and

---

[217] Piaia, "Jacob Bruckers Wirkungsgeschichte," 230. For Diderot's dependence on Brucker, see Fabre, "Diderot et les théosophes"; Jehl, "Jacob Brucker und die 'Encyclopédie'."
[218] Braun, here quoted from the German edition by Jehl, "Jacob Brucker und die 'Encyclopédie'," 241.

the second traces the history of its polemical "Other."[219] This presentation became the normative one for intellectuals throughout the eighteenth century and far into the nineteenth, and was fundamental to how the Enlightenment came to define its very identity.

What, then, are the main outlines of how Brucker describes the history of philosophy's shadow? Quite similar to Heumann's, all his work is marked by the peculiar combination of Protestant biblicism and rational criticism. For Brucker, the truth of the biblical revelation is a matter of faith beyond rational demonstration; but in evaluating historical materials, he thinks and argues entirely as an Enlightenment critic. The history of thought is approached as a history of human opinions, which may be either right or wrong; and like his predecessors, Brucker thinks of them as "systems" of thought that can be described in terms of a limited number of basic doctrinal propositions.[220] With respect to all kinds of pious traditions and ideas concerning ancient wisdom, Brucker typically begins by giving an overview of the arguments that are being adduced, then examines the available evidence, and finally decides whether or not it is reasonable to maintain those beliefs. He argues essentially the way academic historiography still argues today, albeit with a strong normative agenda.

Heumann had used theological criteria to divide the history of philosophy into three main periods: the great caesuras for him were the birth of Christ and the advent of the Reformation.[221] Brucker's subdivision was roughly similar, but used a non-theological nomenclature: the great turning-points were now described as the beginning of the Roman Empire and the "restoration of letters" in the late Middle Ages and early Renaissance. Through all these periods he traced the history of the "philosophica sectaria." In the first period, the central place in that regard is taken by the Chaldaean/Zoroastrian and the Egyptian system, next to the birth and development of true philosophy among the Greeks. The second period is dominated, at least for our concerns, by two great systems: Neoplatonism and Kabbalah. In the third period, finally, both of these systems are revived and combined during the Renaissance, and against their background there emerges yet a third relatively autonomous system of sectarianism, that of Theosophy. Although Brucker clearly distinguishes these various "systems" and treats them separately, his discussion shows that they are essentially branches of one and the same great tree of pagan superstition.

---

[219] Cf. Böhme and Böhme, *Das Andere der Vernunft*.
[220] Catana, *Historiographical Concept*.   [221] Heumann, "Eintheilung."

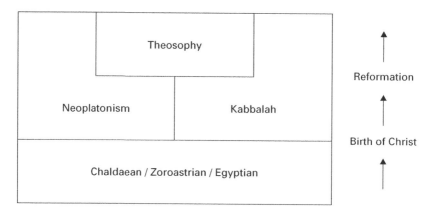

The Chaldaean/Zoroastrian and the Egyptian systems belong to the category of "Philosophia Barbarica." The Chaldaeans are the oldest, and described as wholly drenched in the darkest idolatry and superstition: their system of thought is based not on the light of sound reason but merely on blind tradition and priestly deception, and it is expressed in obscure images and language.[222] Their system combines the basic errors of all false philosophy: atheism, metaphysical dualism, absence of divine providence, and the doctrine of emanation. Again, we see here the lingering influence of Jacob Thomasius: while biblical faith is based on theistic belief in a *creatio ex nihilo*, paganism is based on belief in the eternity of the world, from which derive the false doctrines of dualism, pantheism, or emanationism. As for Zoroaster, Brucker concludes that there is so much confusion about his identity that it is no longer possible to find out the truth; but the many writings attributed to Zoroaster are in fact not by him.[223] Notably this goes for the famous *Chaldaean Oracles*, which Brucker attributes quite correctly to later platonists[224] and describes as a compendium of pagan superstitions. Likewise, the "secret doctrines" of the Egyptians consist of nothing but idolatry and superstition; Brucker discusses Thoth or Hermes as their originator, and emphasizes the spurious nature of the writings attributed to him.[225]

Nothing found in this "philosophia barbarica" actually deserves the name philosophy, and the beginnings of Greek thought are hardly more impressive. The first stirrings of real philosophy come with Thales and Pythagoras, later followed by Socrates;[226] but much of the later development of both

[222] Brucker, *Kurze Fragen* I, 94–117; *Historia* I, 102–142.
[223] *Kurze Fragen* I, 101–105; *Historia* I, 116–127.   [224] *Kurze Fragen* I, 111; *Historia* I, 189.
[225] *Kurze Fragen* I, 160–181; *Historia* I, 244–305.
[226] *Kurze Fragen* I, 345–346, 420; *Historia* I, 457–458.

Pythagoreanism and platonism is in fact a perversion that distorts Plato's teachings by mixing them up with a variety of pagan superstitions derived from Chaldaea and Egypt.

This brings us to the first of the three main systems or clusters of "sectarianism" in Brucker's scheme: that of Neoplatonism. Brucker of course does not use that term: rather confusingly, he speaks of the "secta eclectica"[227] while pointing out on many occasions that it is in fact an example of "syncretism that puts a knife to the throat of healthy philosophy."[228] Neoplatonism is crucial to Brucker's story, because it succeeded in becoming the most successful and influential of all the sects. He discusses it in great detail, and sees it as part of a deliberate pagan strategy to counter the rise of Christianity:

Since the pagan theology, through its many fables and other absurd teachings about the gods, had come to be a horror not only for the Christians, who were now spreading all over the world, but even for the philosophers themselves . . . they sought to give themselves a better image by explaining the fables in a mystical manner and thereby free them from the accusation of absurdity. And because, moreover, they saw that the Christian religion, being a highly reasonable philosophy, was accepted widely, also by great and respected men, and was defended by good people with clear proofs, they put much effort into plundering the philosophical doctrines of the ancients and bringing them into a system in such a way that they looked more similar to the Christian teaching, and more reasonable as well. And this is how the *ratio philosophandi eclectica* came into existence.[229]

Since most of the neoplatonists had a melancholic temperament, they were continuously led astray by the products of their overheated imagination; in short, their entire system rested on an "unfounded enthusiasm."[230] They deliberately sought to infiltrate Christianity and corrupt it from within, for example by promoting their own theurgical theories as the true explanation for the miracles of Jesus and his apostles, and by introducing fraudulent texts – such as the Hermetica – that superficially looked Christian but were in fact grounded in paganism. As for the ancient philosophers whose authority they claimed, their true doctrines were completely distorted by the neoplatonists:

they also hatched all kinds of books, as scandalous and harmful miscarriages of their weird brains, and put them as strange eggs into the nest of the ancient philosophers, presenting them as Chaldaean, Egyptian, Zoroastrian, Hermetic, or

---

[227] *Kurze Fragen* III, 427–873; *Historia* II, 189–462.   [228] *Kurze Fragen* III, 506.
[229] *Kurze Fragen* III, 431–432; cf. corresponding discussion in *Historia* II, 192.
[230] *Kurze Fragen* III, 506–508; cf. *Historia* II, 363–367.

Orphic monuments, and thereby made the entire history of philosophy extremely uncertain.[231]

In fact, the neoplatonists produced so many dangerous "eggs" of their own, that finally their teachings spread as an infectious plague all over Europe and Asia, while absorbing most of the other sects in the process.[232]

What, then, is the essential doctrine of Neoplatonism? It teaches that there is one God with whom the human soul has a natural connection and to whom he therefore seeks to return. There are hierarchies of higher, spiritual beings, such as gods, spirits, and angels, which are invisibly present everywhere. The purpose of prayer is to get in contact with these beings, and this happens by means of ecstatic trances. Fortune-telling is an important part of such rituals, and, in sum, one can clearly see that the real purpose of this system is to promote "all the horrors of pagan superstition" and idolatry.[233] The great problem, of course, is that it succeeded. This was partly due to the naivety of Christians, who used platonic terminology to convert the heathens, and thereby unwittingly welcomed the virus, which ended up infiltrating the very body of Christian theology.

We can be much briefer about the second great system, the "esoteric philosophy" of Judaism known as Kabbalah, not because Brucker gives it any less attention[234] but because it is based upon essentially the same process: biblical faith being infected by pagan thought:

and so there were famous Jewish teachers, who expounded the Kabbalah, that is to say, the secret tradition, and who applied the pythagorean, platonic and other pagan inventions to the Law and the Book of Moses, and in so doing introduced a special and secret . . . dark and confused theology and philosophy. And they did it the way all philosophical and theological deceivers have always done it . . . : they attributed a great antiquity to this kabbalistic teaching, presented it as the true Tradition and secret doctrine of the Patriarchs, of Abraham, of Moses and others, and even attributed to them writings whose plumage taken from the pagan flower-garden of philosophers clearly betrays their true assumptions and the nature of the deception.[235]

Kabbalah relates to the Old Testament as Neoplatonism relates to the gospel: in both cases, the purity of the biblical revelation is heavily compromised by the pernicious influence (the "syncretic pest,"[236] as Brucker calls it) of paganism, derived from the Chaldaeans and Egyptians, and from

---

[231] *Kurze Fragen* III, 520.   [232] *Kurze Fragen* III, 521.   [233] *Kurze Fragen* III, 574.
[234] *Kurze Fragen* IV, 428–466, 622–955; *Historia* II, 916–1069 ("De philosophia Iudaeorum esoterica, sive cabbalistica").
[235] *Kurze Fragen* IV, 428–429.   [236] *Kurze Fragen* IV, 428.

degenerated Pythagoreanism and platonism as well. In both cases the result was, in Brucker's opinion, an impenetrable mass of irrational speculation, expressed by means of obscure language and imagery.

The revival of Neoplatonism and Kabbalah in the Renaissance is meticulously analyzed by Brucker,[237] with separate chapters for central figures such as Plethon,[238] Ficino,[239] Pico della Mirandola,[240] Reuchlin,[241] Giorgio da Veneto,[242] Agrippa,[243] Patrizi,[244] and so on. These authors dug up the old neoplatonic writings, along with the spurious texts attributed to Hermes, Zoroaster or Orpheus and the Jewish kabbalah, as far as they understood it, and out of it patched together a new philosophical system. It should be noted that Brucker's analysis here is far more neutral and businesslike than before. Most of these authors are discussed respectfully, as honest Christians who had good intentions but were simply deluded. Brucker refutes their ideas essentially on scholarly grounds, by pointing out philological errors, misdatings, incorrect historical interpretations, and so on. In the end, all these errors can be traced back to the polluted source of Neoplatonism in late antiquity, and to the idea of a *philosophia perennis* or *translatio sapientiae*:

> For because they were of the opinion that the ancient Hebrew, Chaldaean, Egyptian, Orphic, Pythagorean and Platonic philosophy was essentially one and the same thing, and that it all emanated from the ur-ancient divine philosophy, they concluded that everything in it had to be in harmony with the Christian religion, and as a result they attempted to reconcile these teachings – perverted and wrong anyway, and packed together from all kinds of fraudulent texts – with the Christian religion.[245]

Brucker's third great system, finally, that of Theosophy, stands somewhat on its own in his work.[246] He writes that it was created in a more recent period by authors who (quite rightly) abhorred all pagan and sectarian philosophy, but nevertheless ended up inventing a new variation of it. Their systems are based not on the light of reason but on claims of internal, divine illumination; by means of it, they believe they have privileged

---

[237] *Historia* IV, 41–61 ("De restauratoribus philosophiae Platonicae"), 353–448 ("De restauratoribus philosophiae Pythagoreo-Platonico-Cabbalisticae").
[238] *Kurze Fragen* V, 1410–1419.   [239] *Kurze Fragen* V, 1428–1443; *Historia* IV, 48–55.
[240] *Kurze Fragen* V, 1443–1456; *Historia* IV, 55–60.
[241] *Kurze Fragen* VI, 536–537; *Historia* IV, 357–374.
[242] *Kurze Fragen* VI, 573–586; *Historia* IV, 374–386.
[243] *Kurze Fragen* VI, 587–637; *Historia* IV, 386–421.
[244] *Kurze Fragen* VI, 637–655; *Historia* IV, 422–430.
[245] *Kurze Fragen* VI, 678, as part of Brucker's general critical conclusions about the "pythagorean-platonic-kabbalistic philosophy"; and cf. the corresponding section in *Historia* IV, 443–448.
[246] *Kurze Fragen* VI, 1063–1254; *Historia* IV, 644–750.

insight into the deepest mysteries of nature, and know the secrets of magic, alchemy, astrology, and other such sciences. They call their system Theosophy, and also see it as a kind of kabbalah.[247] Strictly speaking, in Brucker's opinion, they belong to the history of theology rather than of philosophy; but he discusses them nevertheless, with his usual attention to detail and an impressive apparatus of notes and references. The most important representatives are Paracelsus and his pupils,[248] Valentin Weigel,[249] Robert Fludd,[250] Jacob Böhme and his followers,[251] father and son van Helmont,[252] Pierre Poiret,[253] and the Rosicrucians.[254] In evaluating Theosophy as a whole, Brucker highlights its rejection of healthy rationality in favor of inner illumination, and its underlying system of emanation, which teaches that all comes from God and returns to it.[255] Taken together, it all clearly comes down to a dangerous doctrine of *Schwärmerei* and self-deification, grounded in the "secret hybris"[256] of the human heart, which undermines sound reason along with Holy Scripture.

With that, we return to the very foundations of Brucker's history of philosophy, which, as should now be clear, likewise contains a complete history of its polemical "Other," that is to say, all the currents and ideas that are nowadays studied under the rubric of Western esotericism. The internal logic of Protestant anti-apologeticism had now resulted in a clear distinction between three main domains in the history of thought:

(1) *History of philosophy*: the central concern for Heumann and Brucker. According to them, it had to be written according to a methodology of eclecticism; that is to say, the historian's task was to survey the entire history of thought, and select from it only those traditions that were in accord with sound human reason. It is on this basis that these seventeenth-/eighteenth-century authors laid the foundations for the modern history of philosophy as an autonomous academic discipline.

(2) *Biblical revelation*. We have seen that, their professional interest in rational philosophy notwithstanding, all the authors in this German Enlightenment tradition were deeply pious Lutherans, convinced of the superiority of the Christian revelation. They were not Voltairean critics

---

[247] *Kurze Fragen* VI, 1064.   [248] *Kurze Fragen* VI, 1067–1137; *Historia* IV, 646–689.
[249] *Kurze Fragen* VI, 1138–1144; *Historia* IV, 689–691.
[250] *Kurze Fragen* VI, 1144–1152; *Historia* IV, 691–695.
[251] *Kurze Fragen* VI, 1152–1183; *Historia* IV, 695–709.
[252] *Kurze Fragen* VI, 1183–1210; *Historia* IV, 709–725.
[253] *Kurze Fragen* VI, 1210–1229; *Historia* IV, 725–735.
[254] *Kurze Fragen* VI, 1229–1242; *Historia* IV, 735–741.
[255] *Kurze Fragen* VI, 1242–1254; *Historia* IV, 741–750.   [256] *Kurze Fragen* VI, 1246.

of religion, on the contrary: they strictly distinguished between biblical faith as the absolute and exclusive foundation of religion, and human reason as the no less exclusive foundation of philosophy. Reason and revelation could not be contradictory, but they were autonomous and incommensurable: each should keep strictly within its own domain, to avoid the "apologetic" confusion and crypto-paganism that had been the very essence of Roman Catholic theology.

(3) *(Crypto)Pagan religion*. As a result of the radical anti-apologetic separation between revelation and reason, late seventeenth-century historiography found itself left with a very large domain of currents and ideas that belonged to neither of the two camps, because they were characterized precisely by syncretic mixtures between the two. Essentially, this third domain represented *the continuation of pagan religion concealed as Christianity*. With philosophy it shared its pagan foundations, but it differed from philosophy in not being based on reason. With Christianity it shared its religious nature, but it differed from Christianity in that it was false religion, not based on Revelation. In short, it was the non-rational "natural religion" of humanity. It is in this late seventeenth-century, Protestant, anti-apologetic concept of pagan religion concealed as Christianity that we find both the historical origin *and* the theoretical core of our current concept of "Western esotericism" as a specific domain of research.

Brucker's work is representative of the historical moment at which the memory of the various currents and ideas belonging to this third domain was still intact among intellectuals; but at the same time, it laid the foundations on which this memory would be marginalized by later generations. Not only did Brucker himself and all his anti-apologetic predecessors still pay serious, sustained, and critical attention to all the main currents and personalities that belong to the study of Western esotericism – even more important is that they did so on the basis of a consistent theoretical concept, which allowed them to think of the field as an essentially unitary tradition. However, the very nature of their theoretical concept implied that its representatives were the negative counterpart of both reason and faith, and therefore could not claim to remain a legitimate part of the history of either. Once their non-philosophical and non-Christian nature was clearly recognized, there was no further need to dignify them with much attention in the history of either philosophy or Christianity. From now on, they began to vanish from the textbooks of history of philosophy and church history, where they still have the status of mere footnotes today.

THE PARTING OF THE WAYS

In his indispensable study of the anti-apologetic current, Sicco Lehmann-
Brauns catches the essence of what happened to the ancient wisdom narrative under the impact of Enlightenment criticism:

> The defense of a historical perspective that was modeled after the *prisca theologia*
> and refused to distance itself historically from the now much-criticized tradition
> of Christian platonism had certainly not become wholly obsolete with the arrival
> of the Enlightenment: by way of pietism, it continued its career as an alternative
> model in competition with the new, critical-progressive philosophy of history. But
> because this view of history could not keep its ground against the rational standard
> of historical-philological criticism and against the progressive thrust of Enlight-
> enment philosophy of history, it found itself increasingly pushed into the esoteric
> sub-currents of intellectual history . . . [With the liberation of philosophy from its
> theological context], the critical potential of a rationality free of theology was able
> to flourish, and to establish itself as criticism of metaphysics [*Metaphysikkritik*].
> Its eventual success finally resulted, during the eighteenth century, in the esoteri-
> cization of the ancient model of *philosophia adepta*, which was pushed towards
> marginal circles.[257]

In other words, the ancient wisdom narrative now lost its status as a serious
option in mainstream intellectual discourse, but survived as the historiographical model to which most modern esoteric currents adhere. As we saw
at the end of the previous chapter, Platonic Orientalism remained, and still
remains, fundamental to how modern and contemporary esotericists imagine their own tradition. But in this chapter we now have also investigated
the other side of the coin. The anti-pagan and anti-platonic tradition of the
Renaissance, particularly under the influence of the witchcraft debate, had
the effect of turning the ancient wisdom narrative into its radical opposite:
far from representing the light of divine truth, it came to be imagined as
its sinister enemy, up to the extreme imaginary of a demonic "genealogy
of darkness" originating in the machinations of "the ancient serpent," the
devil. This alarmist narrative, with its paranoid and conspiratorial connotations, has survived notably in the (still insufficiently studied) anti-occultist
and anti-satanist literature of Christian evangelical and fundamentalist
authors.[258]

---

[257] Lehmann-Brauns, *Weisheit*, 6, 19.
[258] On evangelical and fundamentalist depictions of the New Age movement, see Saliba, *Christian
Responses*, 39–88, esp. 51–53; Kemp, "Christians and New Age"; Kemp, *New Age*, 133–137. The term
"genealogy of darkness" is actually used in Carl Raschke's attempt to present modern Satanism as
the outcome of the history of Western esotericism (*Painted Black*, Part Two).

Due to their utter incompatibility with the findings of modern historical criticism, these two traditional perspectives were unable to keep up with scholarly progress in the study of ancient religions, and they have lost all credit in modern academic discourse: it is hardly an exaggeration to say that modern academic research in all relevant domains of history (such as Egyptology, or the study of ancient Iran) begins where these narratives end, and continued adherence to them is the easily recognized mark of the dilettante. But in the decades around 1700, two new paradigms evolved out of these traditional models, and these have become highly successful in establishing foundations of how "Western esotericism" came to be conceptualized in academic contexts after the Enlightenment. The first of them has been referred to here as "religionism," and traced to Gottfried Arnold's innovative construct of the history of Christianity. Religionism may be defined as an approach to religion (in Arnold's case: Christian religion) that presents itself explicitly as "historical" but nevertheless denies, or at least strongly minimizes, the relevance of any questions pertaining to historical "influences," and hence of historical criticism, because of its central assumption that the true referent of religion does not lie in the domain of human culture and society but only in a direct, unmediated, personal experience of the divine. In Arnold's case, this was a highly effective strategy for ignoring any line of argumentation that might threaten the integrity of Christian religion by relating it to "pagan" influences. In its later development, as will be seen, the essential logic of religionism would allow academics to ignore, or reject, any argumentation that might threaten the integrity of "religion" as such by relating (and thereby potentially reducing) it to historical or social factors. In all its phases of development, the crucial reference of religionist approaches is to an irreducible experience of "the sacred," considered as a reality *sui generis*. We will see how important this perspective was to become to modern academic understandings of "Western esotericism."

The second new paradigm emerging in the decades around 1700 was based upon Enlightenment eclecticism, and clearly emerges in the work of authors such as Heumann and Brucker. Whereas the core concept of religionism is direct, personal, unmediated religious experience, its Enlightenment counterpart is autonomous human rationality and "sound judgment." The basic assumption of the Enlightenment paradigm is that Reason is the universal yardstick for evaluating the truth or seriousness of any worldview, whether religious or philosophical. Religious or philosophical currents and ideas that are perceived as not satisfying the criterion of rationality lose their right to be taken seriously in intellectual discourse:

they are delegated to the categories of "prejudice," "superstition," "foolishness," or "stupidity." In that process of exclusion – and this point is particularly important to emphasize – they are tacitly divested of their traditional status as players in the field of history, and transformed into non-historical universals of human thinking and behavior. In other words, one no longer needs to discuss them as traditions, such as "platonism," "hermeticism," or even "paganism," but can dismiss them as synonymous with irrationality as such.

The Enlightenment paradigm and its religionist counterpart have more in common than one might think at first sight. Both are ideological, not empirical: they do not start by investigating historical evidence, but by stipulating "absolute" criteria of truth *a priori*, and whatever does not satisfy those criteria is without any further interest to them. Applied to historical materials, this necessarily results in highly selective procedures: the goal is that of finding the treasures of truth hidden in the forests of history – *not* that of exploring those forests for their own sakes! As a result, the religionist and Enlightenment paradigms both fall short, and seriously so, as methodological frameworks for historiography proper. With respect to the study of Western esotericism specifically, we will see that the former has tended to "reify" it as an autonomous spiritual tradition *sui generis* at the expense of historical and social context, while the latter has either ignored its very existence, or simply treated it with contempt as the pariah of Western thought.

In contrast to both paradigms, it is the anti-apologetic current – from Jacob Thomasius through Colberg, and even up to and including Brucker – that appears to have created the essential foundations for a properly historical/empirical and therefore non-ideological study of Western esotericism.[259] Such a thesis might seem counter-intuitive at first sight: after all, these staunch Protestants were declared enemies of anything that we might categorize as "esoteric," and far from wanting to turn it into a separate field of research, they would much rather have seen it disappear altogether. It is also true that the essentially non-historical Enlightenment perspective on Western esotericism emerged from the same anti-apologetic current, in the writings of Christian Thomasius, Heumann, and Brucker; and that the latter prepared the eclipse of Platonic Orientalism, and everything it had come to imply, by carefully separating each of its single components

---

[259] For the basic argument in favor of an "empirical" and historical perspective based upon "methodological agnosticism," against the religionist and reductionist alternatives, see Hanegraaff, "Empirical Method."

from "true philosophy" along Heumannian lines, and thus readying it for exclusion by the next generation. However, none of this detracts from the lasting achievements of the anti-apologetic school: the combination of a *methodology* of historical criticism with a *theoretical focus* on the "Hellenization of Christianity" as the conceptual core and historical origin ("the platonic egg," to quote their own favorite metaphor) of everything that is nowadays known as "Western esotericism."

If the history of anti-apologeticism finally ended in large-scale suppression and neglect of that domain in mainstream intellectual and academic culture, this did not follow with any compelling logic from its basic theoretical and methodological perspectives – on the contrary, the latter demanded close historical study and critical analysis of the encounter between Hellenistic "paganism" and Christian religion, and its historical effects. It happened, rather, because of the strong normative and ideological biases of its main proponents and their audience: the combination of a dogmatic Protestant stereotyping of anything "pagan" with the no less dogmatic Enlightenment assumption that only rational beliefs deserve to be taken seriously by historians. Hence Enlightenment ideology eventually trumped historical criticism, leading to endless cases of historians showing deep embarrassment about the fact that their objects of research so often failed to live up to modern standards of rationality. Such embarrassment is clearly based on anachronistic projections, and does nothing to help us understand the historical realities under scrutiny. Indeed, if one of the most lasting achievements of the Enlightenment has been its insistence that "prejudice" in any form should be subjected to critical investigation, then there is no good reason to make an exception for the anti-"pagan," anti-"mystical" and even anti-"religious" prejudice ingrained in the Enlightenment itself, partly derived from its Protestant roots,[260] or to refrain from

---

[260] It might seem strange to suspect not just the Enlightenment, but even Protestantism of an anti-religious prejudice, but that assertion is made here deliberately. What it means is that "religion" is understood as a human phenomenon, in sharp contrast to the truth believed to be revealed by God himself in the Jewish and Christian traditions: a distinction that amounts to treating "religion" as an equivalent of "paganism," thereby deliberately including Roman Catholicism under the latter rubric. This basic perspective was famously formulated by Karl Barth in the seventeenth paragraph of his *Kirchliche Dogmatik*, where he presented the absolute authority of "Revelation" over "religion" in the most extreme form possible, leading to the notorious conclusion "Religion ist Unglaube" (Religion is unbelief). Barth left no doubt that his concept of Christian theology was the polar opposite of any scholarly study of religion (*Religionswissenschaft*), because the latter, instead of accepting the absolute truth of Revelation, reduced it to just another hegemonic claim made by a religion, Christianity in this case. The "reversal of revelation and religion" was traced by Barth to Salomon van Til and Johann Franz Buddeus in the decades around 1700, and was held

questioning the long-standing effects it has had on the practice of academic historiography.

From this point of view, the study of Western esotericism that will be defended here might be characterized as *anti-eclectic historiography*. It questions the selective procedures by which historians since the period of the Enlightenment have been narrowing the study of philosophy down to what they consider "real" philosophy, the study of Christianity to that of "real" Christianity, the study of science to that of "real" science (as will be seen in Chapter 3), and even the study of religion to that of "real" religion or the study of art to that of "real" art. Anti-eclectic historiography seeks to correct the attenuated and ideology-driven pictures of Western history that result from such forms of eclecticism, by calling attention to the historical role and significance of the various currents and ideas that have ended up in the reservoir of "rejected knowledge" since the period of the Enlightenment. In short, it questions the canon of modern intellectual and academic culture and emphasizes that our common heritage is of much greater complexity than one would infer from standard academic textbooks. Obviously this program does not reflect an apologetic agenda in favor of "paganism" or "Western esotericism," but a historiographical one: its goal is neither to defend nor to attack "pagan" or "esoteric" claims, but to ensure that the currents to which these labels refer are recognized as significant *historical* factors in the development of Western culture. I will get back to this program in more detail in the Conclusion, but first we need to continue our story from the period of the Enlightenment into the nineteenth and twentieth centuries.

responsible for the "catastrophe" of Protestant theology since the eighteenth century by which it had fallen into "heresy" (Barth, *Church Dogmatics* I.2, 288, 291–292, 294). From an academic point of view the argument of Barth's seventeenth paragraph is supremely bizarre, and would be difficult to take seriously at all, if it were not for the enormous influence it has exerted in twentieth-century theology.

CHAPTER 3

The error of history
Imagining the occult

> Why are you afraid... for a magnetic quality to be felt by the iron?... If generation and corruption are seen as nothing more than local motion of atoms... it's all over for substantial forms... What then will become of the sacred mysteries of our religion?
>
> Pierre de Cazrée to Pierre Gassendi (1642)[1]

The history of philosophy has been our dominant framework, up to this point, for studying how intellectuals, from the Renaissance to the Enlightenment, tried to come to terms with the presence of "paganism" in Christian culture. We have become acquainted with the protagonists of the ancient wisdom discourse as highly erudite, professional scholars who held strong religious convictions and were sincerely concerned with preserving and defending the basic truths of the Christian faith, as each of them understood it. In very different ways, they all used their extensive knowledge of the traditional canons of classical and humanistic learning to understand the historical emergence and subsequent development of a specific cluster of currents and ideas that are studied today under the label "Western esotericism." In short, *pace* existing stereotypes about this field, we have been concerned with learned debates over a philosophical "religion of intellectuals."[2]

This picture is going to change dramatically in the present chapter, as we enter a period in which Christianity slowly but surely loses its hegemonic position in intellectual discourse, while academic historians of philosophy abandon the currents and ideas associated with "Platonic Orientalism" as unworthy of serious study. Although the frameworks and background

---

[1] Gassendi, *Petri Gassendi Diniensis... opera omnia*, vol. VI, 450–451 ("cur qualitatem magneticam... à ferro sentiri times?... Si ortus atque interitus nihil aliud videntur, praeter locales Atomorum... motiones; de formis rerum substantialibus conclamatum est... Quid sanctioribus igitur nostrae Religionis mysteriis fiet?"); see discussion in Copenhaver, "Occultist Tradition," 469–473, here 472. Cf. George Berkeley in his notebooks for 1707–1708 (*ibid.*, 502): "Anima mundi. Substantial Forms. Omniscient radical Heat. Plastic vertue. Hylarchic principle. All these vanish."

[2] Rudolph, "Intellektuelle, Intellektuellenreligion"; Kippenberg, "Intellektuellen-Religion."

assumptions typical of the ancient wisdom discourse would continue to exert a strong residual influence,[3] a radically new perspective established itself during the eighteenth century: that of *science and natural philosophy* as the dominant framework for interpretation in all domains of thought.[4] With respect to the study of "Western esotericism," this resulted in a momentous shift of attention away from metaphysical questions concerning theology and philosophy, such as the nature of the soul, towards a new concentration on the "secrets of nature." For reasons that will be analyzed below, this development went hand in hand with a process of critical reorientation in which the intellectual and academic elites abandoned the field almost completely, leaving its study – including its historiography – to whomsoever else might happen to take an interest in it. As a result, it became the domain of amateur scholars.

The attitudes of these authors covered the complete spectrum from utter skepticism and hostility to "the occult" via antiquarian curiosity about the quaint beliefs of bygone ages to an enthusiastic embrace of "higher religious truths," but their common emphasis on the natural sciences led all of them to perceive the field from a new angle: rather than (crypto)pagan philosophy or "Platonic-Hermetic Christianity," what they saw was a set of traditional ways of understanding *nature*, exemplified by what now came to be known as the "secret" or "occult" sciences of natural magic, astrology, and alchemy. Such a shift of emphasis was easy enough, for the first two of these – and particularly their combination in the form of astral magic – had been part and parcel of the worldviews defended in the context of the ancient wisdom narrative since Ficino, and we will see how the final one had become practically inseparable from it somewhat later, particularly in the wake of Paracelsus and his followers.

Because of their focus on philosophy and theology, the anti-apologists had mentioned these arts or sciences only in passing, without assigning them a very important role in their constructs of pagan heresy. But this would no longer do for a new generation of authors whose worldviews were deeply impacted by the new natural sciences and philosophies. To them, it was becoming evident that the decisive battle over religious truth and error would be decided over the question of what, exactly, was to be understood

---

[3] For the persistence of "Platonic Orientalist" assumptions in classicist scholarship from the eighteenth through the nineteenth and twentieth centuries, see Jaap Mansfeld's fascinating and extremely well-documented analysis of how an Anaximander fragment has been interpreted from secular as well as "mystical" or "pantheist" perspectives (Mansfeld, "Bothering the Infinite").

[4] As programmatically formulated in Gladigow, "Pantheismus als 'Religion' von Naturwissenschaftlern," 219–220.

by "nature," what its limits were (if any), and what the answers implied for the status of spiritual and divine agency, and hence for the Christian religion: in short, did nature leave any room for the divine? Feelings of acute anxiety over these questions are evident for example in the quotation introducing this chapter, from a Jesuit scholar deeply concerned about Pierre Gassendi's corpuscularianism; and they were central to the uproar over the "disenchantment of the world" proclaimed by the Dutch Calvinist minister and Cartesian Balthasar Bekker in his bestseller *De betoverde weereld* (The World Enchanted), published in 1691 and translated into German, French and English within four years. The furor over Bekker's thesis was, as Jonathan Israel reminds us, "assuredly the biggest intellectual controversy of Early Enlightenment Europe, producing a stupendous 300 publications for and against."[5]

If Bekker has become indirectly responsible for Max Weber coining his famous notion of *Entzauberung* – central to which is the disappearance of mysterious and unpredictable powers and forces from the natural world[6] – his own brand of Cartesian philosophy represented only one of the many ways in which nature could be understood from the perspective of the new science. The familiar standard narrative, according to which belief in witchcraft and other forms of immaterial or spiritual agency simply declined in direct proportion with the advance of modern science,[7] has been thoroughly deconstructed by historians during the last three decades, who have pointed out that many of the most central pioneers of the scientific revolution were preoccupied with avoiding atheism by preserving immaterial agency (exemplified by the activities of witches, demons and spirits) as a significant factor even – or rather, especially – in the context of the mechanical philosophy.[8] Far from reflecting any simple dualism of science against magic or superstition, learned opinion appears to have varied along a wide scale. Mechanical concepts of nature as reducible to

[5] Israel, *Radical Enlightenment*, 382 (and see the rest of his extensive and detailed analysis). On Bekker and his significance, see also Knuttel, *Balthasar Bekker*; Attfield, "Balthasar Bekker"; Stronks, "Significance"; and particularly the comprehensive recent study of Nooijen, *"Unserm grossen Bekker."* Specifically on Bekker's "cartesian disenchantment," see van Ruler, "Minds, Forms and Spirits."

[6] Weber introduced the term *Entzauberung* in several publications between 1913 and 1920 (see overview in Dassen, *Onttovering*, 194), but most famously in *Wissenschaft als Beruf* (1917/1919), 9.

[7] The classic reference for this now outdated perspective is, of course, Keith Thomas, *Religion and the Decline of Magic*. For an excellent short description of the "scientific triumphalism" typical of this narrative, exemplified by Charles Singer, Marie Boas, Preserved Smith, Bertrand Russell, and Karl Popper, see Styers, *Making Magic*, 149–151.

[8] Among many important recent studies, see, for example, Jobe, "The Devil in Restoration Science"; Schaffer, "Occultism and Reason"; Coudert, "Henry More and Witchcraft." For a very useful synthetic overview, see Clark, *Thinking with Demons*, 294–311.

matter in motion could be defended on religious grounds because they emptied the world of demonic beings while preserving the divine transcendence of its Creator and sovereign Ruler; but they could also be criticized as a danger to religion because, along with any other spiritual agency, they were seen as driving God himself out of his own world, making him into an irrelevancy while emptying his creation of any mystery. On the other hand, "enchanted" concepts of nature as a kind of organism animated by a spiritual force could be defended precisely because they seemed to preserve God's universal presence and activity in the world; but they were vulnerable to the criticism that they did so by blurring any distinction between God and his creation, leading to the dreaded position of pantheism. It will be remembered that precisely such a concept (the co-eternity of God and the world) had been highlighted by Jacob Thomasius as the core doctrine of all pagan error, and sharply contrasted with the doctrine of *creatio ex nihilo*. This basic theological perspective, of which Thomasius Sr. was only one representative, was particularly prominent in Protestant circles, and eventually came to dominate the mainstream of Enlightenment thought even among atheist thinkers. That it greatly facilitated the acceptance of the mechanical philosophy is an understatement, and it certainly made it easy to perceive any panentheist concept of "living nature" as tainted with pagan superstition. The "victory of science," then, was more than just scientific: to a considerable extent, the new science succeeded because it supported the theological battle against paganism.

To understand how, against these backgrounds, the traditional *artes* or *scientiae* of astrology, natural magic and alchemy came to be conceptualized as "secret" or "occult" sciences since the eighteenth century, we now need to take a closer look at their historical origins and the nature of their relation to the ancient wisdom discourse. In doing so, we must first confront a cluster of three loaded concepts that are basic to the eventual status of Western esotericism as "rejected knowledge."

TAINTED TERMINOLOGIES I: SUPERSTITION

Since the eighteenth century, the substantives "superstition" and "magic," as well as various terminological coinages around the adjective "occult" (occult qualities, occult philosophy, occult sciences, occultism), have often been seen as mutually interchangeable, even to the point of being used as near or complete synonyms in mainstream scholarly research. From a historical point of view, this is regrettable not just as evidence of sloppy language, but, much more importantly, because it reflects and perpetuates fundamental misconceptions about the ideas and historical currents to which these terminologies are supposed to refer. We will see that anachronistic distortions, and hence bad scholarship, are not just likely but unavoidable if the three terms are used in an uncritical manner to interpret the past.[9] Each of them has a very long and complex history, and none of them should be used innocently or naively on the assumption that "everyone knows what is meant": the fact is that almost nobody does, although most people think they do. Most important of all, these three terms are qualitatively different from more straightforwardly descriptive (although, as will be seen, by no means unproblematic) ones such as, notably, "astrology," "alchemy," and "divination," in that most of their current meanings and connotations are relatively recent *and* intrinsically biased. Although the terms "superstition," "magic," and "occult" have long histories, they were essentially *reinvented* during the period of the Enlightenment, in such a manner that they could serve to demarcate "the Other of science and rationality." This has two important implications. One is that applying them to earlier periods leads to anachronistic distortions, because Enlightenment preoccupations are thereby projected upon materials that have very little to do with them. A second is that they are wholly unsuitable as neutral instruments in scholarly interpretation: they belong to the category of value judgments[10] and political *Kampfbegriffe* (battle concepts),[11] not of valid "etic" terminology. In this chapter, I will therefore analyze them strictly as "emic" terms.[12] One

---

9 Curry, *Prophecy and Power*, 3–4, with nn. 10–11.   10 Jonathan Z. Smith, *Relating Religion*, 218.

11 Hagner, "Bye-bye Science," 22.

12 Briefly stated, the adjective "emic" refers to statements, terminologies, concepts, or technical perspectives as used and understood by those who are being studied, while "etic" refers to statements, terminologies, concepts, or technical perspectives as used by scholars (in their attempts to interpret emic statements, terminologies, concepts, or technical perspectives). Hotly debated by anthropologists since its introduction in 1954 (Pike, *Language*), the emic/etic distinction remains indispensable if we wish to avoid, or at least minimize, the risk of conceptual anachronism in disciplines like the history of religion or of science. As formulated by Nick Jardine, "etics without emics is empty, emics without etics is blind" (Jardine, "Etics and Emics," 275): one needs to study the exact meaning of terms as used in their original historical context, but very often one also needs new terminologies to make better sense of them. For example, in Chapter 1, I analyzed a historical discourse that used emic terms such as *prisca theologia* or *philosophia perennis*, but argued that the etic concept "Platonic Orientalism" may be useful as a tool for understanding the nature of that discourse. It is important to understand that the emic/etic distinction is not static and closed, but dialectic and open-ended: by definition, the moment a given scholar's etic terminology is made into an object of study by other scholars, it is thereby turned into emic language. As such, its implications, subjective connotations, underlying agendas, and so on, can be critically evaluated by the scholars doing the investigation, who may well be using etic terminology of their own to do so – which can likewise be turned into an object of critical investigation by others, and so on *ad infinitum*. The implication does not need to be one of complete relativism. It is true that since all terminology, etic as well as

would like to be able to say that they succeeded in becoming part of common academic discourse in spite of their clear dependence on ideological agendas, but, sadly, such a conclusion would be mistaken. On the contrary, they undoubtedly succeeded *because* of that dependence. We will see that this fact is a major key to understanding much that has gone wrong in academic research on Western esotericism, as indeed in several other areas of the study of religion.

The term "superstition"[13] is undoubtedly the most uniformly pejorative of the three key terms, although that is not how it began its career. Current ideas about superstition are still strongly influenced by the legacy of the founder of cultural anthropology Edward Burnett Tylor, and his discussion of "magic" and "survivals" in his famous *Primitive Culture* of 1871. Tylor found the term "superstition" too strongly loaded with pejorative connotations to be used as a scholarly concept, and hence coined the term "survivals" as an alternative.[14] In so doing, he actually adopted the etymological root of the very word "superstition," *superstes*, which refers to "surviving."[15] Tylor himself carefully distinguished "survivals" from "magic," and discussed them in separate chapters; but later readers were less precise, and have frequently treated the two concepts as coming down to one and the same thing. This has had the unfortunate result that, on the tacit assumption that there is little difference between magic and superstition anyway, Tylor's definition of magic (discussed below) has often been applied to superstition as well, so that the latter came to stand for beliefs and practices that presuppose a faulty understanding of cause and effect.[16] However, projecting the Tylorian concept back into periods earlier than the nineteenth century results in serious anachronisms, for the various meanings of superstition in pre- and early modern periods turn out to be entirely different, and their influence on modern concepts of superstition is both more subtle and more pervasive than usually appreciated.

emic, is contextual, etic language can never claim any perfect "objectivity"; but subjective biases and anachronistic projections can be recognized for what they are, and replaced by alternatives that are less distorting, more neutral, and therefore more suitable for "etic" discourse. The analogy with translation from one language to another is close and instructive: perfection will forever elude us, but this does not imply the impossibility of replacing bad translations with superior ones.

[13] For the historical developments summarized here, see Schmitt, "Les 'superstitions'"; Pott, *Aufklärung und Aberglaube*, 1–77. Essential for the period of antiquity are Koets, Δεισιδαιμονία; Moellering, *Plutarch on Superstition*; and particularly Martin, *Inventing Superstition*. The standard work for the medieval period is undoubtedly Harmening, *Superstitio*. On "superstition" in the Enlightenment, see Dompnier, *La superstition à l'âge des lumières*; and Shorr, *Science and Superstition in the Eighteenth Century.*

[14] Tylor, *Primitive Culture*, vol. 1, 72; see discussion in Hanegraaff, "Emergence of the Academic Science of Magic," 254–265.

[15] Harmening, *Superstitio*, 14.   [16] Martin, *Inventing Superstition*, 10.

The Latin *superstitio* and its earlier Greek equivalent *deisidaimonia* both began their career as neutral or positive terms. *Deisi* could mean fear, but also "awe" or "respect," and *daimones* could be gods, goddesses, semi-divinities, or any other kind of superhuman being, regardless of their good or evil intentions. Hence, *deisidaimonia* could mean an appropriate awe or respect for the gods (for example, the apostle Paul respectfully addressed the Athenians as *deisidaimones* in Acts 17:22).[17] However, as pointed out by Dale Martin, it was turned into a negative term in the context of a new and revolutionary concept introduced by Plato and Aristotle, who "taught that the ontological hierarchy of nature was matched by an ethical hierarchy: beings who were superior in nature and power were assumed to be superior ethically."[18] Based upon this axiom, the gods were good and benevolent by definition, and there could not be any reason to be afraid of them. Thinking otherwise was a clear sign of ignorance. It was from this perspective that the term *deisidaimonia* came to be used by the later philosophical elite (from the fourth century BC on) as a term of disdain for popular and irrational beliefs about harmful deities, and the various cultic practices based upon misguided fear of the gods.[19] The early *locus classicus* for "superstition" in this sense is Theophrast's amusing sketch of "The Superstitious Man" (fourth century BC).[20] However, cracks in the philosophical concept of a matching ontological and ethical hierarchy had begun to appear by the beginning of the Common Era, as philosophers began to doubt whether *daimones* were really all good and benevolent;[21] and in their polemics against pagan intellectuals, Christians turned the tables on their pagan opponents by arguing that the so-called gods were actually evil demons.[22] Hence the notion of *deisidaimonia* as "fear of demons" became firmly enshrined in Christian thinking.

As for the Latin *superstitio*: like its Greek equivalent it was originally a positive or neutral term, referring in this case to the practices of soothsaying, divination or prophecy, which, in traditional Roman religion, were perfectly acceptable.[23] However, from the first century on, it acquired new connotations of political danger. The Greek philosophical elite considered superstitious behavior as shameful, ridiculous and perhaps blasphemous,

---

[17] See Grant, *Gods and the One God*, 19.   [18] Martin, *Inventing Superstition*, 76.
[19] Note that positive or neutral understandings of *deisidaimonia* did not vanish right away, but continued to exist next to negative ones (Martin, *Inventing Superstition*, 83; Koets, Δεισιδαιμονία, 99; Diggle, in Theophrast, *Characters*, 349).
[20] Theophrast, *Characters*, 110–113 (and commentary: 348–375).
[21] Martin, *Inventing Superstition*, 93–108.   [22] *Ibid.*, 160–186, 207–225.
[23] Martin, *Inventing Superstition*, 126; Harmening, *Superstitio*, 15; Calderone, "Superstitio," 387–389.

but not as particularly dangerous; in the Roman Empire, however, *super-stitio* came to be seen as referring to the "depraved, strange, spooky and dishonorable" religious practices imported from foreign peoples, such as the Egyptians, Druids or Chaldaeans.[24] In short, it referred to the "religion of the Other," whose presence might pose a threat to political stability. This perception of *superstitio* as politically subversive and socially dangerous could only be further enhanced by its association with individual, private rites instead of the public and officially sanctioned rituals of Roman state religion: in this respect, *superstitio* overlaps strongly with Roman concepts of magic.[25] As the term was adopted by Christians, its original reference to practices like soothsaying, divination and prophecy inevitably mingled with the "fear of demons" central to its Greek equivalent; and because those demons were seen as none other than the gods of the pagans, the practices traditionally known as *superstitio* became all but synonymous, in the minds of Christians, with the religious sin *par excellence*, idolatry. As demonstrated in great detail by Dieter Harmening in his standard work on the subject, the notion of idolatrous practice grounded in fear of demons became central to how superstition was understood in church regulations and theological discussions throughout the Middle Ages (with Augustine and Thomas Aquinas as particularly influential voices).[26] The term was applied to a very wide spectrum of practices, subdivided by Harmening into the categories *superstitio observationis* (such as the reading of signs and omens, visions, dreams, oracles, and the observation of "good or bad times"), *superstitio divinationis* (including notably astrology, but also necromancy and a variety of other mantic arts), and *superstitio artis magicae* (to which we will return). All of these were therefore seen as implying contact with pagan deities, or demons, whose persistent goal was to get human beings to turn away from God and worship them instead.

Next to "fear of demons" and "idolatry," there is yet a third central dimension to the concept of superstition, which goes back again to the Greek *deisidaimonia*. Under the influence of Aristotle's notions of "moderation," "balance," and "the mean," it came to be seen, by the philosophical elite, as referring to immoderate, excessive, unbalanced forms of ritual practice inspired by, again, an unfounded fear of the gods.[27] The element of ritual "excess" remained a central element of superstition throughout

---

[24] Martin, *Inventing Superstition*, 132–133.
[25] For some of the extremes to which the imagination of the demonic Other could lead, see, for example, Stratton, *Naming the Witch*, 71–105.
[26] Harmening, *Superstitio*, 34, 43, and *passim*.
[27] Martin, *Inventing Superstition*, esp. 26–27, 67–72.

the Middle Ages,[28] and one finds it still routinely referred to far into the modern period. For example, village priests by the end of the seventeenth century received instructions about how to explain to ignorant peasants that the evil of superstition consisted in their belief that prayer is not just freely offered to God, but requires precisely "such a number of candles, for example, of such a color, such a number of prayers, or breads [etc.] which they offer for themselves or for their flock by means of false or superfluous worship."[29] Even in Diderot's *Encyclopédie*, superstition is still defined as "any excess in religion in general."[30]

The Reformation, of course, had turned this traditional notion of superstition against the same Roman Catholic Church whose theologians had developed it in the first place. As formulated by Stuart Clark, "that [Roman Catholicism] was the quintessence of superstition was a view so general to Protestant cultures that it ranks as the merest of commonplaces in the history of early modern religion."[31] This fact is documented by innumerable passages in the oeuvres of Luther and Calvin, but also in an enormous range of polemical or satirical writings by lesser-known Protestants, where the terms "idolatry" and "superstition" (or *Aberglaube*) are used as wholly interchangeable, and turned with a truly incredible vehemence against such examples of "excessive" ritual as the Roman Catholic Mass, the adoration of the host and the sacraments in general, the veneration of images of Mary or the saints and their relics, the belief in purgatory, Masses for the dead, vigils and funeral services, fasting, the baptism of church bells or candles, relics, indulgences, pilgrimages, and so on and so forth.[32] Luther, Calvin and their followers essentially adopted the authoritative perspectives of Augustine and Aquinas, but with an added emphasis on justification by faith alone and the supreme grandeur of God: the superstitious man searches for salvation and consolation in his own "good works," and thereby hopes to earn (or even "force") his salvation instead of giving himself over to God's mercy, while relying on idols made by his own hands which diminish the absolute sovereignty of his Creator. The Reformers developed their full-scale attack on Roman Catholic "superstition and idolatry" in the context of a frightening demonology and a vivid expectation of the imminent Judgment, after which the damned would be facing an eternity

---

[28] Harmening, *Superstitio*, 16–25, 39–40, and *passim*.
[29] *Conférences du dioceze du Puy* (1673), in Dompnier, "Les hommes d'église," 22.
[30] D. J. [Louis de Jaucourt], "Superstition," 669; and cf. "Superstitieux."
[31] Clark, *Thinking with Demons*, 534.
[32] For an extremely useful discussion and overview of relevant passages in Luther, Calvin, and other Protestant writers, see Delumeau, "Les réformateurs et la superstition."

in hell – in short, instilling fear definitely remained central to their discourse, as had been the case throughout the Middle Ages.[33] Catholics after
Trent, for their part, reacted by attempting to demarcate Christian faith
from superstition far more sharply than before.[34] The traditional notion
of ritual "excess" combined with that of idolatrous worship still remained
the backbone of normative Roman Catholic literature by the end of the
seventeenth century,[35] as well as Enlightenment reference works such as
Chambers' *Cyclopedia* in the early eighteenth.[36]

Although superstition is thus a conceptual compound, it was easy to
see its different connotations as part of one single psychological *Gestalt*,
for example by suggesting that out of fear of invisible beings, a superstitious man engages in excessive ritual acts (or an excessive obsession with
performing them correctly) and is therefore bowing to them to win their
favor, instead of relying on simple faith in the one true God. It required
just a small step – but a very important one – to move from this dominant
Christian, and more specifically Protestant, understanding of superstition
to one that clearly reflected an Enlightenment perspective. A particularly
clear example of this shift is the entry "Aberglaube" in Johann Heinrich
Zedler's monumental *Grosses vollständiges Universal-Lexikon* (1732–1754).
Although grounded explicitly in all the traditional elements mentioned
above (fear, excess, idolatry), it defined the concept itself in terms that
were entirely different from anything we have seen so far, namely that of
confusion between natural and supernatural causation:

The word [superstition] is generally used to indicate an error, in which to natural
and human things something divine is attributed, which they do not possess, from
whence an unreasonable affect emerges in the soul [*Gemüt*].[37]

What we see here is that from a *religious* error, superstition has become an
intellectual one: rather than being religiously wrong, or sinful, it is simply
mistaken. The essence of the mistake is a failure to keep nature and the
divine separate, and the result of such failure is that the mind becomes

---

[33] For the Middle Ages, see the pertinent remarks by Harmening, *Superstitio*, 246; and for the
Reformation, see the examples in Delumeau, "Les réformateurs," 460–467.
[34] Lebrun, "Le *Traité des Superstitions*," 108–109.
[35] See for example the quotations from *Conférences du dioceze du Puy* (1672 and 1673; quoted in Dompnier, "Les hommes d'église") and Jean-Baptiste Thiers' extremely influential *Traité des superstitions*
(1679).
[36] See, for example, Chambers, *Cyclopedia*, vol. II, 153. Cf. Shorr, *Science and Superstition*, 12–34,
who points out that many of the beliefs and practices covered by the concept were still discussed
remarkably seriously in the same reference work.
[37] Zedler, *Grosses vollständiges Universal-Lexikon*, I, 107–108. Generally on "superstition" in the *Zedler*,
see extensive discussion in Shorr, *Science and Superstition*, 35–73.

vulnerable to emotional excess: fear of invisible beings, vain imaginations, and religious fanaticism. The idea that God is immanent in the natural world is seen as opening the door to a belief in invisible beings present everywhere in nature; but instead of being condemned as sin, the pagan idolatry implied by such belief is lampooned as an illusion. On such foundations, it became easy to conclude, as did the *Encyclopédie*, that superstition is "the unhappy daughter of the imagination":[38] after all, the natural world may be empty of numinous presences, but seems filled with them if only we imagine them to be there. One sees how easily we arrive, by this route, at what Lorraine Daston and Katherine Park refer to as the Enlightenment's "Unholy Trinity: Enthusiasm, Superstition, Imagination."[39]

What conclusions may be drawn from the above? Although highly innovative in defining superstition as an intellectual error and opposing it to science, Enlightenment constructs of superstition remained firmly rooted in traditional *theological* concepts of paganism as fear of demons, idolatry, and ritual excess. It is no exaggeration to say that the basic error Enlightenment ideologues tried to remove from Christian culture *was* paganism, but now redefined as its long-standing weakness for imagining the presence of spiritual realities in nature (the very same concept that would famously be labeled "animism" by Tylor at the end of the nineteenth century).[40] For thinkers with Christian commitments, and Protestants in particular, this was an extremely attractive perspective, for it allowed them to align themselves with scientific progress in a joint campaign to finish the job of purifying Christianity from its ancient nemesis. Although we have learned to think of the Enlightenment crusade against superstition as a battle of science against nonsensical "pseudo-science," this perception is therefore misleading. Rather, it was a straight continuation of the old battle of Christian theology against paganism, but now fought with a potent new weapon. This weapon was *not*, as usually assumed, that of scientific and rational argument, for even the decline of astrology cannot be convincingly attributed to those factors,[41] and Enlightenment thinkers hardly bothered

---

[38] D. J. [Louis de Jaucourt], "Superstition," 669–670.   [39] Daston and Park, *Wonders*, 334–343.

[40] Tylor presented animism ("belief in spiritual beings") as basic to "religion" and tried to keep it sharply apart from "magic" (defined as grounded in a confused understanding of causality), but significantly, these two domains actually blurred and overlapped precisely in the manifestation *par excellence* of paganism, that of "idolatry" (Hanegraaff, "Emergence of the Academic Science of Magic"). This neglected fact strongly underlines the point that is made here: although Tylor was trying to avoid the pejorative concept of "superstition," it remained inseparable from *both* his central categories, animism and magic.

[41] Tester, *History*, 214, 225, 240; Curry, *Prophecy and Power*, 138–139; Meinel, "Okkulte und exakte Wissenschaften," 38; Rutkin, "Astrology"; von Stuckrad, *Geschichte der Astrologie*, 242–286, esp.

to refute "superstitious" beliefs.[42] They had discovered a simpler and much more effective tool to rid the world of invisible spirits: ridicule.

We will encounter many illustrations of these basic points, but, for now, the representative case of Voltaire must suffice. Essentially, his battle was not against Christianity, or against religion as such, but against the pagan errors that had crept into it. Thus, in his treatise on tolerance he followed tradition in seeing astrology as *superstitio*, but did so by setting it against religion, not science: "Superstition is to religion what astrology is to astronomy: that is the very foolish daughter of a wise and intelligent mother."[43] Less well known than this oft-quoted witticism, which praises both science and religion as "wise and intelligent," is the entry "Superstition" in his *Dictionnaire philosophique*, where he states that "Almost everything that goes beyond the worship of a supreme Being and the submission of the heart to his eternal orders is superstition,"[44] and emphasizes its relation to fanaticism. And as far as history was concerned, Voltaire appears to have been entirely in line with the anti-apologist perspective: "Born in paganism, adopted by Judaism, superstition infected the Christian Church from the very beginning."[45]

TAINTED TERMINOLOGIES 2: MAGIC

If historical and conceptual analyses of "superstition" have been relatively rare, *magic* is undoubtedly one of the most heavily theorized concepts in the study of religion. As noted by Marco Pasi, there seem to be almost as many definitions of "magic" as there have been scholars writing about it.[46] Nevertheless, on closer scrutiny, most of these definitions turn out to be variations on a few extremely influential theories.[47] (1) "Intellectualist" approaches are linked to the names of Edward Burnett Tylor, who defined magic as based upon "the error of mistaking ideal analogy for real analogy"

253–260. Notice, however, that von Stuckrad's post-Foucauldian methodology (see Chapter 4, pp. 362–367) has the effect of reducing any critical debate to an instance of discursive competition, which is then automatically about power rather than content, so that the very question of the scientific status of astrology becomes a non-issue for him (for the logic of this line of argument, against the background of skepsis over the demarcation criterion of science in the wake of Kuhn, Lakatos, and Feyerabend, see Hagner, "Bye-bye Science," 31–41). But content was important and the force of arguments did matter: they were not just convenient weapons in power competition, but had (and have) the ability to convince. Whiggish or "presentist" interpretations by which current concepts of "science" are projected back into the seventeenth century are certainly misleading, but it remains possible to analyze historically how the scientific status of astrology changed in parallel with the development (!) of what seventeenth-century authors understood by "science."

[42] For example, Thorndike, "*L'Encyclopédie*," 376.   [43] Voltaire, *Treatise on Tolerance*, 83.
[44] Voltaire, *Dictionnaire philosophique*, 394.   [45] *Ibid.*, 396.   [46] Pasi, "Notion de magie," 38.
[47] For a more detailed discussion, see Hanegraaff, "Magic I."

(that is, the erroneous assumption of "primitive man" that things associated in his thinking must be connected in actual fact),[48] and James G. Frazer, who simplified Tylor's approach into his famous evolutionist triad: humanity had evolved from magic, through religion, to science. For Frazer, magic actually meant *sympathetic* magic, based upon the assumption that "things act on each other at a distance through a secret sympathy" or "an invisible ether."[49] Both definitional approaches were based upon science, not religion, as the theoretical opposite of magic: it was seen as grounded in merely imaginary analogies, correspondences, and invisibles forces, in contrast to the causal mechanisms basic to positivist science.[50] (2) "Functionalist" approaches to magic are linked to the names of Marcel Mauss and Emile Durkheim, and concentrate on ritual action. Mauss used the term magic for "any rite that is not part of an organized cult: a rite that is private, secret, mysterious, and ultimately tending towards one that is forbidden."[51] Along very similar lines, Durkheim defined religious beliefs as shared by, and constitutive of, a social group (referred to as a "Church"), whereas magic was inherently non-social: "*There is no Church of magic.*"[52] Functionalist approaches are therefore based upon religion, not science, as the theoretical opposite of magic: as formulated by Durkheim, "there is something inherently anti-religious about the maneuvers of the magician."[53] (3) A third approach, finally, derives from a theoretical concept central to the oeuvre of Lucien Lévy-Bruhl – remarkably, since he himself saw it as equally applicable to magic and religion.[54] It was based upon the perceived contrast between a worldview or mentality grounded in "instrumental causality" (which assumes the presence of secondary causes or mechanisms that mediate between causes and effects) and one grounded in "participation" (where causes and effects are seen as associated, or merging, to the point of identity or consubstantiality, without assuming the presence of mediating links).[55] At first Lévy-Bruhl considered it to be typical of

---

[48] Tylor, *Primitive Religion*, vol. 1, 116.   [49] Frazer, *Golden Bough*, vol. 1, 54.

[50] See detailed analysis of Tylor and Frazer in Hanegraaff, "Emergence of the Academic Science of Magic."

[51] Mauss, "Esquisse," 16.

[52] Durkheim, *Les formes élémentaires*, 61 (emphasis in the original). For Durkheim's blatant sins of circular reasoning in this famous passage, see Hanegraaff, "Defining Religion," 341–345. His way of defining all forms of "religion" after the evidently Christian model of a "church" is so transparently ethnocentric that one is amazed how easily it has been taken for granted by generations of sociologists.

[53] *Ibid.*, 59–60. The Mauss/Durkheim approach clearly reflects ancient Roman concepts of superstition and magic as the "religious Other" (see text).

[54] See esp. Lévy-Bruhl, *Fonctions mentales*, 341–351.

[55] See analysis in Hanegraaff, "How Magic Survived," 371–374.

"primitive" cultures, but he eventually came to understand participation as a primary and irreducible human constant in *any* society, including our own. Based largely on caricatures such as those found in Bronislaw Malinowski's criticism of Lévy-Bruhl,[56] and a neglect of his late *Carnets*, later scholars came to assume that participation and magic were meant to be equivalent terms, leading to a spate of theories that interpret magic as grounded in a "different kind of rationality."[57] In theories of this kind, it is clearly science, not religion, that serves as the theoretical opposite of magic: alternatives to instrumental causality are believed to be the heart of the matter.

The basic theoretical approaches represented by Tylor, Mauss, and Lévy-Bruhl have been mixed, combined, adapted, and reinterpreted by later authors in manifold ways, but almost without exception on the basis of a tacit acceptance of the triad "magic – religion – science" as universal concepts. As noted by Jonathan Z. Smith, this fact is highly problematic from a theoretical point of view, as it breaks conventional definitory rules and leads to interpretational frameworks that are riddled with inconsistencies. His conclusion is that magic cannot be salvaged as an etic term; and in fact, in the study of religion since the 1990s it seems to be in the process of vanishing from standard terminology.[58] However, it is not just for reasons of strict conceptual logic that "magic" is losing its traditional status as a "second-order" or etic term, defined by its opposition to both "religion" and "science." This development also reflects a general trend, after the fall of the Berlin wall, of widespread disaffection among intellectuals with the "grand narratives" of modernity, and critical attention to their implicit ideological agendas.[59] Although radical "postmodern" versions of this phenomenon have received most attention in the popular media, many historians have found that one does not need the theoretical machinery of French post-structuralism to understand a very basic point about much of traditional terminology in the study of religion: its thorough dependence on normative modernist ideologies and implicit hegemonic claims

---

[56] Malinowski, "Magic, Science and Religion"; cf. Hanegraaff, "How Magic Survived," 375 and n. 33.
[57] As representative of this trend, see, for example, Horton, *Patterns of Thought*; and the good overview in Luhrmann, *Persuasions*, 345–356.
[58] Smith, *Relating Religion*, 216–218. In a much-noted article from the early 1990s, H. S. Versnel still considered the term indispensable ("Some Reflections," for example, 181) but, significantly, many of the most important recent reference works on basic terminology in the study of religion seem to be doing just fine without it (Taylor, *Critical Terms in Religious Studies*; Braun and McCutcheon, *Guide to the Study of Religion*).
[59] Cf. Hanegraaff, "Study of Western Esotericism," 509–511.

of Western superiority rooted in missionary and colonialist mentalities. Scholarly theorizing about magic is a (arguably even *the*) paradigmatic example, in that it has typically perpetuated and lent academic legitimacy to traditional heresiological stereotypes about the alleged horrors of paganism, and served as "scientific" justification for converting non-European peoples from benighted superstition to the superior truths of Christianity, Enlightenment, and science.[60]

The historical evidence for this basic point is overwhelming, and has been presented and analyzed by Randall Styers in a landmark study published in 2004.[61] Styers shows in meticulous detail how the reification of "magic" as a supposedly universal category *sui generis*, defined by its very contrast with the (likewise reified) categories of "religion" and "science," has been subservient to the goal of elaborating the project of modernity and selling its values and worldviews to Western and non-Western audiences. Scholars have been extraordinarily successful in convincing their readers and themselves about the universal applicability and scientific legitimacy of theories and concepts of magic that are, in actual fact, transparently culture-specific, normative, and ideology-driven. The evidence in this regard, as laid out in detail by Styers, is so abundant and straightforward that one can only marvel at how long, and how effectively, this essentialist and total-izing discourse on "magic versus religion and science" has kept academics spellbound, as if they were trapped themselves in a magic circle without escape:[62] "you cannot talk about magic without using the term magic,"

---

[60] *Ibid.*, 512–516; and see in particular the thoroughly convincing discussion in Styers, *Making Magic*, 14–21, 69–119.

[61] Styers' *Making Magic* analyzes academic theories of magic as reflective of three basic modernist concerns: the regulation (social, political, discursive) of piety, of reason, and of desire. As pointed out by Pasi ("Notion de magie," 41–50), an important predecessor of Styers' basic approach was the Italian scholar of religion Ernesto de Martino, in his *Magia e civiltà* (1962). Whereas Styers concentrates on the process of modernization, de Martino emphasized that the "anti-magical polemic" has been central to the historical process of Western identity-formation since the early Christian period, so that modernist discourses of magic should be seen within a larger historical context and related to discursive formations that go back to the origins of Christianity if not even further. Pasi points out that while his conclusions confirm de Martino's pioneering intuitions, Styers himself seems to underestimate the extent to which his own work results in a relativization – more precisely, perhaps, deconstruction – of the very concept of "magic" understood as a reified category of universal application ("Notion de magie," 49; and on the "magical" reification of "magic" by scholars, see, for example, Styers, *Making Magic*, 223). One sign of this is the fact that whereas Styers thoroughly deconstructs the term "magic," he speaks of "superstition" as if its meaning and its relation to magic are unproblematic and not in need of any explanation (for example, *ibid.*, 43, 48, 51–55, 165–167).

[62] My metaphors are inspired by Styers, *Making Magic*, 3: "The core of my argument is that these theories of magic are, in essential respects, magical." Cf. *ibid.*, 216–217.

as exclaimed by Versnel in 1991.[63] The vicious circle is broken, however, once we recognize that the magic "out there" is believed to "exist" only because *we* have first decided to call it "magic." It is literally a creature of the theoretical imagination, conjured into existence by the same intellectual fallacy that has so often been considered the very essence of magic: the confusion of mental concepts with actual realities, so that what we believe we understand in our mind seems to exist in the external world.

The conclusion would seem inevitable. The term "magic" is an important object *of* historical research, but definitely unsuitable as an etic instrument *for* doing research. It should simply not be used as a general category, as happens whenever a scholar states or implies that this or that practice or belief "is" magic or magical. Unfortunately, however, scholars have been every bit as active as "believers" in promoting this culture-specific terminology as if it were universal, or naively believing in its universality; and all along the line they have fallen prey, again like believers, to the temptation of presenting normative biases and subjective convictions as if they were "disinterested" observations and "objective" truths. Once the famous "magic – religion – science" triad has been demystified as the academic ghost it is, what we are left with is writing the history, not of magic as such, but of emic *concepts* of magic, and of how these have been applied to a wide range of practices and beliefs in different periods of history.[64] As

---

[63] Versnel quite rightly observes about his colleagues that "practically no one escapes moments of reduced concentration when they suddenly fall into using unsophisticated common sense concepts, though they sometimes betray their awareness of the lapse by putting the term magic between inverted commas or adding 'so-called'" ("Some Reflections," 181). For example, even a very careful scholar like de Jong does not manage to evade circular reasoning entirely, when he writes that the Greeks came to use the term μαγεία and its cognates to denote something already known as γόης, meaning "sorcerers, quacks, *magicians*" (emphasis added) and their activities (*Traditions of the Magi*, 387); similarly, Jan Bremmer seems to suggest that magic is an unproblematically universal human phenomenon existing already long before it was named, when he writes that "The practice of magic probably goes back several millennia, but the origin of the term has its roots in ancient Greece" ("Birth of the Term 'Magic'," [2002 version], 1). The point here is *not* to deny that commonalities between certain kinds of religious behavior may be sufficiently strong to consider them as belonging to one and the same general category: that such a category did exist in antiquity is argued convincingly, for example, by Dickie (*Magic and Magicians*, 27). Rather, the point is that our modern term "magic" is unsuitable as a label for that category, because it has acquired so many *new* connotations after antiquity, and these are so tightly bound up with our own post-Reformation and post-Enlightenment identities, that even by the wildest stretch of imagination they cannot be applicable to, for example, the fifth century BCE. For that reason (*contra* Dickie, Versnel, or Bremmer) we should resist the temptation of using our term "magic" in discussing what may have been known as μαγεία or *magia* in Greek and Roman antiquity. Again, the problem is *not* the use of etic terminology as such (which is often indispensable in scholarly analysis, as pointed out, for example, by Dickie, *Magic and Magicians*, 18–20, in agreement with Versnel and Bremmer, as well as Jardine, "Etics and Emics"), but the use of *this* particular terminology.

[64] See also Pasi, "Theses de magia," 2 (thesis 0 and 0.1). Logically, the same approach should be followed with regard to emic concepts of "religion" and "science."

with the related case of "superstition," it is a complex story, but fortunately it has been much better researched.[65]

The Greek complex of words relating to magic (μάγος, μαγεία, μαγικός, μαγεύω, etc.) is derived from the Old Persian *magu-*, the exact meaning of which is unclear although it must have referred to a religious functionary of some kind. The terminology was imported into Greek no later than the sixth century BCE, and while a positive understanding of *mageia* as "worship of the gods" (Plato, *Alcibiades* I.122A) survived at least as late as Apuleius in the second century,[66] it seems to have rapidly acquired a set of negative connotations that already adhered to the native term γόης.[67] These origins became highly important from the Renaissance on, as seen in the attempts by authors like Giovanni Pico della Mirandola or Cornelius Agrippa to promote a positive understanding of magic understood as the "ancient wisdom" of Zoroaster by juxtaposing it sharply against its negative and demonic counterpart, *goetia*:[68] a distinction that became an almost unavoidable cliché in discussions of magic up to the eighteenth century. However, prior to the fifteenth-century revival of the ancient wisdom narrative and the earlier emergence of the concept of *magia naturalis* around the thirteenth century, to which we will turn in a moment, the notion of magic (as μαγεία in Greek and *magia* in Latin) was dominated entirely by its negative connotations with the sinister or threatening, demon-ridden or simply fraudulent practices attributed to "others." Jan Bremmer rightly points out that magic was contrasted not with religion *tout court*, but with normative religious practice, so that it became all but indistinguishable

---

[65] The main lines of development can be traced through the entries on magic in the *Dictionary of Gnosis and Western Esotericism*: Graf, "Magic II: Antiquity"; Fanger and Klaassen, "Magic III: Middle Ages"; Brach, "Magic IV: Renaissance–17th Century"; Hanegraaff, "Magic V: 18th–20th Century." On the origins of the term "magic," see Bremmer, "Birth of the Term 'Magic'"; Bremmer, "Persian *Magoi*"; de Jong, *Traditions of the Magi*, 387–394; de Jong, "Contribution of the Magi." More generally for antiquity, see Graf, *Gottesnähe und Schadenzauber*; Dickie, *Magic and Magicians*. For the Middle Ages, see Kieckhefer, *Magic in the Middle Ages*; Kieckhefer, "Specific Rationality of Magic"; Flint, *Rise of Magic*. On magic in the Renaissance there are many relevant titles (see bibliography in Brach, quoted *supra*), but surprisingly few synthetic works attentive to the terminological problem. See, nevertheless, Walker, *Spiritual and Demonic Magic*; Zambelli, *L'ambigua natura della magia*; Zambelli, *White Magic, Black Magic*.

[66] See Chapter 1, n. 33.

[67] De Jong, *Traditions of the Magi*, 387–394, here 387–388; and, in more detail, de Jong, "Contribution of the Magi," 85–88. See also Graf, *Gottesnähe und Schadenzauber*, 24–25; Bremmer, "Birth of the Term 'Magic'," and the updated version "Persian *Magoi*" plus separate appendix "Magic *and* Religion." A particularly useful discussion of early Greek terminologies is Dickie, *Magic and Magicians*, 12–16, who emphasizes that persons called *goetes*, *epodoi*, *magoi*, and *pharmakeis* may originally have pursued distinct callings, but the terms had become wholly interchangeable by the fifth century BCE.

[68] For example, Pico della Mirandola, *De hominis dignitate* (Garin ed., 54–55); Agrippa, *De occulta philosophia*, Preface to Trithemius (Perrone Compagni ed., 68–71).

from *deisidaimonia* and *superstitio* especially in the Christian medieval context.[69] As emphasized by Richard Kieckhefer, "Up through the twelfth century, if you asked a theologian what magic was you were likely to hear that demons began it and were always involved in it. You would also be likely to get a catalogue of different forms of magic, and most of the varieties would be species of divination."[70]

The decisive change in these traditional understandings occurred around the thirteenth century, with the emergence of *magia naturalis* as an alternative to demonic magic. The historical backgrounds to this development are well known, and will only be sketched here very briefly.[71] With the disintegration of the Roman Empire, knowledge of Greek had vanished from Western Europe almost completely; and by the time of Boethius' death in 524, only a limited number of classic philosophical and scientific works had been translated into Latin. With the relative exception of medicine, secular learning declined in the West for a period of 600 years. However, it survived in the eastern parts of the former empire, and, with the rapid expansion of Islam after Muhammad's death in 632, much of the regions where Greek learning was still intact came under Muslim rule. A large-scale undertaking of translating the philosophical and scientific texts into Arabic got under way during the eighth century, eventually leading to a vibrant intellectual culture in which scores of Muslim authors revised and further developed the Greek sciences, thereby transforming them into Islamic ones.[72] This wealth of Arabic science rooted in classic Hellenistic culture remained unknown to the Latin West until the later Middle Ages. Gerbert of Aurillac (the later Pope Sylvester II) in the tenth century and Constantine the African in the eleventh studied in Islamic Spain, and began making translations, but it was only after the monarch Alfonso VI of Castile took control of Toledo in 1085 that Christian intellectuals gained full access to the magnificent collections of the Iberian peninsula. The caliphal library of Cordoba, for example, is believed to have held no fewer than 400,000 volumes, in a period when even the largest libraries in Christian Europe

[69] Bremmer, "Magic *and* Religion?" (2002), 269–270 / (2008), 349–351.

[70] Kieckhefer, *Magic in the Middle Ages*, 10–11. On the important stream of angelic and necromantic ritual magic practiced by a "clerical underworld" during the Middle Ages, see *ibid.*, 151–176, and the landmark volume edited by Fanger, *Conjuring Spirits*.

[71] For general overviews, see, for example, Lindberg, "Transmission"; Pingree, "Diffusion of Arabic Magical Texts." An older but still very important analysis of the Islamic corpus is Ullmann, *Natur- und Geheimwissenschaften im Islam*. On Arabic Hermetica, see now van Bladel, *Arabic Hermes*; and on the reception into Latin, see Burnett, *Arabic into Latin*.

[72] The creative and innovative character of medieval Islamic science is strongly emphasized by David Pingree, against "the false claim that medieval Islam only preserved Greek science and transmitted it as Muslims had received it to the eager West" ("Hellenophilia," 555).

did not have more than 400.[73] From the twelfth century on, multiple texts from the corpus of Greek natural philosophy and science and its medieval Islamic elaborations began to be translated from Arabic into Latin, leading to an unprecedented revival of classical materials concerning the sciences of nature.

Astrology and alchemy were central to this development of medieval science, and, as will be seen, these two traditional disciplines are the supreme examples of how thoroughly mainstream academic scholarship can be led astray by an anachronistic use of basic concepts.[74] Reacting to the standard post-eighteenth-century image of astrology as "pseudoscience," Lynn Thorndike pointed out as early as 1955 that modern historians of science have been "strangely blind" to the fact that classical astrology was grounded in a concept of universal, immutable natural law.[75] As formulated more recently by the leading contemporary specialist David Pingree, the union of some aspects of advanced Babylonian celestial divination with aristotelian physics and Hellenistic astronomy had resulted, in Egypt by the second century BCE, in

the supreme attempt made in antiquity to create in a rigorous form a causal model of the *kosmos*, one in which the eternally repeating rotations of the celestial bodies, together with their varying but periodically recurring interrelationships, produce all changes in the sublunar world of the four elements that, whether primary, secondary, or tertiary effects, constitute the generation and decay of material bodies and the modifications of the parts or functions of the rational and irrational souls of men, animals and plants. In other words, ancient Greek astrology in its strictest interpretation was the most comprehensive scientific theory of antiquity, providing through the application of the mathematical models appropriate to it predictions of all changes that take place in the world of cause and effect . . . [76]

However, such an "internalist" approach focused on the actual nature of astrology, no matter how justified in itself, does not suffice for understanding its career in Western culture: at least as important is its social status and the way it was perceived by the wider culture. As a divinatory art and

[73] For a beautiful evocation of the richness of this medieval Spanish culture, see Menocal, *Ornament of the World*, here 33.

[74] Because alchemy will be discussed separately in the next section, the argument about the concept *magia naturalis* will here be made with reference to astrology, which is most central to it in any case.

[75] Thorndike, "True Place of Astrology," 276. Even Thorndike's opponent George Sarton (see below, Chapter 4, pp. 318–323) agreed on this point: "Pure astrology was a very remarkable scientific system; it provided a congruous explanation of the world" (Review of Lynn Thorndike [1924], 85).

[76] Pingree, "Hellenophilia," 560 (this does not mean that Pingree believes astrology is true: "on the contrary, I believe it to be totally false" [*ibid.*, 559]). On astrology as science, see also von Stuckrad, *Geschichte der Astrologie* [index: under "Empirie" and "Astrologie und wissenschaftliche Methode"] (cf. von Stuckrad, "*Astrologia Hermetica*," 54).

as a practice linked to traditional understandings of the heavenly bodies as living and divine beings, astrology tended to be seen, as early as Roman antiquity, as falling under the categories of *superstitio* and *magia*. I have already discussed the mingling of those two categories and its continuation in Christian culture, as well as the common medieval understanding of astrology as *superstitio observationis*. Patristic polemics against astrology largely focused on fatalism, seen as incompatible with the notion of free will, and this would remain an important issue through the Middle Ages;[77] but already in Tertullian's *De idolatria*, astrology was presented as a species falling under the more general genus of magic, condemned as an idolatrous practice invented by the fallen angels.[78] From the fourth century on, with the establishment of Christianity as the official religion of the empire, this understanding of astrology as a form of superstition and idolatrous magic became dominant, at least in the Latin West:[79] in fact, there is a remarkable contrast between the paucity of condemnations leveled specifically and exclusively against astrology, and the copious number of sources in which astrology is ranged under the larger rubric of superstition.[80]

This was the perspective inherited by the late medieval intellectuals who began to rediscover the treasures of ancient science from the Islamic libraries, and they naturally needed to find a way to legitimate the serious study of such "wretched subjects."[81] Fortunately for them, they could profit

---

[77] Von Stuckrad, *Das Ringen*, 771–782; Laistner, "Western Church and Astrology," 254–256.

[78] Tertullian, *De idolatria* 9.1–2 and especially 7–8.

[79] For the suppression of astrology by the Christian Church, see von Stuckrad, *Das Ringen*, 767–800 (and for the association of astrology with magic, esp. 782–787, 791, 794–797). For the period from Constantine to the end of the ninth century, see Laistner, "Western Church and Astrology." Against the traditional thesis that Christianity was hostile to astrology from the very beginning (Gundel and Gundel, "Astrologumena," 332; Blume, *Regenten des Himmels*, 8; cf. von Stuckrad, *Das Ringen*, 767; and von Stuckrad, Review of Blume, 213) von Stuckrad emphasizes the plurality of Christianities before Constantine, concentrating on astrology in Gnostic and Manichaean contexts (implicitly confirming the wholly negative attitude among what eventually became mainstream or "centrist" Christianity). Thorndike's thesis that during the Middle Ages "even the most educated men believed in astrology" (*Place of Magic*, 5) is mildly misleading since the revival of astrology happened only with the translations from Arabic sources in the *later* Middle Ages (cf. Thorndike, *History*, vol. 1, 551–782).

[80] Laistner, "Western Church and Astrology," 263, 265.

[81] The allusion is to the famous but half-hearted one-page article by Neugebauer, "The Study of Wretched Subjects," published in the journal *Isis* in 1951. Although Neugebauer criticized George Sarton's characterization of the Mandaean "Book of the Zodiak" as "a wretched collection of omens, debased astrology and miscellaneous nonsense" and the whole field as "the superstitious flotsam of the Near East," he himself also remained under the spell of the medieval Christian categorization of astrology as *superstitio* (as shown by his characterization of Sarton's language as "factually correct," and his adoption of similar language in the rest of the article). A more consistent criticism would have emphasized the anachronism of projecting Christian concepts of *superstitio* back on to Hellenistic astrology, and the inappropriateness for modern historians of science of adopting ancient Roman and medieval theological categories as "factually correct."

from a terminological loophole that had been opened by Isidore of Seville in his authoritative *Etymologiae*. Although Isidore, too, had ranged the various kinds of divination under "magic" and condemned all of them as involving contact with demons,[82] in his section on "astronomy" he had also distinguished between *astrologia superstitiosa* and an acceptable *astrologia naturalis*.[83] Only a very small step was required to apply a similar distinction to the category of magic as a whole, and argue that the demon-ridden and idolatrous practices known under that name should not be confused with the legitimate study of the workings of nature: *magia naturalis*. This new term should therefore be understood *not* as an attempt to present magic as scientific, but as an apologetic concept intended to protect the study of the ancient sciences against theological censure.

Among the earliest authors to use this new terminology was the Parisian bishop William of Auvergne (Guillelmus Alvernus) in the thirteenth century, and it had become well established by the end of the fourteenth.[84] Significantly, William's assertion that part of the domain known as "magic" was actually concerned with the legitimate study of natural processes went hand in hand with a renewed, and extremely formulated, emphasis on pagan idolatry as its demonic counterpart that must be exterminated "with fire and sword."[85] For the later development of the debate on magic, it is highly important that the same author was responsible for reviving the memory of Augustine's largely forgotten condemnation of the "godmaking passages" in the hermetic *Asclepius*, where Hermes praised the ancient Egyptian practice of creating statues and drawing the souls of divine entities down into them.[86] In intellectual debate since William of Auvergne and throughout the Renaissance, *Asclepius* 23–24/37–38 became a virtually unavoidable *locus classicus* for discussions of "astral magic" (the drawing down of "powers" or "virtues" from the stars), or, more specifically, the use of astrological images or talismans.[87] If talismans were intended to be "addressed"[88] to some kind of spirit or intelligence, associated with a

---

[82] Isidore of Seville, *Etymologiae* 8.9; cf. Kieckhefer, *Magic in the Middle Ages*, 11.

[83] Isidore of Seville, *Etymologiae* 3.27; cf. Tester, *History of Western Astrology*, 124–126; von Stuckrad, *Geschichte der Astrologie*, 187–188.

[84] Kieckhefer, "Specific Rationality of Magic," 818–819, with reference to William of Auvergne, *De universo* 1.50.43 (*Opera Omnia* I, 648); and Thorndike, *History*, vol. II, 346–349, with reference to various passages in *De legibus*.

[85] De Mayo, *Demonology of William of Auvergne*.

[86] For Augustine on Hermes, and his legacy, see Hanegraaff, "Hermetism." For William of Auvergne's role, see Porreca, "Hermes Trismegistus"; cf. Gilly, "Überlieferung," esp. 345–346.

[87] See Weill-Parot, "Astral Magic," and the exhaustive study by the same author, *Les "images astrologiques"* (with pp. 175–213 devoted to William of Auvergne).

[88] Hence Weill-Parot's coinage of the term "addressative magic" for this type ("Astral Magic," 169).

heavenly body, whose power could then be channeled down into the material receptacle, the practice could be condemned as an idolatrous attempt to contact astral demons. However, if the image derived its virtue solely from the natural powers of the stars, as suggested in the extremely influential thirteenth-century *Speculum Astronomiae*, it could be accepted as natural magic.[89] As explained by Nicolas Weill-Parot, the distinction is one of semiology versus etiology:[90] illicit magic depended on signs addressed to intelligences, whereas licit natural magic depended on chains of causality in a naturalistic framework.

This basic opposition was part of the strict classifications typical of scholastic rationality, and developed in paradigmatic fashion by Thomas Aquinas.[91] While legitimating natural magic in principle, it nevertheless forced its defenders into a defensive position, for they always needed to convince theological critics that what they claimed were natural processes did not actually involve some "addressative" and hence illicit dimension. However, alternative neoplatonizing theoretical frameworks coming from the Islamic world, such as, notably, al-Kindi's *De radiis* (available in Latin since the thirteenth century) implied exactly the opposite logic, as explained by Weill-Parot: since all events were supposed to be governed by the universal celestial harmony and connected by a network of invisible "rays," the efficacy of magic depended on natural processes *even* if the practitioner believed himself to be addressing demons![92] *De radiis* is among the major influences on Marsilio Ficino's novel Renaissance understanding of natural magic as working by means of the universal *spiritus* (described as a "very tenuous" intermediary substance, more soul-like than the body but more bodily than the soul, and permeating the whole of reality);[93] and

---

[89] *Speculum Astronomiae* 11 (in: Zambelli, *Speculum Astronomiae*, 246–247); and the extensive discussion in Weill-Parot, *Les "images astrologiques"*, 27–90.

[90] Weill-Parot, "Astral Magic," 176.

[91] See discussion in Weill-Parot, *Les "images astrologiques,"* 223–259.

[92] Weill-Parot, "Astral Magic," 177–178; and extensively in Weill-Parot, *Les "images astrologiques,"* 155–174. See also d'Alverny and Hudry, "Al-Kindi: De Radiis"; and Travaglia, *Magic, Causality and Intentionality*. Weill-Parot points out that the al-Kindian position was unacceptable in a Christian scholastic framework, as shown by the attack on *De radiis* by Giles of Rome in his *Errores philosophorum*: pushed to the limit, it could be used to undermine even the possibility of prayers addressed to God!

[93] Ficino, *De vita* 3.3.31–33 (Kaske and Clark ed., 256–257): "corpus tenuissimum, quasi non corpus et quasi iam anima, item quasi non anima et quasi iam corpus." On Ficino's concept of magic and the centrality of *spiritus*, see Kaske and Clark, "Introduction," 45–55 (and 50–51 for the importance of al-Kindi). A classic discussion remains Walker, *Spiritual and Demonic Magic* (whose term "spiritual magic" is technically correct given the centrality of *spiritus*, but perhaps misleading today, in view of current connotations of "spirituality"), but his analysis must be complemented by more recent ones, such as notably Copenhaver, "Scholastic Philosophy and Renaissance Magic"; "Renaissance Magic and Neoplatonic Philosophy"; "Iamblichus, Synesius and the Chaldaean Oracles."

the extremely influential discussions of astral magic and talismans in his *De Vita Coelitus Comparanda* were, of course, thoroughly grounded in a platonic worldview. It is therefore hardly surprising that the phenomenon known as Renaissance magic, beginning with Ficino, is characterized by profound ambiguities on the theoretical level: drawing on a great variety of Latin, Greek and Arabic sources, it had to combine aristotelian with platonic strands of natural philosophy and metaphysics, it needed to present both of them as compatible with Christian doctrine, it had to convince the theologians that magic was strictly natural, but nevertheless, it also wanted to see that same natural magic as the supreme *religious* wisdom derived from Zoroaster![94]

As remarked by Jean-Pierre Brach, the Renaissance saw a series of famous attempts at theorizing and systematizing magic against the background of the scholastic distinction between natural and ritual (angelic or demonic) magic, but "the elaboration of a synthetic approach had, in many cases, the not-so-paradoxical effect of partially blurring the basic differences that were assumed to exist between them."[95] This ambiguity is already evident in the case of Ficino, whose main discussion of "natural" (that is, astral) magic took the form, very significantly, of a crypto-commentary on the hermetic "god-making passages" which, as we have seen, had been precisely the paradigm of idolatrous magic since William of Auvergne.[96] In the wake of Pico della Mirandola's magical theses, it was strongly enhanced by a tendency of associating magic with kabbalah, sometimes to a point where they became virtually identical.[97] With Cornelius Agrippa's famous *De occulta philosophia* (originally meant to be titled *De magia*) this development reached its logical conclusion. Magic was explicitly presented here as the "ancient wisdom," whose reputation needed to be purified from the common association with illicit practices of evil sorcery, superstition,

---

[94] Zambelli, *L'ambigua natura della magia*; Weill-Parot, "Astral Magic," 178–179; and for the complexity of Ficino's talismanic magic and its sources, see in particular Weill-Parot, "Pénombre Ficinienne."

[95] Brach, "Magic IV," 732.

[96] Hanegraaff, "Lodovico Lazzarelli," 73 n. 193. The crucial point was whether the beneficial "gifts" drawn down from the stars by means of astral magic were in fact demonic, in line with Augustine's censure of *Asclepius* 23–24/37–38, or natural, as suggested by a closely equivalent passage in Plotinus' *Ennead* 4.3.11. *De Vita Coelitus Comparanda* was presented as a commentary on the latter (title above chapter I, see Kaske and Clark ed., 242–243), but any well-informed reader would have recognized the parallel with the notorious *Asclepius* passage, and Ficino himself made it explicit in his chapter 26.77–89 (Kaske and Clark ed., 388–389).

[97] See, for example, Pico's Magical thesis 9>15 (Farmer, *Syncretism*, 498–499): "No magical operation can be of any efficacy unless it has annexed to it a work of Kabbalah, explicit or implicit." Cf. discussion in Brach, "Magic IV," 733.

and demonism.[98] Agrippa adopted Reuchlin's categorization of the *ars miraculorum* as consisting of three levels (physics, astrology, and magic, the latter subdivided into a negative *goetia* and a positive *theurgia*),[99] but he made *magia* into the umbrella term, subdividing it into (1) "natural magic," concerned with the sublunar world of the elements, (2) "celestial magic," pertaining to the realm above the moon but below the fixed stars, and mostly concerned with numbers and astrology, and (3) "ceremonial magic," concerned with demonic and angelic entities above the fixed stars, and dominated by kabbalah. The brilliance of this scheme was that it could encompass all the ancient materials that were now available, while assigning to each discipline its proper place in an orderly hierarchy: from the natural arts and sciences recovered from Arabic sources, via the religious speculations attributed to the ancient sages in Greek manuscripts, to the supreme Mosaic revelations known as kabbalah from the Hebrew sources. Extremely influential through the following centuries, Agrippa's scheme reflects his awareness that, while a distinction between "good" and "bad" magic remained crucial, the term *magia naturalis* was no longer convincing as a general term for the former category: the ancient *mageia* linked to the name of Zoroaster was too obviously concerned with metaphysical realities, not just physical ones, and its true origin was the kabbalistic revelation coming from the Creator himself. In short, even if many authors kept referring to *magia naturalis*, in fact there was no real distinction any more between a *prisca theologia* and a *prisca magia*.

The "metamorphosis of magic"[100] from late antiquity to early modernity is a remarkable phenomenon, somewhat reminiscent of the beggar who became a millionaire. Notwithstanding some vague claims of a remote and noble ancestry, it had begun its life as a wholly negative term for despicable demonic and idolatrous practices; in due time, however, it had managed to gain a degree of respectability by setting itself off sharply against its former identity, as *magia naturalis*; and once having carved out that securer niche for itself, it finally set out to conquer the world by proclaiming itself universal, all-encompassing, and related to the Highest Good. Once having attained its highest reputation by the sixteenth century among certain circles of humanist intellectuals, it became a natural target

---

[98] For example, Agrippa, *De occulta philosophia*, "Ad lectorem" and dedication to Trithemius (Perrone Compagni ed., 65–71).

[99] Reuchlin, *De verbo mirifico* Bk. 2 (Ehlers *et al.* ed., 142–143); and see Perrone Compagni, "Introduction," 17–18.

[100] Bremmer and Veenstra, *Metamorphosis of Magic*.

for critics. Many of them kept calling attention to its doubtful origins, suggesting that its splendid garb was just a show, and the old heart of darkness was still beating underneath. Others suggested that it was over-reaching itself, and should be satisfied with a respectable existence limited to the realm of nature. But even though it gradually began to concede much of its power to competitors from the seventeenth century on, and was finally ridiculed as a fool and a fraud after the eighteenth, ever since its Renaissance moment of glory there have been those (as will be seen) who kept on believing in its superior spiritual mission, and in the authority derived from its ancient nobility.

This complicated career explains much of the confused status of "magic" since the period of the Enlightenment: the term could mean very different things to different parties, and each participant in the discourse had a wide choice of connotations to highlight or play down at will, according to his particular religious, scientific, or philosophical agenda. However, the general playing field in which these discussions took place was the one sketched in the introduction to this chapter: since the later seventeenth century, it was always concerned with the status of "nature" and its relation to the divine, and, more particularly, the question of whether science left any room for the presence of "spiritual" forces or entities in the natural world. Within that context, the concept of "natural magic" came to play a central role *because* of its profound ambiguity: it could be used to disenchant the world by claiming that magic was really just a natural phenomenon, but it could also be used to re-enchant the world by claiming that nature was inherently "magical" (now in the sense of being permeated by mysterious forces). Most confusing of all, the former argument could turn out to be a Trojan horse: an author might stress his agreement with naturalists that magic was just another term for natural philosophy, only to continue by endowing "nature" with all the invisible forces and presences otherwise associated with the supernatural and the demonic! It is to those forces and presences that we must now turn.

TAINTED TERMINOLOGIES 3: OCCULT

Having sketched the life and career of "magic" up to the sixteenth and into the seventeenth century, we must make one further excursion back into time before we are ready to move back to the eighteenth and the nineteenth. We have seen that, in its original time and cultural setting, astrology was perfectly able to qualify as a scientific system insofar as it was based upon a concept of universal natural law: its later rejection as *superstitio* and demon-inspired *magia* was not based upon scientific arguments but on the theological battle against paganism. The same is true for the ancient sciences more generally. One has to wait until the seventeenth and eighteenth centuries to observe the process, which should begin to sound familiar by now, of such theological censure being translated into scientific terms. In order to understand that development, we now have to turn to a third key term: the adjective *occult* (literally: hidden, concealed) and its cognates.

At the very origin of this terminology, we find the common recognition that there are certain forces and connections in nature that remain invisible or "hidden," and are bound to strike us as mysterious because they are hard to account for in rational terms. Although we are no longer used to thinking about phenomena such as the power of the magnet, the force of gravity, or even the ability of our mind to move our body, as mysterious or occult forces, a philosopher like David Hume in the eighteenth century was still perfectly aware of the connection, and made a point of emphasizing that the ideas of "power, force, energy, or necessary connection" were "more obscure and uncertain" than any other.[101] His very terminology went back, once again, to the science and philosophy of Greek antiquity, where such "hidden" forces were discussed notably by means of the concepts of δύναμις and ἐνέργεια (to which we owe our "dynamics" and "energy"), συμπάθεια and ἀντιπάθεια (sympathy and antipathy), and the peculiar notion of ἰδιότητες ἄρρητοι.[102] Literally meaning "unspeakable qualities," the adjective had a double set of connotations, roughly similar to contemporary usage: "unexplainable" or "unnatural" on the one hand, and "morally reprehensible," "horrible," or "abnormal" on the other.[103] According to Julius Röhr, ἰδιότητες ἄρρητοι was used more exclusively than the other terms for forces in nature that we would nowadays tend to see as

---

[101] Hume, *Enquiry Concerning Human Understanding* 7.49 (part of the chapter "On the Idea of Necessary Connexion"). The elusiveness of the concept of "force" is captured very nicely by a quotation from the nineteenth-century philosopher Otto Liebmann: "Kräfte sind Kausalgespenster, aber reale, nicht imaginäre" ("Forces are phantoms of causality, but they are real, not imaginary": *Zur Analysis der Wirklichkeit*, 287). Note that apart from invisible "forces" connecting causes and effects, non-causal connections usually referred to as "correspondences" fall under the "occult" umbrella as well (cf. n. 110, below), and can be traced from ancient concepts of "sympathy/antipathy" and "macrocosm/microcosm" to rationalist theories in Enlightenment thinking. A particularly instructive example of how correspondences could be developed as a rational (definitely not "mystical") concept in post-Cartesian natural philosophy is Emanuel Swedenborg in his scientific phase, a few years before Hume's *Enquiry*: see his *Clavis Hieroglyphica* (1741 or 1742), and analysis in Hanegraaff, *Swedenborg, Oetinger, Kant*, 3–11.

[102] The indispensable reference, with copious quotations for all the relevant terms, remains Röhr, *Der okkulte Kraftbegriff im Altertum*.

[103] *Ibid.*, 101.

"occult";[104] and it was probably as a translation of this specific terminology that the crucial medieval concept of *qualitates occultae* (occult qualities) emerged in a scholastic context, closely connected with the peripatetic concept of "substantial form," during the later Middle Ages.[105]

The key importance of "occult qualities" to the history of science has been clearly demonstrated in recent scholarship, and almost every contributor has warned against anachronistic confusion with modern ideas about "the occult" or "occultism."[106] In the medieval reception of aristotelian natural philosophy, a distinction was made between the manifest, directly observable qualities of things (such as colors or tastes), and their occult qualities, which were not directly observable and therefore could not be accounted for in terms of the four elements. Many important natural effects of which the reality was not in doubt – such as magnetic and electrostatic attraction, the curative virtues of specific herbal, animal or mineral substances, or the influences of the sun and moon – were impossible to account for in terms of the primary elemental qualities (moist/dry, warm/cold) and their mixtures or combinations. Their efficient cause therefore had to be some "hidden" (occult) quality: hidden not only because the senses could not perceive it, but, even more importantly, because it was beyond the reach of scientific investigation altogether. The reason was that, by definition, occult qualities could only be studied indirectly through their effects, but not directly as causes, as required by medieval *scientia*. This made them into the black box of scholastic science: a necessary part of the technical apparatus, but also a reminder that God had set limits to man's curiosity.[107]

---

[104] *Ibid.*, 96.

[105] *Ibid.*, 96 and 105 (notwithstanding Röhr's careful distinctions between *qualitas, potentia*, and *proprietas occulta*). See Copenhaver, "Occultist Tradition," 459, for how the concepts of ἰδιότητες ἄρρητοι and "substantial form" came to be connected by Galen and his followers. On Thomas Aquinas and substantial form, cf. Blum, "Qualitates occultae," 50–51.

[106] As observed by Ignaz Wild in his pioneering article of 1907 (mostly consisting of quotations from Latin sources), "in the eighteenth century . . . the true meaning of the expression [*qualitates occultae*] was no longer known, and misguided opinions are still reflected in current historiography" ("Zur Geschichte der Qualitates Occultae," 344). Few specialists of scholasticism even knew the expression, except as a "scientific term of abuse" (*ibid.*, 307–308). Although Lynn Thorndike discussed the role of "occult virtues" in all the eight volumes of his *magnum opus*, they were put back on the agenda due to a provocative article by Keith Hutchison in 1982 ("What happened to Occult Qualities"), followed by John Henry in 1986 ("Occult Qualities"), both focused on the scientific revolution. Fundamental for the medieval context are two articles by Paul Richard Blum published in 1989 and 1992 ("Qualitas occulta"; "Qualitates occultae"). Important recent contributions are Meinel, "Okkulte und exakte Wissenschaften"; Millen, "Manifestation of Occult Qualities"; and Copenhaver, "Occultist Tradition." For a general overview of the terminological problematics, see Hanegraaff, "Occult/Occultism." A parallel and previously neglected alchemical tradition concerning occult/manifest is analyzed in Newman, "The Occult and the Manifest."

[107] In his seminal article of 1982 ("What happened to Occult Qualities"), Keith Hutchison argued that not the concept of *qualitates occultae* as such, but their banishment into the category of the

The concept of *qualitas occulta* came to play a key role in the project of emancipating the ancient sciences from the domain of *superstitio*, and legitimating them as *magia naturalis*. The reason is that it provided a cogent scientific argument for claiming that many "wondrous" or "marvelous" phenomena of nature, which the common people tended to attribute to demonic or supernatural agency, were in fact purely natural. In other words: far from suggesting an "occultist" worldview according to modern understandings of that term, it was originally an instrument for disenchantment, used to withdraw the realm of the marvelous from theological control and make it available for scientific study. To theological critics, however, the concept might look like a Trojan horse, for if it could account for unquestionable realities such as magnetic attraction or the connection between the moon and the tides, it could be used quite as easily to legitimate more doubtful influences, such as those emanating from the stars – not to mention an enormous range of other "occult" powers, such as the evil eye, monstrous births caused by the *imaginatio*, or "sympathetic" cures at distance, like the famous weapon salve.[108] In principle, all these strange and marvelous phenomena could now be seen as legitimate objects of scientific research, and they did indeed become a major preoccupation of scientists in the early modern period.

The emergence of the concepts of "occult philosophy" and the "occult sciences" during the sixteenth century becomes not just understandable, but almost predictable against these backgrounds. We have seen that, in the wake of the platonic revival, the original concept of *magia naturalis*

---

unknowable by definition (their confinement in an "asylum of ignorance," as famously formulated by Julius Caesar Scaliger in 1557 and often repeated since then; see Blum, "Qualitates occultae," 58 and nn. 44–45) was unacceptable to the new science of the seventeenth century. Far from rejecting occult qualities, as has traditionally been assumed by historians of science, philosophers and scientists in the wake of Descartes were arguing that they could and should be made into an object of research, and sought to account for them in mechanical terms (cf. d'Alembert's positive notion of "physique occulte" in the entry on experimental method in the *Encyclopédie*: d'Alembert, "Expérimental," 298; cf. Thorndike, "*L'Encyclopédie*," 379). Even more than that, they rejected "manifest qualities" and argued that *all* qualities were occult, but nevertheless knowable!

[108] For a provocative discussion of Renaissance magic focused particularly on these dimensions, see Couliano, *Eros and Magic*. On the powers attributed to the *imaginatio*, see van den Doel and Hanegraaff, "Imagination." For the "sympathetic" cure and its remarkable tenacity in serious medical debate, see, for example, van den Elsen, "The Rotterdam Sympathy Case." The most famous example of sympathetic treatment was the weapon salve, for example the belief that wounds could be cured at distance by treating the weapon that had caused them; but it could take many other forms, as in the controversy of 1696–1697 (analyzed by van den Elsen) around Henricus Georgius Reddewitz, who claimed to have cured patients in their absence, by stirring a "secret powder" in their urine. See especially the extremely popular book by Kenelm Digby, *Discours* (twenty-nine editions in five languages; cf. Thorndike, *History*, vol. VII, 498–512; Copenhaver, "Occultist Tradition," 480–482).

was expanded and transformed into a much more all-encompassing and explicitly religious *prisca magia*, with Agrippa's great compendium as the paradigmatic example. Furthermore, in the first chapter we saw how – particularly under the influence of Pico della Mirandola and his Christian kabbalah – references to secrecy and concealment became increasingly prominent within the same discourse of ancient wisdom, culminating, again, in Agrippa's notion of *occulta philosophia*:[109] the hidden philosophy of the ancients, now revealed to the Christian world. And finally, Pico was at the origin of a strong Renaissance revival of "correlative thinking," focusing on the notion of hidden non-causal correspondences (as distinct from hidden causal connections) between all parts of reality.[110] It was practically inevitable that the traditional notion of mysterious "hidden" powers that are somehow "secretly" at work in nature would now be expanded and transformed together with the original notion of *magia naturalis*, so that from the black box of scholastic naturalism they became the privileged sanctuary of divine mystery in the world.

This subtle but important process of conceptual transformation amounted, in other words, to a re-enchantment of *magia naturalis*. How the term "occult" could transmute from technical scholastic terminology into something closer to current understandings of the word may be illustrated by many examples. For instance, Giovanni Battista della Porta, in the first edition of his *Magia Naturalis* (1558), discussed the occult qualities as follows:

They are occult and hidden because they cannot be known with certainty by way of demonstration. This is why the ancient sages considered it good to establish a certain limit, beyond which one cannot pass in researching the reasons of things. Since in Nature there are many inner sanctuaries, hidden and full of energy, whose causes the conjecture of the human mind can neither search out nor understand.

---

[109] See Chapter 1, pp. 64–68. The term "occulta philosophia" was picked up by various authors later in the sixteenth century: a pseudo-paracelsian *Occulta philosophia* was printed in 1570, followed by several other works under that title, and by 1600 the term was also commonly used as a synonym for alchemy (Telle, "Astrologie und Alchemie," 242–243, with n. 64). It also appears, for example, in the subtitle of Campanella's *De sensu rerum et magia*.

[110] Concepts of "occult causality" assume the existence of some kind of hidden medium by which influences are transmitted from cause to effect (for example al-Kindi's "rays"), whereas concepts of "correspondence" assume that things can be connected by some kind of pre-established harmony, without a need for mediating forces (see, for example, Plotinus, *Ennead* 4.4.41–42). Already in Ficino's *De Vita Coelitus Comparanda* we find mixtures between the two concepts (Kaske and Clark, "Introduction," 48–49), and "correlative thinking" became a fundamental notion in the "occulta philosophia" beginning with Pico della Mirandola (Farmer, *Syncretism in the West*, 18–29, 91–96; cf. Brach and Hanegraaff, "Correspondences"). Of particular importance in that context was the Renaissance revival of arithmology started by Pico and Reuchlin (Brach, "Mathematical Esotericism"; "Number Symbolism").

For Nature is obscure and full of a hidden majesty, which one should better admire rather than wish to penetrate.[111]

Even more instructive is the work of a minor but representative sixteenth-century poet, mythographer, cryptographer, Christian kabbalist, and alchemist, Blaise de Vigenère (1523–1596). Throughout his *Traicté des chiffres* (1586), the term "occult" is used according to its normal diction-ary sense, whenever de Vigenère is referring to his main topic, "secret writing" by means of codes or ciphers. However, he also uses it to refer to *qualitates occultae*, and more generally to the "most occult and inti-mate secrets of nature."[112] In so doing, he was merely repeating a common medieval topos;[113] but of considerable importance is the fact that he may well have been the first author to refer to sciences concerned with those secrets of nature as *occult sciences*.[114] He does this within a more general context entirely dominated by the ancient wisdom narrative and its central authors; and under the explicit influence of Agrippa's *De occulta philosophia*, the term "occult" now suggests religious mysteries hidden from the vulgar but revealed to the wise as "higher knowledge."[115] From that perspective, Kabbalah, Magic, and Alchemy are presented by de Vigenère as the three "occult and secret sciences" (occasionally also "mystical sciences"),[116] and he was evidently thinking of them in terms of Agrippa's "three worlds": "May nobody be scandalized by these appellations, which have such a bad reputation everywhere, and are so much abused. Rather, I will give them other names: that of the elemental science, the celestial one, and the super-mundane or intelligible one."[117]

---

[111] Della Porta, *Magia Naturalis* 1.8.
[112] De Vigenère, *Traicté des chiffres*, 7v (the "occulte proprieté" of magnetism as an analogy for family cohesion), 17v, 27r–v (referring to a quotation in Giorgio da Veneto about a "very occult and hidden [caché] spirit" by which metals are connected to a superior force of "life"), 66v, 106r–v (alchemical), 143v.
[113] Eamon, *Science and the Secrets of Nature* (apart from the technical term *qualitas occulta*, "occultus" according to its normal dictionary meaning was used along with equivalent terms such as *arcanum*, *secretum*, etc.).
[114] De Vigenère, *Traicté des chiffres*, 18v ("the occult and secret sciences, buried [*ensevelies*] at present"), 77r (on "the three worlds, of which the three occult sciences are the key"), 112r ("one must turn to the Prophets to encounter the true sources of all the philosophies and occult sciences"), 340r (reference to Antonio de Fantis as a "person of high renown in all the occult sciences"). That the term "occult sciences" originated with de Vigenère is suggested, although not explicitly stated, by Secret, "De 'De occulta philosophia' à l'occultisme," 57 (1988 edn, 7).
[115] De Vigenère, *Traicté des chiffres*, 37v, 39r, 45r, 59v. The term "occult philosophy" is used regularly, evidently in Agrippa's sense.
[116] In line with original connections of "mystical" with "secret": see Bouyer, "Mysticism," 43.
[117] *Ibid.*, 19r. De Vigenère is a sloppy writer, and evidently the order of the three sciences is meant to be reversed: alchemy belongs to the world of the elements, "magic" is understood here as pertaining to

The notion of occult sciences therefore emerged in the specific context of the ancient wisdom narrative, and reflected the Renaissance project of a synthetic *occulta philosophia* in particular. It is of critical importance to understand that, in this framework, it was much more than just a pragmatic umbrella category for covering a range of otherwise diverse and relatively autonomous sciences. On the contrary: from the outset, the term implied an underlying, "hidden" unity and coherence, ultimately grounded in the "ancient wisdom" (of Hermes Trismegistus in particular). Seen merely "from the outside," the domains of magic, astrology, kabbalah, and alchemy might look like relatively distinct disciplines; however, referring to them as "occult sciences" carried the deliberate suggestion that they were unified at a deeper level, because they reflected one and the same, comprehensive, hidden, but universal knowledge about the true nature of reality. A particularly clear example of this perspective comes from the Paracelsian Gérard Dorn (1584):

Adam was the first inventor of the *artes*, because he possessed knowledge of all things, both before and after the Flood . . . His successors drew up two stone tablets, on which they inscribed all the natural arts, in hieroglyphic characters . . . After the Flood, Noah . . . found one of these tablets under mount Ararat. It showed the course of the superior firmament, and of the inferior globe, and of the planets. Finally, being divided into different parts, this universal knowledge was diminished in power, and as an effect of this separation, one [person] became an astronomer, another a magus, yet another one a kabbalist, and the fourth an alchemist . . . The monarchy of the true *artes* was divided up into diverse and various democracies, that is, into astronomy, magic, kabbalah, alchemy, etcetera. But in their perfect form they all came from one single fountain of truth, and from the knowledge of the two lights, natural and supernatural.[118]

Understood from such unifying perspectives, the various "occult sciences" eventually came to be presented, polemically and apologetically, as alternatives to the normal, non-occult sciences: by way of contrast, the latter could then be dismissed as relatively superficial pursuits concerned merely with the external surface of things, but blind to their deeper spiritual essence. At the same time, the concept of a "unity of the occult sciences" was quite acceptable for opponents as well, even welcome, for they could use it to

the celestial world, and kabbalah to the supercelestial world. On 128v, de Vigenère defends his use of the term "magic" for the celestial world, describing it as "the natural and licit occult philosophy: definitely not that detestable acquaintance and commerce of evil spirits that one has wanted to color with the name of magic, where there are only shadows and confusion."

[118] Dorn, *In Theophrasti Paracelsi Aurorum philosophorum*, 10–11, 16; see Mandosio, "La place de l'alchimie," 280–281.

oppose them wholesale against "real" science. We will encounter many examples further on in this chapter.

Of course, the term "occult sciences" is common in modern scholarship as well, as a convenient shorthand category for astrology, alchemy, and natural magic, occasionally expanded so as to include witchcraft. But it is important to emphasize that, whether intentionally or not, any such usage still implies the unifying perspective inherited from the Renaissance project of *occulta philosophia*: after all, these sciences or practices are classed together only because all of them are seen as "occult." This, of course, begs the question of what that means for modern scholars. How convincing is the assumption of unity? What are its underlying assumptions? And what are its effects on our ways of studying the phenomena in question? It is fair to say that modern scholars and critics have very rarely asked themselves these questions, let alone answered them. Rather, they have tended to take the category for granted, usually on the basis of an implicit (often unconscious) acceptance of "magic" as a universal category *sui generis*. A classic example is Keith Thomas' celebrated *Religion and the Decline of Magic* (1971), which made a point of emphasizing "the unity of magical beliefs" such as astrology, alchemy, witchcraft, natural magic, and the various divinatory arts.[119] In a truly extreme form, the modernist bias underlying that perspective can be studied in Wayne Shumaker's much-quoted study *The Occult Sciences in the Renaissance* (1972).[120] But by far the most explicit and sustained defense of the "unity of the occult sciences," understood as the essentially irrational and superstitious counterpart to reason and science, comes from a contemporary scholar of English literature and history of science, Brian Vickers. As formulated by him in 1988:

There are sufficient internal resemblances among astrology, alchemy, numerology, iatromathematics, and natural magic for one to be able to describe the occult

---

[119] Thomas, *Religion and the Decline of Magic*, 755–761 (and cf. 767 for the motifs of "closed system" and "resistance to change": "Such systems of belief possess a resilience which makes them virtually immune to external argument").

[120] It is hard to find a scholar who expresses his contempt for anything "occult" as explicitly as Shumaker. If Keith Thomas famously claimed in his foreword that "Astrology, witchcraft, magical healing, divination, ancient prophecies, ghosts and fairies, are now all rightly disdained by intelligent persons" (*Religion and the Decline of Magic*, ix), Shumaker went as far as stating that anyone holding such beliefs today was "the victim of some special psychological need" (*Occult Sciences*, xiv, 7), and kept emphasizing their status as "delusions," the prominence of which in early modern thinking had "shocked" him (*Occult Sciences*, xiv, cf. 198). Shumaker's study must be seen against the background of his moral concerns about the contemporary "crisis" of society and the resurgence of the occult among his students, reflective of the 1960s counterculture (*Occult Sciences*, xiii, xv). That Shumaker's perspective remained essentially unchanged is clear from the extreme whiggishness and anachronistic reasoning that pervades his *Natural Magic and Modern Science* (1989).

sciences as forming a unified system. They all invoke a distinction between the visible and invisible worlds; they all depend on the designation of symbols relating to this dichotomy; they all make great use of analogies, correspondences, and relations among apparently discrete elements in man and the universe. As a system the occult sciences were imported into Greece from various oriental cultures, and were systematically codified in the Hellenistic period, following the death of Alexander in 323 BC. Once codified they retained their essential assumptions and methodology through the Middle Ages, into the Renaissance, and beyond – indeed, one of the most remarkable features of the occult tradition is its static nature, its resistance to change.[121]

It would seem, then, that Vickers does not see the alleged "unity of the occult sciences" as a relatively recent phenomenon grounded in the Renaissance synthesis from Ficino through Agrippa, but as one that can be traced all the way back to its origins in the ancient Near East. However, such an impression would ultimately be misleading, for, in its essence, "the occult" according to Vickers is not a historical phenomenon at all, but a universal tendency of the human mind. In all his publications on the subject, he argues that the fundamental unity, homogeneity, continuity, and "resistance to change" of the occult sciences is based upon a basic "mentality," which they share with non-scriptural cultures studied by anthropologists. In short, the occult sciences are grounded not in experimentation, explanatory theories, or even just ideas, but in abiding pre-rational mental habits that are structurally similar to those of "primitive" peoples. This is why they are not supposed to change and develop, as science does. Vickers makes a strong plea for the use of anthropological categories in the study of history, and mentions a range of authorities; but as pointed out by Patrick Curry, his approach is based essentially on what was highlighted above as one of the three basic theoretical approaches to "magic," Lucien Lévy-Bruhl's theory of "participation" versus "causality."[122] In sharp contrast with the

---

[121] Vickers, "Function of Analogy," 265; on the same page, see Vickers' emphasis on the "fundamental homogeneity and continuity" of the occult sciences. Vickers' two other major statements on the topic were published four years earlier in his edited volume *Occult and Scientific Mentalities* ("Introduction"; "Analogy versus Identity").

[122] Curry, "Revisions of Science and Magic," 307. For Vickers' anthropological references, see "Introduction," 32–43, with long discussions of Robin Horton and Ernest Gellner. Vickers refers to Robin Horton for describing science and the occult as respectively "open" and "closed" systems, but as pointed out by Curry (*ibid.*, 306; referring to Horton, *Patterns*, 319), Horton himself has eventually rejected that dichotomy as "ripe for the scrap heap." Vickers' reception of Lévy-Bruhl's theories seems mostly indirect, through authors such as Stanley Tambiah (Vickers, "Analogy versus Identity," 96–97; "Function of Analogy," 280). Note that the notion of "resistance to change" is an anthropological cliché so common as to be shared even by Lévy-Bruhl's opponent Malinowski: "Follow one rite, study one spell, grasp the principles of magical belief, art and sociology in one case, and . . . adding a variant here or there, you will be able to settle as a magical practitioner in any part of the world" ("Magic, Science and Religion," 70).

instrumental causality basic to rational science, the occult sciences have their foundation, according to Vickers, in the *reification of symbols and analogies*: that is to say, the tendency of the human mind to project mere mental connections into the real world, and confuse linguistic signs with their signified objects.[123] The result is a view of the world as permeated by non-causal correspondences (reified analogies), in sharp contrast with the instrumental causality basic to science.[124] Accordingly, Vickers concludes, there can be no question of any historical influence of the "occult sciences" on the development of real science:[125] on the contrary, science is based upon "the rejection of occult symbolism."

This stringent application of the traditional "magic versus science" argument to the historiography of science has been sharply attacked by representatives of the "new historiography" in these fields,[126] who reject it as a fundamentally anachronistic and unhistorical perspective out of touch with current scholarship.[127] If the "occult sciences" are really a homogeneous unity, there would seem to be no point in seeking to differentiate between its various manifestations or studying their historical development in detail. But recent scholarship emphasizes that, to the contrary, the residual influence of the unifying Renaissance concept of *occulta philosophia* has caused a sort of blindness with regard to the relative independence and autonomy of disciplines such as astrology and magic;[128] and it points out

---

[123] For the collapse of analogy into identity, see especially Vickers, "Analogy versus Identity," 118, 122, 125–127 (quoting Paracelsus as the example *par excellence*, cf. *ibid.*, 131); "Function of Analogy," 276–277, 283–284, 289. For the confusion of signifier and signified, with reference to de Saussure, see Vickers, "Introduction," 97; "Function of Analogy," 277.

[124] On correspondences, see "Analogy versus Identity," 120, 122; "Function of Analogy," *passim*.

[125] Vickers, "Introduction," 31, 44 ("The error . . . lies in arguing that the occult sciences in the Renaissance were productive of ideas, theories, and techniques in the new sciences"); "Function of Analogy," 288 ("I cannot see that any constructive borrowing took place").

[126] Curry, "Revisions of Science and Magic"; Newman, "Brian Vickers." For some less trenchant criticisms, see, for example, Feldhay, "Critical Reactions"; von Greyerz, "Alchemie, Hermetismus und Magie," 423–427. The "new historiography of alchemy" (Principe, "Reflections"; Vickers, "The 'New Historiography'") is representative of a wider phenomenon, and the notion is therefore expanded here so as to include new approaches to the study of astrology (see, for example, Newman and Grafton, *Secrets of Nature*) and natural magic. It represents an important "paradigm change" in the historiography of science, as reflected emblematically in the removal, in 2002, of the category "pseudosciences" from the classification scheme of the famous "Current Bibliography of the History of Science" in the leading scholarly journal for the history of science *Isis* (Weldon, "Table of Contents & Introduction"). The new scheme has separate categories for "Occult sciences and magic," "Astrology," and "Alchemy."

[127] Newman, "Brian Vickers," 483, 502. Vickers' defense against the charge of anachronistic "Whig" reasoning can be found in the final paragraph of an article published in German in 1988 ("Kritische Reaktionen," 226–229) but deleted from the English version in 1992 ("Critical Reactions").

[128] Newman and Grafton, "Introduction," 26; Newman, *Promethean Ambitions*, 54; Newman, "Brian Vickers," 488–491, 502; Kahn, *Alchimie et Paracelsisme*, 2, 8–9, 11. For a detailed analysis, see Telle, "Astrologie und Alchemie"; and cf. Halbronn, "Résurgences."

that, far from being uniform and static, each discipline has gone through highly complex processes of change, transformation, and innovation over time. Again, if the specificity of the "occult sciences" according to Vickers resides in a basic mentality typical of "primitive thought," not in any rational attempt at studying and understanding the natural world, and if this mentality is merely the result of conceptual confusion and delusionary mental projections, then they cannot possibly be seen as relevant to the history of science: they will never be more than "proto-scientific" dead ends, or "pseudo-sciences" pure and simple. But recent scholarship has pointed out again and again that, contrary to popular assumptions, each of the disciplines in question has been deeply and centrally concerned with rational models of causality and empirical study of the natural world, and that they have made significant contributions to the history of what we consider as science today.[129] Furthermore, as correctly noted by Newman, Vickers' argument is strictly identical with that of Edward Burnett Tylor in his famous definition of "magic" as based upon "mistaking an ideal for a real connexion."[130] Against the background of my previous discussions, this in itself suffices to expose Vickers' construct of "occult sciences" as yet another example of the common but deeply ironic phenomenon of a "magical" reification of mental concepts by the very scholars who believe that they are doing the opposite.[131] For exactly the same reasons as "magic," then, the concept of "occult sciences" must indeed be rejected as valid scholarly terminology. It forces very different historical phenomena into the straitjacket of an artificial and reductive *sui generis* concept, thereby causing us to lose sight of their actual complexity and development over time. It falsely suggests that the disciplines in question have no interest in empirical observation or experimentation, and that they refuse to recognize causal connections because their deep involvement in pre-rational, "primitive" modes of thought allegedly makes them blind to any genuinely scientific concerns.[132] In short: by calling them "occult sciences," scholars inevitably

---

[129] Representative are the many recent studies by Newman and Principe (for example, Newman, *Gehennical Fire*; Newman, *Promethean Ambitions*; Newman and Principe, *Alchemy Tried in the Fire*; Principe, *Aspiring Adept*). For the criticism of Vickers' concept of "occult sciences" from this perspective, see Newman, "Brian Vickers," esp. 485–497 (focusing on the elements of "unity," reified analogy and symbolism, and "resistance to change").

[130] Newman, "Brian Vickers," 492–494; referring to Tylor, *Primitive Culture*, vol. I, 115–116, 129–131.

[131] See above, pp. 167–168. Newman ("Brian Vickers," 502) ends his article with drawing exactly the same conclusion: "In Vickers' work on the occult we have a striking example of the very reification of mental concepts that forms the central subject of his own complaint."

[132] The mistake is identical with the one committed by Malinowski in his famous critique of Lévy-Bruhl, who was supposed to have claimed that "primitive man has no sober moods at all, that he is hopelessly and completely immersed in a mystical frame of mind. Incapable of dispassionate and consistent observation, devoid of the power of abstraction, hampered by 'a decided aversion towards

end up endorsing an argumentative logic that, against the weight of historical evidence, is designed to exclude them from the history of science.[133]

The argument is persuasive, and backed up by superior scholarship in the history of science. But as happens so often in the heat of "scientific revolutions," there is always a risk of throwing out some babies with the bathwater. Vickers' suggestion that representatives of the "new historiography" are "apologists" for the occult sciences confuses partisanship with the legitimate defense of a field of study against hostile and distorting interpretations;[134] but admittedly, in their zeal for getting fields like astrology and alchemy back on the core agenda of history of science, the "new historians" sometimes overshoot the mark. In Newman and Grafton's defense for the independence of astrology and alchemy, one cannot help noticing a certain degree of impatience with the "occult philosophy" of the Renaissance, held responsible for the "hackneyed" thesis of a "unity of the occult sciences," and constantly evoked by scholars of "the Hermetic Tradition" since Frances Yates in the 1960s.[135] One understands the irritation of specialists about how that perspective still dominates any discussion in the field, even when it comes to medieval astrology or alchemy.[136] Nevertheless, there was certainly a very widespread concern in the sixteenth and seventeenth centuries with integrating astrology, alchemy, and natural magic, along with such fields as kabbalah and number symbolism, as parts

reasoning' . . . unable to draw any benefit from experience, to construct or comprehend even the most elementary laws of nature" ("Magic, Science and Religion," 25). Malinowski's refutation of that thesis, by demonstrating that the Trobriand Islanders showed an acute understanding of natural law while fishing or hunting, was directed against a straw man, for the summary is a caricature of Lévy-Bruhl's work, and "instrumental causality" and "participation" are not mutually exclusive but can easily coexist (see discussion in Hanegraaff, "How Magic Survived," 371–378).

[133] Vickers could respond with a variation on Tylor's view of magic as proto-science: "the very reason why magic is almost all bad is because when any of it becomes good it ceases to be magic" (Tylor, "Magic," 206; for the importance of this neglected article, see Hanegraaff, "Emergence of the Academic Science of Magic," 262–265). The occult sciences would then be not scientific, because when anything in them becomes scientific, it automatically ceases to be occult. But this would not save Vickers' argument, for if so, we are no longer dealing with "occult sciences" as an umbrella concept: instead, "occult" becomes a simple synonym for "unscientific," resulting in an empty tautology.

[134] Vickers, "The 'New Historiography'," 144, 154; Newman, "Brian Vickers," 482–484.

[135] Newman and Grafton, "Introduction," 21, 26: "Even during the heyday of Renaissance neoplatonism, astrology and alchemy lived independent lives, despite the vast inkwells devoted to the rhetorical embellishment of occult philosophy." Newman, *Promethean Ambitions*, 44, 54: "The hackneyed modern view that automatically equates alchemy with witchcraft, necromancy, and a potpourri of other practices and theories loosely labeled 'the occult' has little historical validity before the nineteenth century." On Yates and her approach, see Chapter 4, 323–334.

[136] Newman, "Technology and Alchemical Debate," 425: medieval alchemy was "a perfectly reasonable and sober offshoot of Aristotle's theory of matter," as opposed to "the eclectic, Neoplatonic alchemy of the Renaissance, suffused with theosophy and cabalism." Cf. Obrist, "Die Alchemie in der mittelalterlichen Gesellschaft."

of one unified worldview grounded in correspondences and occult forces,[137] and Renaissance adherents of *philosophia occulta* can hardly be blamed for what rationalists and occultists (not to mention twentieth-century historians) did with that idea two centuries later. In a historiography that wishes to avoid essentialism, the *occulta philosophia* project of the Renaissance just cannot be dismissed as marginal to what astrology or alchemy were "really" about: rather, it must be studied as an important historical phenomenon that resulted in creative and extremely influential new ways of understanding these disciplines and their relationship to one another.[138] If this somewhat blurs their fresh scientific image in the context of the "new historiography," so be it.

If Vickers' complex of reified analogy, symbolism, and correspondences (in short, "analogical thinking")[139] cannot be used to define a unified concept of "occult sciences," what then is the nature of its relation to the fields of astrology, alchemy, and natural magic? Nobody denies that they do have their roots in an ancient Hellenistic culture permeated by belief in hidden correspondences and analogical thinking; as "textually cumulative disciplines"[140] they clearly retained those dimensions as a vital part of their theoretical apparatus; and as we have seen, there is no doubt at all that such analogical modes of thought experienced an enormous boost in the wake – again – of the Platonizing tendencies of the Renaissance *occulta philosophia*. Nor does the "new historiography" deny these facts: for example, Lawrence Principe calls specific attention to the doctrine of similitudes in medieval works like Pseudo-Arnaud of Vilanova's *Tractatus parabolicus*

---

[137] This is correctly pointed out not only by Vickers ("The 'New Historiography'," 130) but even by Newman and Grafton themselves: they trace the "unifying" perspective to authors like Ficino, Agrippa, and Elias Ashmole ("Introduction," 24–26), thereby contradicting Newman's own thesis that it is a modern nineteenth-century invention.

[138] At issue here is the risk of an implicit essentialism even among strong and explicit defenders of strictly historical research: see discussion, with reference to a different but strictly comparable field of research, in Hanegraaff, "Origins of Occultist Kabbalah." Gershom Scholem's refusal to take the study of occultist and contemporary kabbalah seriously (Huss, "Ask No Questions") stood in sharp conflict to his explicit historical methodology.

[139] There is no agreement even about basic terminological conventions in this extremely complex domain of overlapping concepts, speculative systems, worldviews, and mental habits. Alternative terms are, for example, "correspondences" (see overview in Brach and Hanegraaff, "Correspondences"), "correlative thinking" (Needham, *Science and Civilization*; Farmer, Henderson and Witzel, "Neurobiology, Layered Texts, and Correlative Cosmologies"), *"ressemblance"* (Foucault, *Les mots et les choses*), "participation" (Lévy-Bruhl, *Les fonctions mentales*; Lévy-Bruhl, *Carnets*; cf. Tambiah, *Magic, Science, Religion*, 84–110) and in all cases there is a close interwovenness with traditional concepts such as sympathy/antipathy, micro/macrocosm, ἐνέργεια, and the ἰδιότητες ἄρρητοι mentioned above (for example, Röhr, *Der okkulte Kraftbegriff*; Conger, *Theories of Macrocosms and Microcosms*; Allers, "Microcosmus").

[140] The formulation is taken from Vickers, "The 'New Historiography'," 132. See similar emphasis in Ehrard, "Matérialisme et naturalisme," 197; Newman, "'Decknamen'," 164–165.

or Petrus Bonus' *Pretiosa margarita novella*,[141] stresses that Heinrich Khunrath's Renaissance concept of *harmonia analogica* was not just an arbitrary
or merely decorative conceit but something seen as existing independently
in the world itself, and discusses similar examples of "analogical thinking"
in authors like Kepler and Kircher.[142] In his formulation, there was indeed
a "virtually ubiquitous reliance of alchemical authors on metaphor, similitude, and analogy in both their thinking and their ways of encoding their
writings."[143]

The delicate task for historians consists in recognizing and analyzing
these dimensions as integral to much of pre-modern thinking, and to
the Renaissance *philosophia occulta* in particular, and yet to do so without falling prey to the bad dualistic habit of playing them out against
"science" (whether it is to denigrate their irrationality or to defend their
poetic beauty).[144] What makes this task so difficult is the fact – keenly
perceived by many scholars from Lévy-Bruhl to Vickers, and not to be
underestimated – that "analogical thinking" can, indeed, take forms that
violate our most basic canons of logic and common sense. A particularly
clear example is the pervasive fascination with a "natural language" of "real
symbols" (highly relevant to astrology and talismanic magic) in which signs
are treated as *being* what they signify, so that names or images do not just
"refer" to persons or things, but are assumed to somehow contain their very
essence.[145] Among many other instances, one might mention the peculiar

---

[141] Principe, *Secrets of Alchemy*, chapter 3.

[142] *Ibid.*, chapter 9. For the case of Khunrath, see Principe's reference to Forshaw, "'Alchemy in the
Amphitheatre'," here 209.

[143] Principe, *Secrets of Alchemy*, chapter 9. A famous statement of this basic point is of course Foucault's chapter "La prose du monde" in *Les mots et les choses*. How close Foucault's "archaeological"
perspective really is to the type of structuralist theorizing basic to Vickers' approach is demonstrated by Huppert, "*Divinatio et Eruditio*," 191–196. The rest of the article responds to Foucault's
exaggerations concerning the ubiquity of "ressemblance" before Descartes by erring in the opposite
direction and dismissing "magical thinking" as wholly marginal; but neither Foucault's dogmatic
and anti-historical insistence on mentalities as massive "blocks" separated only by sudden discon-
tinuous ruptures nor Huppert's attempt to marginalize the role of *occulta philosophia* in intellectual
discourse (with reference, amazingly, to Yates and Walker) can be seriously maintained in the light
of current scholarship.

[144] Vickers' approach was discussed as typical of the former, "Enlightenment" perspective. A classic
example of its "Romantic" counterpart is the poet Novalis (for his references to "correspondences,"
see Versluis, "Novalis"). Novalis' vision is brilliant and impressive, but the point here is that it
also constitutes a Romantic idealization which leads to anachronistic misreadings if projected back
onto the past to interpret Renaissance texts.

[145] Apart from Vickers, see, for example, Coudert, "Some Theories" (with a helpful overview of
examples from Plato's *Cratylus* to Franciscus Mercurius van Helmont's *Alphabet of Nature*) or
the classic article by Gombrich, "*Icones Symbolicae*," esp. 175–177. The *Cratylus* discusses "real
symbolism" at length but ends up rejecting it. However, as pointed out by Coudert, "In the
following centuries many people forgot Socrates' conclusion. What impressed them most was the
suggestion that a language which mirrored nature would be the most perfect" (*ibid.*, 65).

non-linear logic that informs Agrippa's elaborate tables of correspondences, systematically linked to elaborate numerical systems and "magical squares," talismanic images, and angelic and demonic hierarchies.[146] One might also think of the deliberate paradoxes of kabbalistic speculation, the coincidence of opposites in Cusanian metaphysics, or Paracelsus' tendencies to radicalize the theory of microcosm and macrocosm to a point where the former seems to contain the latter in which it is itself contained.[147] The list could go on. The fact is that such concepts were proclaimed, not just as a frivolous afterthought but deliberately and persistently, by highly trained intellectuals. Even allowing for the power of traditional authority, it therefore makes no sense to dismiss them as instances of irrationality, lack of logical competence, primitive thinking, or plain stupidity. Nor are they representative of some "occult" subculture out of touch with mainstream intellectual discourse, as popular clichés would have it. Rather, they are the reflection of intellectual traditions that have become unfamiliar to us, such as arithmology,[148] and of basic modes of thinking that are grounded in sets of priorities (metaphysical instead of physical) entirely different from those of modern science and philosophy. Both frameworks are equally capable of rejecting the other as fundamentally false and misleading.[149] There is no reason to continue the habit of calling early modern ones "occult," except as an admission of ignorance on our part: if they have become a closed book to most of us, that is because we have forgotten its language.

ALCHEMY BETWEEN SCIENCE AND RELIGION

In the first chapter, I argued that the famous "Hermetic Tradition" grounded in Ficino's 1471 translation of the *Corpus Hermeticum* should

---

[146] Agrippa, *De occulta philosophia libri tres* II.4–14; and cf. Lehrich, *Language of Demons and Angels*, 98–146; Nowotny, "Construction of Certain Seals and Characters."

[147] For the centrality of paradox in Jewish kabbalah, see especially Wolfson, *Language, Eros, Being*. For paradox and analogy in Cusanus, see Schulze, *Zahl, Proportion, Analogie*; Miller, *Reading Cusanus*; and for his influence and relevance to the ancient wisdom discourse, Meier-Oeser, *Präsenz des Vergessenen*. On Paracelsus, see Conger, *Theories of Macrocosms and Microcosms*, 55–60; Vickers, "Analogy versus Identity," 126–132 (relying heavily on Koyré, "Paracelse"); Müller-Jahncke, "Makrokosmos und Mikrokosmos bei Paracelsus"; Weder, "'das jenig das am subtilesten ...'."

[148] Apart from Jewish kabbalah, arithmology, or the symbolism of numbers (not to be confused with numerology), is arguably the most important key tradition here, indispensable for decoding much that seems weird or obscure in the context of *occulta philosophia*. Highly technical in nature, and part of the standard training of intellectuals in the Renaissance, its very existence has fallen into near-complete oblivion among modern academics. For introductory overviews, see Brach, *Simbolismo dei numeri*; "Number Symbolism" (and bibliography there). For a representative example of Renaissance arithmology, illustrative of its difficulty, see Brach's edition of Postel, *Des admirables secrets*.

[149] On this point, see Hanegraaff, "Under the Mantle of Love," 177 (here illustrated at the example of Ficino's metaphysics of eros as opposed to modern psychoanalysis).

better be seen as just one strand, although an important one, within the larger context of "Platonic Orientalism" and its revival in Renaissance culture: after all, the foundational narrative of ancient wisdom looked back not just to the Egyptian wisdom of Hermes Trismegistus, but at least as strongly to the "Chaldaean" wisdom of Zoroaster and the kabbalistic wisdom of Moses. With hindsight, if "hermeticism" nevertheless assumed a predominant profile in the imagination of later scholars of the Renaissance, this seems to have been caused not just by the reception of the *Corpus Hermeticum* and the *Asclepius* alone, but probably even more by the influence of a quite different tradition strongly linked to the name of Hermes: that of alchemy. It is also this tradition, grounded in the study of natural processes, that became central to the contextual shift of the later seventeenth century and the eighteenth century, emphasized at the beginning of the present chapter. As science and natural philosophy began to take the place of theology and metaphysics as the dominant framework of interpretation in all domains of thought, those who believed in the superiority of ancient wisdom naturally began to emphasize what they saw as Hermes' teachings about the workings of nature.

With reference to this development, it is useful to look back for a moment at the entire complex of currents and ideas described by Colberg as "Platonic-Hermetic Christianity." Colberg's choice for the double adjective seems to have reflected a quite correct intuition on his part. Although he was trying to describe one unified tradition of heresy, it really consisted of two different strands: a "Platonic" one grounded in the ancient wisdom narrative and a "Hermetic" one consisting of the "chymical" *Naturphilosophie* associated with Paracelsus, Weigel, Böhme, and the Rosicrucians. In the context of the *occulta philosophia* (not yet in Agrippa's work, but certainly in the later development of that synthetic project), these two had come to be thoroughly intermingled in the writings of countless authors until, finally, they were widely seen as mutually implying one another as part of one single worldview.[150] Nevertheless, on closer scrutiny, we appear to be dealing with a very uneasy marriage (or, if one prefers, a series of only partly successful marriage attempts) between two strongly different, even logically incompatible intellectual paradigms or styles of thinking.

Analytically, I would propose to distinguish the two along the following lines. The first, "Platonic" paradigm was concerned with ancient wisdom and emerged in the wake of Ficino, as we have seen; the second, "Alchemical" paradigm was concerned with alchemical transmutation and emerged

---

[150] See, for example, Mandosio, "Quelques aspects."

as a major force in the wake of Paracelsus. The first was grounded primarily in Platonic frameworks and assumptions; the second came to be known as Hermetic but combined a largely aristotelian framework of natural philosophy with innovative paracelsian concepts. The first reflected a top-down and hierarchical mode of thinking, starting from general metaphysical principles and approaching the lower domain of physical realities from that perspective; the second took a bottom-up approach, starting with the physical world but capable of working its way up from there towards the realm of the soul. The first was dominated by concepts of universal harmony, starting with a vision of the whole and assigning to everything its proper place in an essentially static "great chain of being";[151] the second was inherently dynamic, linear, and dialectic, starting with the simple unity of primal matter and working its way up from there, by means of dramatic and painful processes of growth and development full of violent conflicts between opposed forces or principles. The first implied some "downward" notion of a Fall, as it needed to explain how the darkness of matter and spiritual ignorance could have emerged from the original bliss, perfection and unity of divine Harmony and Light; the second implied "upward" notions of birth and generation, as it tried to describe how an original state of darkness could be the matrix of superior and even divine realities. Finally, the first was conservative and backward-looking, as it argued essentially by accumulating the testimonies of past authorities; the second was less focused on erudition and more open to discovery and new insights, as it relied primarily on direct, personal experience.[152] If the first strand developed in the context of the Renaissance narrative of ancient wisdom, anchored in the Roman Catholic culture of the Italian Renaissance, the second one had its cultural, geographical and linguistic center in German culture in the sixteenth and seventeenth centuries, and has been strongly associated with native terms such as *Naturphilosophie* and *Pansophie*.[153] Although grounded in alchemical models and practice, its scope went far

---

[151] See the classic study of Lovejoy, *Great Chain of Being*.

[152] "Experience" should be understood here in its double meaning, as retained in the French *expérience*: it may refer to empirical experimentation (see, for example, Paracelsus' emphasis on direct investigation of nature; cf. Halleux, "Pratique de laboratoire et expérience de pensée," 116–118) or to personal religious experience (see, for example, Böhme's emphasis on direct interior revelation). In both cases, "experience" is opposed to "blind" reliance on traditional authority, such as Galenism in medicine or the Patristic tradition in Protestantism.

[153] On the concept of *Naturphilosophie*, see Faivre, "Nature" (cf. Hanegraaff, *New Age Religion*, 64–67); Faivre, *Access*, 61–66; and the important collective volume by Faivre and Zimmermann, *Epochen der Naturmystik*. In the wake of Joël, *Ursprung der Naturphilosophie*, it has been under this heading that the origins of the Romantic natural sciences in the context of German idealism have been traced to the Renaissance and the pre-Socratics.

beyond that of laboratory alchemy and medicine, and came to encompass a wide variety of theosophical speculations with or without a direct relation to scientific experimentation.

"Platonic" paradigm	"Alchemical" paradigm
Platonic	Hermetic/Aristotelian/Paracelsian
From metaphysics to nature	From nature to metaphysics
Static harmony	Dynamic process
Fall: from light to darkness	Birth: from darkness to light
Tradition	Experience

Again, these distinctions are meant as an analytical instrument, *not* as historical description. Throughout the sixteenth and seventeenth centuries one can observe continuous attempts at mixing and combining the two models, or elements of them; but because they were based on logically contradictory forms of reasoning, no truly satisfying and lasting synthesis was achieved. We are dealing with a very complex dialectics between models of reality, played out in a historical context where the perspectives of natural science, philosophy, theology, and religion were themselves engaged in continuous conflicts, negotiations, and attempts at conciliation. In Chapters 1 and 2, we have seen that the ancient wisdom narrative emerged specifically as a Roman Catholic perspective in the century before Trent, and its agenda of integrating pagan wisdom in the theology of the One Church was an unacceptable heresy for Protestants. Due to its very "catholicity," the vision of ancient wisdom always remained rather alien to the Protestant mind,[154] but, interestingly, the "alchemical" alternative did find a very receptive audience precisely among Lutherans. There is no doubt that the fertile combination of Lutheranism and alchemical modes of thought became responsible for the most important forms of creative innovation in what we now see as "Western esotericism" after the sixteenth century, those of Rosicrucianism and the Christian Theosophy associated with Jacob Böhme and his followers.[155] The question of why alchemical modes of thinking could be so appealing to Lutherans (but rarely to Calvinists) is important, and should be explored in greater detail than is possible here.[156] It seems

---

[154] Walker, *Ancient Theology*, 144–148 (mentioning Philippe Duplessis-Mornay, Georges Pacard, and Petrus Ramus as exceptions).

[155] Gilly and Niewöhner, *Rosenkreuz als europäischen Phänomen*; Faivre, "Christian Theosophy."

[156] On the surprising scarcity of serious research concerning the relation between religion and alchemy in the seventeenth century, cf. Trepp, "Religion, Magie und Naturphilosophie," 482–490, esp. 487.

reasonable to suggest, however, that the last three dimensions of the "Platonic" and the "Alchemical" paradigm respectively have much to do with it. In sharp contrast with images of broken harmony and fragmented unity that were obviously congenial to the recent Roman Catholic experience, the cultural identity of Lutheranism rested upon narratives of a very different kind, for which alchemical transmutation provided a natural model. For generations now, the experience of Lutherans had been one of a desperate, violent, life-and-death struggle in which the religious individual could no longer fall back on any authoritative traditions or institutions to give him guidance, but had to trust his personal conscience in attempting to find the path of "regeneration" (rebirth) by which, through Christ's grace, his very being could be transmuted from the natural darkness of his sinful and fallen humanity into the spiritual light of divine truth. In the case of Lutherans who took such a narrative to its logical conclusion, the salvation of the soul could not be thought of in platonic terms, as an escape from the prison of the body: on the contrary, in the tradition of Jacob Böhme it was believed to continue its existence after death as a regenerated spiritual *body* of light.[157]

That alchemical models came to be applied to religious contexts by many authors at least after the sixteenth century is impossible to deny, and we will see how important this fact is for the study of Western esotericism. But does this imply that religious or "spiritual" dimensions are inherent or essential to alchemy as such? Scholarly controversies about this question since World War II have been dominated to a remarkable degree by the legacy of Carl Gustav Jung, which will be discussed in detail in Chapter 4. At this point, we can be brief. There is no doubt that alchemical symbolism can be used for illustrating Jungian psychology, but it is a common mistake to conclude from this that Jung's theories provide a valid framework for the historiography of alchemy, or that alchemy is "really" about spiritual transformation. Both assumptions are false, as will be seen.[158] If we wish to understand the relation between alchemy and religion in Western culture, we must therefore begin by trying to forget contemporary Jungian notions of "spiritual alchemy" and make an effort to understand the sources in their original historical and intellectual context. As already noted by the earliest reviewers of Jung's writings on alchemy, "putting a modern psychological pattern over a system of thought

---

[157] On the spiritualization of the body in the Böhmian tradition (F. C. Oetinger's *Geistleiblichkeit*), see Deghaye, "Jacob Boehme and his Followers"; *Naissance de Dieu*.
[158] See discussion in Chapter 4, pp. 289–294.

based on totally different premises" is a perfect recipe for anachronistic misunderstandings.[159]

At the same time, we must try to avoid the anachronisms that result from what is known as the "Conflict Thesis."[160] This essentially nineteenth-century belief in an inherent hostility between "science" and "religion" is based upon the same type of essentialism and reification of mental categories that I have already discussed with reference to "magic" – their competitor within the well-known "magic–religion–science" triad. The Conflict Thesis remains popular among the general public, but has been widely discarded by historians of science since the 1980s. Nevertheless, its tenacity is almost as strong as that of "magic," and its residual influence can be observed even in the "new historiography of alchemy." To understand why, one must understand that scholars like Principe and Newman are in the difficult position of doing battle on a double front: they emphasize the scientific legitimacy of alchemy against popular Jungian interpretations (which see it as essentially spiritual)[161] *and* against the old historiography (which sees it as an "occult" pseudoscience). Their emphasis on alchemy as early modern science and natural philosophy is entirely justified in itself, and an important corrective to earlier approaches, but it appears extremely difficult to avoid the subtle but crucial shift of meaning that is implicit in statements suggesting that alchemy is therefore "really" science (and not religion). Logically, such a shift implies that although religious elements may be found in the relevant textual corpus, these are not "really" alchemical, and may thus be marginalized as relatively unimportant or even dismissed as wholly irrelevant. As a result, in spite of the anti-positivist thrust of the "new historiography," one will still end up with a (crypto)essentialist position reminiscent of the Conflict Thesis: alchemy may sometimes look like religion, but it is really science.

This effect may well be unintentional: against the "whiggish" or "presentist" projections of normative modernist agendas upon the past, the "new historiography" emphasizes the study of primary sources within their own

---

[159] G. H., Review of Jung's *Alchemie und Psychologie*, 66; and see the analogous remarks in Pagel, "Jung's Views on Alchemy," 48.

[160] The "Conflict Thesis" is linked to the names of John William Draper, *History of the Conflict between Religion and Science* (1874) and Andrew Dickson White, *History of the Warfare of Science with Theology in Christendom* (1896). See discussion in Russell, "Conflict of Science and Religion"; Wilson, "Historiography of Science and Religion."

[161] For the criticism of Jungian concepts of "spiritual alchemy," see Obrist, *Débuts*, 11–36; Newman, "'Decknamen'"; Principe and Newman, "Some Problems"; Newman and Principe, *Alchemy Tried in the Fire*, 35–38; Principe, "Alchemy I," 13–14. So far, the most outspoken critics of Principe and Newman's position are Tilton, *Quest for the Phoenix*, 1–34; and Călian, "*Alkimia operativa* and *alkimia speculativa*."

historical context, and its proponents are well aware that unlike twentieth-century science, "natural philosophy" as understood in the seventeenth century incorporated and spoke to a range of religious ideas and speculations. If we take the "new historiography" to its logical end, it is possible to reach a conclusion that avoids the implicit essentialisms and either/or logic that the Conflict Thesis shares with its Jungian or Eliadean counterpart (which says exactly the opposite: "alchemy may sometimes look like science, but it is really psychology or religion"). Acknowledging the presence of religious elements throughout the alchemical corpus does not commit us to occultist or Jungian ideas of "spiritual alchemy," and emphasizing alchemy as a scientific pursuit does not need to imply that religious references are marginal or secondary to what alchemy is "really" all about. Instead, I would propose to look at alchemy as a complex historical and cultural phenomenon that does *not* have a conceptual core or essence (whether scientific, rational, religious, spiritual, or psychological) but is characterized by basic procedures of transmutation that can be pursued in laboratory settings *and* function as narratives in religious or philosophical discourse.[162] From such a perspective (to give just one example), questions such as whether the famous "visions" of Zosimos are essential or marginal to his alchemy become not just irrelevant, but meaningless; however, the fact that those visions appear together with strictly technical descriptions in one and the same textual corpus becomes an important fact that cries out for interpretation.[163] Implicit in such a comprehensive, radically historical, and (therefore) anti-eclectic[164] perspective is the recognition of alchemy as a "textually cumulative"[165] tradition that has kept acquiring new dimensions (scientific, philosophical, religious, eventually literary, artistic, or psychological) and has therefore been *evolving* throughout the many stages of its long history, not just until the eighteenth century but up to the present day.[166]

---

[162] Similarly, Didier Kahn describes the history of alchemy as obviously pertaining to the history of science and natural philosophy, but also embracing such domains as emblematics, the arts, mythology, architecture, moral philosophy, philosophy of language, and philology: "Reconstituer l'histoire de l'alchimie, c'est nécessairement replacer cette dernière dans l'intégralité du context culturel de son temps" (Kahn, *Alchimie et Paracelsisme*, 6–8).

[163] See Mertens, *Zosime de Panopolis*, 207–212.   [164] See Chapter 2, page 152.

[165] See page 189, with note 140.

[166] The tenacity of the Conflict Thesis is again demonstrated by a widespread tendency of seeing the history of alchemy as ending in the eighteenth century. Not only does this reflect the crypto-essentialist thesis that alchemy is "really" science; but by suggesting that alchemy ended when modern chemistry came into its own, it ironically lends support to the very notion of alchemy as "proto-science" that is rejected so emphatically, and with so much justification, by the "new historiography" (Newman and Principe, "Alchemy *vs.* Chemistry"; cf. Principe, *Chymists and Chymistry*; but see now Principe, *Secrets*, Chapter 4). For an instructive overview of the history of alchemy in the nineteenth and twentieth centuries, see Caron, "Alchemy V." Of course, if alchemy

Let us see how far such an approach takes us. In a seminal article on the philosophical foundations of medieval alchemy, Barbara Obrist has shown how the very fact that the *qualitates occultae* were considered inaccessible to the human intellect led to the idea, as early as the second half of the thirteenth century, that they could be accessed by means of other and "higher" faculties for gaining knowledge: those of direct intuition or divine revelation.[167] As alchemists failed to be successful in achieving transmutation, they reacted with a proliferation of theoretical models and an increasing emphasis on the difficulty of understanding the ancient authorities, who must have intentionally hidden their true meanings. To have any chance at achieving certain knowledge in the domain of alchemy, one therefore needed to submit oneself to the divine truth by means of faith, which in thirteenth-century Western society meant the eucharistic theology of God's incarnation and the resurrection of Christ.[168] The new status of alchemy from such a perspective, as explained by Obrist, is shown exemplarily in Petrus Bonus of Ferrara's *Pretiosa margarita novella* from the first part of the fourteenth century, which states explicitly that alchemy is "partly natural and partly divine or supernatural" and speaks of an invisible "divine hidden stone" (*lapis divinus occultus*) that is indispensable for completing the Great Work. This stone cannot be apprehended by the human intellect but can only be known through divine inspiration or revelation, and is what enabled the ancient sages to prophesy.[169]

One understands how attractive such a notion must have been to hermetic enthusiasts in the wake of the translation of the *Corpus Hermeticum*. Thus, Lodovico Lazzarelli and his mentor, the apocalyptic prophet Giovanni da Correggio, already saw Petrus Bonus as the conveyor of a "sacred mystery"[170] and began to study laboratory alchemy for evidently religious and eschatological rather than scientific reasons by the end of the fifteenth century. Lazzarelli transcribed the *Pretiosa margarita novella* and a collection of alchemical recipes from what is known as the "Pseudo-Lullian" tradition,[171] and Correggio wrote an original text based upon the same

    evolves or mutates through history, this implies that nineteenth-century occultist and "spiritual" understandings of alchemy as well as their further developments in Jungian psychology, and so on, are legitimate objects of study (which is not the same thing as methodological perspectives *for* study) in the history of alchemy.

[167] Obrist, "Les rapports d'analogie," 52–54. Of course, this is another example of the "re-enchantment" of the *qualitates occultae* discussed earlier.

[168] *Ibid.*, 54–56.   [169] Petrus Bonus, *Pretiosa margarita novella*, 38r–39r; and Obrist, *ibid.*, 56–57.

[170] Lazzarelli, "Epigram," in: Hanegraaff and Bouthoorn, *Lodovico Lazzarelli*, 278–279.

[171] Florence, Biblioteca Riccardiana, MS 984 (Lami III xx). Cart. In 8°, sec. XVI (1°); Modena, Biblioteca Estense, MS. Est.lat. 299 (M 8, 16). Lazzarelli, "Vade Mecum," in: Hanegraaff and Bouthoorn, *Lodovico Lazzarelli*, 274–277, and discussion in *ibid.*, 96–99. On Pseudo-Lullian alchemy, see Pereira, *The Alchemical Corpus attributed to Raymond Lull*.

perspective.[172] As explained by Chiara Crisciani, pseudo-Lullian alchemy was characterized by a greatly expanded understanding of transmutation: the real goal of the alchemist-philosophers, or "sons of Hermes" (*filii Hermetis*) was that of restoring man to his original Adamic purity and the whole of nature to its pristine state before the Fall.[173] For a thinker like Lazzarelli this made perfect sense, for his earlier *Crater Hermetis* consisted of a brilliant interpretation of the *Corpus Hermeticum* as concerned with exactly the same goal: reversing the effects of the Fall by means of a "literal" transformation or interior regeneration (rebirth) that restored man to his original divine nature.[174] In a period when Hermes Trismegistus' status as one of the most ancient teachers of wisdom had not yet been called into doubt, there is nothing surprising about the fact that alchemical materials attributed to him or linked to his name assumed great interest for intellectuals with such religious and eschatological agendas. On the contrary: alchemical practice could be seen as a necessary part of interior regeneration. Lazzarelli's case makes this perfectly clear: alchemy is identified as *magia naturalis* and concerned with "the conjunction of a body with a body," *magia celestis* is concerned with "the conjunction of a soul with a body," and *magia sacerdotalis & divina* with "the conjunction of a soul with a soul."[175] In this manner, alchemy becomes the first stage in a universal "magical" process of transformation that links the body to the soul and leads like a "stairway to heaven" from material nature all the way up to the divine. Addressing his own book of pseudo-Lullian recipes in the second person, Lazzarelli writes:

> You will show me the forces and secrets of nature;
> You will lead me to the sanctuaries of the Word-begotten God.
> Each thing is a step to the next: while making known her Maker,
> Nature clears for us a highway to the stars,
> And clearly reveals to us that all things are one, and one is all;
> That heaven is on earth, and that God is present in things.[176]

---

[172] See Hanegraaff, "Pseudo-Lullian Alchemy and the Mercurial Phoenix."

[173] Crisciani, "Hermeticism and Alchemy," 148.

[174] Lazzarelli, *Crater* Hermetis 25.4, in Hanegraaff and Bouthoorn, *Lodovico Lazzarelli*, 246–247. The term "spiritual alchemy" would not be applicable to Lazzarelli, for two reasons. First, because of his evident interest in the practical alchemy of Petrus Bonus and Pseudo-Lull. Second, because his talk of "interior regeneration" was not meant as a metaphor for purely "spiritual" processes, but referred to a literal transformation of the entire person understood as an organically integrated unity of body, soul, and spirit. See detailed analysis in Hanegraaff, "Lodovico Lazzarelli and the Hermetic Christ," esp. 70–71; and for the crucial impact of these concepts on Agrippa, see Hanegraaff, "Better than Magic."

[175] Hanegraaff, "Lodovico Lazzarelli and the Hermetic Christ," 96–99.

[176] Lazzarelli, "Vade Mecum," in: Hanegraaff and Bouthoorn, *Lodovico Lazzarelli*, 274–275.

Lazzarelli and Correggio are minor figures in the history of alchemy, but very important here as illustrations of how early alchemy came to be included in the religious framework of the ancient wisdom narrative, at least by some of its defenders, and how natural it was for this to happen. As for the much more influential writings of Marsilio Ficino, alchemy played a very minor role in them. However, as has been shown in impressive detail by Sylvain Matton, Ficino's references (in his *De Vita*) to alchemy in relation with his central concept of *spiritus mundi*, in the context of a vitalist worldview that saw even metals and stones as endowed with "life," came to exert a truly extraordinary influence on alchemists from the end of the sixteenth century on. Mixed with the paracelsian concept of "Aerial Niter," Ficino's *spiritus* finally gained an overwhelming influence in the alchemical and iatrochemical literature of the seventeenth century.[177]

With this, we have come to the intellectual tradition that is chiefly responsible for the fact that alchemical models were developed, from the sixteenth century on, into a full-blown "paradigm" of *Naturphilosophie* or *Pansophie* with both religious and scientific dimensions, always in complex interaction with the Platonizing models proper to the Renaissance narrative of ancient wisdom. The contributions of Paracelsus and Paracelsianism to the history of medicine, chemistry, and religion have been recognized for a long time, leading to an extensive and still rapidly growing body of research that need not be summarized here.[178] The importance of what is known as the "Chemical Philosophy" for seventeenth- and eighteenth-century scientific debate can hardly be overstated,[179] and the same must be said about its religious significance in the same period. In a seminal article grounded in decades of archival research, Carlos Gilly has described how Paracelsianism became an alternative religion in conflict with the established churches, with Paracelsus in the role of a divinely inspired Seer. Known under the name *Theophrastia Sancta* since Adam Haslmayr and Benedictus Figulus, and understood as a kind of perennial religion practiced by the apostles and revived by "German Trismegistus, Philippus

---

[177] Matton, "Marsile Ficin et l'alchimie." Cf. Newman and Grafton, "Introduction," 24.

[178] For general introductions with reference to the essential literature, see Benzenhöfer and Gantenbein, "Paracelsus," and Moran, "Paracelsianism." A classic older study is Pagel, *Paracelsus*; an important recent one is Webster, *Paracelsus*. Of foundational importance are the works by Allen G. Debus, *Chemical Philosophy*; *English Paracelsians*; *French Paracelsians*; *Chemical Promise*. For the German context, the writings of Wilhelm Kühlmann and Joachim Telle are indispensable: see especially their multi-volume *Corpus Paracelsisticum* project and Telle, *Parerga Paracelsica*. For France, the standard reference is now Kahn, *Alchimie et Paracelsisme*. For a good sample of modern studies, see Grell, *Paracelsus*; Schott and Zinguer, *Paracelsus und seine internationale Rezeption*.

[179] Debus, "Paracelsians in Eighteenth Century France"; "Alchemy in an Age of Reason"; *French Paracelsians*, chs. 4 and 5.

Theophrastus," its theological opponents finally came to refer to it as "Weigelianism" (with reference to Valentin Weigel).[180] This current, of course, is central to the "Hermetic" wing of Colberg's "Platonic-Hermetic Christianity," and the alchemical paradigm sketched at the beginning of this section.

As already suggested, alchemy was extremely attractive to Lutheran and other Protestant authors. Among the earliest examples is Heinrich Khunrath, famous for the impressive illustrations of his *Amphitheatre of Eternal Wisdom* (1609).[181] The Rosicrucian *Fama Fraternitatis* (1614) criticized "the ungodly and accursed gold-making" but presented Christian Rosenkreutz as adept at metallic transmutation and placed Paracelsus' work in his inner sanctuary;[182] and alchemical models and narratives of transmutation were central to the famous *Chymische Hochzeit Christiani Rosenkreuz* (1616), as they were to the theosophical and cosmosophical writings of later self-proclaimed Rosicrucians such as Michael Maier and Robert Fludd. Likewise, alchemy and Paracelsianism provided the essential models used by the theologies, or theosophies, of "reintegration" developed by Jacob Böhme and his followers.[183] The role of practical alchemy in this current could range from very important, as in Khunrath, to negligible or non-existent, as in Böhme; but it is important to emphasize that even in the latter case, references to alchemical transmutation were *not* just metaphors for purely "spiritual" processes. On the contrary: against the docetist implications of platonic idealism, Böhme's perspective was thoroughly incarnational and rooted in organic concepts (not just metaphors) of birth and generation. He described how out of the mysterious and unknowable *Ungrund* before all manifestation, God himself had been born as a *body*, constituted of the darkness of "wrath" (*Zorn*, associated with the God of the Old Testament) redeemed by the light of "love" (associated with Christ). In an original state beyond time and space, God had thus come into existence as a perfect body of Light, referred to as "eternal nature" (*die ewige Natur*), in which the potentially destructive darkness of wrath was immanent but rendered harmless and invisible by the redemptive light of love. Due to the fall of Lucifer, however, who was born in "eternal nature" as a perfect being of

---

[180] Gilly, "*Theophrastia Sancta*" (quotation on p. 173); *Adam Haslmayr*. Gilly points out that "Weigelianism" was preferred over "Theophrastia" or "Paracelsism" to avoid "misunderstandings amongst the medical profession and other professional groups," where Paracelsus' merits had to be acknowledged regardless of his theological views ("*Theophrastia Sancta*," 184).

[181] Forshaw, "'Alchemy in the Amphitheatre'"; Szulakowska, *Alchemy of Light*, 79–152.

[182] Andreae, *Fama Fraternitatis* (van Dülmen ed., 20, 26, 29).

[183] Faivre, "Christian Theosophy"; Faivre, *Theosophy, Imagination, Tradition*; Faivre, *Philosophie de la Nature*; Versluis, *Wisdom's Children*.

light but tried to be reborn out of light and thereby turned into a being of darkness, "eternal nature" itself had fallen into disintegration, thereby giving birth to a "temporal nature" existing in time and space: our world of division and suffering, in which the darkness of wrath is unleashed as a diabolic force in mortal combat with the light of divine love. In this dark and threatening world, Man is born as a mortal creature; but in an exact "microcosmic" parallel to God's own birth, Christ can be literally (again: not just metaphorically!) born within his own being as a body of light. The universal process of "reintegration" involves the salvation not just of human individuals, but of Nature itself: the fallen body of God should be restored by being transmuted into its original perfection as an eternal world of light. This entire theosophical scheme based on alchemical/paracelsian models was resolutely incarnational and anti-idealist,[184] and can therefore be called "spiritual" only with reservations. "The great lesson of the theosophy of Böhme," as formulated by Pierre Deghaye, is that "it is the devil who denies the body. The devil is an idealist."[185] Precisely this concept of nature as a spiritual body that could be transmuted into divine light made it highly attractive to eighteenth-century thinkers who rejected Enlightenment rationalism as a dualist heresy that pitted empty rational abstractions against an equally empty world of mere matter-in-motion.[186]

A comprehensive understanding of alchemy, as a cultural phenomenon that evolves and mutates through history, has the advantage of embracing both its religious and scientific dimensions without playing them out against one another according to an either/or logic. However, like any model, it comes at a price: it may be evident to us that theosophical speculations such as in Böhmenism are grounded in alchemical narratives, but this does not imply that, in their own time, they were known as "alchemy" or "chemistry" or seen as connected to science (that is, etic does not coincide here with emic terminology). They functioned as religious perspectives known by other names, and we have seen that when

---

[184] Hanegraaff, "Reflections," 27–30; cf. Deghaye, *Naissance de Dieu*; Deghaye, "Jacob Boehme and his Followers"; Koyré, *Philosophie de Jacob Boehme*. The conflict between Christian theosophical and idealist modes of thinking (opposed as "incarnational" versus "docetic") is perfectly exemplified, in the eighteenth century, by the case of Oetinger in relation to Swedenborg: see Hanegraaff, *Swedenborg, Oetinger, Kant*, 67–85.

[185] Deghaye, "Jacob Boehme and his Followers," 241; and cf. Deghaye, *Naissance de Dieu*, 54: "The demons do not incarnate. They have no flesh. Their doom is that of being disembodied."

[186] On the milieus of eighteenth-century theosophical illuminism and Martinism, emerging from Martines de Pasqually's *Traité de la réintegration* and developing into a European network centered around Louis-Claude de Saint-Martin (for example Saint-Martin, *Theosophic Correspondence*; and Jacques-Lefèvre, *Louis-Claude de Saint-Martin*), see the many publications by Antoine Faivre, especially *Kirchberger* and *Eckartshausen*.

they were eventually excluded from intellectual discourse, this happened in the domain of history of philosophy. The parallel process by which "alchemy" came to be excluded from "genuine science" during the eighteenth century occurred, however, in the domains of science and history of science; and for that story, we can ignore the purely theosophical lines of speculation and concentrate on what was known explicitly as "alchemy" or "chemistry" in the seventeenth century. As emphasized by many scholars, these terms (chimie/alchimie, chemie/alchemie, chymia/alchymia) were still used interchangeably, so that it was simply impossible to draw the lines of demarcation familiar to us.[187] For this reason, Newman and Principe have proposed to use the seventeenth-century term "chymistry" as a general inclusive term at least for this period.[188] Of course, the adoption of such a terminological convention strengthens their agenda of studying alchemy as a normal part of natural philosophy, while highlighting the polemical opposition of chemistry versus alchemy as a later invention that should not be projected back onto the past.

For our concerns, the crucial question is why that polemical opposition emerged in the first place, and why it became so singularly successful. Attempts to answer this question have been surprisingly scarce: if scholars of alchemy refer to it at all, it is usually clear that their thinking stands under the spell of the "magic versus science" dualism, and hence they seldom suggest much more than that alchemy was separated from chemistry due to the rise of experimental science.[189] Clearly this will not do. If alchemy did not exist apart from chemistry, even terminologically, then there *was* no such entity for scientists to reject in the first place! And since the alchemy/chemistry distinction is clearly modeled upon the magic/science distinction, using the latter to explain the former amounts to explaining a phenomenon in terms of the very thing that needs to be explained. A much more convincing solution has been suggested, almost in passing, by Allen G. Debus in 1985. Discussing the controversy between the anti-Paracelsian Hermann Conring and his opponent Olaus Borrichius – which was given wide publicity in the world of science and learning through the

---

[187] Rocke, "Agricola, Paracelsus, and 'Chymia'"; Mandosio, "Quelques aspects de l'alchimie"; Newman and Principe, "Alchemy *vs.* Chemistry"; Abbri, "Alchemy and Chemistry"; Halleux, *Les textes alchimiques*, 47–49. Halleux and Newman/Principe both criticize Dietlinde Goltz's 1968 attempt at demarcation ("Versuch einer Grenzziehung").

[188] Newman and Principe, "Alchemy *vs.* Chemistry," 141. They also propose to use the term "chrysopoeia" specifically for the procedures concerned with making gold (*ibid.*, 141–142).

[189] See, for example, the section on "the separation between chemistry and alchemy" in Halleux, *Textes alchimiques*, 47–49. Newman and Principe note that "in the early eighteenth century, the domain of 'alchemy' was for the first time widely restricted to gold making" ("Some Problems," 386), but this seems to be an effect of the polemical distinction rather than its fundamental cause.

Journal des Sçavans and the *Philosophical Transactions* of the Royal Society
in the 1660s and 1670s[190] – Debus pointed out that whereas the French
chemical textbooks of the seventeenth century paid scant attention to the
historical backgrounds of their discipline, the Paracelsians and alchemists
were marked by a strong interest in presenting themselves as the inheritors
of an ancient and venerable tradition going back to Hermes Trismegistus,
if not all the way to Adam.[191] Admittedly, Debus' own formulation already
assumes the distinction ("chemists" versus "alchemists") that is in need
of explanation, but what counts is his way of defining the two basic
approaches. The one that would generally come to be known as "alchemy"
has been nicely described by M. J. Ehrard in the early 1960s: "When the
chimiste is not at his furnace and his flasks, he is collating, with a passion
full of respect, the precious texts of the Ancients: his ambition is less that
of making science progress than that of recovering a lost *secret*."[192]

The search for the historical origins of (al)chemy became systematic
in the sixteenth and seventeenth centuries.[193] However, in the wake of
Casaubon and the general decline of the *prisca theologia*, such attitudes of
antiquarian scholarship grounded in historiographies of ancient wisdom
seem to have turned into a serious liability for Paracelsians and, more
generally, for chymists who understood themselves as *Filii Hermetis*. If
there was certainly no clear distinction between *chymia* and *alchymia* in
the early modern period, then, it may be useful to draw a distinction along
a different axis: between chymists who thought of themselves primarily as
belonging to a learned *tradition* whose forgotten secrets they tried to recover
from the texts and test in the laboratory, and those who saw themselves

---

[190] *Philosophical Transactions* 3 (1668), 779–788; 10 (1675), 296–301; *Journal des Sçavans* 3 (1675),
209–211.

[191] Debus, "Significance of Chemical History," 3. For suggestions that point in a similar direction,
see Ganzenmüller, "Wandlungen," 152; Halleux, *Textes alchimiques*, 50–51; Mandosio, "Quelques
aspects," 21–22; Abbri, "Alchemy and Chemistry," esp. 218–221, 224. The historiographical tradition begins with the Paracelsian Bostocke, *Difference* (see Debus, "Elizabethan History"; *Chemical
Promise*, 219–228). The criticism of such historiographies seems to have begun in 1661 with Ursi-
nus, *De Zoroastre Bactriano* (Ganzenmüller, "Wandlungen," 145), but the confrontation between
Conring and Borrichius has been more important historically. See Halleux ("La controverse,"
812–813) on the initially surprising focus on ancient hermetic origins even among the followers
of Paracelsus, known for his rejection of ancient authorities like Aristotle, Galen, or Avicenna. In
practice, Paracelsians do not seem to have seen any contradiction: their discipline was considered
at least as ancient as whatever could be claimed by their aristotelian and Galenic rivals, but superior
precisely because of its method of studying nature directly instead of learning about it from books.

[192] Ehrard, "Matérialisme et naturalisme," 197. The same point was made very recently by Robert
Halleux: "First of all, the alchemist is a man alone in front of a book. The book affirms that the
Ancients have realized the magisterium (*expertum*), and the alchemist believes it. But the alchemist
does not understand how" (*Savoir de la main*, 137).

[193] Halleux, "La controverse," 807 and *passim*.

primarily as experimental scientists and could therefore dispense with a historical pedigree. Both were doing science, but they looked differently at what they were doing, and were perceived differently. The distinction is reminiscent of what would become known, in the terms of C. P. Snow, as the "two cultures" of humanities and sciences in the modern academy: one primarily historical and hermeneutical, the other primarily concerned with direct experimental study of the natural world. My suggestion is that, by and large, the former trend was discredited along with the general decline of the ancient wisdom narrative and was eventually rejected under the label of "alchemy," while the latter trend developed into what we now recognize as "chemistry." Such a separation was all the more logical because, as explained by Robert Halleux, the basic assumptions of the former were becoming a serious obstacle from the perspective of the latter:

the main point of *experientia* – that is to say, of putting the procedure into practice in the laboratory – consists in demonstrating to the operator that he has understood the art. If the experiment goes wrong, one must start over. For while the success of the procedure provides "experimental" confirmation of the theory, its failure never disconfirms it. Here we touch upon the main weakness of alchemical *experientia*: reduced to the role of illustrating the theory, it never questions the correctness of the latter. The Ancients are right, no matter what happens in the laboratory. [194]

The argument becomes even more compelling if we look at what had happened to the discourse of "secrecy" during the seventeenth century. In Chapter 1, I discussed the Renaissance idea that the *prisci theologi* had spoken about divine things under the guise of mythological fable: the ancient wisdom was a hidden wisdom. Furthermore, we saw that the fascination of Pico della Mirandola's kabbalah lay in the fact that he seemed to have discovered a universal hermeneutic key grounded in the original Mosaic revelation, which promised to reveal the secret, hidden, invisible connections between all domains of knowledge. The result was an enormously increased emphasis on secrecy and concealment in the context of the ancient wisdom discourse and the *occulta philosophia*;[195] and naturally, this development affected alchemy as well. William Newman and Lawrence Principe have emphasized the function of alchemical *Decknamen* and symbolic imagery, often derived from Greek mythology, as straightforward codes for technical recipes since the Middle Ages and through the early modern period.[196] This is a welcome correction of Jungian interpretations,

[194] Halleux, "Pratique de laboratoire et expérience," 120; cf. Halleux, *Savoir de la main*, 136.
[195] See Chapter 1, pp. 64–68.
[196] See, for example, Newman, "'*Decknamen*'"; Principe, "Revealing Analogies."

but it does not exhaust the topic. Firstly, alchemists since the fifteenth century also began to interpret ancient monuments and mythological as well as biblical stories as alchemical allegories, suggesting that this was how the Ancients had concealed their secrets:[197] in such cases, we are not dealing with recipes concealed by symbols and mythological references, but with an alchemical hermeneutics of architecture and mythology inspired by the search for "ancient wisdom." Furthermore, alchemical techniques of dissimulation took on a life of their own during the Baroque era: partly under the influence of kabbalah, they developed into a full-blown "mystery discourse" that could go far beyond the relatively straightforward procedure of coding chemical contents.[198] In Frank Greiner's formulation, by adopting the "obscure style of the philosophers," one identified oneself as part of "a prestigious tradition that could sometimes provide mediocre works with a halo of mystery so as to mask their poverty even better."[199] Finally, very much in line with the literary tastes of the Baroque, some alchemical authors developed incredibly complicated tricks and techniques of dissimulation to mystify the reader and lead him through a labyrinth full of enigmas and false turns, in search of an answer that kept eluding him forever.[200] In such cases, the dialectics of concealment and discovery became an end in itself, and alchemical emblematics could function in a manner somewhat reminiscent of modern cryptograms: sophisticated intellectual games for the pleasure of the erudite, here with an additional dimension of moral edification.

The emphasis on secrecy led to a distinction between two basic styles of writing in chymical literature, much *earlier* than the terminological separation between alchemy and chemistry. An excellent example is David de Planis Campy's *Opening of the School of Metallic Transmutational Philosophy* (1633), devoted specifically to this question, where we read the following:

Those who have discussed the Arts & Sciences have taken care to give them a very clear & intelligible order, beginning with general matters so as to end with special ones. But in this Art [of metallic transmutation] one does the complete opposite, for sometimes one has begun at the end & ended at the beginning, & all that with so little order that, not at all having determined what it is, they have driven their readers into despair about never understanding nothing of it. [201]

---

[197] Halleux, "Le mythe de Nicolas Flamel," 237; "La controverse," 811–812.
[198] For many examples, see Greiner, "Art du feu, art du secret."   [199] *Ibid.*, 210.
[200] See the many examples given by Greiner, *ibid.*, 217–223.
[201] Planis Campy, *Ouverture de l'escolle*, 8–9. An interesting case from a few decades later (1672) is J. M. D. R. (Jean Maugin de Richebourg), *Bibliothèque des philosophes chimiques*, vol. 1, cvj–cxliv ("On the Obscurity of the Chemical Philosophers").

In sum, I am suggesting here that texts that presented chymistry as concerned with recovering ancient secrets – typically concealed by obscure language, enigmatic symbolism, or other techniques of dissimulation – became perceived as "alchemy." In contrast, texts that used clear and sober language to speak about experimental science became "chemistry." Even in the domain of natural science, then, it was still the ancient wisdom narrative and its concern with recovering the forgotten secrets of the past – and not, as so often assumed, the perceived irrationality, unscientific attitude, factual incorrectness, or superstitiousness of certain disciplines in the "chymical" study of nature – that functioned as the mark of "otherness" by which acceptable discourses were demarcated from unacceptable ones.

Still, what the academy rejected as false science could be a source of endless fascination for an audience with other concerns than scientific research. With this, we have come to a final core dimension of what would come to be known as Western esotericism after the eighteenth century.

THE ORGANIZATION OF SECRECY

Central to the ancient wisdom discourse of the Renaissance was the idea of a superior wisdom that had been known to the Ancients, but had been forgotten and needed to be rediscovered and restored. Similarly, the alchemists were perceived as searching for the lost secret of their art, hidden by enigmatic symbols that needed to be deciphered. Both highlighted the Egyptian Hermes Trismegistus as one of the earliest authorities, if not the very origin of the lost knowledge; and both believed that it had been transmitted, in a veiled and hidden manner, by divinely inspired sages or by alchemical "adepts" from generation to generation. Remarkably, however, the idea that the transmission of secret knowledge required some kind of formal *organization* does not seem to have occurred to anyone before the early seventeenth century. It is only in the first of the Rosicrucian manifestoes, the *Fama Fraternitatis* (1614), that we encounter the concept of a secret brotherhood founded for the express purpose of ensuring the transmission of superior knowledge through the centuries. Already in this earliest instance, the knowledge was concerned with the secrets of *nature* studied by what was becoming known as the "occult" sciences.[202] As the legend of the Rosicrucians developed, in parallel and close interaction with the spread of Paracelsianism, alchemy came to assume a central role in

---

[202] See Andreae, *Fama Fraternitatis*; and as a first introduction, Edighoffer, "Rosicrucianism I" (and bibliography there).

it. As suggested earlier, it provided an excellent model for narratives of spiritual rebirth and regeneration, which could be applied to individuals and even to the hoped-for transformation of society as a whole; and the idea of "hermetic adepts" passing on the secrets of their art by means of symbolic language was eminently applicable to the concept of a secret brotherhood passing on the true secrets of nature and the divine.[203] It was only a small step to suggest that their mastery of the "occult sciences" gave the members of this invisible brotherhood extraordinary magical powers; and in the context of growing tensions between the Protestant Union and the Catholic League within the Holy Roman Empire, the Rosicrucians came to exist in the popular imagination as a "conspirational Protestant fraternity" working in secret as a counterpart to the Jesuit order.[204] The fascinating question of when and where, exactly, the legend of a Rosicrucian brotherhood led to the emergence of *actual* Rosicrucian organizations can only be answered on the basis of precise archival researches and must be left here for specialists to decide.[205] For our concerns, we can concentrate on the uncontroversial fact that the concept of a secret brotherhood of initiates did become a historical reality with the establishment of Freemasonry.

But when did it get established? Traditional research in this field presents Freemasonry as an essentially rationalist and humanitarian movement created in 1717 with the foundation of the Grand Lodge of England. Having spread to France, it is supposed to have taken an embarrassing turn towards the "irrational," with a proliferation, beginning in the 1740s, of higher degrees of initiation filled with references to esoteric or occult beliefs that were alien to the original spirit of Freemasonry.[206] This point of view remains extremely popular among contemporary Freemasons and historians of Freemasonry.[207] However, in a seminal study of 1988, David Stevenson has shown that the date of 1717 is "almost an irrelevance in the

---

[203] Le Forestier, *Franc-Maçonnerie templière et occultiste*, vol. I, 31–33.

[204] Tilton, "Rosicrucianism."

[205] Carlos Gilly's eagerly awaited *Bibliographia Rosicruciana*, announced as comprising six volumes, will be decisive. In the meantime, see Gilly and van Heertum, *Magia, alchimia, scienza*, vol. II, 221–230; De Dánann, *La magie de la Rose-Croix d'Or*; Vanloo, *L'utopie Rose-Croix*, 209–215; Faivre, "Fictuld"; Faivre, *Access*, 178–186; McIntosh, *Rose Cross and the Age of Reason*, 30–33; Tilton, "Rosicrucianism" (about the *Testamentum der Fraternitet Roseae et Aureae Crucis . . . Anno 580* preserved in the Austrian National Library); Barbierato and Malena, "Rosacroce, libertini e alchimisti."

[206] The thorough deconstruction of this traditional perspective by René le Forestier in his *Franc-Maçonnerie templière et occultiste*, 25–48, seems to have been largely ignored by researchers in the anglophone world.

[207] See, for example, Hamill, *The Craft*, esp. 27–40 (published before Stevenson, see text); Piatigorsky, *Freemasonry*; Jacob, *Origins of Freemasonry* (but see also her more nuanced discussion in *Living the Enlightenment*, 35–38); Dachez, "Véritables origines," esp. 10–11.

long process of development of the movement,"[208] which can be traced back to the period around 1600.

To understand that argument, one must first go back even further, to the Middle Ages. Most of the medieval craft guilds were locally based, but the stonemason's trade was unusual because it required craftsmen to move around from job to job and often stay for extended periods at a building site far from home. To accommodate their special needs, working places called "lodges" were instituted, where the workmen could meet, eat, rest, and even sleep. If unknown strangers arrived who claimed to be masons, admission procedures were needed to decide whether they were qualified members of the craft who could be accepted as colleagues. Prior to admission to the lodge, they would therefore be examined, perhaps by asking them to give a demonstration of their skill, answer questions about the practice of masonry or the legendary lore of the craft, or give standard responses amounting to identification codes or passwords.[209] If they satisfied the requirements, they would be asked to swear obedience to the rules of the craft and preserve its secrets.

This legendary lore of the craft is particularly important for our concerns. It is contained in the so-called Old Charges, which have survived in many versions but all share a similar form and message.[210] They equate masonry with one of the seven liberal sciences or arts, that of geometry. This supreme art had allegedly been invented by Jabal, one of the sons of Lamech mentioned in the Old Testament. Jabal had inscribed the secrets of the art on a pillar that survived the great Flood and was discovered by Hermarius, a great-grandson of Moses and in fact none other than Hermes Trismegistus. From him, the knowledge of masonry/geometry spread throughout the world. Abraham and his associate Euclid taught it to the Egyptians, and it eventually reached the Holy Land, where King David and his son Solomon used it to build the great temple of Jerusalem. Masons who had worked on that supreme project spread the craft to other countries, including England, where it arrived thanks to St. Alban.[211] Fanciful as these legendary histories might be, there was nothing extraordinary about them. The other crafts, too, used to claim supremacy by boasting of their great antiquity: in fact, another son of Lamech, Tubal-Cain, was often invoked

---

[208] Stevenson, *Origins of Freemasonry*, 4. See also Snoek, "Researching Freemasonry," 10; Snoek, "Freemasonry"; Bogdan, *Western Esotericism*, 67.

[209] *Ibid.*, 13–18.

[210] Hamill, *The Craft*, 27–40; Stevenson, *Origins of Freemasonry*, 18–25; Bogdan, *Western Esotericism*, 67–69.

[211] Stevenson, *Origins of Freemasonry*, 19–21.

as having invented alchemy and passed it on to Hermes Trismegistus, in a
very similar manner. But the lore of the masons was particularly impressive, reflecting a degree of pride and self-confidence that had to do not
only with their conviction that geometry was the fundamental discipline
underlying all others, but also with their awareness of being responsible for
the astonishing feats of the great medieval cathedrals and abbeys.[212]

Against these backgrounds, what would eventually become Freemasonry
seems to go back at least as far as the Scottish "master of works" William
Schaw (1550–1602) at the end of the sixteenth century.[213] As reflected in
two sets of Statutes (1598–1599), Schaw set up a new system of organization
for the craft in Scotland, which contained most of the features still typical
of Freemasonry today.[214] In describing this development, David Stevenson
has provided substantial confirmation for what Frances Yates suggested
already in 1964, namely that Masonic symbolism emerged from a context
strongly influenced by the "hermetic philosophy" of the Renaissance.[215]
This made it all the more natural that the craft got associated with the
Rosicrucian brotherhood and its alchemical concerns, particularly as it
began to accept "non-operative" masons (members who were not masonic
craftsmen) during the seventeenth century.[216] A famous case is that of
Elias Ashmole, who was initiated in October 1646.[217] Ashmole was an
antiquarian, editor of the major alchemical collection *Theatrum Chemicum
Britannicum* (1652), and a typical believer in the unity of the occult sciences:
"Iudiciall Astrologie is the Key of Naturall Magick, and Naturall Magick the
Doore that leads to [the] Blessed Stone."[218] René le Forestier has suggested

---

[212] *Ibid.*, 23.
[213] On the question of origins, and Stevenson's claim that Freemasonry was created in Scotland instead
of England, cf. Snoek, "Earliest Development."
[214] Stevenson, *Origins of Freemasonry*, 26–76. Cf. *ibid.*, 215: the only two aspects of modern Freemasonry still absent in seventeenth-century Scotland were (1) a grand lodge supervising the whole,
and (2) lodges composed *entirely* of non-operatives. Stevenson is explicit in refuting the common
assumption that "speculative" interests imply non-operative lodges, so that the Scottish operative
tradition before 1717 could not have included speculative elements (*ibid.*, 10, 215; *First Freemasons*,
8–9).
[215] Yates, *Giordano Bruno*, 273–274; Stevenson, *Origins of Freemasonry*, 77–124; Stevenson, *First
Freemasons*, 6–8; cf. Bogdan, *Western Esotericism*, 70–76. Stevenson highlights article 13 in Schaw's
second set of statutes, about the requirement of testing every Entered Apprentice and Fellowcraft
in "the art of memorie and science thairof" (*Origins of Freemasonry*, 49, 95, and cf. Yates, *Art of
Memory*; but cf. Snoek, "Earliest Development," 5). Cf. the review by Margaret Jacob, who is critical
of Stevenson for reasons less relevant here, but applauds him for demonstrating that seventeenth-
century Freemasonry was "one link between the more esoteric doctrines of the Renaissance and
the beliefs and values of the Enlightenment" (review of Stevenson, 326–327; and Jacob, *Living the
Enlightenment*, 35–38).
[216] Stevenson, *Origins of Freemasonry*, 96–105 (Rosicrucianism), 196–208 (non-operatives).
[217] *Ibid*, 219. Josten, *Elias Ashmole . . . Autobiographical Writings*, vol. I, 33–34; vol. II, 395–396.
[218] *Theatrum Chemicum Britannicum*, 443. Cf. Newman and Grafton, "Introduction," 15–16, 19–21.

that Ashmole may have joined the craft for a perfectly logical reason: if the secret of the alchemical process was encoded in architecture of the cathedrals, as suggested by the widely dispersed legend of Nicolas Flamel, then these operative masons might have preserved the key to the secret![219]

This brings us to the core of the matter. Freemasonry was not originally the rationalist and humanitarian movement that it eventually became, at least in England. Even during the early decades of the eighteenth century, it was still strongly associated with "Rosy-Crucians and Adepts, Brothers of the same Fraternity, or Order, who derived themselves from Hermes Trismegistus, which some call Moses," and accordingly, its initiates were widely believed to be alchemical practitioners.[220] There is nothing surprising about this, for several reasons. Like the legendary Rosicrucian brotherhood, the Order was at first still resolutely Christian (Jews, Muslims or pagans were excluded; oaths were sworn on the Bible; the demand of tolerance was limited to the various Christian sects).[221] Furthermore, alchemy and masonry were similar in that both were grounded in medieval arts or crafts, and both boasted legendary histories of a very similar kind, with a central role for Hermes and Egypt. Since the Rosicrucians were believed to harbor the ancient and secret knowledge of the occult sciences, alchemy in particular, it was quite natural to have similar suspicions about the Freemasons. And finally, alchemists were looking for the great secret of transmutation that had been known to the Ancients and that some believed might be coded in myths and architecture; and Freemasons, too, were searching for a lost secret, whether it was the "Mason Word" or (eventually) the secret of Hiram Abiff, the legendary architect of Solomon's temple.[222] For many

---

[219] Le Forestier, *Franc-Maçonnerie templière et occultiste*, vol. 1, 32. For the Flamel legend, see Halleux, "Le mythe de Nicolas Flamel."

[220] Anon., *Secret History* (1725), iii (quotation) and iii–iv for the amusing description of how the landlady of a Freemason discovered his secret: she was missing some "Pewter Pots and Dishes," and found them back in her tenant's room "all converted into Gold and Silver." See also Eugenius Philalethes, *Long Livers* (1722; cf. le Forestier, *Franc-Maçonnerie templière et occultiste*, vol. 1, 32–33; Bogdan, *Western Esotericism*, 74–75; on the author Robert Samber, see Blom, "Life and Works of Robert Samber"). Concerned with the universal alchemical medicine attributed to Arnaud of Vilanova, this text is dedicated to the "Grand Master, Masters, Wardens and Brethren, of the Most Antient and most Honourable Fraternity of the Free Masons of Great Britain and Ireland." Finally, there is a pamphlet "The Knight" of 1723, and a letter by "A. Z." in *The Daily Journal* of September 5, 1730 (see Knoop, Jones and Hamer, *Early Masonic Pamphlets*, 26–27, 110, 233–236).

[221] Le Forestier, *Franc-Maçonnerie templière et occultiste*, vol. 1, 29; cf. Chakmakjian, "Theological Lying."

[222] The Hiram myth is first attested in Samuel Prichard, *Masonry Dissected* (1730) and there are some references to Hiram from the 1720s.

would-be initiates, the conclusion must have been obvious: the great secret held by this brotherhood of initiates must be the secret of the Rosicrucians. If so, it must have to do with alchemy – or even better, the two secrets might turn out to be one and the same.[223]

Seen from this perspective, the mushrooming of "higher degrees" in French Freemasonry from the 1740s (significantly,[224] although confusingly, known as *Maçonnerie Ecossaise*: Scottish Masonry), with its constant references to the occult sciences and religious pursuits of all kinds, or the alchemical practice central to the Order of the *Gold- und Rosenkreuz* somewhat later, become simple continuations of basic masonic tradition rather than exceptions or aberrations. In fact, if anything represented a departure from the tradition, it was the rationalist, humanitarian and deist outlook that came to dominate English Freemasonry. Very similar to how modern chemistry established its identity by splitting off from chymistry, then, modern Freemasonry did so by renouncing parts of its own tradition; in the former case, the rejected part became known as "alchemy," in the latter (as will be seen) it became the archetype of "occult brotherhoods." For our discussion we need not trace this process as it took place in Freemasonry, but it would seem to have started in the early period after 1717: very significantly, the historical genealogies of Freemasonry in Freemasonry's foundational document, James Anderson's *Constitutions* (first edition 1723, second expanded edition 1738), had already become entirely biblical in that no more mention was made of Hermes Trismegistus. All the credit for Egyptian masonry went to Moses.[225] English Freemasonry needed an impressive historical pedigree, but had apparently decided that it could dispense with a "hermetic" one.

Decisive for our concerns is the fact that, once the Rosicrucian *legend* of a secret brotherhood had given rise to actual initiatory *organizations* in the shape of Freemasonry, this new phenomenon became a model that could be projected back into the past: the legendary histories of ancient wisdom, to which we have given so much attention, now came to be reinterpreted in terms of such initiatory organizations as well. The historical importance of this development is almost impossible to overstate. Even the more extreme anti-pagan polemicists discussed in Chapter 2, with their ideas of a heretical counter-tradition inspired by the devil, had not

[223] Le Forestier, *Franc-Maçonnerie templière et occultiste*, vol. 1, 31–33.
[224] "Significantly" in view of Stevenson's argument (contested as overly chauvinistic, however, by, for example, Margaret Jacob) that Freemasonry was born in Scotland.
[225] Anderson, *Constitutions* (1723), 5–8; (1738), 8–9; and see the excellent article by Stevenson, "James Anderson."

imagined the transmission of "ancient wisdom" as taking place by means of secret underground organizations. The implications of this novel idea were enormous, not least from a political perspective, for it implied that hidden ("occult") conspiracies might be silently at work to subvert and overthrow the existing order – for good or evil, depending on one's perspective. The concept became highly important for the "imagination of the occult" during the nineteenth and twentieth centuries, from pulp fiction in the genre of Dan Brown's *Da Vinci Code* to the very real politics of paranoia focused on Jewish, Masonic, or Satanist conspiracies (and their various combinations).

The exciting fantasy of a secret society of initiates, working behind the scenes of history to further their benevolent or sinister aims, developed into a discourse of staggering complexity during the eighteenth century and later. Its many twists and turns are fascinating, but for our present concerns we only need to summarize the main components. With respect to the early history of the lineage that was supposed to lead from antiquity to the present, many authors developed a fascination with the ancient Jewish sect of the Essenes that had been described by Philo of Alexandria and Josephus.[226] Through a mistaken identification with the Therapeutae, the latter were widely seen as the Egyptian counterpart of the Palestinian Essenes; and Eusebius (*Ecclesiastical History* II.17) had interpreted the Therapeutae as early Christian monastics. This idea became important in debates about monasticism after the Reformation: many Catholic authors defended monasticism by tracing it to the "Christian" Essenes, against Protestants who insisted that they had been Jews. In the heat of these debates, Catholics made Jesus, Mary, John the Baptist and the apostles into Essenes, and this notion has never vanished since.[227]

The modern phase of the Essene legend began with Johann Georg Wachter, most famous for his *Der Spinozismus im Jüdenthumb* (1699). In an influential text of 1707, revised in 1717, he described the Essenes as representatives of a strictly natural theology on deist foundations that could be traced back to Egypt and the kabbalah.[228] Jesus had been an Essene, and far

---

[226] On this topic, see Wagner, *Essener*; Hammer and Snoek, "Essenes"; Maurice, "Mysterien der Aufklärung," 282–286. For the Essene legend in modern and contemporary esotericism, see also Kranenborg, "Presentation of the Essenes"; Hanegraaff, *New Age Religion*, 314–319.

[227] Wagner, *Essener*, 3–8. Carmelites in the seventeenth century had a particularly strong investment in the Essene legend: they wanted to trace their own order back to Elijah/Elisa and saw the Essenes as the missing link. Jesus and his apostles were made into Essenes, and thus into Carmelites (*ibid.*, 5). This Carmelite–Essene connection has even found its way into twentieth-century New Age literature, by way of the American seer Edgar Cayce (Hanegraaff, *New Age Religion*, 316–317).

[228] Wachter, *De primordiis Christianae religionis* 15 (Schröder ed., 62).

from being based upon divine revelation, his religion was a purely historical phenomenon. This thesis was taken up by Enlightenment thinkers as
famous as Voltaire and Frederick the Great: "Jesus was in fact an Essene; he
was imbued with the morality of the Essenes, which is much like Zeno's.
His religion was a pure deism, and see what we have made of it [*voyez
comme nous l'avons brodée*]."[229] As suggested by this last sentence, when
seen as the original source of "pure Christianity," the Essenes could easily be
used as ammunition in the Protestant/Enlightenment attack on the "Hellenization of Christianity." In the formulation of Andreas Riem in 1792,
"Christianity is therefore really 'Essaism,' which retained its purity until
Paul accepted the heathens into Christianity."[230] The idea of the Essenes
as a brotherhood devoted to a reasonable religion on deist foundations
made them irresistible to English Freemasonry. Beginning with a *Defense
of Masonry* published in 1730/31, they came to be described first as a kind
of Freemasons avant la lettre, and soon as the original form of masonic
tradition.[231] But non-masonic Enlightenment thinkers, too, began to look
at the Essenes/Therapeutae as a secret brotherhood with enlightened ideals
that had had its representatives everywhere. How strongly the masonic
model came to affect the imagination of contemporary theologians can
be seen, for example, from a book by Carl Friedrich Stäudlin about Jesus'
moral teachings (1799):

The Essenes were not just a sect, but a kind of Order of a partly public and
partly secret society. They existed in great numbers... spread through Palestine, Syria and, apparently, wherever there were Jews... Whoever wanted to
be admitted into the sect, had to go through several grades... The practicing
Essenes... were apparently a kind of secret Order, which was not just very similar
to the Pythagoreans, but greatly participated in its origins as well as in the doctrine and school of Pythagoras. They were not just a school, a sect, or a society,
but a Brotherhood [*Bund*] and Order... Whoever wanted to enter the society
was first tested for a long time about his opinions and morals, and when he had
been admitted, he slowly rose through three grades up to the fourth and highest... The Order must also, mainly in the higher grades, have had mysteries,
of which Josephus and Philo knew nothing, and which have not become publicly known... They probably traced their institution and its mysteries back to
Moses.[232]

[229] Frederick II, Letter to d'Alembert, October 18, 1770 (Schröder, "Einleitung," 13).
[230] Riem, *Christus und die Vernunft*, 704 n. 2, here quoted according to Wagner, *Essener*, 23.
[231] Hammer and Snoek, "Essenes," 341; Wagner, *Essener*, 21–39; Le Forestier, *Franc-Maçonnerie tem-
       plière et occultiste*, vol. 1, 72.
[232] Stäudlin, *Geschichte der Sittenlehre Jesu*, vol. 1, 456, 459, 478–479, 483. On the Pythagorean
       backgrounds, cf. 484–485.

Inevitably the Essenes/Therapeutae were made into the inheritors of ancient "Platonic Orientalist" traditions, and were widely associated with the mystery religions of the ancient world. For Freemasons, with their focus on geometry, Pythagoreanism was particularly attractive in that regard.[233] But to present Freemasonry convincingly as the inheritor of ancient initiatic orders, a large historical gap still needed to be bridged. Enter the Order of the Knights Templar.

Since the Temple of Jerusalem plays such a central role in masonic symbolism, it cannot surprise that Freemasons developed a special interest in the chivalric Order that had been charged with its defense. In a famous speech of 1736, the "chevalier" Andrew Michael Ramsay presented the Crusaders as the ancestors of Freemasonry; and in the years that followed, connections with the medieval Knights Templar began to be suggested.[234] Still before 1750, this led to the creation of a Templar high degree, the "Ordre Sublime des Chevaliers Elus,"[235] followed by an entire system of Templar Freemasonry in the so-called Strict Observance that became dominant in Germany from the 1750s through the 1770s.[236] At being admitted into the "Inner Order," it was revealed to the candidate that the original order of the Knights Templar had not vanished, but survived in Freemasonry, and was governed in an occult manner by the "Unknown Superiors." Out of these masonic contexts, a whole series of non-masonic "neo-Templar" traditions has emerged since the early nineteenth century, continuing up to the present day.[237]

As the Templars established themselves in the Holy Land, so it was argued, they had made contact with secret Essenian and Pythagorean traditions that had managed to survive there since antiquity.[238] When Phillip IV cracked down on the Knights Templar in 1307, followed by the dissolution of the Order by Pope Clement V, their Grand Master Jacques de Molay had managed to bring the secrets of the Order into safety. In the oldest document about this legend, from around 1760, one reads that he passed them on to his cousin De Beaujeu, who passed them on to

---

[233] Wagner, *Essener*, 27–29.

[234] Mollier, "Neo-Templar Traditions," here 850–851; Mollier, "Des Franc-Maçons aux Templiers," here 97–99; Le Forestier, *Franc-Maçonnerie templière et occultiste*, vol. 1, 68–82; Faivre, *Access*, 186–193; Schiffmann, *Entstehung der Rittergrade*.

[235] Mollier, "Neo-Templar Traditions," 851. The order may even have been created before Ramsay's speech: see Snoek, "Researching Freemasonry," 17–18, with reference to Kervella and Lestienne, "Un haut-grade templier."

[236] Le Forestier, *Franc-Maçonnerie templière et occultiste*, vol. 1, 83–270 and *passim*.

[237] Mollier, "Neo-Templar Traditions," 852–853; Introvigne, "Ordeal by Fire"; cf. Caillet, *L'ordre rénové du Temple*.

[238] Wagner, *Essener*, 28–29.

another Templar, Aumont, who had fled to Scotland – the homeland of Freemasonry. Ever since, there has been

an unbroken series of Grand Masters of the Order up to our own days, and if the name and the residence as well as the location of the true Grand Master and the true Superiors who rule the Order and direct [its] sublime works is today a mystery, known only to the true *illuminés* and kept an impenetrable secret, that is because the hour of the Order has not yet come and the time is not yet fulfilled at which the doors will open and the light will shine for all, and because it is prudent still to hide the domicile of him who is in charge of it from the profane, even if they would have seen a few beams of the light that illuminates the true Freemasons.[239]

In an early and still embryonic form, we have here the typical elements of a discourse that has continued to flourish in "occultist" milieus up to the present day. Note that we are dealing with an alternative version of the transmission of spiritual knowledge from the Orient to the West: from Pythagorean sources, the ancient wisdom is believed to have been adopted by the Essenes in the Holy Land, from where the surviving Templars brought it to Scotland. Since the eighteenth century, this Pythagorean–Essenian–Templar–Masonic filiation has given rise to an endless and still expanding series of further historical fantasies and conspiracy theories about secret networks and societies searching for the Ultimate Secret or suspected of possessing it.[240]

The contents of that secret have obviously remained unknown. However, we have seen that, in the early days, it was often thought to be alchemical. Hence, for example, the famous wealth of the medieval Knight Templar: surely they had discovered the secret of the Stone! Hence, also, the strong concern with practical alchemy in eighteenth-century organizations like the *Illuminés d'Avignon*[241] or the *Gold- und Rosenkreuz*.[242] But as primarily or even exclusively religious interpretations of alchemy flourished, the alchemical secret of transmutation could also come to be understood in terms of a process of spiritual transformation or reintegration, leading to the attainment of a superior gnosis. In this manner, Christian theosophical interpretations of the alchemical quest could furnish an ideal model for the goals of spiritual development pursued by a plethora of new esoteric

---

[239] Strasbourg manuscript, *c.* 1760, as published in Schiffmann, *Entstehung der Rittergrade*, 178–191 (here 188–190); cf. le Forestier, *Franc-Maçonnerie templière et occultiste*, vol. 1, 68–73.

[240] For an introduction to the mental labyrinth of these speculations, the best reference remains Umberto Eco's extremely well-informed novel *Foucault's Pendulum*. For a recent historical overview, see Frenschkowski, *Geheimbünde*.

[241] Snoek, "Illuminés d'Avignon"; Meillassoux-Le Cerf, *Dom Pernety*.

[242] Geffarth, *Religion und arkane Hierarchie*, 242–265.

and occultist organizations that developed in the wake of Freemasonry. With the increasing separation of Church and state during the nineteenth century, it became possible for such organizations to establish themselves as new religious movements in competition with the traditional ecclesiastical institutions.[243] As such, we will see, participants in the "cultic milieu"[244] of esotericists and occultists needed to establish their own historical pedigree.

At the same time, as already noted, the developing "mythology of the secret societies"[245] created a new genre of conspiracy literature with obvious political implications. For example, the announcement in the previous quotation that "the doors will open and the light will shine for all" clearly echoes the prophecy of the Rosicrucian *Fama Fraternitatis* that "a door will open for Europe," leading to a "general reformation" of the world. However, for anybody who disliked or distrusted the religious perspectives in question, such predictions were bound to sound like a threat rather than a promise. By the end of the eighteenth century, the Jesuit Abbé Barruel was claiming in his famous *Mémoires pour servir à l'histoire du Jacobinisme* (1798–1799) – which has been described as "the bible of the secret society mythology"[246] – that the threat had indeed become a catastrophic reality with the French Revolution. Ever since, conservatives of every ilk have been tempted to follow his lead in blaming the modern world and its democratic institutions on a demonic conspiracy of underground organizations.[247] This, too, would become an essential part of how "the occult" came to be imagined in the modern world.

Where does this bring us? In the first two chapters, I outlined the ancient wisdom narrative that emerged in the Roman Catholic culture of the Italian Renaissance, and its counterpart, the anti-pagan/anti-platonic narrative that culminated in largely Protestant polemics in seventeenth-century Germany. As pointed out at the end of Chapter 2, due to their incompatibility with the findings of modern historical criticism, neither of the two perspectives has been able to keep up with scholarly progress. Having lost all credit in modern academic discourse, the former survived only in a typical dilettante genre of occult literature for the popular market, the latter

---

[243] For introductory historical overviews, see, for example, the two classic studies by Webb, *The Occult Underground* and *The Occult Establishment*. A more recent landmark study is Godwin, *The Theosophical Enlightenment*. For an extremely well-informed overview continuing through the twentieth century, see Introvigne, *Cappello del Mago*. Entries devoted to all the major currents, with bibliographies, can be found in Hanegraaff, *Dictionary*.
[244] Campbell, "The Cult, the Cultic Milieu and Secularization"; Hanegraaff, *New Age Religion*, 14–18.
[245] Roberts, *Mythology of the Secret Societies*.   [246] *Ibid.*, 204.
[247] For the original conspiracy thesis, see, for example, Rogalla von Bieberstein, "These von der freimaurerischen Verschwörung"; Roberts, *Mythology* (199–213 on Barruel).

in the genre of anti-occultist and anti-satanist writings popular in Christian evangelical and fundamentalist circles. However, two new paradigms emerged in the decades around 1700: a "religionist" approach grounded in the centrality of direct, unmediated, personal experience of the divine, and a skeptical Enlightenment alternative grounded in rationality and "sound judgment." Both positions are ideological rather than empirical, and essentially non-historical: for the former, the centrality of religious experience makes the outcomes of historical criticism ultimately irrelevant to what religion is "really" all about, whereas the latter treats the historical currents and ideas with which we are concerned as non-historical universals of human thinking and behavior ("prejudice," "superstition," "foolishness," or "stupidity"). In spite of their clearly non-historical assumptions – or perhaps, more worryingly, because of them – these new paradigms have both been remarkably successful in academic culture: the Enlightenment paradigm has been dominant through the nineteenth and much of the twentieth century, and we will see how important the religionist option would become particularly in the twentieth century.

To these two sets of alternatives, we must now add a third one, based upon the novel concept of secret organizations. Understood positively, it argues for the presence of a hidden, "underground" lineage of adepts who have kept the true wisdom alive through the ages; and understood negatively, it is based upon the sinister concept of demonic "dark brotherhoods" who, through the ages, have been conspiring against the religious and moral order of society. Contrary to the second set, this one is compatible with a historical approach at least in theory. In practice, however, we are typically dealing with the products of amateur scholarship, in which historical fantasies flourish due to a deficient use of sources and a lack of understanding about the basics of historical criticism. All three sets of opposites have become highly important for the history of Western esotericism since the eighteenth century, and their underlying assumptions have been mingled in very complicated ways. In the remainder of this chapter I will try to outline their impact on the "imagination of the occult" in popular fiction and scholarship up to the early twentieth century.

THE OCCULT MARKETPLACE

In *The Radical Enlightenment*, Jonathan Israel has emphasized the crucial role that the popular media came to play in the process of Enlightenment. Due to a combination of cultural, social and economic factors, the European universities after the middle of the seventeenth century were plunged into a deep crisis, and their educatory function was largely taken over by various forms of private initiative focused on the general market. With just a few exceptions like Oxford and Halle, university libraries were unable to keep their collections up to standard, and private libraries in places "where there was no Court, no university, and no great aristocrats" now developed into powerful centers for the discussion of new ideas.[248] Furthermore, Europe during the final decades of the seventeenth century witnessed a "veritable mania" of encyclopedias, lexicons and dictionaries that made intellectual discussion and new scientific knowledge available to the general public. Bayle's *Dictionnaire* (1697), Ephraim Chambers' *Cyclopaedia* (1728), Zedler's stupendous *Grosses vollständiges Universal-Lexicon* (1732–1754), and of course Diderot's *Encyclopédie* (1751–1772), along with many less famous but similar works, all targeted a broad popular audience of "scholars and philosophers, certainly, but also the new élites of officials, diplomats, patricians, professionals, and courtiers, and even their wives and daughters."[249] Reaching all classes of society, and dominated by the new philosophy and science, they have been called "a philosophical engine of war which massively invaded the libraries, public and private, of the whole continent."[250] And finally, there was the phenomenon of learned journals: "an even more powerful machine" of Enlightenment ideas, even though they tended towards more moderate Christian perspectives halfway between traditional religion and the radical Enlightenment.[251]

But there was an obvious flip side to the "media revolution" of the later seventeenth and the eighteenth century. Following the laws of supply and demand, it worked not just in favor of Enlightenment agendas, whether radical or moderate, but also led to an unprecedented wave of popular literature in the domains associated with "superstition," "magic" and the "occult sciences."[252] It did not matter that many authors or compilers of such publications professed a wish to expose the dangers or stupidity of superstition, or just wanted to amuse their readers: regardless of their intentions, part of the public undoubtedly read them from a different perspective, and took an interest in these materials for their own sake. The fact is that – in sharp contrast with popular images of the "Age of

[248] Israel, *Radical Enlightenment*, 131: "until around 1750 the large private library covering all fields was one of the prime motors of the Enlightenment."
[249] *Ibid.*, 135.   [250] *Ibid.*, 137.
[251] *Ibid.*, 142–155. On the treatment of "occult" topics in the learned journals, see, for example, van den Elsen, *Monsters*; Daston and Park, *Wonders*.
[252] See, for example, Bila, *Croyance à la magie*; Doering-Manteuffel, *Das Okkulte*, 17–33; Kemper, "Aufgeklärter Hermetismus," 149–151; Debus, "Alchemy in an Age of Reason," 244–246; Kirsop, "Collections."

Reason" – esotericism in all its forms was extremely fashionable during the eighteenth century, culminating in a very large wave dominated by illuminism and mesmerism during its final decades.[253] In 1784, just five years before the Revolution, a critic of the latter current summarized the situation as follows:

> There exist secret societies in Paris, where one pays large sums of money to occupy oneself with the mystical sciences. One is convinced that nature is filled with powers, invisible spirits, and sylphs that can be at man's disposal; that most of the phenomena of nature and all our actions can be reduced to hidden causes and to an order of unknown entities; that not enough credence is given to talismans, judicial astrology, and magical sciences; that our fates and destinies are determined by particular spirits that guide us without our knowledge, by threads that we do not notice; and finally, that all of us, in this mean world, are really like marionettes, like ignorant and perfectly blind slaves. They strongly impress on everyone's minds that it is time to be illuminated, that man must begin to enjoy his rights, shake off the yoke of the invisible powers, and at least become conscious of who is directing him. This taste for concealed things, with mystical and allegorical meanings, has become ubiquitous in Paris and nowadays occupies almost all the well-to-do. It is not a question of associations shrouded in great mystery. The lyceums, the clubs, the museums, the societies of harmony: all are sanctuaries where one can occupy oneself only with abstract sciences. All books of secrets, all those that are dealing with the Great Work, with mystical and kabbalistic science, are in great demand.[254]

This popular demand for occult literature continued right into the nineteenth century. By 1825, Collin de Plancy could speak hyperbolically of "twenty thousand volumes" on such "bizarre matters," and although most of it was little more, in his opinion, than "ridiculous heaps of extravagances, or imperfect compilations, or dry discussions without aim or coherence,"[255] the important point is that there was a large market for them.

Most of those who catered to this demand were no longer intellectual professionals and academics but amateur scholars, or autodidacts. We have seen that the intellectual elites had still been discussing "platonic-hermetic"

---

[253] A well-known literary reference to the "superstitions" of Paris in the early eighteenth century is Montesquieu's *Lettres Persanes* no. 58. The prominence of esotericism in the "Age of Reason" still seems capable of surprising contemporary historians, but is by now too well documented to require further proof or discussion. See, for example, Viatte, *Sources occultes du romantisme* (2 vols.); le Forestier, *Franc-Maçonnerie occultiste*; Zimmermann, *Weltbild*, vol. 1, 19–43; Faivre, *L'ésotérisme au XVIIIe siècle*; Faivre, *Mystiques, théosophes et illuminés*; Mozzani, *Magie et superstitions*; Frick, *Erleuchteten*; Darnton, *Mesmerism*; Leventhal, *In the Shadow of the Enlightenment*; Jacob, *Living the Enlightenment*; Neugebauer-Wölk, *Aufklärung und Esoterik* (1999); Neugebauer-Wölk, *Aufklärung und Esoterik* (2008).

[254] Paulet, *L'antimagnétisme*, 3–5.

[255] Collin de Plancy, *Dictionnaire Infernal* (2nd edn 1825), vol. 1, i.

religion and the history of its various affiliated currents with perfect seriousness through most of the seventeenth century, but began abandoning the field during the eighteenth. To be sharply dismissive of these traditions, as a domain below one's contempt and undeserving of serious discussion, was now becoming a crucial identity marker for intellectuals affiliated with the emerging modern academy. In other words, if the early Church had once needed a concept of "heresy" (gnostic or otherwise) to define its own "orthodox" identity, and Protestantism had needed the concept of a "pagan" opponent (Roman Catholic or otherwise) to define its own identity as true Christianity, the newly developing academic orthodoxies created reified "Others" more suitable to their own needs of self-definition: irrational "superstition" based on human ignorance, credulity, prejudice, and sheer stupidity in the case of Enlightenment philosophers, "alchemy" in the case of modern chemists, "astrology" in the case of modern astronomers, "magic" and "occult philosophy" in the case of scientists in general. In this manner the category of "the occult" emerged during this period as a conceptual waste-basket for "rejected knowledge," and it has kept functioning as the academy's radical "Other" to the present day.[256]

The near-complete dominance of amateur scholars from the eighteenth and through the nineteenth centuries had predictably negative results as regards the quality of research, and this in turn made the field look even less respectable for academics. Most materials available in print during this period were lacking in any sense of historical criticism or scholarly contextualization, and these failings were matched by an increasing state of ignorance among professional scholars. The result of this combination was a self-reinforcing downward spiral: the lower the quality of printed information, the less reason for scholars to take an interest, but since ever fewer of them knew anything about it, this meant that the book market became even more dependent on dilettante scholarship, and so on. By the later nineteenth century, it had become very hard for anybody to get reliable information about the actual nature, historical development, or cultural significance of "hermetic," "magical" or "occult" ideas and traditions – but rather than experiencing this as a research hiatus, academic professionals were more likely to take pride in not knowing anything about such things. Under these conditions, it was obviously hard to tell fiction apart from

---

[256] The politics of identity that are basic to this process will be discussed at greater length in the Conclusion. The terminology of "rejected knowledge" derives from James Webb, *Occult Underground*, 191–192; cf. Barkun, *Culture of Conspiracy*, 23–24.

reality; and as a result, the "study of the occult" became a fertile field for historiographical fantasies unchecked by historical criticism.[257]

ELEMENTAL FICTION

Popular nineteenth-century images of "the occult" – and even, eventually, new forms of occultist practice – have been influenced to a remarkable extent by literary fiction for the general public. Throughout the "age of reason," as in our own days, there was a flourishing market for pulp fiction and initiatic novels capitalizing on the theme of mysterious secret societies, kabbalists, Templar knights, dark magicians, and alchemical adepts.[258] Of central importance for our concerns is an early example of this type of literature, which spawned an entire sub-genre of its own, and the influence of which can be traced through the centuries: Nicolas Pierre Henri Montfaucon de Villars' *Comte de Gabalis*, first published in 1670 and reprinted in numerous editions and translations up to the present.[259] The author, a libertine and *abbé de salon*,[260] lived a short but troubled life: condemned to death, together with his sister and two brothers, for having murdered an uncle (in revenge for his murder of their father), he managed to avoid capture but was killed by a relative on the road to Lyon in 1673, at the age of thirty-five. Of the several novels that he managed to publish in his lifetime, *Comte de Gabalis* was an instant hit. For our concerns, it is important because of its remarkably innovative and extremely influential concept of "the occult."

The title is a clear reference to the paracelsian concept of *Gabalia*. According to Paracelsus, this term stood for the ancient "ars caballistica":

---

[257] Pasi ("Notion de magie," 95–102) likewise emphasizes the special importance of literary fiction, next to "works of erudition," for conceptualizations of the occult in the nineteenth century.

[258] See, for example, Bila, *La croyance à la magie*; Thalmann, *Trivialroman* (badly written but extremely useful for its extensive documentation of esoteric dimensions in a forgotten sub-genre of popular literature, and notable for its influence on Thomas Mann: see Hanegraaff, "Ironic Esotericism"); Faivre, *L'ésotérisme au XVIIIe siècle*, 187–190; Faivre, "Genèse d'un genre narratif"; Vernière, "Un aspect de l'irrationnel." This genre is a clear research desideratum: who still remembers authors like Cajetan Tschink (*Geschichte eines Geistersehers*, 3 vols., 1790–1793), Wilhelm Friedrich von Meyern (*Dya-Na-Sore*, 3 vols., 1787), or Veit Weber ("Die Teufelsbeschwörung," or "Brüder des Bundes" in *Sagen der Vorzeit*, 1792), to give just a few random examples from Germany alone?

[259] De Villars, *Comte de Gabalis* (and see now the critical edition by Didier Kahn, 2010). See Treske, *Rosenkreuzerroman*; Laufer, "Introduction"; Peuckert, *Gabalia*, 497–504; Kilcher, *Sprachtheorie der Kabbala*, 213–214, 318–319; Nagel, "Marriage with Elementals." For the editions and translations, see Laufer, "Introduction," 55–61, and Nagel, "Marriage," 64–68. For the novel's reception and its remarkable influence on the history of literature and art, see Laufer, "Introduction," 47–54; Nagel, "Marriage," 28–39.

[260] Laufer, "Introduction," 54.

a subcategory of magic that had emerged among the pagans and had been transmitted through the Chaldaeans and the Hebrews.[261] De Villars' novel is subtitled "conversations on the secret sciences," and begins by describing how the protagonist got involved with mysterious circles of "adepts." They are said to consist of people from all orders of society, male and female, including noblemen, princes, priests, monks and doctors. "Some were interested in angels, others in the devil, others in their familiar spirit, others in incubi, others in the healing of all illnesses, others in the stars, others in the secrets of Divinity, and almost all in the Philosophers' Stone."[262] Note that these lines were written more than half a century after the Rosicrucian manifestoes, but still in a period from which we have no irrefutable evidence for the actual existence of such more or less organized circles concerned with alchemy and the "occult arts."[263] Whether or not they existed in Villars' time, they certainly did so in his literary imagination, and many readers would come to believe that he was describing the secrets of real esoteric organizations under the veil of fiction. The novel announces in grandiose terms what the occult philosophy is supposed to be all about: "to become the master of Nature, have power over the elements, converse with the supreme Intelligences, command demons, bring forth giants, create new worlds, speak to God on his awesome throne, & obligate the cherubim."[264] The protagonist describes himself as a skeptic who is masquerading as an enthusiast to get himself admitted among these "elect" and satisfy his curiosity.

His companions are anxiously awaiting the arrival of a great kabbalist from Germany, and the protagonist decides to write this Count of Gabalis a letter. He includes his horoscope, so that the great man will be able to decide whether he is fit to receive "the supreme Wisdom." After some correspondence about the harmony of the world, the Pythagorean numbers, the Apocalypse and the book of Genesis, they finally meet face to face. Already in their first conversation, the Count tells him that he may indeed

---

[261] Paracelsus, *Theologische Werke* 1, 311 (annot. Gantenbein); cf. Kahn, "L'alchimie sur la scène française," 94 with nn. 79–80.

[262] De Villars, *Comte de Gabalis* (1715 edn), 8.

[263] See above, p. 208, with n. 205. The rumor of a Rosicrucian group founded by a certain Jacob Rose in 1660 is a good illustration of how easily myths are created in these domains, by authors who keep copying one another's statements without checking the original source: see Kahn, "L'alchimie sur la scène française," 70 n. 25.

[264] De Villars, *Comte de Gabalis*, 5–6; cf. 19: "You will learn to command the whole of Nature; God alone will be your Master, & the Sages alone will be your equals. The supreme Intelligences will be proud to obey your wishes; the demons will not dare to be where you are; your voice will make them tremble in the pits of the abyss, & all the invisible Peoples that inhabit the four elements will consider themselves happy to be the Servants of your pleasure."

receive "the kabbalistic lights," and will soon experience the interior rebirth that will make him into a new creature.[265] During their next meeting, however, it becomes clear that he will only attain these "great mysteries" if he chooses a life of celibacy. Fortunately – and here we come to the central theme that will dominate the rest of the novel – there is a compensation. By partaking of the alchemical elixir, the protagonist's eyes will be opened, and he will discover that the four elemental realms of nature are inhabited by "very perfect creatures":[266] salamanders (fire), nymphs (water), sylphs (air), and gnomes (earth). De Villars was using a concept with origins in Proclus, Michael Psellus, Trithemius, and Knorr von Rosenroth's *Kabbala denudata*, but developed most extensively in a (pseudo)paracelsian treatise, *Liber de nymphis, sylphis, pygmaeis et salamandris et de caeteris spiritibus*.[267] The important point about these beings, the Count explains, is that they are born, to their great sorrow, without an immortal soul. However, there is a possibility for them to attain immortality: by marrying a human being.

In other words, the "sages" may have to abstain from intercourse with earthly women, but they are offered an alternative! Female elementals are far more beautiful than earthly women, they never develop "horrible wrinkles," and they are all ready to throw themselves into the arms of their human saviors: "Think of the love and gratitude of these invisible Mistresses, & with how much passion they seek to please the charitable philosopher who does his best to immortalize them."[268] What is more, they are not jealous among themselves, so human men are free to love as many of them as they wish.[269] Very interestingly, the *Comte de Gabalis* appears to have adopted Cornelius Agrippa's heretical belief that the Fall consisted in sexual intercourse,[270] but with a novel twist: Adam sinned by having sex with another human being instead of with elementals! If he had chosen the latter alternative, he would not have fallen, but would have produced a superior offspring of "heroes" and "giants" full of power and wisdom.

---

[265] *Ibid.*, 14.   [266] *Ibid.*, 23; cf. 48 about the "Catholic Kabbalistic Medicine."
[267] Paracelsus, *Sämtliche Werke*, Abt. I, vol. xiv, sect. 7. For the origins of the concept in Psellus, Knorr von Rosenroth, and Paracelsus, see Laufer, "Introduction," 26–31; for Proclus and Trithemius, see Strebel, "Prolegomena," 173–175; see also Stauffer, "Undines Sehnsucht." The elemental beings already appear in an alchemical table of correspondences as early as 1602 (Bernard Georges Penot, *alias* B. à Portu, Aquitanus, in *Theatrum Chemicum* [1613], vol. ii, 114; see Kahn, "L'alchimie sur la scène française," 91–92).
[268] De Villars, *Comte de Gabalis*, 30.   [269] *Ibid.*, 94.
[270] *Ibid.*, 84–85: "children of sin" means "all children conceived through the will of the flesh and not through the will of God; children of wrath & malediction; in one word, children of man & woman." On Agrippa's innovative doctrine of original sin, possibly inspired by Lodovico Lazzarelli (*Crater Hermetis* 14:3), see van der Poel, *Cornelius Agrippa*, chapter 7, esp. 227–228; and Hanegraaff and Bouthoorn, *Lodovico Lazzarelli*, 211 n. 110.

Great sages like Zoroaster were, in fact, such children born from the union of humans and elementals.[271]

Underneath the bizarre and often quite funny conversations that make up the *Comte de Gabalis*, there is a message congenial to its author's libertine beliefs. The erotic connotations are obvious, and go hand in hand with an implicit polemics against established Christianity and its suppression of pagan nature-worship. The protagonist keeps protesting that these elementals are in fact demons and pagan deities, but the Count always responds that theologians have corrupted the truth by turning the elemental spirits of nature into evil demons. The so-called "fallen angels" who fell in love with the daughters of man were really elementals, and superior children ("giants") were born from their union.[272] The stories of witches, the sabbath, and incubi and succubi having intercourse with human beings are tragic distortions of the marriages between elements and humans and their festive assemblies in honor of the "Sovereign Being."[273] The elementals had also been behind the ancient pagan oracles; and the voice lamenting the death of the great god Pan, famously recorded in Plutarch's *Cessation of the Oracles*, belonged to a sylph.[274] But the oracles have returned:

"And in what place of the world?," I said. "In Paris," he replied. "In Paris?," I exclaimed. "Yes, in Paris," he continued. "You are a Master of Israel, & and you do not know that? Doesn't one consult the Water Oracles in glasses of water each day; or in basins; & the Aerial Oracles in mirrors & in the hands of virgins?"[275]

So the ancient spirits of the natural world – that is, the so-called pagan deities – are behind the popular practices of "superstitious" divination. Prominent in the *Comte de Gabalis* are several oracles attributed to Porphyry, and actually taken by Montfaucon de Villars from Agostino Steuco's *De perenni philosophia*: "Above the celestial fire there is an incorruptible flame, ever sparkling, the source of life, fountain of all beings, & principle of all things. This Flame produces everything, & nothing perishes except what is consumed by it . . . All is full of God, God is everywhere."[276]

---

[271] De Villars, *Comte de Gabalis*, 86–88. [272] *Ibid.*, 28–29. [273] *Ibid.*, 46, 130–131.
[274] *Ibid.*, 41. [275] *Ibid.*, 54.
[276] *Ibid.*, 60. On the source of the quotation in Steuco (*De perenni philosophia* III.16), see Roger Laufer's commentary, in de Villars, *Comte de Gabalis*, 166–167. I am grateful to Dylan Burns for having identified the Greek passage quoted by Steuco as a combination of fragments from two oracles preserved in the fifth-century oracle collection nowadays known as the Tübingen *Theosophy*: following the edition of Hartmut Erbse, lines 1–3 in Steuco (*De perenni philosophia*, 196) can be found in § 15 (Erbse, *Theosophorum graecorum fragmenta*, 10 = Beatrice, *Anonymi monophysitae Theosophia*, 10), and lines 4–10 in § 21 (Erbse, 15 = Beatrice, 15–16). The sentence "All is full of God, God is everywhere" comes from § 43 (Erbse, 28 = Beatrice, 21), quoted by Steuco in *De perenni philosophia*, 197–198.

Presented as fictional satire meant for entertainment, the *Comte de Gabalis* contained most of the elements that would come to determine popular images of "the occult" through the eighteenth and, particularly, the nineteenth century. It hinted at secret organizations (never referred to as Rosicrucian, but easily recognizable as such) focused on the occult practices of magic, astrology, alchemy, and contact with invisible spiritual beings. At the core of these practices, it suggested, there was the prospect (in fact central to Agrippa's *occulta philosophia*) of a profound spiritual transformation that reverses the effects of the Fall and makes it possible for man to regain the supra-human knowledge and power that had been his original birthright.[277] The underlying metaphysics was a platonic panentheism directed towards γνῶσις τῶν ὄντων: the very perspective that Jacob Thomasius had highlighted, only five years earlier, as the doctrine at the heart of all pagan heresy.[278] The combination with Paracelsianism and the "occult sciences," alchemy in particular, resulted in exactly the kind of "platonic-hermetic" religion that Colberg would attack in his foundational synthesis twenty years later. But to all these traditional notions, the *Comte de Gabalis* added something new, congenial to anti-clerical sentiments among his readers: the notion of a superficially Christian but essentially pagan religion grounded in a profoundly spiritual "intercourse" with *nature*. In eroticizing the idea of contact between human beings and spiritual entities that inhabit the natural world, Villars had turned his novel into a perfect reversal of the current witchcraft discourse. The Church had distorted the truth by turning the benevolent spirits of nature into evil demons, prohibiting any contact with them as pagan idolatry, and rejecting sex between humans and demons (incubi or succubi) as the *non plus ultra* of moral depravity.[279] But the Count of Gabalis defended exactly the opposite: he was denouncing "normal" sex as carnal practice that kept us in our fallen and sinful state, while praising "marriage" with the spirits of nature as the royal road towards spiritual regeneration.

We do not know whether Montfaucon de Villars just meant to write an amusing novel with a sexy theme, or may have had somewhat more serious intentions: his protagonist seems to hover between skepticism and credulity, and never clearly makes up his mind. But readers certainly did. Within ten years, in 1680, the first English translation was published in London by one "B. M. (printer to the Cabalistical Society of the Sages, at the Sign

---

[277] Surprisingly, the religious beliefs that are at the core of Agrippa's work – and thereby indirectly of the *Comte de Gabalis* and its many heirs – can be traced to the little known Christian Hermetist Lodovico Lazzarelli and his *Crater Hermetis* (Hanegraaff, "Better than Magic").

[278] See Chapter 2, p. 106.   [279] See, for example, Stephens, *Demon Lovers*.

of the Rosy Crucian)," and since the original made no explicit reference to Rosicrucians, they were simply inserted into the text by the translator, Philip Ayres.[280] Alexander Pope took inspiration from this version for his *Rape of the Lock*, and intimated that the novel might be not just what it seemed: "both in its title and size [it] is so like a novel, that many of the fair sex have read it for one by mistake."[281] As novelists and playwrights, beginning with Thomas Corneille in 1681, began to explore the humorous and romantic possibilities of elemental spirits falling in love with human beings, and the reverse,[282] and elementals were even turned into mouthpieces of the Enlightenment by the Marquis d'Argens in his multi-volume *Lettres cabalistiques* (1737),[283] readers in search of mysteries, for their part, appeared to be quite willing to take the teachings of the *Comte de Gabalis* seriously. Eventually, many occultists during the nineteenth and twentieth centuries became convinced that its author had been an "initiate" who revealed great secrets under the guise of fiction,[284] and some even lent credence to popular jokes (shared, among others, by Voltaire) to the effect that he had been murdered by Rosicrucians or elementals as punishment for revealing too much![285] In the wake of Helena Blavatsky, occultists in the final decades of the nineteenth century began to report that they had themselves seen elementals, and some of them drew the ultimate conclusion: they began to experiment with ritual techniques for attracting and even marrying elementals.[286]

---

[280] For example, de Villars, *Count of Gabalis*, 169 (Nagel, "Marriage with Elementals," 29; cf. McIntosh, *Rosicrucians*, 108).

[281] Pope, *Poetical Works*, 87.

[282] On Corneille's comedy *La pierre philosophale* (starring the Comte de Gabalis' son, along with two Rosicrucians, all the four classes of elementals, plus "a speaking shadow"), see Kahn, "L'alchimie sur la scène française," 66–76.

[283] See the excellent analysis in Kilcher, "Orakel der Vernunft," esp. 192–193, 196.

[284] See for example the 1913 edition by "The Brothers," with a foreword by one Lotus Dudley, who described the *Comte de Gabalis* as "a book of light," whose pages stated "in terms of exact science the goal and means of man's finer or spiritual growth and identify his position and purpose in evolution."

[285] For example, Eliphas Lévi, *Histoire de la magie*, 1.7 (in: *Secrets de la magie*, 419).

[286] Nagel, "Marriage with Elementals," 40–58; Greer, *Women of the Golden Dawn*, 160–163. See especially Blavatsky, "Thoughts on the Elementals," 181 (*Collected Writings*, vol. xii, 193: since it is undeniable that spirits can interact with the physical world, "*why should not those same Spirits perform matrimonial duties as well?*" [emphasis in original]); ritual for attracting elementals reproduced in Godwin, Chanel, and Deveney, *Hermetic Brotherhood of Luxor*, 109–120; correspondence on elemental marriage in Howe, *Magicians of the Golden Dawn*, 119–123. This entire development may well have its origin in Georgy Henry Felt's much-discussed lecture on "The Lost Canon of Proportion of the Egyptians" on September 7, 1875. Felt claimed to be able to make the elementals visible by means of a "chemical and kabbalistic" process, and it was in response to this lecture that Colonel Olcott seems to have conceived the idea of founding a Society "for this kind of study." The eventual result was the Theosophical Society (Santucci, "Forgotten Magi," 132–138; Deveney,

The *Comte de Gabalis* and its remarkable reception history might seem merely amusing at first sight, but are highly relevant if seen against the background sketched in the introduction to this chapter: the widespread feelings of anxiety, among intellectuals and the general public, about whether the advances of the new science left any room for the presence of divine or spiritual forces in nature. Many Protestants, scientists and Enlightenment thinkers were arguing that the "disenchantment of the world" would liberate humanity from its unfounded fear of non-existent ghosts and witchcraft practices. But for others, the presence of spiritual forces in the natural world inspired positive feelings of awe and wonder, and what *they* were afraid of was alienation: the emptiness of a world of mere matter in motion, wholly indifferent – as famously expressed by Pascal[287] – to the thoughts, hopes, or feelings of human beings. Much of esoteric and occultist religion since the eighteenth century is grounded in the argument that a science leading to such a conclusion necessarily had to be false. Thus, the crucial occult novel of the nineteenth century (and most important sequel to *Comte de Gabalis*), Edward Bulwer-Lytton's *Zanoni*,[288] emphasized a panvitalist cosmology with direct reference to the elemental beings, as a radical alternative to the specter of an empty universe as evoked by Pascal:

[C]an you conceive that space which is the Infinite itself is alone a waste, is alone lifeless, is less useful to the one design of universal being than the dead carcass of a dog, than the peopled leaf, than the swarming globule? The microscope shows you the creatures on the leaf; no mechanical tube is yet invented to discover the nobler and more gifted things that hover in the illimitable air . . . Not without reason have the so-styled magicians, in all lands and times, insisted on chastity and abstemious reverie as the communicants of inspiration. When thus prepared, science can be brought to aid it; the sight itself may be rendered more subtle, the nerves more acute, the spirit more alive and outward, and the element itself – the air, the space – may be made by certain secrets of the higher chemistry, more palpable and clear. And this, too, is not magic as the credulous call it . . . It is but the science by which Nature can be controlled. Now, in space there are millions of beings, not literally spiritual, for they have all . . . certain forms of matter, though matter so delicate, air-drawn, and subtle, that it is, as it were, but a film, a gossamer that clothes the spirit. Hence the Rosicrucian's lovely phantoms of sylph and gnome . . . He who would establish intercourse with these varying beings, resembles the traveller who

---

Paschal Beverly Randolph, 289–295). Theosophists may therefore have been pursuing elementals from the very beginning.

[287] Pascal, *Pensées*, III.205: "abîmé dans l'infinie immensité des espaces que j'ignore et qui m'ignorent, je m'effraie . . . "

[288] On the centrality of Bulwer-Lytton and *Zanoni* to Victorian occultism, see Godwin, *Theosophical Enlightenment*, 123–130, 192–196.

would penetrate into unknown lands . . . the very elixir that pours a more glorious life into the frame, so sharpens the senses that those larvae of the air become to thee audible and apparent . . . [289]

Over the course of almost two centuries, then, a deeply ironical reversal had taken place. From a humorous satire about "kabbalah," the teachings of *Comte de Gabalis* were turned into the paradigm *par excellence* of an "occult philosophy" of nature directed against the disenchantment of the world. This feat was accomplished by what might be called an esoteric hermeneutics of suspicion: occultists assumed that the adepts had been so smart as to conceal their superior "kabbalistic" knowledge under the veil of a satire against themselves – and as usual, they concluded, this trick had fooled everybody except the true initiates.

If Montfaucon de Villars' type of satire was just a bit too subtle to prevent such interpretations, there was nothing subtle about the intentions of its most famous counterpart: the *History of the Extravagant Imaginations of Mr. Oufle*, published in 1710 by yet another *abbé*, Laurent Bordelon. The very name of the protagonist, a transparent anagram of "le fou" (the fool), sets the tone: Mr. Oufle is the very archetype of the superstitious erudite. He owns a big library devoted to demonology and the occult sciences (Bordelon provides a lengthy and very interesting list of titles)[290] and is ready to believe anything he reads, no matter how outrageous. He is blind to reason and common sense, and keeps making a fool of himself throughout the novel because of his limitless credulity and utter inability to learn from his mistakes. In a desperate last attempt to cure him of his folly, a letter is fabricated in which his own familiar spirit threatens him with the worst if he does not stop practicing astrology. In this manner, Oufle is cured of one superstition by means of another one, but of course he returns to his old habits as soon as he discovers the deception. It should be noted that there is nothing disconcerting or frightening about his persona: unlike many Enlightenment thinkers, Bordelon did not connect Oufle's folly with such serious factors as fear, fanaticism or mental illness, but just made fun of his credulity and ignorance.[291]

Even the main specialist of Bordelon admits his mediocrity,[292] but the popularity of *Mr. Oufle* – it was often reprinted, and translated into English, German, and Italian[293] – made it an early classic in the "debunking" genre. The book was not meant just for amusement: its author, an

---

[289] Bulwer-Lytton, *Zanoni*, 252–254.   [290] Bordelon, *L'histoire des imaginations*, chapter 2.

[291] De la Harpe, *L'abbé Laurent Bordelon*, 161–162.

[292] *Ibid.*, 197 ("it must be admitted: his oeuvre leaves an incontestable impression of superficiality").

[293] *Ibid.*, 199.

enlightened cleric,[294] was using the fictional genre for explicit didactic purposes, inspired by serious worries about the dangers of superstition. This
agenda is demonstrated by the many footnotes, full of erudite references,
that he added to his novel, and by the many lengthy (and boring) discourses
through which his skeptical protagonists make their fruitless attempts to
make Mr. Oufle see reason.

Gabalis and *Oufle* are representative of the two main types of fiction
relevant for our concerns. In spite of its satirical intentions, the former
created a classic image of "the occult" as a mysterious science of transformation, practiced by "adepts" and focused on the hidden forces and spirits
of nature; in the latter, the occult appeared quite simply as the summit
of superstition and credulity. Both images would recur in non-fictional
contexts as well.

COMPENDIA OF REJECTED KNOWLEDGE

We have seen that in the gradual shift from a dominantly theological to an
Enlightenment perspective, superstition was transformed from a religious
error into an intellectual one: from a sin it became a mistake, and the
essence of the error was a failure to keep nature and the divine separate.
As demonstrated by the case of Bordelon and countless other examples,
Christian and rationalist commitments could easily join forces in the battle
against "superstition," "magic" or "the occult" – terms which now all came
to refer to the emerging waste-basket category of "rejected knowledge," and
tended to be used interchangeably. If Christian hardliners interpreted the
belief in spiritual presences in nature as paganism and idolatry, rationalists
could denounce the same belief as incompatible with new post-Cartesian
perspectives in science and natural philosophy, and those who considered
themselves enlightened Christians felt free to combine both perspectives.
From the eighteenth century on, this development can be studied in a
newly emerging genre of popular compendia intended to enlighten the
masses about "the occult" and, eventually, similar reference works that no
longer tried to warn the public but rather sought to provide information,
leaving it to the readers to make up their own minds or even trying to
convince them.

The development of the genre can be traced most clearly in France.
In 1702, a generation after Jean-Baptiste Thiers' normative *Traité des*

---

[294] *Ibid.*, 190–191.

superstitions,[295] Pierre Le Brun (a member of the congregation of the Oratory of St. Philip Neri) published an equally influential *Histoire critique des pratiques superstitieuses*, eventually followed by a greatly expanded second edition in three volumes that appeared posthumously in 1732.[296] Le Brun's work, preceded by a long series of endorsements by ecclesiastical authorities, was intended for Christians[297] and remained firmly rooted in the theological doctrine of the Tridentine Church. Superstition was still defined along traditional lines as rooted in idolatrous worship,[298] and Le Brun was therefore free to demarcate it from legitimate belief in the possibility of divine as well as demonic intervention. Inevitably, this led to conclusions that would be considered bizarre from an Enlightenment perspective. For example, Le Brun had originally been led to his investigations by an article on the dowsing rod in the *Journal de Savans* in 1700, and he discussed that topic through no fewer than seventeen chapters of his second volume, concluding that dowsing undoubtedly worked, but not by natural causes: its effects therefore had to be attributed to demons.[299] For Enlightenment critics such a conclusion alone would of course suffice to see him as representative of the very error he claimed to be fighting, and this in spite of all his attempts to use scientific argument wherever possible. For Le Brun himself, the "enchantment of the world" was evidently the very heart of superstition. Following the now familiar narrative, he traced it back to the ancient Oriental nations, who had misunderstood the belief in "intelligent spirits" that they had received from the Hebrews. Their fundamental mistake was that they had "placed these intelligences in almost all the bodies," so that they "found mystery everywhere." Inevitably, this had resulted in the idolatrous worship of spiritual presences in nature, and a whole range of "most absurd fables and most extravagant practices."[300] For Le Brun, the battle against "prejudice" in favor of "straight reason" implied an attack on the credulous belief in the ancient authorities that kept being quoted as historical sources: "how unpleasant to be always obliged to defy the Compilators & the Historians who have had a reputation in the world," he complained, and went on to quote Seneca: "to be a historian & a liar is almost the same thing."[301] Having established these foundations in his first book, the rest of Le Brun's work consisted in lengthy chapters devoted to

[295] See Le Brun, "Le *Traité des superstitions*"; Dompnier, "Les hommes d'église," 22–28.
[296] Dompnier, "Les hommes d'église," 29–30. A fourth volume largely filled by other authors was added in the edition of 1750–1751.
[297] Le Brun, *Histoire critique*, vol. I, 80–81.   [298] *Ibid.*, vol. I, 83–84.
[299] *Ibid.*, vol. II, 140. For an alternative attempt to explain dowsing in terms of corpuscularian physics, see de Vallemont, *Physique occulte*.
[300] Le Brun, *Histoire critique*, vol. I, 2–3, 6.   [301] *Ibid.*, vol. I, 15–17.

such topics as the dowsing rod, magic and witchcraft, astrology and divination, cataleptic trances, and magical practices such as the use of talismans and amulets. Interestingly, alchemy is absent entirely; and apart from their origin in the ancient Orient, there was no further attempt to place the various "superstitions" in any historical context.

Le Brun's ambivalent attempts at using naturalist arguments within a general context dominated by traditional Christian demonology remained very much the norm in similar works during the rest of the century. A certain De Saint-André, a medical consultant of King Louis XV of France, published his much noted "Letters on Magic" in 1725, and the *abbé* Claude-Marie Guyon devoted the eighth volume of his *Bibliothèque Ecclésiastique* (1771) to the same domains, but although they were almost half a century apart, their approaches were still very similar. Both showed the influence of Gabriel Naudé, who in his well-known *Apologie* (1625, plus later editions and translations) had defended a whole range of famous men against the accusation of magic. Like Naudé, De Saint-André and Guyon argued that many phenomena attributed to magic by the common people could in fact be explained by purely natural causes; but both made a point of emphasizing that supernatural causation and demonic intervention were nevertheless possible and real. They differed from Le Brun in adopting Agrippa's distinction between a pure and noble magic of the ancients that had only later degenerated into "criminal and condemnable" practices.[302] For our concerns, the main point to be retained from these writings is that the "waste-basket category" of superstitious arts was now firmly in place. In Guyon's formulation, his book was meant as

a summary of what one should know about judicial astrology, the power of demons, the commerce that they can have with men, by means of the different forms of magic, about enchantments, marvels, amulets and talismans, prophecies, sorcery, dreams, the various ways by which men have tried to know the future, divination and the ordeals of the Middle Ages . . . [303]

As for De Saint-André, at the end of his preface he announced that if anyone were interested, he was ready to continue with even more letters, "on Ghosts, Phantoms, judicial Astrology, Talismans, the Philosophers' Stone, Sympathy, Antipathy, & some other things of this nature [*de cette nature*]."[304] The important point to notice is that his audience evidently no longer needed him to explain what was meant by "of this nature": *that* it somehow all hung together was clear to everyone, even though perhaps none of his readers would be able to explain how and why. Eventually,

---

[302] De Saint-André, *Lettres*, 3–7.   [303] Guyon, *Bibliothèque ecclésiastique*, vol. VIII, 90.
[304] De Saint-André, *Lettres*, Preface [unpag.].

during the nineteenth century, this situation found its reflection in a strategy of book marketing that tried to catch customers' interest by simply mentioning as many terms as possible on the title-page, related or not – as long as one could expect them to be associated with things "of this nature." To give a typical example, a popular book by "J. S. F." (1827) looked as follows:

DEMONOLOGIA; or
NATURAL KNOWLEDGE REVEALED;
being an exposé of
Ancient and Modern Superstitions,
CREDULITY, FANATICISM, ENTHUSIASM, & IMPOSTURE,
as connected with the
DOCTRINE, CABALLA, AND JARGON, of

amulets,	hell,	predictions,
apparitions,	hypocrites,	quackery,
astrology,	incantations,	relics,
charms,	inquisition,	saints,
demonology,	jugglers,	second sight,
devils,	legends,	signs before death,
divination,	magic,	sorcery,
dreams,	magicians,	spirits,
deuteroscopia,	miracles,	salamanders,
effluvia,	monks,	spells,
fatalism,	nymphs,	talismans,
fate,	oracles,	traditions,
friars,	physiognomy,	trials, &c.
ghosts,	purgatory,	witches,
gipsies,	predestination,	witchcraft, &c. &c.

By the beginning of the nineteenth century, the contents of this wastebasket category were turning into favorite objects of antiquarian curiosity about the "strange and forgotten" beliefs and practices of bygone ages.[305] With some notable exceptions,[306] the domain no longer evoked strong feelings of religious or moral concern; but publishers knew how to use its associations with the demonic to attract readers. One sees this in the opportunistic title of Jacques Collin de Plancy's *Dictionnaire infernal*: in fact a pioneering reference work that intended to fill a gap left by Diderot's *Encyclopédie*[307] and treated all imaginable aspects of the field in thousands of lemmata from A to Z. The author was working in the publishing

---

[305] On the antiquarian impulse among students of "the occult," see the humorous and perceptive comments in Deveney, "Ozymandias," and cf. Deveney, "Paschal Beverly Randolph," 355–357.
[306] See, for example, the entirely traditional demonology in Abbé Fiard, *La France trompée*, and the dry commentary by Ferdinand Denis: "a curious work, mostly because of the time in which it came out" (*Tableau*, 271). On Fiard, see also Pasi, "Notion de magie," 104–105.
[307] Céard, "Démoneries," 297–298.

business, and his dictionary is a typical example of nineteenth-century antiquarian erudition. It first appeared in two volumes in 1818, then in a greatly revised edition in four volumes in 1825–1826, and again in 1844. Finally, it was republished as *Dictionnaire des sciences occultes* in volumes 48–49 of the *abbé* Migne's monumental *Encyclopédie*, in 1846–1848, and the title-page took the "waste-basket" approach to a new level:

DICTIONARY

of the

OCCULT SCIENCES

CONCERNING

AËROMANCY, ALCHEMY, ALECTRIOMANCY, ALEUROMANCY, ALFRI-
DARY, ALGOMANENCY, ALOMANCY, ALOPECIE, ALPHITOMANCY,
AMNIOMANCY, ANTHROPOMANCY, APANTOMANCY, ARITHMANCY, ARMOMANCY,
ASPIDOMANCY, ASTRAGALOMANCY, BASCANY, BELOMANCY, BIBLIOMAN-
CY, BOTANOMANCY, BOUZANTHROPY, BRIZOMANCY, CABALOMANCY, CAPNOMANCY,
CARTOMANCY, CATROPTOMANCY, CAUSIMOMANCY, CEPHALONOMANCY, CERAUNO-
SCOPY, CEBOMANCY, CHEMISTRY, CHIROMANCY, CLEDONISMANCY, CLEIDOMANCY, CLEROMANCY,
CO-QUINOMANCY, CRISTALLOMANCY, CRITOMANCY, CROMNIOMANCY, CYNANTHROPY, DACTY-
LOMANCY, DAPHNOMANCY, DEMONOCRACY, DEMONOGRAPHY, DEMONOMANCY, ENGASTRIMISM, FANTASMA-
GORIA, FATALISM, GAROSMANCY, GELOSCOPY, GEMATRIA, GEOMANCY, GYROMANCY, HEPATOSCOPY,
HIPPOMANCY, HYDROMANCY, ICHTHYOMANCY, ILLUMINISM, LAMPADOMANCY, LECANOMANCY, LIBANOMANCY, LITHO-
MANCY, LYCANTHROPY, LYSIMAGHIA, MAGIC, MAGNETISM, MARGARITOMANCY, MATRIMONANCY, MEGA-
NOMANCY, MEGALANTHROPOGNY, METOPOSCOPY, MIMIQUE, INFERNAL MONARCHY, MYOMANCY, NAYRAN-
CY, NECROMANCY, NIGROMANCY, OCULOMANCY, OECONOMANCY, OLOLYGMANCY, OMOMANCY,
OMPHALOMANCY, ONEIROCRITICISM, ONOMANCY, ONYCHOMANCY, OOMANCY, OPHIOMANCY, OPHTHAL-
MOSCOPY, ORDALY, ORNITHOMANCY, OVINOMANCY, PALINGENESIS, PALMOSCOPY,
PARTHENOMANCY, PEGOMANCY, PETCHINANCY, PELTIMANCY, PHARMACOLOGY, PHRENOLOGY,
PHYLLORHODOMANCY, PHYSIOGNOMY, PHILOSOPHERS' STONE, PYRO-
MANCY, RABDOMANCY, RHAPSODOMANCY, SCIAMANCY, SEXOMANCY, SIDERO-
MANCY, SOMNAMBULISM, SPODOMANCY, STEGANOGRAPHY,
STERNOMANCY, STOICHEOMANCY, STOLISOMANCY, SUPERSTITIONS,
SYCOMANCY, SYMPATHY, TACITURNAMANCY, TAUPO-
MANCY, TEPHRAMANCY, TERATOSCOPY, THALMUDANCY,
THEOMANCY, THEURGY, THURIFUMY, TI-
ROMANCY, UROTOPEGNY, UTESETURE, VAMPI-
RISM, VENTRILOQUISM, VISIOMANCY,
XYLOMANCY, ZAIRAGY

or

UNIVERSAL REPERTORY,

OF BEINGS, PERSONS, BOOKS, FACTS AND THINGS THAT HAVE TO DO WITH APPARITIONS, DIVINATIONS, MAGIC,

CONTACT WITH HELL, DEMONS, SORCERERS, OCCULT SCIENCES, GRIMOIRES,

THE KABBALAH, ELEMENTAL SPIRITS, THE GREAT WORK, PRODIGIES, ERRORS, PREJUDICE,

IMPOSTURES, ARTS OF THE GYPSIES, VARIOUS SUPERSTITIONS, POPULAR STORIES, PROGNOSTICS,

AND GENERALLY WITH ALL THE FALSE BELIEFS THAT ARE MARVELLOUS, SURPRISING,

MYSTERIOUS OR SUPERNATURAL

This is just a small collection of terms that appear in Collin de Plancy's dictionary: amazingly, they all seem to really exist, and the author discussed them with an impressive show of erudition. That his work could appear with Migne had to do with Collin de Plancy's personal itinerary: he had started out as a Voltairean freethinker but converted to Catholicism in 1841. His *Dictionnaire* contained pretty much everything associated with magic or the occult sciences, but the leading concept was still that of superstition, presented as a kind of perennial parasite that always saps the life-force of religion:

Superstition, which attaches itself to all religions, always ends up destroying it. It, alone, reigns eternal; the centuries go by without enfeebling it, and time does not break its leaden scepter; it gains mastery over all hearts; and even he who no longer believes in God still believes in predictions and dreams. One could find the source of all superstitions in these four causes: ignorance, pride, fanaticism, and fear.[308]

Collin made quite some revisions after his conversion, but, significantly, his basic view of "superstition" remained the same.[309] Notwithstanding an explicit agenda of "exterminating" superstition by bringing its evils to light,[310] most of the entries in *Dictionnaire infernal* just provided factual information, and it became an indispensable reference work.

During the first few decades of the nineteenth century, the term "occult sciences" was turning into the label of preference. Thus Eusèbe Salverte, a civil servant working in the French magistracy,[311] published a volume *Des sciences occultes, ou essai sur la magie, les prodiges et les miracles* in 1829. Salverte has been hailed as an early pioneer of the "theorization of the occult sciences,"[312] but this gives too much credit to his singularly muddle-headed discussions of badly digested bits of information.[313] More serious

---

[308] Collin de Plancy, *Dictionnaire*, vj.   [309] Céard, "Démoneries," 298–300.

[310] Collin de Plancy, *Dictionnaire*, xxiii–xxiv.

[311] On Salverte's career, see the obituary by his friend François Arago, in Salverte, *Des sciences occultes*, xi–xvi.

[312] Laurant, *L'ésotérisme chrétien*, 63–65.

[313] On Salverte's understanding of magic, see the short discussion in Pasi, "Notion de magie," 99–101.

and readable was the work of his competitor Ferdinand Denis, a pioneer of Latin-American exploration who later settled down as a librarian in Paris.[314] His *Tableau historique, analytique et critique des sciences occultes* was published in 1830 in the very small format of a series for the general public, known as the "portable encyclopedia." The title-page (see bibliography) was yet another example of the "waste-basket" approach, but his discussions were clear and reasonably well informed, and his book provided the reader with at least a rudimentary historical overview. The perspective was clearly skeptical: Denis emphasized "the nothingness of the occult sciences" but argued that there is a certain value in looking back to "take an objective look at the fantastic edifice that has vanished into thin air before the lights of civilization."[315] During the earliest "childhood of humanity," it had all begun with dream interpretation and necromancy, followed by astrology, and finally magic. In the ancient cultures of India, Egypt or Chaldaea, what went by the name "magic" often had a basis in purely physical or chemical processes.[316] These ancient sciences of the Orient reached Europe mainly due to the crusades, and Muslims in Spain had developed "the taste for studying the occult sciences and the high kabbalah, which was probably cultivated by the Templars and whose principles were mingled with those of the gnostics."[317] The influence of the occult sciences has been both negative and positive, for although much of it is based on superstition and credulity, they have also been a stimulant of genuine science: "it is easy to understand how inspiring, to an exalted medieval spirit, must have been the idea that by studying the sciences, he was entering step by step into an intimate contact with mysterious spirits who transmitted to him divine thoughts about earthly things . . . "[318] Those who studied the occult sciences deserve our respect, even though their ideas are false. And on these foundations, Denis then launches into a chapter-by-chapter description of divination and oracles, the kabbalah, faeries, magic, sorcery, demonology, and possession, leading finally to a roughly historical chapter on "gnosticism, secret societies, illuminism, animal magnetism,

---

[314] On Denis, his contacts and his sources, see Laurant, *L'ésotérisme chrétien*, 65–69; and cf. the short discussion in Pasi, "Notion de magie," 101–102. Denis participated in the salons of Countess Marie d'Agoult (a.k.a. Daniel Stern), a meeting-place of Catholic Traditionalists and authors with an interest in French illuminism and related forms of esotericism, including George Sand, Paul Leroux, Baron Ferdinand d'Eckstein, Charles Nodier, and his friend Pierre-Simon Ballanche (Laurant, *L'ésotérisme chrétien*, 54; on these milieus, cf. McCalla, *Romantic Historiosophy*, 216–225).

[315] Denis, *Tableau*, xi.   [316] *Ibid.*, 1–7 (with reference to Eusèbe Salverte).

[317] *Ibid.*, 11.   [318] *Ibid.*, 23–24.

and ecstasy." Gnosticism is based upon a mixture of Christianity with "the dogmas of a high oriental kabbalah," and their oriental cult was passed on by secret societies through the Middle Ages.[319] By way of the Templars, the gnostic/kabbalistic teachings reached Freemasonry (which, too, is "wholly oriental")[320] and the Rosicrucians. Denis continues with a discussion of the various esoteric currents that had flourished since the later eighteenth century: illuminism, Swedenborgianism, and Mesmerism, finishing with a chapter on the "hermetic philosophy" of alchemy and a demonstration that there are natural explanations for seemingly miraculous events. The final parts of his volume contained an alphabetical list of biographical entries on the "most illustrious men who have occupied themselves with the occult sciences," an annotated bibliography, and an analytical vocabulary/index. About twenty years later, a more condensed overview based upon the same historical outline and approach to "the occult sciences" was published in the fourth volume of Paul Lacroix's widely disseminated *Moyen âge et Renaissance.*[321]

In the country of the *philosophes* and the French Revolution, popular compendia of the occult tended to be somewhat more polemical in tone than across the Channel. The most prominent eighteenth-century author in this domain, Ebenezer Sibly, was even a convinced defender. From 1784 to 1788 he published a huge *New and Complete Illustration of the Celestial Science of Astrology* in four volumes, later republished (presumably for commercial reasons) as *A New and Complete Illustration of the Occult Sciences*; and in 1792 it was followed by *A Key to Physic, and the Occult Sciences, opening to Mental View the System of the Interior and Exterior Heavens; the Analogy betwixt Angels and Spirits of Men; and the Sympathy between Celestial and Terrestrial Bodies.* As suggested by the very title, Sibly was a very late heir of Renaissance polymaths like Athanasius Kircher and Robert Fludd, but, interestingly, he was entirely familiar with the new scientific literature as well, and was seriously trying to combine their perspectives.[322] In his personal life he worked as a physician and was involved in Swedenborgianism and Freemasonry, and while his emphasis was very clearly on astrology, his large compilations gave

---

[319] *Ibid.*, 180. Denis refers here to the academic studies by Matter and Tennemann.
[320] *Ibid.*, 182.
[321] Denis, "Sciences Occultes." In 1843, Denis also published a volume titled *Le monde enchanté*, focused on the "marvelous and fantastic" dimension of the Middle Ages.
[322] Debus, "Scientific Truth and Occult Tradition"; Curry, *Prophecy and Power*, 134–137; Godwin, *Theosophical Enlightenment*, 106–111 (also on Ebenezer's brother Manoah).

his readers access to the much wider context of Renaissance *philosophia occulta.*

Sibly's personal library provided Francis Barrett with what he needed to compile *The Magus* (1801):[323] a digest of plagiarized materials taken from already existing translations of, most importantly, Agrippa's *De occulta philosophia*, ps.-Agrippa's *Fourth Book of Occult Philosophy*, ps.-Peter of Abano's *Heptameron*, and Giovanni della Porta's *Magia Naturalis*. It could not make any claim to originality other than for its hand-tinted portraits of demons, but the book was a success. Its author, a shadowy entrepreneur best known as a balloon adventurer,[324] offered the reader his services as a teacher in "Natural Philosophy, Natural Magic, the Cabala, Chemistry, the Talismanic Art, Hermetic Philosophy, Astrology, Physiognomy, &c. &c." and "the Rites, Mysteries, Ceremonies, and Principles of the ancient Philosophers, *Magi*, Cabalists, Adepts, &c." Of course, the repeated "&c's" once more reflect the waste-basket approach to things "of this nature." The purpose of his school was "to investigate the hidden treasures of Nature; to bring the Mind to a contemplation of the Eternal Wisdom; to promote the discovery of whatever may conduce to the perfection of Man..."[325] We know of only one student, a Dr. John Parkins, but for later occultists this was enough to imagine Barrett as an important link in the initiatic chain by which the occult sciences were supposed to have been handed down from the Renaissance through the "dark ages" of the early nineteenth century to the Victorian era.[326]

A final name that must at least be mentioned here is Robert Cross Smith, an astrologer who published his works under the pseudonym "Raphael." His case was similar to that of Sibly, in that his works were focused on astrology but in fact introduced their readers to a much wider domain of "occult sciences." In 1824, Smith started a magazine called *The Straggling Astrologer*, followed by *Urania; or, the Astrologer's Chronicle, and Mystical Magazine*; and after both had failed, he began selling their contents as books. In spite of the title, his *Astrologer of the Nineteenth Century* (1825) was concerned with the occult sciences in general, and with spirit invocations

---

[323] Godwin, *Theosophical Enlightenment*, 118; Hamill, *Rosicrucian Seer*, 20–21; Pasi, "Notion de magie," 150–155.

[324] King, *Flying Sorcerer*.   [325] Barrett, *The Magus*, Bk. II, 140.

[326] In the grey area of publications half way between occultism and scholarly research, one still finds such ideas even today: see, for example, Butler, "Beyond Attribution," 9, 21, 24–25, who manages to praise *The Magus* as "one of the most original and valuable additions to western occultist literature" (*ibid.*, 7) although even her own evidence demonstrates its derivative nature.

in particular, and it has been called "the occult compendium of its time" next to Barrett's *Magus*.[327]

There would be no point to analyzing these and similar compendia in any further detail. In mentioning just some of the most well known among them, we have merely looked at the tip of an iceberg;[328] but if the genre demonstrates anything, it is that the field now widely known as "the occult" had lost all academic respectability, and had become an intellectual wasteland dominated by trivial literature meant for the largest audience possible. As mentioned earlier, its authors were typically autodidacts (one would like to add "well-meaning," but the fact is that many were just trying to make money), and what they chose to publish was determined largely or exclusively by the demands of this particular niche in the popular reading market. Given that fact, a critical or historical approach to the masses of derivative information on "occult" beliefs and practices was not just unnecessary but unwanted: readers did (and still do) not buy such books to learn, or to ask themselves difficult questions about the development of science, religion, or philosophy, but to be amused by bizarre facts and anecdotes, thrilled by stories about demons, excited at the vague idea that there might be something to magic after all, or intrigued by the suggestion that it might be possible to know the future. At most, readers with a more intellectual or scholarly interest might browse through this literature to satisfy themselves, like the scholarly pedant Wagner in Goethe's *Faust*, about "wie wir's denn zuletzt so herrlich weit gebracht" ("how wonderfully far we have come at last"). In short, these nineteenth-century compendia of the occult represent the lowest ebb of "Western esotericism" as a possible topic of intellectual exploration or academic interest. Ever since, there has been a continuous market for books of this general kind. In the absence of serious scholarship, they have played a dominant role in determining how the field was perceived both by the general public and by academics.

SECRET TRADITIONS AND HIDDEN HISTORIES

For many decades after Brucker's *Historia critica philosophia*, it is very hard to find anything that looks like a history of the various currents that would be recognized today as falling under the rubric of "Western

---

[327] Godwin, *Theosophical Enlightenment*, 143–147, here 145.
[328] For the countless nineteenth-century publications on "the occult," the indispensable bibliography is Caillet's three-volume *Manuel bibliographique*. A useful short guide through this labyrinth is Galbreath, "History of Modern Occultism."

esotericism." When historical approaches finally began to appear, most of them[329] were building upon the general legacy of the ancient wisdom narrative, or on historiographical models that had been developed in the contexts of alchemy and Freemasonry. As we have seen, alchemists and freemasons shared a strong interest in the historical origins of their respective crafts, and both were trying to recover a "lost secret" that had been known to the ancients. It was therefore logical for them to develop a special interest in how those ancient secrets had been passed on through history, and their overviews could serve as a model for historiographies of "the occult." A history of the separate historiographies of alchemy or Freemasonry (and of other fields, such as astrology) falls beyond the scope of this study, but it is important for us to take a brief look at the general models that they bequeathed to later authors with a more comprehensive agenda.

The outstanding eighteenth-century example of a history of alchemy was Nicolas Lenglet Dufresnoy's three-volume *Histoire de la philosophie hermétique*, first published in 1742 and reprinted twice in 1744. Interestingly, it was intended as the prequel of a much larger work on the history of philosophy, philosophers, and their opinions, which never saw the light of day.[330] Lenglet was a learned érudit and former diplomat who left a large oeuvre mainly on historical and geographical topics, and he had republished Jean Maugin de Richebourg's important collection *Bibliothèque des philosophes chimiques* one year before.[331] He claimed, with some exaggeration, to be the first author ever to have written a "history of hermetic philosophy": "the learned [sçavans] who busy themselves with history distrust everything that has to do with this science, and rightly so; & the philosophers, occupied exclusively with their operations, neglect its history & confuse all the terms."[332] Lenglet, for his part, was addressing those among the general public who might want to satisfy their curiosity and amuse themselves by learning about the "illustrious fools" who had occupied themselves with alchemy.[333]

Lenglet's historical overview was quite unremarkable in itself. Still firmly grounded in biblical chronology, and attempting (in vain) to make sense of

[329] The important exception to this rule – historical overviews that constructed "magic" as the historical precedent for mesmerism – will be discussed separately in Chapter 4.
[330] Lenglet Dufresnoy, *Histoire*, vol. I, iv.
[331] On Lenglet Dufresnoy and his alchemical writings, see Sheridan, *Nicolas Lenglet Dufresnoy*, 178–187; Debus, "French Alchemy in the Early Enlightenment," 51–55 (repr. 2006, 416–419).
[332] Lenglet Dufresnoy, *Histoire*, vol. I, iii; cf. Debus, "French Alchemy in the Early Enlightenment," 51 (repr. 2006, 416–417) with n. 25.
[333] Lenglet Dufresnoy, *Histoire*, vol. I, v–vj; cf. Sheridan, *Nicolas Lenglet Dufresnoy*, 180.

the conflicting reports in ancient sources, he traced the history of alchemy from Noah's son Ham to Hermes Trismegistus in Egypt, and from there to the Hebrews, Greeks, and Romans. From late antiquity on, the narrative turns into an author-by-author description of the major alchemists, culminating in the seventeenth century, "the century of folly,"[334] when the mad dreams of alchemy begin to carry their fruits to the fullest. In spite of many disparaging remarks of this kind, contemporary reviewers noticed, quite correctly, that Lenglet's attitude to alchemy was in fact rather ambiguous:

It is true that, from time to time, he insinuates that this hermetic Philosophy is false, chimerical and ruinous. But more often, he presents it to us as a sublime science, and as an admirable art, and the great work as something real. Accordingly, it is not easy to know what the Author thinks of this metallic transmutation, which modern physics judges to be impossible. Sometimes he takes the trouble to refute what is being said against the vain arguments of the Alchemists. If he is a partisan of the hermetic philosophy, he does not say so sufficiently, and if he disdains it, his disdain is not clear enough: sometimes he mentions the pros, sometimes the cons, which is not agreeable to all readers.[335]

Hence the difference was not so very great with the perspective of a convinced "adept" like Antoine-Joseph Pernety, in his *Fables Egyptiennes et Grecques dévoilées et réduites au même principe* (1758), where he alluded to the universal medicine, "this treasure," "fruit of life," "remedy to all ills" that had been known already to the first philosophers.[336] The secret knowledge about it had been passed on from Hermes Trismegistus to the Druids, Gymnosophists, *Magi*, Chaldaeans, Homer, Thales, Orpheus, Pythagoras, and so on; and to be able to pass it on without revealing the true secret, they had all used hieroglyphs, symbols, allegories, and fables.[337]

Masonic historiographies were similar in that they, too, liked to trace the secret knowledge to the Orient and as far back into history as possible,

---

[334] *Ibid.*, 322.
[335] Review in *Observations sur les écrits modernes* 28 (1742), 190–191, here quoted according to Sheridan, *Nicolas Lenglet Dufresnoy*, 181. Cf. the quite defensive statements in Lenglet Dufresnoy, *Histoire*, vol. 1, xvj ("I hope one will not believe . . . that I wish to affirm the truth of the Hermetic Science; I speak as a historian, & not as a Philosopher; I offer what I have read, & not what I have practised"); vol. 11, iv–v ("Oh, if I would give free rein to my imagination, what strange things I could tell! One would almost take me for an Adept"); vol. 11, 118–119 ("I affirm nothing, I leave it to the readers to judge. I do not want to be blamed if one works without result; I give no guarantee for the examples that I give; I am not a judge, I am content with being a Historian without prejudice; so nobody should accuse me of having led them into error, if someone makes crazy expenses in this kind of thing. I report facts of history . . . ").
[336] Pernety, *Fables*, vol. 1, iv–v.   [337] *Ibid.*, v–x.

and placed strong emphasis on symbols; but as already suggested, the difference was their additional interest in initiatic *organizations*. As we have seen, the ancient Mysteries, the Pythagorean brotherhood, and the order of the Essenes were attractive candidates for the early period, followed by the Knights Templar for the Middle Ages and the transmission of masonic secrets from the Middle East to Europe, where the lineage was believed to have continued with the Rosicrucians and modern Freemasonry. As more information became available about India and its religions since the early nineteenth century, it became possible for masonic authors to push the oriental origins of the order even further eastward; and as the antagonism between Freemasonry and Roman Catholicism (the Jesuit order in particular) grew stronger, the gnostic and Manichaean heretics moved increasingly into the picture as well: according to the logic of "my enemy's enemy is my friend," the more they were demonized by Catholics, the more attractive they were bound to become for masons.[338]

If the concept of "secret societies through the ages" had its origin in Freemasonic attempts to construct a pedigree for the Craft, it eventually got divorced from masonic agendas and developed into an autonomous sub-genre of its own. Its foundational classic, *The Secret Societies of All Ages and Countries*, was published by Charles William Heckethorn in 1875 (revised and expanded edn 1896), but was in fact modeled upon a large Italian work, *Il mondo secreto* (fifteen books in nine volumes) published by Giovanni de Castro in 1864. De Castro began with the "ancient initiations" (the Zoroastrian *Magi*, the Mithras cult, the Brahmans and Gymnosophists, Egyptian and Eleusinian mysteries, and so on) and the "Christian initiations" (from the Essenes and Therapeutae to Jesus himself), continuing with the "emanationist" schools of the kabbalah and the gnostics, medieval currents like the Cathars, the Templars and the Ismaelites, moving on from there to the alchemists and Rosicrucians, so as to finally reach Freemasonry, which was clearly the heart and center of his work. Having discussed its various manifestations over several volumes, he continued with other "secret societies," such as the Martinists, the Illuminati, the Carbonari, and a variety of smaller Italian sects.

---

[338] Some examples of the genre are Marconis de Nègre's *Sanctuaire de Memphis ou Hermès*, which imagined the first initiations as having taken place on "the banks of the Ganges and the Nile," and accorded a central role to Mani (identified with Hiram); Ragon de Bettignies' *Maçonnerie occulte* (published as the second part of *Orthodoxie maçonnique*), which emphasized that the masonic secret was alchemical in nature (*ibid.*, 3–5, 418); or, from a later period, John Yarker's *The Arcane Schools*, which shows a clear influence of then current theories about "Indo-Aryan" culture.

Heckethorn – an English bibliophile, probably of Swiss descent, who earned his living as an estate agent[339] – claimed that his own work began as a translation of de Castro, but had "speedily assumed a more independent form" as he decided to delete parts of the original and add many new sections to it.[340] In so doing, he in fact changed the entire concept of de Castro's work, which evolved under his hands from a history of predecessors and descendants of Freemasonry into a general overview of each and every secret society about which he could find some information, including the Thugs, the Mafia, the Ku-Klux-Klan, or the Jesuits, but also German and French Workmen's Unions, anarchist and nihilist societies, the "Know-Nothings," African Hemp-smokers, "Mumbo-Jumbo," "Wahabees," and so on and so forth. Many similar overviews of "secret societies of all times and places" have been published ever since.[341] Their relevance for our concerns consists mainly in the fact that such works added considerable plausibility to the general idea that "Western esotericism" could be described in terms of secret organizations or hidden brotherhoods.

Outside the sphere of masonic publication, however, that idea remained no more than a vague suggestion at best, and this has much to do with the remarkable influence of Roman Catholic perspectives on French occultism in the nineteenth century. In this regard, it is useful to adopt Joscelyn Godwin's distinction between an "occultism of the left" and an "occultism of the right."[342] As described in Godwin's groundbreaking study *The Theosophical Enlightenment*, occultism in the English-speaking world was very strongly indebted to an anti-Christian mythographical tradition grounded in the work of Enlightenment libertines, who had argued that religion had its origin not in divine revelation but in a "natural religion" of solar worship and phallicism. It was on these intellectual foundations that spiritualists like Emma Hardinge Britten and occultists like Helena P. Blavatsky developed their idiosyncratic forms of "comparative religion" as an alternative for traditional Christian narratives.[343] Godwin's "occultism of the left" was hostile

---

339 For the scanty biographical information on him, see Eve Juster's Introduction to the 1965 edition of Heckethorn, *Secret Societies*, vol. 1, ix–xi.
340 *Ibid.*, vol. 1, xxiii.
341 For example Schuster, *Die geheimen Gesellschaften*; Lepper, *Famous Secret Societies*; Peuckert, *Geheim-Kulte*; Frenschkowski, *Die Geheimbünde*.
342 Godwin, *Theosophical Enlightenment*, 204.
343 Godwin, *Theosophical Enlightenment, passim*. For the Enlightenment theories of phallicism and solar mythology, the most central authors were Richard Payne Knight, Charles François Dupuis, Constantin François de Volney, and William Drummond. By mediation of authors such as Samson Arnold Mackey and Godfrey Higgins, the tradition reached the occultists of the later nineteenth century. Emma Hardinge Britten's trance lectures on "the Origin of All Religious Faiths" (published

towards traditional Christianity and tended to support liberal and progressive causes,[344] and this makes it strikingly different from the "occultism of
the right" that was dominant in France. If anything emerges with perfect
clarity from the best-informed study of these milieus, Jean-Pierre Laurant's
L'ésotérisme chrétien en France au XIXe siècle, it is that French occultism
was dominated by countless *abbés* (pretended or real) and other Catholics
who were trying to come to terms with the legacy of the Revolution and
its sensationally successful assault on the traditional authority of "altar and
throne." Their attitudes towards modernization and progress were of great
complexity, and can by no means be characterized simply as "conservative"
and "traditionalist," but they all shared an obsessive nostalgia for the lost
unity of a universal Tradition that had expressed itself by means of spiritual
symbolism.[345] We will return to this perspective in Chapter 4; but at this
point, it is important to emphasize that the dream of a universal "Catholic"
Tradition that preserved the Truth under a veil of symbolic language and
imagery was central to how they imagined the history of what now began
to be referred to, sometimes, as "esotericism."

By far the most influential example was published in 1860 by the *abbé*
Alphonse-Louis Constant, better known under his pseudonym Eliphas
Lévi. Born in poor circumstances, Constant had attended seminary to
study for the priesthood, but never made it to the ordination due to a
series of events and conflicts that have been described by his biographers
but do not need to detain us here.[346] Suffice it to say that, during the
first part of his life, he maintained a highly complex relation with the
Church, while at the same time getting involved in various movements
working for social and political reform: his socialist and utopian writings,
including high-minded ideals about the emancipation of woman, led to
conflicts with the authorities and several prison sentences. It was in the
wake of the revolution of 1848 that he made his decisive move towards

in 1860 as *Six Lectures on Theology and Nature*) "achieved the marriage of spiritualism with
the mythography of the Enlightenment" (Godwin, *Theosophical Enlightenment*, 203), and in
combination with the new vogue of "occult sciences," this novel synthesis would come to full
development in Blavatsky's *Isis Unveiled* of 1877. For a useful list of Blavatsky's mythographical
(and other) sources, see Coleman, "Sources of Madame Blavatsky's Writings."

[344] See Pasi, "Modernity of Occultism."

[345] Laurant, *L'ésotérisme chrétien*, 17–18; and see the useful short summary of nineteenth-century
"Catholic Science" in Brach, review of Laurant (with primary reference to the strange story of
Dom Jean-Baptiste Pitra's failed attempt to attribute a medieval Latin manuscript to the second-
century bishop Meliton of Sardis, and present it as the "Key" to the "symbolic tradition" of the
Roman Catholic Church: see Laurant, *Symbolisme et écriture*).

[346] Most complete in this regard is Chacornac, *Eliphas Lévi*. Another good monographic treatment is
McIntosh, *Eliphas Lévi*.

study of the occult. The three central works documenting his worldview were published in 1854–1856, 1860, and 1861 respectively, and established his name as a popular authority of "magic and kabbalah."[347]

Constant *alias* Lévi was an enthusiastic amateur scholar of considerable but unsystematic erudition (he had, of course, learned Latin as part of his seminary training), and while his occultist synthesis certainly cannot pass the test of historical scholarship, it is the reflection of a remarkably original mind, presented in brilliant romantic prose.[348] His *Histoire de la magie* of 1860 is based (in spite of the title) upon a universalist understanding of "kabbalah," presented as the key that unlocks the secrets of all religions and philosophies. Like the main academic scholar of kabbalah in France at this time, Adolphe Franck,[349] Lévi did not see it as a specifically Jewish phenomenon: along the lines of a Christian kabbalah on patristic foundations, he described it as the direct reflection of the *Logos* that has created the world according the Gospel of John. On the highest level of creation, kabbalah manifests itself as a symbolism of numbers; and their meaning and dynamics can serve as a universal hermeneutic key at all lower ontological levels of reality, according to the logic of correspondences or universal analogy.

What makes Lévi's work intellectually interesting is the fact that he does not present magic and kabbalah dualistically, as a counterculture against Christianity (let alone a "secret tradition" of initiates), but dialectically, as the hidden truth of Roman Catholicism which both reveals *and* conceals itself in the very *coincidentia oppositorum* of light and darkness. Lévi's basic law of equilibrium (the law of two) implies, as he often repeats, that there can be no truth without error, no light without darkness, and no concept of God without a concept of Satan. The hidden unity of the divine is revealed to us under the sign of the ternary, Lévi's number of "manifestation," and obviously linked to the Trinity, which paradoxically reconciles these opposites without sacrificing either one of them to the other. It is only from the divine perspective of absolute Unity that all these dualities are mysteriously resolved. The temptation for us as creatural beings is to misunderstand the law of equilibrium and thereby lapse into

---

[347] My earlier remarks on the lack of academic expertise in the nineteenth century are illustrated by the fact that Lévi was apparently seen as an authority even outside occultist circles, as he was asked to contribute articles on kabbalah and Knorr von Rosenroth to a reference work as famous as the *Larousse* (see Kilcher, "Verhüllung und Enthüllung," 354–355).

[348] For an analysis of Lévi's oeuvre, see Hanegraaff, "Beginnings of Occultist Kabbalah."

[349] For Franck's concept of a "universal kabbalah" with Persian/Zoroastrian rather than Jewish origins, and the resonances of his perspective with the Martinist current of Papus (Gérard Encausse), see Hanegraaff, "Beginnings," 111–118.

a Manichaean dualism of good and evil as independent absolutes. Because the dualistic doctrine destroys the very law of equilibrium, it necessarily destroys the very unity of the divine, of reality, and of truth as well. It is against this fundamental heresy of heresies, Lévi argues, that the Church has defended its trinitarian doctrine, grounded in unity and the universal law of equilibrium.

From this perspective it becomes much easier to understand the internal logic that governs Lévi's history of magic. Like Adolphe Franck, but for different reasons, Lévi traced magic and the true kabbalah (which to him were one and the same) to Zoroaster; but he distinguished the latter from a *second* Zoroaster, the inventor of the material fire-cult and of the "impious dogma of divine dualism," who is ultimately responsible for the later decline of true magic.[350] This topos of the two Zoroasters was an old one, but Lévi's use of it was new.[351] If the false Zoroaster was the father of materialism and dualism, the true Zoroaster was his exact opposite. The former taught the cult of material fire, but the latter revealed what Lévi referred to as a "transcendental pyrotechnique,"[352] focused on the great agent of magic: a universal invisible fluid called the astral light. Lévi supported this view by extensive quotations in French from Francesco Patrizi's *Magia philosophica* (1593),[353] which contains a Latin translation of the *Chaldaean Oracles*. As a late believer in Gemistos Plethon's attribution of the *Chaldaean Oracles* to (the true) Zoroaster, it was easy for Lévi to conclude that when Abraham left Ur of the Chaldaeans, he must have taken the Zoroastrian kabbalah with him, and this is how it entered Jewish culture. The doctrine also spread to Egypt, where it was translated into the hieroglyphic language of images and symbols, leading to an elaborate science of correspondences between gods, letters, ideas, numbers, and signs; and just as Abraham had saved the doctrine before it began to degenerate in Chaldaea, Moses did the same for Egypt. This is how the kabbalah became the hidden doctrine of the Hebrew Bible.

And then everything changed. "[A] breath of charity descended from the sky,"[354] Lévi writes, with the birth of Christ. From that moment on, the magic of the "ancient world" became obsolete: "a sad beauty spread over its dead remains . . . a cold beauty without life."[355] And as for Judaism: just like Rachel died at the birth of her youngest son Benjamin, the birth

[350] Lévi, *Histoire de la magie*, in: *Secrets*, 383.   [351] Stausberg, *Faszination Zarathushtra*, 334.
[352] Lévi, *Histoire de la magie*, in: *Secrets*, 383–384.
[353] *Ibid.*, 384–385. The quotation is from Patrizi, *Magia philosophica*, 43v–45r.   [354] *Ibid.*, 456.
[355] *Ibid.*, 457.

of Jesus as the youngest son of Israel meant the death of his mother.[356] Henceforth Christianity became the legitimate carrier of the true kabbalah, and its survivals outside the Church, whether Jewish or pagan, lack such legitimacy. As a logical result, the rest of Lévi's history of magic turns out to be essentially a history of heresies: the teachings of the false Zoroaster lived on in such currents as gnosticism and the Order of the Knights Templar, in witchcraft and black sorcery, and in various kinds of ecstatic cults up to and including the contemporary current of spiritualism. In other words: Eliphas Lévi, who is often regarded as the founding father of occultism, did *not* defend any concept of "secret traditions" or underground organizations that had kept the truth alive against the suppression of the Church. On the contrary, he maintained that only Roman Catholicism itself has been the legitimate carrier of kabbalah and true magic since its very origins, and all competitors were sectarian heretics by definition. However, the true nature of Catholicism still remained hidden even to its adherents: "Considered as the perfect, realized and living expression of kabbalah, that is to say, of the ancient tradition, Christianity is still unknown, and that is why the kabbalistic and prophetic book of the Apocalypse remains unexplained. Without the kabbalistic keys, it is perfectly inexplicable, because incomprehensible."[357] In other words: there is no such thing as a secret tradition of initiatic organizations, but there does exist a hidden, secret, "esoteric" dimension to the exoteric church, and by preaching the great "dogma" of kabbalah and magic, Lévi was trying to lead his readers to the one universal truth of Roman Catholicism as he saw it. This is why his *Histoire de la magie* even contains several formal declarations of submission to the authority of the Church,[358] and his later *Cléf des grands mystères* abounds in references to the absolute truth of hierarchical authority.

　　Eliphas Lévi's works were introduced to the English-speaking world through the translations of Arthur Edward Waite, who, unfortunately, misunderstood them on a basic level and thereby bequeathed a warped interpretation to his occultist readers and the general public.[359] Waite seems to have had no antenna for the dialectical nature of Lévi's thinking,

---

[356] *Ibid.*, 461.

[357] *Ibid.*, 458. Cf. Lévi, *Clef*, in: *Secrets*, 865: "The Catholic dogma comes entirely from the kabbalah, but under how may veils and with what strange modifications!"

[358] Lévi, *Histoire*, in: *Secrets*, 358 ("we submit our work in its entirety to the supreme judgment of the Church"), 421 ("We do not dogmatize, we submit our observations and our studies to the legitimate authorities"), 481 ("We pretend here neither to deny not to affirm the tradition of the fall of the angels, referring as always, in matter of faith, to the supreme and infallible decisions of the holy catholic, apostolic, and roman Church").

[359] See the "Biographical and Critical Essay" in Waite, *Mysteries of Magic*; see also the Preface to his later translation of Lévi, *History of Magic*.

and perceived a great contradiction in the fact that after first presenting himself as "an initiate in possession of the Great Arcanum," the French magus was trying in his later works "to stultify himself by attempting to pose as a faithful and humble child of the Catholic Church."[360] However, the underlying assumption that Lévi's "magical" or "kabbalistic" beliefs had to be heretical from a Catholic perspective, thereby forcing him to make a choice, is unwarranted in view of our discussions in Chapter 1: these occultist beliefs might be perceived as incompatible with Christian orthodoxy by nineteenth-century outsiders, but we have seen that a Catholic like Constant, whose seminary training had made him familiar with patristic tradition, could provide excellent arguments for defending their orthodoxy.

Arthur Edward Waite's failure to grasp Lévi's perspective is all the more interesting because his own belief in a "Secret Tradition" was ultimately closer to his French counterpart than might appear at first sight. More than any other author in the English-speaking world, this scholarly autodidact, poet, occultist and self-made mystic has been responsible for establishing and popularizing the concept of an "esoteric tradition" in Western culture,[361] by means of an impressive series of large and erudite books, published from the mid-1880s through the 1930s, on the history of alchemy, magic, kabbalah, mysticism, Rosicrucianism, Freemasonry, the Tarot, and the Graal legend, plus many editions and translations of sources.[362] As summarized by Waite's biographer,

During his years of multifarious reading at the British Museum, Waite had acquired an immense fund of knowledge on the history and practice of the occult sciences, and in the late 1880s he began to put it to good use. He realized that if his speculative writing was to be taken seriously he must first establish a reputation among the "occult" public as a sound scholar; he must do what had not previously been done in the field of occultism – he must write carefully reasoned historical

---

[360] Waite, *Mysteries of Magic*, 12, and discussion on the following pages. Waite's ten-point summary of Lévi's message and his four-point summary of its implications (*ibid.*, 12–14) says more about his own religious preoccupations than about the contents of Lévi's *Dogme et rituel*, and the same is true of the series of "contradictory passages" discussed in parallel columns on pp. 15–20.

[361] Cf. Gilbert, *A. E. Waite*, 12, 161.

[362] On Waite's life and career, see Gilbert, *A. E. Waite*; on his publications, see Gilbert, *A. E. Waite: A Bibliography*; for a short introduction, see Gilbert, "Waite." Among the most important titles for our concerns are *The Real History of the Rosicrucians* (1887), *Lives of the Alchemistical Philosophers* (1888), *The Occult Sciences* (1891), *Devil-Worship in France* (1896), *The Book of Black Magic and Pacts* (1898), *The Life of Louis-Claude de Saint-Martin* (1901), *The Doctrine and Literature of the Kabbalah* (1902), *Studies in Mysticism and Some Aspects of the Secret Tradition* (1906), *The Hidden Church of the Holy Graal* (1909), *The Pictorial Key to the Tarot* (1911), *The Secret Tradition in Freemasonry* (1911), *The Secret Doctrine in Israel* (1913), *A New Encyclopedia of Freemasonry* (1921), *The Brotherhood of the Rosy Cross* (1924), *The Secret Tradition in Alchemy* (1926), *The Holy Kabbalah* (1929), *The Holy Grail, its Legends and Symbolism* (1933), *The Secret Tradition in Freemasonry* (1937).

and critical studies. Studies, moreover, that quoted original sources and argued from established facts to rational conclusions – a method of working quite alien to the occultists who were (as they still are) in the habit of setting out preconceived opinions and selecting just those facts to support them as required the least amount of distortion.[363]

In the absence of any serious competitors, Waite's prodigious output did make him the virtually unavoidable authority, until far into the twentieth century, for anybody who wished to place the various currents associated with "the occult" in some kind of historical framework. To assess Waite's achievements fairly, one must recognize that his schooling was minimal, he never attended university, and had virtually no models or predecessors for his detailed historical studies in what he himself preferred to call "the Secret Tradition" of the West. One can therefore have respect for his labors, even while acknowledging that his legacy is highly problematic. Discussing Waite's editions of alchemical treatises, Principe and Newman conclude that

[t]hey are almost invariably based upon corrupt editions and offer texts butchered to unrecognizability by the silent excision of large portions of material and adulterated by the addition of occultist elements and slants completely alien to the originals. The fact that there are in many cases no other modern translations with which to compare or replace them has intensified their ill effects over time. Waite's corrupt translations were used regularly by historians of science until the middle of [the twentieth] century, as witnessed by their frequent citation in articles in *Ambix* and *Isis*, as well as in scholarly books; some authors still continue to refer to them. Nearly all have been reprinted and are currently available in inexpensive editions.[364]

More even than on Waite's failings, this criticism is a reflection on the remarkable extent to which the scholarly study of alchemy was still being neglected by the academy: the fact is that enthusiastic autodidacts like Waite were doing the work that should have been done by philologically trained historians, and the result of this neglect was a flood of unreliable and misleading publications that still keep influencing popular and academic perceptions of the field. For another central domain, that of kabbalah, the situation was very much the same, as remarked by Gershom Scholem in his ground-breaking *Major Trends in Jewish Mysticism*:

It is not to the credit of Jewish scholarship that the works of the few writers who were really informed on the subject were never printed, and in some cases were not even recorded, since there was nobody to take an interest. Nor have we reason to

---

[363] Gilbert, *A. E. Waite*, 91.   [364] Principe and Newman, "Some Problems," 395.

be proud of the fact that the greater part of the ideas and views which show a real insight into the world of Kabbalism, closed as it was to the rationalism prevailing in the Judaism of the nineteenth century, were expressed by Christian scholars of a mystical bent, such as the Englishman Arthur Edward Waite in our days... [I]t is all the more regrettable that [Waite's *Secret Doctrine in Israel*] is marred by an uncritical attitude towards facts of history and philology...[365]

In spite of the millions of words that he devoted to its outward manifestations, Waite's ideas about "the Secret Tradition" are not so easy to discern. His strange, difficult and ponderous style of writing, his infuriatingly vague way of referring to what he saw as the mysterious reality at work in religious history, his continuous revisions of earlier writings, the fact that he never attempted a synthetic overview of "the Secret Tradition" as a whole, and his refusal to disclose his intimate thought and its development over time, even in his autobiographical *Shadows of Life and Thought*, are factors that all conspire to keep his basic perspective frustratingly elusive. After having known him for thirty-eight years, even his close friend Arthur Machen had to admit "I have not the faintest notion as to his real beliefs."[366] One of Waite's clearest statements appears in his autobiography:

I believe to this day ... that there is a Church behind the Church on a more inward plane of being; and that it is formed of those who have opened the iridescent shell of external doctrine and have found that which abides within it. It is a Church of more worlds than one, for some of the Community are among us here and now and some are in a stage beyond the threshold of the physical senses.[367]

At least in his mature years, Waite does not seem to have thought of the "Secret Tradition" as some esoteric school or initiatory organization. Rather, he saw it as the invisible community of all those – in this life or the next – who were striving to reverse the fall from divine union by means of interior regeneration, or had achieved that goal. He referred to the latter category as the "Holy Assembly," and saw it as working in a hidden, "inward" manner through historical traditions such as alchemy or kabbalah. Waite was raised as a Catholic and had a great love of ceremony, but did not believe that the "exoteric" church – or any other organization – possessed the

[365] Scholem, *Major Trends*, 2, 212.
[366] Arthur Machen to Colin Summerford (1925), quoted in Gilbert, *A. E. Waite*, 163.
[367] Waite, *Shadows*, 170–171. Waite seems to have derived his notion of a "Hidden Church" from Karl von Eckartshausen and Ivan V. Lopukhin (cf. Faivre, *Eckartshausen*, 151–153, 378–386, with reference to Lopukhin, *Quelques traits de l'église intérieure* [1799] and various works by Eckartshausen). To get an impression of Waite's personal doctrine, his scholarly books are less instructive than the rituals for the orders he founded and the texts he contributed to obscure and now almost unobtainable periodicals like *The Unknown World*, *The Occult Review*, and *The Seeker* (for a useful selection, see Gilbert, *Hermetic Papers of A. E. Waite*, and see his remarks on p. 10).

power or authority to initiate members into the hidden or "esoteric" Community: "There are no admissions – at least of the ceremonial kind – to the Holy Assembly, but in the last instance the candidate inducts himself."[368]

The combination of this mystical belief with a historical approach to alchemical, magical, or kabbalistic materials resulted in a type of occultist scholarship that has become remarkably influential in the twentieth century. Even today, it remains a very significant factor in the grey area of writings halfway between esoteric religiosity and strictly academic research. Its basic assumption is that the term "esotericism" refers not primarily to initiatic organizations (although these may be included too), but to the "inner" spiritual dimensions that are believed to be discreetly present under the surface of "exoteric" traditions. The implicit concept of two parallel "planes of reality" was crucial to the worldview of Victorian occultism and has remained a bedrock of occultist belief and practice to the present day. As explained by the anthropologist Tanya Luhrmann in her seminal study *Persuasions of the Witch's Craft*, its significance lies in the fact that it allows modern occultists to accept the limitations of a thoroughly disenchanted world ruled by the laws of physics: by means of ritual and symbols, they can always make a temporary escape from its restrictions to a "magical plane," ruled by the laws of the imagination. In other words: the dissipation of mystery in *this* world is compensated for by a separate magical world of the reified imagination, where the everyday rules of science and rationality do not apply,[369] and this is how occultists manage to secure a "place of enchantment" in a disenchanted world.[370]

We will encounter a very similar perspective in the work of Carl Gustav Jung and some other scholars associated with Eranos, and its significance for the study of Western esotericism will be discussed in Chapter 4. At this point, all that needs to be emphasized is the impact that Arthur Edward Waite's voluminous oeuvre has had on how that field has been perceived by enthusiasts as well as scholars in the English-speaking world. It

---

[368] Waite, *Hidden Church of the Holy Graal*, 641. On Waite's concept of the "Secret Tradition" and the "Holy Assembly," see Gilbert, *A. E. Waite*, 96–99, 134, 163–165. While Waite did not subscribe to orthodox biblical concepts of the Fall, his belief system was grounded in the general idea of "a loss which has befallen humanity" and the possibility of restitution, restoration, or regeneration (*ibid.*, 97–98).

[369] Luhrmann, *Persuasions*, 274–283; Hanegraaff, "How Magic Survived," 369–371. Contrary to, for example, Christopher Partridge (*Re-Enchantment*, vol. 1, 40–41) I see "disenchantment" as an unavoidable reality even for contemporary magicians, resulting in attempts at "(re)enchantment" that are qualitatively different from pre-Enlightenment ones.

[370] Owen, *Place of Enchantment*. Waite's development from a magical to a mystical interpretation of this worldview is of minor importance for our concerns.

introduced them to a wide range of historical traditions that were difficult
to get access to otherwise, and even provided them with editions and
translations of primary sources, while subtly but persistently suggesting
to them that all these traditions and materials were merely the outward
face of a mysterious, "inward" reality known only to "initiates." From a
modern academic perspective, the most ambiguous aspect of Waite's legacy
consists in his position halfway between mystical or esoteric commitment
and critical scholarship. More than almost anyone else in his generation, he
was making a sincere and persistent effort to establish standards of critical
historiographical research; but although the quality of his work improved
as he developed a more critical attitude in his later writings,[371] he still failed
to do so in a manner that could satisfy professionals. However, because it
took those professionals so long to appear on the scene at all, the weaknesses
of Waite's historiography became almost inseparable from how the field
itself was perceived by the general public.

THE WASTE LAND

I began this chapter by emphasizing the shift from a predominantly philosophical and intellectual discourse concerned with ancient wisdom and
the virtues or dangers of paganism, to a new perspective in which science
and natural philosophy became the dominant framework of interpretation in all domains of thought. The process known since Max Weber as
"disenchantment" – the disappearance of "mysterious and incalculable"
forces from the natural world – is of absolutely central importance in this
new context, as we have seen throughout this chapter. Major examples are
the Enlightenment reinterpretation of superstition, which from fear and
worship of pagan deities and demons active in this world became redefined
as an intellectual failure to keep nature and the divine separate; the complicated development of *magia naturalis*, from a concept meant to protect
the study of the ancient natural sciences from theological censure into an
"animistic" or "participatory" worldview that divinized nature itself and
endowed it with spiritual or even divine powers and presences, thereby
rendering it unacceptable for adherents of the new science; the parallel
development of "occult qualities" from the black box of scholastic naturalism into the privileged sanctuary of the divine within the natural world,

---

[371] This is acknowledged by Principe and Newman in their discussion of Waite's *Secret Tradition in
Alchemy* of 1926: "a degree of skepticism and historical discretion appears," and it even looks as if
"the occultist has marvelously transmuted himself into a positivist" ("Some Problems," 395).

studied by what came to be known as the "occult sciences" as an alternative to the new scientific disciplines; the fundamental ambiguity of alchemical transmutation, hovering between its status as an experimental science and its common perception as involving a spiritual process by which Man and even Nature itself could be "regenerated" from their fallen state and restored to their original bodily-spiritual perfection; the belief that such a "science" of spiritual regeneration had been known to the ancients and pursued by secret societies through the centuries; the fictional reversal of traditional demonology by which incubi and succubi were transformed into elemental beings through which one might actually enjoy an intimate "intercourse with nature"; or the late nineteenth-century idea of a "magical plane" ruled by the laws of the imagination, corresponding as a separate, parallel reality with the "physical plane" ruled by physics and thus providing a means of escape from the disenchanted world.

To recognize the true significance of the disenchantment process, it is useful to return for a moment to Max Weber's original formulations. Having pointed out to his audience that "the savage" has a better knowledge about the working tools or processes of exchange on which his life depends, than we do about the functioning of our tramlines or our economy, he continued as follows:

Increasing intellectualization and rationalization . . . does *not* mean an increasing general knowledge concerning one's conditions of life. It means something different: the knowledge, or faith, that if only one *wished* to, one could always find out; hence, that as a matter of principle, there are no mysterious incalculable powers that play into it; but rather, that – as a matter of principle – one can *have power* over all things by means of *calculation*. That, however, means the disenchantment of the world. No longer does one need – like the savage, for whom such powers did exist – to have recourse to magical means to gain power over the spirits or pray to them. Technical instruments and calculation are doing the job. This is the principal meaning of intellectualization as such.[372]

The indispensable foundation of modern natural science does indeed consist in the conviction that, in principle and by definition, nothing in the natural world can be essentially "mysterious" and "incalculable," that is to

---

[372] Weber, *Wissenschaft als Beruf*, 9. Weber's matter-of-course references to "the savage" and "magic" as the counterpart to rationalization and disenchantment are obvious examples of the type of discourse criticized in my section on magic, with primary reference to Randall Styers' work. This does not, however, invalidate the correctness of his observations about the nature of "disenchantment": one can support his analysis without subscribing to a *sui generis* concept of "magic" as opposed to "science" or "religion."

say, forever out of reach for intellectual understanding and human control. In very general terms, the conceptualization of "Western esotericism" that took place in the wake of the Enlightenment, and continued in the twentieth century, can be seen as a direct outcome of the disenchantment process as formulated by Weber. As a "waste-basket category" of exclusion, it contained everything now seen as incompatible with a disenchanted worldview grounded in science and rationality; but by the same token, the category came to be reified as a positive counter-tradition of enchantment (or, eventually, re-enchantment) by those who felt that the evaporation of mystery emptied the world of any deeper meaning. It is significant, in this regard, that the famous definition of Western esotericism as a "form of thought," presented by Antoine Faivre in 1992 (and to which we will return) reads like a definition of "enchantment": the notion of "correspondences" is clearly an alternative to instrumental causality, "living nature" stands against a mechanistic worldview, "imagination/mediations" implies a multi-leveled neoplatonic cosmology as opposed to a cosmos reducible to only matter in motion, and "transmutation" implies the theosophical/alchemical process of regeneration by which fallen man and nature are reunited with the divine.

Modernization is therefore the key to understanding the emergence of Western esotericism (or whatever alternative term one might prefer) as a concept or a category in the study of Western culture. Understood in terms of disenchantment, the core identity of modern post-Enlightenment society and its appointed representatives (such as, notably, academics) *requires and presupposes* a negative counter-category consisting of currents, practices and ideas that refuse to accept the disappearance of incalculable mystery from the world. Moreover, the new science and post-Enlightenment society define themselves as "modern" by way of contrast with any appeal to the authority of "ancient wisdom." This combination makes the domain nowadays known as "Western esotericism" into much more than just a collection of currents and ideas that happen to have been neglected or overlooked: rather, by being conceptualized as "the Other of science and rationality" it functions as the dark canvas of presumed backwardness, ignorance or irrationality that modernity needs in order to paint the outlines of its own identity in shining colors of light and truth. In short: modern identities imply the occult.

But every new development comes at a price, and therefore evokes a reaction. As will be seen in the fourth and final chapter, highly influential academics during the twentieth century revolted against the implications of disenchantment by promoting a new kind of scholarship on Romantic, Idealist, and Traditionalist foundations. For intellectuals of such a persuasion, it was obvious that disenchantment had turned the world into a spiritual Waste Land abandoned by the gods. For them, it was as if the famous prophecy of the hermetic *Asclepius* had become a literal reality in post-industrial Europe:

A time will come when . . . divinity will withdraw from earth to heaven and Egypt will be deserted. The land which used to be the seat of religion will be abandoned by the gods and become void of their presence . . . Then to men, tired of living, the cosmos will no longer seem an object of wonder or adoration . . . People will find it oppressive and scorn it . . . The dark will be preferred to the light, and death thought better than life. No one will look up to heaven. A religious person will be considered mad, and an irreligious one wise. The lunatic will be thought brave, the scoundrel will be taken for a decent person . . . How grievous will be the withdrawal of the gods from humanity! Only the evil angels will remain. Mingling with humanity they will force these wretches into all the evils of violence: wars, robbery, fraud and all those things which are contrary to the nature of souls. In those days the earth will not be stable, nor will the sea be navigable . . . Every divine voice will of necessity be stopped. The fruits of the earth will rot, and the land will no longer be fertile. The very air will hang heavy in gloomy lethargy. Such will be the old age of the world: irreligion, disorder, and unreason concerning all that is good.[373]

The Waste Land metaphor can be applied not only to the image of a thoroughly disenchanted secular world, as in T. S. Eliot's famous poem. It is also relevant to the situation of "Western esotericism" as a topic for intellectual reflection and scholarly research in what may well be called the "Age of the Amateur." While the gods were abandoning the world, intellectuals and scholars were abandoning the study of historical currents and ideas associated with "Platonic Orientalism," and everything associated with "magic" or the "occult sciences" was likewise abandoned by the emerging academy during the same period. Thus the domain came to be dominated almost exclusively by amateur scholars and their popular writings for the general market, with predictably negative results as regards historical sophistication, critical analysis, and factual knowledge pure and simple. The mediocre quality of most publications on "the occult," in combination with the ignorance of academics about its actual contents and historical backgrounds, were two factors that mutually reinforced one

---

[373] *Asclepius* 24–26 (translation inspired partly by Copenhaver, *Hermetica*, 81–82; partly by Salaman, *Asclepius*, 78–81).

another in a downward spiral: reliable information was hard or impossible to come by, critical editions of primary sources were unavailable, and the intellectual elites saw no reason why anybody should take an interest in what they saw as no more than irrational nonsense. It would take the better part of the twentieth century for this situation to improve.

CHAPTER 4

The truth of history
Entering the academy

> We wished to immerse ourselves in the study of the finest detail. We were seized by a compulsion to deal with the dry details, the small things of the great things, so as to develop therein the closed well of turbulent vitality, for we knew that this was its place and there it was hidden, and that from there we could draw upon its waters and quench our thirst . . . And we thereby became specialists, masters of one trade. And if we did not struggle with God . . . we struggled with the Satan who danced among us. This was the Satan of irresponsible dilettantism, who does not know the secret of construction, because he does not know the secret of destruction.
>
> Gershom Scholem[1]

We have come a long way since the days when Renaissance humanists could think of history in terms of grand and glorious designs, through which divine providence was working out its mysterious plan for the salvation of humanity. Gemistos Plethon had expected the imminent restoration of an ancient and universal religion on Platonic Orientalist foundations, Ficino believed that he was in fact witnessing the return of the Golden Age, and Pico della Mirandola envisioned the final unification of all religion and philosophy in his own time. But nothing in their intellectual culture could have prepared them for the avalanche of unprecedented events and revolutions that was about to hit Europe instead, and would end up transforming its culture and society beyond recognition. We have seen that Christians had once been accused of cutting out for themselves "a new kind of track in a pathless desert,"[2] but new revolutionaries were about to go even much more boldly where no one had ever gone before. We all know what happened. During the three centuries after Ficino, radical reformers rejected the tradition of the Church itself and ended up destroying the unity of Western Christendom forever; new philosophies in the wake of Descartes,

---

[1] Scholem, "Reflections on Modern Jewish Studies," 69.
[2] Porphyry, in Eusebius, *Praep. Evang.* 1.2.4 (see page 25, with n. 81).

Spinoza, or Kant dared to make the unaided human intellect into the only reliable instrument for knowledge, authorizing it to judge even divine revelation; sensational scientific breakthroughs and technological innovations began to work "magic" and "miracles" beyond anything imaginable in previous periods of history; and violent political and social revolutions attacked the traditional authority of "altar and throne," paving the way for democratic mass societies on secular, non-religious foundations. All this happened because countless thinkers and activists were willing to attempt what no adherent of the ancient wisdom narrative could ever have considered: to ignore tradition and start from scratch.

It is important to prevent misunderstandings about the nature of the relation between "tradition" and "innovation" in the context of Western esotericism. Contrary to the stereotype that sees them as inherently static and "resistant to change" – a kind of insulated anomaly, somehow exempt from history and time – the various intellectual currents and practices associated with magic and the occult have always gone through processes of creative development, transformation, and innovation.[3] In this regard they are, of course, like any other product of human culture. However, no matter how creative their representatives may have been, they never saw themselves as making a new start and heading in an entirely new direction towards an unknown future. On the contrary, those who followed the logic of a "platonic paradigm"[4] sought to restore the ancient wisdom, return to a universal tradition, recover forgotten secrets, or find the way back to a lost unity. And even the more linear, dynamic, process-oriented logic of the alternative "alchemical" paradigm implied that any process – including history – had to be conceived of as an organic unfolding of pre-existing potentials or seeds that predetermined its possible outcomes. Jacob Thomasius was even more right than he probably realized himself: concepts of *creatio ex nihilo* have always been alien to Western esoteric modes of thought.

Modern culture, in sharp contrast, is grounded in an acute awareness of its own historical novelty and uniqueness. It is impossible to think of our secular and democratic mass societies, with their enormous technological achievements, in terms of restitution, return, or even transformation or unfoldment: in essential respects they are a new phenomenon for which no traditional script was available, and that developed as a revolution, or series of revolutions, rather than an organic development from previous

---

[3] See above, Chapter 3, pp. 184–189 (with reference to Brian Vickers).

[4] For my distinction between a "Platonic" and an "Alchemical" paradigm, see above, Chapter 3, pp. 192–195.

conditions. As a result, our dominant historical perspectives assume a timeline that is linear, irreversible, and open-ended. Even if we are not convinced that modern society and its dominant values are to be preferred over the past, we still know that we have *progressed* in the literal sense of the word – "moved forward," or "advanced" – towards something that had never existed before, and are on our way towards an uncertain future for which no historical models are available either.

Such a perspective is capable of inspiring positive feelings of freedom, even exhilaration: as human beings we are not conditioned by the past but can always start over again, we therefore have unlimited possibilities ahead of us, and it is up to us to shape our future! However, it can also lead to feelings of disorientation, anxiety, and spiritual malaise: if we do not know from where we have come, where we are going, or whether we are going anywhere at all, then history becomes meaningless and futile – a pointless series of random events that might as well have happened differently, without any deeper significance, goal, or direction, beginning with nothing and leading nowhere, for no particular reason at all. Many modern thinkers have attempted to avoid such nihilist conclusions, and esotericism is an important part of that story.[5] In this fourth and final chapter, we will see how high-level intellectuals and academics inspired by modern esoteric traditions, and much else besides, developed new and highly influential scholarly perspectives as antidotes against the course of modern history and the world that had been its result. These new theoretical frameworks have been enormously successful in the study of religion after World War II, and are essential to the emergence of Western esotericism as a field of academic research in that same period.

The cultural impact of these new theories is easy to understand: created by some of the great minds of twentieth-century intellectual culture, their conceptualizations were sophisticated, sometimes brilliantly creative, and emotionally appealing to readers in search of a deeper meaning in human existence. Nevertheless, we will be forced to draw a disappointing conclusion: whatever other virtues they may have, most of these theoretical approaches are inadequate as a framework for historical research, and hence unsuitable as a foundation for the study of Western esotericism. If

---

[5] For an excellent overview of the famous "crisis of historicism," see Oexle, "Krise des Historismus"; and for an equally impressive philosophical analysis, see Bambach, *Heidegger, Dilthey, and the Crisis of Historicism*. On "historicism" and evolutionism in relation to Western esotericism, see, for example, Hanegraaff, *New Age Religion*, 158–168, 411–421, 462–482; "Romanticism and the Esoteric Connection." For essential remarks on Romantic evolutionism and its relation to esotericism, see McCalla, "Evolutionism."

we wish to do justice to that field in its full historical complexity, then, we must resist their seductive attractions. This conclusion is bound to upset some readers and colleagues active in this field; but my discussion of the alternatives will hopefully show not only why the price needs to be paid, but also why it is worth paying. As a first step towards this argument, we now need to return one last time to the late eighteenth and early nineteenth centuries.

MAGNETIC HISTORIOGRAPHY: GERMAN ROMANTIC MESMERISM AND EVOLUTIONISM

Some time during the later 1760s, a German physician retreated into the wilderness. He had published a new scientific theory that he considered revolutionary in its implications, but his colleagues had reacted with cold indifference. Hurt and disappointed, he now wondered what to do.

A devouring fire filled my entire soul. I was searching for the truth no longer full of tender devotion – I was searching for it full of the extremest unrest. Only fields, woods and the most remote wildernesses still appealed to me. There I felt closer to Nature. In my most vehement emotions I sometimes believed that my heart, tired of having been seduced by her in vain, wildly rejected her. "O Nature!" I exclaimed during such moments, "what do you want from me?" Then again I believed to be tenderly embracing her, imploring her, full of impatience, to fulfill my wishes. Fortunately, only trees were the witnesses of my outbursts in the solitude of the woods, for I must really have resembled a madman. All other occupations became hateful to me. To devote even a single moment to them seemed to me like a crime against truth. I regretted the time that I needed to give expression to my thoughts. I found that we are used to clothing each thought immediately, without long reflection, in the language best known to us: and so I made the strange decision to free myself from this slavery . . . For three months I thought without words.

When I ended this deep thinking, I looked around in amazement. My senses no longer betrayed me as before. All things looked different to me . . . Gradually peace returned to my soul, for now it was wholly convinced that the truth I had been pursuing so vehemently really existed. Admittedly I still perceived her only from afar, still surrounded by a faint nebula, but I clearly saw the road that led towards her . . . Now a long and difficult journey through the realm of other people's opinions lay ahead of me.[6]

---

[6] [Mesmer], *Kurze Geschichte*, 42–47. Cf. Benz, *Franz Anton Mesmer*, 23–24; Baier, *Meditation und Moderne*, vol. I, 183.

Although the author of this autobiographical fragment, Franz Anton Mesmer, is known as a man of the Enlightenment, the description makes him look rather like a Romantic visionary. His claim of "thinking without words" confirms the importance attached to "higher knowledge" even among representatives of the German *Aufklärung*:[7] Mesmer is saying that he struggled with Nature until she revealed her secrets to him through an ecstatic state beyond rational discourse.[8]

Mesmer's theory of "animal magnetism" posited the existence of a universal "fluid" or life-force intermediary between spirit and matter, permeating the planetary atmosphere and all organic life, and moving harmoniously along with the tides of gravitation. Illness had to do with blockages in the natural flow of this fluid through the human body, but harmony could be restored by various techniques, such as the laying on of hands or making "passes" over the patient's body. In Mesmer's original approach, patients typically went through a violent "crisis" as part of the healing process; but one of his followers, the marquis de Puységur, developed a technique through which the patient fell into a peculiar trance that became known as artificial somnambulism. The complicated further development of "mesmerism" and somnambulism has been documented extensively, and there is no longer any doubt about its key importance for a whole series of extremely influential, and closely interrelated, developments in nineteenth- and twentieth-century culture, including spiritualism and occultism, the American New Thought movement and its many offshoots up to the present day, and – most relevant for the present discussion – the "discovery of the unconscious" leading to modern psychology and psychiatry.[9] To understand that connection, and its importance for the academic study and historiography of Western esotericism, we must now take a closer look at the somewhat neglected history of mesmerism in German Romantic culture.

---

[7] Neugebauer-Wölk, "'Höhere Vernunft' und 'Höheres Wissen'," 170–172.

[8] Mesmer confirms this himself: in a footnote, he identifies such "thinking without words" as leading to a form of "enthusiasm," and warns the reader against its risks: the highest level of ecstasy is very close to madness, and the extreme mental exertion needed to achieve such a state may be dangerous to the brain (*Kurze Geschichte*, 43 n. 10).

[9] Succinct overview with bibliographies in Méheust, "Animal Magnetism/Mesmerism." Comprehensive histories of mesmerism and its many ramifications are Ellenberger, *Discovery of the Unconscious*, 53–253; Crabtree, *From Mesmer to Freud*; and Gauld, *History of Hypnotism*. For mesmerism in the German-speaking countries, see Gauld, *History of Hypnotism*, 75–110; Hammoud, *Mesmérisme*; and Baier, *Meditation und Moderne*, vol. 1, 179–243 (followed, on pp. 253–290, by a very important discussion of the influence of mesmerism on occultism). For Victorian England, see Winter, *Mesmerized*. For France, see Méheust, *Somnambulisme et médiumnité*; Edelman, *Voyantes* (concentrating on mesmeric visionaries); and Darnton, *Mesmerism*. For the United States, see Fuller, *Mesmerism*.

As emphasized by Karl Baier in a seminal discussion, the specific development of mesmerism in German Romanticism was based entirely upon a medical theory proposed in 1807 by the respected physician Johann Christian Reil, and adopted by Carl Alexander Ferdinand Kluge in his influential textbook of animal magnetism published in 1811.[10] This theory distinguished between two separate but mutually complementary nerve systems, the "cerebral system" (brain and spinal marrow) and the "ganglion system" (centered on the solar plexus), presented as the organs of the conscious and the unconscious soul.[11] The basic concept was quickly adopted by a whole series of major authors, including Gotthilf Heinrich von Schubert, Georg Wilhelm Friedrich Hegel, Joseph Ennemoser, Johann Carl Passavant, Dietrich Georg Kieser, Carl Joseph Hieronymus Windischmann, and Justinus Kerner.[12] They appear to have agreed that through the ganglion system, we have access, in Schubert's influential formulation, to the mysterious "nightside" of nature.[13] The cerebral system, associated with rational thinking and discursive language, is dominant during our waking life; but its ganglionic counterpart takes over when we fall asleep, and our soul then starts speaking to us in its own "hieroglyphic" and poetic language of images and symbols.[14] However, it was only in the artificial state of somnambulic sleep, or trance, that the ganglion system was seen as revealing its full potential: countless contemporary observers described how patients in such a condition displayed a range of spectacular "occult" or "psychic" abilities, including action-at-distance, hypersensitivity, perception by a "sixth" or inner sense, precognition, clairvoyance, the perception of spirits and angelic beings, speaking and writing in archaic or unknown languages and scripts, and mystical visions of higher worlds and divine realities. The most famous of all these somnambulic patients was Friederike Hauffe, known as "the Seeress of Prevorst," whose case was described in detail by the poet and physician Justinus Kerner in a bestselling book of 1829;[15] but similar phenomena appear to have been

---

[10] Baier, *Meditation und Moderne*, vol. 1, 190, with reference to Reil, "Über die Eigenschaften"; and Kluge, *Versuch einer Darstellung*, 217–219, 223–267. On the latter, see Gauld, *History of Hypnotism*, 99–110. The connection between the ganglion system and magnetism/somnambulism was made by Reil himself ("Über die Eigenschaften," 231–235).

[11] The terminology is Reil's own, although he speaks of "bewusstlos" rather than "unbewusst" (see, for example, "Über die Eigenschaften," 216, 236, 239).

[12] On these authors and their use of the theory, see Baier, *Meditation und Moderne*, vol. 1, 179–246; Faivre, "'Eloquence magique'"; Magee, "Hegel on the Paranormal"; Hanegraaff, "A Woman Alone"; Hanegraaff, "Versuch über Friederike Hauffe."

[13] Schubert, *Ansichten*.   [14] Schubert, *Symbolik des Traumes*, 1.

[15] Kerner, *Seherin von Prevorst*. For detailed analysis, see Hanegraaff, "A Woman Alone" and "Versuch"; and Gruber, *Seherin von Prevorst*.

observed in countless other patients (almost all of them female), leading to a copious literature and intense discussions among physicians and philosophers.[16]

In the German Romantic literature on somnambulism, the theory of two complementary nerve systems was developed into a full-blown counter-metaphysics directed wholesale against Enlightenment rationalism. In the paradigmatic formulations of Justinus Kerner, the shallow "daylight" world of the rationalist, whose hard "glass skull (*tabula vitrea*)" keeps him isolated from intuitions of a higher world, stands against the profoundly meaningful "nocturnal" world of the somnambules, who know from direct experience that behind the brutal realities of social and material existence there is a much larger, all-encompassing, and deeply meaningful life. Hence there are two complementary worlds, or levels of reality, each with its own specific mode of experience and expression: while the Enlightenment reduces everything to cold logic and discursive prose, its alternative expresses itself through profound symbols and poetic language. When our bodily senses shut down temporarily, and we descend into dream or somnambulic trance, our soul "wakes up" to the larger world whence it has come and where it really belongs.[17] The rationalist, in contrast, is spiritually asleep. He lives in a state of artificial isolation from his own soul and its powers of perception, incapable of understanding the language of symbols and poetry. He naively believes that his brain and his senses show him all there is, never realizing that they are obstacles rather than reliable instruments for discovering the deeper "secrets of nature." Blind as he is to her spiritual dimensions, he can only dismiss belief in occult powers and supra-normal abilities as irrational "superstition." Such abilities are, however, neither miraculous nor supernatural: they are *natural* human faculties, potentially available to us all. Hence, the remarkable feats of somnambules reveal the powers that are latent in humanity, and the first step towards developing them is to reject the limited and limiting reductionist superstitions that have claimed the name of science and reason for themselves.

[16] For the wider context in Germany, with discussion of several case studies, see Sawicki, *Leben mit den Toten*, 131–225. Among the many intellectuals who traveled to Weinsberg to visit Friederike Hauffe were (next to those mentioned in the text) such famous names as Franz von Baader, Joseph Görres, Friedrich Schelling, Friedrich Schleiermacher, and David Friedrich Strauss (for the latter's account, see Hanegraaff, "A Woman Alone," 246). Important periodicals devoted to somnambulism and related topics were the *Blätter aus Prevorst: Originalien und Lesefrüchte für Freunde des inneren Lebens* (1831–1839) and *Magikon: Archiv für Beobachtungen aus dem Gebiet der Geisterkunde* (1839–1853), both edited by Kerner.

[17] This basic Romantic notion has its origin in Reil as well: "Dream is a partial waking; rest in waking is a partial sleep" ("Über die Eigenschaften," 236).

In appealing to recent medical theories and discoveries, and insisting that these were grounded in empirical facts (*Thatsachen*) ignored by Enlightenment thinkers, German Romantic intellectuals were defending the scientific superiority of an "enchanted" and poetic worldview on paracelsian and theosophical foundations.[18] The organic center of the ganglion system was in the hypochondrium (the upper region of the abdomen, marked by the lower ribs), now usually linked to the solar plexus but known in nineteenth-century Germany as the *Herzgrube*: the heart cavity. For Paracelsus and Johannes Baptista van Helmont, this was the seat of the *archaeus* or "life spirit," and it assumed a crucial importance in German Romantic mesmerism as well. An earlier mesmerist, Tardy de Montravel, pointed to the *Herzgrube* as the location of the "interior sense" through which direct perception was possible independent of the five exterior senses;[19] and in fact, this region was constantly highlighted as the main organ of clairvoyant perception in virtuoso somnambulists such as Friederike Hauffe. In other words: against the cold rational knowledge of the brain associated with the cerebral system, the German Romantic mesmerists highlighted the superior spiritual "knowledge of the heart" associated with its ganglionic counterpart. This knowledge included "paranormal" or clairvoyant perception, but went far beyond it to embrace metaphysical realms. Following the micro/macrocosmic correspondence thinking of paracelsian and swedenborgian theory, the heart as the center of the human organism corresponded with the sun as the center of the solar system; and this center, in turn, corresponded with the unfathomable light of divinity at the heart of all creation.[20] Ultimately, then, the somnambulic knowledge of the heart was understood as a gnosis about divine things, infinitely superior to the merely rational knowledge of the brain and the testimonies of the exterior senses.[21]

By presenting "daylight" rationality as a limited instrument – powerless to grasp the deeper "nightside" truths accessible to the soul, or explain

---

[18] On the intellectual origins of Romantic *Naturphilosophie* in what I have called the "alchemical" paradigm, dominated by Paracelsianism and Boehmian theosophy, see, for example, Faivre and Zimmermann, *Epochen der Naturmystik*; and Faivre, *Philosophie de la nature*. For the historical backgrounds of mesmerism specifically, see, for example, Benz, *Franz Anton Mesmer*.

[19] Baier, *Meditation und Moderne*, vol. 1, 189–190; Crabtree, *From Mesmer to Freud*, 58.

[20] For excellent examples, see Friederike Hauffe's so-called "Solar Circle" and "Circle of Life": circular diagrams that represented her outer and inner life, and revolved around the "Gnadensonne" (sun of grace) in the center. See discussion in Hanegraaff, "Versuch" (part 1), 31–36; "Human Potential before Esalen," 30–38 (with reproductions of the circles). The correspondence of "heart" and "sun" as the centers of the individual organism, the physical solar system, and metaphysical reality, were undoubtedly influenced by the teachings of Emanuel Swedenborg (see Hanegraaff, *Swedenborg, Oetinger, Kant*, 51–55).

[21] See Hanegraaff, "Magnetic Gnosis."

the empirical facts of consciousness revealed in somnambulic trance – the Romantic mesmerists had discovered a line of argumentation that stood all the principles of Enlightenment philosophy and science on their head. One century later, its essence would be formulated in all simplicity by their most influential modern successor, Carl Gustav Jung: "my soul cannot be the object of my judgment and knowledge – rather, my judgment and knowledge are objects of my soul."[22] Anybody who accepted such an epistemological hierarchy was forced to rethink a whole series of dualisms constitutive of Enlightenment rationalism, as will be seen. Most important for our present concerns, however, are the historiographical implications: anything that Enlightenment historiography had sought to consign to the waste-basket of history – magic, divination, clairvoyance, symbolism, the occult – now came to be perceived as manifestations of the soul and its hidden powers, and highlighted as *central* to the historical development of human culture! At the same time, however, because anything pertaining to the soul was believed to be of universal and eternal validity, historicity and temporality themselves were downplayed in favor of timeless truths, and mere "external events" in favor of their "inner essence." One can see this clearly, for example, in one of the earliest German Romantic authors who attempted to sketch a history of "magnetism," Johann Carl Passavant. Along Hegelian lines, he introduced that history as follows:

Of the history of humanity we know almost nothing but the outer occurrence, the dead letter, the skeleton of times. The life-giving spirit that moved individuals and entire generations, and is expressed only as half-understandable ciphers in deeds and world-events, remains inaccessible to historical research. This is why the more we investigate the wellsprings of human spiritual activity, out of dissatisfaction with mere external phenomena, and descend into the deeper recesses of our inner self, where spiritual treasures lie hidden, the more often do we find the books of the past to be closed to us, the more hieroglyphic does their writing appear to us. For example, we hear of men who, through their profound insights into the essence of things, through their inspired speech, or through their laudable deeds, were like bright stars to their contemporaries; but what is most important – the spiritual roots of these phenomena, the light that illuminated those elect ones, the power that inspired them, the motivation for their great deeds – we can hardly guess. The mortal eye perceives only the dial of time, not the clockwork that moves the hour hands.[23]

In the second part of his monograph on magnetism and somnambulism, Passavant sketched its historical antecedents among the Israelites, Indians,

---

[22] Jung, *The Red Book*, Liber Primus, vol. ii, cap. i.
[23] Passavant, *Untersuchungen über den Lebensmagnetismus*, 271–272. Generally on Passavant and his importance, see Baier, *Meditation und Moderne*, vol. i, 210–218.

Greeks and Romans, Nordic peoples, and in Christianity. In what sounds like a far echo of Augustine he emphasized that Christianity "should not be seen as a new doctrine," and hence cannot be compared with any other historical religion, but was the fullest and purest manifestation of "the absolute and eternal religion."[24]

The most influential and representative "magnetic historiographer" from the German Romantic period was, however, the Tyrolean physician Joseph Ennemoser (1787–1854).[25] Raised in a pious Roman Catholic environment, as a young man he traveled through Italy and Austria but returned to Innsbruck to study physics and medicine. In 1809 he took part in the Tyrolean war of liberation against France and Bayern, and after some further peregrinations ended up in Berlin, where he continued his medical studies under Fichte, Reil (the inventor of the ganglionic theory), and other major authorities on mesmerism including Christoph Wilhelm Hufeland and Karl Christian Wolfart. After further military adventures – he was rewarded for his courage with an iron cross – in 1814 he returned to Berlin to finish his studies in medicine. In the following years he worked on his large history of magnetism, published in 1819,[26] and in the same year was appointed professor in the medical faculty of the University of Bonn – the center of German Romantic *Naturphilosophie*. From 1837 on he worked as a physician, first in Innsbruck and from 1841 to his death in Munich, during which time he cultivated his contacts with thinkers like Kerner and Schubert. A completely reworked version of his history of magnetism appeared in 1844 under the new title *Geschichte der Magie*, and it is on this work that I will further concentrate.[27]

In Chapter 2, we saw that the earliest attempts at a historical conceptualization of "Western esotericism" emerged from the anti-apologeticism of Jacob Thomasius, in the form of Colberg's Protestant heresiological construct of "Platonic-Hermetic Christianity" and Brucker's history of "philosophia sectaria." From this perspective, the domain as a whole was interpreted as the continuation of pagan religion concealed as Christianity. Against these Protestant and Enlightenment approaches, the Roman Catholic and Romantic physician Ennemoser now presented a history

---

[24] *Ibid.*, 413. My reference is again to Augustine, *Retractationes* I.12.3 (see Chapter 1, page 9).
[25] For Ennemoser's biography, see Boegner, "Joseph Ennemosers Leben und Werk"; de Rachewiltz, *Joseph Ennemoser*. His anthropology has been analyzed in detail by Schweizer, *Anthropologie der Romantik*, 610–693.
[26] Ennemoser, *Der Magnetismus*.
[27] Ennemoser, *Geschichte der Magie*. A systematic comparison with the first version of 1819 would be extremely interesting, but because the final 1844 edition (and its English translation of 1854) has been much more influential, I must here concentrate on the latter.

based on entirely different foundations: his ambition was to show that magnetic phenomena and somnambulic states had been central to the development of human consciousness since the beginning of history. The question of platonic or pagan influences on Christianity played no structural role in his story; but in line with the general shift of emphasis highlighted in Chapter 3, science and natural philosophy had become the basic framework. In sharp contrast with Enlightenment naturalism or positivism, however, Ennemoser's Romantic/mesmerist *Naturphilosophie* was based upon a concept of "living nature" (Faivre) permeated by invisible, occult, "mysterious and incalculable powers" (Weber). He emphasized that these powers were neither supernatural nor demonic in origin, as claimed by traditional Christianity, but no superstitious illusions either, as claimed by Enlightenment rationalism: rather, they should be seen as manifestations of the "inner" and more profound nightside of nature, that reveals itself only when "daylight consciousness," dominated by the rational brain and the exterior senses, is temporarily suppressed. It is important to realize how easily such a thesis harmonized with the pietist sensibilities that had been cultivated in German culture since the seventeenth century. Somnambulic states were extremely similar to the "divine ecstasies" (*göttliche Entzückungen*) that had been highlighted by Spener with reference to the apostle Paul, and criticized as *Schwärmerei* or "enthusiasm" by opponents; and already Colberg had emphasized the tendency of the "enthusiasts" to distinguish each and every thing into "external" and "internal" (the Inner Church, inner word, inner heaven, and so on).[28] Add to this the evident dependence of Romantic mesmerism and *Naturphilosophie* on the German traditions of Paracelsianism and Christian theosophy, and it is clear that in Ennemoser's history of magic, we have the "Hermetic-Platonic" answer to Colberg and Brucker.

Ennemoser's understanding of *Magie* or *Magismus* comes straight out of the Renaissance tradition of *magia naturalis* understood as a *prisca magia*, obviously including its emphasis on the classic concept of ἰδιότητες ἄρρητοι (which had already included magnetism in antiquity) or occult qualities in the wider context of *philosophia occulta*. He never gives a sharp definition of magic, but clearly presents it as the "ancient wisdom" as such, referring to it as the "sum of all secret wisdom," and adopting the conventional distinction between true divine magic and evil or superstitious *goeteia* (*Zauberei*, or sorcery).[29] The most significant innovation lies

---

[28] See Chapter 2, page 111.
[29] Ennemoser, *Geschichte der Magie*, 65–66 (including the terminology of "white" versus "black" magic).

in his emphasis – which announces the progressive psychologization of mesmerism through the nineteenth century – that the true magic "lies in the most secret and innermost powers of the mind."[30] Suggesting a notion of progress "from magic to science" while adapting it to his own ends, Ennemoser states that the genuinely scientific study of these powers began only with Mesmer, and hence his history of magic proper is restricted to the previous, pre-scientific stage.[31] His emphasis on the mind is evident in his general introduction "on magic and its parts in general," which is dominated by three long chapters about visions, dreams, and prophecy/divination (*das Wahrsagen*) as the central manifestations of "magic": although Ennemoser believes strongly in action at a distance and the power of mind over matter, and distinguishes between "visionary" (*schauende*) and "active" (*wirkende*) magic,[32] he is ultimately most interested in magic as a means of achieving "higher (or deeper) knowledge" of the world.

Clearly representative of German historiographical approaches in the wake of Herder, Ennemoser thinks of history in terms of the achievements of successive "peoples." He divides it into three parts: the "ancient world" (the Oriental peoples, the Egyptians, the Israelites), the world of the Greeks and Romans, and the "Germanic world" (from the ancient Germans and Nordic peoples through the Middle Ages and the Renaissance, continuing into the present). If one steps back to consider the course of "history as a whole," in a visionary *Gesamtschau*,[33] its events appear to be far from random and can be described in terms of lawful organic development. History then reveals itself as a deeply meaningful drama in several acts: it narrates the story of how, with many twists and turns, the inborn potential of human consciousness slowly but certainly comes to full realization, according to God's providential design.[34] Similar to Lessing's famous *Erziehung des Menschengeschlechts*, Ennemoser's leading metaphor is that of an individual's life: humanity progresses from birth and childhood through adolescence to full maturity. But he also keeps using the metaphor of a tree that develops from its seeds and roots into a trunk that finally bears branches and flowers, and that of a stage drama: at given moments in time, a new people "steps on to the stage of history" to play the part that Providence has written for it. Ennemoser never thinks of "external" events

---

[30] *Ibid.*, xxvii. See also, for example, xix, xxvii, 273–275, 278–281, 752.
[31] Ennemoser's *Geschichte der Magie* was presented as the first part of a larger *Geschichte des thierischen Magnetismus*, but the second part devoted to the "scientific" stage was never published.
[32] For example, *ibid.*, 67, 69, 277.   [33] For example, *ibid.*, 29, 264–267.
[34] For example, *ibid.*, 264–266, 441–442, 467–468.

as causal factors in history: on the contrary, the true cause of any outward "manifestation" always lies in an inward necessity, "essence," or germinal "idea,"[35] and, in true Hegelian fashion, individuals and their actions are ultimately just the instruments through which the World Spirit is realizing itself:

with steady pace, like a succession of a kingdom's dynasties, history marches forward in a chain of peoples [*Völkern*], each one of which, in increasing power and at ever greater length, builds upon the ruins of its predecessor to claim world domination and represent the peak of the World Spirit for the length of its existence, until it is ousted by the next.[36]

The most ancient peoples were literally in an infantile state. Humanity still "hung on to nature by the umbilical cord and sat in the Creator's lap":[37] it lived in a barely conscious, dreamlike state of innocence, intimately one with nature. "Magical" states of mind were more common than today, and because man's inner sense, "yet undisturbed by reflection, was still more open to the voice of nature," he lived his life in the peaceful harmony of "the endless depth of an untroubled mind."[38] The presence of divinity was still experienced everywhere in nature, humanity stood under the benevolent guidance of an ideal priesthood, and "God, the Seers, and the Poets" spoke through a superior Ur-language of symbolic images.[39] Ennemoser has to admit that there was also "superstition and idolatry," but hardly dwells on it: "Faith, love and obedience were everywhere the pillars."[40]

Because Ennemoser sees magic as a universal phenomenon rooted in natural human abilities, he does not trace it back to Persia but emphasizes its presence throughout the ancient Orient, including India and China.[41] His long discussions of magic among the oriental peoples focus on ecstatic visionary states and healing arts practiced in temples by a spiritually enlightened priesthood. Ennemoser argues that the ancient forms of temple healing were based upon a "natural science" whose basic principles were the same as those of modern mesmerism.[42] The "secret doctrines" (*Geheimlehren*) concerning such practices were preserved by priestly elites and transmitted through mystery initiations and mythical narratives. Egypt represents the highest development of magic during this first, oriental

---

[35] For example, *ibid.*, 45–46, 260–263, 357, 479, 705.
[36] *Ibid.*, 706 (quoting Carl Friedrich Haug, *Allgemeine Geschichte* [1841], without page no.).
[37] *Ibid.*, 300.   [38] *Ibid.*, 32–33.   [39] *Ibid.*, 41–52.
[40] *Ibid.*, 46 (cf. 65 about the necessary qualities of the ancient sages: "Justice, truth and a spirit of service").
[41] *Ibid.*, 64–68 (including criticism of Brucker), 300, 303.   [42] *Ibid.*, 281–399.

period, and it is from here that many later Greek philosophers derived much of their wisdom.[43] Ultimately, however, the great oriental cultures had no future, because they lacked any sense of history and development: Ennemoser compares them with a mummy, whose body has neither decayed nor grown and developed through the centuries.[44] There was, however, one exception. The people of Israel were destined to become the oriental "root" or "stem" from which humanity would grow through adolescence to maturity:

In the ancient, true sense of the word, Judaism is the real tree of life of the inner, genetically progressing development of culture. All the other pagan peoples with their various religious systems are twigs torn off from the great tree of life: although they vegetate, they are capable of no inner development [*Wachsthum*]. Judaism is the real Mysterium, which in Christianity attained the ideal state of sanctity and reunion with God [*Gottesvereinigung*].[45]

The Jews, with their forward-looking mentality, developed a new kind of magic based upon a humble reliance on divine grace rather than the *hubris* of human autonomy.[46] Since Ennemoser always emphasizes "inner" processes rather than external causality, it is easy for him to avoid a dependence of Judaism on pagan Egypt: although they spent so much time in that country, the Jews adopted very little of its magical traditions.[47] The role of kabbalah in Ennemoser's narrative remains somewhat unclear: he discusses it not in his chapter on "the Old Covenant" (which concentrates on dreams, visions, and trances in the Old Testament), but in the introductory parts of his book,[48] and his understanding of the topic appears to be based entirely on Franz Joseph Molitor's famous *Philosophie der Geschichte oder über die Tradition* (1827–1839), which is quoted extensively.[49] In line with this source, Ennemoser hardly bothers to differentiate between Jewish and Christian manifestations: to explain what kabbalah is all about, he freely refers to such authorities as Reuchlin, Knorr von Rosenroth, Paracelsus, Böhme, Pordage, Pasqually, Saint-Martin, Henry More, Schelling, and von Baader.

---

[43] *Ibid.*, 222–226, 364–366.   [44] *Ibid.*, 282, cf. 264.

[45] *Ibid.*, 62. For the idea of pagan religions "breaking off" from the main trunk, see also 120–122 about the Sons of Noah, where Ennemoser quotes Jacob Böhme as the key to understanding the "true development of history." The descendants of Ham are the worst of the worst: "Nowhere does one find such spiritual numbness, such a coarse soul and such alienation from God [*Gottesverlassenheit*] as among the black race of Africa and, as seems certain, among the wild tribes of South America and Australia that were transported from there" (123).

[46] *Ibid.*, 429–432.   [47] *Ibid.*, 426.   [48] *Ibid.*, 71–96.

[49] *Ibid.*, 72–85. On Molitor's many connections with contemporary Christian theosophy and *Naturphilosophie*, see Koch, *Franz Joseph Molitor*.

The central event in Ennemoser's history of consciousness is the appearance of Jesus Christ, through whom Judaism fulfills its historical destiny: that of giving birth to the "absolute religion," which is limited no longer to just one people but brings together humanity as a whole.[50] Through another instrument of Providence, Alexander the Great, the political foundations for this unity had already been created, and the capital of Alexandria became the nodal point for the further development of magic. Ennemoser's discussions of Greek culture demonstrate how strongly he associates the Greeks with myth, rather than with rational philosophy: for him, Greek culture is essentially "poetic," which means that it is thoroughly "magical."[51] With constant reference to the physicist and chemist Johann Salomo Christoph Schweigger and his influential *Einleitung in die Mythologie* (1836), he argues that myth uses the "poetry of nature" to speak about natural forces:[52] symbols are "archetypal [*urbildliche*] representations of how the spirit reveals itself, and truer than the knowledge of systematic reflection."[53] The true source of poetry is nature herself:

For Nature is essentially poetic, higher and deeper than anything of which human fantasy is capable; in her wondrous manifestations she is the expression, by means of images, of the divine creations; a voice of God, to which man should give attention, in order to be aware of the wonders that occur all the time in the world around him. Only the faithful observer and worshipper of Nature, who traces her signs and listens to her voices, gets to know the hidden laws of Nature . . . while the rest of the world, as if half asleep, gets ever more alienated from the divine and sinks away in illusion and superstition. That is why all the great natural scientists have always been truly pious people; that is why the magnetic clairvoyant, waking up in sleep from the daylight dream, through his deeper insight into the secret workings of Nature and her symbols breaks out in ecstatic admiration, in poetic utterings and songs of praise – just as in the poetic time of beginnings, when knowledge about Nature, poetry, and religion were still one.[54]

Flourishing in Alexandria, neoplatonic "eclecticism" was the essential medium through which all the magical traditions of the declining pagan world were transmitted to Christianity.[55] In evaluating this phenomenon positively, as a crucial step in the continuation of ancient magical wisdom,

---

[50] Ennemoser, *Geschichte der Magie*, 461.
[51] *Ibid.*, 484: "Das ganze Griechenthum ist eine lebendige Magie . . . denn das Griechenthum ist durchaus poetischer Natur."
[52] *Ibid.*, 616–703. On Schweigger's work, see von Engelhardt, "Naturforschung als Mythologie und Mission."
[53] Ennemoser, *Geschichte der Magie*, 621.   [54] *Ibid.*, 635–636.
[55] *Ibid.*, 599–601, and cf. 714–715.

Ennemoser integrates the *philosophia perennis* into a novel framework of providentialist evolutionism.

Ennemoser states that Christianity's task was to "disenchant the world" while "restoring the true magic,"[56] and this may sound puzzling unless one is familiar with the specifics of German terminology. *Entzauberung* uses the term *Zauberei*, conventionally translated as "sorcery" and associated with the negative counterpart of natural magic: the idolatrous and superstitious practices known as *goeteia*. In the final part of his book, Ennemoser traces the history of true magic (*Magie*) – that is to say, the natural magic based on magnetism – in what he sees as the "Germanic" period, but much of his attention goes to its negative counterpart: the various forms of demonic or idolatrous superstition of the Middle Ages, culminating in the witchcraft craze. In these discussions, his essentially scientific agenda becomes more and more evident. It is clear to Ennemoser that belief in witchcraft was a tragic mass delusion, and he does not want to spend much time on phenomena that may be associated with "magic" but cannot easily be interpreted in terms of magnetism, such as "spirit-conjurors and exorcists, treasure-diggers and alchemical goldmakers, astrological and hermetic mystagogues like the Rosicrucians etc., horoscope-makers, Illuminati and cartomancers, necromancers, and mirror-prophets etc."[57] He does devote some discussion to Christian theosophers known for their ecstatic or trance-like states, like John Pordage, Thomas Bromley, Antoinette Bourignon, Jane Leade, Pierre Poiret, and Emanuel Swedenborg, but his ambivalence is obvious: he admits that most of what they do pertains to magic in the good sense, but feels he has to warn against the risk of getting lost "in the fanatical darkness of spiritual adepts."[58] Not surprisingly, the true lineage of post-medieval magic up to Mesmer begins with the physicians Paracelsus and the elder van Helmont, continuing from there to authors like Agrippa, Fludd, Campanella, Kircher (important because of his work on the magnet) plus a range of Paracelsians, and ending with Gassner, Cagliostro and Swedenborg in the eighteenth century. However, Ennemoser ends his book with "the arch-magus in the true sense," who has gained a deeper insight into "the life and spirit of humanity" than anyone else: the "true German and Christian theosopher" Jacob Böhme.[59] Now that Böhme's work has been rediscovered[60] and Mesmer has put "magic" on a scientific foundation, Enlightenment rationalism will soon prove to be a transitory phenomenon, and we can look towards the future with the greatest confidence:

---

[56] *Ibid.*, 709.   [57] *Ibid.*, 836.   [58] *Ibid.*, 879.   [59] *Ibid.*, 966.
[60] On the rediscovery of Böhme in German Romanticism, see, for example, Viatte, *Sources occultes*; Benz, *Sources mystiques*; Mayer, *Jena Romanticism*; Magee, *Hegel and the Hermetic Tradition*.

The ancient Orient . . . appears to us, so to speak, as a living image of the primitive childhood of the past. The Graeco-Roman world was a fleeting phenomenon, like the contemporary moment, but an endless future still lies ahead for the German spirit. The history of the world so far has merely provided it with the elements for an endless spiritual activity. Therefore, if the Orient has often been compared with childhood, the time of the Greeks and Romans with the living movement and vitality of the adolescent, and the Germanic one with mature manhood, this comparison is true insofar as with German history, maturity is only just beginning: Germanhood has a whole new future ahead of it, first to complete its own formation, and then to become a leader and teacher of the peoples and the times . . . [T]he Greeks and Romans were just the momentary means of transmission between old and new; and the Orient, already sunk into stagnation and into the night of the past, is dreaming in a thousand-year sleep of death, until one day, stirred up by the new Germanic spirit of the future, it will wake up to fresh new life again.[61]

This must suffice as an overview of Ennemoser's German Romantic vision. Its importance for the general argument of this book has to do with no fewer than three innovative features: (1) his use of *mesmerism/somnambulism* as the heuristic "key" for tracing the history of magic, (2) his *evolutionist/ providentialist* vision, and (3) the *religionist* nature of his approach in general.

The first point stands in stark contrast with previous historiographies of "Western esotericism," which had concentrated essentially on philosophical or religious ideas and opinions, and had been concerned with the history of the true religious doctrine or the conflict between pagan or heretical concepts and biblical theology. None of that was of any importance to Ennemoser: his concern was, quite simply, to show that the phenomena of magnetism and somnambulic trance were nothing new but had existed since the earliest childhood of humanity. In making that claim, he became the chief pioneer of a new genre of "occult historiography." Within ten years, his book was published in an English translation,[62] and, by that

---

[61] Ennemoser, *Geschichte der Magie*, 264–265.

[62] Ennemoser's history was translated in 1854 by William Howitt, as *History of Magic*, with an appendix devoted to stories of "apparitions, dreams, second sight, somnambulism, predictions, divination, witchcraft, vampires, fairies, table-turning, and spirit-rapping" compiled by his wife Mary (on this remarkable couple and their work, see Oppenheim, *The Other World*, 36–38). Ennemoser became one of the most frequently plagiarized sources of Helena P. Blavatsky's *Isis Unveiled*: with no fewer than 107 passages, Emmette Coleman ("Sources of Madame Blavatsky's Writings," 356) ranked him second place, after the 134 passages from Dunlap's *Sod: The Son of Man*. For the influence of Ennemoser on Blavatsky, see also Baier, *Meditation und Moderne*, vol. 1, 258–261; and for the more general influence of German mesmerism on occultism, see Baier, *Meditation und Moderne*, vol. 1, 277–282. The relation between German Romantic mesmerism and Blavatsky, by mediation of English authors who had studied the sources in the original language, deserves further study: in *The*

time, the Scottish lawyer John Campbell Colquhoun – who had studied in Germany and was deeply familiar with the tradition of *Naturphilosophie* – had already published his own *History of Magic, Witchcraft, and Animal Magnetism* in two volumes (1851).[63] Along very similar lines as Ennemoser, he traced the history of magnetism a.k.a. magic from the Chaldaean *Magi* to Mesmer, but without the heavy evolutionist/providentialist slant. In the "Waste Land" of the later nineteenth century, his book was one among the very few that made it possible for readers to place the various manifestations of "the occult" within a reasonably clear historical narrative from antiquity to the present.

In the last decade of the century, we find essentially the same approach in a series of large and erudite works on the history of "occultism" and the "occult sciences" published by an elusive private scholar, Carl Kiesewetter (1854–1895).[64] Similar to A. E. Waite in the anglophone world, Kiesewetter's impressive erudition made him into the virtually unavoidable German authority for history of "the occult." In the Introduction to his first large volume, *Geschichte des neueren Occultismus* (1891), he defined "occultism" as concerned with "all those phenomena of nature and the soul [*des Natur- und Seelenlebens*] that have not yet been generally recognized by official science [and] whose causes are hidden from the senses."[65] In other words: writing the history of "occultism" meant tracing how earlier generations had practiced and theorized about the "psychic" or "paranormal" phenomena that were currently the object of parapsychology or psychical research. Thus, for example, Kiesewetter's first chapter focused on Agrippa's ideas about such topics as telepathy, dreams, clairvoyance, hypnosis, ecstasy,

---

Theosophical Enlightenment, Joscelyn Godwin has highlighted Blavatsky's debt to Enlightenment mythography, but to understand her evolutionism and her pervasive references to the mesmeric fluid, sources such as Wilkins' Ennemoser translation or the works of John Campbell Colquhoun (see text) may be equally important. In 1836, the latter had even published a study of animal magnetism under the title *Isis Revelata*!

[63] On Colquhoun, see also Baier, *Meditation und Moderne*, vol. 1, 212, 245, 258, 282.

[64] Almost nothing is known about Kiesewetter's life and career. He lived with his mother in a small town, Meiningen, and was a regular contributor to the important occultist journal *Die Sphinx*. Max Dessoir remembered him as a large bald man with a red face, who was "anything but an ascetic or navel-gazer" but, rather, "was living quite a wild life" and had no patience for pious upper-class ladies swooning over the occult: "Remarkable about Kiesewetter is that he was faithful like a child when it came to ancient manuscripts, but a stubborn and mocking skeptic about reports from his own time" (*Buch der Erinnerung*, 129–130). Emil Bock claims that Kiesewetter "ate and drank himself to death" (*Rudolf Steiner*, 173–174), but according to a persistent rumor that I have been unable to confirm or disconfirm, his premature death at age forty-one was caused by a failed experiment with the witches' salve.

[65] Kiesewetter, *Geschichte des neueren Okkultismus*, 13. The formulation echoes the third objective of the Theosophical Society, of which Kiesewetter was a member: "To investigate unexplained laws of Nature and the powers latent in man."

the magical power of the will, and the mesmeric or magnetic life force; and he went on to trace these themes through essentially the same series of sixteenth- to eighteenth-century authors that had been discussed by Ennemoser. But he also discussed Ennemoser himself, and continued with nineteenth-century spiritualism and psychical research up to and including Carl du Prel. After three smaller books on the Faust figure, John Dee, and Mesmer himself (all published in 1893), Kiesewetter began to push his investigations ever farther back into the past, resulting in a large volume on the history of alchemy, astrology, and magic (*Die Geheimwissenschaften*, 1895) and another one on the occult in antiquity (*Der Occultismus des Altertums*, vol. I, 1896). Kiesewetter's books became standard references in the field, at least in the German-speaking world, and deserve more study in their own right, but for our present concerns we can dispense with a detailed analysis. It suffices that, similar to A. E. Waite's volumes, they are essentially works of erudition that give the reader access to otherwise obscure materials, often by means of lengthy quotations; and that, like Ennemoser's and Colquhoun's, their intention is to provide contemporary research into the "paranormal" with a solid historical pedigree. From such a perspective, "Western esotericism" was no longer understood in terms of a syncretism between pagan/platonic ideas and biblical Christianity, but as comprising the sum of historical evidence for the mysterious powers of nature and the human mind prematurely discarded by the Enlightenment.

Moving on to the second innovative feature of Ennemoser's *Geschichte der Magie*: as far as the history of "Western esotericism" is concerned, it was the exemplary and pioneering example of a new type of historiography typical of the Romantic period. It was neither a narrative of decline or continuity of the "ancient wisdom" (as in the *prisca theologia* and *philosophia perennis* tradition); nor was it an exercise in intellectual history, based on the assumption that to understand the ideas of specific authors or currents, one must put them in their historical context and investigate the influences upon them (as in the histories of Colberg and Brucker). Contrary to the former approach, Ennemoser presented his readers with a teleological narrative of spiritual progress by means of evolution, which endowed the very fact of historical change and development with profound spiritual meaning and import; and contrary to the latter, he rejected "external" causation in favor of the "inner" drives and dynamics of divine providence, or God's plan with humanity. As far as academic research is concerned, historiographies of this type would only very gradually lose their credibility along with the general decline of Romanticism and German idealism during and after the nineteenth century. They were, however, adopted with great enthusiasm by occultist authors, and have remained popular in esoteric and New Age circles to the present day.[66]

For the third innovative feature of Ennemoser's work, it is useful to look back at the discussion of Gottfried Arnold's history of Christianity in Chapter 2. As we have seen, it was grounded in a radical pietist rejection of sterile dogmatic dispute in favor of direct spiritual experience. Following exactly the same logic, Ennemoser attacked the "cerebral thinking" of the self-appointed "schoolmasters" and "policemen" of reason,[67] with their endless quarreling over mere words and abstractions. Both authors agreed that what mattered in history was not the dead letter but the living spirit, not outward doctrines but inward experience, not the knowledge of the brain but the knowledge of the heart. This similarity is not accidental, but reflects a structural commonality grounded in German pietist sensibilities. Arnold's historiography was based upon the concept of a radical incommensurability between "Athens" (reason) and "Jerusalem" (faith), which simply do not speak the same language and share no common ground; and the same logic of incommensurability governs Ennemoser's contrast between the discursive "daytime" consciousness of the brain and the experiential "nightside" consciousness of the soul. Arnold argued that faith had nothing in common with reason; and similarly, Ennemoser saw no point in using the language of the brain to speak about the truths of the soul. Both authors would have readily agreed that when it comes to spiritual realities, critical debate is useless: there is simply no alternative to direct spiritual experience.

As a result, neither of our two authors was able (or willing) to look at historical developments from the perspective of social context, external influences on the genesis or development of ideas, or contingent factors: all those were clearly irrelevant or, at best, of secondary importance. But nevertheless, both claimed to be writing history. Above, I referred to this peculiar combination as typical of "religionism," and it should now be clear

---

[66] On the importance of Romantic evolutionism to nineteenth-century esotericism, see Hanegraaff, *New Age Religion*, 462–482, and cf. 302–330 for the point that even New Age visions of historical evolution still tend to focus on a "Platonic Orientalist" lineage through Egypt and the Essenes to Christianity: "the Christian west is consistently highlighted as the center stage for those historical events which have been essential to humanity's spiritual evolution" (*ibid.*, 303). For Ennemoser's influence on H. P. Blavatsky's evolutionist theosophy, see above, n. 62. On the role of Romantic evolutionism in Jung's work, see text (below, pp. 284, 292). A particularly clear example of latter-day Romantic (neo-Hegelian) evolutionism is Ken Wilber's transpersonal historiography in *Up From Eden* (1983).

[67] For invectives against such thinking, see, for example, Ennemoser, *Geschichte der Magie*, VII–X, 36, 63, 265, 271.

that Ennemoser's work represents an important new development in the history of that phenomenon after Arnold. The principal difference between the two is Ennemoser's evolutionism, which was really something new. Arnold's perspective had allowed for no real development of "Christianity" at all, because absolute truth has no history; Ennemoser, however, could claim that whereas the truths of nature and the soul were indeed eternal, man's capacity to *understand* them had developed dramatically over the course of the centuries. A very similar vision would be defended in the twentieth century from the perspective of psychology.

THE ARCHETYPE OF ERANOS:
CARL GUSTAV JUNG AND THE WESTERN UNCONSCIOUS

Around 1930, a wealthy woman of Dutch descent, Olga Fröbe-Kapteyn (1881–1962), began organizing summer conferences in her beautiful villa in Ascona on the shore of the Lago Maggiore, Switzerland. Originally influenced by modern theosophy and other forms of contemporary esotericism,[68] these gatherings quickly evolved towards an academic format, and became known as the Eranos meetings from 1933 on.[69] The lectures were published in an annual book series, the Eranos Year Books, edited by Fröbe-Kapteyn until her death in 1962, when the organization and editorship passed to Rudolf Ritsema and Adolf Portmann. Eranos meetings are still being organized today, by several competing organizations, but the original series came to an end in 1988, when Ritsema decided to abandon

---

[68] For the influences on Fröbe-Kapteyn, see Hakl, *Verborgene Geist*, 33–79. Her lifelong fascination with myth, symbolism, and the mystery religions of antiquity seems to have been kindled by her friendship with the Christian esthete and mystagogue Ludwig Derleth, who introduced her to the Romantic mythographers Friedrich Creuzer and Johann Jacob Bachofen (Helbing, "Ludwig und Anna Maria Derleth," 70; and extensive discussion in Hakl, *Verborgene Geist*, 38–51). She was also interested in Vedanta, and had contact with the Ramakrishna movement and the Theosophical Society, but disliked the bohemian lifestyle of nearby Monte Verità. Fröbe-Kapteyn's first summer conferences were dominated by the theosophist Alice Bailey, who left in 1933 when "the place was overrun by German professors and the whole tone and quality of the place altered" (Bailey, *Unfinished Autobiography*, 225).

[69] By far the best-informed history of Eranos was published in German by Hans Thomas Hakl in 2001 (*Verborgene Geist von Eranos*), and I am grateful to Dr. Hakl for granting me access to the expanded and updated English translation, due for publication in the near future. Hakl describes a gradual development from the early "esoteric" meetings, with a prominent presence of Alice Bailey, towards the eventual academic format, and calls attention to the importance of Graf Hermann Keyserling's *Schule der Weisheit* in Darmstadt as a model for Eranos (*Verborgene Geist*, 33–99, 101). An indispensable source alongside Hakl's work is McGuire, *Bollingen*. A very useful study focused on Jung, Eliade, and Campbell is Ellwood, *Politics of Myth*. The much-noted study by Wasserstrom, *Religion after Religion*, concentrates on the postwar period dominated by Eliade, Corbin, and Scholem. For a particularly evocative overview of Eranos in its heyday, see the thematic issue of the Swiss illustrated monthly *Du* (vol. 15, April 1955).

the existing format.[70] The history of Eranos may be divided up into two halves, before and after the end of World War II. The first period might well be called the "Jung Era": without any doubt, the Swiss psychologist was the dominant figure, next to a range of other important thinkers including the indologist Heinrich Zimmer, the theologian Friedrich Heiler, the historian of religion Jakob Wilhelm Hauer, the philosopher Martin Buber, the Islamicist Louis Massignon, and scholars of mythology such as Walter F. Otto and Karl Kerényi. As a new development, the second, postwar period began by a broadening of scope, with the invitation of natural scientists such as the biologist Adolf Portmann and the physicist Erwin Schrödinger; but the heyday came in the 1950s and 1960s, when Eranos attracted a truly remarkable series of scholars of religion from all over the world, many of whom became celebrities. Among the most famous names are the pioneer of Jewish kabbalah Gershom Scholem, the Islamicist Henry Corbin, and the scholar of religion Mircea Eliade, next to the Japanese zen Buddhist D. T. Suzuki, the historian of gnosticism Gilles Quispel, the second-generation Jungian Erich Neumann, the phenomenologist of religion Gerardus van der Leeuw, the historian of religion Raffaele Pettazzoni, the historian of Christianity Ernst Benz, the theologian Paul Tillich, the scholar of symbolic anthropology Gilbert Durand, the psychologist James Hillman, and, last but not least, the pioneering scholar of Western esotericism Antoine Faivre.

Formulated in the most general terms, a willingness to take *myth and symbolism* seriously and explore their relevance to history and modern culture is what the Eranos meetings were all about. However, against the background of my conclusions at the end of the previous chapter, these basic concepts should not be considered in isolation or understood according to narrow scholarly definitions. In practice, they were understood as intimately connected with a whole range of other terms that shared one thing in common: the fact that they had ended up in the "waste-basket" category of exclusion against which the Enlightenment had been defining its own identity as rational and scientific. In the wake of this process of identity-formation by means of binary simplification, it had become practically impossible to speak about "myth" or "symbolism" without touching upon, or at least suggesting, things associated with "mysticism," "esotericism," "magic," or "the occult" as well. This post-Enlightenment tendency of conflating all terms and categories that were seen as contrary to "science and rationality" into one diffuse counter-category had a paradoxical

---

[70] For all the details about this change of direction and later developments, see Hakl, *Verborgene Geist*, 359–373.

result: it made the domain very hard to pin down because no single term seemed to cover the whole, but it nevertheless produced a clear sense of coherence and direction as well. Eranos, in other words, was concerned with an area of research that might be difficult or even impossible to define in positive terms, but was easily recognized by its *alterity* with respect to Enlightenment rationality and modern science.[71]

The core speakers of Eranos appear to have been animated by feelings of urgency and grave intellectual responsibility, occasionally leading even to a sense of messianic vocation to resolve "the crisis of the modern world." But what was the nature of that crisis, and what was the danger? Basic to the characteristic Eranos perspective, I suggest, was a conviction that the representatives of Enlightenment and positivism had committed a serious error of judgment in assuming that just by dumping "myth," "magic," or "the irrational" into the waste-basket of history, one could make them go away. In 1871, in the midst of the positivist era, Edward Burnett Tylor had still been supremely confident in that regard: "the growth of myth has been checked by science, it is dying of weights and measures, of proportions and specimens – it is not only dying, but half dead, and students are anatomising it."[72] Just a few decades later, however, James Frazer had expressed a very different sentiment:

It is beneath our feet – and not very far beneath them – here in Europe at the present day . . . This universal faith, this truly Catholic creed, is a belief in the efficacy of magic . . . [T]he permanent existence of such a solid layer of savagery beneath the surface of society, and unaffected by the superficial changes of religion and culture [is] a standing menace to civilization. We seem to move on a thin crust which may at any moment be rent by the subterranean forces slumbering below.[73]

Less than fifteen years later, the abyss had opened, and naive confidence in rationality, civilization, and progress was being ground to pieces in the trenches of the World War. These traumatic events, and their worrying

---

[71] This, I suggest, is why the two main scholars of Eranos both seem to agree about its "esoteric" nature although their understandings of that term are completely different. Hakl defines it as concerned with a process of individuation focused on achieving self-knowledge or gnosis (*Verborgene Geist*, 21). Wasserstrom strongly associates Eranos with "esoterism" as well, but never defines the term: sometimes he seems to adopt Corbin's understanding of esotericism as concerned with "the reintegration of the human being in symbols" (*Religion after Religion*, 37–38), sometimes he associates it with Traditionalist concepts in the lineage of Guénon (*ibid.*, 45–46, 49–50), sometimes with Romantic theosophy (*ibid.*, 55), sometimes simply with secrecy and concealment (*ibid.*, 59), sometimes with an "aggressively antidemocratic bias" and "a narrowly exclusivist elitism" (*ibid.*, 351 n. 11), and sometimes he just seems to assume the term is self-explanatory (*ibid.*, 36, 147).

[72] Tylor, *Primitive Culture*, vol. 1, 317. On Tylor's ambivalence about "mythopoeic" thought, and its implications for his theoretical framework, see Hanegraaff, "Emergence of the Academic Science of Magic."

[73] Frazer, *Golden Bough*, vol. 1, 235–236.

implications with respect to the European dream of modernization, civilization, and progress, had a deep impact on intellectuals across the entire political spectrum.[74] Arguing from the perspective of a psychologist, Carl Gustav Jung, the foundational figure of Eranos, concluded that the suppressed "Other" of Western rationality was never going to vanish and disappear because its ultimate source was the human unconscious itself. On the collective as well as on the individual level, the "primitive" or "savage" energies of the unconscious psyche could be kept under the surface for some time, but their pent-up energy might erupt and wreak havoc again at any moment.[75] Some of Jung's contemporaries, such as Ludwig Klages, Alfred Schuler, or Stefan George, in fact embraced such a prospect with enthusiasm, because they hated instrumental rationality and bourgeois society and hoped for its violent destruction.[76] On the other side of the political spectrum, Marxist critics like Horkheimer and Adorno associated myth and the irrational with dangerous regression and barbarism, but finally reached the worrying conclusion that it could not be destroyed because it was part of the dialectics of Enlightenment itself.[77] Somewhere between these two poles, many thinkers saw myth as a deeply ambivalent phenomenon: in the great novels of Thomas Mann, for example, myth and the irrational are recognized as the very sources of life and creativity, which, however, manifest themselves as demonic forces of death and destruction if they are embraced at the expense of "humanity."[78] In spite of their

---

[74] On the pervasive "sense of crisis" in German intellectual culture after the loss of World War I, see Ringer, *Decline of the German Mandarins*, 241–434. For an interesting analysis focused on Eranos, see Wasserstrom, *Religion after Religion*, 112–124.

[75] Concerning the use of geological metaphors, similar to Frazer's, cf. Richard Noll's discussion of "Bodenbeschaffenheit" (*Jung Cult*, 95–103); cf. Ellwood, *Politics of Myth*, 44.

[76] On Ludwig Klages, Alfred Schuler, and the "Cosmic Circle" in Munich, see, for example, Plumpe, "Alfred Schuler und die 'Kosmische Runde'"; Faber, "Schwabinger Imperatorenstreit"; Müller, *Kosmik*. For Stefan George and his remarkable influence on German culture in the interbellum, see the important biography by Norton, *Secret Germany*, which emphasizes the metaphorical violence against bourgeois society and all its values that became increasingly prominent in the work of "the Master" and his disciples.

[77] Horkheimer and Adorno, *Dialectic of Enlightenment*. On the complicated and not simply antithetical relation between critical theory and the kind of *Lebensphilosophie* represented by Klages, see Grossheim, "'Die namenlose Dummheit'."

[78] See, for example, Mann's *Zauberberg*, especially the crucial chapter "Schnee," based upon Nietzsche's opposition of Apollonian and Dionysian, against the background of the protagonist's attempts to find a way for "humanity" between Settembrini's Enlightenment humanitarianism and Naphta's dark Romantic totalitarianism. Whereas *Der Zauberberg* ends in the sudden eruption of violence of World War I, Mann's *Doktor Faustus* describes a composer who buys the spark of true creative genius by selling his soul to the devil, as a metaphor for the descent of Germany into the demonic darkness of the Third Reich. The most extended reflection of Mann's concern with myth, in the dialectical tension between "pagan" Egyptian polytheism and Jewish monotheism, is found in his *Joseph und seine Brüder* (cf. Assmann, *Thomas Mann und Ägypten*).

considerable differences, all these interbellum intellectuals, and many others thinking along similar lines, had recognized something that the Enlightenment had apparently overlooked, ignored, or underestimated: that neither the individual nor the collective was capable of living by "reason" alone. Tylor had been mistaken, and Frazer's fears had been proven correct. If this was true, then what role should be accorded to "myth," "symbolism," and the non-rational (always understood in an inclusive sense) in modern culture and society?

At bottom, this is the question that animated the Eranos meetings and accounts for their remarkable coherence over more than half a century. The answers varied greatly, ranging from an emphasis on the need for achieving some kind of "integration" between the unconscious and conscious layers of the individual and collective psyche (as in Jung) to radical declarations of war against the modern world (as in Corbin). An enormous amount of critical – and less than critical – literature has been devoted to the central figures of Eranos, and they have been the center of scholarly controversies of a particularly emotional kind.[79] In the present section and the next, I will have to limit my discussion strictly to the question of how Eranos should be situated *vis-à-vis* "Western esotericism," and to the influence of its specific perspective on how that field came to be conceptualized and understood after World War II.

Carl Gustav Jung dominated the Eranos approach during the first phase of its existence, but to understand the nature of his contribution, we must begin by recognizing the problem of the "Jung legend."[80] Generations of Jungians have cultivated an idealized, even sanctified image of the Swiss psychologist, paradoxically combining an emphasis on his claim to being a strict empirical scientist with the mysterious and romantic image of Jung as a kind of modern shaman or initiate into numinous mysteries. The latter dimension was based essentially on the famous volume *Memories, Dreams, Reflections* (1962), which was marketed as Jung's autobiography but is in fact a heavily manipulated product of his secretary, Aniela Jaffé.[81]

---

[79] As regards Jung, see, for example, the attacks by Jungians, Jung scholars, and historians of alchemy on Richard Noll, *The Jung Cult* (for example, Shamdasani, *Cult Fictions*; Segal, review of Noll; Tilton, *Quest for the Phoenix*, 18–21). As regards Eliade, a particularly strong example is Daniel Dubuisson's vendetta in *Twentieth Century Mythologies*, 173–288, and *Impostures et pseudo-science*. For controversy over Corbin, see Wasserstrom, *Religion after Religion*, and responses such as Lory, "Note sur l'ouvrage *Religion after Religion*," and Subtelny, "History and Religion."

[80] In spite of their differences, this point is emphasized by Richard Noll (*Jung Cult*, 6, 13–15) as well as Sonu Shamdasani (*Jung and the Making of Modern Psychology*, 1–3).

[81] For the amazing details, see Shamdasani, "Memories, Dreams, Omissions"; *Jung Stripped Bare*, 22–38. On the "sacralization" or "canonization" of Jung in the wake of *Memories, Dreams, Reflections*, see Noll, *Jung Cult*, 13–15; Shamdasani, "Memories, Dreams, Omissions," 116.

Furthermore, what has become known as "Jungian psychology" after the war is often far removed from what Jung had in mind himself, resulting in all kinds of anachronistic distortions when the ideas of contemporary Jungians, including New Age interpretations with little resemblance to the original, are projected back onto the person who supposedly invented them.[82] At the same time, our view of the historical Jung has been heavily compromised by non- or anti-Jungian ideologies as well. Even today, Jung is usually seen primarily from the perspective of his relation to Freud, and the dominant "Freud legend" has pictured him as the renegade student who abandoned psychoanalysis for a speculative worldview more akin to mysticism than to science. In fact, however, Jung was indebted at least as much, and arguably more, to the tradition of William James, Frederic Myers, and his Swiss compatriot Théodore Flournoy.[83] The neglect of this lineage in favor of a Freudocentric one has resulted, as Sonu Shamdasani puts it, in "nothing less than the complete mislocation of Jung and complex psychology in the intellectual history of the twentieth century."[84] Add to this the more sensationalist perceptions of Jung as a *völkisch* racist and antisemite,[85] a thinly disguised occultist,[86] or the guru of a modern cult,[87]

---

[82] Shamdasani, *Jung and the Making of Modern Psychology*, 13–18.

[83] Shamdasani, *Jung and the Making of Modern Psychology*, 11–13; "Misunderstanding Jung," 460–462 (also with reference to the researches of Eugene Taylor); Noll, *Jung Cult*, 31–32; and for a general introduction to Flournoy and "subliminal psychology," see Shamdasani, "Encountering Hélène." The only section in *Memories, Dreams, Reflections* named after an individual is that on Freud, but in the original editorial typescript it was followed by a section on Flournoy and James. In the German edition these authors were still present in appendices, but these were deleted from the English and American edition, thus leaving only Freud (Shamdasani, "Memories, Dreams, Omissions," 121).

[84] Shamdasani, *Jung and the Making of Modern Psychology*, 13; cf. Noll, *Jung Cult*, 43.

[85] On Jung's *völkisch* roots, see Noll, *Jung Cult*, 40–137. Note that Noll is explicit in refuting the "association fallacy" of assuming that since Jung had certain backgrounds in common with National Socialism, this suffices to make him into a fascist or Nazi (*ibid.*, 102–103, 130–133, 135–136). For a refutation of this type of *reductio ad Hitlerum* or *argumentum ad nazium*, and an analysis of its roots in the critical theory of the Frankfurt School, see the excellent article by Fisher, "Fascist Scholars, Fascist Scholarship," 264–271. For the clash between critical theory and Jungian thought, see the interesting study by Evers, *Mythos und Emanzipation*. On Jung and antisemitism, see Maidenbaum, *Jung and the Shadow of Antisemitism*. On Jung and National Socialism, see Lewin, *Jung on War, Politics and Nazi Germany*.

[86] In this regard, everything depends on how one defines one's terms (for a general overview of terminological options, see Hanegraaff, "Occult/Occultism"). If "occultism" is seen as including spiritualism and psychical research (for example Treitel, *Science for the Soul*), then it was certainly a strong influence on Jung. If understood as a historical current that tried to demarcate itself *from* spiritualism (for example Pasi, "Occultism," 1367), then Jung has very little to do with it. In an earlier discussion of Jung, I interpreted his perspective as a Romantic as opposed to an occultist form of esotericism, with reference to a novel definition of occultism introduced by myself (Hanegraaff, *New Age Religion*, 422–423, 500–501).

[87] This was the central thesis of Noll, *Jung Cult*. I find Noll's historical contextualization of Jung's intellectual development much more important than the question of whether or not he or his

and one understands Shamdasani's complaint that "C. G. Jung has almost become completely fictional."[88]

In his acclaimed *Discovery of the Unconscious* (1970), Henri F. Ellenberger created the foundations for a more adequate historical contextualization of the Swiss psychologist and his work. He showed that Jung must be seen as a "late offshoot of Romanticism" who "returns to the unaltered sources of psychiatric romanticism and philosophy of nature."[89] Even more specifically, Jung was a direct twentieth-century descendant of the German Romantic form of mesmerism discussed in the previous section, including its further roots in Paracelsianism and Christian theosophy. For anybody who can recognize the references, and takes the trouble of going back to the German original, this is immediately evident from the opening chapter of the pivotal work that marked the beginning of his mature oeuvre, *Wandlungen und Symbole der Libido* (1912).[90] Titled "On the Two Ways of Thinking," it is based entirely upon the distinction of "daytime" and "nightside" consciousness pioneered by Schubert, Kerner, and his contemporaries. Significantly, the second type is not described as something different *from*, but as a different kind *of* thinking. Jung writes that the dreamlike and associative type was more prominent in antiquity, and resulted in mythology instead of science.[91] The same type of thinking is known to all of us from childhood, and is equally typical of the "lower races, like the negroes."[92] From here, Jung proceeds to draw the famous parallel between ontogenesis and phylogenesis – the psychological development from earliest childhood to maturity is a "repetition" of the development of human consciousness as a whole, from archaic to logical thinking – concluding that our dreams are therefore an avenue towards better understanding of our remote cultural past.[93] Jung's use of this theory

---

followers may have exhibited "cult-like" characteristics. Unfortunately, Noll's historical scholarship is simply discarded along with the "cult"-thesis by his critic Shamdasani, who refuses to even acknowledge his existence in his important *Jung and the Making of Modern Psychology*, and summarily dismisses his historical contributions, without arguments, in *Cult Fictions*, 7–8 and n. 20.

[88] Shamdasani, "Misunderstanding Jung," 459; and cf. Shamdasani, *Jung Stripped Bare*.

[89] Ellenberger, *Discovery of the Unconscious*, 657, and cf. 728–730. For a contextualization "along similar lines, although focused on "mysticism" rather than mesmerism, see Maillard, "'Mystique' de la psyché."

[90] Jung, *Wandlungen*, 7–35 (numbered as chapter II, but chapter I is only a four-page introduction). The English translation in Jung's Collected Works is completely unreliable if one wishes to understand the original text.

[91] *Ibid.*, 21–22.

[92] *Ibid.*, 22–24. This passage was removed from the standard English translation (*Symbols of Transformation*, 21). On Jung and race, cf. Pietikäinen, *C. G. Jung and the Psychology of Symbolic Forms*, 157–165.

[93] *Ibid.*, 25.

is usually explained with reference to Ernst Haeckel;[94] but in fact, we have seen with the example of Joseph Ennemoser that exactly the same parallel between the development of humanity and that of the human individual (modeled on Lessing's *Education of the Human Race*) was already a natural one in early German Romanticism. The idea that myth is a reflection of the archaic "childhood of the human race" was a commonplace, and it was easy for Jung to adopt Herbert Silberer's conclusion that "Myth is the dream of the people – the dream is the myth of the individual."[95]

Hence the basic logic underlying Jung's *Wandlungen* is essentially quite simple. If the interpretation of dreams is the key to psychological healing on the level of the individual, then the interpretation of myths is the key to such healing on the level of the collective. If a healthy development implies that unconscious material be taken seriously and integrated, then it is vitally important for the peoples of modern Europe to take the contents of their own phylogenetic unconscious seriously, so as to integrate rather than repress them. Both on the individual and on the collective levels, failure to do so results in pathology.[96] One sees how naturally the concepts of archetypes and the collective unconscious result from this logic: the images and narratives that we remember as dreams must be based on the same structural patterns as the symbols and myths that are remembered by the human race as a whole. The general assumption underlying this entire parallelism is a Romantic evolutionism extremely similar to Ennemoser's.[97] In both cases, human consciousness is seen as evolving through history from the "lower races" and cultures to the higher ones, and contemporary European/Germanic culture is believed to be its most advanced manifestation so far. However – and it is here that Jung introduces an important element of innovation – this does not mean that it is necessarily healthier. On the contrary: the growth towards maturity means that rational "daytime consciousness" emancipates itself from the dreamlike state of childhood, but this carries the risk of suppressing the latter rather than integrating it harmoniously. The result will be a misbalanced, neurotic culture continually threatened by destructive eruptions of libidinal energy.

[94] Noll, *Jung Cult*, 51–54; Shamdasani, *Jung and the Making of Modern Psychology*, 184; Pietikäinen, *C. G. Jung and the Psychology of Symbolic Forms*, 68–70.

[95] Silberer, "Phantasie und Mythos," 118; Jung, *Wandlungen*, 26 (quotation from Karl Abraham, *Traum und Mythos*).

[96] For excellent examples of this parallelism between the healing of individuals and of the collective, see, for example, Jung, "Bedeutung der Psychologie."

[97] See also Pietikäinen, *C. G. Jung and the Psychology of Symbolic Forms*, 171–180 (with primary reference to Hegel). Pietikäinen notes that the reason for Jung's belief in a "psychological-evolutionary determinism" is not clear (*ibid.*, 171); but Jung had a copy of Ennemoser's *Geschichte der Magie* in his library (Anon., *C. G. Jung Bibliothek Katalog*, 21), and this may well have been his direct source.

We know that Jung was familiar with the literature of German Romantic mesmerism from early on;[98] but in spite of Ellenberger's work, that intellectual milieu still seems *terra incognita* to most scholars of his oeuvre, and the connection has not been explored nearly as seriously as one might expect.[99] This is unfortunate, for precisely this connection provides us with the key to understanding much that might otherwise seem puzzling in Jung's range of interests, including his persistent fascination with "the occult." Jung knew that the somnambulic and "hysterical" patients treated by psychologists like Charcot, Janet, Flournoy, and many others displayed the same kinds of "supranormal" abilities, and reported the same kinds of entranced visions, as had been described already by Justinus Kerner and many other German Romantic mesmerists. He also knew that the phenomena of modern spiritualism had evolved straight out of the same mesmeric tradition, used similar techniques, led to similar trance states, and resulted in similar "paranormal" phenomena and spirit visions. Hence he was bound to consider it bizarre that Freud expected him to set up the sexual theory as a "bulwark" against the "black tide of mud" of occultism: "what Freud seemed to mean by 'occultism'," he objected, "was virtually everything that philosophy and religion, including the rising contemporary science of parapsychology, had learned about the psyche."[100] Jung's insistence on "the occult" therefore cannot be dismissed as of secondary importance, or as just the superficial effect of contemporary fashions: on the contrary, it was central to how he conceived of psychology. As convincingly argued by Sonu Shamdasani, Jung's ambition was not just to create a particular school of psychotherapy, but to establish psychology *in general*, as the fundamental scientific discipline upon which all other disciplines should henceforth be

---

[98] Jung, *Memories, Dreams, Reflections*, 120: "Kant's *Dreams of a Spirit-Seer* came just at the right moment, and soon I also discovered Karl Duprel...I dug up Eschenmayer, Passavant, Justinus Kerner, and Görres, and read seven volumes of Swedenborg." See also Charet, *Spiritualism*, 49 n. 25, 131.

[99] German Romantic mesmerism is as good as absent from Noll's *Jung Cult* (see mainly 146), but his *Aryan Christ* devotes a few pages to Jung–Stilling and Justinus Kerner (32–38). The second part of Shamdasani's impressive *Jung and the Making of Modern Psychology* is titled "Night and Day," but surprisingly ignores the Romantic theory of nightside/daytime consciousness (mesmerism is mentioned only in passing, on 110, 115; Jung's relation to Romanticism as such is briefly discussed, on 166–168). Charet touches upon German Romantic mesmerism briefly (*Spiritualism*, 31–32), but is dependent entirely on Ellenberger and quotes no German sources.

[100] Jung, *Memories, Dreams, Reflections*, 150–151. For background, see Shamdasani, "Encountering Hélène." Jung's dissertation of 1902 (*Zur Psychologie und Pathologie*) was, of course, based entirely on the same perspective. It described the case of a medium, Jung's cousin Hélène Preiswerk, who in fact seems to have copied the behavior and phenomena of Friederike Hauffe from Justinus Kerner's *Seherin von Prevorst*, which Jung had given her to read (Gruber, "Romantische Psychoanalyse?," 350).

based.[101] The conceptual foundation for this universal and encyclopedic project, I suggest, was the German Romantic mesmerist view of the soul and its mysterious powers that has been neglected almost completely by Jung specialists to the present day.

Among other things, this background may help resolve the seeming paradox that the man who appears as a kind of initiate into numinous mysteries in *Memories, Dreams, Reflections* and *The Red Book*, never ceased to insist that he was a strictly empirical scholar. The German Romantic mesmerists insisted that they were exploring facts of consciousness (*Thatsachen*) that belonged to the *natural* order and had nothing to do with "miracles" or the supernatural.[102] If anybody was guilty of neglecting empiricism, they argued, it was the Enlightenment ideologue, who denied the phenomena of mesmerism and somnambulism *a priori*, dismissing them out of hand as superstitious or supernatural illusions instead of taking the trouble to study them first. Jung took the same approach: like William James, he subscribed to a radical empiricism that "concedes no a priori or preconceived limits to what constitutes a 'fact'," and therefore saw psychology as concerned with "the entire field of consciousness including its margins or fringes."[103] Hence, even his most sensational visionary experiences, or encounters with spiritual guides like Philemon, were understood by him within an empirical framework: like the German Romantic mesmerists (but unlike modern theosophists, whom he disliked), he did not see them as attempts to contact supernatural beings or metaphysical realities pertaining to the afterlife, but as demonstrations that the realm of Nature itself included a mysterious *Nachtseite*, now conceptualized as the unconscious, that had been arbitrarily ignored in the wake of the Enlightenment but belonged to the proper domain of scientific investigation.

Returning now to our specific concerns in this chapter: what were the implications of Jung's vision for the Eranos approach to the study of religion, and more specifically for the historical study of what we now call Western esotericism? As already noted, with reference to Shamdasani, Jung believed that psychology should become the foundation of all other disciplines, including history: its role should be "to counter the fragmentation of the sciences, and to provide a basis for a synthesis of all knowledge."[104]

[101] Shamdasani, *Jung and the Making of Modern Psychology*, 15, 18–22.
[102] Hanegraaff, "A Woman Alone," 216; "Versuch," 23–24, with reference to Schubert, *Ansichten*, 2; Kerner, *Seherin von Prevorst*, 40, 73, 174, 284; Kerner, *Geschichte Besessener*, 128–129; von Meyer, "Die Schutzgeister," 160; and Anon. [Kerner?], "Lavater's Äusserungen," 16–17: "Das Wort *Wunder* hat *Alles* verdorben" ("The word *miracle* has spoiled *everything*").
[103] As formulated by Fuller, *Americans and the Unconscious*, 85 (cf. Hanegraaff, *New Age Religion*, 492).
[104] Shamdasani, *Jung and the Making of Modern Psychology*, 22.

Against the trend of increasing specialization, Eranos should be a plat-
form for interdisciplinary collaboration paving the way for such a universal
science of the soul. Psychologists like Jung himself could provide reliable data from the clinical perspective, but scholars in all domains of the
humanities were needed to administer data about the development of consciousness in all cultures across the globe, from remote antiquity to the
present.

Now, if one looks at Jung's approach to exploring the historical record
from that perspective, it appears to be remarkably similar, once again, to
what we find in Ennemoser's *History of Magic*. For the Tyrolean physician,
the revolutionary new science was mesmerism; for his Swiss colleague,
it was a further development of mesmerism, now known as psychology.
What the German Romantics had described as the "nightside of nature" had
become "the unconscious" for Jung. Both were concerned with studying
the basic "facts of consciousness" empirically, in contemporary patients,
and historically, by exploring the records of the past for evidence of the
same types of phenomena and experiences. In both cases, the result was
that everything that had been consigned to the waste-basket of history
by the Enlightenment returned to center stage; but Ennemoser and Jung
both argued that this domain should be understood in a new way, as a
manifestation of the soul and its hidden powers, and should therefore
be recognized as *central* to the historical development of human culture.
Ennemoser spoke of a "history of magic," from the primitive childhood of
humanity through the ancient mystery cults, and from Renaissance authors
like Agrippa, Paracelsus, Campanella, Böhme, van Helmont, Kircher, and
Fludd up to the new German *Naturphilosophie* associated with authors
like von Baader or Schelling. Jung, for his part, provided a very similar
pedigree for his own psychology, including the same collection of currents
and central personalities, with a similar emphasis on antiquity.

There are, however, at least two important differences between Jung and
his German Romantic predecessors. First, Ennemoser's story was typical
of his time in that it was grafted upon a traditional concept of Christian salvation: he was thinking in terms of a providentialist *Heilsgeschichte*
focused on Judaism as the central tradition of human evolution, culminating in the appearance of Christ as the pivotal event of history. Jung's story,
in contrast, was based upon the concept of an inherent tension between
the deeper "pagan" strata of consciousness derived from the earliest pre-
Christian periods, and the later sediments added on to it by the emergence
of Judaeo-Christian thought: to a very large extent, in other words, the
psychological predicament of modern man could be understood as the

struggle of his Christian consciousness with his pagan unconscious.[105] This idea of associating the "nightside of nature" with paganism, and "daytime consciousness" with Christianity, had not occurred to the German Romantic mesmerists. By making such a link, perhaps under the influence of Nietzsche,[106] Jung reintroduced the basic theme of a struggle between "paganism" and biblical Christianity that has occupied us through the first two chapters of this book.

Second, Ennemoser's story had left a large historical gap between antiquity and the Renaissance: from his account, the medieval period appears as a "dark age" largely dominated by "goetic" *Zauberei*, such as witchcraft, but more or less devoid of healthier phenomena reminiscent of mesmerism or somnambulism. Jung, however, wanted an unbroken historical continuity from antiquity to his own time, and created one by postulating a lineage from gnosticism and neoplatonism through alchemy up to modern psychology:

> As far as I could see, the tradition that might have connected Gnosis with the present seemed to have been severed, and for a long time it proved impossible to find any bridge that led from gnosticism – or neo-platonism – to the contemporary world. But when I began to understand alchemy, I realized that it represented the historical link with gnosticism, and that a continuity therefore existed between past and present. Grounded in the natural philosophy of the Middle Ages, alchemy formed the bridge on the one hand into the past, to gnosticism, and on the other into the future, to the modern psychology of the unconscious . . . [107]

Jung came to understand gnosticism in terms of his theory of individuation: the goal of the gnostic was that of "finding his true self," symbolized by the image of an "interior sun" or star.[108] It is significant that this imagery has in fact no parallel in the ancient gnostic sources,[109] but is typical of

---

[105] Obviously this logic would not hold for Jews. Hence, in his notorious essay "Über das Unbewusste" (1918), Jung stated that "Christianity split the Germanic barbarian into its upper and a lower half, and enabled him, by repressing the dark side, to domesticate the brighter half and fit it for civilization," but this split-consciousness problem did not exist for Jews. Jews were therefore "domesticated to a higher degree," whereas the barbarian unconscious was still present "in dangerous concentrations in Germanic man" (*ibid.*, 470–471; see discussion in Ellwood, *Politics of Myth*, 57–67; Noll, *Jung Cult*, 97–103).

[106] For Nietzsche's influence on Jung, see Bishop, *Dionysian Self*. Jung was struck by the similarity between a passage from Nietzsche's *Also sprach Zarathustra* and a report from 1686 reprinted in Kerner's *Blätter aus Prevorst*. He went as far as contacting Nietzsche's sister, who confirmed that Nietzsche knew Kerner's work and had read it together with her when she was eleven years old (Bishop, *Dionysian Self*, 83–84).

[107] Jung, *Memories, Dreams, Reflections*, 227; cf. Pietikäinen, *C. G. Jung and the Psychology of Symbolic Forms*, 130–144.

[108] Hanegraaff, *New Age Religion*, 501–508. As rightly emphasized by Noll, the influence of G. R. S. Mead on Jung's understanding of gnosticism is an important research desideratum (*Jung Cult*, 69).

[109] Quispel, "Hesse, Jung und die Gnosis," 257.

German Romantic mesmerism and its references to the *Herzgrube* as the seat of the paracelsian *archaeus*, corresponding with the sun as the "heart" of the universe according to Swedenborg's system.[110] The whole point was that the "two ways of thinking" distinguished in Jung's *Wandlungen* could be seen as corresponding to two kinds of knowledge: a rational or cerebral type expressed by discursive language, and a non-rational type (gnosis) consisting of direct intuition and perception "with the heart," expressed by means of symbols.

Hence, gnosticism related to official Christianity as the unconscious related to consciousness: with its rich mythology and symbolic language, it represented the suppressed "nightside" counterpart of the religion that had carried the day. After antiquity, the gnostic quest for self-knowledge by individuation was continued, according to Jung, by the alchemical tradition; and it is here that we encounter the notorious problem of "spiritual alchemy." The idea that alchemy is essentially a spiritual pursuit, not a scientific one, had first been proposed by Mary Atwood in 1850, from a perspective permeated by German Romantic mesmerism and Boehmian theosophy.[111] A similar thesis was presented by Ethan Allen Hitchcock just a few years later, and it was also adopted by Traditionalists like René Guénon and Julius Evola in the early twentieth century.[112] Reacting to the enormous popularity of such interpretations in post-war Jungian milieus and alchemical scholarship, Principe and Newman have sharply criticized Jung for effectively writing laboratory alchemy out of the picture and claiming that "alchemy's real concern was the transformation of the psyche."[113] We must, however, be careful with this interpretation. There is no doubt that in his studies of alchemical symbolism, "*Jung's* real concern was the transformation of the psyche," but it is important not to confuse the two statements. The former amounts to a massive, and manifestly untenable, claim about alchemy as a historical phenomenon. The latter merely indicates the focus

---

[110] See above, page 264. For the further influences of solar mythology on Jung's thinking, see Noll, *Jung Cult*, 109–137; and cf. Hanegraaff, *New Age Religion*, 501–508.

[111] Atwood, *Suggestive Inquiry*. For the remarkable story of this book and its author, see Wilmhurst, "Introduction"; and for the formative influence of mesmerism and Boehmian theosophy, mediated by the circle of James Pierrepoint Greaves, see Godwin, *Theosophical Enlightenment*, 227–246.

[112] Hitchcock, *Remarks*; Evola, *Hermetic Tradition*. See Principe and Newman, "Some Problems," 391–392 and 422 n. 25. Herbert Silberer, the pioneer of Jung's way of connecting alchemy to psychology, gave credit to the "profound" Hitchcock for having "rediscovered" the psychological content of alchemy (Tilton, *Quest for the Phoenix*, 23–29, here 25). The influence of the Traditionalists on twentieth-century ideas of "spiritual alchemy" seems to be underestimated by all participants in the debate, perhaps because of a failure to differentiate between occultism and Traditionalism.

[113] Principe and Newman, "Some Problems," 402.

of Jung's interest, as a psychologist, in studying alchemical symbolism as a reflection of unconscious mental processes.[114]

In the heat of debate between critics and defenders of Jung, such nuances easily get lost; and both sides tend to underestimate the differences between Jung's original statements and what we find in translations and interpretations by later followers. Thus, Principe and Newman quote from the English translation by Stanley Dell, published in 1940, of an article originally published in the Eranos Yearbooks: "we are called upon to deal, not with chemical experimentations as such, but with something resembling psychic processes expressed in pseudo-chemical language."[115] This might look like the proverbial "smoking gun" that proves Jung's adherence to "spiritual alchemy," but Tilton dismisses it as a misrepresentation of the original. He refers the reader to the parallel passage in Jung's chapter on the "psychic" nature of alchemy, in his book *Psychologie und Alchemie* (orig. 1944), which actually reads as follows: "In the alchemical work, we are dealing *for the greatest part not only* with chemical experiments, but *also* with something resembling psychic processes expressed in pseudo-chemical language" [italics added].[116] Unfortunately, however, neither Tilton nor Principe/Newman seem to have looked at the original Eranos lecture, which undermines both their positions. It begins with a statement that is remarkably *negative* about the purely "spiritual" understanding of alchemical symbolism in the wake of Jacob Böhme:

---

[114] Tilton points out that the "projection" of psychical contents onto the matter in the alembic was understood by Jung not as a conscious process, as assumed by Principe and Newman, but as an unconscious one. The alchemists were therefore not seen as engaging in strange practices of psychic projection, but were "largely *un*aware of the course of their psychic life during laboratory practice," and not at all "indifferent to the chemical nature of the substances in their retort" (*Quest for the Phoenix*, 12–13; cf. Pietikäinen, *C. G. Jung and the Psychology of Symbolic Forms*, 140–141).

[115] Jung, "Idea of Redemption in Alchemy," 210; quoted in Principe and Newman, "Some Problems," 402. Note that although Dell's version is presented as a translation of Jung's Eranos lecture, it completely changes the structure by reshuffling the various parts of the text. Whether Dell might have worked from a revised manuscript by Jung is unknown to me.

[116] "Im alchemischen Opus handelt es sich zum größten Teil nicht nur um chemische Experimente allein, sondern auch um etwas wie psychische Vorgänge, die in pseudochemischer Sprache ausgedrückt werden" (Jung, *Psychologie und Alchemie*, 282; quoted in Tilton, *Quest for the Phoenix*, 12 with n. 51). It should be noted, however, that Jung adds a footnote quoting the Italian Traditionalist Julius Evola, of all people: a reference that hardly inspires confidence in Jung's historical rather than "spiritual" intentions, but further strengthens my suspicion that not occultism but Traditionalism, probably more than Atwood or Hitchcock, and certainly more than Jung, is at the origin of twentieth-century notions of "spiritual alchemy." Similarly, Principe and Newman see Jung's understanding of alchemy as derived from occultism, especially A. E. Waite ("Some Problems," 393–395, 402), but this is questioned by Tilton (*Quest*, 18–19) and deserves further study: note that Waite's *Azoth*, central to Principe and Newman's argument, is not among the seven volumes by Waite in Jung's private library (Anon., *C. G. Jung Bibliothek Katalog*, 79, 116).

Gradually, during the course of the eighteenth century, alchemy fell victim to its own obscurity... The inner decay of alchemy began more than a century earlier, already in the time of Jacob Böhme, when many alchemists left their retorts and crucibles and devoted themselves exclusively to the hermetic philosophy. At that time, the *chemist* separated himself from the *hermeticist*. Chemistry became natural science, but hermeticism lost the empirical ground under its feet and lost its way in allegories and speculations that were as bombastic as they were empty of content, and merely lived off the memories of a better time. This better time, however, was when the spirit of the alchemist still truly struggled with the problems of matter, when the investigating mind was facing the realm of the unknown and believed to perceive forms and laws in it.[117]

In other words, Jung calls purely "spiritual" alchemy a degenerate phenomenon! Further on in the article, we find the original version of the contested sentence: "The decisive thing is, however, that we are dealing not at all [*gar nicht*], or at least for the greatest part not [*wenigstens zum größten Teil nicht*] with chemical experiments, but probably [*vermutlich*] with something like psychic processes expressed in pseudo-chemical language."[118] Of course, these differences are significant. In revising the Eranos lecture for his *Psychologie und Alchemie*, Jung removed the radical "not at all" (which conflicted with the quotation just given) but also the cautious "probably." As for the passage criticized by Newman and Principe: it was never there at all, but represents a mistranslation by Stanley Dell. Hence, we are dealing with a classic example of a scholarly "ghost." Jung's American audience was led astray by the defective English version; and since most of his followers were reading him with little or no interest in history of science anyway, they came away with the absurd idea, which Jung never seems to have held, that alchemy as a historical phenomenon was essentially unconcerned with laboratory processes. It would seem, then, that Principe's and Newman's criticism is applicable to the drift of popular Jungian (mis)interpretations of alchemy – and to radical Traditionalist views such as Evola's, which they do not discuss – rather than to Jung's own work; and the "spiritual alchemy" highlighted by Tilton was in fact dismissed by the Swiss psychologist as "bombastic" and "empty of content." All these are effects of what Shamdasani calls the "fictionalization" of Jung by later generations.

The real problem of Jung's perspective lies not in his attempt to interpret alchemical or gnostic symbolism as a reflection of unconscious processes,

---

[117] Jung, "Erlösungsvorstellungen," 13–14.
[118] "Das Entscheidende ist aber, daß es sich gar nicht oder wenigstens zum größten Teil nicht um chemische Experimente handelt, sonder vermutlich um etwas wie psychische Vorgänge, die in pseudochemischer Sprache ausgedrückt wurden" (*ibid.*, 17).

but in its adoption as a methodology by historians. It is in the nature of psychology to look for general patterns in the functioning of the mind, and therefore a psychology that claims to be applicable to the collective psyche and its development through history will try to reduce specific events to underlying dynamics of a more general and universal kind. The essence of the historical approach, in contrast, consists in moving away from such theoretical generalizations and insisting on what can be empirically ascertained on the basis of primary sources: the specificity of unique events as they have occurred in the "external" world, in all their detail and contextual complexity. This in itself makes Jungian psychology into an "antithesis to the historical approach."[119] What has not been sufficiently noted, however, is that the most direct models for Jung's approach to history are to be found, once again, in the literature of German Romantic mesmerism. Thus, in a classic text by Jung on "The Meaning of Psychology for Modern Man" (1934), we seem to be reading a remarkably close paraphrase of the passage from Passavant that was quoted in the previous section:

When we look at the history of humanity, we see only what happens on the outermost surface of events – and even that distorted by the turbid mirror of tradition. But what has *really* been happening eludes the inquiring gaze of the historian, for the true historical event lies deeply hidden, experienced by all and observed by none... Wars, dynasties, social upheavals, conquests, and religions are but the most superficial symptoms of a secret basic attitude [*Grundhaltung*] of the soul of the individual, unknown to himself and hence transmitted by no historian; the founders of religions are perhaps still most instructive. The great events of world history are, at bottom, profoundly unimportant.[120]

Unlike second-generation Eranos scholars such as Eliade and Corbin, Jung does not seem to have felt a strong emotional resistance against "history."[121] Rather, he believed in a general evolution of human consciousness "from childhood to maturity," but simply accorded so little importance to critical historiography as an autonomous discipline that it never seems to have occurred to him to see it as a threat. The work of the historian was evidently subordinate to that of the psychologist, because specific external events were dependent by definition on more universal and fundamental "internal" dynamics; and in the end, only the latter were truly important

[119] Pietikäinen, *C. G. Jung and the Psychology of Symbolic Forms*, 114.
[120] Jung, "Bedeutung der Psychologie," 55; and cf. Passavant, above, page 265. Jung clearly means that history is "made" by "great men," who are ultimately unconscious instruments of what Hegel would have called the Absolute Spirit.
[121] On the differences between Jung's and Eliade's approaches to history, see, for example, Pietikäinen, *C. G. Jung and the Psychology of Symbolic Forms*, 125–129.

to him. Of course, such a perspective condemns the specialized historian to the subservient role of providing the psychologist with data suitable for illustrating the dynamics of the unconscious: the result is a "paint-by-numbers history of religions," as humorously formulated by Arthur McCalla, "in which [psychologists] provide the picture with its color-code and invite historians to sit quietly and color it in."[122] That historiography might in fact be the more fundamental science of the two – since it can demonstrate, as formulated by Shamdasani, how "particular psychologies became dominant through historically contingent events, and, not least, through the rescripting of history"[123] – is inconceivable within a Jungian paradigm.

The incompatibility of Jungian psychology with the most basic principles of historical research is acknowledged even by scholars who are otherwise sympathetic towards Jung's work,[124] and is hardly in need of further demonstration.[125] Nevertheless, many historians of alchemy after World War II seem to have found Jung's perspective so attractive that they were willing to overlook this fact. It is not so hard to understand why. The study of alchemy was barely beginning to recover from its near-universal perception as "pseudo-scientific" nonsense by positivist historiography,[126] so specialists in this domain had a hard time explaining to their readers (or even to themselves) why it should be taken seriously at all. As Walter Pagel admitted in his 1948 review of Jung, the vast literature on alchemy still left the reader with a "feeling of frustration" because it did not seem to amount to more than "a well illustrated catalogue of what appears to be yet another human folly."[127] Under such circumstances, Jung's work was bound to come as a breath of fresh air: all of a sudden, a "new and startling perspective"[128] had become available, developed by a psychologist who commanded respect for having studied more alchemical sources than anyone else, and who demonstrated that one could look at them from an angle that suddenly made the entire science/pseudoscience problematic look irrelevant. In short, while historians had been struggling against a

---

[122] McCalla, "When is History not History?," 447.

[123] Shamdasani, *C. G. Jung and the Making of Modern Psychology*, 9.

[124] For example, Dobbs, *Foundations of Newton's Alchemy*, 40; Halleux, *Les textes alchimiques*, 55; Tilton, *Quest for the Phoenix*, 10, 13, 16; Călian, "*Alkimia operativa* and *alkimia speculative*," 172–173; and cf. Chapter 3, n. 159. The shift from a relatively mild criticism of Jung's unhistorical methodology towards a sharp rejection of it occurred only as late as 1982, with Obrist, *Débuts*, 15–18, followed more recently by Principe and Newman, "Some Problems," 401–408.

[125] For a useful analysis, see Pietikäinen, *C. G. Jung and the Psychology of Symbolic Forms*, 114–129; cf. 18–19, 26–27.

[126] Ganzenmüller, "Wandlungen"; Weyer, "Image of Alchemy."

[127] Pagel, "Jung's Views on Alchemy," 48.   [128] *Ibid.*, 45.

sense of futility, Jung seemed to have found the key that could "make sense" of alchemy, and even endow it with meaning and significance for modern man. One must not forget that in the 1940s and 1950s, when his first works on alchemy became available, Jung was a well-known psychologist but had not yet become the almost mythical hero of the post-1960s imagination. Nobody could yet predict that this new perspective was on its way towards becoming the new orthodoxy.

Jung's impact did not remain limited to alchemy alone. Academic study of the "occult sciences" had seemed all but dead by the end of the nineteenth century, but Jung's psychology seemed capable of making the Waste Land revive, by causing "magic" and astrology to appear in a new light as well. In this regard, his theory of "synchronicity" played a central role. Presented explicitly as an alternative to instrumental "causality," it questioned the most fundamental assumptions of post-Cartesian philosophy and Newtonian physics, replacing them with a psychological reformulation of analogy and "correspondences": the very thing that positivist anthropology had rejected as the epitome of "magical superstition."[129] Obviously this amounted to a systematic assault on the entire fabric of nineteenth-century positivism,[130] and illustrates Jung's ambition of setting up psychology as the master-science relevant not just to the humanities, but perhaps even to physics. At the same time, the theory of synchronicity sought to rehabilitate the *magia naturalis* of the Renaissance, by interpreting it in modern psychological terms and harmonizing it with quantum mechanics as a more advanced alternative to post-Newtonian science. In short, avant-garde physics and depth psychology had joined forces to unmask positivism as "superstition" and announce the return of "magic" as science! Again, the success of this argument was remarkable. Apart from the fact that Jungian psychology has been adopted by the great majority of practicing astrologers as their chief theoretical framework, resulting in

[129] Jung, "Synchronizität" (and cf. his short Eranos lecture "Über Synchronizität"). Against the Cartesian dualism of *res extensa* and *res cogitans*, synchronicity assumes a principle of non-causal connection between mind and matter; against Newtonian physics it embraces the implications of quantum mechanics as undermining classic materialism. Jung's essay was published together with a text by the physicist Wolfgang Pauli, who applied archetypal psychology to Kepler's scientific theories. Jung himself discussed Taoism, Theophrast, Plotinus, Pico della Mirandola, Agrippa, Paracelsus, Kepler, and Leibniz as "predecessors" of synchronicity ("Synchronizität," 69–90). On analogy and correspondences as the epitome of magical superstition, see above, pp. 164–165, 186, 189–190 (Tylor's theory of magic), and cf. Lévy-Bruhl, who was a significant influence on Jung (see, for example, Pietikäinen, *C. G. Jung and the Psychology of Symbolic Forms*, 151–154).

[130] As such, the Jung/Pauli theory of synchronicity is in fact a late offshoot of the assault on "causality" typical of the *Lebensphilosophie* that came to dominate Weimar intellectual culture, including the milieus of mathematicians and theoretical physicists, immediately after Germany had lost the war (Forman, "Weimar Culture, Causality, and Quantum Theory").

the widespread popular phenomenon of "psychological astrology,"[131] Jung's theory of "synchronicity" has proved attractive as a theoretical framework even for modern historians of ancient astrology, as will be seen.

Summing up: from the perspective of the academic study of "Western esotericism," Jung's essential contribution is that he took the basic idea (invented by German Romantic mesmerism, with Ennemoser as the paradigmatic example) of a history of the magical "nightside of nature" and its experiential manifestations, but repackaged it in modern psychological terms as the history of Western culture's suppressed unconscious. The result was an extremely attractive narrative with an internal logic all of its own, which has been widely adopted in popular culture since World War II and – in spite of its evidently non-historical foundations – has deeply influenced scholars as well. Its basic concept is that of an esoteric "counter-tradition,"[132] that has always been present as the hidden – occult – "shadow" of the mainstream: from gnosticism and the ancient mystery cults, through alchemy and the other "occult sciences" (natural magic and astrology), to early modern thinkers like Paracelsus and his followers, to Romantic *Naturphilosophie*, mesmerism and, finally, modern psychology. In this narrative, the official representatives of the mainstream (Christian theologians, rational philosophers, modern scientists) have always tried to suppress it, but never with any lasting success, because, like the unconscious, it is the hidden secret of their own existence, the vital source without which they could not exist. The positive religions, particularly the monotheistic ones, are "external" products of time and historical circumstance – they have had a beginning, and will have an end – but underneath them, there has always been this permanent and universal substratum: a kind of objective paganism expressing itself by symbols and myths, and grounded in the universal human search for self-knowledge, or gnosis.

ERANOS AND RELIGIONISM: SCHOLEM, CORBIN, ELIADE

The importance of Eranos for the study of "Western esotericism" lies in a specific approach to religion that came to dominate its proceedings and publications, and was adopted as a matter of course by many of the scholars who became interested in "hermetic" or "occult" traditions as an object of

---

[131] Von Stuckrad, *Geschichte der Astrologie*, 337, 339–340, 345. Jung was interested in astrology already before the break with Freud: see, for example, his letter to Freud of June 12, 1911 (Freud and Jung, *Briefwechsel*, 470–471).

[132] Cf. Pietikäinen's concept of "counter-myth" (*C. G. Jung and the Psychology of Symbolic Forms*, 130–144).

study from the 1960s onwards. In line with my earlier discussions, I will refer to this approach as "religionism." Rooted in the impossible dream of a "history of truth," it may be defined as the project of exploring historical sources in search of what is eternal and universal. The paradoxical nature of any such attempt is obvious; and at least in its more sophisticated representatives, this sometimes lends religionism a quality of intellectual daring bordering on the heroic. Each in their own way, and with particular vehemence after World War II, the religionists of Eranos were rebelling against the finality of history and time, change and impermanence – in short, they refused the nihilist verdict that all things that appear to be meaningful and true in human existence are just finite and transitory, ending in dissolution and death.

The relative emphasis placed on either temporality or eternity was, however, different with each of these scholars. On the farthest "historical" side of the spectrum we find a thinker like Gershom Scholem (1897–1982), the pioneering scholar of Jewish kabbalah, who stood for critical philology and historiography and only very rarely allowed his readers to catch a glimpse of his deepest motivations. His clearest statement is in a famous letter to his publisher, Zalman Schocken:

For the Mountain, the body of things, needs no key; it is only the nebulous wall of history, which hangs around it, that must be traversed. To traverse it – that is what I have tried. Will I remain stuck in the nebula, so to speak, falling victim to "death by professorship?" But even where it requires sacrifice, there is just no alternative to the necessity of historical criticism and critical historiography.

True, history may at bottom be an illusion, but an illusion without which no perception of the essence is possible in time. The wondrous concave mirror of philological criticism makes it possible for the people of today first and most purely to receive a glimpse, in the legitimate orders of commentary, of that mystical totality of the system, whose existence, however, vanishes in the very act of being projected onto historical time.

From the first day to the present, my work has lived in this paradox, out of such a hope for a true message from the Mountain – for that most trivial, tiniest shift of history that makes truth erupt from the illusion of "development."[133]

---

[133] Scholem, "Birthday Letter," in: Biale, *Gershom Scholem*, 216, and Scholem, *Briefe* I, 472; and cf. Scholem, "Zehn unhistorische Sätze." On the connection of these texts and their role in Scholem's development, see the excellent analysis by Peter Schäfer, "'Philologie der Kabbala'." See also the important passage from a highly perceptive article on Scholem by his pupil Joseph Weiss, published in *Yedioth hayom* (December 5, 1947; reproduced in Schäfer, "'Philologie der Kabbala'," 22 n. 69), and Scholem's affirmative reaction in a Hebrew letter to Weiss (March 31, 1960; not included in the printed correspondence), reproduced in German translation by Schäfer ("'Philologie der Kabbala'," 22–23). See also the quotation at the heading of this chapter.

Like all other central Eranos figures, Scholem had absorbed the basic message that metaphysical Truth cannot be found in history and will never be discovered by the historian *qua* historian. But whereas colleagues with Christian backgrounds like Corbin or Eliade saw historical existence as a prison or nightmare and "historicism" as the enemy, for a Zionist Jew like Scholem such an attitude was impossible. He was deeply convinced that the very identity of contemporary Judaism was determined "by historical consciousness, by the feeling of a continuity with the past and a common hope for the future,"[134] and his understanding of history was therefore inseparable from a dimension of messianic expectation. From a Jewish perspective, history is the very condition that makes messianic fulfillment possible, even if it provides no guarantee about when, or how, or perhaps even whether the hope for a "message from the mountain" will be fulfilled. But at the same time, the fact that eternity cannot appear in time means that the hope that sustains Jewish identity through history can only be called an "aspiration to the impossible."[135] Under these conditions, the historian must have the courage to "descend into the abyss" of history, knowing that he might encounter nothing but himself, and guided by nothing but a desperate hope for the impossible: that against all human logic, the transcendent might inexplicably "break through into history" one day, like "a light that shines into it from altogether elsewhere."[136]

---

[134] Hamacher, *Gershom Scholem*, 66. Hamacher points out that for Scholem, historical consciousness in this sense was all the more important because, for him, it replaced *Halakhah* as the basis of modern Jewish identity.

[135] Mosès, *L'ange de l'histoire*, 189.

[136] Scholem, "Zum Verständnis der messianischen Idee," 25 (and cf. 7–8 for how Scholem contrasted Jewish ideas of salvation with Christian ones, which he deeply disliked because of what he called the "horrible smell" and "swindle" of pure interiority [letter to Georg Lichtheim about Simone Weil, 1950, in: *Briefe* II, 16]). My understanding of Scholem's perspective is informed by a manuscript from 1921 that contains an earlier version of the ideas expressed in the letter to Schocken (Scholem Archive of the Jewish National and University Library, Arc. 4° 1599/282, as reproduced in Schäfer, "Philologie der Kabbala," 4–7). Here, the passage "without which no perception of the essence is possible in time" ends as "in an unmessianic time"; and about the mountain without a key, one reads that "What we are missing is not a key, but only one thing: courage. Courage to descend into an abyss that, against expectation, might end with ourselves. Courage to go through a plane, a wall – history . . ." (Schäfer, "Philologie der Kabbala," 5; and cf. Scholem's letter to Hugo and Escha Berman of December 15, 1947, responding to Hugo's criticism of Scholem's sharp distinction between "prophets" and "professors" in the final sentences of *Major Trends in Jewish Mysticism*: "I live in despair [*Verzweiflung*], and only from the position of despair can I be active" [*Briefe* I, 331]). About correct and incorrect interpretations of the letter to Schocken, see the excellent analysis in Hamacher, *Gershom Scholem*, 62–72. On "the spiritual quest of the philologist," see also Mendes-Flohr, "Introductory Essay." Finally, see Burmistrov, "Gershom Scholem und das Okkulte," 34: in his *9½ Mystics*, Herbert Weiner writes that for Scholem, "a reference in a kabbalistic document to an 'Elijah appearance' may be hallucination, or simply a technical term . . . but it cannot mean what most kabbalists took it to mean, that Elijah actually did appear

In the meantime, Jews are condemned to the exilic situation of strictly historical existence, guided only by myths and symbols that, by their very nature, provide a glimpse of the transcendent only by concealing it at the same time. In his understanding of symbolism and myth in relation to kabbalah, Scholem owed much to the perspectives of German Romanticism, notably Molitor (a major influence on Ennemoser, as we saw earlier) and Novalis, but also Schelling and von Baader; and the exact nature of his debt to A. E. Waite deserves further study.[137] These backgrounds make it easier to understand why Scholem's strict insistence on philology and historical criticism as the only legitimate approach to the study of Jewish mysticism did not prevent him from feeling at home in Eranos,[138] with its emphasis on myth and symbolism as reflections of meta-historical truth, and did not prevent him from expressing feelings of deep spiritual kinship even with a declared enemy of historicism like Henry Corbin.[139] It remains, nevertheless, that in his published writings he appears as the very model of a "historian's historian,"[140] and in this regard it would have made little difference if he had chosen never to reveal his personal hopes and motivations. Scholem is therefore best interpreted as a scholar who felt the temptation of religionism but resisted it, explicitly and largely successfully.

with a message" ($9^{1/2}$ *Mystics*, 81). However, in the margin of his personal copy, Scholem wrote "I NEVER SAID SO!"

[137] Kilcher, *Sprachtheorie der Kabbala*, 331–345; Schulte, "'Die Buchstaben'." Mostly during the 1920s, Scholem took the trouble to read everything that occultists (Eliphas Lévi, Blavatsky, de Guaita, Papus, Saint-Yves d'Alveydre, Waite, Westcott, Crowley, Regardie, Pullen-Burry, MacGregor Mathers, Steiner) had to say about "kabbala." Usually the verdict was negative, as shown by his many marginal notes ("Lying and deceitful," "Nonsense," "No!" and so on); but Scholem's attitude towards Waite is more complex than one might perhaps expect (Burmistrov, "Gershom Scholem und das Okkulte").

[138] *Contra* Dan, "Gershom Scholem," 53–56, and "Foreword." Dan is very convincing when he describes the sharp contrast between Jungian/Eliadian approaches and Scholem's historical approach ("Foreword," 8–9); but he too easily reduces Eranos to just a "Jungian/Eliadean" project, and contrasts it with Scholem's historicism in terms of simple opposition rather than dialectical tension. Whereas Dan considers Scholem's participation in Eranos as "belonging probably to the most difficult questions of his biography" ("Gershom Scholem," 53; cf. Wasserstrom's initial "perplexity" about the same point: "Response," 460), I would see Eranos as an indispensable key. Idel emphasizes that most of Scholem's writings on the phenomenological aspects of kabbalah were written rather late in his career, and do reflect the influence of Eranos and its audience (*Kabbalah: New Perspectives*, 11). For Scholem's ironic dialectics, see his own reflections on Eranos, significantly titled "Identifizierung und Distanz."

[139] See Scholem's letter to Corbin on April 5, 1973 (*Briefe III*, 69) and to his widow Stella Corbin on October 26, 1978 (*ibid.*, 193), where he writes that, for him, Corbin's death meant "the loss of a spiritual brother." These passages refute Wasserstrom's contention that Scholem was "spiritually unrelated" to the "esoteric blood brothers" Eliade and Corbin (*Religion after Religion*, 13, but cf. 53). As far as their published *scholarship* is concerned, however, Corbin's influence on Scholem appears to have been quite minor (Fenton, "Henry Corbin et la mystique juive," 161–162).

[140] Wasserstrom, *Religion after Religion*, 64.

Privately he may well have believed, or hoped, that events in time could be symbolic reflections of the eternal and universal; but he also knew that, if so, the very act of "projection" concealed their source from the historian's gaze.

If Scholem was situated on the farthest "historical" side of the Eranos spectrum, Henry Corbin (1903–1978) certainly exemplified the opposite, radically "anti-historical" alternative. This does not mean that he disregarded the study of primary sources: on the contrary, he spent his life studying the works of Suhrawardī, Ibn ʿArabi and a range of other important Iranian theosophers in their original language, and his enormous contribution to the study of medieval Islamic mysticism is undisputed. What it does mean is that he adopted the metaphysical perspective of his favorite authors as his own, and opposed it in the strongest possible wordings against the "disease," "profanation," "corruption," even "satanic inversion" represented by historical reductionism.[141] In so doing, he explicitly took the perspective not of a historian, but of a philosopher in the phenomenological tradition of Husserl and Heidegger:[142] "visible, apparent, outward states, in short, phenomena, can never be the causes of other phenomena. The agent is the invisible, the immaterial."[143] In other words, whatever appears in empirical reality has its origin in a transcendent realm: "any *history* that happens in this visible world is the *imitation* of events that happened first in the soul, 'in Heaven,' and hence the *place* of hierohistory . . . cannot be perceived by the senses, for their signification refers to another world."[144] When Corbin spoke of "esotericism," as he frequently did, he meant a spiritual perspective – the only true one, in his

[141] For example, Corbin, "L'*imago Templi*," 368 (all references are to the complete edition of 1980, not the abridged version published in the Eranos Yearbook). "Historical reductionism" captures most exactly what Corbin rejected under the term "historicism": a kind of "historical consciousness that cannot conceive of a reality otherwise than from the perspective of its material genesis" (Corbin, "Science traditionnelle," 30). See Faivre, "La question," 91 n. 11, and for the problematics of "historicism," cf. his reference to Hanegraaff, *New Age Religion*, 413–417. There is also a theological dimension to Corbin's anti-historicism: for him, an eschatological and docetist theology associated with the early "Johannite community" represented the very antithesis of the historical and incarnational theology of the "Great Church" ("L'*imago templi*," 354–358).

[142] As pointed out *contra* Wasserstrom (who did, however, acknowledge the fact: *Religion after Religion*, 145) by Lory, "Note sur l'ouvrage," 109; and Subtelny, "History and Religion," 93. On Corbin's use of phenomenology and his refusal of history, see Cheetham, *World Turned Inside Out*, 1–15; and see, for example, Corbin's application of Heideggerian categories in "De Heidegger à Sohravardî," 28, where he speaks of "the refusal to let ourselves be inserted into the historicity of History" and the demand "to tear ourselves loose from the historicity of History. For if there is a 'meaning of History,' in any case it does not reside in the historicity of historical events; it resides in this *historiality*, in these existential, secret, esoteric roots of History and the historical."

[143] Corbin, *Creative Imagination*, 119.

[144] Corbin, *En Islam Iranien*, vol. 1, 163. Cf. Jambet, "Henry Corbin et l'histoire," 145.

opinion – grounded in this distinction between external reality and a more fundamental "inner" dimension hidden from the senses. As explained by his close friend and colleague Seyyed Hossein Nasr,

> For Corbin, the essential distinction in Islamic esotericism, and notably in Sufism, between the exterior (*zâhir*) and the interior (*bâtin*), as well as the process that relates the exterior to the interior – the *ta'wîl*, translated by him as hermeneutics, in reference to the original meaning of the term – together constitute *the only method* for accessing the truth, a method which is also the real meaning of phenomenology.[145]

All this makes it pointless to judge Corbin's work by the criteria of academic historiography: as Maria E. Subtelny bluntly puts it, he was simply "not interested in historical truth."[146] Overwhelming evidence for this fact can be found in Corbin's fundamental text "The *imago templi* in Confrontation with Profane Norms," presented in abridged form at Eranos shortly before his death. Discussing a "filiation" from the original Judaeo-Christian community and the Essenes, through the Templars and the Graal legend to the illuminism of eighteenth-century Masonic Templarism and Swedenborg's "New Jerusalem,"[147] Corbin kept emphasizing that in order to understand it properly, one must take a position "beyond becoming and historical causality, beyond the norms of chronology, of filiations that require archives and notarial documents to justify themselves."[148] The *imago* of the Temple is claimed to exist at a level of reality – the *mundus imaginalis* – that is ontologically prior to its earthly manifestation, and hence it is this transcendent image that conditions and determines its historical manifestations, never the reverse.[149] Historical causality is therefore irrelevant by definition. This is why Corbin's elaborate claims about "hidden connections" between early Christianity, the Essenes, Islamic mysticism, the medieval Templars, the legend of the Graal, and Masonic neo-Templar traditions are declared by him, *ex cathedra*, to be immune against any historical falsification. By the same token, although Corbin's own dependence on modern and contemporary esotericism is obvious to the historian,[150] any critical objection on

---

[145] Nasr, "Henry Corbin, 'L'exil occidental'," 13–14.   [146] Subtelny, "History and Religion," 93.

[147] Corbin, "L'*imago templi*," 190–191. Interestingly, the specialist of Jewish mysticism Elliot Wolfson appears to accept Corbin's perspective as a valid textual hermeneutics in the study of religion and uses it to include Zoharic kabbalah as well (Wolfson, "*Imago Templi*").

[148] Corbin, "L'*imago templi*," 188. Cf. *ibid.*, 190: "although there are historical traces, always hidden under the veil of what is known as 'legends,' it is not by these uncertain traces that we find the knights of the Temple," for the true connections "are not of the kind that leave traces in archival documents."

[149] *Ibid.*, 191.

[150] See notably his relation to Traditionalism (below, nn. 155–156) and his involvement in the Martinist *Rite Ecossaise Rectifié* (below, page 341 with n. 305).

that basis would automatically be declared inadmissible and misguided. Corbin was not speaking about what, on the basis of his studies, he had come to see as the truth: Truth itself was being spoken through Corbin, and any objection therefore had to be false by definition.[151]

Corbin had understood the depth of the conflict between "history" and "truth" perhaps more profoundly than any of his colleagues, with the exception of Scholem. This conflict goes to the very heart of the modern study of religion, and hence of "Western esotericism" as well,[152] and has accompanied us like a red thread throughout this book. It is therefore important to understand it correctly. We are dealing with two types of reasoning that are internally consistent but mutually exclusive. Both are capable of rejecting the alternative on their own terms, but they share no common measure that would make it possible to decide which one is ultimately true or false.[153] When all is said and done, they are a matter of choice. Scholem chose the path of historiography, more congenial to modern thinking, and accepted that the transcendent was thereby reduced to only a glimmer of hope at the very limit of the human horizon. Corbin chose the narrow path of metaphysics, and accepted that this made him into an "occidental exile,"[154] speaking on behalf of a spiritual world that had become alien and incomprehensible to practically all his contemporaries. One understands the attraction of his work among modern students of "Western esotericism," for his vision of reality has an undeniable beauty, and his oeuvre commands respect for the depth of its intellectual vision. But admirers should not be fooled about its unflinching dogmatism: no less radically than the Traditionalist school of René Guénon and Frithjof Schuon, Corbin rejected "the modern world" along with all its basic assumptions,[155] claiming exclusive

---

[151] More precisely, Corbin saw the historian's objections as based upon the blind assumptions of a world that is not only in exile, but refuses, or is unable, to recognize that fact (*ibid.*, 198–204). Living in this world, the "gnostic" is a "stranger" to it, because he has at least discovered the true nature of his condition, and knows that his true home is elsewhere.

[152] See Hanegraaff, "Empirical Method."

[153] Cf. Hanegraaff, "Under the Mantle of Love," 176–177, about the strictly comparable case of Marsilio Ficino's platonic theory of love as compared to modern psychoanalysis.

[154] Nasr, "Henry Corbin, 'L'exil occidental'" (and cf. above, n. 151).

[155] For the core argument against modernity, see Corbin, "*L'imago templi*," 196–200, and cf. 251. Wasserstrom associates Corbin's antimodernism with fascism and antisemitism but, by his own admission, fails to find any evidence (*Religion after Religion*, 155, 179). Regarding the type of discourse and rhetoric basic to Wasserstrom's argument, see below, n. 160; for a critical assessment of his moral agenda, see Benavides, "Afterreligion after Religion." On the complex relation between Corbin and Guénonian Traditionalism, see the excellent analysis by Accart, "Identité et théophanie"; and *Guénon*, 203–204, 1012–1019. Corbin's very first published article (under the pseudonym Trang-Ni) already contained a long discussion of Guénon, who was praised for presenting an India free of Romantic and occultist distortions, and showing "what true esotericism consists of." But Corbin did not share Guénon's rejection of "all Western philosophy . . . and

truth for only his own worldview and presenting his hermeneutics as the only correct method. Critical discussion about these foundations was out of the question.[156]

Representing two extreme options in the polar dynamics of religionism, Scholem ultimately sacrificed "truth" in the interest of history, while Corbin sacrificed history in the interest of "truth" (the former with regret, the latter with relish). The third central figure of Eranos in the postwar period, Mircea Eliade (1907–1986), rather seems to represent the unresolved paradox of religionism as such: as has often been noted, the discipline that he referred to as "history of religions" was in fact notable for its attempt to transcend history.[157] Unlike Scholem and Corbin, Eliade was not a deep specialist in any particular religious tradition, and did not spend his life reading primary sources in their original languages. He relied essentially on secondary sources to provide him with information on a wide variety of religious traditions, and his sympathizing ex-student Robert Ellwood describes him quite correctly as "not at heart a scholar, much less a politician or social scientist, but a litterateur, a writer and literary critic."[158] It belongs to this profile that Eliade had little concern for questions of methodology, as noted by another of his ex-students, Douglas Allen: "He simply looks at the religious phenomena, and he just 'sees' these essential structures and meanings."[159] It is therefore somewhat ironic – understandable though it may be, given the dominance of his "Chicago school" in the American study of religion, not to mention the posthumous scandal of his political past – that precisely Eliade's oeuvre has become the focus of intense methodological debate in the study of religion.[160]

European scientific methods," and highlighted the importance of German philosophers who would always remain alien to Guénon (Trang-Ni [Henry Corbin], "Regard vers l'Orient"; see Accart, "Identité et théophanie," 179–180). For Corbin's criticism of Guénon, see his response in 1963 to a review of his work by the Guénonian Mohammad Hassan Askari (Corbin, "Correspondance"; Accart, "Identité et théophanie," 189–195).

[156] Corbin, "L'*imago templi*," 213: "between 'those who see' and 'those who do not see,' debate is pointless." Corbin's reasoning exhibits the same "no-win logic" as Traditionalism: "if you understood, you would agree; if you disagree, obviously you don't understand" (Bowman, "Status of Conceptual Schemata," 12). See also Hakl's remarks about Corbin's problems with accepting disagreement (*Verborgene Geist*, 347).

[157] See, for example, McCalla, "When is History not History?," 435 ("History is not history when it is the history of religions") and 437–438; Rudolph, "Mircea Eliade and the 'History' of Religions"; Alles, "Ist Eliade Antihistorisch?."

[158] Ellwood, *Politics of Myth*, 124.

[159] Allen, "Encounters," 14; and cf. Turcanu, *Mircea Eliade*, 429–430.

[160] The number of publications on this debate is overwhelming. As *partes pro toto*, I just mention here Dudley, *Religion on Trial*, and McCutcheon, *Manufacturing Religion*. The methodological debate is inseparable from the question of Eliade's politics. Against the background of the "Eliade scandal" that erupted in the 1990s, when Eliade's enthusiastic pre-war engagement with Romanian

Rather than looking for an implicit method in Eliade's writings, I believe it is more fruitful to emphasize the *absence* of method in his work. At the very core of his oeuvre we do not find some theoretical conviction about the correct way to study religion, but, very simply, a deep emotional need to find meaning in human existence. Eliade's obsessive activity as a writer, beginning in his teenage years and continuing until his death, reflects a profound awareness of transitoriness and death: "Everything passes. That is my immense pain . . . an intimate and never admitted obsession."[161] Temporary relief from this oppressive awareness was granted only by special moments of "grace": evident models of what Eliade would later refer to as "hierophanies." Perhaps the most impressive example occurred one afternoon, when, as a small child, he discovered a room in the house that was normally closed:

The emotion that I felt then nailed me to the ground. I found myself transported into a palace of legend. The blinds had been lowered and through the heavy curtains of green velvet filtered a pale light of emerald colour, rainbow-like and almost supernatural. I felt as if I were inside a gigantic green grape. I stayed like that for a long moment, motionless in the middle of the room, holding my breath . . . Like great surfaces of clear water . . . the venetian mirrors reflected my image, but larger, and more beautiful, more noble above all, surrounded by that light that seemed to me to come from another world.[162]

---

fascism and antisemitism became impossible to deny (see Turcanu, *Mircea Eliade*, 251–301 and *passim*; for perhaps the most shocking piece of evidence, see the journal of Eliade's Jewish friend Mihail Sebastian for March 2, 1937: *Journal 1935–1944*, 113–114), scholars like Russell McCutcheon and Daniel Dubuisson have claimed that fascism and antisemitism are structurally *encoded* in Eliade's scholarship. For a convincing deconstruction of the underlying procedures of discourse and rhetoric (which are typical also of Wasserstrom's analysis of Eranos in his *Religion after Religion*, and the earlier analysis by Holz, "ERANOS") see Fisher, "Fascist Scholars, Fascist Scholarship." As pointed out by Fisher, the taken-for-granted associations between fascism and concepts such as "gnostic," "esoteric," "platonic," or "neopagan" (along with, for example, "totalizing," "antinomian," "aesthetic," "elitist," "syncretist," "Nietzschean," "Faustian," "amoral," "lawless," "organic," and "antimodernist": *ibid.*, 264) are ultimately derived from the "Critical Theory" of the Frankfurt School, which came to enjoy great moral and intellectual prestige after World War II (Fisher, "Fascist Scholars, Fascist Scholarship," 271–281; and see below, pp. 312–313).

161 Eliade, *Journal des Indes*, 24 (Turcanu, *Mircea Eliade*, 96, 128). On the young Eliade's obsession with writing and reading, see Turcanu, *Mircea Eliade*, 23–24, 27–30, 71, 78. For some time, he even tried to win more time by reducing his hours of sleep to four each night (*ibid.*, 29).

162 Eliade, *Promesses de l'équinoxe*, 14. This experience served as a model for Stefan's "secret room" in Eliade's novel *Noaptea de Sânzienze*, later translated as *The Forbidden Forest* (von Stuckrad, "Utopian Landscapes," 96–97). Eliade writes that for years, he trained himself in prolonging and artificially evoking such states of mind, always with success, but it finally brought unbearable sadness because he now knew that the world of the secret room was gone forever (*Promesses de l'équinoxe*, 11, 14–15). Particularly illuminating in this regard is a passage attributed to Eliade by his friend Corbin: "To be like a child means being a newborn, being re-born to another spiritual life; in short, being an initiate. Contrary to all other modes of being, the spiritual life knows of no law of becoming, for it does not develop in time. The 'newborn' is not a baby who will grow up in

Referring to the great importance that such "magical moments" had for Eliade, Ellwood speaks of him as having lived "a life governed by nostalgia: for childhood, for historical times past, for cosmic religion, for paradise,"[163] and his biographer Florin Turcanu concurs that "the famous *illud tempus* that Eliade talks about, the primordial time evoked by myths, is identified on another level with the time of childhood and its particular relation to the world."[164] Whereas Corbin was inspired by very similar emotions and personal experiences[165] but went on to embrace a consistent metaphysical worldview, I see no indication that Eliade ever did so. At bottom, his famous notion of the "terror of history" does not refer to any specific form of "historicism" either, but quite simply to the painful experience that in the prosaic reality of adult human existence, it appears that "things just happen," without any apparent reason or deeper meaning. The experience of war during his childhood, including the bombing of Bucharest in 1916,[166] seems to have affected him deeply, and his frantic workpace can be explained at least partly as reflecting a continuous struggle against his depressive tendencies.[167] In his pivotal *Myth of Eternal Recurrence*, written under the impact of the traumatic events of World War II and Eliade's own exile from Romania, we find him reacting with deep emotion to the terrors and atrocities of history, and stressing that human beings somehow need to "defend" themselves against the nihilistic view that "everything that happens is 'good,' simply *because* it has happened."[168]

Eliade never says that historical events *do* have a meaning, either in themselves or as a reflection of some "deeper" or "inner" dynamics, and contrary to Corbin and even Scholem, he never developed any concept of a "meta-historical" reality: his many references to "the Sacred" remain

order to die one day. He is a *puer aeternus*. He remains a child *in aeternum*: he participates in the atemporal beatitude of the Spirit, and not in the becoming of history" (Corbin, "L'université de Saint-Jean de Jérusalem," 11 [without source reference]).

163   Ellwood, *Politics of Myth*, 99. For strong confirmation, see Olson, "Theology of Nostalgia"; and cf. McCutcheon, *Manufacturing Religion*, on what he calls the "politics of nostalgia."

164   Turcanu, *Mircea Eliade*, 13.

165   For a very similar "hierophanic" experience reported about Corbin, see Shayegan, "L'homme à la lampe magique," 31.

166   Eliade, *Promesses de l'équinoxe*, chapter 2 ("War at Age Nine").   167   *Ibid.*, 28.

168   Eliade, *Myth of the Eternal Return*, 152 n. 11, and cf. 149–150: the various "historical philosophies" all claim that "every historical event finds its full and only meaning in its realization alone." Nevertheless, Eliade also writes that even Hegelianism and Marxism still preserve some dimension of "transhistorical significance" or meaning in history, and can therefore serve as a means of "defense" against it (*ibid.*, 148–149). I find little theoretical depth and consistency in this famous chapter on "The Terror of History," which ends even more strangely with a simple appeal to Christian faith in God as modern man's only defense against "despair" (*ibid.*, 159–162). Like his novel *The Forbidden Forest*, Eliade's *Myth of the Eternal Return* must evidently be seen as a response to the recent historical horrors: see Turcanu, *Mircea Eliade*, 340–342, 376–383.

extremely vague,[169] and imply little else than that some kind of "absolute" reality *must* exist because the alternative is nihilism and despair. Essentially, then, his oeuvre appears to be based upon a life-long search for psychological "defenses" against such despair: they are not so much "solutions," "explanations," or "justifications" of suffering as ways to make it bearable. Myths and rituals of periodic cyclical renewal and rebirth as an antidote against the finality of events in irreversible chronological sequence, the concept of an irreducible religious reality *sui generis* as an antidote against historical reductionism (that is, against religions as mere contingent products of historical circumstance), ecstatic techniques for entering an "other reality" and the imaginal return to "archaic" and primordial worlds as antidotes against the sense of being imprisoned in time: all have the same function of providing a measure of existential relief and emotional comfort, by suggesting that the dream of escaping historical reality is not altogether hopeless. In short, for Eliade, the revival of myth as a counterbalance to history became a kind of "therapeutic" necessity for modern man:

Until recently, all personal dramas or collective catastrophes found their justification in some kind of cosmology or soteriology ... Today history terrorizes purely and simply, for the tragedies that it produces no longer find a justification or absolution ... The cosmic alteration, the day that invariably, *in spite of everything*, follows the night, the spring that follows the winter: the eternal return. This myth must be re-invigorated if life still has some meaning, if it still deserves to be lived.[170]

Elsewhere in his private journal, Eliade was even more implicit about his work as a means of "escaping History, of saving myself through symbol, myth, rites, archetypes."[171]

In his search for "escapes" from historical reality, Eliade explored a wide variety of ancient and contemporary "esoteric" currents as well. German Romantic culture always remained somewhat alien to him, but occultist authors played a role in awakening the youthful Eliade's interest in comparative religion and the Orient, and convincing him of the reality of paranormal phenomena.[172] Alchemy was another early fascination, likewise

---

[169] Faivre, "L'ambiguità della nozione del sacro," 368: the ontological status of the Sacred "remains ambiguous by lack of precision. What, then, is this Being that manifests itself by means of hierophanies and is situated beyond any religious phenomenon properly speaking?" On the ambivalence of Eliade's sacred/profane distinction (as compared with Rudolf Otto, Emile Durkheim, and Roger Caillois), cf. Hanegraaff, "Defining Religion," 356.

[170] Eliade, unpublished diary fragments (Eliade Papers, Box 3, Regenstein Library, University of Chicago) for April 6, 1944, and March 15, 1945, as quoted in Turcanu, *Mircea Eliade*, 340–341. Emphasis in original.

[171] Eliade, *Caete de Dor* 8 (1954), 27, as quoted in Ierunca, "Literary Work of Mircea Eliade," 351.

[172] Turcanu, *Mircea Eliade*, 37–41 (focusing on Eliade's youthful reception of Edouard Schuré, H. P. Blavatsky, and Rudolf Steiner); cf. Faivre, "Modern Western Esoteric Currents in the Work

linked in his mind with "the Orient"; it was sparked by Marcelin Berthelot's *Collection des anciens alchimistes grecs*, but Eliade became a firm believer in "spiritual alchemy" under the influence of Guénon and Evola, as we will see shortly.[173] While studying in Italy from 1927 to 1928, he developed an interest in Renaissance philosophy, resulting in an unfinished thesis that discusses, *inter alia*, Ficino and Pico della Mirandola; but this remained no more than an episode.[174] References to contemporary esoteric currents are scattered through Eliade's literary and scholarly works,[175] and during his Parisian period after World War II he frequented French esoteric milieus, including the alchemist Eugène Canseliet, the Gurdjieffian Louis Pauwels, and (somewhat later) the "neo-gnostic" writer Raymond Abellio.[176] But by far the most important "esoteric" factor in Eliade's intellectual development was the Traditionalism of René Guénon, Ananda K. Coomaraswamy, and Julius Evola. While he tried to conceal his debt to these thinkers,[177] Paola Pisi has demonstrated beyond any doubt that they were decisive influences on a range of central concepts in Eliade's mature oeuvre, notably the symbolism of the "center," his notion of "reintegration," and his understanding of "archetypes."[178] The two most important theoretical chapters of his

of Mircea Eliade," 150. In an early article in a school journal, titled "Știinṭă și ocultism" ("Science and Occultism"; 1925), he reacted to a skeptic schoolmate by expressing his firm belief in paranormal phenomena while trying (characteristically) "to crush his adversary under the weight of a bibliography" dominated by occultists and parapsychologists (Turcanu, *Mircea Eliade*, 40).

[173] For the general development of Eliade's interest in alchemy, see Turcanu, *Mircea Eliade*, 42–43, 85–86, 232–234, 251. Eliade's brochure *Alchimia asiatică* (1935) was "based upon one master-idea: alchemy is not a 'proto-chemistry,' it is not a 'proto-science,' but an autonomous spiritual discipline whose reasonings and goals have nothing to do with the intellectual instruments and the results of modern chemical experiments" (Turcanu, *Mircea Eliade*, 233). This belief developed prior to and independently of Jung (whose views were more ambivalent in any case, as seen above, pp. 289–291). Already Eliade's teacher Nae Ionescu appears to have presented alchemy as mysticism, probably under the influence of Evelyn Underhill (Pisi, "I 'traditionalisti'," 92 n. 36), but Eliade's "panvitalist" and soteriological interpretation was dependent on Guénon and Evola (*ibid.*, 49–51).

[174] Eliade, *Contribuţii la filosofia Renaşterii* (1928), available in French translation as *Contributions à la philosophie de la Renaissance*; see discussion in Turcanu, *Mircea Eliade*, 112–115. Looking back at this dissertation at the end of his life, Eliade clearly projected post-Yatesian understandings of "Renaissance hermeticism" back onto his own early work.

[175] See overview in Faivre, "Modern Western Esoteric Currents in the Work of Mircea Eliade," 150–154.

[176] Turcanu, *Mircea Eliade*, 360–361.

[177] For example, Eliade, *Viaṭă Nouă*, 212 (as quoted/translated in Spineto, "Mircea Eliade and Traditionalism," 68 n. 48): "Tuliu [the hero of his novel] will say things which . . . I have never had the courage to express in public. I have only, at times, confessed to a few friends my 'traditionalist' views (to use René Guénon's terms)."

[178] Pisi, "I 'tradizionalisti'," 51–60, 64–72. Pisi shows that, again, Eliade's understanding of archetypes is not derived from Jung but from Coomaraswamy (*ibid.*, 66–69). On Evola's political ideas, his failed attempts to become the philosopher of Italian fascism and German National Socialism, and his antisemitism, see the exhaustive analysis by Hansen [Hakl], "Julius Evolas Politisches Wirken."

Myth of Reintegration even turn out to be summaries of, and partly literal quotations from, an article by Coomaraswamy![179] Nevertheless, Eliade never became a convinced Traditionalist. He did not accept the notions of a "primordial tradition," an initiatic transmission of traditional knowledge, and cyclical decline, and, most importantly, he interpreted Traditionalist beliefs not as metaphysical truths, but as expressions of the fundamental needs of *homo religiosus*: man's (and Eliade's) desire for unity and reintegration in the life of the cosmos, as an emotional response to the existential anguish of temporal being.[180]

As suggested by his enormous popularity, Eliade's books do seem to have been experienced as "therapeutic" by a wide postwar readership, including many academics.[181] They clearly answered a widely felt need for alternatives to the dominant trends of thought – notably, in Eliade's own words, existentialist pessimism and "the chaos and meaninglessness of modern life"[182] – and became essential parts of the *Zeitgeist* of the 1960s.[183] Achieving world fame in this period, the Romanian exile with his unfamiliar approach ended up dominating the academic study of religion in the United States. As all his previous books now began to be translated, at least one new title by Eliade appeared in English every year between 1958 and 1965, and almost all of them became bestsellers.[184] This boom coincided with the no less spectacular popularity of Carl Gustav Jung, along with a range of further authors associated with Eranos, all made widely available in English by the financial support of the Bollingen Foundation.[185] The result was a remarkable transference of Eranos scholarship concerned with religion, myth and symbolism from Europe to the United States. Remarkably, at the same time when anything related to this domain was being declared

---

[179] Detailed analysis in Pisi, "I 'tradizionalisti'," 54–57, with reference to Eliade's *Mitul Reintegrării* (1942) and Coomaraswamy's essay "Angel and Titan" (1935). Furthermore, Pisi argues that Eliade's chapters are not just a summary of Coomaraswamy's work, but a "banalization" of it ("I 'tradizionalisti'," 57 and n. 80).

[180] Pisi, "I 'tradizionalisti'," 52, 57, 59, 60.

[181] For testimonies about the impact that Eliade's work made on members of this generation, see, for example, the cases of Jonathan Z. Smith, Robert Ellwood, Norman Girardot, and Bruce Lincoln (Turcanu, *Mircea Eliade*, 449–452; Ellwood, *Politics of Myth*, 5; Ellwood, *Sixties Spiritual Awakening*, 94), and a range of further memories by former students collected in Gligor and Ricketts, *Intalniri cu / Encounters with Mircea Eliade*.

[182] Eliade, *Occultism, Witchcraft and Cultural Fashions*, 8–11, 63–65, here, 64. Eliade discussed the French magazine *Planète*, Teilhard de Chardin, and structuralism as contemporary "cultural fashions," and he could easily have gone on to analyze the wave of fascination with his own work along similar lines.

[183] Ellwood, *Sixties Spiritual Awakening*, 90–100 (on Eliade as one typical representative of the religious *Zeitgeist* next to, for example, Pierre Teilhard de Chardin, Nikos Kazantzakis, Carl Gustav Jung, Joseph Campbell, Thomas Merton, Paul Tillich, or John A. T. Robinson).

[184] Turcanu, *Mircea Eliade*, 439.   [185] McGuire, *Bollingen*.

taboo in German-speaking countries,[186] the "spirit of Eranos" flourished like never before on the other side of the Atlantic, further strengthened by a series of American intellectuals strongly connected with Eranos and its agendas, such as, notably, the mythologist Joseph Campbell and the archetypal psychologist James Hillman.[187] This is how a range of basic assumptions originating in European interbellum scholarship on "myth" came to be accepted as a matter of course, not just by a wide international audience, but also by many of the scholars who, from the 1960s onwards, began to become interested in "hermetic" or "occult" traditions as an object of study.

In spite of this fact, however, the range of currents and ideas that we have been discussing as relevant to "Western esotericism" in the previous chapters of this book did *not* play any central role in the Eranos agenda up to the 1970s, at least not explicitly, and they were not conceptualized as manifestations of one continuous tradition or as belonging to a more or less coherent field of research. It is only in 1974 that Eliade briefly sketched the general outlines of such a historiographical project, under the influence of Frances Yates' concept of the Hermetic Tradition and probably of Antoine Faivre's work: in his essay "The Occult and the Modern World" (1974) he referred to a "secret 'occult' tradition" represented by gnosticism and hermeticism in antiquity, reviving in the Italian Renaissance and its "longing for a universalistic, transhistorical, 'mythical' religion," continued by the "vogue of occultism" in nineteenth-century France, and culminating in the "occult explosion" of the 1970s.[188] Prior to this, Scholem had been devoting his life to recovering the "esoteric" dimensions of Judaism, and from a very different perspective, Corbin had done the same for Islam;[189] but perhaps surprisingly, a similar project focused on the third of the great scriptural religions, Christianity, had not taken shape, and began to emerge only during the 1970s in the work of Antoine Faivre.

If Judaism and Islam were believed to have their own "esoteric" traditions, what exactly did that mean in the context of Eranos prior to Faivre?

---

[186] In this regard, the essential factor was the "Critical Theory" of the Frankfurt School: discussion below, pp. 312–313, and cf. above, n. 160.

[187] On the role of these two authors at Eranos, see Hakl, *Verborgene Geist*, 232–240 and 329–337.

[188] Eliade, *Occultism, Witchcraft, and Cultural Fashions*, quotations on 49, 55–56, 58. Yates and Faivre are mentioned on 55–56.

[189] It must be noted that Hebrew has no term for "mysticism," and Scholem spoke of *ba'aley sod*, "esoterics" (Dan, "In Quest," 122), so that his famous historical overview of 1946 should perhaps have been titled more appropriately *Major Trends in Jewish Esotericism*. As seen above, Corbin adopted the emic terminology *batîn* ("hidden," or "inward"; cf. Lory, "Sexual Intercourse," 49–50).

As pointed out by Moshe Idel, Scholem's understanding was based upon the idea of a sharp antagonism between "a Kabbalistic mode of thought motivated by a mythical universe, and the 'history-saturated' consciousness of the rabbinic mind";[190] and, moreover, Scholem maintained that this mythical universe, deeply informed by the paganism of the ancient Near East, had entered Judaism "from outside," so to speak, by way of gnosticism.[191] In short, Scholem saw Jewish "esotericism" as an eruption of mythical consciousness into the historical consciousness of rabbinic Judaism, triggered by contact with non-Jewish sources. But at the same time, it is precisely in these products of pagan–monotheistic syncretism that he perceived the true, "living heart" that had kept Judaism alive, as opposed to the dry and stifling legalism of the rabbinic counterpart:[192] somehow, then, its essence was not exclusively Jewish, for the mythical dimension lent a more universal quality to it. In the case of Corbin, the situation is easier to summarize: he saw "esotericism" quite simply as the true, hidden or inward dimension of exoteric Islam, known only to the mystics and visionaries and imperceptible to the historian. What we find, then, is that both thinkers claimed, for their respective fields, that the true "vital essence" of monotheistic religions was *not* to be found in their external, historical, doctrinal, and legalistic[193] manifestations, but only in a more universal, experiential dimension dominated by myth, symbolism, and the religious imagination, and ultimately focused on a superior knowledge of divine mysteries, or "gnosis." This "inner" ("esoteric") dimension was seen as the true secret – the "well of turbulent vitality" in Scholem's words – of "outward" ("exoteric") religion.[194] We will see that until the early 1990s, very much the same perspective dominated Antoine Faivre's understanding of "esotericism" in Christian culture.

[190] Idel, "Rabbinism versus Kabbalism," 289. [191] *Ibid.*, 283, 291.

[192] On the centrality, in Scholem's oeuvre, of the idea "that Judaism was kept alive by the revival, in mysticism, of the mythical-magical worldview," in the context of his organic understanding of Judaism as "living religion" and its roots in Romanticism and contemporary *Lebensphilosophie*, see Hamacher, *Gershom Scholem*, 195–227 (here 195); on the "regenerating" virtue of myth and mysticism, see also Biale, *Gershom Scholem*, 113–147.

[193] On the anti-legalistic dimension in both Scholem and Corbin, see Wasserstrom, *Religion after Religion*, 57–59.

[194] See the opening quotation. If we go back to the last paragraph of the previous section, and compare this perspective with the narrative that emerged from Carl Gustav Jung's approach, one can see how easily the two can merge. Nevertheless, Scholem did not accept Jung's theory of archetypes, and was irritated about David Biale's suggestions concerning Jungian leanings in his work (Biale, *Gershom Scholem*, 145–146; Scholem, *Briefe III*, 199), but see the perceptive remarks by Wolfson, *Through a Speculum*, 56–57 n. 21. As for Corbin, see, for example, "*L'imago templi*," 288, 290, 322: Corbin was respectful towards Jung and quotes him from time to time in his writings, but saw archetypes as metaphysical (celestial), not psychological realities.

The ambitions of Scholem and Corbin were therefore *not* limited to the straightforward agenda of "filling in the gaps" of traditional historiography, by calling attention to a series of historical currents that had been neglected by previous scholars (merkabah mysticism, medieval kabbalah, Lurianic theosophy, Suhrawardī's *ishrāqi* school, Ibn 'Arabi's mysticism, Ismaelism, Sufism, and so on). They were after something bigger as well: nothing less than an answer to the question of what is true and of lasting value in Judaism and Islam, and ultimately in the scriptural religions as such. In other words, underneath the historiographical project there was a normative one, which valuated "myth and mysticism" much higher than mere "legalism and doctrine." Now, the problem is that such normative judgments may be appropriate for philosophers or theologians, but cannot be supported on the basis of historical evidence. In the sources available to the historian, one simply does not discover anything about the truths or values of Judaism or Islam: all one will ever find is a wide variety of conflicting *claims* and *opinions* about such truths and values. One may perhaps regret this fact, but it cannot be avoided: the moment a scholar leaves the position of impartiality or "methodological agnosticism" and starts favoring some of these claims and opinions as more true or valuable than others, he starts practicing what I have been referring to as "eclectic historiography" on the basis of some philosophical or theological *a priori*.

Even Scholem, the "historian's historian," did not entirely succeed in avoiding this temptation. As pointed out by Steven Wasserstrom, in Scholem's writings and, much more extremely, those of Corbin, the "esoteric" dimensions were promoted from a position of marginality to one of centrality with Judaism and Islam, at the expense of the purely doctrinal, legalistic, and other "exoteric" dimensions that have in fact dominated much of the beliefs and practices of ordinary Jews and Muslims.[195] This emphasis is understandable as a reaction against the eclecticism of previous scholars, who had marginalized and suppressed "mysticism" as irrelevant to *their* ideas of "true" Judaism and Islam;[196] but this does not make it any more correct as a general statement about those religions. Presenting

---

[195] Wasserstrom, *Religion after Religion*, 52, cf. 98, 174, 180–182, 239–241 (one need not share the author's polemical stance to appreciate the basic point); Wasserstrom, "Response," 461–462; Algar, "Study of Islam"; cf. Masuzawa, "Reflections on the Charmed Circle," 435–436. Provoked by Idel's "Rabbinism versus Kabbalism," Joseph Dan recognizes Scholem's "strict, almost ascetic concentration on the field of Jewish mysticism" and his complete avoidance of such dimensions as Jewish philosophy, Halakhah, or Talmud, but claims that he was merely restricting himself to his own field of expertise ("Gershom Scholem," 36 with n. 36 referring to Idel).

[196] For the paradigmatic case of Heinrich Graetz in the case of Judaism, see Schäfer, "'Adversus cabbalam'."

"esoteric" dimensions as the true "vital core" of a religion is possible only by adopting some kind of "essence versus manifestation" scheme, in which the great majority of believers have supposedly been oblivious to the true nature of their own religion, which is known only to a mystical elite – and some scholars studying them.[197] Such essentialism is a belief, not a fact of history. By adopting it nevertheless, one replaces the historian's perspective with that of the metaphysician or theologian. The "study of esotericism" then becomes a crypto-philosophical or crypto-theological pursuit that feels free to move beyond history towards a "higher knowledge" about what, behind the surface of events or on a deeper and more "inward" level, is supposed to be "really" going on. One might be tempted to conclude that quite a lot of what has been presented as the "study of esotericism" since the 1960s has, to a greater or lesser extent, fallen prey to this religionist temptation. But it is perhaps more correct that many scholars embraced it with enthusiasm, because at some level of consciousness they shared the dream of escaping from history.

Originating in Jungian approaches and developing into new directions after World War II, Eranos may be considered the classic example of "religionism," and a predominant model for how Western esotericism has come to be understood from the 1960s. In Chapter 2, discussing its emergence in the decades around 1700, I referred to religionism as an approach to religion that presents itself as "historical" but nevertheless denies, or strongly minimizes, the relevance of questions pertaining to historical "influences," and hence of historical criticism, because of its central assumption that the true referent of religion does not lie in the domain of human culture and society but only in a direct, unmediated, personal experience of the divine;[198] and at the beginning of this section, I referred to it more briefly as "the project of exploring historical sources in search of what is eternal and universal." But we have seen that in the same period that saw the emergence of religionism, there also emerged a counter-paradigm based upon Enlightenment assumptions, which saw Reason as the universal yardstick for evaluating the truth or seriousness of any worldview. Religious or philosophical currents that were perceived as not satisfying the criterion of rationality lost their right to be taken

---

[197] On history of religions as a disclosure of hidden meanings, see the pertinent remarks by Hugh Urban, who points out how closely Wasserstrom's attempt to unveil the "secrets" of Eranos scholarship resembles the approach that he criticizes ("Syndrome of the Secret," 439–440). Cf. the "gnostic study of religion" (practiced by scholars who claim to understand "secrets" about religion that escape the common practitioner) advocated by Jeffrey J. Kripal, and my critical objections in Hanegraaff, "Leaving the Garden."

[198] Above, Chapter 2, pp. 126–127, 149.

seriously in intellectual discourse, and were relegated to the waste-basket category of "prejudice," "superstition," "foolishness," or "stupidity." In that process, they were tacitly divested of their traditional status as players in the field of history, and transformed into non-historical universals of human thinking and behavior: they no longer needed to be discussed as traditions ("platonism," "hermeticism," even "paganism"), but could be dismissed as synonymous with irrationality as such.

If Eranos was the main twentieth-century manifestation of religionism, the alternative Enlightenment paradigm was continued in the decades before and after World War II by a philosophical school associated with the *Institut für Sozialforschung* in Frankfurt, and known as Critical Theory or the Frankfurt School.[199] Grounded in Marxist assumptions and dominated by Jewish intellectuals, its moral prestige after 1945 was above any suspicion; and its understanding of totalitarianism would remain remarkably authoritative in Germany and the United States in spite of the Cold War, even after the full extent of the Stalinist terror was revealed to the Western public by the publication of Solzhenitsyn's *Gulag Archipelago* in 1973. The history of how Critical Theory has impacted the perception of "Western esotericism" among intellectuals after World War II, particularly in Germany, deserves a major study; but for our present concerns, it suffices to point out that the background assumptions of critical theorists about concepts such as "magic" or "the occult"[200] display no theoretical originality but are derived straight from the "waste-basket" approach of the Enlightenment as analyzed in the previous chapter. The element of innovation in Critical Theory was that it posited a straight connection between such "irrationalism" and fascism, thereby suggesting that the entire field of myth, symbolism, mysticism, gnosis, or esotericism was, by definition, tainted with dangerous political and immoral implications. Georg Lukács developed the basic argument about "irrationalism" and fascism in his classic study *Die Zerstörung der Vernunft*, based upon the Marxist adaptation of Hegelian belief in an inseparable connection between Reason and historical progress.[201] From this perspective there could be no such thing as a "history of esotericism" in any strict sense, for irrationalism has no autonomous existence by definition: as Lukács put it, it can never be more

---

[199] Jay, *Dialectical Imagination*; Wiggershaus, *Frankfurt School*; Bottomore, *Frankfurt School and its Critics*.

[200] For example, Adorno, "Theses Against Occultism"; Horkheimer and Adorno, *Dialects of Enlightenment*.

[201] Lukács, *Zerstörung der Vernunft*, 111. For the definition of "irrationalism" as the attempt to bridge the distance between thinking and reality by appealing to "higher knowledge," see *ibid.*, 88–89, 93.

than a "form of reaction (reaction here in the double meaning of secondary and regressive) to the dialectical development of human thought."[202] In other words, it lacks independent validity and is inextricably linked to "reactionary" politics. In the wake of Lukács, Horkheimer, and Adorno, these basic assumptions became a dominant factor in the thinking of left-leaning intellectuals and academics after World War II; and particularly in Germany, the result was a virtual taboo on the study of anything related to esotericism or the occult, except of course from a perspective of *Ideologiekritik*. Any wish to do research in such domains from a strictly historical perspective became suspicious by definition, as it seemed to reflect an unhealthy fascination with the perennial enemy of reason and progress, and could always be interpreted as a front for covert apologeticism on behalf of dangerous anti-democratic ideas. Most of the critical attacks on Eranos by academics have been inspired, directly or indirectly, by these assumptions typical of Critical Theory and the Frankfurt School;[203] and many scholars of Western esotericism have, at some point in their career, been forced to defend themselves against the suspicion of holding far-right sympathies.[204]

Although the religionist and Enlightenment paradigms are one another's counterpart, we have seen that they have more in common than one might think. Already in their original manifestations around 1700, they were based upon ideological axioms rather than empirical research, and as a result they were seriously deficient as methodological frameworks for the study of history. The anti-apologetic alternative to both, which combined a methodology of historical criticism with a theoretical focus on the "Hellenization of Christianity," could have developed into a proper academic study of Western esotericism; but its potential never came to fruition because the entire domain was dropped from the history of philosophy after Brucker, no other discipline took it up, and the Enlightenment paradigm came to dominate how it was perceived by intellectuals and academics. The result was a sharp decline of serious scholarship in the field, as we have seen,

---

[202] *Ibid.*, 92–93. Cf. James Webb's notion of occultism as a "flight from reason" (*Occult Establishment*, 8 and *passim*).

[203] Evident examples are Wasserstrom, *Religion after Religion*; Dubuisson, *Twentieth Century Mythologies*; McCutcheon, *Manufacturing Religion*. In my opinion, the academic debate about these influential studies will remain unsatisfactory unless their underlying theoretical and methodological assumptions are made into an object of critical analysis. For a first step in that direction, see Fisher, "Fascist Scholars, Fascist Scholarship."

[204] See, for example, Laurant, "*Politica Hermetica*." Obviously I do not mean to suggest that such suggestions are never correct, although they often are. My point is that they tend to be based on an ideology that makes study of Western esotericism "tainted" by default, so that scholars can be attacked for fascist tendencies even in the absence of any demonstrable evidence.

finally resulting in the Waste Land of the nineteenth century. Eranos was the first major reaction to this state of affairs, but turned into the vanguard of a new form of religionism that studied history in the hope of finding ways to transcend it. Critical Theory, for its part, perpetuated the unhistorical ideology of the alternative Enlightenment paradigm, thereby nipping historical research in the bud and declaring it politically suspect by definition. Caught in the middle between religionist and rationalist ideologies, the historiographical tradition in this field was therefore abandoned for two centuries, resulting in alarming levels of ignorance among intellectuals and academics. But fortunately, it had not vanished for good. In the 1960s the core approach of the anti-apologetic tradition began to return to the academy at last, under the flag of "the Hermetic Tradition."

THE RETURN OF THE HISTORIANS: FROM PEUCKERT AND THORNDIKE TO FRANCES YATES

The preceding discussions might almost make one forget that specialized historians working in specific fields were continuing quietly to go about their core business of exploring the sources of the past, usually without much concern for such things as the "crisis of the modern world," existential anxieties about being imprisoned in time, or crypto-metaphysical projects of transcending history in view of some kind of salvational gnosis. Since the final decades of the nineteenth century, classicists and philologists began the work of recovering the manuscript sources of ancient hermetism, magic, astrology, and alchemy;[205] and on those foundations, serious historical research in these domains began to flourish around the turn of the century, with scholars such as Auguste Bouché-Leclercq, Franz Boll, Richard Reitzenstein, Wilhelm Bousset, Wilhelm and Josef Kroll, Walter Scott, and many others: a tradition that culminated finally in classics such as, notably, André-Jean Festugière's monumental four-volume study *La révélation d'Hermès Trismégiste* (1944–1954). However, research of a similar kind focused on the period *after* antiquity developed only piecemeal and gradually; and with the notable exception of historically corrupt overviews for the general market written by esoteric or occultist authors, mostly of French provenance,[206] comprehensive or synthetic works remained rare.

---

[205] For example, Berthelot and Ruelle, *Collection des anciens alchimistes grecs* (1887–1888); the multi-volume "Codex Codicum Astrologorum Graecorum" (from 1898 on); Preisendanz, *Papyri graecae magicae* (1928); Nock and Festugière, *Corpus Hermeticum* (1946, 1954).

[206] See, for example, Bosc, *La doctrine ésotérique à travers les âges* (1899); Jollivet-Castelot, Ferniot, and Redonnel, *Les sciences maudites* (1900); Durville, *La science secrète* (1923); Hall, *Secret Teachings*

Next to the research tradition associated with the "Warburg School" and the famous oeuvre of Frances A. Yates, which will be the main topic of this section, only two authors produced works of such a kind on a high scholarly level.

The first of these two, Will-Erich Peuckert (1895–1969), has remained virtually unknown outside the German-speaking domain. None of his works were translated, and he left no pupils to continue his approach, so that his oeuvre has remained an isolated phenomenon in spite of its pioneering importance.[207] In the present context, Peuckert deserves at least a brief discussion because he was the first modern scholar to take up the prematurely abandoned historiographical tradition that had led from Ehregott Daniel Colberg to Jacob Brucker, and to make a new attempt at reconstructing the forgotten world of "Platonic-Hermetic Christianity" from the original sources.[208] Like Frances Yates after him, he pointed towards the Italian humanism of Florence as the origin of a new tradition of "magic" that had become central to Renaissance culture; and, like Antoine Faivre, he traced this lineage further through the predominantly German traditions of Paracelsianism, Christian theosophy, and *Naturphilosophie* from the sixteenth century through the eighteenth. Peuckert's primary field was that of *Volkskunde* ("folkloristics," or "European ethnology"), but his importance for us lies in his series of monographs on Paracelsus, Sebastian Franck, Jacob Böhme, Rosicrucianism, astrology, and, most important of all, his best-known book *Pansophie* and its sequels, *Gabalia* and *Das Rosenkreutz*.[209]

In spite of his explicit references to Colberg, the conflict between "pagan" philosophies and biblical Christianity did not loom very large in Peuckert's perspective. Instead, what he perceived was a momentous conflict between the declining rural world of the medieval farmers (*die bäuerliche Welt*), and the newly emerging bourgeois world (*die bürgerliche Welt*) dominated by

---

(1928); Grillot de Givry, *La musée des sorciers, mages et alchimistes* (1929); de Campigny, *Les traditions et les doctrines ésotériques* (1939).

[207] Apart from an unpublished Ph.D. dissertation that concentrates on other aspects of Peuckert's oeuvre (Jacobsen, "Boundary Breaking and Compliance"), the only discussion of Peuckert in English is Hanegraaff, "Will-Erich Peuckert." The only important discussion in German is Zimmermann, "'Ich gebe die Fackel weiter!'."

[208] Peuckert was explicit about placing himself in this lineage: see *Pansophie*, VIII. On his pioneering labors in primary-source research, without benefit of critical editions, see Hanegraaff, "Will-Erich Peuckert," 287–289 (including the reference to Carlos Gilly's recognition of Peuckert as a "master": Gilly, "Comenius und die Rosenkreuzer," 95 n. 21).

[209] Peuckert, *Theophrastus Paracelsus*; *Sebastian Franck*; *Das Leben Jacob Böhmes*; *Die Rosenkreutzer*; *Astrologie*; *Pansophie*; *Gabalia* (= *Pansophie* vol. II); *Das Rosenkreutz* (= *Pansophie* vol. III). For Peuckert's general view of early modern history, as a context for his other monographs, see *Die grosse Wende*.

the city and the new merchant class. In describing how these "two streams burst upon one another"[210] in the early modern period, Peuckert was still thinking in the organic and teleological terms of Romantic historiography: throughout his work, historical periods and cultures are described as if they are living organisms whose potentials and destinies are already implicit in their seeds, and that possess an inner drive towards attaining their full potential. The magical worldview described in *Pansophie* and *Gabalia* is seen as organically rooted in the rural Middle Ages, and Peuckert wants to show that, far from simply declining or vanishing in the face of modernity, "only now, stirred by some impulse, it unfolded its most seductive blossom . . . [F]rom this 'decay,' there emerged an unheard-of world that still remains wholly unknown to us."[211]

This new spiritual worldview or religious mentality, which Peuckert calls "pansophy," began to emerge in Renaissance Florence but was lacking in vitality there and might have remained no more than an unfulfilled promise.[212] It only revealed its full potential after having been transported to German soil, in the *Naturphilosophie* of Paracelsus and his followers, finally culminating in the Christian theosophy of Jacob Böhme, and continuing through a string of later and lesser representatives as far as into the eighteenth century. Highlighting Goethe's *Faust* as its archetypal expression, Peuckert described pansophy as a quintessentially German perspective ultimately grounded in the platonic notion, as expounded by Ficino, of the two "wings of the soul": the wing of the intellect that allows us to penetrate the secrets of nature, and the wing of mystical contemplation by which we are lifted directly to the Absolute.[213] Once transposed to the German context, the two wings are transformed into a doctrine of two *lights* (the "Light of Nature" and the "Light of Grace") and two *books* (the "Book of Nature" and the Bible). This notion of two complementary ways of knowledge was the Ariadne's thread by which Peuckert led his readers through the labyrinth of forgotten "pansophical" texts, often by means of long quotations. He did so with an infectious enthusiasm and very impressive erudition, and his books remain a pleasure to read for those who can appreciate his inimitable style of writing; but although Peuckert became

---

[210] Peuckert, *Pansophie*, x.   [211] *Ibid.*, xi.

[212] On Peuckert's description of Florentine platonism as a beautiful but somewhat decadent *fin-de-siècle* estheticism, in contrast to the healthy, practical, earthy mentality of the German common man, as exemplified by Paracelsus, see Hanegraaff, "Will-Erich Peuckert," 296–297.

[213] Peuckert, *Pansophie*, 12–15, quoting Walser, *Gesammelte Studien*, 277–278. The central reference for Peuckert and Walser is Lorenzo de' Medici's poem "Altercazione," in which Ficino appears as a musician singing Orphic hymns, and responds to Lorenzo's melancholy by evoking the platonic image of the two wings (Lorenzo de' Medici, *Poemi*, 71–102).

a recognized authority of *Volkskunde* during the final decades of his life, appointed to what would remain the only German chair in that discipline for many years, his name was already met with "an apathetic reserve" two years after his death in 1969,[214] and he left no pupils to continue his researches into the "pansophical" tradition. One may reasonably assume that this had to do with the virtual taboo on such areas of research in Germany after World War II, to which I referred earlier. Although Peuckert's personal reputation was spotless – unlike most colleagues in the field of *Volkskunde* he had always refused to compromise or collaborate with the Nazis, who deprived him of his right to teach in 1935[215] – he just happened to have specialized in a field that was tainted with the double charge of "irrationality." It was dismissed as irrelevant and superseded *Schwärmerei* by rationalists in any case; and, in addition, the historical links of *Volkskunde* and "German mysticism" with the *völkisch* nationalist movements of the interbellum were much too close for comfort in the eyes of left-leaning intellectuals, who, under the influence of the neo-Marxism of the Frankfurt School, tended to associate anything pointing in this direction with some kind of implicit "Ur-fascism."[216] As a result, what could have become the beginning of a genuine academic tradition in the field of "Western esotericism" remained stillborn, so to speak: it never progressed beyond the works of Peuckert himself.

The second major author of comprehensive or synthetic works prior to Frances Yates in fact exerted a significant influence on her thinking. The American historian Lynn Thorndike (1882–1965) devoted his life to exploring the role of "magic" in the intellectual history of Europe, starting with his dissertation defended at Columbia University in 1905,[217] at the age of twenty-three, and culminating in the monumental eight-volume work known as *A History of Magic and Experimental Science*, published between 1923 and 1958.[218] Although most of the critical reception of Thorndike's oeuvre has taken place in the field of history of science, it is important to emphasize that he was in fact an intellectual historian specializing in the Middle Ages: his successive professorships at Western Reserve

---

[214] Zimmermann, "'Ich gebe die Fackel weiter!'," vii.

[215] For the details, see Jacobsen, "Boundary Breaking and Compliance," 57–59.

[216] For this notion, see Eco, "Ur-Fascism."

[217] Thorndike, *The Place of Magic in the Intellectual History of Europe*. The very title shows Thorndike's debt to the pioneer of intellectual history James Harvey Robinson, one of his chief teachers at Columbia University (see Thorndike, review of Robinson).

[218] For Thorndike's scholarly career, see Clagett, "Éloge: Lynn Thorndike"; Boyer and Boyer, "Memorial: Lynn Thorndike"; and Kibre, "Lynn Thorndike" (with bibliography up to 1952). For a good critical discussion of his oeuvre, see Durand, "Magic and Experimental Science."

University in Cleveland and, from 1924 until his retirement in 1950, at
the Faculty of Political Science of Columbia University were all in "history." His oeuvre – not only his eight-volume *summa*, but his *Catalogue
of Incipits*[219] and an impressive flood of articles as well – was grounded
in painstaking archival research during a series of research trips that made
him "one of the best known American names in European manuscript
rooms."[220] As rightly noted by the contemporary specialist of medieval
magic Claire Fanger, his remarkable achievements in this domain will be
appreciated – in spite of many gaps and errors that are evident from the
more advanced perspective of contemporary research – by "anyone who
has had the humbling experience of extracting evidence even from much
smaller quantities of manuscript material."[221] The sheer amount of forgotten material unearthed, edited and commented upon by Thorndike
was daunting indeed. His first two volumes dealt with the first thirteen
centuries, going systematically through a large string of authors and anonymous works; the next two volumes showed an increasing expansion of the
scale of treatment, dealing with the fourteenth and fifteenth centuries
alone; and this trend was continued in two further volumes about the
sixteenth century and two final ones devoted to the seventeenth. To this,
one should add a "veritable forest of Appendices"[222] (sixty-two in number)
and very detailed Indices that made the set into an encyclopedic work of
almost inexhaustible richness. Although the scope of Thorndike's *magnum
opus* might seem to make him into a specialist of the Renaissance and early
modernity as much as of the Middle Ages, he in fact disliked the concept
of a "Renaissance," and emphasized the continuity of ancient and medieval
thought into modernity.[223]

In spite of its obvious contribution to scholarship, Thorndike's work
was initially received with considerable harshness, even hostility, from the
direction of classical philology and history of science.[224] For our concerns,
it is particularly important to look at the reaction to his work by the
doyen of history of science, George Sarton. In a large review of the first
two volumes of Thorndike's *History*, in 1924, Sarton had to admit that
by studying "an enormous amount of repellent material" the author had

[219] Thorndike and Kibre, *Catalogue of Incipits*; and supplement published in *Speculum* 14 (1939),
93–105. On its importance, see Durand, "Magic and Experimental Science," 691; Clagett, "Eloge,"
88.
[220] Durand, "Magic and Experimental Science," 692.   [221] Fanger, "Medieval Ritual Magic," x.
[222] Durand, "Magic and Experimental Science," 693.
[223] Thorndike, "Renaissance or Prenaissance?," 65: "Legacies from the past? Yes. Inheritances from
previous period? Yes. Survivals? Yes. Resemblances to our forebears? Yes. Reformations? Perhaps.
Reactions? Unfortunately. But no rebirths or restorations!"
[224] For the former perspective, see Riess, review of Lynn Thorndike.

made a valuable contribution to scholarly research;[225] but in fact, almost the entire review was devoted to an emotional attack on the implications of the title and on Thorndike's basic historiographical program. These eleven pages of high rhetoric drama – at one point, Sarton describes the history of science as "a growing light eating up the darkness"[226] – are an ultimate example of the reification of "magic" and "science" as mutually exclusive universal categories; and they illustrate not only how important these categories are as identity markers from a perspective of Enlightenment ideology, but also how decisively they can determine the very parameters of historical research. Sarton emphasized (italics in the original) that "*science is essentially a cumulative, a progressive activity,*" characterized by rationality and skepticism.[227] Magic was presented as its radical opposite: "[o]ne irrational idea is as good as another. To speak of evolution of magic is thus a contradiction in terms."[228] We have encountered this type of argument before, and need not analyze it again.[229] In Sarton's formulation,

science is essentially progressive, while magic is essentially conservative. There can be no compromise between them; they cannot possibly walk together – for one is going forwards, and the other backwards. All that they can do is to hinder and fight one another. One might thus properly write a history of the warfare of experimental science and magic, but it should be noted that Thorndike's thesis is exactly the opposite. He would make us believe that the magician . . . was the ancestor of the modern investigator; that reason is the fruit of unreason; and truth, of superstition and occultism.[230]

---

[225] Sarton, review of Lynn Thorndike (1924), 88–89.

[226] *Ibid.,* 83. See also p. 79 ("to call such a book a 'history of experimental science' is a joke, and a very bad one at that"; most readers' familiarity with scientific knowledge will unfortunately be "on the same level as the author's and [they] will thus be unable to realize how completely they are deceived"; the work will "become an abundant source of misunderstanding, and will work considerable harm"), 81 ("the confusion of Thorndike's ideas"), 83 ("this elaborate parody of the history of medieval science"), 84 ("Nonsense!"). Even Sarton's close collaborators appear to have been shocked by his outburst, and it is remarkable that, somehow, the two scholars still "continued in friendly disagreement" (see Thorndike, "Some Letters of George Sarton," 324–325). In his review of volumes 3 and 4, Sarton acknowledged that as "a palaeographic virtuoso," Thorndike had "placed himself in the foreground of scholarship with the first two volumes" (review of Lynn Thorndike [1935], 471), but went on to repeat his fundamental criticism in milder terms. In 1957, two years after Sarton's death, Thorndike received the George Sarton medal of the History of Science Society (Anon., "Award of the George Sarton Medal").

[227] Sarton, review of Lynn Thorndike (1924), 78, 80.   [228] *Ibid.,* 81.

[229] See above, Chapter 3, pp. 167–168 (the reification of "magic"); pp. 184–189 (discussion of Brian Vickers), p. 196 (the "Conflict Thesis"). See also Chapter 4, pp. 312–313 (Lukács' notion that "irrationality" can have no history), and cf. Chapter 2, p. 150 (conclusions about the "Enlightenment paradigm").

[230] Sarton, review of Lynn Thorndike (1924), 84. The "warfare" metaphor is, of course, a reference to one of the founders of the "Conflict Thesis," Andrew Dickson White (see above, Chapter 3, n. 160).

Sarton had good reasons to be alarmed, and his remarks were sharpsighted. Even though Thorndike still had one foot planted firmly in the positivist camp,[231] his basic approach did point towards a new perspective that would come to fruition after World War II, first in the type of historiography represented by Frances Yates, and eventually in the "new historiography" whose representatives succeeded, in 2002, in having the term "pseudo-sciences" removed from the authoritative annual bibliography of Sarton's journal *Isis*.[232] With hindsight, the revolution announced in Thorndike's work may be summarized as follows:

(1) Thorndike was willing to consider a constructive rather than antithetic relation between history of magic and history of science, in which elements of the former might have influenced the latter. By implication, "magic" was seen as a historical phenomenon capable of change and development; and as such, it would have to be taken seriously by historians of science.

(2) Once this step was taken, a further one was bound to follow: even the very distinction between magic and experimental science no longer appeared to be so clearcut. Particularly in the medieval context, the boundaries became blurred: rather than with a situation of magic influencing science, one might be dealing with a situation where the two could no longer be distinguished. As a result, not only would historians of science have to take magic seriously, but they would inevitably become historians of magic themselves!

(3) It followed, furthermore, that the Middle Ages could no longer be seen as an age of darkness and decline into superstition and ignorance – "ancient science gradually smothered by the luxuriant growth of medieval magic,"[233] in Sarton's words – but had to become an entirely legitimate period of continuous scientific exploration.

(4) As a further implication, the sharp boundary between medieval "magic" and modern "science" became blurred as well. While the Middle Ages began to look more like a period of experimental science, medieval magic appeared to continue straight into the early modern period, and

---

[231] On Thorndike's own use of "magic" and "science" as reified general categories, clearly modeled after Tylor and Frazer, see Durand, "Magic and Experimental Science," 698–699 (with reference to Thorndike, *History*, vol. v, 12–13). Interestingly, both Riess and Sarton criticized him for including alchemy and astrology under the general "magic" umbrella (Riess, review of Lynn Thorndike, 210; Sarton, review of Lynn Thorndike [1924], 85).

[232] See above, Chapter 3, n. 126.

[233] Sarton, review of Lynn Thorndike (1924), 84 (*ibid.*: "the beautiful garden of ancient thought was gradually overrun with superstitions").

even many of the great "heroes" of scientific progress were considerably indebted to it.[234]

Contrary to Sarton, Thorndike was thinking not as a partisan of modern science, but as an intellectual historian interested in contextuality and complexity.[235] His job, as he saw it, was not that of protecting the project of modernity and progress against the perceived specter of irrationalism or superstition, or engaging in "hero worship or debunking,"[236] but simply that of trying to describe and interpret the past as faithfully as possible:

Frankly, it is not for this contribution towards modernity that we most prize these writings of two remote centuries which we have been at some pains to decipher and to set forth. We have taken them as we found them and we esteem them for what they are in their totality, their fourteenth and their fifteenth century *complexio* – a chapter in the history of human thought. Read it and smile or read it and weep, as you please. We would not credit it with the least particle of modern science that does not belong to it, nor would we deprive it of any of that magic which constitutes in no small measure its peculiar charm. Perhaps it would be well to read it and think of what the future historian may say of the mentality and scholasticism of the present era and with what sympathy or antipathy he would be justified in regarding us.[237]

Precisely this kind of relativism typical of the "pure historian"[238] is what must have worried Sarton most, but it also defines the nature of Thorndike's contribution to the history of "rejected knowledge." At one point, Sarton blamed him for being more interested in the "weeds" than the "flowers" in the garden of history;[239] and one might readily agree that Thorndike's

---

[234] On Thorndike's aversion to the obsession with "great names," who often receive more credit than they deserve, at the expense of the "solid achievements of obscure scientists," see Durand, "Magic and Experimental Science," 702–703 (here n. 22). See also her remarks on Thorndike's distaste for "historical generalizations about *Zeitgeist*," particularly in relation to the Renaissance and humanism (*ibid.*, 704).

[235] For the underlying conflict between a partisan of the "hard sciences" and of the "humanities" respectively, it is instructive to compare Thorndike, *History*, vol. II, 983, with Sarton's response in his review (1924), 83. Thorndike emphasized the inherent conservatism of human thought: "Even the most intellectual men seem to have a limited number of ideas, just as humanity has a limited number of domesticated animals. Not only is man unable by taking thought to add one cubit to his stature, he usually equally fails to add one new idea to humanity's small collection. Often men seem to be repeating ideas like parrots." Sarton responded by presenting history of science as a "heroic and stupendous tale" full of "victories and conquests; permanent conquests over the chaos; a growing light eating up the darkness... Men of letters have no conception of this; in their little world, indeed, the number of ideas is limited, and every one of them has long been domesticated..."

[236] Thorndike, "Whatever Was, *Was* Right," 268.   [237] Thorndike, *History*, vol. IV, 615.

[238] Durand, "Magic and Experimental Science," 712.

[239] Sarton, review of Lynn Thorndike (1924), 84.

concern, like Peuckert's, was with the complete biosystem in its full diversity. If Sarton was thinking like a gardener, then, Thorndike was thinking like a biologist.[240]

Each from their own perspective, both Peuckert and Thorndike were still concerned with "survivals" – in the classic Tylorean sense, including its reference to the etymological root of superstition, *superstes* – of "medieval magic" into the early modern period; and it remained possible to read their work as merely documenting the stubborn tenacity of magical thinking faced with the inevitable forward march of modern science and progress. With the famous studies published by Frances A. Yates in the 1960s and 1970s, such interpretations were no longer possible. What provoked traditional historians of science, and fascinated the general public, was that she boldly entertained the very ideas that Sarton had already feared as an implication of Thorndike's historiography: "that the magician . . . was the ancestor of the modern investigator; that reason is the fruit of unreason; and truth, of superstition and occultism."[241] Contrary to Thorndike, Yates was quite traditional in pitting the Middle Ages as a period of darkness and stagnation against the Renaissance as an age of light and progress that led the way towards the momentous rise of "genuine science" in the seventeenth century.[242] However, instead of simply associating the former period with magic and the latter with reason and science, she made the surprising move of applying the contrast *to magic itself*: far from being static and "resistant to change," magic was capable of creative renewal and reform, and Yates even went as far as to suggest that it might be the real key to the phenomenon of the Italian Renaissance as such.[243] The result was a strikingly new perspective that placed the "old dirty magic" of the Middle Ages against the new, beautiful, elegant magic of Italian humanists like Ficino and Pico della Mirandola:

How remote is the gibberish of [the] demonic invocation to Sol in *Picatrix* from Ficino and his "natural" planetary songs! Or if we think of the flowers, jewels, scents with which Ficino's patients are advised to surround themselves, or the

---

[240] For an equivalent metaphor with reference to Peuckert, see Hanegraaff, "Will-Erich Peuckert and the Light of Nature," 301–302.

[241] Sarton, review of Lynn Thorndike (1924), 84.

[242] See, for example, with how much pathos she described the rise of modern science: "no one will deny that the seventeenth century represents that momentous hour in the history of man in which his feet first began to tread securely in the paths which have since led him unerringly onwards to that mastery over nature in modern science which has been the astonishing achievement of modern European man . . ." (Yates, *Giordano Bruno*, 432).

[243] See the critical assessment, from a medievalist's perspective, in Kieckhefer, "Did Magic have a Renaissance?".

charmingly healthy and wealthy way of life which they are to follow, and compare this with the filthy and obscene substances, the stinking and disgusting mixtures recommended in *Picatrix*, the contrast is again most striking between the new elegant magic, recommended by the fashionable physician, and that old dirty magic.[244]

Such an approach implied that magic was an intellectual tradition in its own right, capable of historical change and development, even progress, and possibly leading towards "genuine" science: a revolutionary notion that must surely have caused scholars like Sarton to turn in their graves. Like all representatives of her generation, Yates was still far from immune to traditional Enlightenment notions of "magic" versus "genuine science" as general reified categories, and the closely related idea of "survivals"; but, just as in Thorndike's case, her approach in fact undermined these concepts. As formulated by Margaret Jacob and Edward Gosselin on the occasion of Yates' death, the true reason why her work made such an impact is that it "destroyed whole categories of analysis" that were "once held by some historians of science with such complacency," and "in the process forced a rewriting... of the standard accounts of the origins of early modern science."[245]

The woman who accomplished this revolution was born in a typical late Victorian family in 1899,[246] and went on to study French at the University of London, where she earned her M.A. degree in 1926. After this, she "missed the career bus"[247] and embarked on many years in virtual academic isolation, pursuing research as a private scholar while continuing to live with her parents and sisters. As regards her central interests, Frances Yates was essentially self-educated, and this helps explain her remarkable independence of mind, her willingness to explore unconventional pathways of research, and her lifelong refusal to be intimidated by established disciplinary boundaries.[248] Her first monograph, *John Florio* (1934), was read by Fritz Saxl and Edgar Wind, who invited her in 1936 to use the library of the Warburg Institute, then still unknown to her.[249] This library had been founded in Hamburg by the art historian Aby Warburg, and transformed into a semi-public research institute during the 1920s. Associated

---

[244] Yates, *Giordano Bruno*, 80. Yates continues by emphasizing that, nevertheless, there is "absolute continuity between the old magic and the new" as well (*ibid.*, 81). See also her chapter on Agrippa, who is described quite negatively as an "irresponsible magician," whose "trivial" books on magic risk "slipping back towards the old necromancy and conjuring" (*ibid.*, 130, 141–142).

[245] Jacob and Gosselin, "Dames Frances Yates," 424.

[246] On this background, which determined much of her outlook, see Yates, "Autobiographical Fragments"; and Jones, *Frances Yates*, 1–22.

[247] Yates, "Autobiographical Fragments," 307.   [248] *Ibid.*, 306–307.   [249] *Ibid.*, 308, 313.

with a range of important scholars, including Fritz Saxl, Erwin Panofsky, Ernst Cassirer, Raymond Klibansky, and Edgar Wind,[250] its focus was on the "afterlife of antiquity" (*Nachleben der Antike*) in Christian and especially Renaissance culture, and the collection was ordered according to an unusual, flexible system that strongly stimulated interdisciplinary research. Most members of the Warburg circle were Jews who had to flee from Germany in 1933, and the library itself was moved to England at the same time, where it became the center of an independent research institute affiliated to the University of London.[251] Frances Yates began working there from 1936 on, and was offered a position by Fritz Saxl in 1941. Yates later claimed to have learned the Warburg approach from Jean Seznec's *La survivance des dieux antiques* (1940),[252] and it proved a natural fit. For her, the new "Warburgian history" meant "history in the round, encyclopedic history, the history of symbolism and imagery integrated with general history,"[253] but such a degree of interdisciplinarity was still very uncommon at the time. It is illustrative, for example, that when Yates decided to use slides in a lecture in 1945 about English literature, it "fell absolutely flat" because "it was an absolutely unheard-of thing in those days to use pictures in connection with a talk on poetry (poetic imagery having then absolutely no connection with pictures in the minds of the literary)."[254]

Frances Yates' fame rests upon her *Giordano Bruno and the Hermetic Tradition* (1964) and a further series of influential monographs that followed in its wake, notably *The Art of Memory* (1966), *The Rosicrucian Enlightenment* (1972), and *The Occult Philosophy in the Elizabethan Age* (1979). This remarkable burst of scholarly creativity at a late stage of her career had its origin in 1961, when she was working on Giulio Camillo's *L'idea del theatro*. Yates had been fascinated by Giordano Bruno's *Cena de le ceneri* since the mid-1930s, but always felt that "some major clue was missing."[255] As shown by her unpublished diaries, the answer came to her like a sudden revelation, while she was working on Camillo: "In doing this saw that Hermeticism is clue to Bruno. Saw whole view in history of renaissance magic in relation to Bruno."[256] Everything fell into place, and

[250] *Ibid.*, 227–230.
[251] On the German phase of the Warburg Library, see Michels, "Die Kulturwissenschaftliche Bibliothek Warburg."
[252] Yates, "Autobiographical Fragments," 317. Note the implicit reference in Seznec's title to a theory of "survivals," similar to Warburg's emphasis on the "afterlife" of antiquity.
[253] *Ibid.*, 315.   [254] *Ibid.*, 321.   [255] Yates, *Giordano Bruno*, ix.
[256] Yates, Note after diary entry for December 31, 1961 (unpubl.), as quoted in Gatti, "Frances Yates's Hermetic Renaissance," 203; Jones, *Frances Yates*, 120. Cf. Yates, *Giordano Bruno*, x.

in less than one year she drafted the manuscript of *Giordano Bruno and the Hermetic Tradition*, "the most important thing I have ever done."[257]

That this book made such an impression, on scholars as well as on the general public, has much to do with its unique style of exposition: Yates' prose was bubbling with almost childlike enthusiasm and excitement, but somehow managed to combine this with a tone of quiet authority that commanded respect for the opinions of what was obviously a very experienced scholar. Most of all, however, this passionate historian who seemed to have burst on the scene almost out of nowhere at the age of sixty-five, "seemingly exploding with brain-power, ideas, and hairpins,"[258] was challenging some of the most basic assumptions of mainstream science and scholarship, *and* happened to do so at the very moment when the scientific establishment and its basic values were coming under attack from the rebellious generation of the 1960s. Yates' book hit the *Zeitgeist* at exactly the right moment, and continued to ride the wave of countercultural dissent within the academy and outside it.[259]

Most of the critical debate about Frances Yates' oeuvre has taken place in the fields of history and philosophy of science, and focused on her ideas about the relation between hermeticism and the scientific revolution as expressed with particular clarity in an article published by her in 1967.[260] A first source of worry for many scholars was Yates' suggestion that since hermeticism had played an important role in the scientific revolution, hermetic "magic and superstition" henceforth had to be taken seriously as objects of research in the history of science. We have seen that this implication had already been a source of deep worry for Sarton in his review of Thorndike; and since the 1960s it became a major issue not only due to Frances Yates' work, but also because it was becoming impossible to ignore the importance of "hermetic" currents such as the *prisca theologia* and alchemy in the oeuvre of Isaac Newton.[261] Responding to Yates in 1970,

---

[257] *Ibid.* [258] Sydney Anglo at Yates' memorial service (Jones, *Frances Yates*, 107).
[259] See analysis in Hanegraaff, "Beyond the Yates Paradigm"; and note how frequently participants in the debate about magic and hermeticism in this period mention how "the values of science" are presently "under attack from sections of the rebellious young" (for example Rattansi, "Some Evaluations," 149; Rossi, "Hermeticism, Rationality," 266; cf. above, Chapter 3, n. 120 for the case of Wayne Shumaker).
[260] Yates, "The Hermetic Tradition in Renaissance Science."
[261] Pioneering publications in this regard were McGuire and Rattansi, "Newton and the 'Pipes of Pan'," and Dobbs, *Foundations of Newton's Alchemy*. How emotional an issue this was for historians of science at the time may be gauged from a memory fragment of Margaret Jacob: "I was in the audience in the 1970s when Richard Westfall, speaking at one of the big international congresses in the history of science, presented his early work on Newton's alchemy. There were audible gasps, and under a barrage of hostile questioning, Westfall retorted in exasperation, 'I did not write

the philosopher of science Mary Hesse tried (in vain) to turn the tide by defending an "internal" historiography of science – essentially what would now be called a "whiggish" or "presentist" perspective – against the claim, with its relativistic implications, that science is "an irreducibly social and cultural phenomenon, subject alike to rational and irrational influences, to magic as well as mathematics, religious sectarianism as well as logic, politics and economics as well as philosophy."[262] Essentially, these two opposed "historiographies" were representative of a philosopher's and a historian's perspective respectively; and as the hegemonic claims of rationalism found themselves increasingly under attack after the 1960s, historical research began to move ever more clearly into the latter direction.

A second line of critical debate was historical rather than philosophical. In an influential article published in 1977, Robert S. Westman claimed that Yates had advanced a "thesis" about how magical interpretations of the Copernican cosmos had prepared the way for the mathematization and mechanization of that cosmos during the seventeenth century, and proceeded to deconstruct it in great detail.[263] His argument came in for sharp criticism,[264] but succeeded in popularizing the notion of a "Yates thesis," now understood much more broadly as the claim that "hermeticism" had been a significant or even crucial influence on the scientific revolution. It is doubtful, to say the least, whether Yates ever intended to present any such "thesis";[265] but the beneficial effect was that, under the general although vague umbrella of "hermeticism," historians of science did begin to pay serious attention to the role of natural magic, astrology, alchemy,

---

these manuscripts,' or words to that effect" (Jacob, "Introduction," x). Significantly, even in his monumental Newton biography of 1980, this great scholar still felt he needed to defend himself for doing his job as a historian: "I am not an alchemist, nor do I believe in its premises . . . Nevertheless, I have undertaken to write a biography of Newton, and my personal preferences cannot make more than a million words he wrote in the study of alchemy disappear" (Westfall, *Never at Rest*, 21 n. 12).

[262] Hesse, "Hermeticism and Historiography," here 135. See also Hesse, "Reasons and Evaluations." In both articles, Hesse took issue with Butterfield's famous rejection of "Whig history," while embracing the view that "what counts as rational at any period is a timeless characteristic which shows itself to the historian . . . and which transcends the cultural peculiarities of particular historical periods" ("Hermeticism and Historiography," 142). As noted by Floris Cohen, precisely the typical Enlightenment idea that "there is something perennial to science" was criticized as unhistorical by those who explored the hermeticist approach (*The Scientific Revolution*, 176).

[263] Westman, "Magical Reform" (formulation of the "Yates thesis" on p. 8).

[264] Schmitt, "Reappraisals"; Copenhaver, "Essay Review"; Rattansi, review of Westman and McGuire.

[265] Schmitt, "Reappraisals," 202; Copenhaver, "Natural Magic," 290 n. 3; Rattansi, review of Westman and McGuire, 393. Cf. Yates' own ironic comment in 1979: "[M]y next book . . . will not be a 'Yates thesis' but only another Yates attempt at laborious digging, or a sign-posting of fields in the hope that others will dig more deeply" (article in *Encounter* 3 [1979], 61, quoted in Jacob and Gosselin, "Dame Frances Yates," 425).

and kabbalah in relation to early modern science. As this trend developed from the 1970s on, simplistic notions of a causal relation between "magic" and "science" were gradually discarded in favor of more subtle historical/contextualist perspectives on early modern science. As an ultimate outcome of this development, it has now become quite normal and accepted for historians of science to discuss topics like alchemy, astrology, and natural magic.

For our specific concerns, by far the most important aspect of Yates' mature oeuvre is her basic claim that such a thing as "the Hermetic Tradition" had existed in the first place, and that "hermeticism" was an important but neglected dimension of early modern intellectual and cultural history. Not only did Yates "destroy whole categories of analysis," then, but she created new ones as well. What made her books so exciting was the startling revelation that at the very origins of the modern world, a large and multifaceted, vibrant and fascinating intellectual tradition had once flourished – and that somehow, even its very existence had been entirely overlooked, forgotten, or suppressed. Yates introduced her readers to "hermeticism" as a cultural and intellectual universe all of its own, parallel to but different from the well-known worlds of established theology and Christianity, rationality and science: a universe with its own laws and dynamics, its own intellectual giants and lesser figures, its own intellectual roots and traditions, its own victories and tragedies – in short, with a history all of its own. Moreover, the worldview and aspirations of this rediscovered "Hermetic Tradition" resonated powerfully with a whole range of concerns that were central to the *Zeitgeist* of the 1960s and 1970s. As presented by Frances Yates, it was a tradition dominated by magic, personal religious experience, and the powers of the imagination; it promoted a world-affirming mysticism consonant with an "enchanted" and holistic science that looked at nature as a living, organic whole, permeated by invisible forces and energies; and it reflected a confident, optimistic, forward-looking perspective that emphasized humanity's potential to operate on the world and create a better, more harmonious, more beautiful society.

All of this made "the Hermetic Tradition" look like a kind of traditional counterculture, inspired by beliefs and aspirations that seemed very similar to those that animated the post-World War II generation in its revolt against established science and religion.[266] But Yates' story was also a tragic

---

[266] See Hanegraaff, "Beyond the Yates Paradigm." The prominence of all these elements in what may broadly be called the countercultural milieus of the 1960s and 1970s, often rooted in the 1950s, is too well known to require extensive documentation. For general overviews, see Ellwood, *Fifties*

one, full of "hopes never materialized":[267] Bruno had been burned at the
stake in 1600, the hopes for Rosicrucian renewal had not survived the short
reign of Elizabeth and Frederick V in the Palatinate, and the authority of
the Hermetic Tradition had come to an end in 1614 when Isaac Casaubon
refuted the great antiquity of the Hermetica.[268] For general readers, it was
easy to give this story a slight twist that made it relevant to the contemporary situation. At the dawn of modernity, so they understood, the magical
and enchanted worldview of the Renaissance had lost the battle against
the Christian and scientific establishment, after which the very memory of
its existence had been suppressed and almost deleted, and its representatives and their ideas had been dismissed and ridiculed as obscurantists and
fools. It was only now, after several centuries of oblivion and neglect by the
intellectual and academic establishment, that the forgotten counterculture
of the West had been rediscovered at last, thanks to the researches of an
academic outsider. The message was clear: Yates' master-narrative appeared
to expose mainstream accounts of science and progress as ideological constructs by means of which the establishment had attempted, and was still
attempting, to suppress and silence its rivals. For many of Yates' readers,
moreover, the step from rediscovery to restoration was easy to make: the
hermeticists of the seventeenth century might have lost the battle against
establishment religion and science, but perhaps their contemporary heirs
could get it right! If the new generation was calling for a "re-enchantment
of the world," then Frances Yates' Hermetic Tradition provided an excellent
model.

But did that tradition ever exist? Or, more precisely: did it exist in the
manner that Yates believed it did? To answer these questions, we first need
to look at her chief sources of inspiration. As far as academic research is concerned, the emergence of the idea of a "Hermetic Tradition" can be traced

---

Spiritual Marketplace; Ellwood, *Sixties Spiritual Awakening*; Sounes, *Seventies*. Classic manifestoes
of the counterculture are Roszak, *Making of a Counter Culture*, and *Where the Wasteland Ends*.

[267] Cohen, *Scientific Revolution*, 171; Trapp, "Introduction," xxi ("a preoccupation, which was
to become almost her trademark, with great possibilities denied"); Jones, *Frances Yates*, 101–
102, 117.

[268] Yates' idea that the reign of Elizabeth and Frederick V was a "hermetic golden age" was central to
her much-criticized *Rosicrucian Enlightenment* (here xiii; cf. the review by Vickers, "Frances Yates
and the Writing of History"). For the strong claim that Casaubon's dating of the Hermetica spelt
the end of the Hermetic Tradition, because it "shattered at one blow the build-up of Renaissance
Neoplatonism," leading to a sharp distinction between a "pre-Casaubon era" and a "post-Casaubon
era," see Yates, *Giordano Bruno*, chapter 21, here 398. The centrality of Casaubon's dating has
been much relativized in recent research (Mulsow, *Das Ende des Hermetismus*, and summary in
Hanegraaff, review of Mulsow), and in 1967, Yates herself already accepted Allen Debus' argument
that the "real collapse of Renaissance magical science" occurred only in the period after 1660
(Debus, review of Yates, 391; Yates, "Hermetic Tradition," 272).

very precisely to the year 1938, when the great Renaissance scholar Paul Oskar Kristeller published a ground-breaking article in Italian (and never translated) on Marsilio Ficino and Lodovico Lazzarelli.[269] While working on his two-volume *Supplementum Ficinianum* in the Italian libraries and archives,[270] Kristeller had come to the realization that the great importance of the *Corpus Hermeticum* to Marsilio Ficino and to Renaissance culture in general had been sorely neglected by historians.[271] He therefore exhorted his colleagues that the history of the reception of the hermetic writings should urgently be put on the agenda of Renaissance research and, in so doing, laid the foundations for the academic recovery of the "Hermetic Tradition." In 1955, this led to a pioneering edition titled *Testi Umanistici su l'Ermetismo*, with texts by Lazzarelli, Giorgio da Veneto and Agrippa;[272] and the truth is that by the time that Frances Yates published her book on Bruno in 1964, the general story of Renaissance hermetism that she told through its first ten chapters was already a familiar one among Italian specialists. As concluded by Hilary Gatti, what made her book "in some way canonical for the English-speaking world" was therefore not so much the originality of this story as the "remarkable stylistic *tour the force*" by which she succeeded in making it available "in a language that avoided the dryness and tedium of so much academic prose."[273] Moreover, not just the basic story of the rediscovery, translation, and reception of the *Corpus Hermeticum* was derived straight from available scholarship, most of it Italian, but the same was true of Yates' understanding of Renaissance magic, its relation to hermetism, and its significance for "man the operator." In the 1955 volume just quoted, Eugenio Garin already highlighted the basic elements that were to become central to Yates' grand narrative;[274] and in two important essays from 1950, we find the entire magical universe to which his English colleague introduced her readers fourteen years

---

[269] Kristeller, "Marsilio Ficino e Lodovico Lazzarelli." On Kristeller's importance to the study of Renaissance hermetism, see Celenza, "Paul Oskar Kristeller and the Hermetic Tradition."

[270] Kristeller, *Supplementum Ficinianum*; and see Kristeller and King, "Iter Kristellerianum."

[271] For the bibliographical material central to Kristeller's discovery, see *Supplementum Ficinianum*, vol. II, lvii–lviii, cxxix–cxxxi.

[272] Garin, Brini, Vasoli, and Zambelli, *Testi Umanistici su l'Ermetismo*.

[273] Gatti, "Frances Yates's Hermetic Renaissance," 196.

[274] See Hanegraaff, "Lodovico Lazzarelli and the Hermetic Christ," 6 (with quotation in English translation from Garin, "Note sull'ermetismo del Rinascimento," 12). Cf. Gatti, "Frances Yates's Hermetic Renaissance," 196: "those who are familiar with the work of Eugenio Garin and his Florentine school might find it difficult to discern any essential difference between his picture of the renaissance drawn in the light of its Hermetical and magical doctrines and the whole of the first half of Yates's book on Bruno." For the notion of a "Yates narrative," see Hanegraaff, "Beyond the Yates Paradigm."

later.[275] In other words, it seems that Garin essentially created the paradigm that was later linked to Yates and her work. Although he recognized the differences between the "philosophical" and "technical" Hermetica, Garin saw them as sharing the same animated universe in which all things were interconnected by means of correspondences:

During the Quattrocento, the new image of man was gradually outlined and acquired its characteristic dimensions under the sign of Hermes Trismegistus. It came to be modeled along the lines that had already been established in the hermetic books. Now, if one may draw a clear distinction between the *Pimander*, the *Asclepius*, and the theological writings on the one hand, and the innumerable magical-alchemical treatises on the other, one still must not forget the subtle and profound subterranean connection that unites the former to the occultist, astrological, and alchemical tradition of the latter. The link consists in the idea of a universe that is wholly alive, wholly made of secret correspondences, of occult sympathies, where the spirit is blowing everywhere, where signs with a hidden significance are interwoven everywhere. A universe where every thing, every being, every force is like a voice yet to be understood, a word suspended in the air; where every word that is pronounced has innumerable echoes and resonances; where the stars are looking, listening, and exchanging signs among themselves the way we do ourselves. A universe, finally, that is an immense dialogue; one with diverse and multiple forms, sometimes murmuring, sometimes speaking loudly, sometimes confidentially and obscurely, sometimes in clear language. And in the middle of it stands man: an admirable and changeable being, capable of speaking any word, of remaking all things, writing in all languages, responding to all requests, and invoking all the gods.[276]

Frances Yates must have been aware of how much she owed to Garin: in fact, her diaries show that when *Giordano Bruno and the Hermetic Tradition* appeared in 1964, he was the recipient of the first copy.[277] This makes it all the more interesting to observe Garin's deep irritation twelve years later,

---

[275] As already noted by Rossi, "Hermeticism, Rationality and the Scientific Revolution," 256. The two essays were Garin's "Considerazioni sulla Magia" and "Magia e Astrologia nel Pensiero del Rinascimento," later included in his *Medioevo e Rinascimento*. To this formative influence, we must certainly add D. P. Walker's *Spiritual and Demonic Magic*, published in 1958.

[276] Garin, *Medioevo e rinascimento*, 154. The final sentence obviously refers to Pico della Mirandola's *Oratio*, which emphasizes man's unique status as a "creature of indeterminate nature" placed by God "in the middle of the world," and to Pico's famous quotation from *Asclepius* 6, which speaks of man as a "great miracle" placed "in the happier state of a middle status." These elements are central to Yates' work as well. For a sharp criticism of Garin's interpretation, which "miscast Giovanni Pico, an ascetic Christian mystic, as the herald of human freedom and dignity," see Copenhaver, "A Grand End for a Grand Narrative," 218 (and cf. Copenhaver, "Studied as an Oration"). According to Copenhaver, this understanding of Pico became the "canonical" one after World War II but is based upon neo-Kantian projections and entirely mistaken.

[277] Gatti, "Frances Yates's Hermetic Renaissance," 204. For March 18, 1960, the year before her breakthrough discovery, Yates' diary says "Garin – Lunch," without further comment (*ibid.*, 202).

about how the concept of "the Hermetic Tradition" had become reified in the meantime, taking on a life of its own among legions of scholars who knew little or nothing about it:

To the debate on Renaissance -*isms* (platonism, aristotelianism, neoplatonism, etc.), especially after Frances A. Yates' provocative books, a new personality has been added: hermetism. But unfortunately, the discussion, as far as this new element is concerned, appears not always to be conducted with the rigor that the problem of the origins of modern thought would require . . . In all these [i.e. Yates'] works the notion of "Hermetic Tradition" tends to be broadened enormously, to the extent of becoming both all-encompassing and elusive.[278]

Although Garin had planted the seeds of this phenomenon himself, he was right to call for caution and emphasize the need for terminological precision. In the light of recent scholarship, Frances Yates' "grand narrative" of the Hermetic Tradition turns out to be extremely problematic, for at least two interconnected reasons that must be briefly outlined here.

First of all, we have seen that Hermes Trismegistus was only one among a whole series of oriental sages who were important within the ancient wisdom discourse of the Renaissance. If one were to name the various ancient wisdom narratives after the wise man who was believed to be at their origin, then Plethon and Ficino were clearly defending not a Hermetic but a "Zoroastrian" Tradition, and Pico a "Mosaic" one.[279] Only Lodovico Lazzarelli believed in a specifically "Hermetic" Tradition, and this fact had been recognized by Italian scholarship from the beginning. However, in a bizarre turn away from the existing academic consensus and sheer textual evidence, Yates chose to marginalize precisely this purest available example of a Renaissance Hermetist, because he did not fit her narrative.[280] In

---

[278] Garin, "Divagazioni ermetiche," 462–463. In the rest of the article, see the critical discussions, full of irritation about scholars who do not know what they are talking about, of Richard Westfall, Mary Hesse, Jean Zafiropulo and Catherine Monod, and Thomas Kuhn.

[279] This "Zoroastrian Tradition" has in fact been traced in consummate detail by Stausberg, *Faszination Zarathushtra*. My discussion in Chapter 1 implies that Christian kabbalah was in fact equivalent to the parallel notion of a "Mosaic Tradition" within the broader ancient wisdom narrative of the Renaissance.

[280] Lazzarelli and his spiritual master Giovanni "Mercurio" da Correggio, who saw himself as the "Hermetic Christ," were central to Kristeller's pioneering Italian publications ("Marsilio Ficino e Lodovico Lazzarelli"; "Ancora per Giovanni Mercurio da Correggio"; "Lodovico Lazzarelli e Giovanni da Correggio"), and Lazzarelli was the first and most important of the three authors selected for the 1955 volume *Testi umanistici su l'Ermetismo*. In sharp contrast, Yates called Lazzarelli "a most ardent Hermetist" and "a most enthusiastic and exaggerated Hermetist" but devoted just one long footnote to him and Correggio (*Giordano Bruno*, 50 and 171 with n. 2). As I have suggested elsewhere (Hanegraaff, "Lodovico Lazzarelli and the Hermetic Christ," esp. 2–8, 101–104; "La fin de la tradition hermétique"), Yates must have realized that the case of Lazzarelli messed up her narrative of what "hermeticism" should be: hermetic as he might be, his work had nothing to do

marked contrast to Lazzarelli (and, as I would argue, Agrippa: another *bête noire* for Yates),[281] none of Yates' heroes can reasonably be called Hermetists: contrary to common assumptions, Ficino did not place Hermes at the center even in the famous preface to his *Pimander*, Pico saw him as only one of the ancient sages after Moses, and even Bruno just occasionally refers to him.[282] In short: Yates wrote the real hermetists out of her story, and replaced them by a set of more famous protagonists who hardly fit the description. These facts lead to an unavoidable conclusion: while the history of the reception of the Hermetica in the Renaissance remains as important as ever, Frances Yates' concept of a "Hermetic Tradition" is simply impossible to uphold.[283] As I have argued in Chapter 1, "Platonic Orientalism" would be a much more adequate umbrella for the general phenomenon to which she rightly called attention, and of which hermetism is only a part.

Second, there is Yates' ruling idea of a close connection between hermeticism and magic. Renaissance hermeticism was presented by her as beginning with Ficino's translation of the *Corpus Hermeticum* and receiving the lethal blow with Casaubon's refutation of its great antiquity; and she interpreted it as essentially a magical tradition that stimulated man to operate on the world. However, there is a fatal flaw to the argument: it just so happens that the *Corpus Hermeticum* contains virtually nothing that, by any definition, could be construed as "magic!"[284] The optical illusion

---

with astral magic (*contra* Walker, *Spiritual and Demonic Magic*, 64–72; see Hanegraaff, "Lodovico Lazzarelli," 45 n. 143, 84–86, 94, 102) but amounted to an ascetic Christian mysticism that aimed at transcending nature rather than "operating" on it. The notorious "god-making passages" of the *Asclepius* on which Yates built most of her narrative (see n. 285, below) were central to Lazzarelli as well; but he interpreted them allegorically as referring to the ability of spiritually regenerated man to literally participate in God's creative powers.

[281] On the centrality of Lazzarelli's understanding of hermetism to Agrippa's worldview, see Hanegraaff, "Better than Magic." Yates realized that she could not ignore Agrippa in a book on Renaissance magic, but although she devoted a whole chapter to him, she did so with obvious distaste (see above, n. 244).

[282] Bruno, *Spaccio della bestia trionfante*, dialogue 3; cf. Yates, *Giordano Bruno*, chapter 12.

[283] I suggest that the broad but vague category of "hermeticism" should better be discarded along with that of "the Hermetic Tradition," in favor of the relatively restricted but much more precise category of "hermetism," understood as referring strictly to the ensemble of the late antique Hermetica and the literature inspired by them during the Middle Ages, the Renaissance, and later periods. The term "hermetism" should thus be used strictly for the reception history of the Hermetica (Hanegraaff, "Lodovico Lazzarelli and the Hermetic Christ," 2 n. 1; cf. Faivre, "Questions of Terminology"). I have tacitly been using this terminological distinction already in my discussions above.

[284] For what fifteenth-century readers could and could not find in Ficino's *Pimander*, see Hanegraaff, "How Hermetic was Renaissance Hermetism?" How easily historians of science accepted Yates' assumptions without bothering to check the evidence at first hand is shown, for example, by the case of Westman, "Magical Reform," 7: Yates "has provided one element that was generally lacking

according to which Ficino's *Pimander* nevertheless laid the foundations for a magical discourse was largely created by Yates' considerable rhetorical skills: if one studies *Giordano Bruno and the Hermetic Tradition* carefully, one discovers that in her efforts to explain the revival of magic as a revival of hermetism, she was systematically referring not to Ficino's *Pimander* but to the *Asclepius*. More particularly, within that relatively lengthy treatise, she strategically highlighted only a few – admittedly notorious – idolatrous passages that, along with the rest of the *Asclepius*, had been known in Latin throughout the Middle Ages and could hardly be called great news for intellectuals in the second half of the fifteenth century.[285] In sum, the "magical" dimension of hermetism was not new in the Renaissance; and what was new (the *Corpus Hermeticum*) was not "magical." Again, the conclusion would seem to be unavoidable: while Renaissance magic is a real and obviously important historical phenomenon, it makes no sense to label it specifically "hermetic" or connect it to the impact of Ficino's *Pimander*.

Regretfully, then, we must say goodbye to the grand narrative of "the Hermetic Tradition" created by Frances Yates. It must be emphasized that all the elements that she managed to place back on the agenda of international scholarship were important indeed and remain of the greatest interest to historians: this is true of topics such as Ficino's translation of the *Corpus Hermeticum* and its reception, the importance of astral magic in the Renaissance, the cultural significance of the dating of the *Hermetica*, the importance of mnemonics as an intellectual tradition, the phenomenon of Christian kabbalah and *occulta philosophia*, John Dee and his impact in

in earlier studies of Renaissance magic and science, namely a concrete *textual* locus to which might be referred an explanation of the changed view of the Renaissance towards man and nature. This textual corpus was the collection of occult works [i.e. the *Corpus Hermeticum*]." One can only conclude that Westman had not actually looked at this "concrete textual locus" but took Yates at her word.

[285] At her very first mention of the text, Yates puts the reader on the wrong foot by stating that "the *Asclepius* purports to describe the religion of the Egyptians, and by what magic rites and processes the Egyptians drew down the powers of the cosmos into the statues of their gods" (*Giordano Bruno*, 3), whereas this description fits only *Ascl.* 23–24/37–38. How strongly these short passages came to dominate her idea of the Hermetic Tradition as a whole becomes clear if one simply counts her references to the Hermetica. C.H. II–XVIII are quoted or discussed only rarely, with a slight prominence given to treatises X–XIII (no references at all to VII–VIII, XIV, XVII–XVIII). Only C.H. I is quoted regularly (I counted twenty-four text references, most of them in Chapter 3, and three in footnotes). The *Picatrix* is mentioned twenty-three times in the text, seventeen times in footnotes; but the *Asclepius* appears no fewer than eighty times in the text, twenty-nine times in footnotes. Moreover from these text references to the *Asclepius*, at least forty-five are about the idolatrous passages in *Ascl.* 23–24/37–38 (and the number will expand considerably if one adds the many references to "godmaking," "idolatry," or "bad magic" that do not mention the treatise by name), next to seven about the "magnum miraculum" sentence famously quoted by Pico.

Elizabethan England, the Rosicrucian phenomenon, and so on. But Yates' terminology, her general framework of interpretation, and its underlying assumptions simply fail to do justice to the true complexity of the sources, and create a misleading picture of the field as a whole. Among the most important of these problematic aspects are the opposition of Middle Ages versus Renaissance as darkness and stagnation versus light and progress, the reification of "hermeticism" as a quasi-autonomous or independent tradition opposed to an ascetic and world-denying Christian orthodoxy, the essentially "magical" nature of this entire Hermetic Tradition, its dominant focus on "man the operator," its basic cast of characters, its central importance to Giordano Bruno and early modern science, and its essential optimism, progressiveness, or "modernity."

As I hope to have shown, all these various problematic areas in Yates' "grand narrative" follow from how she looked at two central concepts in Renaissance culture: that of an ancient wisdom tradition, and that of magic. Interestingly, these are precisely the topics about which her close colleague and intimate friend Daniel P. Walker wrote his two major monographs: *Spiritual and Demonic Magic from Ficino to Campanella* (1958) and *The Ancient Theology* (1972). Walker was a more careful scholar than Yates, but did not have her literary flair and large vision, and never achieved the fame that she came to enjoy late in life. As a result, his works remain indispensable as classics in their field, but his formidable female counterpart succeeded in a way that he could not: to her lasting credit, she found a way of breaking through the barriers of academic resistance and rejection, thereby making it possible for an entire neglected field of research to return to the arena of scholarship. From the 1960s through the 1980s, "hermeticism" was the magic word that allowed academics to be taken seriously while exploring the "waste-basket of historiography." It is only during the 1990s that this terminology slowly began to give way to a new one, that of "Western esotericism," along with the emergence of a new research paradigm pioneered by the French scholar Antoine Faivre.

ANTOINE FAIVRE AND WESTERN ESOTERICISM

The adjective "esoteric" made its first appearance in Lucian of Samosata's satire *Vitarum Rustio* 26 (second century). It was picked up by patristic authorities such as Clement of Alexandria, Hippolyte of Rome, Origen, and Gregory of Nyssa, and generally came to refer to secret teachings reserved for a mystical elite, as exemplified by the Pythagorean brotherhoods in particular.[286] The substantives "esotericist" and "esotericism" appear to be of much more recent origin. In his *Revision der Philosophie*, published anonymously in 1772, the German philosopher and historian Christoph Meiners drew a distinction between "exoteric" and "esoteric" philosophy, referring to practitioners of the latter as *Esoteriker* (esotericists); and in a critical footnote to Meiners' work in Johann Gottfried Eichhorn's *Urgeschichte* (1792), Johann Philipp Gabler coined the novel substantive *Esoterik* (esotericism).[287] Interestingly, Meiners and Eichhorn were far from believing that the ancient Pythagorean brotherhoods had been concerned with an "enthusiastic" or mystical doctrine derived from Egypt: rather, they imagined their ancient "esotericists" as rationalists and freethinkers with a Republican program, similar to enlightened Freemasons and Weishaupt's Illuminaten, who had kept their beliefs secret out of sheer political necessity.[288] It was Gabler who objected that "imitation of the Egyptian and Greek mysteries" had, after all, played a role in the "esotericism" of the ancient Pythagoreans, and this is how the substantive came to be understood in Jacques Matter's *Histoire critique du gnosticisme* of 1828.[289]

The Elsassian scholar Jacques Matter (1791–1864) held professorships in history, philosophy, and religion at the University of Strasbourg, and married a granddaughter of the important Christian theosopher Frédéric-Rodolphe Saltzmann. Clearly representative of the illuminist milieu during the Romantic era, he published general works on the history of Christianity and mysticism as well as monographs on Saint-Martin and Swedenborg.[290] In his important book of 1828, he used "gnosticism" and "gnosis" as mutually interchangeable terms for "the introduction into Christianity of all the cosmological and theosophical speculations that had formed the most important part of the ancient religions of the Orient, and which the new platonists had adopted in the Occident as well."[291] In other words, Matter

---

[286] Hanegraaff, "Esotericism," 336; and see exhaustive documentation in Riffard, *L'ésotérisme*, 63–88.

[287] [Meiners], *Revision*, 131–132; Eichhorn, *Urgeschichte*, vol. II:1, 326–327 n. 146. That the substantives "esotericist" and "esotericism" have their origins in German Enlightenment historiography rather than in Jacques Matter's *Histoire critique du gnosticisme* of 1828 (Laurant, *L'ésotérisme chrétien*, 19; Laurant, *L'ésotérisme*, 40–41; Hanegraaff, "Esotericism," 337; Hanegraaff, "Birth of Esotericism," 201–203) was discovered by Monika Neugebauer-Wölk in 2010: see her detailed analysis of the relevant sources in "Der Esoteriker und die Esoterik." Note that whereas *Esoterik* was coined by Gabler, Matter's German translator Christian Heinrich Dörner could find no equivalent for *ésotérisme* in any dictionary, and came up with the parallel version *Esoterismus* ("Der Esoteriker und die Esoterik," 227).

[288] Neugebauer-Wölk, "Der Esoteriker und die Esoterik," 219–222.

[289] *Ibid.*, 222–227.   [290] Laurant, "Matter, Jacques."

[291] Matter, *Histoire critique*, 16 (cf. the slightly different formulation in the second edition of 1843, as quoted in Hanegraaff, "Birth of Esotericism," 202).

saw "gnosis/gnosticism" as grounded in what I have been referring to as "Platonic Orientalism," and as resulting from what the anti-apologists had criticized as the "Hellenization of Christianity." The main difference – but obviously a crucial one – was that Matter, a Protestant strongly influenced by illuminist theosophy, simply noted the fact that Christianity had been fertilized by the "ancient wisdom," but saw no reason to attack the result-ing worldviews as heresies. In view of the later career of "esotericism" as a scholarly term, it is significant that, in fact, Matter's description of its basic worldview might as well have been taken straight from the writings of Martines de Pasqually, the foundational author of the "martinist" current of theosophical illuminism to which Matter himself was affiliated:

The emanation of all spiritual beings out of God, the progressive degenera-tion of these emanations, redemption and return to the purity of the Cre-ator, re-establishment of the original harmony of all beings, the felicitous and truly divine life of all in God himself: those are the fundamental teachings of gnosticism . . . Behold, it tells you, here, the light that emanates from an immense source of light, that spreads its beneficent rays everywhere: this is how all the pure spirits emanate from the divine light. Behold, again, it cries out, how all the sources that feed the earth, that beautify it, that fertilize and purify it, emanate from one single and immense ocean: this is how, from the center of divinity, emanate so many *rivers* (*genii* pure like watery crystal) which shape and fill the world of intelligences. Behold, it finally says, the numbers, which all emanate from an original number, which all resemble it, are made from its essence, and are nevertheless infinitely diverse; and behold the voices, which are made of so many syllables and elements, all enclosed in the original voice, and nevertheless of an unlimited variety: thus it is that the world of intelligences has emanated from the first intelligence, resembling it, and still results in an infinite variety of beings.[292]

What Matter described as "gnosis/gnosticism" was essentially an illuminist credo in the lineage of Pasqually's theosophy. It should be noted, however, that, technically at least, "esotericism" had not yet become a synonym for it: in Matter's work, the term still referred to secret teachings concerned with superior knowledge, reserved for an elite and passed on from the ancient mystery traditions, or the "inner" dimensions of religion as opposed to mere external doctrine and religious observance. For the basic worldview in question, or the various currents that represented it, it was rather the term "gnosis" that was now beginning to gain some currency.[293] In a large

---

[292] Matter, *Histoire critique*, 18–20 (and cf. again the 1843 edition: Hanegraaff, "Birth of Esotericism," 201). For Martines de Pasqually, see his *Traité sur la réintégration des êtres*; and overviews of his life and doctrine in Var, "Martinism: First Period"; "Pasqually."

[293] On the first "timid" beginnings of "gnosis" as a positive term, see Faivre, "Le terme et la notion de 'gnose'." Non-pejorative use of the term can be traced to Abraham von Franckenberg's apology of 1627, published in 1703 (see Chapter 1, n. 21).

study a few years after Matter, whose work he knew well, the historian of Christianity Ferdinand Christian Baur defined *die Christliche Gnosis* quite simply as "philosophy of religion."[294] This was a smart move: it acknowledged the anti-apologetic argument (from Thomasius through Brucker) that its representatives were trying to bring human reason to bear upon the mysteries of the divine, but went on to argue that far from being punishable *hubris*, this intellectual ambition was simply what defined the discipline's specificity and demarcated it from other types of philosophical inquiry. Baur discussed the various gnostic systems of antiquity, then jumped to Jacob Böhme, and from there drew a line to Schelling, Schleiermacher, and finally Hegel as the triumphant culmination of Christian gnosis: the result was, again, a Christian theosophical worldview (Böhmian dialectics interpreted from an Idealist point of view) presented as the core of a long tradition from antiquity to the present. Baur's book did much to popularize the concept of "gnosis" as a general, quasi-historiographical category, but while this notion can be traced through many esoteric or esotericizing authors through the nineteenth and twentieth centuries, its impact on academic literature remained limited at least until the period after World War II.[295]

In the wake of Matter's book, the term "esotericism" began to spread as well, first in French and eventually crossing over to various other languages.[296] For our concerns, the French context remains the most relevant by far, because it is here that *l'ésotérisme* eventually mutated from a term for secrecy and concealment or interiority into a historiographical concept, and came to be taken seriously by academics. Two factors appear to have been crucial to this phenomenon: the explosion after

---

[294] Baur, *Christliche Gnosis*, vii.

[295] For occultist notions of gnosis, see, for example, H. P. Blavatsky, *Isis Unveiled*, vol. II, 38: "the *Gnosis*, based on the secret science of sciences . . . was never without its representatives in any age or country" (i.e. Zoroaster, Abraham, Henoch, Moses, the three Hermeses Trismegisti, Pythagoras, Plato, Jesus, Philo, and the Kabbalah). A special although isolated case is that of the Christian anarchist philosopher Eugen Heinrich Schmitt (see Stöckelle, "Eugen Heinrich [Jenő Henrik] Schmitt") and his two-volume work *Die Gnosis* (1903), subtitled "foundations of the worldview of a nobler culture," which devotes one volume to the gnostics of late antiquity and then traces a lineage up to the end of the nineteenth century in the second volume. For further twentieth-century examples, see Faivre, "Le terme et la notion de 'gnose'." On modern academic constructs of "gnosis" or "gnosticism" as general categories, see Hanegraaff, "Gnosticism," 794–796; and for a criticism of Eric Voegelin's influential theory of "gnostic politics," see Hanegraaff, "On the Construction," 29–36. A useful overview of the many understandings of "gnosis/gnosticism" is Sloterdijk and Macho, *Weltrevolution der Seele*; and for the eventual degeneration of "gnosticism" into a term that seems capable of meaning "all things and their opposite," see the apt and humorous remarks by Culianu, "Gnostic Revenge," 290.

[296] Hanegraaff, "Esotericism," 337. The theosophist A. D. Sinnett seems to have introduced the term in English in 1883 (*ibid.*). In general reference works, the German *Esoterik* does not seem to appear before 1920 (Neugebauer-Wölk, "Der Esoteriker und die Esoterik," 227–228).

1928 of French research into eighteenth-/nineteenth-century illuminism and theosophy, and the personal involvement of a few influential scholars with modern and contemporary esoteric practice and speculation. To begin with the first: the boom in French illuminism studies after 1928 was described in the following words by Mircea Eliade in a book review of 1973:

The publication of Auguste Viatte's two-volume work, *Les sources occultes du romantisme: Illuminisme-Théosophie* (Paris, 1928), marked an important date in the investigation of esoteric literature. It revealed an unknown or perhaps carefully neglected dimension of the Enlightenment – the religious concern of a great section of European intelligentsia, considered until that time antireligious or religiously indifferent. Professor Viatte was the first savant to examine an immense number of documents, mostly unpublished, buried in administrative and private archives. The sensation caused by this work among literary historians and critics as well as among historians of ideas stimulated a number of researches on the esoteric and occult movements of the eighteenth and nineteenth centuries.[297]

As examples, Eliade went on to list the publications by Gérard van Rijnberk (1935), Alice Joly (1938), Jacques Roos (1953), Léon Cellier (1953), Louis Guinet (1962), Robert Amadou (1962), Max Geiger (1963), Paul Arnold (1970), and the subject of his book review, René le Forestier (posthumously published by Antoine Faivre, 1970).[298] To understand the importance, for our concerns, of this post-Viatte development of French illuminism studies, we should remember that the research paradigm grounded in Frances Yates' concept of "the Hermetic Tradition" described a domain that was limited essentially to the fifteenth through the seventeenth centuries, and thereby suggested that the triumph of modern science and rationality had put an end to it. This made "hermeticism" a thing of the past, which could play no role of any real importance in the modern world. In marked contrast, we will see that when "esotericism" began to make its entrance in the academy by means of Faivre's writings, it emphasized how illuminism and Christian theosophy, grounded in Renaissance "hermeticism," had not only survived but had flourished during the ages of the Enlightenment and Romanticism. Once it became evident how successfully these traditional currents had managed to cross the epistemological barrier of the eighteenth century, the way was open for scholars to explore their further development as well. As a result, the field was eventually broadened so as to include the entire period from the Renaissance to the present day. This development

---

[297] Eliade, "Occultism and Freemasonry," 89.
[298] Le Forestier, *Franc-Maçonnerie templière et occultiste.*

might have sufficed, by its own logic, to get "esotericism" established as an inclusive historiographical concept that not only covered everything called "hermeticism" by Frances Yates but, in addition, explored the actual development and transformation of the field under modern and contemporary secular conditions as well. In fact, this is what the term would eventually come to mean in academic research from the 1990s on. First, however, it went through a lengthy religionist phase, due to the personal esoteric commitments of a few influential francophone scholars affiliated with Eranos. To describe how this happened, we must now turn to the central protagonist of this section.

Born in 1934, Antoine Faivre[299] studied German and North American literature and history of religions at the Sorbonne, where he continued to pursue a doctorate in German studies. His very earliest publications were marked by a fascination with "gothic" and fantastic literature, and in 1962 he published a book on vampire mythology that is now considered the first genuinely scholarly study of that topic.[300] It would appear that fantastic literature was his point of entrance into the domain that the French call *l'Imaginaire*, and a love for myths, images, and symbols was to remain a constant factor in his scholarly oeuvre. The year 1961 was decisive for Faivre on both a personal and a professional level. Having been raised in a Roman Catholic family, he became a convinced Christian during his army service in Algeria;[301] and around the same time, Auguste Viatte's *chef d'œuvre* inspired him to specialize in the illuminist and theosophical milieus of eighteenth-century Germany.[302] Back in France, Faivre went on to earn his doctorate with two large and meticulously documented studies of Niklaus Anton Kirchberger (1966) and Karl von Eckartshausen (1969), and detailed historical research into the primary sources of illuminism, Christian theosophy, and the closely related current of German Romantic *Naturphilosophie* would remain the backbone of his voluminous oeuvre through the years.

---

[299] Previous accounts of Faivre and his scholarship include Davis, "Hermes on the Seine"; Giegerich, "Antoine Faivre"; and, most importantly, McCalla, "Antoine Faivre and the Study of Esotericism." I am deeply grateful to Antoine Faivre for giving me generous and unrestricted access to his private *Journal* (1973–present) and his voluminous correspondence.

[300] Faivre, *Les vampires*. See analysis in Introvigne, "Antoine Faivre: Father of Contemporary Vampire Studies." As early as 1955, Faivre had been co-founder of an organization for young French writers, "Jeunesses Littéraires de France," and a journal *Cahiers d'action littéraire* (Faivre, *Journal*, December 31, 1973).

[301] Faivre, *Journal*, Good Friday 1977.

[302] *Ibid.*, July 10, 1982. The work of Gabriel Marcel played an important role in that decision, by helping him overcome philosophical idealism and lending legitimacy to a "concrete" philosophy that included the body (Faivre, *Journal*, May 6, 1974).

The early Faivre was a fairly typical representative of the post-Viatte tradition in French academic research. He might well have spent the rest of his career as a specialized historian in Germanic studies, had it not been for a second factor: the impact on his thinking of the Eranos approach to religion, and of Henry Corbin and Gilbert Durand in particular. In Faivre's contribution to Corbin's *Festschrift* in 1977, we read the following lines:

I am given the opportunity to thank a Master to whom I owe it to distinguish between a thriving chaff – destined, however, to be collected as well – and a good grain, the quality of which is overlooked by the researcher interested too exclusively in the diachronic history of events. About eight years ago, an article by Henry Corbin devoted to the Divine Wisdom, as well as his preface to C. G. Jung's book (*Response to Job*) and the work devoted to Ibn 'Arabi, revealed to me what one cannot summarize in ten lines, and made suddenly clear to me that it is possible to work as a philosopher without thereby neglecting history. The latter, like the Sleeping Beauty woken up from her night, is then no longer just an archeologist's business.[303]

Characteristically combining a biblical with a fairy-tale metaphor, and without forgetting to point out that even the "chaff" deserves to be collected, Faivre was thanking Corbin for showing him how to find truth in history: what might seem to be mere collections of dead facts could be brought back to life by the scholar who understood that there was more to reality than a mere succession of diachronic events. As will be seen, this insight derived from Corbin – and strongly supported by the leading French scholar of the *imaginaire* Gilbert Durand, whom he met around the same time – marked the beginning of Faivre's religionist period.

At the same time, in 1969, that Corbin's work was opening up a new approach to history for him, Faivre's studies of illuminism and Christian theosophy were crowned with the doctorate and the publication of his large study of Eckartshausen; and without passing through the usual lower university positions, he got a full professorship at the University of Paris in the same year, followed by one at the University of Bordeaux in 1972. Moreover, still in 1969, he was initiated as a Freemason in the *Grand Loge Nationale Française* and began to practice the Martinist *Rite Ecossais Rectifié* (Rectified Scottish Rite), a Christian chivalric system created by Jean-Baptiste Willermoz in 1778.[304] Faivre's studies of eighteenth-century

---

[303] Faivre, "Ternaire alchimique," 613–614. The references are to Corbin, "La Sophia éternelle"; "Post-face"; and the 1953 French original of *Creative Imagination*.

[304] For a short description, see Mazet, "Chevaliers Bienfaisants de la Cité Sainte," 256–257. Interestingly, it was a Jesuit priest, R. P. Riguet, an old friend of his father, who introduced Faivre to the *Rite Ecossais Rectifié* and allayed his concerns about its compatibility with Roman Catholicism

illuminism had therefore inspired him to join one of the most important masonic high-degree systems, whose historical origins he had been studying in depth; and four years later, in 1973, he introduced his friends and colleagues Henry Corbin and Gilbert Durand into the same system.[305] This was also the year when Faivre made his first appearance as a speaker at Eranos, with a lecture on "mystical alchemy and spiritual hermeneutics";[306] and one year later, in 1974, he participated in the foundation of a specifically French and militantly religionist offshoot of the Eranos perspective – the *Université Saint-Jean de Jérusalem*.[307]

Because of its importance to Faivre's religionist period, and its considerable impact on how he came to develop his notion of "Western esotericism," we must take a somewhat closer look at this remarkable initiative. It was the brainchild of Henry Corbin, and the most explicit vehicle of his personal understanding of "esotericism." Like most Eranos thinkers, Corbin and Faivre shared a deep interest in German intellectual culture and Romantic philosophers in particular;[308] and Corbin, a pupil of Alexandre Koyré, saw his own worldview as perfectly consonant with the (actually quite divergent) Christian theosophies of Jacob Böhme, Friedrich Christoph Oetinger, and Emanuel Swedenborg.[309] Corbin's initiation into the *Rite Ecossais Rectifié* and its inner order, the *Chevaliers Bienfaisants de la Cité Sainte*, seems to have filled him with deep enthusiasm, as reflected in his great study on the *Imago Templi* discussed above: he was enchanted by its neo-Templar symbolism inspired by the theosophy of Martines de Pasqually, and his understanding of neo-Templar Freemasonry, Graal mythology, the "Inner Church," and the "Celestial Jerusalem" was profoundly indebted to these currents and the scholarship about them – from

---

(Faivre, *Journal*, May 6, 1975). The young Faivre had been initiated in the *Ordre Martiniste* in 1963 (*Journal*, April 22, 1975), but he began to withdraw around the time he became a Freemason.

[305] Faivre, personal communication, July 21, 2010. For the remarkable story of Corbin's masonic career, and the problems concerning its "regularity," see the analysis by Clergue, "En quête de Henry Corbin." As shown by this author, extraordinary measures were taken by those in Corbin's retinue to make it possible for him to advance with record speed towards the inner order of the *Rite Ecossais Rectifié*, the *Chevaliers Bienfaisants de la Cité Sainte*.

[306] He had been a regular visitor since 1967, and was known to the audience for his German summaries of Corbin's difficult French contributions (Hakl, *Verborgene Geist*, 346).

[307] See Hakl, *Verborgene Geist*, 407–411; Eliade, "Some Notes," 172–176.

[308] For example, Nasr, "Henry Corbin, 'L'exil occidental'," 5; Soster, *Le développement*, chapter 2. Corbin highlighted the country of "Faustian man" already in his very first published article (Accart, "Identité et théophanie," 180).

[309] For Swedenborg, see Corbin's Eranos lectures "Herméneutique spirituelle comparée" (1965) and "L'imago templi," 239–248. Koyré is, of course, the author of a standard work on Böhme (*La philosophie de Jacob Boehme*); and it was his chair at the École Pratique des Hautes Études that was changed into a chair for "Christian Esotericism" in 1964, at Corbin's suggestion (see below, page 348).

Arthur Edward Waite to Antoine Faivre himself.[310] Given the very title of the *Université Saint Jean de Jérusalem* and his great study of the "Image of the Temple," it should be noted that ritual progress through the order of the *Chevaliers Bienfaisants de la Cité Sainte* is supposed to culminate in a vision of the celestial Jerusalem and the announcement that the candidate has now reached the doors of its Temple.[311]

Spurred on by these spiritual commitments, and deeply concerned about the "crisis" of contemporary intellectual life, Corbin decided (together with Faivre and a few other academics, supported by an impressive group of international scholars)[312] to found an "international center for comparative spiritual research," focused on the three "religions of the book" and devoted to the "restoration and revival of the traditional studies and sciences in the occident."[313] Like Eranos, this "counter-university" took the form of an annual seminar, and the papers were published in a series of *Cahiers* from 1975 to 1988. What makes the *Université Saint Jean de Jérusalem* unique and fascinating is that it combined academic scholarship on a high intellectual level with a very explicit profession of Christian theosophical, illuminist, and related "esoteric" beliefs. In his opening address, Corbin left no doubt about the religious and spiritual nature of his initiative, or its uncompromising hostility towards the evils of the modern world. The *Université* was placed under the auspices of a priory belonging to the "Sovereign Order of Saint John of Jerusalem," one of the many neo-Templar organizations claiming the heritage of the "Knights Hospitaller"

---

[310] Apart from le Forestier's *Franc-Maçonnerie templière et occultiste* (criticized for its "tone": "L'*imago templi*," 274 n. 200), Corbin's principal references for Templar Masonry in "L'*imago templi*" are Waite's *New Encyclopaedia of Freemasonry* and *Emblematic Freemasonry*. Given the topic, Corbin's use of the scholastic terminology *a parte ante* and *a parte post* ("L'*imago templi*," 291 and *passim*) and his frequent references to the "Inner Church" (cf. Schimmel, "Einleitung," 16–17) would suggest Waite's *Hidden Church of the Holy Graal* as another significant source.

[311] Mazet, "Chevaliers Bienfaisants de la Cité Sainte," 257. For detailed discussions, see le Forestier, *Franc-Maçonnerie templière et occultiste*; and especially Faivre, "Temple de Salomon" (and repr. in *Accès* [1986], 174–192 and *Accès* [1996], vol. i, 178–197).

[312] The founding committee consisted of Henry Corbin (President), Gilbert Durand (Vice-President), Antoine Faivre (Chancellor), Richard Stauffer (Treasurer), and Robert de Chateaubriant (General Secretary). The list of supportive academics reads like a "who's who" of French and international scholarship in esotericism and Eranos-inspired study of religion, and included the philosopher of Judaism Armand Abecassis, the ethnologist Jean Servier, the scholar of Renaissance hermeticism Jean-François Maillard, important scholars of Christian theosophy such as Ernst Benz, Pierre Deghaye, and Bernard Gorceix, the philosopher and scholar of theosophy and *Naturphilosophie* Jean-François Marquet, the scholar of German idealism Jean-Louis Vieillard-Baron, and last but not least, Mircea Eliade (who incorrectly claimed to have been a founding member in his *Journal* iii, 201).

[313] Corbin, "L'Université Saint-Jean de Jérusalem," 8.

or "Knights of Malta,"[314] and devoted itself to defending "the unique sovereignty of the spirit":

The evil that it intends to confront is the total confusion in the spirits, souls, and hearts, a confusion resulting from the disaster of the secular institutions of the West. Its task is directed towards a goal more profound than that of replacing the latter by other institutions... In saying that a spiritual oecumenicalism cannot be pursued by the exoteric path of a confrontation with the dogmas or institutions, one essentially bestows the meaning of *interiorism* upon the "esoteric" quest.[315]

In other words, the *Université* should be a visible reflection of the "Inner Church." Corbin went on to point out that, in contrast to the great theological and philosophical systems of Western culture, "the treasure of the spiritual sciences, which can be grouped under the more or less happy or adequate term 'esotericism'" was still buried in libraries, without adequate institutional settings to safeguard and promote it. As a result, it had become easy prey for ignorant "improvisers without discernment," as shown by the current wave of "pseudo-esotericisms."[316] The *Université Saint Jean de Jérusalem* intended to remedy this situation by providing a context where the true meaning of esotericism could be discussed on a high level by competent academics. But such a project could not be pursued from a perspective of scholarly detachment: "the level of spiritual reality proper to the traditional sciences remains inaccessible if the researcher does not himself go through a new birth."[317] In its fight against historicism, agnosticism, and any other doctrine that sought to prohibit humanity from referring to the "beyond," the *Université* expected each of its participants (speaker or listener) to be "a believer" committed to "the spiritual life."[318] In this connection it should be noted that Corbin and Faivre have always seen their Christian beliefs[319] as perfectly compatible with their commitment to the "Inner Church" of theosophy or the masonic chivalry and neo-Templarism of the Rectified Scottish Rite.

---

[314] On this affiliation, see de Chateaubriant, "L'université Saint-Jean de Jérusalem" (in the first issue of the *Cahiers*).

[315] Corbin, "L'Université Saint-Jean de Jérusalem," 8–9.   [316] *Ibid.*, 10.   [317] *Ibid.*, 11.

[318] *Ibid.*, 12. Note that Corbin himself originally conceived the *Université* as a private gathering of no more than about twenty carefully selected "esotericists in perfect spiritual accord with one another." That it finally took a more public and academic shape was due only to the strong opposition of Faivre, Durand, and de Chateaubriant against this idea (Faivre, *Journal*, March 4, 1974).

[319] Corbin was raised a Catholic but had converted to Protestantism, partly under the influence of Karl Barth's *Römerbrief* (on this conversion and the young Corbin's participation in the Barthian group *Hic et Nunc*, see Soster, "Le développement de la pensée d'Henry Corbin," chapter 2).

Prior to 1969, Antoine Faivre's references to "esotericism" were still in line with the conventional usage of that term by French scholars in the post-Viatte tradition: it was mainly associated with the distinction of "inner" (esoteric) and "outer" (exoteric). His true concern was with defining the category of "illuminism," and here he emphasized the notions of an Inner Church, initiation, the myth of fall and reintegration, and the centrality of nature as a web of correspondences.[320] In his first general overview devoted to "Christian esotericism" from the sixteenth to the twentieth century (1972), one sees him struggling with the various connotations of the word and the difficulties of demarcating the field. His proposal ("perhaps artificial, but methodologically useful") was to define as "esotericist" any thinker, "Christian or not," who emphasized three points: analogical thinking, theosophy, and the Inner Church.[321] Interestingly, Faivre made a point of demarcating esotericism not only from witchcraft, but also from magic, astrology, and the mantic arts: these "occult" arts qualified as "esotericism" only insofar as they appeared in a theosophical context. While Faivre's definition of theosophy itself remained a bit vague here, it was clearly central to his understanding of "esotericism"; and his historical overview showed that he looked at the field from a perspective dominated by the illuminist context and its immediate roots in Paracelsianism, Christian kabbalah, and Jacob Böhme. At the end of the article, Henry Corbin was singled out as an essential author for understanding Christian esotericism, and it finished with a statement typical of the Eranos perspective:

comprehending the spiritual events of esotericism is not possible without a hermeneutics that always leads back to the archetypal plane, for a meaning has its own proper value, independently from all the explications that one can – and must – give it; as such, this meaning should neither be reduced to one fixed literal interpretation, nor enclosed in a history that is seen as belonging to the past.[322]

In a slightly earlier contribution to the journal *Annales* (special issue on structuralism and historiography, 1971), we find Faivre's first attempt at putting such a program into action himself, by moving beyond strict historiography and towards a general philosophical hermeneutics. As could be expected, it showed the dominant influence of Henry Corbin, Gilbert Durand, and Mircea Eliade, alongside another crucial influence on Faivre's thinking in this period, the philosopher of non-aristotelian logic Stéphane

---

[320] Faivre, *Kirchberger*, xiii–xvii; *Eckartshausen*, 13–14. The first longer discussion of "esotericism" occurs in *Eckartshausen*, 374–382, where it denotes the "interiorism" of the "Inner Church" (the human heart as the true temple of divinity) as opposed to the exotericism of the established churches (*ibid.*, 378–380).
[321] Faivre, "L'ésotérisme chrétien," 1304–1307.   [322] *Ibid.*, 1360.

Lupasco.[323] Faivre discussed alchemical texts as reflections of an underlying worldview, and applauded Eliade for having demonstrated that "the historical perspective alone, although absolutely indispensable in any serious study, is powerless to give an account of certain spiritual facts."[324] To truly understand alchemy, which "'imagines' always in space, almost never in time," one needed a non-aristotelian and non-Cartesian logic as developed by Lupasco and supported by modern physics.

In his *L'ésotérisme au XVIIIe siècle* (1973) this perspective was applied to eighteenth-century esotericism as a whole. Its Introduction was based roughly upon the article of 1972, but Faivre now stated confidently that "esoteric thought appears to be of an essentially contradictorial type, that is to say, it is made up of symbolic mechanisms that belong to the logic of contradiction."[325] In line with contemporary debate about "different rationalities,"[326] and referring specifically to Lévi-Strauss, he was arguing that esotericism must be understood in terms of the "analogical thinking" proper to myth and symbolism, not the "aristotelian" logic proper to philosophy and doctrinal theology. The theosophers or esotericists tended to be badly understood because they either speak their own language, which is understood only by their peers and by poets, or try to make themselves understood in the inadequate language of the philosophers and theologians.[327] Faivre tried to demarcate his own approach from two types of dogmatic either/or thinking, those of traditionalist esotericism and rationalist reductionism;[328] and presented "esotericism" as a kind of mental space mediating between the radical "homogenizing" extremes of dualism, ecstatic mysticism, and the established churches.[329] In conclusion, he emphasized that next to Eliade's oeuvre, Corbin's notions of the "imaginal" and the creative imagination and Durand's studies of the "regimes of the imaginary" provided the key to his Introduction, and hence to his understanding of esotericism.[330] In Faivre's first Eranos lecture, also in 1973, the same set of ideas was applied to alchemy. Referring to Schelling's notion of "tautegory" as used by Corbin, Faivre stated that the true meaning of alchemical images such as those in Michael Maier's *Atalanta Fugiens* lies in an independent and autonomous spiritual reality that

---

[323] Faivre, "Pour un approche figuratif de l'alchimie" (repr. in Faivre, *Mystiques, théosophes et illuminés*, 201–213); and cf. the description of Faivre's lecture "Alchimie occidentale et logique aristotélicienne" in the same year.

[324] *Ibid.*, 202.   [325] Faivre, *L'ésotérisme au XVIIIe siècle*, 15, cf. 19.

[326] See above, Chapter 3, pp. 165–166 (third approach to "magic").

[327] Faivre, *L'ésotérisme au XVIIIe siècle*, 19.   [328] *Ibid.*, 26–27.

[329] See the diagram in *ibid.*, 21.   [330] *Ibid.*, 28–29.

cannot be deduced from their textual explanations or reduced to historical analyses.[331]

One year later, in Faivre's first contribution to the *Université Saint Jean de Jérusalem*, we find an ambitious attempt at interpreting the general course of Western culture in terms of a basic "divorce" between analogical thinking and aristotelian logic since the later Middle Ages. The crucial event was that Aristotle's principles of identity, non-contradiction and the excluded middle had come to be applied not only to the created world, where they were indispensable to the development of science and technology, but to metaphysical reality as well. As a result, aristotelian logic turned into an "intolerant master" that excluded any other approach to reality as deficient *a priori*;[332] and as a result of this process, what we now call "esotericism" emerged as a category of exclusion:

the principles of formal aristotelianism, having wrongly become the foundation *a priori* of all official metaphysics in theology – and later, in secularized philosophy – have, by the same token, banished the other forms of logical (hence analogical) thinking into a no man's land that is still imagined as if surrounded by sulphuric vapours. Piled up all together, always on the peripheries of the churches and universities, and condemned perpetually to either use cunning or defend themselves openly, little by little these [forms of thinking] have coalesced into a strange mass that, for lack of a better term, has been called *esotericism* since about a century ago, and is still seen by many as just a cabinet of curiosities where the best rubs shoulders with the worst. Sometimes without any transition, next to the low magic or the delirious divination of a sorcery inherited by last century's occultism, one discovers there the summits of human thinking, intuitions on man and the universe that are capable of bursting open the deadlocks in which our modern philosophers have indifferently allowed themselves to get imprisoned: one discovers theosophy there, and at the same time – which is hardly surprising – all kinds of instructive speculation on themes that are considered "esoteric" in the Latin Occident but have acquired *droit de cité* elsewhere.[333]

Faivre's history of the "divorce" emphasized how the repression of analogical thinking resulted in an artificial opposition that left room only for two extremes: either an abstract idealism focused only on pure divine essences, or a concrete visible universe cut off from any spiritual reality (finally leading to materialism). The decisive event in this disjunctive process – and here Faivre depended heavily on Corbin – had been

---

[331] Faivre, "Mystische Alchemie und geistige Hermeneutik," 343, 355.
[332] Faivre, "Philosophie de la nature et naturalisme scientiste," 92. Cf. 97 ("a science that is actually a form of superior technology had the pretension of turning itself into a metaphysics and ended up considering itself as the absolute norm"), and 107 ("epistemological totalitarianism").
[333] Faivre, "Philosophie de la nature et naturalisme scientiste," 92–93.

the triumph of Averroism over the thinking of Avicenna.[334] The destruction of an organic harmony uniting God, man, and the world resulted in a continuing situation of existential malaise that remains characteristic of the "idealist and schizomorphous intellectualism of modernity."[335] Against this dominant intellectual trend, "the analogical and theosophical tradition" continued in Renaissance currents such as Christian kabbalah and Paracelsianism, leading finally to a *Naturphilosophie* that was now making its comeback in the thinking of modern physicists like Werner Heisenberg.[336]

Faivre's article culminated in a passionate plea for "remythologization" and revaluation of the "creative and participatory imagination," against contemporary trends such as existentialist pessimism, the abstract formalism of structuralism, the "superstition" of materialism, and the nihilism of an "archaeology of knowledge" that tries to convince us "that knowledge sounds hollow, man is dead, nature is meaningless, and no philosophy has any sense."[337] Here and in a few other publications around the mid-1970s, Faivre was speaking explicitly as a Christian;[338] and like other participants of Eranos and (particularly) the *Université Saint Jean de Jérusalem*, he was now lashing out at the desacralization of the world, the reversal of values that made "above" a reflection of "below" instead of the reverse, historicist concepts of linear causality, the blind faith in secular evolution and progress, and so on: against all forms of "reductionism," he was affirming that myth should have precedence over history, metaphysics over physics, correspondences over causality, analogical thinking over aristotelian logic, and images over concepts.[339] One can only conclude that at this point in his intellectual career, Faivre was speaking as a Christian theosopher, deeply concerned about the *Umwertung aller Werte* that had caused the crisis of the modern world.

---

[334] Corbin, *Creative Imagination*, 10–18. For a short summary and critical evaluation of Corbin's view of Avicenna, see Sebti, "Avicenna," 145–146.

[335] Faivre, "Philosophie de la nature et naturalisme scientiste," 94.

[336] *Ibid.*, 103–105.   [337] *Ibid.*, 105–107.

[338] *Ibid.*, 110; Faivre, "Église intérieure et Jérusalem céleste," 77, 88–89; "Théosophie chrétienne et prophétie," 149.

[339] For example, Faivre, "Les normes," 313–314 ("the norm is not that we have ten fingers but that the number ten incarnates itself in nature"), 317 ("subordinating the future to the past comes down to denying that life tends towards liberty" and "the valorization of linear time, the affirmation that everything, starting from nothing, is created by increasing complexification privileges the 'simple' as norm of departure at the expense of the polyvalence of the real"), 320 (in terms of Schelling's notion of tautegory, "mythology appears to be the first term, and history only a secondary and derivative term. It is mythology that determines history and not the inverse"). Cf. "Théosophie chrétienne et prophétie," 141–144, with its strong affirmation of Eliade's *in illo tempore* and Corbin's view that history is subordinate to a "metahistory."

Interestingly, the lecture was not all that well received at Eranos;[340] and over the next years, such explicit religionist fervor slowly began to recede into the background even in Faivre's lectures at the *Université Saint Jean de Jérusalem*.[341] Parallel to this development, he began to distance himself from Eranos because of its elitist and authoritarian tendencies, which left no room for open discussion with the audience and showed no interest in addressing a younger generation.[342] The religionist approach by no means vanished from Faivre's scholarship, as will be seen, but by the end of the 1970s it was becoming less explicit. A convenient marker in this process of transition is the year 1979, when Faivre was elected to the chair for "History of Esoteric and Mystical Currents in Modern and Contemporary Europe" at the École Pratique des Hautes Études (Sorbonne), a highly prestigious research institute with a strong secular focus in the French tradition of *laïcité*.[343] Once again, although almost by accident, it was Henry Corbin who had been at the origin of this unique academic position, which was to become crucial to the establishment of "Western esotericism" as an academic field of research. In 1964, as one of the EPHE's professors, Corbin had suggested the new title "History of Christian Esotericism" for a chair that had just become vacant, because it seemed to correspond more or less to the competences of the favorite candidate, the specialist of Christian kabbalah François Secret. Coming at the end of a long and exhausting faculty meeting, Corbin's idea was accepted by his colleagues for want of anything better.[344] Secret got the position in 1965, but was in fact embarrassed by the title of his chair, and never attempted to conceptualize "esotericism" (Christian or not) as a specific field of research.[345] At his retirement in 1979, the title of the chair was modified: it should no longer

---

[340] Faivre, *Journal*, August 29, October 10, 1974; see Hakl, *Verborgene Geist*, 346.

[341] In "Les 'Noces Chymiques'" (1977) he restricted himself to simply pointing to "the existence of a certain type of occidental spirituality . . . generally suppressed, occulted, by the intellectual fashions, stagnations, and totalitarianisms that have hardly ceased to prevail over the last centuries" (o.c, 139). The religionist message was implicit rather than explicit in "Les métamorphoses d'Hermès" (1978, the year after Corbin's death), devoted largely to the "new physics" as *Naturphilosophie*, with much attention to Raymond Ruyer's bestseller *La Gnose de Princeton* (1974). The following four years Faivre gave no lectures at the *Université*, and when he returned in 1983, it was with entirely historical lectures on chivalric imagery in eighteenth-century alchemy, Freemasonry, and literature (Faivre, "Miles redivivus") and elements of Christian theosophical thought two years later ("Pensées de Dieu, images de l'homme").

[342] Faivre, *Journal*, August 29, 1974, August 21, 1976; Hakl, *Verborgene Geist*, 346–348. In 1975 Faivre unsuccessfully tried to change the Eranos format by offering a petition signed by many long-standing participants.

[343] Faivre, "From Paris to Amsterdam and Beyond," 123.

[344] Faivre, personal communication, March 29, 2008.

[345] *Ibid.*, 123–124; Hanegraaff, "Birth of Esotericism," 189–201.

be limited to Christianity alone, but restricted to the European context from the Renaissance to the present, and the adjective and plural "esoteric currents" was chosen to avoid suspicions of essentialism. Furthermore, the adjective "mystical" was added so as to broaden the range of applicants, leading eventually to a job competition between Faivre and the specialist of mysticism Michel de Certeau.[346]

Illuminism, Christian theosophy, and *Naturphilosophie* remained Faivre's chief domain of research in the period from 1979 to 1992, but he was concerned to situate those currents within a larger historical framework, and spent considerable effort discussing the specificity of "Western esotericism" as a field of research. Of fundamental importance in his publications during this period[347] remains the notion of esotericism as a worldview pitted against the "desacralization of the cosmos," still understood in terms of the late medieval triumph of Averroism and its application of aristotelian logic to the domain of metaphysics. Instead of assuming an ontological "rupture" between pure spirit and material bodies – and hence ultimately, in biblical terms, between Creator and creation – esotericism in this understanding is predicated on the simultaneous incarnation of spirit and spiritualization of body on an intermediary plane of reality accessible by the imagination (which, on these assumptions, is understood not as a fabricator of illusions but as an organ of perception). This fundamental notion was derived from Corbin, but there always remained an unresolved tension between the latter's docetist understanding of his *mundus imaginalis* on the one hand, and Faivre's decidedly incarnational perspective on the other. Whereas Corbin ultimately privileged the spiritual dimension and thereby had to make the body into an "illusion" by comparison, Faivre was more consistent in emphasizing the centrality of "nature" (understood very much in terms of German Romantic *Naturphilosophie*) as a living body intermediary between the dead weight of pure matter and the cool abstractions of pure spirit. Corbin's preference for Swedenborg[348] and Faivre's for Paracelsus and his successors[349] exemplified this fundamental difference between two

---

[346] Dosse, *Michel de Certeau*, 382–384.

[347] Key publications regarding his understanding of "esotericism" are Faivre, "L'imagination créatrice" (1981, later reprinted in significantly revised versions under the title "Vis Imaginativa" in *Accès* [1996], vol. II, 171–219, and *Theosophy, Imagination, Tradition*, 99–136); Faivre, "Sources antiques et médiévales" (1984, repr. in *Accès* [1986], 51–135; *Accès* [1996], vol. I, 50–137; and Faivre and Needleman, *Modern Esoteric Spirituality*, 1–70); Faivre, "Introduction: Définitions et positions" in *Accès* (1986), 13–49.

[348] Corbin, *Swedenborg and Esoteric Islam*.

[349] In Faivre's key text "L'imagination créatrice," Paracelsus' concepts play a central role both in the general historical overview and in the special discussion of alchemy (*ibid.*, 358–360, 368).

worldviews predicated on models derived from Islamic and Christian theosophy respectively.[350]

A religionist program in the line of Eranos and the *Université Saint Jean de Jérusalem*, with a strong emphasis on the incarnationist perspectives of Christian theosophy and *Naturphilosophie*, was still very much in evidence in Faivre's *Accès de l'ésotérisme occidental* published in 1986. Apart from a new introduction, it consisted of revisions of earlier articles, four of which came from the USJJ's *Cahiers*. Faivre now distinguished between esotericism in a restricted sense, understood as an attitude of "interiorism" leading to a salvational gnosis, and in a large sense, defined by the addition of a theosophical dimension pertaining to the mysteries of divinity, man, and the universe: "theosophy opens esotericism up to the entire universe, thereby making possible a philosophy of nature."[351] Such "esotericism properly speaking" should not be confused with general and popular understandings of the term:[352] Faivre was very concerned to make his readers distinguish between the many forms of "trivial esotericism" flourishing in contemporary society and the profound meaning of the true esoteric Tradition as he saw it.[353]

To contextualize these discussions properly, it is important to understand that popular contemporary "esotericism" played no role of any importance in Faivre's work until the 1980s. In the academic context to which he was used, the term was functioning in erudite discussions on a high intellectual level, among sophisticated scholars and philosophers who, more than anything, shared an abhorrence of the dogmatic Marxism that had come to dominate much of French academic life since the events of 1968. In their fight against "historicism" and "reductionism," they were reacting to what was experienced as a stifling new totalitarianism that sought to suppress freedom of thought and left no room for any religious or spiritual

---

[350] Corbin misinterpreted the anti-docetic theosophies of Böhme and Oetinger as docetic theosophies similar to Swedenborg's: on this point, see the clash between Corbin and Ernst Benz in 1975 as summarized by Faivre, "La question," 96; and cf. Hanegraaff, *Swedenborg, Oetinger, Kant*, 132–133 n. 116. Faivre deliberately emphasized incarnationism at the *Université Saint Jean de Jérusalem*, and his disagreement with Corbin was well known among the participants (Faivre, *Journal*, July 8, 1975, December 24, 1975, July 23, 1976; March 18, 1980; June 18, 1986). Note that while Erik Davis ("Hermes on the Seine") correctly recognizes the Roman Catholic subtext in Faivre's work, he spectacularly misinterprets him as promoting an ascetic rejection of the body and sexuality.
[351] Faivre, *Accès* (1986), 14, 19.   [352] *Ibid.*, 7.
[353] See especially *ibid.*, 28–30, 33–48. Faivre's frequent references, in this period, to Tradition (capitalized) reflect the influence of Guénonian perspectives in the French intellectual milieu, but he was at pains to demarcate his own understanding from their "severe" and "purist" views (*ibid.*, 33–39). Rather confusingly, he referred to popular New Age perspectives as adhering to an "historical" perspective because they were exploring a multitude of "traditions" rather than the single Tradition (*ibid.*, 36).

values. The specter that they feared was an imminent communist takeover reminiscent of the fascist dictatorship in recent memory.[354] One can therefore imagine Faivre's initial puzzlement in the early 1980s, when a series of annual guest professorships at the University of Berkeley introduced him first-hand to the phenomenon of a decidedly left-wing and liberal "esotericism" flourishing among students and professors on the American West Coast. Faivre's unpublished diaries show how, almost immediately after arrival, he found himself confronted with the vogue of "new religious movements" and the alternative lifestyles nowadays associated with the New Age – not to mention a general expectation among students and colleagues that this European professor of "esoteric and mystical currents" would certainly know all about them! In fact, Faivre's understanding of "esotericism" was quite far removed from that of his new American audience, and adjustments proved necessary on both sides.

It is no exaggeration to say that Faivre fell in love with San Francisco, and he kept returning to the Berkeley campus each year during most of the 1980s. As a result of these lengthy sojourns and his many discussions with American colleagues, the phenomenon of contemporary "popular" esotericism became a serious topic of reflection. He began to broaden the scope of his research beyond the domains of Christian theosophy, illuminism and *Naturphilosophie*, and his studies of such topics as animal magnetism, spiritualism, Traditionalism, or new religious movements forced him to revise and broaden his theoretical understanding of the field. His initial approach appears to have been one of trying to educate his audience about the differences between popular and superficial forms of "New Age" esotericism and the more profound and meaningful Tradition of esotericism "properly speaking," that is to say, the core perspective represented by Christian theosophy and *Naturphilosophie*.[355] Its ideas and traditions appeared to be utterly unknown to his students and colleagues, but could be made more

---

[354] Faivre, *Journal*, February 2, April 1, November 18, 1974; March 15 and 20, 1977; March 15, 1978; January 23, 1980; April 25, 1981; February 8, 1982. The similarity between fascist and communist totalitarianism was obvious both for Durand, who served in the French resistance during World War II, and Faivre, whose father was likewise in the resistance and spent seven months in a German concentration camp (Faivre, *Journal*, September 26, 1976).

[355] See, for example, the many pejorative references to popular and contemporary esotericism in the Introduction of Faivre's *Accès* (1986) and the parallel English entry "Esotericism" in Eliade's *Encyclopedia of Religion* (1987). See also Faivre's first large article in English, "Children of Hermes" (1988), with references to, for example, "malicious writers" like Erich von Däniken or the "pseudo-initiatic discourse" prominent in Californian new religious movements. On the other hand, when the theosophist and scholar Jean-Louis Siémons severely criticized an old article by Faivre on "Theosophy" (*Encyclopaedia Universalis*, 1973), in 1985, Faivre surprised him by readily admitting its weaknesses and pointing out that his opinions had evolved in the meantime (Faivre, *Journal*, March 8, 1985).

understandable thanks to the main intellectual framework that they shared
with Faivre: that of the Eranos-inspired study of religion and myth, prominently represented in American academic culture by such famous names as
Jung and Eliade, next to Joseph Campbell, James Hillman, and a range of
other authors in the same tradition. In these years, Faivre was much concerned with the mythical figure(s) of Hermes, "the antitotalitarian god par
excellence,"[356] and was vigorously defending what he now called a "hermesian" program of remythologization, against the reign of empty abstraction
and the false "ideologies and pseudophilosophies of history."[357]

Nevertheless, the tension between such religionist engagement and the
requirements of historiography proper became an increasingly pressing
issue for Faivre during the later 1980s. It would appear that this happened
mainly as a result of academic internationalization: combinations of historical and philosophical erudition with a spiritual message, of the kind
that he was used to in his own French context (and that also went down
well among American audiences influenced by Eliadian, Jungian, and other
Eranos-inspired perspectives), appeared to be puzzling, to say the least, for
specialized American, Italian, or German historians working in the emerging fields of hermeticism and alchemy,[358] and this eventually led him to
reconsider his own approach. Furthermore, Faivre's growing irritation with
the dogmatic antimodernism and intolerant attitudes of the "perennialists"
at the annual conferences of the American Academy of Religion[359] would
appear to have contributed to a renewed appreciation for the virtues of
the French tradition of *laïcité* ingrained in his home institution, the École
Pratique des Hautes Études, and the merits of secular historiography in
general.[360] The results of this process of reorientation became visible in his
small but seminal volume *L'ésotérisme* of 1992.

The publication of that 127-page booklet, written for a famous French
series of pocket introductions, marks both the end of Faivre's religionist period and the beginning of the study of Western esotericism as an
academic field of research.[361] Written deliberately from a perspective of
descriptive neutrality, its five main chapters were devoted to the ancient

---

[356] Faivre, "Children of Hermes," 432.

[357] *Ibid.*, 431. In *Accès*, 49, Faivre defines as "Hermesian" the "spiritual attitude common to all Western esotericism placed under the sign of the god with the caduceus," i.e. Hermes. For Faivre's analyses of Hermes as a mythical figure, see his *Eternal Hermes*.

[358] Notable examples were the large conference on hermeticism in Washington, 1982, and a conference on alchemy in Wolfenbüttel in 1984 (Faivre, *Journal*, March 27, 1982; April 4 and 13, July 19, 1984).

[359] For an overview of the sessions on esotericism at the AAR, see Hanegraaff, "Study of Western Esotericism," 505 n. 13. For perennialism in American academic life and in the AAR, cf. Houman, *De la philosophia perennis au pérennialisme américain*, esp. 491–575.

[360] Faivre, *Journal*, November 20, 1989.   [361] Cf. Hanegraaff, "Birth of Esotericism."

and medieval sources of "modern esoteric currents," esotericism in the Renaissance and Baroque period, esotericism in the period of the Enlightenment, the developments from Romanticism through nineteenth-century occultism, and esotericism in the twentieth century. As such, it was the first scholarly publication of its kind that covered the entire field from early modernity to the present day, with due attention to its sources in antiquity, combining the broad scope of the generalist with an unparalleled level of historical expertise concerning the relevant primary sources. In his Introduction, moreover, Faivre confronted the considerable problems of defining and demarcating "esotericism" as a domain of academic research. This, too, had never been done before. He discussed the advantages and disadvantages of various approaches and solutions, and presented his own proposal as a "methodological tool susceptible of being completed and corrected" by future research.[362] The heart of his Introduction consisted of a soon-to-be-famous definition of esotericism as a "form of thought" that can be recognized by the presence of four intrinsic characteristics (correspondences; living nature; imagination/mediations; transmutation) and the possible presence of two non-intrinsic ones (practice of concordance; transmission).[363]

Seen in the context of Faivre's intellectual development, as briefly sketched above, it is clear that this definition was not invented from scratch. The notion of correspondences was inseparable from the "analogical thinking" that he had highlighted from the start, and had figured as a crucial dimension of "hermeticism" in Faivre's own writings as well as those of thinkers like Durand.[364] We have seen that the crucial notion of imagination/mediations was derived straight from Corbin's concepts of the *mundus imaginalis*; but by combining it with living nature, Faivre steered away from any docetic understanding towards an incarnational perspective in line with the central notion of *Naturphilosophie*. Transmutation was perhaps the most innovative aspect: obviously inspired by Faivre's long-standing interest in "spiritual" alchemy and paracelsian thought, it lent a dynamic and developmental aspect to what might otherwise have been a somewhat static picture of "esotericism."[365] In addition, most of

---

[362] Faivre, *L'ésotérisme* (1992), 4.

[363] *Ibid.*, 13–21. In the same year, 1992, the definition was presented in English in Faivre and Needleman, *Modern Esoteric Spirituality* (Faivre, "Introduction 1"). The notion of a "form of thought" was suggested by Faivre's colleague Émile Poulat (Faivre, "Émile Poulat," 211–212).

[364] See notably Durand's large contribution to the Eranos meeting of 1973 devoted to correspondences ("Similitude hermétique").

[365] In terms of my distinction between two paradigms as outlined above (Chapter 3, pp. 192–195), Faivre's definition clearly favors the "Alchemical" one over its "Platonic" alternative, which may

the elements that were central to his earlier conceptualizations (esotericism as hermeneutics, the notion of interiority, the autonomization of "esotericism" after the twelfth century, the centrality of mythical thinking, and esotericism as a "counterpart of our scientific and secularized vision of the world")[366] all figured prominently in his Introduction, although no longer as parts of a polemics against "modernity."

Faivre has always emphasized that the four intrinsic characteristics are more or less inseparable by nature; and, as a result, it is clear that the central tradition of an incarnational Christian theosophy has remained the heart and core of what he sees as "esotericism." It is consistent with this focus that, to give just a few examples, such phenomena as *magia naturalis* and sophiology are accepted as belonging to the field only insofar as they appear within a theosophical discourse; that nineteenth-century spiritualism may often have been "intimately mingled" with esotericism but is not seen as belonging to that domain "properly speaking"; or that the contemporary "New Age," in spite of its dependence on traditional esoteric currents, is seen as pertaining to the field of new religious movements rather than esotericism. Faivre has maintained these demarcations and exclusions in all later revisions and translations of *L'ésotérisme*.[367] This leads us to an unavoidable conclusion: his definition of esotericism – now deliberately presented as strictly heuristic and open to criticism and future revision – originated as a Christian and religionist notion of "true" esotericism, and retains its fundamental anti-docetic, anti-idealist, and anti-dualist perspective. Therefore it comes at a price: it is hard to see how, for instance, the docetic and post-Cartesian theosophy of Swedenborg, the pure idealism of Guénonian Traditionalism, or the gnostic/cathar dualism of the *Lectorium Rosicrucianum*, could consistently be seen as forms of "esotericism" in terms of Faivre's definition. Moreover, the latter describes essentially an "enchanted" worldview pitted against the "secularization of the cosmos,"[368] and this makes it doubtful, to say the least, whether it can account for the secularization *of* esotericism itself since the nineteenth century.[369] In fairness to Faivre, he has never denied that his approach does

---

contain elements of "mediation" such as Ficino's *spiritus*, but nevertheless tends to highlight the pure intellect and look negatively at nature and the body.

[366] Faivre, *L'ésotérisme* (1992), 6 (hermeneutics), 9 (interiority), 9–10 (autonomization), 11 (mythical thinking as opposed to modern science and secularization).

[367] Faivre, *L'ésotérisme* (1992), 12, 86. For spiritualism and the New Age, see the recent edition of *L'ésotérisme* (2007), 26–27, 87, and *Western Esotericism*, 28, 87 (and cf. Faivre, "Émile Poulat," 210).

[368] See above, Chapter 3, page 254.

[369] Hanegraaff, "The Study," 507–508. In the third part of *New Age Religion and Western Culture*, I described the emergence during the nineteenth century of a "secularized esotericism": a contradiction in terms if one follows the logic of Faivre's definition! Faivre recognizes this as a legitimate problem but does not further address it (*L'ésotérisme* [2007], 17; *Western Esotericism*, 17).

indeed limit the scope of what is popularly understood by "esotericism."[370] The question is whether these restrictions, based upon the centrality of Christian theosophy and *Naturphilosophie*, are still as important to the new generation of scholars as they clearly are for him.

ESOTERICISM IN THE ACADEMY

During the 1970s and 1980s, not only did the study of "hermetic" currents in early modern history develop rapidly under the impact of the Yatesian revolution, but the phenomenon of "new religious movements" and alternative spiritualities stimulated a new scholarly interest in the post-eighteenth-century "occult" as well. When James Webb published his two seminal volumes on what he called the "occult underground" and the "occult establishment" in the mid-1970s, he still presented them as examples of a rearguard "flight from reason."[371] Other pioneers in this domain, such as Christopher McIntosh, Ellic Howe, or Nicholas Goodrick-Clarke,[372] did not feel a need to condemn the supposed "irrationality" of occultism but simply emphasized its significance as a historical factor whose presence and influence could not be denied. Yet others were inspired by explicit commitment to the "inner traditions" of the West, and hoped that bringing them to the attention of a wider audience might stimulate a new spiritual revival.[373] What set these new trends of scholarly and popular writing apart from the predominantly sociological concern with new religious movements was their attention to history, and especially the history of ideas. With various degrees of emphasis, all these authors noted that the "occult" milieus since the nineteenth century had to be understood as continuations of older traditions that went back to early modern times and ultimately late antiquity.

While a flood of new scholarship in these domains emerged during the 1970s and 1980s, the academy did not yet have any institutional settings or disciplinary frameworks that were able to accommodate them as belonging to a distinct field of research. As a result, specialists were working in relative isolation, scattered over a variety of disciplines, with very few opportunities to meet and discuss their research, present it to the wider

---

[370] For his most recent formulation, see, for example, *Western Esotericism*, 3–4.
[371] Webb, *Occult Underground*; *Occult Establishment*. Cf. an early collective volume like Kerr and Crow, *Occult in America*.
[372] For example, McIntosh, *Eliphas Lévi and the French Occult Revival*; Howe, *Magicians of the Golden Dawn*; Möller and Howe, *Merlin Peregrinus*; Goodrick-Clarke, *Occult Roots of Nazism*.
[373] Highly representative for this approach was the popular magazine *Gnosis* (1985–1999) and various books published by its founder Jay Kinney and his close associate Richard Smoley. See short analysis in Hanegraaff, "Kabbalah in *Gnosis* Magazine."

academic community, or introduce it to students. It was only in the years after 1992 that this situation began to improve. As Antoine Faivre's writings began to be translated into English, his concept of "Western esotericism" appeared to be capable of accommodating the new wave of scholarship in "the occult" as part of a much wider historical vision that encompassed the entire period from the Renaissance on, with due recognition of its ultimate sources in late antiquity. As increasing emphasis came to be placed on critical historiography and empiricism – instead of scholarship with covert apologetic or even missionary pro-esoteric agendas – this made it possible for the study of "Western esotericism" to be admitted into the academy as a legitimate field of scholarly research.[374]

As usual in such cases, this development has been accompanied by vigorous theoretical and methodological debate among a relatively small number of specialized scholars.[375] In this final section I will not analyze these discussions in technical detail: doing so with any degree of accuracy would result in a disproportionately lengthy microhistory, out of balance with the broader scope of this book. Moreover, far from being closed or resolved, the academic debate on "esotericism" is very much alive and evolving at the time of writing, and the author of these lines is himself strongly involved in it. Standing too close to historical events always makes it difficult to evaluate them with a sufficient measure of critical distance or objectivity, and obviously even more so if the historian finds himself and his ideas among the topics being studied. It would be pointless to deny that my own publications and activities have played a considerable role in the development of "Western esotericism" as a field of research since the early 1990s, or that this book in its entirety reflects my present vision of its nature and importance. But it would be equally pointless, and rather pretentious, to try and use this final section to "demonstrate" the superiority of my theoretical and methodological approaches over those of colleagues with whom I disagree: that debate must be carried out elsewhere,

---

[374] For overviews, see Hanegraaff, "Study of Western Esotericism" (until 2004) and Pasi, "Correnti esoteriche occidentali."

[375] In chronological order, see especially Hanegraaff, "Empirical Method" (1995); Faivre, "L'ésotérisme et la recherche universitaire" (1996); Hanegraaff, "On the Construction" (1998); Gruber, "Mystik, Esoterik, Okkultismus" (1998); Neugebauer-Wölk, "Esoterik in der frühen Neuzeit" (2000); Hanegraaff, "Beyond the Yates Paradigm" (2001); Versluis, "What is Esoteric?" (2002); Hanegraaff, "Dreams of Theology" (2003); Neugebauer-Wölk, "Esoterik und Christentum" (2003); Hanegraaff, "Study of Western Esotericism" (2004); Hanegraaff, "Introduction" (2005); Hanegraaff, "Forbidden Knowledge" (2005); von Stuckrad, "Western Esotericism" (2005); Hanegraaff, "Trouble with Images" (2006); Faivre, "Kocku von Stuckrad" (2006); Pasi, "Il problema della definizione" (2008); Bergunder, "Was ist Esoterik?" (2008); Kilcher, "Seven Epistemological Theses" (2009); Santamaria, "Etude de l'ésotérisme" (2010); Bergunder, "What is Esotericism?" (2010).

and the arguments should be judged by my peers rather than myself. I will therefore restrict myself to a short outline of the main developments that have taken place on an institutional level, and of the main developments on a theoretical level. While I cannot presume to be neutral in presenting such an account, I will at least try to be fair.

At a conference in 1992, I made the acquaintance of Antoine Faivre, and in the wake of this meeting we decided to try and organize a series of sessions on "Western esotericism" at the quinquennial conference of the International Association for the History of Religions (IAHR) in Mexico City, 1995. We collaborated on this project with Karen Voss, an American scholar of religions in the tradition of Eliade; and to raise awareness in view of the Mexico event, Faivre and Voss co-authored a programmatic article on "Western Esotericism and the Science of Religions" published in the IAHR's journal *Numen* in 1995.[376] Around the same time, we had intensive discussions about a methodological article published by me in the same year, in which I defended an "empirical" approach to the study of Western esotericism.[377] Responding to current debates between defenders of sociological "reductionism" and the *sui generis* approach of "religionist" scholars in the tradition of Eliade, I argued for a third approach grounded in "methodological agnosticism": regardless of a scholar's personal beliefs (or lack of them), the existence or non-existence of divine or sacred realities is simply beyond empirical verification or falsification by scholars *qua* scholars. Therefore a scholar may or may not personally share the beliefs of those he studies, but in his research he should limit himself to what can be verified empirically and historically: he can describe, analyze, interpret, or even seek to explain what people believe, but cannot affirm that they are either right or wrong. Applied to the study of esotericism, this simple principle ruled out both religionist and reductionist perspectives, while making room for consistently historical research. It was also meant to imply a healthy dose of modesty with regard to the scholarly enterprise, which is limited to the empirical and can neither presume to make statements about the existence or non-existence of metaphysical realities, nor strictly rule out the possible legitimacy of such statements made by believers.[378]

---

[376] Faivre and Voss, "Western Esotericism."

[377] Hanegraaff, "Empirical Method." For a further application to Western esotericism, see Hanegraaff, "On the Construction"; "Some Remarks."

[378] Of course such an "empirical" approach does not imply any naive belief in "detached" objectivity. It does not deny the subjectivities of the scholar, but advocates a critical attitude towards one's own biases as well as those of others ("Empirical Method," 107–108; "On the Construction," 16). For a very similar perspective, cf. Max Weber, *Wissenschaft als Beruf*.

In his subsequent writings, Faivre embraced methodological agnosticism as a basic principle, and thereby made a final and clean break with religionism.[379] During the sessions in Mexico City, presided over by Faivre and myself, the effect of our commitment to empirical/historical research became evident almost immediately: it resulted in a clear distance between the "religionist" participants, who found it natural to use their research as a vehicle for expressing esoteric or spiritual commitments, and their "historically-oriented" counterparts who had no wish to do so. The selected proceedings of the Mexico volume were published in 1998,[380] and sessions on Western esotericism became a normal part of subsequent IAHR conferences (Durban 2000, Tokyo 2005, Toronto 2010). The religionist perspective became very much a non-issue at least in this venue; and a similar development took place in the context of the American Academy of Religions.[381]

A breakthrough event for the academic legitimation of Western esotericism as a field of research occurred in 1999, when the University of Amsterdam decided to create the world's second academic chair devoted to this field (after the one held by Faivre at the EPHE), together with two assistant professorships, two Ph.D. positions and a secretary.[382] I had the honor of being appointed to this chair, which now made it possible to create a complete academic curriculum for Western esotericism. Since then, my colleagues for Western esotericism in the early modern period (subsequently Jean-Pierre Brach, Kocku von Stuckrad, and Peter J. Forshaw) and in the eighteenth to twenty-first century (Olav Hammer, then Marco Pasi) and I have had the privilege of teaching a new generation of young academics from all over the world,[383] many of whom have continued to pursue Ph.D. positions and will therefore contribute to the future development of the field on an international scale. Furthermore, the success of the Amsterdam chair encouraged several other academic institutes

---

[379] See in particular "L'ésotérisme et la recherche universitaire" (trans. in *Theosophy, Imagination, Tradition*, xiii–xxxv). In his earlier work, Faivre had followed the common religionist assumption that "historicism" implies reductionism and "agnosticism" is a polite term for unbelief; but from an empirical perspective there is no binding logic to either of these assumptions, so that the scholar remains free to hold any personal belief that does not conflict with demonstrable empirical and historical facts.

[380] Faivre and Hanegraaff, *Western Esotericism and the Science of Religion*.

[381] Hanegraaff, "Study of Western Esotericism," 505–506. The AAR now has annual "Western esotericism" sessions with protected "group" status.

[382] For all the details about the creation of this chair, which was made possible by a generous donation by Rosalie Basten, see Hanegraaff and Pijnenburg, *Hermes in the Academy*, especially van den Broek, "The Birth of a Chair"; Hanegraaff, "Ten Years"; and Faivre, "From Paris to Amsterdam and Beyond."

[383] See testimonies in Hanegraaff and Pijnenburg, *Hermes in the Academy*.

to venture similar initiatives: thus, the University of Exeter created the third chair in the field in 2005 (held by Nicholas Goodrick-Clarke), with a distance-learning curriculum; and a successful, although unfortunately temporary, research group on esotericism and the Enlightenment was created by Monika Neugebauer-Wölk at the University of Halle in 2004.[384] One hopes that this process will continue.

Alongside the University of Amsterdam, the well-known academic publishing house Brill played a major role in the establishment of the field. From 2001 on, Brill began publishing the new peer-reviewed journal *Aries: Journal for the Study of Western Esotericism*, followed from 2006 on by a parallel "Aries Book Series" that brings out monographs, collective volumes, and text editions. And last but not least, due to the initiative of one of its senior editors, Hans van der Meij, a comprehensive *Dictionary of Gnosis and Western Esotericism* (over 1200 pages, with *c.* 150 contributors) was published by Brill in 2005.[385] The combined effect of these various efforts, and the insistence on historical/empirical approaches, was that the term "Western esotericism" has begun to shed its doubtful connotations in academic debate during the first decade of the twenty-first century, particularly in the context of the study of religion, and ever greater numbers of international scholars now present themselves as engaged in research that falls under this umbrella. As a result, numerous conferences on various aspects of esotericism are now being organized each year, and two academic organizations for scholars in this field have been created in Europe and the United States.[386] Finally, whereas Faivre in his entry "Esotericism" for Eliade's *Encyclopedia of Religion* (1987) could still state that "There is no single book on the history of esotericism,"[387] today a choice of introductory textbooks is available.[388]

Institutional and publicational developments apart, the success of Faivre's definition and the "empirical turn" in the study of Western esotericism have been the most crucial factors in this process of academic emancipation: the former by creating a conceptual umbrella covering the

---

[384] Goodrick-Clarke, "Western Esotericism in the United Kingdom"; Neugebauer-Wölk, "From Talk about Esotericism to Esotericism Research"; and see the two volumes edited by Neugebauer-Wölk, *Aufklärung und Esoterik* (1999, 2008).

[385] Hanegraaff (in collaboration with Antoine Faivre, Roelof van den Broek, and Jean-Pierre Brach), *Dictionary*.

[386] The European Society for the Study of Western Esotericism (ESSWE) and the US-based Association for the Study of Esotericism (ASE).

[387] Faivre, "Esotericism," 163.

[388] Von Stuckrad, *Western Esotericism*; Versluis, *Magic and Mysticism*; Goodrick-Clarke, *The Western Esoteric Traditions*; Faivre, *Western Esotericism*.

entire period from the Renaissance to the present, the second by convincing academic communities that this field could be studied without any covert agendas of pro-esoteric apologeticism. Nevertheless, the academic study of "Western esotericism" is still just in its early infancy, and continuous vigilance remains necessary to prevent it from losing what has been gained. A first set of problems has to do with Faivre's definition. Countless scholars have invoked its four/six characteristics over the last two decades, but it is fair to say that very few of them have been aware of its background in a specific type of incarnational Christian theosophy, or cared about the implications. Instead, most of them have been seduced by what I would call "the checklist approach to Western esotericism": simply check whether you can detect something that looks like the four intrinsic characteristics in any type of material, and if you succeed, you have "proven" that it is "esoteric"![389] In doing so, one ignores what the four intrinsic characteristics were supposed to mean in their original context: for example, the incarnational agenda is missed by almost everybody who just looks for references to the "imagination" and likes the idea of seeing it as an "organ of knowledge" rather than just fantasy. Thus taken out of context and turned into abstractions, the Faivrean characteristics become empty containers that may be filled with almost anything, theosophical or otherwise. The result is a strange paradox. While Faivre's definition might be criticized for being too restrictive in suggesting that only the "form of thought" of an incarnational Christian theosophy is truly "esoteric," the way it has actually been *used* produces exactly the opposite effect: rather than demarcating a field, it ends up dissolving its boundaries. Since Faivre himself writes that the components can be distributed quite unevenly, only the scantiest evidence sometimes seems sufficient to magically turn the most disparate materials into species of "esotericism." In addition, the definition is often understood in an essentialist manner, suggesting that it describes some kind of esotericism *sui generis*. The result is, of course, yet another relapse into religionism.

These problems are related to the fact that for many scholars today – especially those working on late modern and contemporary topics – the label "esotericism" seems to have been transformed from an academic liability into a desired commodity: instead of excluding them, it now gives them access to networks and podia where their work will be taken seriously. At first sight it might look encouraging that so many scholars are now eager

---

[389] Hanegraaff, "The Study," 507–508. The phrase "checklist approach to Western esotericism" was suggested to me by Hans van der Meij during a casual conversation.

to "jump on the bandwagon" of esotericism – who could have imagined this just a few decades ago? – but it carries considerable risks as well. In recent years, too many scholars with doubtful credentials have been joining the new community of "esotericism studies" out of pure convenience, if not opportunism. By using the checklist approach, one may easily turn Faivre's definition into an "admission ticket" for whatever one's focus of interest may be, without much concern for the theoretical or methodological issues involved. In order for the study of Western esotericism to have a solid future in the academy, and for the debate on methods and theories to have any sense at all, it will be essential to keep insisting on high scholarly standards and critical debate.

Finally, as the study of "esotericism" began to gain scholarly recognition after 1992, it naturally got involved with wider academic trends and perspectives in the humanities generally, and the study of religion more specifically. Most influential by far has been the notion of *discourse*. As summarized by Olav Hammer in a landmark study of 2001:

Using the term discourse draws attention to the mechanisms of ideology and power that include and accept certain voices, while at the same time excluding others. It implies that certain propositions regarding the human condition and the constitution of reality, which are historically contingent and culturally constructed, are presented within the discourse as if they were natural, trans-historical facts and thus protected from scrutiny. The limits of the discourse also define the boundaries of what may tolerably be questioned.[390]

The relevance to "esotericism" is almost too obvious to need further emphasis. Any reader who has followed the thread of my argument up to this point will recognize how omnipresent such discursive mechanisms of ideology and power have been throughout the story that I have been trying to tell. The same goes, no less obviously, for the three "discursive strategies" highlighted by Hammer, based upon the appeal to "tradition," "rationality and science," and "experience":[391] by and large, they have dominated my chapters 1 and 2, 3, and 4 respectively. While Hammer applied a discursive analysis to the "strategies of epistemology" typical of modern theosophy and the New Age, the intellectual history outlined in the present book would be perfect material for an analysis along similar lines.

While Hammer used discourse analysis within the wider framework of a text-based intellectual history, others have argued that a "discursive study of religion" should become the normative framework for all future research. In fact, for many scholars who feel at home in the post-structuralist academic

---

[390] Hammer, *Claiming Knowledge*, 29.   [391] *Ibid.*, 44–45 and *passim*.

culture currently known as "cultural studies," the notion of discourse has
come to dominate their thinking to an extent where no other perspective
seems to make sense to them. For the field of "esotericism" specifically,
the most vocal proponent of this position in recent years is undoubtedly
Kocku von Stuckrad. I will end this chapter with a short discussion of his
perspective, because it represents currently the most significant challenge
to how "Western esotericism" has come to be understood in the wake
of Faivre's work. As will be seen, von Stuckrad's work converges in an
interesting manner with my own findings in the present book; but his
theoretical and methodological apparatus comes at a price that not all
scholars will be willing to pay.

As he notes himself, von Stuckrad "wrestled with the concept of 'Western esotericism' for years."[392] His early work was focused on the history
of astrology in late antiquity, and at the time he still saw it as representative of an esoteric worldview dominated by "correspondences" in
the sense of Faivre's definition and, particularly, the Jung–Pauli theory of
synchronicity.[393] As von Stuckrad began to broaden his scope of research
in the following years, Faivre's definition remained an important point of
reference; but he began to express reservations particularly about its concentration on Christian esotericism in the early modern period, at the expense
of "the vivid Esoteric discourse in late antiquity and medieval times"[394]
and in Jewish and Islamic culture.[395] Around 2003, several methodological

---

[392] Von Stuckrad, *Locations of Knowledge*, x.

[393] The methodological part of von Stuckrad's large study of Jewish and Christian perspectives
on astrology in late antiquity culminated in a thoroughly affirmative discussion of Wolfgang
Pauli's interpretations of quantum mechanics (*Das Ringen*, 87–101); and in his general history of
astrology, he emphasized Pauli's adoption of Jung's theory of synchronicity (*Geschichte der Astrologie*,
337–343; see also "Entsprechungsdenken"). Noting that historians criticize Jung's approach as a
"tautological construct" whereas it has found support among scholars of religion like Eliade and
Corbin (*Geschichte der Astrologie*, 338–339), he took the latter's side: the historians' objections were
ignored, but the "phenomenological" similarity between synchronicity and an "esoteric" worldview
of correspondences was presented as highly significant for understanding the nature of astrology
(*ibid.*, 339, 341, 343; for an alternative historical perspective, according to which Jung's theory is a
psychological reformulation of theories first formulated by, for example, Pico, Agrippa, Paracelsus,
Kepler, or Leibniz, see Hanegraaff, *New Age Religion*, 501). As noted by Steven Vanden Broecke,
von Stuckrad's theoretical perspective on ancient astrology relied on popular "New Age" mixtures
of synchronicity and quantum mechanics as published by F. David Peat (*Das Ringen*, 95–98), and
his general topic was defined with reference to late twentieth-century manuals of astrology for the
general public (review of von Stuckrad, 104).

[394] Von Stuckrad, "Recent Studies," 213.

[395] *Ibid.*; von Stuckrad, *Schamanismus*, 29; *Was ist Esoterik?*, 14; *Western Esotericism*, 5; "Western
Esotericism," 83. Von Stuckrad also adopted my reservations about whether Faivre's criteriology
could account for the "secularization of esotericism" and about the risk of essentialist interpretations
(cf. Hanegraaff, "The Study," 507–508). Interestingly, in 2005 he still believed that "large parts of
what I understand by esotericism can also be found in other cultures" (*Western Esotericism*, xi–xii),

articles[396] announced von Stuckrad's final break with the "Faivre paradigm" in favor of an ambitious attempt, grounded in post-structuralist theory, "to integrate the study of esotericism into the study of European history of religion."[397] The final outcome of this process of conceptual reorientation was published in 2010 under the title *Locations of Knowledge in Medieval and Early Modern Europe.*

In this book, von Stuckrad rejects the notion of "Western esotericism" as "an objectively identifiable 'tradition' or coherent 'system of thought and doctrine' that can be studied as a separate topic." Instead, he now prefers to speak of "esoteric discourse in Western culture."[398] This terminology should therefore *not* be understood as a label for a specific field of research, in the sense of a collection of specific currents, ideas, or practices that are seen as sharing certain characteristics or historical connections; instead, it functions as an analytical instrument, in the context of von Stuckrad's own discourse (!), for deconstructing the traditional master narrative of "a monolithic Christian occident" and a whole set of closely related assumptions about religion and modernity.[399] As he explains, this "singularizing discourse" can be analyzed in terms of complex processes of identity formation in which important dimensions of Western culture have been

---

thereby suggesting a substantivist and potentially essentialist understanding of "esotericism" that would seem to conflict with his eventual discursive approach.

[396] See notably von Stuckrad, "Discursive Study of Religion"; "Relative, Contingent, Determined"; "Western Esotericism."

[397] Von Stuckrad, *Locations of Knowledge*, xi, 137.

[398] *Ibid.*, x–xi. Accordingly, he gives no definition of esotericism, and suggests that his approach will make the very concept superfluous (*ibid.*, 64). Presumably, this also undermines his own previous attempts at demonstrating "what is esotericism" and writing "its" history (*Was ist Esoterik?* and *Western Esotericism*).

[399] Von Stuckrad, *Locations of Knowledge*, 4, 7–18. Von Stuckrad is right in suggesting that the terminology of "Western esotericism" for a field that is actually dominated by Christianity and modernity risks giving food to a singularizing and hegemonizing discourse of the "Christian occident" that marginalizes Judaism and Islam as somehow less "Western." However, I believe that the approach presented in the present book resolves this problem. Whereas von Stuckrad's concept of "esoteric discourse" is designed to include Judaism and Islam, my analysis implies that whether we like it or not, our very concepts of Western esotericism *did* indeed emerge as a singularizing and hegemonizing construct (directed, however, against "paganism" more than against Judaism or Islam) in the context of specifically Protestant and Enlightenment polemics (see the Conclusion). This brings up the question of whether this process has parallels in the Jewish and Islamic contexts: for example, when Heinrich Graetz constructed kabbalah as a "fungous layer" surrounding the healthy core of Judaism (Schäfer, "'Adversus cabbalam'"; Hanegraaff, "Beginnings of Occultist Kabbalah," 109–110), did this reflect only a post-Enlightenment ideology that he shared with Christian colleagues and projected back on to Jewish history; or did it reflect an autonomous process of polemical exclusion rooted in Jewish history, parallel to but independent from the one that I have been analyzing for the Christian context? These questions lead beyond my competence but should certainly be explored by scholars of Jewish esotericism.

structurally excluded or marginalized as "Other." To correct the simplifying pictures that have been the result, and that still dominate much of the current scholarly and popular discourse,[400] we must sharpen our awareness not just of the plurality of religious options in the history of Europe, but, rather, of religious *pluralism* as a dynamic process that involves the active (polemical and apologetic) negotiation of identity and difference.[401]

Steering away from an emphasis on religious "traditions" and their internal dynamics (including, of course, that of an autonomous "esoteric tradition"),[402] von Stuckrad seeks to demonstrate this agenda by focusing on "esoteric" discourses, in a Foucauldian sense, that transgress or ignore the boundaries between religions (Judaism, Christianity, Islam, and the literary transmission and continuation of "pagan" or "polytheistic" alternatives) as well as between societal systems such as religion, philosophy, science, art, or politics. Concerning the first type of pluralism, his *exempla* are concerned with the "secrets" of direct religious experience, textual hermeneutics, and astrological concepts of time;[403] concerning the second type, they focus on "interferences" between religion and science, art, and politics.[404] To make such an enterprise possible, the notion of "esoteric discourse(s)" is now defined by him in a new way, as "a secretive dialectic of concealment and revelation which is concerned with perfect knowledge."[405] The notions of *secrecy* as social capital (along the lines of Georg Simmel and Pierre Bourdieu) and *claims of perfect knowledge* have therefore become central to von Stuckrad's analysis, within a theoretical framework that operates with "fields, communication, structure, and discourse"[406] and has the goal of trying to "identify genealogies of identities in a pluralistic competition of knowledge."[407]

Von Stuckrad's agenda for the study of religion in Europe is ambitious and interesting, but it comes at a price. The basic notion of a "singularizing discourse" in Western intellectual culture, that constructs its own identity

[400] See, for example, political discussion in the European Parliament about the "Christian roots of Europe," with immediate implications for questions such as whether a country like Turkey should or should not be admitted into the European Union (von Stuckrad, *Locations of Knowledge*, 18).

[401] *Ibid.*, 19–20.

[402] For von Stuckrad's polemics against "tradition" as an analytical term, see his Chapter 2 (*ibid.*, 25–42). Unfortunately, his discussion of *prisca theologia* and *philosophia perennis* ignores their foundations in patristic discourse, and – largely for that reason – overlooks the problematic nature of Idel's unilinear/multilinear theory (see Chapter 1, pp. 58–61). Apart from this, one might argue that the notion of a "twofold pluralism" should be expanded into a threefold one: next to pluralism as the "organization of difference" between religions and between societal systems, why not analyze it *within* religions as well?

[403] *Ibid.*, chapters 4–6.   [404] *Ibid.*, chapters 7–9.   [405] *Ibid.*, 67.

[406] *Ibid.*, 59. Von Stuckrad explains his concept of "esoteric discourse" in *ibid.*, 54–64.

[407] *Ibid.*, 64 (italicized in original).

by means of polemical and apologetic processes of "othering," finds much confirmation by the argument of the present book;[408] but it is important to emphasize that discursive and historical approaches construct their objects of research in very different ways. Von Stuckrad's topic is no longer "esotericism" but "European history of religion": his notion of "esoteric discourse" is an instrument for analyzing it, not an object to be analyzed. Accordingly, von Stuckrad's true concern is with general discursive processes of identity formation by means of exclusion, marginalization, or "othering," *not* with the historical currents or ideas that have been excluded, marginalized or "othered." The latter make their appearance only as *exempla* that are useful to illustrate more "fundamental" discursive processes, not as objects of research that deserve attention in their own right. As a result, it is not just the term "esotericism" that vanishes as a useful concept, but much of the historical material will vanish as well! To pick a random example, if Lodovico Lazzarelli discusses the way towards true felicity in his *Crater Hermetis*, most of his subtle and intricate discussion is bound to be ignored as irrelevant to the specific concerns of discourse analysis; and rather than as making an attempt at formulating his deepest religious beliefs, Lazzarelli will be seen as making "claims of higher knowledge" to improve his strategic position in a pluralistic field of discourse, for example to gain the patronage of King Ferrante or impress his teacher Correggio. The problem is not just the cynicism of such a perspective, which seems blind to anything except competitions over power and capital. More crucially, the problem lies in its approach to textual research: from a consistent discursive perspective as presented by von Stuckrad, the important thing is not what Lazzarelli was trying to tell his readers, but only what his discourse might be telling *us*.

Of course there is nothing wrong with such an analysis in itself: on the contrary, it may yield very interesting insights. The problem lies in an exclusivist and reductionist subtext that automatically devalues "contents and ideas" in favor of "structures," makes history subservient to theory, and ends up promoting discursive approaches as the *only* valid methodology in the study of religion, esoteric or otherwise[409] (while insinuating that failure to comply with such hegemonic claims is proof of some covert "religionist," "essentialist," or "phenomenological" agenda).[410] This brings us back, once

---

[408] From his side, von Stuckrad likewise notes the similarities with my project (first announced in my article "Forbidden Knowledge" of 2005) of reconstructing "a genealogy of what today is referred to as esotericism," with central attention to polemics and identities (*Locations of Knowledge*, 52, cf. 60).

[409] For strong exclusivist claims on behalf of discursive approaches, see, for example, "Discursive Study," 263, 265, 268.

[410] For example, von Stuckrad, *Locations of Knowledge*, 52; "Reflections," 163.

again, to the theme of "history and truth." Like much of current American debate in the study of religion, von Stuckrad's theoretical framework assumes that "theory" (and metatheory) trumps historiography. Only on that basis can one claim that, for example, the subjectivities of the scholar make it "impossible" for him to write a convincing historical narrative, the "recursion of contingency" traps him in an infinite hermeneutical regression, authorial intent is a chimaera, or there are no such things as "facts," "evidence," or "proof."[411] Even where these arguments are philosophically cogent, they still remind one of an archer who claims that one need not even try to hit a target because Zenon's paradox proves that the arrow will never reach it. No responsible historian today is unaware of the theoretical and methodological problems of historiography, or adheres naively to a Rankean ideal of finding out *wie est eigentlich gewesen*.[412] But rather than allowing philosophy to paralyze them, good historians know from working experience that it is possible to improve our knowledge about what happened in the past, that the sources can speak to us and we can understand much of what they tell us, and that misrepresentations of past events can be recognized as such and replaced by better interpretations.[413]

If nothing else, discursive approaches are salutary reminders of how deeply knowledge is implicated with power; and they can be invaluable in analyzing such processes as identity formation and "othering," or exposing the ideological subtexts of scholarly research. But useful though they are, we cannot allow them to dictate or dominate the entire agenda of historical research. If what von Stuckrad calls "esoteric discourse" were to take the

---

[411] For the claimed supremacy of theory over history, and structure over ideas, see, for example, von Stuckrad, "Western Esotericism," 93: "Much of the work in religious studies consists exactly of *reflection* on definitions and tools of analysis" (on the contrary, I hold that important though such reflection certainly is, it concerns only *prolegomena* to the actual "work" of studying religions; cf. Hanegraaff, "Leaving the Garden," 270–271). For von Stuckrad's discussion of various philosophical dilemmas, see his articles mentioned in n. 396; and cf. *Locations of Knowledge*, 195–200, and "Reflections."

[412] See, for example, Evans, *In Defense of History*, 16–26 and *passim*.

[413] My issue is not with the philosophical debate as such (strongly influenced, in von Stuckrad's case, by Richard Rorty's *Philosophy and the Mirror of Nature*), nor would I be so foolish as to deny the importance of philosophical reflection on historiographical method. My point is simply that the theoretical superiority of von Stuckrad's postmodernism is by no means self-evident: as demonstrated for example by Mary Fulbrook (*Historical Theory*, 28–30 and *passim*), historical empiricism does not exclude self-reflexivity and theoretical awareness. As regards Foucauldian discourse, which was intended as an attack against historiography and historians, one cannot ignore the fact that Foucault's philosophical sophistication went at the expense of his historical analyses, which are often wholly mistaken (Huppert, "Divinatio et eruditio"; Hutton, "Foucault Phenomenon"; Maclean, "Foucault's Renaissance Episteme Reassessed"; Windschuttle, *Killing of History*, 121–157; Quétel, *Histoire de la folie*, 89–98, 239–246, 515–520).

place of what others call "Western esotericism," far too many of the historical materials that have barely begun to return to the academic agenda would once again vanish from sight or lose much of their content, depth, and complexity. But if we wish to preserve this strange and elusive field of research from falling prey once more to apologetic or reductive agendas, and make it visible and available for scholarly research, how then should we think of it? What *is* it, really, that we have been talking about? A definitive answer is perhaps neither possible nor desirable; but having reached the end of our long story, we should at least be able now to guess the direction in which to search.

Conclusion
Restoring memory

Definirbar ist nur Das, was keine Geschichte hat.
Friedrich Nietzsche, *Zur Genealogie der Moral* II.13

Can there be a history of Western esotericism? Or can there only be a history of how we have created and developed such an entity in our collective imagination? Does the "hidden continent" really exist, so that all we need to do is explore it, and replace the *hic sunt dracones* by more adequate descriptions of its inhabitants, their practices, and their beliefs? Or is there no such place, and do we only need to ask ourselves why it is that our intellectual culture apparently needed, and still needs, to *believe* in its existence – as a realm that may be mysterious and ill-defined, but in any case is clearly different from the familiar one that we know to be our own? At bottom, this is the old dilemma of realism versus nominalism, and scholars tend to suggest that they are mutually exclusive: thus, one either sets out to write the history of "the Western Esoteric Traditions," or one sees "esotericism" as no more than a social construct reflective of more fundamental discursive processes.[1]

It seems to me that the dilemma is not so absolute as it is sometimes presented. All the historiographies that we have encountered throughout this book are intellectual constructs grounded in the subjective beliefs and individual agendas of the scholars who developed them, and they are evidently reflective of contingent cultural assumptions typical of their own time and place. None of them can claim to be a straightforward description of "esotericism" as an empirical reality out there (a "tradition,"

---

[1] Representative of these polar opposites are Goodrick-Clarke, *Western Esoteric Traditions*, and von Stuckrad, *Locations of Knowledge* (as confirmed by Goodrick-Clarke himself, *Western Esoteric Traditions*, 11–14). Whereas Goodrick-Clarke's approach is modeled after Faivre's definition, and he even defends the religionist notion of "a hermeneutic interpretation of spirit and spirituality as an independent ontological reality" (*Ibid.*, 12), Marco Pasi seeks to defend the reality of Western esotericism as a historical phenomenon by turning Faivre's concept into a "family resemblance" definition ("Il problema").

a "worldview," a "form of thought," a "mode of thinking," etc.): they do not mirror something that is historically given, but construct it.[2] However, and this is the other side of the coin, they do not do so at random. There are very suggestive commonalities that structure the discourse as a whole; and in spite of its great diversity, it refers to real historical currents and ideas that are grouped under a label such as "esotericism" *not* just arbitrarily, but for specific reasons that have as much to do with their own nature and intellectual content as with the discourse that constructs them as such. There is something "out there" after all. What, then, are the historical realities that made it possible, perhaps even inevitable, for "esotericism" to be eventually constructed as a domain of its own?

An obvious red thread runs through my entire narrative in the four chapters of this book: we have seen that an intellectual culture grounded in biblical monotheism and Greek rationality was forced to come to terms with the presence of *paganism*. The development of what we now call Western esotericism is unimaginable without this fundamental fact. I will not try to summarize the argument in my previous chapters, but merely point out that the "wisdom of the pagans" was the heart and core of the ancient wisdom narrative, the central target of Catholic and (especially) Protestant polemicists culminating in the anti-apologetic current, and the principal object of ridicule for Enlightenment critics. The polemical discourse that I have tried to analyze in its historical development resulted first in a historiographical concept of "Platonic-Hermetic Christianity" as the crypto-pagan "Other" of true Christianity and rational philosophy; and having been expelled from intellectual discourse altogether, it ended up as a discredited waste-basket category of rejected knowledge.

The factor of "paganism" has been neglected by modern scholars of Western esotericism to an extent that seems amazing at first sight: while the importance of its specific historical manifestations (particularly hermetism) is obviously recognized, it plays no structural role in how the field has been constructed or defined.[3] This blind spot is understandable in light of my discussions in Chapter 4. When the contents of the "waste-basket" were rediscovered as a serious object of research by modern scholars – from Ennemoser to Faivre – most of them approached it from a religionist

---

[2] In short, "there is no data for esotericism" (cf. Jonathan Z. Smith, *Imagining Religion*, xi).

[3] For example, scholars in the Eranos tradition, including Faivre, thought of their topic in terms of universal categories such as "myth" (versus logos); a scholar like Peuckert in terms of traditional rural culture (versus modern bourgeois culture); and Thorndike or Yates in terms of "magic" (versus science). In all these cases, "paganism" as a concept is hovering in the background without being named or problematized explicitly.

perspective. We have seen that it is typical of such approaches that, even if they are engaged in direct historical study of primary sources, they still tend to downplay the importance of "external" historical influences in favor of the reference to some universal, transcendent, or "inner" spiritual reality associated with the sacred or the divine. From that point of view, to explain esoteric currents in terms of syncretistic processes is bound to be experienced as reductionist and, more generally, as missing the whole point about them. If the ultimate referent of esotericism is some *sui generis* dimension of the sacred, then its "external" manner of manifestation – whether pagan, Christian, Jewish, or even secular – must be of secondary importance by definition, if indeed it has any meaning at all.

The only intellectual approach that took the "pagan" dimension seriously was the anti-apologetic historiography pioneered by Jacob Thomasius, Colberg, and Brucker. As I argued in Chapter 2, it was characterized by a *methodology* of historical criticism combined with a *theoretical focus* on the manifold effects of the encounter between Hellenistic paganism and biblical traditions. This, I suggest, was exactly the right combination. If this basic agenda had been continued and further developed after the Enlightenment (presumably shedding its normative theological assumptions in the process), the study of "Western esotericism" might well have established itself on secure historical foundations already in the nineteenth century. As it happened, this line of inquiry was cut short, for the reasons explained in Chapters 2 and 3, leading to a scholarly "Waste Land" instead. It will come as no surprise, then, that I see this prematurely abandoned intellectual tradition as the one that points in the right direction for the future study of Western esotericism.

In his crucial *Schediasma historicum*, the founder of anti-apologeticism Jacob Thomasius highlighted two elements as fundamental to what he saw as "paganism." The first was a belief that the world was co-eternal with God, as opposed to the doctrine of *creatio ex nihilo*; and this "original fallacy" (Πρῶτον ψεῦδος) led to a second one, the "enthusiastic" belief that human beings could attain direct experiential knowledge (gnosis) of their own divine nature.[4] The sharpsightedness of Thomasius' analysis was such that even today, in my opinion, it may still furnish us with the fundamentals of what can usefully be called Western esotericism.

The first element may take a variety of forms, which can be imagined on a scale between the outer extremes of a strict "manichaean" dualism

---

[4] For the exact reasoning, see Chapter 2, pp. 104–107.

and a strict pantheism; but by far most typical for the context of "Western esotericism" are the many intermediary "panentheist" versions that may be referred to as *cosmotheism*. This term was coined by Lamoignon de Malesherbes in 1782,[5] and adopted by the Egyptologist Jan Assmann as a logical counterpart to monotheism:

The opposite of monotheism is not polytheism, or idolatry, but cosmotheism, the religion of the immanent God and the veiled truth, which both reveals and conceals itself in a thousand images: images that do not logically exclude, but illuminate and complement one another... A divine world does not stand in opposition to the world of cosmos, man, and society; rather, it is a principle that permeates it and gives it structure, order and meaning... The divine cannot be excluded from the world.[6]

This is what Frances Yates called – without further explanation – the "religion of the world"[7] found in the hermetic writings, based upon the fundamental assumption that the divine is at home in the world. As the logical alternative to classic monotheism, where the invisible and eternal Creator is strictly separate from his visible and temporal creation, cosmotheism could never be strictly integrated into a Judaeo-Christian framework; but as an integral part of the "pagan" Hellenistic philosophies that were adopted into Christian theology from the early patristic period on, it could not possibly be kept out of it either. Having analyzed the results of this dilemma through the first two chapters of this book, I suggest that the emergence of what we now call Western esotericism was made possible by a deep structure of conflict between the dynamics of these two mutually exclusive systems and all that they imply. In short, the logical incompatibility of monotheism and cosmotheism has led to an endless series of creative attempts to resolve it. It is within these dynamics that we can locate everything that authors like Colberg and Brucker sought to demarcate from true Christianity and rational philosophy; and when Max Weber defined the eighteenth-century process of disenchantment as the disappearance of "mysterious and incalculable powers" from the natural world, he was describing the attempt by new scientists and Enlightenment philosophers

---

[5] Assmann, *Of God and Gods*, 155 n. 64.

[6] Assmann, *Die mosaische Unterscheidung*, 64, 61, 62; for clarity and convenience I have quoted the passages on page 64 first, followed by those on pp. 61–62, which further explain the nature of Assmann's concept. See Assmann's fundamental discussion in *Moses the Egyptian*, 1–22, and cf. my discussion in Hanegraaff, "Trouble with Images," 114–120. I am not convinced by Peter Schäfer's critique of Assmann's concepts of monotheism and cosmotheism ("Geschichte und Gedächtnisgeschichte," 21–25; "Das jüdische Monopol"; see response in Assmann, "Alle Götter sind eins!"), which seems to reflect a misunderstanding of the concept of mnemohistory (see below, pp. 375–376 and n. 23).

[7] Yates, *Giordano Bruno*, 6 and *passim*.

to finish the job of Protestant anti-pagan polemics, and get rid of cosmo-theism once and for all. The attempt was unsuccessful. Cosmotheism was carried forward by Romantics into the nineteenth and twentieth centuries, as an alternative to the disenchantment of the world;[8] and it appeared capable of adapting even to secular conditions, thereby mutating into strange new forms that would have been unimaginable in previous centuries.[9]

The second element highlighted by Thomasius followed logically from the first. The platonic doctrine of emanation and restitution held that the soul has its origin in an eternal, divine substance and will return to it again. The implication was that human beings have an inborn capacity for knowing the divine: they are not dependent on God revealing himself to them (as in classic monotheism, where the creature is dependent on the Creator's initiative), nor is their capacity for knowledge limited to the bodily senses and natural reason (as in science and rational philosophy), but the very nature of their souls allows them direct access to the supreme, eternal substance of Being. Such direct experiential knowledge, or gnosis, is attained through "ecstatic" states of mind. Thus we see that the intuitive notion of a triad "faith – reason – gnosis"[10] can be given a precise historical meaning: "gnosis" is not just equivalent to a vague notion of higher, absolute, or perfect knowledge, but stands much more specifically for the possibility of direct and unmediated, supra-rational, salvational access to the supreme spiritual level of reality. The aspiration to such knowledge is inseparable from a worldview that makes it theoretically possible: esoteric discourse is characterized not so much by "claims of higher or perfect knowledge"[11] but, rather, by the claim that direct knowledge of ultimate reality is possible and available for those who pursue it. This second element, too, has survived the epistemological rupture of the Enlightenment: we have traced some part of it through Romantic and mesmerist currents during the nineteenth and twentieth centuries, from Ennemoser through Eranos, and outside the academic context it remains crucial to popular and contemporary spirituality.[12]

I do *not* mean to suggest that these two interrelated elements amount to a definition of Western esotericism, which would allow us to write "its" history as a specific historical tradition or domain. What they do is define the

---

[8] For example, Hanegraaff, "Romanticism and the Esoteric Connections."

[9] On the "secularization of esotericism" during the nineteenth century and its survival by means of "evolutionary adaptation," see Hanegraaff, *New Age Religion*, 411–513; "How Magic Survived the Disenchantment of the World."

[10] Hanegraaff, "Reason, Faith, and Gnosis."

[11] As in von Stuckrad, *Locations of Knowledge*, 59–64, here 60–61.

[12] Hanegraaff, "Magnetic Gnosis"; "Gnosis."

theoretical limits within which "esoteric" religiosity may develop while still remaining recognizable as such (not just in Christian and secular contexts but in Jewish and Islamic ones as well),[13] but they have little to say about its actual historical manifestations and its representatives, who seldom attempt to push a massive worldview of "cosmotheism and gnosis" but usually try to negotiate a space where they may survive within a culture dominated by monotheism and the appeal to divine revelation and rationality. In other words, whereas anti-apologetic polemicists and their kindred spirits tend to suspect the existence of a subversive pagan agenda, and try to expose it by bringing its basic "doctrines" to light, esoteric spiritualities are mostly creatures of compromise:[14] their enemies try to sharply exclude them as "Other," but their representatives or sympathizers usually try to remain included. This is why the boundaries of the domain are so vaguely defined and it is so hard to pin down historically: a drift towards cosmotheism and gnosis may be detected with various degrees of emphasis in a variety of cultural contexts (religion, philosophy, science, art), but seldom in a radical and explicit manner that openly attacks the dominant models and demands an either/or choice. If "Western esotericism" is perceived as a relatively separate domain, then, this is not because it in fact represents a kind of hidden gnostic and cosmotheist "counterculture" that existed historically in Christian and secular society but, rather, because it has been polemically constructed as such.

This process of polemical construction, followed by the exclusion of the construct as "rejected knowledge," took place in the second half of the seventeenth and the eighteenth centuries, and is inseparable from the construction of modern identities. Protestantism defined itself against Roman Catholicism, rejecting the latter as a "pagan" degeneration of true Christianity, but "orthodox" – that is, anti-cosmotheist and anti-gnostic – Protestants discovered to their horror that the same heresies began to appear in Protestant contexts as well. The Enlightenment built directly upon these Protestant polemics, and defined its own rational and scientific identity against the same adversary, but no longer granted it the dignity of an intellectual "tradition": cosmotheist worldviews now came to be perceived as vain superstitious belief that nature was inhabited by spirits or

---

[13] Next to my observations in Chapter 4, n. 399 (about studying parallel processes of polemical exclusion in Jewish and Islamic contexts), I see much potential in studying how the dimensions of "cosmotheism" and "gnosis" have functioned in Judaism and Islam, representing a common ground enabling "discursive transfer" across confessional boundaries.

[14] I use the term "spiritualities" here in a specific sense: see Hanegraaff, "Defining Religion in Spite of History," 371–373; "New Age Spiritualities."

ghosts, and references to gnosis became virtually indistinguishable from silly "enthusiasm." The former were unscientific, the latter irrational. Such perspectives no longer needed to be seriously refuted, but could be simply dismissed as "foolishness" and "stupidity."

In this manner, the cultural memory of what we now call "Western esotericism" was constructed during the eighteenth century as the polemical Other of modernity, which was defining its own identity in that very process. The dynamics in question can be usefully analyzed in terms of underlying "grammars" of identity/alterity. The ancient wisdom narrative had been governed by what is known in anthropological theory as a grammar of "encompassment": by being included within a larger framework of *prisca theologia* or *philosophia perennis*, the pagan "Other" could be constructed as really "belonging to us" (that is, Christianity).[15] In their systematic assault on this narrative, Protestant and Enlightenment polemicists argued in terms of a very different, polarizing grammar of "orientalization":[16] here, one defines one's own identity (Christian, rational, or scientific) against the "Other" that is being excluded. However, as explained by Gerd Baumann, this type of binary opposition is always subject to reversal, resulting in a sophisticated dialectics of rejection and desire.[17] Its very alterity can turn the excluded "Other" into an object of attraction, and once it has been constructed as an "alternative option" in the collective imagination, people may well shift their allegiance to it. In this manner, what Enlightenment thinkers rejected as bad could be embraced as good by Romantics, who constructed their identity in conscious opposition against the "Other" of empty rationalism and soulless science. The ultimate example is the German mesmeric concept of the "nightside of nature," grounded in a systematic reversal of all Enlightenment values, leading finally from Ennemoser's historiography to Jungian concepts of the unconscious and a variety of related countercultural perspectives concerned with "re-enchanting the world." It is in this context that the "waste-basket category" created by the Enlightenment was finally turned into a positive category that enabled a variety of "inventions of esoteric tradition" during the nineteenth and twentieth centuries.[18]

---

[15] Baumann, "Grammars of Identity/Alterity," 25–27.

[16] *Ibid.*, 19–21. While this grammar derives its name from Edward Said's *Orientalism*, it is obviously not restricted to constructs of Occident/Orient, but can be applied to the general dynamics of identity/alterity. Baumann's third grammar ("segmentation") is not immediately relevant for our present concerns, in spite of the interesting application to Freemasonry and religious ecumenicism (*ibid.*, 21–24, 29–30).

[17] *Ibid.*, 20–21.

[18] Cf. Lewis and Hammer, *Invention of Sacred Tradition.* The reference is, of course, to Hobsbawm and Ranger's classic *Invention of Tradition.*

In our everyday use of language we are almost never conscious of the grammar that structures our sentences, and, somewhat similarly, scholars or intellectuals are seldom aware of the "orientalizing" grammar that structures discourses of academic identity. In the practice of doing research, and even in explaining that practice and its importance to others or ourselves, this is not a great problem: there is no need to be constantly reminded that our methodologies (whether in the natural sciences, the social sciences, or the humanities) are grounded in the systematic exclusion of such things as clairvoyant perception, religious revelations, intuitive understanding, occult correspondences, spiritual presences, or non-causal influences in nature.[19] The problem lies elsewhere: for eminently scholarly reasons, we need to correct our collective amnesia about large parts of our own intellectual history, and the ideology-driven distortions of what we still remember about it. We have seen how Christoph August Heumann, at the very origin of the modern history of philosophy, advocated a practice of dumping these aspects of the past into "the sea of oblivion," because "superstitious idiocies belong in no better library."[20] Such attitudes finally resulted in a dramatic loss of collective memory – in plain language: ignorance – among the intelligentsia and the wider public from the nineteenth century on.

To help understand this process, Jan Assmann's work is once again useful. In several important publications, he has argued for a distinction between history and "mnemohistory": the former refers to what happened in the past, the latter to how we remember it.[21] To avoid an ambiguity that has led to some unfortunate misunderstandings, I propose to expand the terminology in a logical manner, by distinguishing between "historiography" and "mnemohistoriography" as well: if the former tries to describe what actually happened in the past, the latter tries to describe the genesis and historical development of what a given culture *imagines* has happened. One problem with our collective memories of the past is that they are

---

[19] I am not making any statement about the validity or veracity of these notions, but merely point out that academic research excludes them as methodologies or explanatory theories. One might think of their relation to scholarship or science as similar to the relation between sports, such as, for example, tennis and badminton. Each of them has its own set of rules and restrictions, as well as its own peculiar possibilities and attractive features. One and the same player can be a practitioner of both sports, but *not* at the same time: in order to play tennis he needs to accept its rules at least for the duration of the game, and the same goes for badminton.

[20] See Chapter 2, pp. 132–133.

[21] Assmann, *Moses the Egyptian*, 6–22; *Das kulturelle Gedächtnis*; *Religion und kulturelles Gedächtnis*; cf. Halbwachs, *On Collective Memory*. For the difference between Assmann's use of the concept and mine, cf. Hanegraaff, "Trouble with Images," 112.

highly selective, as pointed out by Assmann: "for a functional communicative memory, forgetting is as important as remembering. Hence it is
not 'photographic.' Remembering means allowing other things to recede
into the background, making distinctions, making many things fade out in
order to highlight others."[22] Furthermore, our collective memories hardly
bother to distinguish between demonstrable facts and fictional constructs,
so that the latter may easily get confused with the former. For example,
it is unlikely that the pure or "classic" monotheism referred to above ever
existed in ancient Israel, or that such an ideology was sharply pitted against
a "cosmotheist" alternative, or indeed that its supposed founder Moses was
a historical personality at all.[23] However, that these are all mnemohistorical
fictions does not make them historically insignificant or irrelevant: on the
contrary, it is precisely the black-and-white simplicity of what Assmann
calls the "mosaic distinction" between monotheism and its "pagan" Other
that has made it so effective in polemical and apologetic discourse – much
more effective, in fact, than any historical facts about what really happened – and a mnemohistoriographical analysis can show in detail how
it has had an impact on real historical events in intellectual and religious
culture.

The relevance to my analysis in the previous chapters should be obvious. In investigating how intellectuals from the fifteenth century to the
present have been constructing a tradition or domain that we would nowadays recognize as "Western esotericism," I have been focusing deliberately
on the mnemohistorical dimension: my concern has been primarily with
the powerful stories that they created, and only secondarily with the true
nature of the historical realities about which they were telling those stories. Throughout my account we have seen evidence for the remarkable

---

[22] Assmann, *Religion und kulturelles Gedächtnis*, 13.
[23] Peter Schäfer has dismissed Assmann's antithesis of monotheism versus cosmotheism as a "historical
fiction" ("Geschichte und Gedächtnisgeschichte," 24), but in my view that is precisely the whole
point. Pure monotheism (or what I call "classic monotheism" in the text of this chapter) is a
*mnemo*historical fiction: like its legendary founder Moses, it is located in the collective imagination
rather than in actual history (see text, above). A mnemohistoriographical analysis can trace how this
fiction has emerged and developed through history, and the results can be critically compared with
historiographical findings about, for example, the religion of ancient Israel. Attacking the "mosaic
distinction" on the level of historiography is therefore missing the point. The terminological
ambiguity that caused this misunderstanding seems to derive from the fact that "mnemohistory"
as used by Assmann could be understood either as an *object* of historical research or as a specific
method for doing research ("doing history"). In my usage, there is only one method or practice,
but it may be called historiography if applied to history and mnemohistoriography if applied
to mnemohistory. Obviously, mnemohistorical fictions eventually become factors in history; and
critical historiography can therefore make use of mnemohistoriographical analysis to interpret and
explain historical developments.

discursive power of mnemohistorical constructs, which largely create the phenomena that they claim to describe while suppressing or distorting any evidence that would undermine the clarity of the narrative. I believe that the conclusion is unavoidable. "Western esotericism" is an imaginative construct in the minds of intellectuals and the wider public, not a straightforward historical reality "out there"; but, as argued above, it does refer to religious tendencies and worldviews that have a real existence and fall within the structural parameters first defined by Jacob Thomasius. These parameters do not reside in a space of mental abstractions or theoretical absolutes, but are grounded in the dynamics of monotheistic religion and the appeal to faith and reason: in a few words, cosmotheism and gnosis emerge as alternatives *because* the divine is held to be separate from the world and inaccessible to human knowledge.

Against the eclecticism ingrained in post-Enlightenment thought, and the highly selective mnemohistorical narratives that resulted from it, I have been advocating an anti-eclectic historiography:[24] one that does not select only what it believes to be "true" or "serious," but questions the established canon of modern intellectual and academic culture (its collective "memory bank") and recognizes that our common heritage is of much greater richness and complexity than one would infer from standard academic textbooks. To give just a few obvious examples, it is simply unacceptable to reduce figures like Marsilio Ficino or Giovanni Pico della Mirandola to mere footnotes in the history of philosophy, as remains standard in most current philosophy programs and textbooks; it is unacceptable to exclude alchemy or astrology from the history of science, as scholars have finally begun to realize; it is unacceptable to reduce the eighteenth century to an "Age of Reason" by silently ignoring the overwhelming evidence that it was an age of illuminism and theosophy as well, where "esoteric" perspectives provided intermediary positions between traditional orthodoxy and radical unbelief; it is unacceptable to dismiss occultist trends as mere survivals that are irrelevant to the culture of modernity; and it is unacceptable to interpret all forms of contemporary esotericism as irrational nonsense or threats to democracy by default. What makes all such approaches, and many similar ones, unacceptable is their systematic selectivity: their unquestioning willingness to recognize only what fits an ideological program, while ignoring or distorting any empirical or historical evidence that might spoil it. Anti-eclectic historiography obviously does not claim to discard mechanisms of selection altogether: it goes without saying that any historian, including the

---

[24] See Chapter 2, page 152.

author of these lines, makes his own choices of what to focus on and what not. The point is, rather, to provide an antidote against the view that historians should select their materials on the basis of normative, doctrinal, or philosophical judgments. More specifically, the point is to be aware of how the hegemonic discourses of modernity are themselves built upon earlier mnemohistorical narratives (mostly concerned, as we have seen, with constructed memories of "paganism") rather than on critical and evenhanded attention to all the available evidence.

This brings me to my conclusions. The study of "Western esotericism" should be firmly grounded, first and foremost, in a straightforward historiographical agenda: that of exploring the many blank spaces on our mental maps and filling them in with color and detail, so that they become integral parts of the wider landscape that we already knew, or thought we knew. In this process, what used to be strange and alien will eventually become normalized as just another dimension of Western culture; and discredited voices concerned with "cosmotheism" and "gnosis" will be taken seriously as representing possible ways of looking at the nature of reality and the pursuit of knowledge. These perspectives may still not be acceptable within academic discourse, which has approaches and methodological principles all of its own, but need not on that account be dismissed as dangerous, stupid, or wrong. Like art or poetry, they may be respected as pursuits and viewpoints that are clearly different from academic ones, but that have their own traditions and legitimacy, and have greatly contributed to the richness of Western culture.

The implications of such a program are considerable. If I am correct in my assessment that what we now call "esotericism" is the Other by which our modern Western identities have been constructed – according to the logic of an "orientalizing" grammar of identity/alterity – then the two depend on each other and cannot exist alone. If dominant historical images of the Other turn out to be simplifications or distortions, then the parallel images of ourselves – our basic identity – will have to be reconsidered and revised as well. How then will we define ourselves, and our essential values, once the enemy or outcast that used to live in our imagination has appeared in the flesh and even joined our own family? Will we use every trick we can think of to prevent such a thing from happening? Will we allow it to happen, but find ourselves unable to live with him? Will we allow him to change us, or will we find ourselves changed without even realizing it? Will we accept him in our midst, and discover that someone else has taken the empty place in our collective imagination? Will that new occupant perhaps look suspiciously like him? These are open questions, to which I have no answer. All that I do know is the prime directive that should guide scholarly research and intellectual exploration: not to hold on to what we already know well enough, allowing it to dominate the whole of our vision and thought, but being ready to discard our prejudices and revise our preconceptions in the light of new knowledge.

Bibliography

Abbri, Ferdinando, "Alchemy and Chemistry: Chemical Discourses in the Seventeenth Century," in: Michela Pereira (ed.), *Alchemy and Hermeticism,* Special Issue of *Early Science and Medicine* 5:2 (2000), 214–226.

Accart, Xavier, "Identité et théophanie: René Guénon (1886–1951) et Henry Corbin (1903–1978)," *Politica Hermetica* 16 (2002), 176–200.

    Guénon ou le renversement des clartés: Influences d'un métaphysicien sur la vie littéraire et intellectuelle française (1920–1970), Edidit / Archè: Paris / Milan 2005.

Adelung, Johann Christoph, *Geschichte der menschlichen Narrheit, oder Lebensbeschreibungen berühmter Schwarzkünstler, Goldmacher, Teufelsbanner, Zeichen- und Liniendeuter, Schwärmer, Wahrsager, und anderer philosophischer Unholden*, 7 vols., Weygand: Leipzig 1785–1789.

Adorno, Theodor W., "Theses Against Occultism" (1950), repr. in: Adorno, *Stars Down to Earth*, 172–180.

    The Stars Down to Earth and Other Essays on the Irrational in Culture, Routledge: London / New York 1994.

Agrippa, Heinrich Cornelius, *Oratio habita Papiae* (Paola Zambelli, ed.), in: Garin et al., *Testi umanistici*, 119–136.

    De occulta philosophia Libri tres (V. Perrone Compagni, ed.), Brill: Leiden / New York / Cologne 1992.

    Opera, quaecumque hactenus vel in lucem prodierunt, vel inveniri potuerunt omnia, in duos tomos concinne digesta & diligenti studio recognita, 2 vols., Georg Olms: Hildesheim 1970.

Albrecht, Michael, "Thomasius – Kein Eklektiker?," in: Schneiders, *Christian Thomasius*, 73–94.

    Eklektik: Eine Begriffsgeschichte mit Hinweisen auf die Philosophie- und Wissenschaftsgeschichte, frommann-holzboog: Stuttgart / Bad Cannstatt 1994.

Alembert, Jean le Rond d', "Expérimental," in: *Encyclopédie*, vol. VI, 298–301.

Algar, Hamid, "The Study of Islam: The Work of Henry Corbin," *Religious Studies Review* 6:2 (1980), 85–91.

Allen, Charlotte, "Is Nothing Sacred? Casting Out the Gods from Religious Studies," *Lingua Franca*, November 1996, 30–40.

Allen, Douglas, "Encounters with Mircea Eliade," in: Gligor and Ricketts, *Întâlniri*, 11–23.

Allen, Michael J. B., *Marsilio Ficino: The Philebus Commentary*, University of California Press: Berkeley / Los Angeles / London 1975.

Marsilio Ficino and the Phaedran Charioteer, University of California Press: Berkeley / Los Angeles / London 1981.

The Platonism of Marsilio Ficino, University of California Press: Berkeley 1984.

Synoptic Art: Marsilio Ficino on the History of Platonic Interpretation, Leo S. Olschki: Florence 1998.

"Ficino, Marsilio," in: Hanegraaff *et al.*, *Dictionary*, 360–367.

Allen, Michael J. B. and Valerie Rees, with Martin Davies (eds.), *Marsilio Ficino: His Theology, his Philosophy, his Legacy*, Brill: Leiden / Boston / Cologne 2002.

Allers, Rudolf, "Microcosmus: From Anaximander to Paracelsus," *Traditio* 2 (1944), 319–407.

Alles, Douglas, "Ist Eliade Antihistorisch?," in: Hans Peter Duerr (ed.), *Die Mitte der Welt: Aufsätze zu Mircea Eliade*, Suhrkamp: Frankfurt a.M. 1984, 106–127.

Alverny, M.-Th. d' and F. Hudry, "Al-Kindi: De Radiis," *Archives d'histoire doctrinale et littéraire du moyen âge* 41 (1974), 139–260.

Amico, John F. d', *Renaissance Humanism in Papal Rome: Humanists and Churchmen on the Eve of the Reformation*, The Johns Hopkins University Press: Baltimore / London 1983.

Anderson, James, *The Constitutions of the Free-Masons. In the Year of Masonry – 5723 / The New Book of Constitutions of the Antient and Honourable Fraternity of Free and Accepted Masons. In the Vulgar Year of Masonry 5738* (Eric Ward, ed.), Facsimile edition Burgess & Son: Abingdon 1976, repr. 1978.

Andreae, Johann Valentin, *Fama Fraternitatis / Confessio Fraternitatis / Chymische Hochzeit: Christiani Rosenkreutz. Anno 1459* (Richard van Dülmen, ed.), Calwer: Stuttgart 1973.

Andresen, Carl, "Justin und der mittlere Platonismus," *Zeitschrift für neutestamentliche Wissenschaft und die Kunde der älteren Kirche* 44 (1952/1953), 157–195.

Logos und Nomos: Die Polemik des Kelsos wider das Christentum, Walter de Gruyter: Berlin 1955.

Angelis, Domenico de, "Vita di Gio. Battista Crispo da Gallipoli," in: de Angelis, *Le vite de' letterati Salentini*, vol. II, Bernardo-Michele Raillard: Naples 1713, 37–56.

Anglo, Sidney (ed.), *The Damned Art: Essays in the Literature of Witchcraft*, Routledge & Kegan Paul: London / Henley / Boston 1977.

Angold, Michael, "Byzantium and the West 1204–1453," in: Angold (ed.), *The Cambridge History of Christianity 5: Eastern Christianity*, Cambridge University Press 2006, 53–78.

Anon., *Testamentum der Fraternitet Roseae et Aureae Crucis...Anno 580*. Ms. Vienna: Österreichische Nationalbibliothek, Cod. SN 2897.

"Zierold (Johann Wilhelm)," in: Zedler, *Grosses vollständiges Universal-Lexikon*, vol. LXII, cols. 653–660.

Histoire critique de l'Éclecticisme, ou des nouveaux Platoniciens, 2 vols., Avignon 1766.

The Secret History of the Free-Masons: Being an Accidental Discovery, of the Ceremonies Made Use of in the several Lodges, London 1724; 2nd edn 1725.

"Lavaters Aeusserungen über den Magnetismus," *Magikon* 4 (1850), 13–21.

"Award of the George Sarton Medal to Lynn Thorndike," *Isis* 49:2 (1958), 107–108.

C. G. Jung Bibliothek Katalog, Küsnacht / Zurich 1967.

Antes, Peter and Donate Pahnke (eds.), *Die Religion von Oberschichten: Religion, Profession, Intellektualismus*, diagonal-Verlag: Marburg 1989.

Apuleius of Madauros, *Pro Se De Magia (Apologia)* (Vincent Hunink, ed., trans. and comm.), 2 vols., J. C. Gieben: Amsterdam 1997.

Arcella, Luciano, Paola Pisi and Roberto Scagno (eds.), *Confronto con Mircea Eliade: Archetipi mitici e identità storica*, Jaca: Milan 1998.

[Aristotle], *The Complete Works of Aristotle: The Revised Oxford Translation* (Jonathan Barnes, ed.), vol. II, Princeton University Press 1984.

Armstrong, A. H., "Pagan and Christian Traditionalism in the First Three Centuries A.D.," in: Elizabeth A. Livingstone (ed.), *Papers Presented to the Seventh International Conference on Patristic Studies held in Oxford 1975*, Part 1, Akademie-Verlag: Berlin 1984, 414–431.

Arnold, Gottfried, *Die Erste Liebe der Gemeinen Jesu Christi, das ist, Wahre Abbildung der Ersten Christen, nach Ihren Lebendigen Glauben und Heiligen Leben*, Frankfurt a.M. 1696.

Unparteyische Kirchen- und Ketzer-Historie, vom Anfang des Neuen Testaments biß auf das Jahr Christi 1688, 2 vols., Frankfurt a.M. 1699–1700.

Historie und Beschreibung der Mystischen Theologie, oder geheimen Gottes Gelehrtheit, wie auch derer alten und neuen Mysticorum, Thomas Fritsch: Frankfurt 1703.

Asad, Talal, "The Construction of Religion as an Anthropological Category," in: Asad, *Genealogies of Religion: Discipline and Reasons of Power in Christianity and Islam*, The Johns Hopkins University Press: Baltimore / London 1993, 27–54.

Assmann, Jan, *Das kulturelle Gedächtnis: Schrift, Erinnerung und politische Identität in frühen Hochkulturen*, C. H. Beck: Munich 1992.

Moses the Egyptian: The Memory of Egypt in Western Monotheism, Harvard University Press: Cambridge, Mass. / London 1997.

"'Hen kai pan': Ralph Cudworth und die Rehabilitierung der hermetischen Tradition," in: Neugebauer-Wölk, *Aufklärung und Esoterik* (1999), 38–52.

Religion und kulturelles Gedächtnis: Zehn Studien, C. H. Beck: Munich 2000.

Die Mosaische Unterscheidung, oder der Preis des Monotheismus, Carl Hanser: Munich / Vienna 2003.

"Alle Götter sind Eins!," *Süddeutsche Zeitung*, September 15, 2004.

Thomas Mann und Ägypten: Mythos und Monotheismus in den Josephsromanen, C. H. Beck: Munich 2006.

Of God and Gods: Egypt, Israel, and the Rise of Monotheism, The University of Wisconsin Press: Madison, Wisc. 2008.

Athanassakis, Apostolos N., *The Orphic Hymns: Text, Translation, and Notes*, Scholars Press: Missoula 1977.

Attfield, Robin, "Balthasar Bekker and the Decline of the Witch-Craze: The Old Demonology and the New Philosophy," *Annals of Science* 42 (1985), 383–395.

Atwood, Mary Anne, *A Suggestive Inquiry into the Hermetic Mystery, with a Dissertation on the More Celebrated of the Alchemical Philosophers, being an Attempt towards the Recovery of the Ancient Experiment of Nature* (1850), William Tait / J. M. Watkins: Belfast / London 1918.

Augustine, Aurelius, *De Doctrina Christiana* (R. P. H. Green, ed. and trans.), Clarendon Press: Oxford 1995.

The City of God against the Pagans (R. W. Dyson, ed. and trans.), Cambridge University Press 1998.

Ayer, A. J., *Part of my Life: The Memoirs of a Philosopher*, Collins: London 1977.

Backus, Irena (ed.), *The Reception of the Church Fathers in the West: From the Carolingians to the Maurists*, vol. II, Brill: Leiden / New York / Cologne 1997.

Baier, Karl, *Meditation und Moderne: Zur Genese eines Kernbereichs moderner Spiritualität in der Wechselwirkung zwischen Westeuropa, Nordamerika und Asien*, 2 vols., Königshausen & Neumann: Würzburg 2009.

Bailey, Alice, *The Unfinished Autobiography*, Lucis Trust: New York 1973.

Baltus, Jean-François, *Défense des SS. Pères accusés de platonisme*, Paris 1711.

Bambach, Charles R., *Heidegger, Dilthey, and the Crisis of Historicism*, Cornell University Press: Ithaca / London 1995.

Barbierato, Federico and Adelisa Malena, "Rosacroce, libertini e alchimisti nella società veneta del secondo Seicento: I Cavalieri dell'Aurea e Rosa Croce," in: Gian Mario Cazzaniga (ed.), *Storia d'Italia, Annali 25: Esoterismo*, Giulio Einaudi: Turin 2010, 323–357.

Barkun, Michael, *A Culture of Conspiracy: Apocalyptic Visions in Contemporary America*, University of California Press: Berkeley / Los Angeles / London 2003.

Barnes, Timothy D., *Constantine and Eusebius*, Harvard University Press: Cambridge, Mass. / London 1981.

Baronius, Cesarius, *Annales Ecclesiastici a Christo nato ad annum 1198*, 12 vols., Rome 1588–1607.

Barrett, Francis, *The Magus, or Celestial Intelligencer; being a Complete System of Occult Philosophy*, Lackington, Allen & Co.: London 1801.

Barth, Karl, *Church Dogmatics, vol. I: The Doctrine of the Word of God, Part 2*, T & T Clark: London / New York 1956.

Baßler, Moritz and Hildegard Châtellier (eds.), *Mystique, mysticisme et modernité en Allemagne autour de 1900 / Mystik, Mystizismus und Moderne in Deutschland um 1900*, Presses Universitaires de Strasbourg 1998.

Baudrillard, Jean, "La part maudite," *Le Courrier* (Unesco), July 1987, 7–9.

Baumann, Gerd, "Grammars of Identity/Alterity: A Structural Approach," in: Baumann and Andre Gingrich (eds.), *Grammars of Identity/Alterity: A Structural Approach*, Berghahn Books: New York / Oxford 2004, 18–50.

Baur, Ferdinand Christian, *Die christliche Gnosis oder die christliche Religions-Philosophie in ihrer geschichtlichen Entwiklung*, C. F. Osiander: Tübingen 1835.

Die Epochen der kirchlichen Geschichtsschreibung (1852), Georg Olms: Hildesheim 1962.

Baxter, Christopher, "Johann Weyer's *De Praestigiis Daemonum*: Unsystematic Psychopathology," in: Anglo, *Damned Art*, 53–75.

Beatrice, Pier Franco, *Anonymi monophysitae Theosophia: An Attempt at Reconstruction*, Brill: Leiden / Boston / Cologne 2001.

Behler, Ursula, "Eine unbeachtete Biographie Jacob Bruckers," in: Schmidt-Biggemann and Stammen, *Jacob Brucker*, 19–73.

Benavides, Gustavo, "Afterreligion after Religion," *Journal of the American Academy of Religion* 69:2 (2001), 449–457.

Benz, Ernst, *Franz Anton Mesmer und die philosophischen Grundlagen des "animalischen Magnetismus"*, Akademie der Wissenschaften und der Literatur / Franz Steiner: Mainz / Wiesbaden 1977.

"Über die Leiblichkeit des Geistigen: Zur Theologie der Leiblichkeit bei Jacob Böhme," in: Nasr, *Mélanges*, 451–520.

Les sources mystiques de la philosophie romantique allemande (1968), Vrin: Paris 1987.

Benzenhöfer, Udo and Urs Leo Gantenbein, "Paracelsus," in: Hanegraaff *et al.*, *Dictionary*, 922–931.

Bergunder, Michael, "Was ist Esoterik? Religionswissenschaftliche Überlegungen zum Gegenstand der Esoterikforschung," in: Neugebauer-Wölk, *Aufklärung und Esoterik* (2008), 477–507.

"What is Esotericism? Cultural Studies Approaches and the Problems of Definition in Religious Studies," *Method & Theory in the Study of Religion* 22 (2010), 9–36.

Berthelot, M. P. E. and C. E. Ruelle (eds.), *Collection des alchimistes Grecs*, 3 vols., Georges Steinheil: Paris 1887–1888.

Biale, David, *Gershom Scholem: Kabbalah and Counter-History*, Harvard University Press: Cambridge, Mass. / London 1979.

Bidez, Joseph and Franz Cumont, *Les mages hellénisés: Zoroastre, Ostanès et Hystaspe d'après la tradition grecque*, 2 vols., Les Belles Lettres: Paris 1938.

Bila, Constantin, *La croyance à la magie au XVIIIe siècle en France dans les contes, romans & traités*, J. Gamber: Paris 1925.

Bishop, Paul, *The Dionysian Self: C. G. Jung's Reception of Friedrich Nietzsche*, Walter de Gruyter: Berlin / New York 1995.

Black, Crofton, *Pico's Heptaplus and Biblical Hermeneutics*, Brill: Leiden / Boston 2006.

Bladel, Kevin van, *The Arabic Hermes: From Pagan Sage to Prophet of Science*, Oxford University Press 2009.

Blau, Joseph Leon, *The Christian Interpretation of the Cabala in the Renaissance*, Columbia University Press: New York / Morningside Heights 1944.

Blaufuß, Dietrich and Friedrich Niewöhner (eds.), *Gottfried Arnold (1666–1714), mit einer Bibliographie der Arnold-Literatur ab 1714*, Harrassowitz: Wiesbaden 1995.

Blavatsky, Helena P., *Isis Unveiled: A Master-Key to the Mysteries of Ancient and Modern Science and Theology*, 2 vols., Bouton: New York 1877.

"Thoughts on the Elementals," *Lucifer* 6:33 (1890), 177–188 (*Collected Writings*, vol. XII, 187–205).

Blom, J. M., "The Life and Works of Robert Samber (1682–plm.1745)," *English Studies* 6 (1989), 507–550.

Blum, Paul Richard, "Qualitas Occulta," in: Joachim Ritter and Karlfried Gründer (eds.), *Historisches Wörterbuch der Philosophie*, vol. VII, Schwabe: Darmstadt 1989, 1743–1748.

"Qualitates occultae: Zur philosophischen Vorgeschichte eines Schlüsselbegriffs zwischen Okkultismus und Wissenschaft," in: Buck, *Die okkulten Wissenschaften*, 45–64.

Blum, Wilhelm, *Georgios Gemistos Plethon: Politik, Philosophie und Rhetorik im spätbyzantinischen Reich (1355–1452)*, Anton Hiersemann: Stuttgart 1988.

Blume, Dieter, *Regenten des Himmels: Astrologische Bilder in Mittelalter und Renaissance*, Akademie Verlag: Berlin 2000.

Bock, Emil, *Rudolf Steiner: Studien zu seinem Lebensgang und Lebenswerk*, Freies Geistesleben: Stuttgart 1961.

Bodin, Jean, *De la démonomanie des sorciers*, Jacques Dupuis: Paris 1587 (Gutenberg facs. repr. l'Imprimerie Centrale de l'Ouest à La Roche-sur-Yon 1979).

Colloquium Heptaplomeres de rerum sublimium arcanis abditis (L. Noack, ed.), Schwerin: Paris / London 1857, repr. Friedrich Frommann Verlag (Günther Holzboog): Stuttgart / Bad Cannstatt 1966.

Boegner, Karl, "Joseph Ennemosers Leben und Werk," in: Joseph Ennemoser, *Untersuchungen über den Ursprung und das Wesen der menschlichen Seele, mit einem Fragment "Mein Leben"* (Karl Boegner and Renate Riemeck, eds.), Die Pforte: Basle 1980, 13–68.

Boer, W. den, "A Pagan Historian and his Enemies: Porphyry against the Christians," *Classical Philology* 69:3 (1974), 198–208.

Boer, W. den, P. G. van der Nat, C. M. J. Sicking, and J. C. M. van Winden (eds.), *Romanitas et Christianitas: Studia Iano Henrico Waszink A.D. VI Kal. Nov. A. MCMLXXIII XIII lustra complenti oblata*, North-Holland Publishing Company: Amsterdam / London 1973.

Bogdan, Henrik, *Western Esotericism and Rituals of Initiation*, State University of New York Press: Albany 2007.

Böhme, Hartmut and Gernot Böhme, *Das Andere der Vernunft: Zur Entwicklung von Rationalitätsstrukturen am Beispiel Kants*, Suhrkamp: Frankfurt a.M. 1983.

Bordelon, Laurent, *Histoire des imaginations extravagantes de monsieur Oufle, servant de préservatif contre la lecture des Livres qui traitent de la Magie, du*

Grimoire, des Démoniaques, Sorciers, Loups-Garoux, Incubes, Succubes & du Sabbat; des Esprits-Folets, Génies, Phantômes & autres Revenans; des Songes, de la Pierre Philosophale, de l'Astrologie judiciaire, des Horoscopes, Talismans, Jours heureux & malheureux, Eclipses, Comettes; & enfin de toutes les sortes d'Apparitions, de Devinations, de Sortilèges, d'Enchantement, & d'autres superstitieuses pratiques, Paris 1710.

Bosc, Ernest, *La doctrine ésotérique à travers les ages*, 2 vols., Chamuel: Paris 1899.

Bostocke, R., *The difference betwene the auncient Phisicke, first taught by the godly forefathers, consisting in unitie peace and concord: and the latter Phisicke proceeding from Idolaters, Ethnickes, and Heathen: as Gallen, and such other consisting in dualitie, discorde, and contrarietie. And wherein the naturall Philosophie of Aristotle doth differ from the trueth of Gods worde, and is iniurious to Christianitie and sounde doctrine*, Robert Valley: London 1585 (partial edition in: Debus, "Elizabethan History," 5–29).

Bottin, Francesco, Luciano Malusa, Giuseppe Micheli, Giovanni Santinello, and Ilario Tolomio, *Models of the History of Philosophy: From its Origins in the Renaissance to the "Historia Philosophica"* (International Archives of the History of Ideas 135: Models of the History of Philosophy 1), Kluwer: Dordrecht 1993.

Bottomore, Tom, *The Frankfurt School and its Critics*, Routledge: London / New York 2002.

Bourdieu, Pierre, *Language and Symbolic Power*, Polity Press: Cambridge 1991.

Bouyer, Louis, "Mysticism: An Essay on the History of the Word," in: Richard Woods (ed.), *Understanding Mysticism*, Image Books: Garden City, New York 1980, 42–55.

Bowman, Len, "The Status of Conceptual Schemata: A Dilemma for Perennialists," *ARIES* (first series) 11 (1990), 9–19.

Boyer, Carl B. and Marjorie N. Boyer, "Memorial: Lynn Thorndike (1882–1965)," *Technology and Culture* 7:3 (1966), 391–394.

Brach, Jean-Pierre, Review of Laurant, *Politica Hermetica* 3 (1989), 159–160.

Il simbolismo dei numeri, Arkeios: Rome 1999 (revised and expanded edn of *La symbolique des nombres*, Presses Universitaires de France: Paris 1994).

"Magic iv: Renaissance–17th Century," in: Hanegraaff *et al.*, *Dictionary*, 731–738.

"Number Symbolism," in: Hanegraaff *et al.*, *Dictionary*, 874–883.

"Patrizi, Francesco (Frane Petric')," in: Hanegraaff *et al.*, *Dictionary*, 936–938.

"Mathematical Esotericism: Some Perspectives on Renaissance Arithmology," in: Hanegraaff and Pijnenburg, *Hermes in the Academy*, 75–89.

Brach, Jean-Pierre and Wouter J. Hanegraaff, "Correspondences," in: Hanegraaff *et al.*, *Dictionary*, 275–279.

Braun, Lucien, *Histoire de l'histoire de la philosophie*, Ophrys: Paris 1973.

Braun, Willi and Russell McCutcheon (eds.), *Guide to the Study of Religion*, Cassell: London / New York 2000.

Bremmer, Jan N., "The Birth of the Term 'Magic'," *Zeitschrift für Papyrologie und Epigraphik* 126 (1999), 1–12; repr. in: Bremmer and Veenstra, *Metamorphosis of Magic*, 1–11, 267–271.

Greek Religion and Culture, the Bible and the Ancient Near East, Brill: Leiden / Boston 2008.

"Persian Magoi and the Birth of the Term 'Magic'," in: Bremmer, *Greek Religion and Culture*, 235–247.

"Magic *and* Religion?," in: Bremmer, *Greek Religion and Culture*, 347–352.

Bremmer, Jan N. and Jan R. Veenstra (eds.), *The Metamorphosis of Magic from Late Antiquity to the Early Modern Period*, Peeters: Louvain / Paris / Dudley 2002.

Broek, Roelof van den, "Hermes Trismegistus I: Antiquity," in: Hanegraaff *et al.*, *Dictionary*, 474–478.

"The Birth of a Chair," in: Hanegraaff and Pijnenburg, *Hermes in the Academy*, 11–15.

Broek, Roelof van den and Wouter J. Hanegraaff (eds.), *Gnosis and Hermeticism from Antiquity to Modern Times*, State University of New York Press: Albany 1998.

Broek, Roelof van den and Cis van Heertum (eds.), *From Poimandres to Jacob Böhme: Gnosis, Hermetism and the Christian Tradition*, In de Pelikaan: Amsterdam 2000.

Broecke, Steven Vanden, Review of von Stuckrad, *Aries* 4:1 (2004), 102–104.

Brown, Peter, *The World of Late Antiquity: From Marcus Aurelius to Muhammad*, Thames and Hudson: London 1971.

Brucker, Jacob, *Kurze Fragen aus der Philosophischen Historie, von Anfang der Welt biß auf die Geburt Christi, mit Ausführlichen Anmerckungen erläutert*, 7 vols., Daniel Bartholomaei & Sohn: Ulm 1731–1736.

Historia critica philosophiae a mundi incunabulis ad nostram usque aetatem deducta (1742–1744), 6 vols., Literis et Impensis Bern. Christoph Breitkopf: Leipzig 1767.

Brun, Pierre le, *Histoire critique des pratiques superstitieuses, qui ont séduit les Peuples & embarrassé les Savans, avec La Méthode & les Principes pour discerner les effets naturels d'avec ceux qui ne le sont pas*, 3 vols., 2nd edn, Jean-Frédéric Bernard: Amsterdam 1733.

Buchholz, Stephen, "Historia Contentionis inter Imperium et Sacerdotium: Kirchengeschichte in der Sicht von Christian Thomasius und Gottfried Arnold," in: Vollhardt, *Christian Thomasius*, 165–177.

Buck, August (ed.), *Die okkulten Wissenschaften in der Renaissance*, Otto Harrassowitz: Wiesbaden 1992.

Buhler, Stephen M., "Marsilio Ficino's *De stella magorum* and Renaissance Views of the Magi," *Renaissance Quarterly* 43:2 (1990), 348–371.

Bulwer-Lytton, Edward, *Zanoni: A Rosicrucian Tale*, Steinerbooks / Garber: Hudson 1989.

Buonosegnius, Johannes Baptista, "Epistola de Nobilioribus philosophorum sectis et de eorum inter se differentia" (Ms Pluteus LXXVI, Cod. LV, 2), in: Stein, "Handschriftenfunde," 540–551.

Burke, Peter, "Witchcraft and Magic in Renaissance Italy: Gianfrancesco Pico and his *Strix*," in: Anglo, *Damned Art*, 32–52.

A Social History of Knowledge: From Gutenberg to Diderot, Polity: Cambridge 2000.

Burmistrov, Konstantin, "Gershom Scholem und das Okkulte," *Gnostika* 33 (2006), 23–34.

Burnett, Charles, *Arabic into Latin in the Middle Ages: The Translators and their Intellectual and Social Context*, Ashgate: Farnham 2009.

Burns, Dylan, "ἄρρητος λόγος τέλειος: 'The Underworld of Platonism' and Esotericism in Late Antiquity," unpubl. Master Thesis, University of Amsterdam 2004.

"*The Chaldean Oracles of Zoroaster*, Hekate's Couch, and Platonic Orientalism in Psellos and Plethon," *Aries* 6:2 (2006), 158–179.

Butler, Alison, "Beyond Attribution: The Importance of Barrett's *Magus*," *Journal for the Academic Study of Magic* 1 (2003), 7–32.

Bywater, I., "Aristotle's Dialogue 'On Philosophy'," *Journal of Philology* 7:13 (1876), 64–87.

Caillet, Albert L., *Manuel bibliographique des sciences psychiques ou occultes*, 3 vols., Lucien Dorbon: Paris 1912.

Caillet, Serge, *L'Ordre rénové du Temple: Aux racines du Temple Solaire*, Dervy: Paris 1997.

Calderone, Salvatore, "Superstitio," in: Hildegard Temporini (ed.), *Aufstieg und Niedergang der Römischen Welt*, vol. 1.2, Walter de Gruyter: Berlin / New York 1972, 377–396.

Călian, George-Florin, "*Alkimia operativa* and *alkimia speculativa*: Some Modern Controversies on the Historiography of Alchemy," *Annual of Medieval Studies at CEU* 16 (2010), 166–190.

Campbell, Colin, "The Cult, the Cultic Milieu and Secularization," *A Sociological Yearbook of Religion in Britain* 5 (1972), 119–136.

Campigny, H.-M. de, *Les traditions et les doctrines ésotériques*, Librairie "Astra": Paris 1939.

Cancik, Hubert, "Apologetik/Polemik," in: Cancik *et al.*, *Handbuch religionswissenschaftlicher Grundbegriffe*, vol. II, Kohlhammer: Stuttgart 1990, 29–37.

Cantimori, D., *Umanesimo e religione nel rinascimento*, Einaudi: Turin 1980.

Cao, Gian Mario, *Scepticism and Orthodoxy: Gianfrancesco Pico as a Reader of Sextus Empiricus. With a Facing Text of Pico's Quotations from Sextus* (Bruniana & Campanelliana suppl. XXII, Materiali 3), Fabrizio Serra: Pisa / Rome 2007.

Caron, Richard, "Alchemy V: 19th–20th Century," in: Hanegraaff *et al.*, *Dictionary*, 50–58.

Caron, Richard and Marco Pasi, "Antoine Faivre: Bibliographie (1960–2000)," in: Caron, Godwin, Hanegraaff, and Vieillard-Baron, *Ésotérisme*, 875–917.

Caron, Richard, Joscelyn Godwin, Wouter J. Hanegraaff, and Jean-Louis Vieillard-Baron (eds.), *Ésotérisme, gnoses & imaginaire symbolique: Mélanges offerts à Antoine Faivre*, Peeters: Louvain 2001.

Carriker, A. J., *The Library of Eusebius of Caesarea*, Brill: Leiden / Boston / Cologne 2003.

Casaubon, Isaac, *De Rebus Sacris & Ecclesiasticis, Exercitationes XVI ad Cardinalis Baronii prolegomena in Annalis et primam eorum partem, de D.N. Iesu Christi Nativitate, Vita, Passione, Assumptione, cum prolegomenis auctoris, in quibus de Baronianis Annalibus candide disputatur*, Johannes Antonius & Samuel de Tournes: Geneva 1614.

Castro, G. de, *Il mondo secreto*, 9 vols., G. Daelli & Co.: Milan 1864.

Catana, Leo, *The Historiographical Concept "System of Philosophy": Its Origin, Nature, Influence and Legitimacy*, Brill: Leiden / Boston 2008.

Céard, Jean, "Démoneries du XVIe siècle et diableries du XIXe: Collin de Plancy et les démonologues de la Renaissance," in: Françoise Lavocat, Pierre Kapitaniak, and Marianne Closson, *Fictions du diable: Démonologie et littérature de saint Augustin à Léo Taxil*, Droz: Geneva 2007, 297–311.

Celenza, Christopher S., "Late Antiquity and Florentine Platonism: The 'Post-Plotinian' Ficino," in: Allen and Rees, *Marsilio Ficino*, 71–97.

"Paul Oskar Kristeller and the Hermetic Tradition," in: John Monfasani (ed.), *Kristeller Reconsidered: Essays on his Life and Scholarship*, Italica Press: New York 2006, 71–80.

"The Revival of Platonic Philosophy," in: James Hankins (ed.), *The Cambridge Companion to Renaissance Philosophy*, Cambridge University Press 2007, 72–96.

Chacornac, Paul, *Eliphas Lévi, rénovateur de l'occultisme en France (1810–1875)*, Chacornac Frères: Paris 1926.

Chakmakjian, Pauline, "Theological Lying and Religious Radicalism in Anderson's Constitutions," *Aries* 8:2 (2008), 167–190.

Chambers, Ephraim, *Cyclopaedia, or, An Universal Dictionary of Arts and Sciences*, 2 vols., London 1928.

Charet, F. X., *Spiritualism and the Foundations of C. G. Jung's Psychology*, State University of New York Press: Albany 1993.

"Understanding Jung: Recent Biographies and Scholarship," *Journal of Analytical Psychology* 45 (2000), 195–216.

"I Beg to Differ," *Journal of Analytical Psychology* 45 (2000), 473–476.

"A Final Reply," *Journal of Analytical Psychology* 45 (2000), 621–622.

Chastel, André, *Art et humanisme à Florence au temps de Laurent le Magnifique: Études sur la Renaissance et l'Humanisme platonicien*, Presses Universitaires de France: Paris 1959.

Chateaubriant, Robert de, "L'Université Saint-Jean de Jérusalem, âme de l'Ordre Souverain," *Cahier de l'Université Saint Jean de Jérusalem 1: Sciences Traditionnelles et Sciences Profanes*, André Bonne: Paris 1975, 13–23.

Cheetham, Tom, *The World Turned Inside Out: Henry Corbin and Islamic Mysticism*, Spring Journal Books: Woodstock, Conn. 2003.

Clagett, Marshall, "Éloge: Lynn Thorndike (1882–1965)," *Isis* 57:1 (1966), 85–89.

Clark, Stuart, *Thinking with Demons: The Idea of Witchcraft in Early Modern Europe*, Oxford University Press 1997.

Clement of Alexandria, *Les Stromates*, 7 vols., Les Éditions du Cerf: Paris 1951–1997.

Clergue, Jean Albert, "En quête de Henry Corbin Franc-Maçon chevaleresque," *L'Initiation* 2 & 4 (2009), 84–114, 245–273.

Cohen, H. Floris, *The Scientific Revolution: A Historiographical Inquiry*, The University of Chicago Press: Chicago / London 1994.

Cohn, Norman, *Warrant for Genocide: The Myth of the Jewish World Conspiracy and the Protocols of the Elders of Zion* (1967), Serif: London 2005.

Colavito, Jason, *The Cult of Alien Gods: H. P. Lovecraft and Extraterrestrial Pop Culture*, Prometheus: Amherst, NY 2005.

Colberg, Ehre Gott Daniel, *Das Platonisch-Hermetisches Christenthum, Begreiffend Die Historische Erzehlung vom Ursprung und vielerley Secten der heutigen Fanatischen Theologie, unterm Namen der Paracelsisten, Weigelianer, Rosencreuzer, Quäcker, Böhmisten, Wiedertäuffer, Bourignisten, Labadisten, und Quietisten*, 2 vols., Moritz Georg Weidmann: Frankfurt / Leipzig 1690–1691.

Coleman, Emmette, "The Sources of Madame Blavatsky's Writings," in: Vsevolod Sergyeevich Solovyoff, *A Modern Priestess of Isis*, Longmans, Green, and Co.: London 1895, 353–366.

Collin de Plancy, Jacques Auguste Simon, *Dictionnaire infernal, ou Bibliothèque universelle sur les Etres, les Personnages, les Livres, les Faits et les Choses qui tiennent aux apparitions, à la magie, au commerce de l'enfer, aux divinations, aux sciences secrètes, aux grimoires, aux prodiges, aux erreurs et aux préjugés, aux traditions et aux contes populaires, aux superstitions diverses, et généralement a toutes les croyances merveilleuses, surprenantes, mystérieuses et surnaturelles*, 2nd edn, P. Mongie: Paris 1825.

Colquhoun, John Campbell, *Isis Revelata: An Inquiry into the Origin, Progress, and Present State of Animal Magnetism*, 2 vols., MacLachlan & Stewart / Baldwin & Cradock: Edinburgh / London 1836.

— *An History of Magic, Witchcraft, and Animal Magnetism*, 2 vols., Longman, Brown, Green & Longmans / Adam & Charles Black: London / Edinburgh 1851.

Conger, George Perrigo, *Theories of Macrocosms and Microcosms in the History of Philosophy*, Columbia University Press: New York 1922.

Coomaraswamy, Ananda K., "Angel and Titan: An Essay in Vedic Ontology," *Journal of the American Oriental Society* 55 (1935), 373–419.

Copenhaver, Brian P., "Essay Review" (Westfall and McGuire, *Hermeticism and the Scientific Revolution*), *Annals of Science* 35 (1978), 527–531.

— "Scholastic Philosophy and Renaissance Magic in the *De Vita* of Marsilio Ficino," *Renaissance Quarterly* 37 (1984), 523–554.

— "Renaissance Magic and Neoplatonic Philosophy: 'Ennead' 4.3–5 in Ficino's 'De Vita Coelitus Comparanda'," in: Garfagnini, *Marsilio Ficino*, 351–69.

— "Iamblichus, Synesius and the Chaldaean Oracles in Marsilio Ficino's *De Vita Libri Tres*: Hermetic Magic or Neoplatonic Magic?," in: James Hankins, John

Monfasani, and Frederick Purnell (eds.), *Supplementum Festivum: Studies in Honor of Paul Oskar Kristeller*, Medieval & Renaissance Texts & Studies: Binghamton, NY 1987, 441–455.
"Natural Magic, Hermetism, and Occultism in Early Modern Science," in: David C. Lindberg and Robert S. Westman (eds.), *Reappraisals of the Scientific Revolution*, Cambridge University Press 1990, 261–301.
"The Occultist Tradition and its Critics," in: Daniel Garber and Michael Ayers (eds.), *The Cambridge History of Seventeenth-Century Philosophy*, vol. 1, Cambridge University Press 1998, 454–512.
"A Grand End for a Grand Narrative: Lodovico Lazzarelli, Giovanni Mercurio da Correggio and Renaissance Hermetica," *Magic, Ritual, and Witchcraft* 4:2 (2009), 207–223.
"Studied as an Oration: Readers of Pico's Letters, Ancient and Modern," in: Stephen Clucas, Peter J. Forshaw, and Valery Rees (eds.), *Laus Platonici Philosophi: Marsilio Ficino and his Influence*, Brill: Leiden / Boston 2011, 149–198.
Copenhaver, Brian P. and Charles B. Schmitt, *Renaissance Philosophy*, Oxford University Press 1992.
Corbin, Henry, "Le récit d'initiation et l'hermétisme en Iran (Recherche angélologique)," *Eranos-Jahrbuch* XVII: *Der Mensch und die Mythische Welt*, Rhein-Verlag: Zurich 1950.
"La Sophia éternelle: A propos de la 'Réponse à Job' de Carl G. Jung," *La revue de culture européenne* 5 (1953), 11–44.
"Post-face," in: Carl Gustav Jung, *Réponse à Job*, Buchet-Chastel: Paris 1964, 247–261.
"Correspondance," *Revue de métaphysique et de morale* 2 (1963), 234–237.
"Herméneutique spirituelle comparée: I. Swedenborg, II. Gnose ismaélienne," *Eranos-Jahrbuch* XXXII (1965), 71–176.
Creative Imagination in the Sufism of Ibn 'Arabi, Princeton University Press 1969.
En Islam iranien: Aspects spirituels et philosophiques, vol. 1: Le shî'sme duodécimain, Gallimard: Paris 1971.
En Islam iranien: Aspects spirituels et philosophiques, vol. II: Sohrawardî et les Platoniciens de Perse, Gallimard: Paris 1971.
"L'Université Saint-Jean de Jérusalem: Centre International de Recherche Spirituelle Comparée," *Cahier de l'Université Saint Jean de Jérusalem 1: Sciences Traditionnelles et Sciences Profanes*, André Bonne: Paris 1975, 8–12.
"Science traditionnelle et renaissance spirituelle," *Cahier de l'Université Saint Jean de Jérusalem 1: Sciences Traditionnelles et Sciences Profanes*, André Bonne: Paris 1975, 25–51.
"L'*Imago Templi* face aux normes profanes," in: Corbin, *Temple et Contemplation*, Flammarion: Paris 1980.
"De Heidegger à Sohravardî," in: Christian Jambet (ed.), *Henry Corbin*, Éditions de l'Herne: Paris 1981, 23–37.
Swedenborg and Esoteric Islam, Swedenborg Foundation: West Chester 1995.
Coudert, Allison P., "Some Theories of a Natural Language from the Renaissance to the Seventeenth Century," in: Albert Heinekamp and Dieter Mettler

(eds.), *Magia Naturalis und die Entstehung der modernen Naturwissenschaften*, Franz Steiner: Wiesbaden 1978, 56–113.

"Henry More and Witchcraft," in: Sarah Hutton (ed.), *Henry More (1614–1687): Tercentenary Studies*, Kluwer: Dordrecht 1990, 115–136.

Alchemy: The Philosopher's Stone (1980), Wildwood House / Bookwise: London / Sydney 2000.

Couliano, Ioan P., *Eros and Magic in the Renaissance*, The University of Chicago Press: Chicago / London 1987.

Crabtree, Adam, *From Mesmer to Freud: Magnetic Sleep and the Roots of Psychologial Healing*, Yale University Press: New Haven / London 1993.

Crisciani, Chiara, "Hermeticism and Alchemy: The Case of Ludovico Lazzarelli," *Early Science and Medicine* 5:2 (2000), 145–159.

Crispo, Giovanni Battista, *De ethnicis philosophis caute legendis disputationum ex propriis cuiusque principiis. Quinarius Primus: De Platone caute legendo Disputationum Libri XXIII, In quibus Triplex Rationalis animi status ex propriis Platonis principiis corrigitur, et catholicae ecclesiae sanctionibus expurgatur*, Aloysius Zannetti: Rome 1594.

Crociata, Mariano, *Umanesimo e teologia in Agostino Steuco: Neoplatonismo e teologia della creazione nel "De perenni philosophia"*, Almo Collegio Capranica: Rome 1987.

Culianu, Ioan P., "The Gnostic Revenge: Gnosticism and Romantic Literature," in: Jacob Taubes (ed.), *Religionstheorie und Politische Theologie, Band 2: Gnosis und Politik*, Wilhelm Fink / Ferdinand Schöningh: Munich 1984, 290–306.

Curry, Patrick, "Revisions of Science and Magic," *History of Science* 23 (1985), 299–325.

Prophecy and Power: Astrology in Early Modern England, Princeton University Press 1989.

Dachez, Roger, "Les véritables origines d'une 'société secrète'," *L'histoire* 256 (2001), 8–14.

Dan, Joseph, "In Quest of a Historical Definition of Mysticism: The Contingental Approach," *Studies in Spirituality* 3 (1993), 58–90.

"Gershom Scholem: Mystiker oder Geschichtsschreiber des Mystischen?," in: Peter Schäfer and Gary Smith (eds.), *Gershom Scholem: Zwischen den Disziplinen*, Suhrkamp: Frankfurt a.M. 1995, 32–69.

"The Kabbalah of Johannes Reuchlin and its Historical Significance," in: Dan (ed.), *Christian Kabbalah*, 55–95.

"Christian Kabbalah: From Mysticism to Esotericism," in: Faivre and Hanegraaff (eds.), *Western Esotericism and the Science of Religion*, 117–129.

"Foreword," in: Gershom Scholem, *On the Mystical Shape of the Godhead: Basic Concepts in the Kabbalah*, Schocken: New York 1991, 3–14.

Dan, Joseph (ed.), *The Christian Kabbalah: Jewish Mystical Books and their Christian Interpreters*, Harvard College Library: Cambridge, Mass. 1997.

Dánann, Alexandre de, *La magie de la Rose-Croix d'Or: Traduction de La Croix d'Or ou Bréviaire de la Confrérie de la Rose-Croix d'Or dans le seul manuscrit connu du XVIIe siècle avec ses psaumes et caractères magiques, une introduction sur l'origine de la Confrérie et la traduction intégrale de ses statuts (1678)*, Archè: Milan 2009.

Dannenfeldt, Karl H., "The Renaissance and the Pre-Classical Civilizations," *Journal of the History of Ideas* 13:4 (1952), 435–449.

"The Pseudo-Zoroastrian Oracles in the Renaissance," *Studies in the Renaissance* 4 (1957), 7–30.

Darnton, Robert, *Mesmerism and the End of the Enlightenment in France*, Harvard University Press: Cambridge, Mass. / London 1968.

Dassen, Patrick, *De onttovering van de wereld: Max Weber en het probleem van de moderniteit in Duitsland 1890–1920*, G. A. von Oorschot: Amsterdam 1999.

Daston, Lorraine and Katherine Park, *Wonders and the Order of Nature 1150–1750*, Zone Books: New York 2001.

Davis, Erik, "Hermes on the Seine: The Esoteric Scholarship of Antoine Faivre" (undated), www.techgnosis.com

Debus, Allen G., "An Elizabethan History of Medical Chemistry," *Annals of Science* 18:1 (1962), 1–29.

Review of Yates, *Isis* 55:3 (1964), 389–391.

The English Paracelsians, Franklin Watts Inc.: New York 1965.

The Chemical Philosophy: Paracelsian Science and Medicine in the Sixteenth and Seventeenth Centuries, Dover: New York 1977.

"The Paracelsians in Eighteenth Century France: A Renaissance Tradition in the Age of the Enlightenment," *Ambix* 28:1 (1981), 36–54.

"Scientific Truth and Occult Tradition: The Medical World of Ebenezer Sibly (1751–1799)," *Medical History* 26 (1982), 259–278; repr. in: Debus, *Chemical Promise*, 353–386.

"The Significance of Chemical History," *Ambix* 32:1 (1985), 1–14.

"Alchemy in an Age of Reason: The Chemical Philosophers in Early Eighteenth-Century France," in: Merkel and Debus, *Hermeticism and the Renaissance*, 231–350.

The French Paracelsians: The Chemical Challenge to Medical and Scientific Tradition in Early Modern France, Cambridge University Press 1991.

"French Alchemy in the Early Enlightenment," in: Caron, Godwin, Hanegraaff, and Vieillard-Baron, *Ésotérisme*, 47–59; repr. in: Debus, *Chemical Promise*, 413–426.

The Chemical Promise: Experiment and Mysticism in the Chemical Philosophy 1550–1800, Science History Publications: Sagamore Beach 2006.

Deghaye, Pierre, *La naissance de Dieu, ou la doctrine de Jacob Boehme*, Albin Michel: Paris 1985.

"Jacob Boehme and his Followers," in: Faivre and Needleman, *Modern Esoteric Spirituality*, 210–247.

Delumeau, Jean, "Les réformateurs et la superstition," in: *Actes du colloque L'Amiral de Coligny et son temps (Paris, 24–28 octobre 1972)*, Société de l'histoire du Protestantisme Français: Paris 1974, 451–487.

Catholicism between Luther and Voltaire: A New View of the Counter-Reformation, Burns & Oates / Westminster Press: London / Philadelphia 1977.

Denis, Ferdinand, *Tableau historique, analytique et critique des sciences occultes, où l'on examine l'origine, le développement, l'influence et le caractère de la Divination, de l'Astrologie, des Oracles, des Augures, de la Kabbale, la Féerie, la Magie, la Sorcellerie, la Démonologie, la Philosophie hermétique, les Phénomènes merveilleux, etc. etc.: précédé d'une Introduction et suivi d'une Biographie, d'une Bibliographie et d'un Vocabulaire*, L'Encyclopédie Portative: Paris 1830.

Le monde enchanté: Cosmographie et histoire naturelle fantastiques du moyen âge, A. Fournier: Paris 1843.

"Sciences occultes," in: Paul Lacroix (ed.), *Moyen Âge et Renaissance: Histoire et description des moeurs et usages, du commerce et de l'industrie, des sciences, des arts, des littératures et des beaux-arts en Europe*, vol. IV, Paris 1851, 32 fols. (unpaginated).

Denyer, Nicholas, "Introduction," in: Plato, *Alcibiades* (Nicholas Denyer, ed.), Cambridge University Press 2001, 1–29.

Dessoir, Max, *Buch der Erinnerung*, Ferdinand Enke: Stuttgart 1946.

Deveney, John Patrick, *Paschal Beverly Randolph: A Nineteenth-Century Black American Spiritualist, Rosicrucian, and Sex-Magician*, State University of New York Press: Albany 1997.

"Ozymandias: Why Do We Do What We Do? Some Ruminations on Theosophical History, Curiosity, Diligence and the Desire to Penetrate the Veil and Find the Inside of History; or, An Attempt to Explain the Feeling that The Truth Is Out There and Lies in the Details," in: Michael Gomes (ed.), *Keeping the Link Unbroken: Theosophical Studies Presented to Ted G. Davy on his Seventy-Fifth Birthday*, TRM: n.p. 2004, 1–21.

"Paschal Beverly Randolph and Sexual Magic," in: Hanegraaff and Kripal, *Hidden Intercourse*, 355–367.

Dickie, Matthew W., *Magic and Magicians in the Greco-Roman World*, Routledge: London / New York 2001.

Digby, Kenelm, *Discours fait en une célèbre assemblée par le chevalier Digby touchant la guerison des playes par la poudre de sympathie où sa composition est enseignée, & plusieurs autres merveilles de la nature sont développées*, A. Courbé: Paris 1658.

Diller, A., "The Autographs of Georgius Gemistus Pletho," *Scriptorium* 10 (1956), 27–41.

Dillon, John, *The Middle Platonists: A Study of Platonism 80 B.C. to A.D. 220*, Duckworth: London 1977.

Diogenes Laertius, *Lives of the Eminent Philosophers* (R. D. Hicks, ed. and trans.), William Heinemann / Harvard University Press: Cambridge, Mass. 1972.

D. J. [Louis de Jaucourt], "Superstition," in: *Encyclopédie*, vol. xv, 669.

Dobbs, Betty Jo Teeter, *The Foundations of Newton's Alchemy, or "The Hunting of the Greene Lyon"*, Cambridge University Press 1975.

Dodds, E. R., *Pagan and Christian in an Age of Anxiety: Some Aspects of Religious Experience from Marcus Aurelius to Constantine*, Cambridge University Press 1965.

Doel, Marieke J. E. van den, *Ficino en het voorstellingsvermogen: Phantasia en Imaginatio in kunst en theorie van de Renaissance*, St. Hoofd-Hart-Handen: Amsterdam 2008.

Doel, Marieke J. E. van den and Wouter J. Hanegraaff, "Imagination," in: Hanegraaff *et al.*, *Dictionary*, 606–616.

Doering-Manteuffel, Sabine, *Das Okkulte: Eine Erfolgsgeschichte im Schatten der Aufklärung, von Gutenberg bis zum World Wide Web*, Siedler: Munich 2008.

Dompnier, Bernard, "Les hommes d'église et la superstition entre XVIIe et XVIIIe siècles," in: Dompnier, *La superstition à l'Age des lumières*, 13–47.

Dompnier, Bernard (ed.), *La superstition à l'Age des lumières*, Honoré Champier: Paris 1998.

Dongen, H. van, *Geen gemene maat: Over incommensurabiliteit*, University of Amsterdam 1999.

Dorez, Léon, "Lettres inédites de Jean Pic de la Mirandole (1482–1492)," *Giornale storico della letteratura italiana* 25 (1895), 352–361.

Dorn, Gérard, *Theophrasti Paracelsi Aurora philosophorum, Thesauram, & Mineralem Oeconomiam, Commentaria, et quibusdam Argumentis*, Frankfurt 1584.

Dörrie, Heinrich, "Was ist 'spätantiker Platonismus'? Überlegungen zur Grenzziehung zwischen Platonismus und Christentum," *Theologische Rundschau* N.F. 36:4 (1971), 285–302.

"Die Wertung der Barbaren im Urteil der Griechen: Knechtsnaturen? Oder Bewahrer und Künder heilbringender Wahrheit?," in: Ruth Stiehl and Gustav Adolf Lehmann (eds.), *Antike und Universalgeschichte: Festschrift Hans Erich Stier zum 70. Geburtstag am 25. Mai 1972*, Aschendorff: Münster 1972, 146–175.

"Platons Reisen zu fernen Völkern: Zur Geschichte eines Motivs der Platon-Legende und zu seiner Neuwendung durch Lactanz," in: den Boer *et al.*, *Romanitas et Christianitas*, 99–118.

Dosse, François, *Michel de Certeau: Le marcheur blessé*, La découverte: Paris 2007.

Droge, Arthur J., "Justin Martyr and the Restoration of Philosophy," *Church History* 56 (1987), 303–319.

Homer or Moses? Early Christian Interpretations of the History of Culture, J. C. B. Mohr (Paul Siebeck): Tübingen 1989.

"Apologetics, NT," in: David Noel Freedman (ed.), *The Anchor Bible Dictionary*, vol. 1, Doubleday: New York 1992, 302–307.

Dubuisson, Daniel, *Twentieth-Century Mythologies: Dumézil, Lévi-Strauss, Eliade*, 2nd edn, Equinox: London / Oakville 1993.

Impostures et pseudo-science: L'oeuvre de Mircea Eliade, Presses Universitaires du Septentrion: Villeneuve d'Ascq 2005.

Dudley III, Guilford, *Religion on Trial: Mircea Eliade and his Critics*, Temple University Press: Philadelphia 1977.

Durand, Dana B., "Magic and Experimental Science: The Achievement of Lynn Thorndike," *Isis* 33:6 (1942), 691–712.

Durand, Gilbert, "Similitude hermétique et science de l'homme," in: Adolf Portmann and Rudolf Ritsema (eds.), *Correspondences in Man and World* (Eranos Yearbook 1973, vol. XLII), Brill: Leiden 1975, 427–515.

"Science de l'homme et islam spirituel," in: Nasr, *Mélanges*, 35–102.

Durkheim, Emile, *Les formes élémentaires de la vie religieuse* (1912), Quadrige/Presses Universitaires de France: Paris 1994.

Durville, Henri, *La science secrète*, Henri Durville: Paris 1923.

Eamon, William, *Science and the Secrets of Nature: Books of Secrets in Medieval and Early Modern Culture*, Princeton University Press 1994.

Ebert, Hermann, "Augustinus Steuchus und seine Philosophia Perennis: Ein kritischer Beitrag zur Geschichte der Philosophie," *Philosophisches Jahrbuch* 42 (1929), 342–356, 510–526; 43 (1930), 92–100.

Eco, Umberto, "Ur-Fascism," *The New York Review of Books*, June 22, 1995, 12–15.

Edelheit, Amos, *Ficino, Pico and Savonarola: The Evolution of Humanist Theology 1461/2–1498*, Brill: Leiden / Boston 2008.

Edelman, Nicole, *Voyantes, guérisseuses et visionnaires en France 1785–1914*, Albin Michel: Paris 1995.

Edighoffer, Roland, "Rosicrucianism I: First Half of the 17th Century," in: Hanegraaff *et al.*, *Dictionary*, 1009–1014.

"Rosicrucianism II: 18th Century," in: Hanegraaff *et al.*, *Dictionary*, 1014–1017.

Ehrard, M. J., "Matérialisme et naturalisme: Les sources occultes de la pensée de Diderot," *Cahiers de l'Association internationale des études françaises* 13:1 (1961), 189–201.

Eichhorn, Johann Gottfried, *Urgeschichte, herausgegeben mit Einleitung und Anmerkungen von D. Johann Philipp Gabler*, vol. II:1, Monath & Kußler: Altdorf / Nuremberg 1792.

Eliade, Mircea, *Le Journal des Indes*, L'Herne: Paris 1992.

Les promesses de l'equinoxe: Mémoire 1 (1907–1937), Gallimard: Paris 1980.

The Myth of the Eternal Return; or, Cosmos and History, Princeton University Press 1954.

Patterns in Comparative Religion (1958), University of Nebraska Press: Lincoln 1996.

"Occultism and Freemasonry in Eighteenth-Century Europe" (review of René le Forestier, *La Franc-Maçonnerie Templière et Occultiste aux XVIIIe et XIXe siècles*), *History of Religions* 13:1 (1973), 89–91.

Occultism, Witchcraft, and Cultural Fashions: Essays in Comparative Religions, The University of Chicago Press 1976.

"Some Notes on *Theosophia Perennis*: Ananda K. Coomaraswamy and Henry Corbin," *History of Religions* 19:2 (1979), 167–176.

Journal III: 1970–1978, The University of Chicago Press: Chicago / London 1989.

Contributions à la philosophie de la Renaissance, suivi de Itinéraire Italien, Gallimard: Paris 1992.

Eliade, Mircea (ed.), *The Encyclopedia of Religion*, 16 vols., MacMillan: New York 1987.

Ellenberger, Henri F., *The Discovery of the Unconscious: The History and Evolution of Dynamic Psychiatry*, Harper Collins: n.p. 1970.

Ellwood, Robert S., *The Fifties Spiritual Marketplace: American Religion in a Decade of Conflict*, Rutgers University Press: New Brunswick 1997.

The Sixties Spiritual Awakening: American Religion Moving from Modern to Postmodern, Rutgers University Press: New Brunswick 1994.

The Politics of Myth: A Study of C. G. Jung, Mircea Eliade, and Joseph Campbell, State University of New York Press: Albany 1999.

Elsen, Juliette van den, "The Rotterdam Sympathy Case (1696–1697): A Window on the Late Seventeenth-Century Philosophical Discourse," *Aries* 2:1 (2002), 34–56.

"Monsters, demonen en occulte krachten: De journalistieke perceptie van magische en wonderbaarlijke verschijnselen in de vroege Verlichting 1684–1727," Ph.D. diss. Catholic University Nijmegen, Tilburg 2003.

Encyclopédie ou Dictionnaire raisonné des sciences, des arts et des métiers, par une Société de Gens de lettres, 17 vols., Briasson, David, le Breton, Durand: Paris 1751–1772.

Engelhardt, Dietrich von, "Naturforschung als Mythologie und Mission bei Johann Salomo Christoph Schweigger (1779–1857)," in: Caron *et al.*, *Ésotérisme*, 249–266.

Ennemoser, Joseph, *Der Magnetismus nach der allseitigen Beziehung seines Wesens, seiner Erscheinungen, Anwendung und Enträthselung in einer geschichtlichen Entwickelung von allen Zeiten und bei allen Völkern wissenschaftlich dargestellt*, F. A. Brockhaus: Leipzig 1819.

Geschichte des thierischen Magnetismus. Erster Theil: Geschichte der Magie, F. A. Brockhaus: Leipzig 1844.

The History of Magic (William Howitt, trans.), 2 vols., Henry G. Bohn: London 1854.

Erbse, Hartmut (ed.), *Theosophorum graecorum fragmenta*, B. G. Teubner: Stuttgart / Leipzig 1995.

Eugenius Philalethes, F. R. S. (Robert Samber), *Long Livers: A Curious History of Such Persons of both Sexes who have liv'd several Ages, and grown Young again: with the rare Secret of Rejuvenescency of Arnoldus de Villa Nova, And a great many approv'd and invaluable Rules to prolong Life: as also, How to prepare the Universal Medicine*, London 1722.

Euler, Walter Andreas, *"Pia philosophia" et "docta religio": Theologie und Religion bei Marsilio Ficino und Giovanni Pico della Mirandola*, Wilhelm Fink: Munich 1998.

Eusebius of Caesarea, *La préparation évangélique*, Les Éditions du Cerf: Paris 1974–1983.

Evans, Richard J., *In Defense of History* (1997), Granta Books: London 2000.

Evans-Pritchard, E. E., *Theories of Primitive Religion*, Clarendon Press: Oxford 1965.

Evers, Tilman, *Mythos und Emanzipation: Eine kritische Annäherung an C. G. Jung*, Junius Verlag: Hamburg 1987.

Evola, Julius, *The Hermetic Tradition: Symbols and Teachings of the Royal Art*, Inner Traditions: Rochester 1971.

Faber, Richard, "Der Schwabinger Imperatorenstreit, (k)ein Sturm im Wasserglas," in: Faber and Holste, *Kreise, Gruppen, Bünde*, 37–64.

Faber, Richard and Christine Holste (eds.), *Kreise, Gruppen, Bünde: Zur Soziologie moderner Intellektuellenassoziation*, Königshausen & Neumann: Würzburg 2000.

Fabre, Jean, "Diderot et les théosophes," *Cahiers de l'Association Internationale des Études Françaises* 13:1 (1961), 203–222.

Facoltà di lettere e filosofia dell'Università degli Studi di Perugia (ed.), *Filosofia e cultura in Umbria tra medioevo e rinascimento: Atti del IV Convegno di Studi Umbri, Gubbio, 22–26 maggio 1966*, Centro di Studi Umbri / Sant'Ubaldo: Gubbio 1967.

Faivre, Antoine, *Les Vampires: Essai historique, critique et littéraire*, Eric Losfeld / Le Terrain Vague: Paris 1962.

Kirchberger et l'illuminisme du dix-huitième siècle, Martinus Nijhoff: The Hague 1966.

Eckartshausen et la théosophie chrétienne, C. Klincksieck: Paris 1969.

"Pour un approche figuratif de l'alchimie," *Annales* 26:3/4 (1971), 841–853.

"Alchimie occidentale et logique aristotélicienne," *Bulletin de la société Ernest-Renan* 20 (1971), included in *Revue de l'histoire des religions* 181:1 (1972), 105–110.

"Le Temple de Salomon dans la maçonnerie mystique au XVIIIe siècle," *Australian Journal of French Studies* 9:3 (1972), 274–289.

L'ésotérisme au XVIIIe siècle en France et en Allemagne, Seghers: Paris 1973.

Journal (unpublished manuscript, in private collection Antoine Faivre), 1973–present.

"Mystische Alchemie und geistige Hermeneutik," in: Adolf Portmann and Rudolf Ritsema (eds.), *Correspondences in Man and World* (Eranos Yearbook 1973, vol. XLII), Brill: Leiden 1975, 323–360.

"Philosophie de la nature et naturalisme scientiste," *Cahiers de l'Université Saint Jean de Jérusalem 1: Sciences Traditionnelles et Sciences Profanes*, André Bonne: Paris 1975, 91–110.

Mystiques, Théosophes et Illuminés au siècle des Lumières, Georg Olms: Hildesheim / New York 1976.

"Église intérieure et Jérusalem céleste: Fondements d'une anthropologie cosmique selon Franz von Baader," *Cahiers de l'Université Saint Jean de Jérusalem 2: Jérusalem la cité spirituelle*, Berg International: Paris 1976, 77–89.

"Le ternaire alchimique et l'Axe Feu Central dans la tradition martinesiste," in: Nasr, *Mélanges*, 613–627.

"Les normes et la sécularisation du cosmos," in: Adolf Portmann and Rudolf Ritsema (eds.), *Norms in a Changing World* (Eranos Yearbook 1974, vol. XLIII), Brill: Leiden 1977, 293–327.

"Théosophie chrétienne et prophétie," *Cahiers de l'Université Saint Jean de Jérusalem 3: La foi prophétique et le sacré*, Berg International: Paris 1977, 139–149.

"Les 'Noces Chymiques de Christian Rosencreutz' comme pèlerinage de l'âme," *Cahiers de l'Université Saint Jean de Jérusalem 4: Les pèlerins de l'orient et les vagabonds de l'occident*, Berg International: Paris 1978, 139–153.

"Les métamorphoses d'Hermès," *Cahiers de l'Université Saint Jean de Jérusalem 5: Les yeux de chair et les yeux de feu (La science et la gnose)*, Berg International: Paris 1979, 95–120.

"L'imagination créatrice (fonction magique et fondement mythique de l'image)," *Revue d'Allemagne* 3:2 (1981), 355–390.

"Miles redivivus (Aspects de l'Imaginaire chevaleresque au XVIIIe siècle: Alchimie, Franc-Maçonnerie, Littérature)," *Cahiers de l'Université Saint Jean de Jérusalem 10: La chevalerie spirituelle*, Berg International: Paris 1984, 98–124.

"Sources antiques et médiévales des courants ésotériques modernes," *Travaux de la Loge nationale de recherches Villard de Honnecourt* 8 (1984), 110–130; 9 (1984), 67–84; 10 (1985), 174–185; 11 (1986), 129–144.

Accès de l'ésotérisme occidental, Gallimard: Paris 1986.

"Pensées de Dieu, images de l'homme: Figures, miroirs et engendrements selon J. Boehme, F. Ch. Oetinger et Franz von Baader," *Cahiers de l'Université Saint Jean de Jérusalem 12: Face de Dieu et théophanies*, Berg International: Paris 1986, 100–119.

"Esotericism," in: Eliade, *Encyclopedia of Religion*, vol. v, 156–163; repr. in: Sullivan, *Hidden Truths*, 38–48.

"Nature: Religious and Philosophical Speculations," in: Eliade, *Encyclopedia of Religion*, vol. x, 328–337; repr. in: Sullivan, *Hidden Truths*, 24–37.

"The Children of Hermes and the Science of Man," in: Merkel and Debus, *Hermeticism and the Renaissance*, 424–435.

"Genèse d'un genre narratif, le fantastique (essai de périodisation)," in: *La littérature fantastique* (Cahiers de l'Hermétisme), Albin Michel: Paris 1991, 15–43.

L'ésotérisme (Que sais-je 1031), Presses Universitaires de France: Paris 1992; 2nd edn 1993; 3rd edn 2002; 4th edn 2007.

"Introduction 1," in: Faivre and Needleman, *Modern Esoteric Spirituality*, xi–xxii.

The Golden Fleece and Alchemy, State University of New York Press: Albany 1993.

Access to Western Esotericism, State University of New York Press: Albany 1994.

The Eternal Hermes: From Greek God to Alchemical Magus, Phanes Press: Grand Rapids, Mich. 1995.

Accès de l'ésotérisme occidental, revised and expanded edn, 2 vols., Gallimard: Paris 1996.

Philosophie de la Nature: Physique sacrée et théosophie XVIIIe–XIXe siècles, Albin Michel: Paris 1996.

"L'ésotérisme et la recherche universitaire," in: Faivre, *Accès* (1996), vol. II, 11–42.

"Questions of Terminology Proper to the Study of Esoteric Currents in Modern and Contemporary Europe," in: Faivre and Hanegraaff, *Western Esotericism and the Science of Religion*, 1–10.

"L'ambiguità della nozione di sacro in Mircea Eliade," in: Arcella, Pisi, and Scagno, *Confronto con Mircea Eliade*, 363–374.

Theosophy, Imagination, Tradition: Studies in Western Esotericism, State University of New York Press: Albany 2000.

"Émile Poulat et notre domaine," in: Valentine Zuber (ed.), *Un objet de science, le catholicisme: Réflexions autour de l'oeuvre d'Émile Poulat*, Bayard: Paris 2001, 209–213.

"Christian Theosophy," in: Hanegraaff *et al.*, *Dictionary*, 258–267.

"Fictuld, Hermann," in: Hanegraaff *et al.*, *Dictionary*, 367–370.

"Kocku von Stuckrad et la notion d'ésotérisme" (review article of Kocku von Stuckrad, *Was ist Esoterik?*), *Aries* 6:2 (2006), 205–214.

"Sensuous Relation with Sophia in Christian Theosophy," in: Hanegraaff and Kripal, *Hidden Intercourse*, 281–307.

"'Eloquence magique,' ou descriptions des mondes de l'au-delà explorés par le magnétisme animal: Au carrefour de la *Naturphilosophie* romantique et de la théosophie chrétienne (première moitié du XIXème siècle)," *Aries* 8:2 (2008), 191–228.

"From Paris to Amsterdam and Beyond: Origins and Development of a Collaboration," in: Hanegraaff and Pijnenburg, *Hermes in the Academy*, 123–127.

"Modern Western Esoteric Currents in the Work of Mircea Eliade: The Extent and Limits of their Presence," in: Wedemeyer and Doniger, *Hermeneutics, Politics, and the History of Religions*, 147–157.

"Le terme et la notion de 'gnose' dans les courants ésotériques occidentaux modernes (essai de périodisation)," in: Jean-Pierre Mahé, Paul-Hubert Poirier, and Madeleine Scopello (eds.), *Les textes de Nag Hammadi: Histoire des religions et approches contemporaines*, AIBI / Diffusion De Boccard: Paris 2010, 87–112.

Western Esotericism: A Concise History, State University of New York Press: Albany 2010.

Faivre, Antoine and Karen-Claire Voss, "Western Esotericism and the Science of Religions," *Numen* 42 (1995), 48–77.

Faivre, Antoine and Rolf Christian Zimmermann (eds.), *Epochen der Naturmystik: Hermetische Tradition im wissenschaftlichen Fortschritt*, Erich Schmidt: Berlin 1979.

Faivre, Antoine and Jacob Needleman (eds.), *Modern Esoteric Spirituality*, Crossroad: New York 1992.

Faivre, Antoine and Wouter J. Hanegraaff (eds.), *Western Esotericism and the Science of Religion: Selected Papers Presented at the 17th Congress of the International Association for the History of Religions, Mexico City 1995*, Peeters: Louvain 1998.

Fanger, Claire, "Medieval Ritual Magic: What It Is and Why We Need to Know More About It," in: Fanger, *Conjuring Spirits*, vii–xviii.

Fanger, Claire and Frank Klaassen, "Magic III: Middle Ages," in: Hanegraaff *et al.*, *Dictionary*, 724–731.

Fanger, Claire (ed.), *Conjuring Spirits: Texts and Traditions of Medieval Ritual Magic*, Sutton: Phoenix Mill 1998.

Farmer, S. A., *Syncretism in the West: Pico's 900 Theses (1486). The Evolution of Traditional Religious and Philosophical Systems*, Medieval & Renaissance Texts & Studies: Tempe 1998.

Farmer, Steve, John B. Henderson, and Michael Witzel, "Neurobiology, Layered Texts, and Correlative Thought: A Cross-Cultural Framework for Premodern History," *Bulletin of the Museum of Far Eastern Antiquities* 72 (2002), 48–90.

Feldhay, Rivka, "Critical Reactions to the Occult: A Comment," in: Ullmann-Margalit, *Scientific Enterprise*, 93–99.

Fenton, Paul B., "Henry Corbin et la mystique juive," in: Mohammed Ali Amir-Mouzzi, Christian Jambet and Pierre Lory (eds.), *Henry Corbin: Philosophies et sagesses des religions du livre*, Brepols: Turnhout 2005, 151–164.

Festugière, André-Jean, *La révélation d'Hermès Trismégiste*, 4 vols. (1950), repr. in one volume Les Belles Lettres: Paris 2006.

Fiard, L'Abbé, *La France trompée par les magiciens et démonolatres du dix-huitième siècle, fait démontré par des faits*, Grégoire / Thouvenin: Paris 1803.

Ficino, Marsilio, *Opera*, Basle 1576; repr. Turin 1959, 1983.

    Three Books on Life: A Critical Edition and Translation with Introduction and Notes (Carol V. Kaske and John R. Clark, ed. and trans.), Medieval & Renaissance Texts & Studies: Binghamton, NY 1989.

    "The Commentary of Marsilio Ficino the Florentine, on Plato's Philebus on the Highest Good," in: Allen, *Marsilio Ficino: The Philebus Commentary*, 70–439.

    Platonic Theology (Michael J. B. Allen, trans.; James Hankins, ed.), 6 vols., The I Tatti Renaissance Library / Harvard University Press: Cambridge, Mass. / London 2001–2006.

Field, Arthur, *The Origins of the Platonic Academy of Florence*, Princeton University Press 1988.

    "The Platonic Academy of Florence," in: Allen and Rees, *Marsilio Ficino*, 369–376.

Firpo, Luigi, "The Flowering and Withering of Speculative Philosophy – Italian Philosophy and the Counter Reformation: The Condemnation of Francesco Patrizi," in: Eric Cochrane (ed.), *The Late Italian Renaissance 1525–1630*, MacMillan: London 1970, 266–284.

Fisher, Elaine, "Fascist Scholars, Fascist Scholarship: The Quest for Ur-Fascism and the Study of Religion," in: Wedemeyer and Doniger, *Hermeneutics, Politics, and the History of Religions*, 261–284.

Flacius Illyricus, Matthias, *Ecclesiastica historia, integram Ecclesiae Christi ideam, quantum ad locum, propagationem, persecutionem, tranquillitatem, doctrinam, haereses, caeremonias, gubernationem, schismata, synodos, personas, miracula, martyria, religiones extra Ecclesiam et statum Imperii politicum attinet, secundum singulas centurias, perspicuo ordine complectens: Singulari diligentia et fide ex vetustissimis et optimis historicis, patribus et aliis scriptoribus congesta per aliquot studiosos et pios viros in urbe Magdeburgica*, Bâle 1560–1574.

Flint, Valerie I. J., *The Rise of Magic in Early Medieval Europe*, Princeton University Press 1991.

Forestier, René le, *La Franc-Maçonnerie templière et occultiste aux XVIIIe et XIXe siècles* (Antoine Faivre, ed.), 2 vols., La Table d'Émeraude: Paris 1987.

La Franc-Maçonnerie occultiste au XVIIIe siècle & L'ordre des Élus Coens (orig. 1928), La Table d'Émeraude: Paris 1987.

Forman, Paul, "Weimar Culture, Causality, and Quantum Theory, 1918–1927: Adaptation by German Physicists and Mathematicians to a Hostile Intellectual Environment," in: Russell McCormmach (ed.), *Historical Studies in the Physical Sciences*, University of Pennsylvania Press: Philadelphia 1971, 1–115.

Forshaw, Peter J., "'Alchemy in the Amphitheatre': Some Considerations of the Alchemical Content of the Engravings in Heinrich Khunrath's *Amphitheatre of Eternal Wisdom* (1609)," in: Jacob Wamberg (ed.), *Art and Alchemy*, Museum Tusculanum Press: Copenhagen 2006, 195–220.

Foucault, Michel, *Les mots et les choses: Une archéologie des sciences humaines*, Gallimard: Paris 1966.

Fowden, Garth, *The Egyptian Hermes: A Historical Approach to the Late Pagan Mind*, Princeton University Press 1986.

Frazer, James G., *The Golden Bough* (1900), 2nd edn, repr. MacMillan & Co: London 1951.

Frenschkowski, Marco, *Die Geheimbünde: Eine kulturgeschichtliche Analyse*, Marix: Wiesbaden 2007.

Freud, Sigmund and C. G. Jung, *Briefwechsel* (William McGuire and Wolfgang Sauerländer, eds.), S. Fischer: Frankfurt a.M. 1974.

Freudenberger, Th., *Augustinus Steuchus aus Gubbio: Augustinerchorherr und päpstlicher Bibliothekar (1497–1548) und sein literarisches Lebenswerk*, Aschendorffschen Verlagsbuchhandlung: Münster 1935.

Freyer, Johannes, *Geschichte der Geschichte der Philosophie im achtzehnten Jahrhundert*, R. Voigtländer: Leipzig 1911.

Frick, Karl R. H., *Die Erleuchteten: Gnostisch-theosophische und alchemistisch-rosenkreuzerische Geheimgesellschaften bis zum Ende des 18. Jahrhunderts: Ein Beitrag zur Geistesgeschichte der Neuzeit*, Akademische Druck- und Verlagsanstalt: Graz 1973.

Licht und Finsternis: Gnostisch-theosophische und freimaurerisch-okkulte Geheimgesellschaften bis an die Wende zum 20. Jahrhundert, 2 vols., Akademische Druck- und Verlagsanstalt: Graz 1975/1978.

Friedman, Maurice, "Why Joseph Campbell's Psychologizing of Myth Precludes the Holocaust as Touchstone of Reality," *Journal of the American Academy of Religion* 66:2 (1998), 385–401.

"Psychology, Psychologism, and Myth: A Rejoinder," *Journal of the American Academy of Religion* 67:2 (1999), 469–471.

Fulbrook, Mary, *Historical Theory*, Routledge: London and New York 2002.

Fuller, Robert C., *Mesmerism and the American Cure of Souls*, University of Pennsylvania Press: Philadelphia 1982.

    Americans and the Unconscious, Oxford University Press: New York / Oxford 1986.

G. H. [Gerard Heym], Review of Jung's *Psychologie und Alchemie*, *Ambix* 3:1–2 (1948), 64–67.

    Review of Jung's *Mysterium Coniunctionis*, *Ambix* 6:1 (1957), 47–51.

Galbreath, Robert, "The History of Modern Occultism: A Bibliographical Survey," *Journal of Popular Culture* 5 (1971), 726–754.

Ganzenmüller, W., "Wandlungen in der geschichtlichen Betrachtung der Alchemie," *Chymia* 3 (1950), 143–154.

Garfagnini, Gian Carlo (ed.), *Marsilio Ficino e il ritorno di Platone: Studi e documenti*, 2 vols., Leo S. Olschki: Florence 1976.

Garin, Eugenio, *Medioevo e Rinascimento: Studi e ricerche*, Gius. Laterza & Figli: Bari 1954.

    "Note sull'ermetismo del Rinascimento," in: Garin *et al.*, *Testi umanistici*, 9–19.

    "Divagazioni ermetiche," *Rivista critica di storia della filosofia* 31 (1976), 462–466.

Garin, E., M. Brini, C. Vasoli, and C. Zambelli, *Testi Umanistici su l'Ermetismo: Testi di Ludovico Lazzarelli, F. Giorgio Veneto, Cornelio Agrippa di Nettesheim*, Fratelli Bocca: Rome 1955.

[Gassendi, Pierre], *Petri Gassendi Diniensis Ecclesiae praepositi . . . opera omnia*, 6 vols., Lyon 1658.

Gatti, Hilary, "Frances Yates's Hermetic Renaissance in the Documents held in the Warburg Institute Archive," *Aries* 2:2 (2002), 193–210.

Gauld, Alan, *A History of Hypnotism*, Cambridge University Press 1992.

Geertz, Clifford, "Religion as a Cultural System," in: Michael Banton (ed.), *Anthropological Approaches to the Study of Religion*, Tavistock: London 1966, 1–46.

Geffarth, Renko, *Religion und arkane Hierarchie: Der Orden der Gold- und Rosenkreuzer als Geheime Kirche im 18. Jahrhundert*, Brill: Leiden / Boston 2007.

Gentile, Sebastiano, "Note sui manoscritti greci di Platone utilizzati da Marsilio Ficino," in: *Scritti in onore di Eugenio Garin*, Pubblicazioni della Classe di Lettere e Filosofia, Scuola Normale Superiore: Pisa 1987, 51–84.

Gentile, Sebastiano, Sandra Niccoli, and Paolo Viti (eds.), *Marsilio Ficino e il ritorno di Platone: Manoscritti, stampe e documenti*, Casa Editrice Le Lettere: Florence 1984.

Gentile, Sebastiano and Carlos Gilly (eds.), *Marsilio Ficino et il ritorno di Ermete Trismegisto*, Centro Di: Florence 1999.

Gerhardt, C. J. (ed.), *Die philosophischen Schriften von Gottfried Wilhelm Leibniz*, vol. III, Olms: Hildesheim 1978.

Geyer, Hermann, *Verborgene Weisheit: Johann Arndts "Vier Bücher vom Wahren Christentum" als Programm einer spiritualistisch-hermetischen Theologie*, 3 parts in 2 volumes, Walter de Gruyter: Berlin / New York 2001.

Giegerich, Eric, "Antoine Faivre: Studies in Western Esotericism," *The San Francisco Jung Institute Library Journal* 20:2 (2001), 7–24.

Gilbert, Robert A., *A. E. Waite: A Bibliography*, The Aquarian Press: Wellingborough 1983.

    A. E. Waite: Magician of Many Parts, Crucible: Wellingborough 1987.

    Hermetic Papers of A. E. Waite: The Unknown Writings of a Modern Mystic, The Aquarian Press: Wellingborough 1987.

    "Waite, Arthur Edward," in: Hanegraaff *et al.*, *Dictionary*, 1164–1165.

Gill, Joseph, *The Council of Florence*, Cambridge University Press 1959.

    Personalities of the Council of Florence, and Other Essays, Blackwell: Oxford 1964.

Gilly, Carlos, *Adam Haslmayr: Der erste Verkünder der Manifeste der Rosenkreuzer*, In de Pelikaan: Amsterdam 1994.

    "'*Theophrastia Sancta*': Paracelsianism as a Religion, in Conflict with the Established Churches," in: Grell, *Paracelsus*, 151–185.

    "Comenius und die Rosenkreuzer," in: Neugebauer-Wölk, *Aufklärung und Esoterik* (1999), 87–107.

    "Die Überlieferung des *Asclepius* im Mittelalter," in: van den Broek and van Heertum, *From Poimandres to Jacob Böhme*, 335–367.

    "Das Bekenntnis zur Gnosis von Paracelsus bis auf die Schüler Jacob Böhmes," in: van den Broek and van Heertum, *From Poimandres to Jacob Böhme*, 385–425.

Gilly, Carlos and Cis van Heertum (eds.), *Magia, alchimia, scienza dal '400 al '700: L'influsso di Ermete Trismegisto / Magic, Alchemy and Science 15th–18th Centuries: The Influence of Hermes Trismegistus*, 2 vols., Centro Di: Florence 2002.

Gilly, Carlos and Friedrich Niewöhner (eds.), *Rosenkreuz als Europäisches Phänomen im 17. Jahrhundert*, In de Pelikaan: Amsterdam 2002.

Gilson, Etienne, *History of Christian Philosophy in the Middle Ages*, Sheed and Ward: London 1955.

Gladigow, Burkhard, "Pantheismus als 'Religion' von Naturwissenschaftlern," in: Peter Antes and Donate Pahnke (eds.), *Die Religion von Oberschichten: Religion, Profession, Intellektualismus*, Diagonal Verlag: Marburg 1989, 219–239.

Glawe, Walther, *Die Hellenisierung des Christentums in der Geschichte der Theologie von Luther bis auf die Gegenwart*, Trowitzsch & Sohn: Berlin 1912.

Gligor, Mihaela and Mac Linscott Ricketts (eds.), *Întalniri cu / Encounters with Mircea Eliade*, Cărții de Știință: Cluj-Napoca 2005.

Godwin, Joscelyn, *The Theosophical Enlightenment*, State University of New York Press: Albany 1994.

    The Pagan Dream of the Renaissance, Thames & Hudson: London 2002.

Godwin, Joscelyn, Christian Chanel, and John Patrick Deveney, *The Hermetic Brotherhood of Luxor: Initiatic and Historical Documents of an Order of Practical Occultism*, Samuel Weiser: York Beach 1995.

Goltz, Dietlinde, "Versuch einer Grenzziehung zwischen 'Alchemie' und 'Chemie'," *Sudhoffs Archiv* 52 (1968), 30–47.

Gombrich, Ernst H., "*Icones Symbolicae*: The Visual Image in Neoplatonic Thought," *Journal of the Warburg and Courtauld Institutes* 11 (1948), 163–192.

Goodrick-Clarke, Nicholas, *The Occult Roots of Nazism: Secret Aryan Cults and their Influence on Nazi Ideology* (1985), I. B. Tauris: London / New York 1992.

The Western Esoteric Traditions: A Historical Introduction, Oxford University Press 2008.

"Western Esotericism in the United Kingdom," in: Hanegraaff and Pijnenburg, *Hermes in the Academy*, 129–133.

Gougenot des Mousseaux, Roger, *Le juif, le judaïsme et la judaïsation des peuples chrétiens*, Henri Plon: Paris 1869.

Graf, Fritz, *Gottesnähe und Schadenzauber: Die Magie in der griechisch-römischen Antike*, C. H. Beck: Munich 1996.

"Magic II: Antiquity," in: Hanegraaff *et al.*, *Dictionary*, 719–724.

Grafton, Anthony, "Protestant versus Prophet: Isaac Casaubon on Hermes Trismegistus," *Journal of the Warburg and Courtauld Institutes* 46 (1983), 78–93; repr. in: Grafton, *Defenders of the Text: The Traditions of Scholarship in an Age of Science, 1450–1800*, Harvard University Press: Cambridge, Mass. / London 1991, 145–161; German trans. in Mulsow, *Ende des Hermetismus*, 283–303.

"Giovanni Pico della Mirandola: Trials and Triumphs of an Omnivore," in: Grafton, *Commerce with the Classics: Ancient Books and Renaissance Readers*, The University of Michigan Press: Ann Arbor 1997, 93–134.

Worlds made by Words: Scholarship and Community in the Modern West, Harvard University Press: Cambridge, Mass. / London 2009.

Grant, Robert M., "Porphyry among the Early Christians," in: den Boer *et al.*, *Romanitas et Christianitas*, 181–187.

Gods and the One God, The Westminster Press: Philadelphia 1986.

Greer, Mary K., *Women of the Golden Dawn: Rebels and Priestesses*, Park Street Press: Rochester 1995.

Greiner, Frank, "Art du feu, art du secret: Obscurité et ésotérisme dans les textes alchimiques de l'âge baroque," in: Greiner, *Aspects*, 207–231.

Greiner, Frank (ed.), *Aspects de la tradition alchimique au XVIIe siècle*, S. É. H. A. / Archè: Paris / Milan 1998.

Grell, Ole Peter (ed.), *Paracelsus: The Man and his Reputation, his Ideas and their Transformation*, Brill: Leiden / Boston / Cologne 1998.

Greyerz, Kaspar von, "Alchemie, Hermetismus und Magie: Zur Frage der Kontinuitäten in der wissenschaftlichen Revolution," in: Lehmann and Trepp, *Im Zeichen der Krise*, 415–432.

Grillot de Givry, Emile Angelo, *La musée des sorciers, mages et alchimistes*, Librairie de France: Paris 1929.

Grossato, Alessandro (ed.), *Forme e correnti dell'esoterismo occidentale*, Medusa: Milan 2008.

Grossheim, Michael, "'Die namenlose Dummheit, die das Resultat des Fortschritts ist': Lebensphilosophische und dialektische Kritik der Moderne," *Logos*, N.F. 3 (1996), 97–133.

Gruber, Bettina, "Mystik, Esoterik, Okkultismus: Überlegungen zu einer Begriffs-diskussion," in: Baßler and Châtellier, *Mystique, mysticisme et modernité*, 27–38.

Die Seherin von Prevorst: Romantischer Okkultismus als Religion, Wissenschaft und Literatur, Ferdinand Schöningh: Paderborn / Munich / Vienna / Zurich 2000.

"Romantische Psychoanalyse? Freud, C. G. Jung und die Traumtheorien der Romantik," in: Peter-André Alt and Christiane Leiteritz (eds.), *Traum-Diskurse der Romantik*, Walter de Gruyter: Berlin / New York 2005, 334–358.

Guillelmus Alvernus (William of Auvergne), *Opera Omnia* (1674), repr. Frankfurt a.M. 1963.

Gundel, W. and H. G. Gundel, *Astrologumena: Die astrologische Literatur in der Antike und ihre Geschichte* (Sudhoffs Archiv 6), Franz Steiner: Wiesbaden 1966.

Guyon, Claude-Marie, *Bibliothèque ecclésiastique, par forme d'instructions dogma-tiques et morales sur toute la religion*, 8 vols., Delalain: Paris 1771.

Häfner, Ralph, "Jacob Thomasius und die Geschichte der Häresien," in: Vollhardt, *Christian Thomasius*, 141–177.

Hagner, Michael, "By-bye Science, Welcome Pseudoscience? Reflexionen über einen beschädigten Status," in: Rupnow *et al.*, *Pseudowissenschaft*, 21–50.

Hakl, Hans Thomas, *Der verborgene Geist von Eranos: Unbekannte Begegnun-gen von Wissenschaft und Esoterik. Eine alternative Geistesgeschichte des 20. Jahrhunderts*, Scientia Nova / Verlag Neue Wissenschaft: Bretten 2001.

Halbertal, Moshe, *Concealment and Revelation: Esotericism in Jewish Thought and its Philosophical Implications*, Princeton University Press: Princeton / Oxford 2007.

Halbronn, Jacques, "Les résurgences du savoir astrologique au sein des textes alchimiques dans la France du XVIIe siècle," in: Greiner, *Aspects de la tradition alchimique*, 193–205.

Halbwachs, Maurice, *On Collective Memory* (Lewis A. Coser, ed. and trans.), The University of Chicago Press: Chicago / London 1992.

Hall, Manly P., *The Secret Teachings of All Ages: An Encyclopedic Outline of Masonic, Hermetic, Qabbalistic and Rosicrucian Symbolical Philosophy*, H. S. Crocker: Los Angeles 1928.

Halleux, Robert, *Les textes alchimiques*, Brepols: Turnhout 1979.

"La controverse sur les origines de la chimie, de Paracelse à Borrichius," in: Jean-Claude Margolin (ed.), *Acta Conventus Neo-Latini Turonensis*, vol. II, J. Vrin: Paris 1980, 807–819.

"Le mythe de Nicolas Flamel, ou les mécanismes de la pseudépigraphie alchim-ique," *Archives internationales d'histoire des sciences* 33:3 (1983), 234–255.

"Pratique de laboratoire et expérience de pensée chez les alchimistes," in: Jean-François Bergier (ed.), *Zwischen Wahn, Glaube und Wissenschaft: Magie, Astrologie, Alchemie und Wissenschaftsgeschichte*, Verlag der Fachvereine: Zurich 1988, 115–126.

Le savoir de la main: Savants et artisans dans l'Europe pré-industrielle, Armand Colin: Paris 2009.

Hamacher, Elisabeth, *Gershom Scholem und die Allgemeine Religionsgeschichte*, Walter de Gruyter: Berlin / New York 1999.

Hamill, John, *The Craft: A History of English Freemasonry*, Crucible: Wellingborough 1986.

Hamill, John (ed.), *The Rosicrucian Seer: Magical Writings of Frederick Hockley*, Aquarian Press: Wellingborough 1986.

Hammer, Olav, *Claiming Knowledge: Strategies of Epistemology from Theosophy to the New Age*, Brill: Leiden / Boston / Cologne 2001.

Hammer, Olav and Jan A. M. Snoek, "Essenes, Esoteric Legends about," in: Hanegraaff *et al.*, *Dictionary*, 340–343.

Hammer, Olav and Kocku von Stuckrad, "Introduction: Western Esotericism and Polemics," in: Hammer and von Stuckrad (eds.), *Polemical Encounters*, vii–xxii.

Hammer, Olav and Kocku von Stuckrad (eds.), *Polemical Encounters: Esoteric Discourse and its Others*, Brill: Leiden / Boston 2007.

Hammoud, Saïd, *Mesmérisme et romantisme allemand (1766–1829)*, L'Harmattan: Paris 1994.

Hanegraaff, Wouter J., "Empirical Method in the Study of Esotericism," *Method & Theory in the Study of Religion* 7:2 (1995), 99–129.

New Age Religion and Western Culture: Esotericism in the Mirror of Secular Thought, Brill: Leiden / New York / Cologne 1996; State University of New York Press: Albany 1998.

"On the Construction of 'Esoteric Traditions'," in: Faivre and Hanegraaff, *Western Esotericism and the Science of Religion*, 11–61.

"The Emergence of the Academic Science of Magic: The Occult Philosophy in Tylor and Frazer," in: Arie L. Molendijk and Peter Pels (eds.), *Religion in the Making: The Emergence of the Sciences of Religion*, Brill: Leiden / Boston / Cologne 1998, 253–275.

"Reflections on New Age and the Secularisation of Nature," in: Joanne Pearson, Richard H. Roberts, and Geoffrey Samuel (eds.), *Nature Religion Today: Paganism in the Modern World*, Edinburgh University Press 1998, 22–32.

"Romanticism and the Esoteric Connection," in: van den Broek and Hanegraaff, *Gnosis and Hermeticism*, 237–268.

"Defining Religion in Spite of History," in: Jan G. Platvoet and Arie L. Molendijk (eds.), *The Pragmatics of Defining Religion: Contexts, Concepts and Contests*, Brill: Leiden / Boston / Cologne 1999, 337–378.

"New Age Spiritualities as Secular Religion: A Historian's Perspective," *Social Compass* 46:2 (1999), 145–160.

"Some Remarks on the Study of Western Esotericism," *Esoterica* 1:1 (1999), www.esoteric.msu.edu

"Versuch über Friederike Hauffe: Zum Verhältnis zwischen Lebensgeschichte und Mythos der 'Seherin von Prevorst'," *Suevica* 8 (1999/2000), 17–38; 9 (2001/2002), 233–276.

"New Age Religion and Secularization," *Numen* 47:3 (2000), 288–312.

"A Woman Alone: The Beatification of Friederike Hauffe *née* Wanner (1801–1829)," in: Anne-Marie Korte (ed.), *Women and Miracle Stories: A Multidisciplinary Exploration*, Brill: Leiden / Boston / Cologne 2001, 211–247.

"Ironic Esotericism: Alchemy and Grail Mythology in Thomas Mann's *Zauberberg*," in: Caron *et al.*, *Ésotérisme*, 575–594.

"Beyond the Yates Paradigm: The Study of Western Esotericism between Counterculture and New Complexity," *Aries* 1:1 (2001), 5–37.

"How Magic Survived the Disenchantment of the World," *Religion* 33:4 (2003), 357–380.

"The Dreams of Theology and the Realities of Christianity," in: J. Haers and P. de Mey (eds.), *Theology and Conversation: Towards a Relational Theology*, Leuven University Press / Peeters: Louvain 2003, 709–733.

"The Study of Western Esotericism: New Approaches to Christian and Secular Culture," in: Peter Antes, Armin W. Geertz, and Randi R. Warne (eds.), *New Approaches to the Study of Religion 1: Regional, Critical, and Historical Approaches*, Walter de Gruyter: Berlin / New York 2004, 489–519.

"La fin de 'La Tradition Hermétique': Frances Yates et Lodovico Lazzarelli," *Accademia* 6 (2004), 85–101.

Review of Mulsow, *Aries* 4:1 (2004), 108–111.

"Lodovico Lazzarelli and the Hermetic Christ: At the Sources of Renaissance Hermetism," in: Hanegraaff and Bouthoorn, *Lodovico Lazzarelli*, 1–104.

"Forbidden Knowledge: Anti-Esoteric Polemics and Academic Research," *Aries* 5:2 (2005), 225–254.

"Introduction," in: Hanegraaff *et al.*, *Dictionary*, vii–xiii.

"Esotericism," in: Hanegraaff *et al.*, *Dictionary*, 336–340.

"Magic I: Introduction," in: Hanegraaff *et al.*, *Dictionary*, 716–719.

"Magic V: 18th–20th Century," in: Hanegraaff *et al.*, *Dictionary*, 738–744.

"Occult/Occultism," in: Hanegraaff *et al.*, *Dictionary*, 884–889.

"Tradition," in: Hanegraaff *et al.*, *Dictionary*, 1125–1135.

"Human Potential before Esalen: An Experiment in Anachronism," in: Jeffrey J. Kripal and Glenn W. Shuck (eds.), *On the Edge of the Future: Esalen and the Evolution of American Culture*, Indiana University Press: Bloomington / Indianapolis 2005, 17–44.

"Idolatry," *Rever: Revista de Estudos da Religião* 5:4 (2005), 80–89.

Swedenborg, Oetinger, Kant: Three Perspectives on the Secrets of Heaven, The Swedenborg Foundation: West Chester 2007.

"The Trouble with Images: Anti-Image Polemics and Western Esotericism," in: Hammer and von Stuckrad, *Polemical Encounters*, 107–136.

"Gnosticism," in: von Stuckrad, *Brill Dictionary of Religion*, vol. 11, 790–798.

"Pseudo-Lullian Alchemy and the Mercurial Phoenix: Giovanni da Correggio's *De Quercu Iulii pontificis sive De lapide philosophico*," in: Principe, *Chymists and Chymistry*, 101–112.

"Altered States of Knowledge: The Attainment of Gnōsis in the Hermetica," *The International Journal of the Platonic Tradition* 2 (2008), 128–163.

"Under the Mantle of Love: The Mystical Eroticisms of Marsilio Ficino and Giordano Bruno," in: Hanegraaff and Kripal, *Hidden Intercourse*, 175–207.

"Reason, Faith, and Gnosis: Potentials and Problematics of a Typological Construct," in: Peter Meusburger, Michael Welker, and Edgar Wunder (eds.), *Clashes of Knowledge: Orthodoxies and Heterodoxies in Science and Religion*, Springer Science & Business Media: Dordrecht 2008, 133–144.

"Leaving the Garden (in Search of Religion): Jeffrey J. Kripal's Vision of a Gnostic Study of Religion," *Religion* 38 (2008), 259–276.

"Better than Magic: Cornelius Agrippa and Lazzarellian Hermetism," *Magic, Ritual & Witchcraft* 4:1 (2009), 1–25.

"The Platonic Frenzies in Ficino," in: Jitse Dijkstra, Justin Kroesen, and Yme Kuiper (eds.), *Myths, Martyrs and Modernity: Studies in the History of Religions in Honour of Jan N. Bremmer*, Brill: Leiden / Boston 2009, 553–567.

"Will-Erich Peuckert and the Light of Nature," in: Arthur Versluis, Claire Fanger, Lee Irwin, and Melinda Phillips (eds.), *Esotericism, Religion, and Nature*, Association for the Study of Esotericism / North American Academic Press: East Lansing 2009, 281–305.

"Ten Years of Studying and Teaching Western Esotericism," in: Hanegraaff and Pijnenburg, *Hermes in the Academy*, 17–29.

"The Beginnings of Occultist Kabbalah: Adolphe Franck and Eliphas Lévi," in: Boaz Huss, Marco Pasi, and Kocku von Stuckrad (eds.), *Kabbalah and Modernity: Interpretations, Transformations, Adaptations*, Brill: Leiden / Boston 2010, 107–128.

"The Birth of Esotericism from the Spirit of Protestantism," *Aries* 10:2 (2010), 197–216.

"Magnetic Gnosis: Somnambulism and the Quest for Absolute Knowledge," in: Andreas Kilcher and Philipp Theisohn (eds.), *Die Enzyklopädik der Esoterik: Allwissenheitsmythen und universalwissenschaftliche Modelle in der Esoterik der Neuzeit*, Wilhelm Fink: Paderborn 2010, 259–275.

"How Hermetic was Renaissance Hermetism? Reason and Gnosis from Ficino to Foix de Candale," in: Jan Veenstra (ed.), *Hermetism and Rationality*, Peeters: Louvain 2011.

"Kabbalah in *Gnosis* Magazine (1985–1999)," in: Boaz Huss (ed.), *Kabbalah and Contemporary Spiritual Revival*, The Ben Gurion University of the Negev Press: Beer Sheeva 2011, 251–266.

"Hermetism," in: Karla Pollmann and Willemien Otten (eds.), *A Guide to the Historical Reception of Augustine*, Oxford University Press 2011.

"Gnosis," in: Magee, *The Cambridge Companion to Western Mysticism and Esotericism*.

Hanegraaff, Wouter J. and Ruud M. Bouthoorn, *Lodovico Lazzarelli (1447–1500): The Hermetic Writings and Related Documents*, Arizona Center for Medieval and Renaissance Studies: Tempe 2005.

Hanegraaff, Wouter J. (ed.) in collaboration with Antoine Faivre, Roelof van den Broek, and Jean-Pierre Brach, *Dictionary of Gnosis and Western Esotericism*, Brill: Leiden /Boston 2005.

Hanegraaff, Wouter J. and Jeffrey J. Kripal (eds.), *Hidden Intercourse: Eros and Sexuality in the History of Western Esotericism*, Brill: Leiden / Boston 2008; Fordham University Press: New York 2011.

Hanegraaff, Wouter J. and Joyce Pijnenburg (eds.), *Hermes in the Academy: Ten Years' Study of Western Esotericism at the University of Amsterdam*, Amsterdam University Press 2009.

Hankins, James, "Cosimo de' Medici and the 'Platonic Academy'," *Journal of the Warburg and Courtauld Institutes* 53 (1990), 144–162.

"The Myth of the Platonic Academy of Florence," *Renaissance Quarterly* 44:3 (1991), 429–475.

Plato in the Italian Renaissance, 2 vols., Brill: Leiden / New York / Copenhagen / Cologne 1991.

"Pletho's Influence in the Later Quattrocento," Appendix 12 in: Hankins, *Plato in the Italian Renaissance*, vol. II, 436–440.

"Ficino's 'Spiritual Crisis'," Appendix 16 in: Hankins, *Plato in the Italian Renaissance*, vol. II, 454–459.

"The Development of Ficino's 'Ancient Theology'," in: Hankins, *Plato in the Italian Renaissance*, vol. II, 460–464.

"The Invention of the Platonic Academy of Florence," *Rinascimento*, 2nd ser., 41 (2001), 3–35.

Humanism and Platonism in the Italian Renaissance, 2 vols., Edizioni di Storia e Letteratura: Rome 2003.

"The Popes and Humanism," in: Hankins, *Humanism and Platonism*, vol. I, 469–494.

"Renaissance Philosophy between God and the Devil," in: *Humanism and Platonism*, vol. I, 591–615.

"Antiplatonism in the Renaissance and the Middle Ages," in: Hankins, *Humanism and Platonism*, vol. II, 27–415.

Hansen, T. H. [Hans Thomas Hakl], "Julius Evolas Politisches Wirken," in: Julius Evola, *Menschen inmitten von Ruinen*, Hohenrain-Verlag: Tübingen / Zurich / Paris 1991, 7–131.

Hanson, Richard P. C., "The Christian Attitude to Pagan Religions up to the time of Constantine the Great," in: Hanson, *Studies in Christian Antiquity*, T & T Clark Ltd: Edinburgh 1985, 144–229.

Hardinge, Emma, *Six Lectures on Theology and Nature*, Scott and Company: Chicago 1860.

Harmening, Dieter, *Superstitio: Überlieferungs- und theoriegeschichtliche Untersuchungen zur kirchlich-theologischen Aberglaubensliteratur des Mittelalters*, Erich Schmidt: Berlin 1979.

Harpe, Jacqueline de la, *L'abbé Laurent Bordelon et la lutte contre la superstition en France entre 1680 et 1730*, University of California Press: Berkeley / Los Angeles 1942.

Hatfield, Rab, "The Compagni de' Magi," *Journal of the Warburg and Courtauld Institutes* 33 (1970), 107–161.

Heckethorn, Charles William, *The Secret Societies of all Ages and Countries*, 2nd edn, University Books: New York 1965.

Helbing, Lothar, "Ludwig und Anna Maria Derleth: Eine Sammlung von Berichten," in: *Ludwig Derleth Gedenkbuch*, Castrum Peregrini Presse: Amsterdam 1958, 5–73.

Henry, John, "Occult Qualities and the Experimental Philosophy: Active Principles in Pre-Newtonian Matter Theory," *History of Science* 24 (1986), 335–381.

Hermonymos, Charitonymos, "Kyrio Georgio to Gemisto," in: J.-P. Migne, *Patrologiae cursus completus, series graecolatina*, vol. CLX, Paris 1866, 806–812.

Hesse, Mary, "Hermeticism and Historiography: An Apology for the Internal History of Science," in: Roger H. Stuewer (ed.), *Historical and Philosophical Perspectives of Science*, University of Minnesota Press: Minneapolis 1970, 134–162.

"Reasons and Evaluations in the History of Science," in: Mikuláš Teich and Robert Young (eds.), *Changing Perspectives in the History of Science*, Heinemann: London 1973, 127–147.

Heumann, Christoph August, *Acta philosophorum, das ist, Gründliche Nachrichten aus der Historia Philosophica, nebst beygefügten Urtheilen von denen dahin gehörigen alten und neuen Büchern* (1715–1727), facs. reprint, vol. 1 parts 1–3, Thoemmes: Bristol 1997.

"Von denen Kennzeichen der falschen und unächten Philosophie," *Acta Philosophorum* 2 (1715), 179–236.

"Von denen vier Cabbalistischen Welten, wie auch von denen zehen Sephiroth," *Acta Philosophorum* 2 (1715), 236–246.

"Von dem Ursprung und Wachstum der Philosophie," *Acta Philosophorum* 2 (1715), 246–314.

"Von dem Nahmen der Welt-Weißheit," *Acta Philosophorum* 2 (1715), 314–321.

"Eintheilung der Historiae Philosophicae," *Acta Philosophorum* 3 (1715), 462–473.

"Von der Barbarey," *Acta Philosophorum* 8 (1717), 204–253.

Hitchcock, Ethan Allen, *Remarks upon Alchemy and the Alchemists*, Boston 1857.

Hobsbawm, Eric and Terence Ranger, *The Invention of Tradition*, Cambridge University Press 1983.

Hoffmann, Philippe, "La fonction des prologues exégétiques dans la pensée pédagogique néoplatonicienne," in: Jean-Daniel Dubois and Bernard Roussel (eds.), *Entrer en matière: Les Prologues*, Les Editions du Cerf: Paris 1998, 209–291.

Hofmann, Michael, *Theologie, Dogma und Dogmenentwicklung im theologischen Werk Denis Petau's*, Herbert Lang / Peter Lang: Bern / Frankfurt a.M. / Munich 1976.

Hofmeier, Thomas, "Cudworth versus Casaubon: Historical versus Textual Criticism," in: Gilly and van Heertum, *Magia, alchimia, scienza*, vol. 1, 581–586.

Holz, Hans Heinz, "ERANOS: Eine moderne Pseudo-Gnosis," in: Jacob Taubes (ed.), *Religionstheorie und Politische Theologie, vol. II: Gnosis und Politik*, Ferdinand Schöningh: Munich / Paderborn 1984, 249–263.

Hopfner, Theodor, *Orient und griechische Philosophie*, J. C. Hinrichs'sche Buchhandlung: Leipzig 1925.

Horkheimer, Max and Theodor W. Adorno, *Dialectic of Enlightenment: Philosophical Fragments*, Stanford University Press 2002.

Horton, Robin, *Patterns of Thought in Africa and the West: Essays on Magic, Religion and Science*, Cambridge University Press 1993.

Houman, Setareh, *De la philosophia perennis au pérennialisme américain*, Archè: Milan 2010.

Howe, Ellic, *The Magicians of the Golden Dawn: A Documentary History of a Magical Order 1887–1923*, Routledge & Kegan Paul: London 1972.

Huppert, George, "Divinatio et Eruditio: Thoughts on Foucault," *History and Theory* 13:3 (1974), 191–207.

Huss, Boaz, "Ask No Questions: Gershom Scholem and the Study of Contemporary Jewish Mysticism," *Modern Judaism* 25:2 (2005), 141–158.

Hutchison, Keith, "What happened to Occult Qualities in the Scientific Revolution?," *Isis* 73 (1982), 233–253.

Hutton, Patrick H., "The Foucault Phenomenon and Contemporary French Historiography," *Historical Reflections/Réflexions historiques* 17:1 (1991), 77–102.

Iamblichus, *De mysteriis* (Emma C. Clarke, John M. Dillon, and Jackson P. Hershbell, ed. and trans.), Brill: Leiden / Boston 2004.

Idel, Moshe, "The Magical and Neoplatonic Interpretations of the Kabbalah in the Renaissance," in: Bernard Dov Cooperman (ed.), *Jewish Thought in the Sixteenth Century*, Harvard University Press: Cambridge, Mass. / London 1983, 186–242.

Kabbalah: New Perspectives, Yale University Press: New Haven / London 1988.

"Kabbalah, Platonism and Prisca Theologia: The Case of R. Menasseh ben Israel," in: Yosef Kaplan, Henry Méchoulan, and Richard H. Popkin (eds.), *Menasseh ben Israel and his World*, Brill: Leiden / New York / Copenhagen / Cologne 1989, 207–219.

"Rabbinism versus Kabbalism: On G. Scholem's Phenomenology of Judaism," *Modern Judaism* 11 (1991), 281–296.

"Jewish Kabbalah and Platonism in the Middle Ages and Renaissance," in: Lenn E. Goodman (ed.), *Neoplatonism and Jewish Thought*, State University of New York Press: Albany 1992, 319–351.

"Introduction to the Bison Book Edition," in: Johann Reuchlin, *On the Art of the Kabbalah / De Arte Cabalistica* (1983), Bison Book / University of Nebraska Press: Lincoln / London 1993, v–xxix.

"Jewish Mystical Thought in the Florence of Lorenzo il Magnifico," in: Dora Liscia Bemporad and Ida Zatelli (eds.), *La cultura ebraica all'epoca di Lorenzo il Magnifico: Celebrazioni dell V centenario della morte di Lorenzo il Magnifico*, Leo S. Olschki: Florence 1998, 17–42.

"Reflections on Kabbalah in Spain and Christian Kabbalah," *Hispania Judaica Bulletin* 2 (1999), 3–15.

Absorbing Perfections: Kabbalah and Interpretation, Yale University Press: New Haven / London 2002.

"Prisca Theologia in Marsilio Ficino and Some Jewish Treatments," in: Allen and Rees, *Marsilio Ficino*, 137–158.

"Jewish Thinkers versus Christian Kabbalah," in: Schmidt-Biggemann, *Christliche Kabbala*, 49–65.

"Italy in Safed, Safed in Italy: Toward an Interactive History of Sixteenth-Century Kabbalah," in: David B. Ruderman and Giuseppe Veltri (eds.), *Cultural Intermediaries: Jewish Intellectuals in Early Modern Italy*, University of Pennsylvania Press: Philadelphia 2004, 239–269.

La Cabbala in Italia 1289–1510, La Giuntina: Florence 2007.

"La Kabbalah in Italia nel XVI secolo: Alcune nuove prospettive," in: Grossato, *Forme e correnti*, 109–123.

Ierunca, Virgil, "The Literary Work of Mircea Eliade," in: Joseph M. Kitagawa and Charles H. Long (eds.), *Myths and Symbols: Studies in Honor of Mircea Eliade*, The University of Chicago Press: Chicago / London 1969, 343–363.

Introvigne, Massimo, *Il cappello del Mago: I nuovi movimenti magici, dallo spiritismo al satanismo*, Sugarco: Carnago 1990.

"Ordeal by Fire: The Tragedy of the Solar Temple," *Religion* 25 (1995), 267–283.

"Antoine Faivre: Father of Contemporary Vampire Studies," in: Caron, Godwin, Hanegraaff, and Vieillard-Baron, *Ésotérisme*, 595–610.

Israel, Jonathan I., *Radical Enlightenment: Philosophy and the Making of Modernity 1650–1750*, Oxford University Press 2001.

Jacob, Margaret, Review of Stevenson, *Eighteenth-Century Studies* 23:3 (1990), 322–329.

Living the Enlightenment: Freemasonry and Politics in Eighteenth-Century Europe, Oxford University Press: New York / Oxford 1991.

"Introduction," in: James E. Force and Sarah Hutton (eds.), *Newton and New-tonianism: New Studies*, Kluwer: Dordrecht / Boston / London 2004, x–xvii.

The Origins of Freemasonry: Facts & Fictions, University of Pennsylvania Press: Philadelphia 2006.

Jacob, Margaret and Edward Gosselin, "Dame Frances Amelia Yates, 28 November 1899–29 September 1981," *Isis* 73:3 (1982), 424–426.

Jacobsen, Johanna Micaela, "Boundary Breaking and Compliance: Will-Erich Peuckert and 20th-Century German Volkskunde," unpublished Ph.D. dissertation, University of Pennsylvania 2007.

Jacques-Lefèvre, Nicole, *Louis-Claude de Saint-Martin, le philosophe inconnu (1743–1803)*, Dervy: Paris 2003.

Jambet, Christian, "Henry Corbin et l'histoire," in: Mohammed Ali Amir-Mouzzi, Christian Jambet, and Pierre Lory (eds.), *Henry Corbin: Philosophies et sagesses des religions du livre*, Brepols: Turnhout 2005, 11–20.

Jardine, Nick, "Etics and Emics (not to mention Anemics and Emetics) in the History of the Sciences," *History of Science* 42 (2004), 261–278.

Jay, Martin, *The Dialectical Imagination: A History of the Frankfurt School and the Institute of Social Research, 1923–1950* (1973), University of California Press: Berkeley / Los Angeles / London 1996.

Jehl, Rainer, "Jacob Brucker und die 'Encyclopédie'," in: Schmidt-Biggemann and Stammen, *Jacob Brucker*, 238–256.

J. M. D. R. (Jean Maugin de Richebourg), *Bibliothèque des philosophes chimiques* (Lenglet Dufresnoy, ed.), vol. 1, André Cailleau: Paris 1741.

Jobe, Thomas Harmon, "The Devil in Restoration Science: The Glanvill–Webster Witchcraft Debate," *Isis* 72:3 (1981), 343–356.

Joël, Karl, *Der Ursprung der Naturphilosophie aus dem Geiste der Mystik*, Friedrich Reinhardt: Basle 1903.

Jollivet-Castelot, François, Paul Ferniot, and Paul Redonnel, *Les sciences maudites*, Éditions de la Maison d'Art: Paris 1900.

Jones, Marjorie G., *Frances Yates and the Hermetic Tradition*, Ibis Press: Lake Worth 2008.

Jong, Albert F. de, *Traditions of the Magi: Zoroastrianism in Greek and Latin Literature*, Brill: Leiden / New York / Cologne 1997.

"The Contribution of the Magi," in: Vesta Sarkhosh Curtis and Sarah Stewart (eds.), *Birth of the Persian Empire*, vol. 1, I. B. Tauris: London / New York 2005, 85–97.

Josephus, Flavius, *Against Apion* (John M. G. Barclay, ed. and comm.), Brill: Leiden / Boston 2007.

Josten, C. H. (ed.), *Elias Ashmole (1617–1692): His Autobiographical and Historical Notes, his Correspondence, and Other Contemporary Sources Relating to his Life and Work*, vols. I–II, Clarendon Press: Oxford 1966.

Jung, Carl Gustav, *Zur Psychologie und Pathologie sogenannter occulter Phänomene: Eine Psychiatrische Studie*, Oswald Mutze: Leipzig 1902.

Wandlungen und Symbole der Libido: Beiträge zur Entwicklungsgeschichte des Denkens (1912), 2nd edn, Franz Deuticke: Leipzig / Vienna 1925.

"Die Bedeutung der Psychologie für die Gegenwart," in: Jung, *Wirklichkeit der Seele: Anwendungen und Fortschritte der neueren Psychologie*, Rascher & Cie: Zurich / Leipzig / Stuttgart 1934, 32–67.

"Die Erlösungsvorstellungen in der Alchemie," *Eranos-Jahrbuch 1936*, Rhein-Verlag: Zurich 1937, 13–111.

"The Idea of Redemption in Alchemy," in: Stanley Dell (ed.), *The Integration of the Personality*, Farrar and Rinehart: New York 1939, 205–280.

Psychologie und Alchemie (1944), Walter-Verlag: Olten / Freiburg i.Br. 1975.

"Über Synchronizität," *Eranos Jahrbuch 20*, Rhein-Verlag: Zurich 1952, 271–284.

"Synchronizität als ein Prinzip akausaler Zusammenhänge," in: *Naturerklärung und Psyche*, Rascher Verlag: Zurich 1952.

Symbols of Transformation: An Analysis of the Prelude to a Case of Schizophrenia, 2nd edn, Princeton University Press 1956.

Memories, Dreams, Reflections (Aniele Jaffé, ed.), Fontana: London 1995.

The Red Book: Liber Novus (Sonu Shamdasani, ed.), W. W. Norton & Co.: New York / London 2009.

Justin, *Apologie pour les chrétiens* (Charles Munier, ed. and trans.), Sources Chrétiennes 507, Les Éditions du Cerf: Paris 2006.

[Justin Martyr], *Writings of Saint Justin Martyr* (Thomas B. Falls, trans.), The Catholic University of America Press: Washington 1948.

Kabbalistes chrétiens, Albin Michel: Paris 1979.

Kahn, Didier, "L'alchimie sur la scène française aux XVIe et XVIIe siècles," *Chrysopoeia* 2:1 (1988), 62–96.

Alchimie et Paracelsisme en France (1567–1625), Droz: Geneva 2007.

Kaske, Carol V. and John R. Clark, "Introduction," in: Ficino, *Three Books on Life*, 3–90.

Kemp, Daren, *New Age: A Guide. Alternative Spiritualities from Aquarian Conspiracy to Next Age*, Edinburgh University Press 2004.

"Christians and New Age," in: Daren Kemp and James R. Lewis (eds.), *Handbook of New Age*, Brill: Leiden / Boston 2007, 453–472.

Kemper, Hans-Georg, *Gottebenbildlichkeit und Naturnachahmung im Säkularisierungsprozeß: Problemgeschichtliche Studien zur deutschen Lyrik in Barock und Aufklärung*, 2 vols., Max Niemeyer: Tübingen 1981.

"Aufgeklärter Hermetismus: Brockes' *Irdisches Vergnügen in Gott* im Spiegel seiner Bibliothek," in: Neugebauer-Wölk, *Aufklärung und Esoterik* (1999), 140–169.

Kerner, Justinus, *Die Seherin von Prevorst: Eröffnungen über das innere Leben des Menschen und über das Hereinragen einer Geisterwelt in die unsere* (1829), Reclam: Leipzig 1846.

Geschichten Besessener neuerer Zeit: Beobachtungen aus dem Gebiete kakodämonisch-magnetischer Erscheinungen, J. Wachendorf: Stuttgart 1834.

Kerr, Howard and Charles L. Crow (eds.), *The Occult in America: New Historical Perspectives*, University of Illinois Press: Urbana and Chicago 1983.

Kervella, André and Philippe Lestienne, "Un haut-grade templier dans des milieux jacobites en 1750: l'Ordre Sublime des Chevaliers Elus aux sources de la Stricte Observance," *Renaissance Traditionnelle* 28 / 112 (1997), 229–266.

Kibre, Pearl, "Lynn Thorndike," *Osiris* 11 (1954), 5–22.

Kieckhefer, Richard, *Magic in the Middle Ages*, Cambridge University Press 1989.

"The Specific Rationality of Magic," *The American Historical Review* 99 (1994), 813–836.

"Did Magic have a Renaissance? An Historiographical Question Revisited," in: Charles Burnett and W. F. Ryan (eds.), *Magic and the Classical Tradition*, The Warburg Institute / Nino Aragno: London / Turin 2006, 199–212.

Kiesewetter, Carl, *Geschichte des neueren Okkultismus: Geheimwissenschaftliche Systeme von Agrippa von Nettesheim bis zu Carl du Prel* (1891–1895), Marix Verlag: Wiesbaden 2007.

Kilcher, Andreas B., *Die Sprachtheorie der Kabbala als ästhetisches Paradigma: Die Konstruktion einer ästhetischen Kabbala seit der frühen Neuzeit*, J. B. Metzler: Stuttgart / Weimar 1998.

"Das Orakel der Vernunft: Poetik und Politik des satirischen Schreibens in Marquis d'Argens' *Kabbalistischen Briefen*," in: Hans-Ulrich Seifert and Jean-Loup Seban (eds.), *Der Marquis d'Argens*, Harrassowitz: Wiesbaden 2004, 179–202.

"Verhüllung und Enthüllung des Geheimnisses: Die *Kabbala Denudata* im Okkultismus der Moderne," in: Kilcher (ed.), *Die Kabbala Denudata: Text und Kontext. Akten der 15. Tagung der Christian Knorr von Rosenroth-Gesellschaft*, published in *Morgen-Glantz* 16 (2006), 343–383.

"Seven Epistemological Theses on Esotericism: Upon the Occasion of the 10th Anniversary of the Amsterdam Chair," in: Hanegraaff and Pijnenburg, *Hermes in the Academy*, 143–148.

King, Francis X., *The Flying Sorcerer: Being the Magical and Aeronautical Adventures of Francis Barrett, author of The Magus*, Mandrake: Oxford 1992.

Kippenberg, Hans G., "Intellektuellen-Religion," in: Antes and Pahnke, *Religion von Oberschichten*, 181–201.

Kippenberg, Hans G., Jörg Rüpke, and Kocku von Stuckrad (eds.), *Europäische Religionsgeschichte: Ein mehrfacher Pluralismus*, 2 vols., Vandenhoeck & Ruprecht: Göttingen 2009.

Kirsop, Wallace, "Les collections de livres alchimiques entre 1700 et 1830: Adeptes, curieux et bibliophiles," in: Caron *et al.*, *Ésotérisme*, 101–111.

Kluge, Carl Alexander Ferdinand, *Versuch einer Darstellung des animalischen Magnetismus, als Heilmittel*, Franz Haas: Vienna 1815.

Klutstein, Ilana, *Marsilio Ficino et la théologie ancienne: Oracles Chaldaïques, Hymnes Orphiques, Hymnes de Proclus*, Leo S. Olschki: Florence 1987.

"Marsile Ficin et les 'Oracles Chaldaïques'," in: Garfagnini, *Marsilio Ficino*, 331–338.

Knoop, Douglas, G. P. Jones, and Douglas Hamer (eds.), *Early Masonic Pamphlets*, Q.C. Correspondence Circle: London 1978.

Knuttel, W. P. C., *Balthasar Bekker, de bestrijder van het bijgeloof*, Bouma's Boekhuis / Bert Hagen: Groningen / Castricum 1979.

Koch, Katharina, *Franz Joseph Molitor und die jüdische Tradition: Studien zu den kabbalistischen Quellen der "Philosophie der Geschichte"*, Walter de Gruyter: Berlin / New York 2006.

Koets, Peter John, Δεισιδαιμονία*: A Contribution to the Knowledge of the Religious Terminology in Greek*, Muusses: Purmerend 1929.

Kohl, Karl-Heinz, "Geschichte der Religionswissenschaft," in: Hubert Cancik, Burkhard Gladigow, and Matthias Laubscher (eds.), *Handbuch religionswissenschaftlicher Grundbegriffe*, vol. 1, W. Kohlhammer: Stuttgart / Berlin / Cologne / Mainz 1988, 217–262.

Köpke, Balthasar, *Sapientia Dei, in Mysterio Crucis Christi abscondita, Die wahre Theologia Mystica oder Ascetica . . . Entgegen gesetzet der falschen aus der heydnischen Philosophia Platonis und seiner Nachfolger*, Verlegung des Waysen-Hauses: Halle 1700.

Koyré, Alexandre, *La philosophie de Jacob Boehme*, J. Vrin: Paris 1929.

"Paracelse," in: Koyré, *Mystiques, spirituels, alchimistes du XVIe siècle allemand*, Gallimard: Paris 1971, 75–129.

Kranenborg, Reender, "The Presentation of the Essenes in Western Esotericism," *Journal of Contemporary Religion* 13:2 (1998), 245–256.

Krause, Carl, *Der Briefwechsel des Mutianus Rufus*, A. Freyschmidt Hof-Buchhandlung: Kassel 1885.

Kraye, Jill, "Ficino in the Firing Line: A Renaissance Neoplatonist and his Critics," in: Allen and Rees, *Marsilio Ficino*, 377–397.

Kripal, Jeffrey J., *Esalen: America and the Religion of No Religion*, The University of Chicago Press: Chicago / London 2007.

Kripal, Jeffrey J. and Glenn W. Shuck (eds.), *On the Edge of the Future: Esalen and the Evolution of American Culture*, Indiana University Press: Bloomington and Indianapolis 2005.

Kristeller, Paul Oskar, *Supplementum Ficinianum: Marsilii Ficini Florentini Philosophi Platonici opuscula inedita et dispersa primum collegit et ex fontibus plerumque manuscriptis edidit*, 2 vols., Leo S. Olschki: Florence 1937.

"Marsilio Ficino e Lodovico Lazzarelli: Contributo alla diffusione delle idee ermetiche nel Rinascimento," Annali della R. Scuola Normale Superiore di Pisa, Lettere, Storia e Filosofia 2 (1938), 237–262; repr. in: Kristeller, *Studies*, vol. I, 221–247.

The Philosophy of Marsilio Ficino (1943), Peter Lang: Gloucester, Mass. 1964.

"Ancora per Giovanni Mercurio da Correggio" (1941), in: Kristeller, *Studies*, vol. I, 249–257.

Studies in Renaissance Thought and Letters, vol. I, Edizioni di Storia e Letteratura: Rome 1956.

"Lodovico Lazzarelli et Giovanni da Correggio, due ermetici del Quattrocento, e il manoscritto II.D.I.4 della Biblioteca Comunale degli Ardenti di Viterbo (1960), in: Kristeller, *Studies*, vol. III, 207–225.

Studies in Renaissance Thought and Letters, vol. III, Edizioni di Storia e Letteratura: Rome 1993.

"Marsilio Ficino as a Beginning Student of Plato," in: Kristeller, *Studies*, vol. III, 93–108.

Kristeller, Paul Oskar and Margaret L. King, "Iter Kristellerianum: The European Journey (1905–1939)," *Renaissance Quarterly* 47:4 (1994), 907–929.

Labriolle, Pierre de, *La réaction païenne: Etude sur la polémique antichrétienne du Ier au VIe siècle*, Les Éditions du Cerf: Paris 2005.

Lactantius, *Divine Institutes* (Anthony Bowen and Peter Garnsey, ed. and trans.), Liverpool University Press 2003.

Lagarde, Bernadette, "Le *De differentiis* de Pléthon d'après l'autographe de la Marcienne," *Byzantion* 43 (1973), 312–343.

Laistner, M. L. W., "The Western Church and Astrology during the Middle Ages," *Harvard Theological Review* 34:4 (1941), 251–275.

Lancre, Pierre de, *On the Inconstancy of Witches: Pierre de Lancre's Tableau de l'inconstance des mauvais anges et demons* (1612) (Gerhild Scholz Williams, Michaela Giesenkirchen, and John Morris, eds.; Harriet Stone and Gerhard

Scholz Williams, trans.), Arizona Center for Medieval and Renaissance Studies / Brepols: Tempe / Turnhout 2006.

Lange, Ursula, *Untersuchungen zu Bodins Demonomanie*, Vittorio Klostermann: Frankfurt a.M. 1970.

Laufer, Roger, "Introduction," in: Montfaucon de Villars, *Le Comte de Gabalis* (1963), 7–64.

Laurant, Jean-Pierre, *Symbolisme et écriture: Le cardinal Pitra et la "Clef" de Méliton de Sardes*, Les Éditions du Cerf: Paris 1988.

L'ésotérisme chrétien en France au XIXe siècle, L'Âge d'Homme: Lausanne 1992.

L'ésotérisme, Les Éditions du Cerf: Paris 1993.

"Ragon de Bettignies, Jean-Marie," in: Hanegraaff *et al.*, *Dictionary*, 976.

"Matter, Jacques," in: François Laplanche (ed.), *Les sciences religieuses: 1800–1914*, Beauchesne: Paris 1996, 462–463.

"*Politica Hermetica*: Une expérience de vingt-cinq ans," *Politica Hermetica* 23 (2009), 13–20.

Laurent, V. (ed.), *Les "mémoires" du Grand Ecclésiarque de l'Église de Constantinople Sylvestre Syropoulos sur le concile de Florence (1438–1439)*, Éditions du CNRS: Paris 1971.

Lauster, Jörg, "Marsilio Ficino as a Christian Thinker: Theological Aspects of his Platonism," in: Allen and Rees, *Marsilio Ficino*, 45–69.

Lazzarelli, Lodovico, "Three Prefaces Addressed to Giovanni 'Mercurio' da Correggio," in: Hanegraaff and Bouthoorn, *Lodovico Lazzarelli*, 151–163.

Lebrun, François, "Le *Traité des superstitions* de Jean-Baptiste Thiers: Contribution à l'ethnographie de la France du XVIIe siècle," in: Lebrun, *Croyances et cultures dans la France d'Ancien Régime*, Les Éditions du Seuil: Paris 2001, 107–136.

Lehmann, Hartmut and Anne-Charlott Trepp (eds.), *Im Zeichen der Krise: Religiosität im Europa des 17. Jahrhunderts*, Vandenhoeck & Ruprecht: Göttingen 1999.

Lehmann-Brauns, Sicco, *Weisheit in der Weltgeschichte: Philosophiegeschichte zwischen Barock und Aufklärung*, Max Niemeyer: Tübingen 2004.

Lehrich, Christopher I., *The Language of Demons and Angels: Cornelius Agrippa's Occult Philosophy*, Brill: Leiden / Boston 2003.

Leijenhorst, Cees, "Francesco Patrizi's Hermetic Philosophy," in: van den Broek and Hanegraaff, *Gnosis and Hermeticism*, 125–146.

Lenglet Dufresnoy, Nicolas, *Histoire de la philosophie hermétique, accompagnée d'un Catalogue raisonné des Ecrivains de cette Science, Avec le Véritable Philalethe, revû sur les Originaux*, 3 vols., Coustelier: Paris 1742.

Lepper, John Heron, *Famous Secret Societies*, Low, Marston & Co.: London 1932.

Leventhal, Herbert, *In the Shadow of the Enlightenment: Occultism and Renaissance Science in Eighteenth-Century America*, New York University Press 1976.

Lévi, Éliphas, *Secrets de la magie (Dogme et rituel de la haute magie; Histoire de la magie; La clef des grands mystères)* (Francis Lacassin, ed.), Robert Laffont: Paris 2000.

Lévy-Bruhl, Lucien, *Les fonctions mentales dans les sociétés inférieures*, Presses Universitaires de France: Paris 1951.

Carnets (1949), Presses Universitaires de France: Paris 1998.

Lewin, Nicholas, *Jung on War, Politics and Nazi Germany: Exploring the Theory of Archetypes and the Collective Unconscious*, Karnac: London 2009.

Lewis, James R. and Olav Hammer (eds.), *The Invention of Sacred Tradition*, Cambridge University Press 2007.

Lewy, Hans, *Chaldaean Oracles and Theurgy: Mysticism, Magic and Platonism in the Later Roman Empire* (Michel Tardieu, ed.), Études Augustiniennes: Paris 1978.

Liber Scha'ar ha-Schamaiim seu Porta Coelorum In quo Dogmata Cabbalistica... Philosophice proponuntur & explicantur, cumque Philosophia Platonica conferuntur, in: Christian Knorr von Rosenroth*, Kabbala Denudata, seu doctrina Hebraeorum transcendentalis et metaphysica atque theologica opus, Antiquissimae Philosophiae Barbaricae variis speciminibus refertissimum: Apparatus in librum Sohar pars tertia & quarta*, Abraham Lichtenthaler: Sulzbach 1678.

Liebmann, Otto, *Zur Analysis der Wirklichkeit: Eine Erörterung der Grundprobleme der Philosophie*, 4th edn, Trübner: Strasbourg 1911.

Lilla, Salvatore R. C., *Clement of Alexandria: A Study of Christian Platonism and Gnosticism*, Oxford University Press 1971.

Lindberg, David C., "The Transmission of Greek and Arabic Learning to the West," in: Lindberg (ed.), *Science in the Middle Ages*, The University of Chicago Press: Chicago / London 1978, 52–90.

Longo, Mario, "La storia della filosofia tra eclettismo e pietismo," in: Santinello, *Storia delle storie*, vol. II, 329–421.

"La teoria della 'historia philosophica'," in: Santinello, *Storia delle storie*, vol. II, 423–476.

"Storia 'critica' della filosofia e primo illuminismo: Jakob Brucker," in: Santinello, *Storia delle storie*, vol. II, 527–635.

"Geistige Anregungen und Quellen der Bruckerschen Historiographie," in: Schmidt-Biggemann and Stammen, *Jacob Brucker*, 159–186.

Lory, Pierre, "Note sur l'ouvrage *Religion after Religion: Gershom Scholem, Mircea Eliade and Henry Corbin at Eranos* par Steven M. Wasserstrom," *Archaeus* 9 (2005), 107–113.

"Sexual Intercourse between Humans and Demons in the Islamic Tradition," in: Hanegraaff and Kripal, *Hidden Intercourse*, 49–64.

Lovejoy, Arthur O., *The Great Chain of Being: A Study of the History of an Idea* (1936), Harvard University Press: Cambridge, Mass. / London 1964.

Luhrmann, Tanya M., *Persuasions of the Witch's Craft: Ritual Magic in Contemporary England*, Harvard University Press: Cambridge, Mass. 1989.

Lukács, Georg, *Die Zerstörung der Vernunft* (1954), Luchterhand: Darmstadt / Neuwied 1974.

Lyon, Gregory B., "Baudouin, Flacius, and the Plan for the Magdeburg Centuries," *Journal of the History of Ideas* 64:2 (2003), 253–272.

MacLean, Ian, "Foucault's Renaissance Episteme Reassessed: An Aristotelian Counterblast," *Journal of the History of Ideas* 59:1 (1998), 149–166.

Magee, Glenn Alexander, *Hegel and the Hermetic Tradition*, Cornell University Press: Ithaca / London 2001.

"Hegel on the Paranormal: Altered States of Consciousness in the Philosophy of Subjective Spirit," *Aries* 8:1 (2008), 21–36.

Magee, Glenn Alexander (ed.), *The Cambridge Companion to Western Mysticism and Esotericism*, Cambridge University Press 2012.

Maidenbaum, Aryeh (ed.), *Jung and the Shadow of Antisemitism*, Nicolas-Hays: Berwick 2002.

Maillard, Christine, "Le 'mystique' de la psyché: De la philosophie du mysticisme à la psychanalyse," in: Baßler and Châtellier, *Mystique, mysticisme et modernité*, 75–93.

Majercik, Ruth, *The Chaldean Oracles: Text, Translation, and Commentary*, Brill: Leiden / New York / Copenhagen / Cologne 1989.

"Introduction," in: Majercik, *Chaldean Oracles*, 1–46.

Malinowski, Bronislaw, "Magic, Science and Religion," in: *Magic, Science and Religion and Other Essays* (1948), Waveland: Prospect Heights, Ill. 1992, 17–92.

Mallary Masters, G., "Renaissance Kabbalah," in: Faivre and Needleman, *Modern Esoteric Spirituality*, 132–153.

Malusa, Luciano, "Renaissance Antecedents to the Historiography of Philosophy," in: Bottin *et al.*, *Models of the History of Philosophy*, 3–65.

"The First General Histories of Philosophy in England and the Low Countries," in: Bottin *et al.*, *Models of the History of Philosophy*, 161–369.

Mandosio, Jean-Marc, "La place de l'alchimie dans les classifications des sciences et des arts à la Renaissance," *Chrysopoeia* 4: 1990–1991 (1993), 199–282.

"Quelques aspects de l'alchimie dans les classifications des sciences et des arts au XVIIe siècle," in: Greiner, *Aspects de la tradition alchimique*, 19–61.

Mansfeld, Jaap, "Bothering the Infinite: Anaximander in the Nineteenth Century and Beyond," *Antiquòrum philosophia* 3 (2009), 9–68.

Marcel, Raymond, *Marsile Ficin (1433–1499)*, Les Belles Lettres: Paris 1958.

Marconis de Nègre, Jacques-Étienne, *Le sanctuaire de Memphis ou Hermès, développements complets des mystères maçonniques*, Bruyer: Paris 1849.

Margolin, Jean-Claude and Sylvain Matton (eds.), *Alchimie et philosophie à la Renaissance*, J. Vrin: Paris 1993.

Markus, Robert A., "Augustine on Magic: A Neglected Semiotic Theory," *Revue des Études Augustiniennes* 40 (1994), 375–388.

Martin, Dale B., *Inventing Superstition: From the Hippocratics to the Christians*, Harvard University Press: Cambridge, Mass. / London 2004.

Masai, François, *Pléthon et le Platonisme de Mistra*, Les Belles Lettres: Paris 1956.

"Pléthon, l'Averroïsme et le problème religieux," in: *Le néoplatonisme*, Éditions du CNRS: Paris 1971, 435–446.

Masuzawa, Tomoko, "Reflections on the Charmed Circle," *Journal of the American Academy of Religion* 69:2 (2001), 429–436.

Matter, Jacques, *Histoire critique du gnosticisme et de son influence sur les sectes religieuses et philosophiques des six premiers siècles de l'ère chrétienne*, 2 vols., F. G. Levrault: Paris 1928.

Matton, Sylvain, "Quelques figures de l'antiplatonisme de la Renaissance à l'âge classique," in: Monique Dixsaut (ed.), *Contre Platon, vol. 1: Le Platonisme dévoilé*, J. Vrin: Paris 1993, 357–413.

"Marsile Ficin et l'alchimie: Sa position, son influence," in: Margolin and Matton, *Alchimie et philosophie*, 123–192.

Maurice, Florian, "Die Mysterien der Aufklärung: Esoterische Traditionen in der Freimaurerei?," in: Neugebauer-Wölk, *Aufklärung und Esoterik* (1999), 274–287.

Mauss, Marcel, "Esquisse d'une théorie générale de la magie" (1902–1903), in: Mauss, *Sociologie et anthropologie* (1950), 6th edn, Quadrige / Presses Universitaires de France: Paris 1995, 3–141.

Mayer, Paola, *Jena Romanticism and its Appropriation of Jakob Böhme: Theosophy – Hagiography – Literature*, McGill-Queens University Press: Montreal and Kingston / London / Ithaca 1999.

Mayo, Thomas B. de, *The Demonology of William of Auvergne: By Fire and Sword*, The Edwin Mellen Press: Lewiston / Queenston / Lampeter 2007.

Mazet, Edmond, "Chevaliers Bienfaisants de la Cité Sainte," in: Hanegraaff *et al.*, *Dictionary*, 255–258.

McCalla, Arthur, "When is History not History?," *Historical Reflexions / Réflexions historiques* 20:3 (1994), 435–452.

A Romantic Historiosophy: The Philosophy of History of Pierre-Simon Ballanche, Brill: Leiden / Boston / Cologne 1998.

"Evolutionism and Early Nineteenth-Century Histories of Religions," *Religion* 28 (1998), 29–40.

"Antoine Faivre and the Study of Esotericism," *Religion* 31:4 (2001), 435–450.

McCutcheon, Russell T., *Manufacturing Religion: The Discourse on Sui Generis Religion and the Politics of Nostalgia*, Oxford University Press 1997.

McGinn, Bernard, "Cabalists and Christians: Reflections on Cabala in Medieval and Renaissance Thought," in: Richard H. Popkin and Gordon M. Weiner (eds.), *Jewish Christians and Christian Jews: From the Renaissance to the Enlightenment*, Kluwer: Dordrecht / Boston / London 1993, 11–34.

McGuire, J. E. and P. M. Rattansi, "Newton and the 'Pipes of Pan'," *Notes and Records of the Royal Society of London* 21:2 (1966), 108–143.

McGuire, William, *Bollingen: An Adventure in Collecting the Past*, Princeton University Press 1982.

McIntosh, Christopher, *Eliphas Lévi and the French Occult Revival*, Rider & Co.: London 1972.

The Rose Cross and the Age of Reason: Eighteenth-Century Rosicrucianism in Central Europe and its Relationship to the Enlightenment, Brill: Leiden / New York / Cologne 1992.

The Rosicrucians: The History, Mythology, and Rituals of an Esoteric Order, Samuel Weiser: York Beach 1997.

Medici, Lorenzo de', *Poemi* (G. Papini, ed.), R. Carabba: Lanciano 1911.

Méheust, Bertrand, *Somnambulisme et médiumnité (1784–1930)*, 2 vols., Institut Synthélabo: Le Plessis-Robinson 1999.

"Animal Magnetism/Mesmerism," in: Hanegraaff *et al.*, *Dictionary*, 75–82.

Meier-Oeser, Stephan, *Die Präsenz des Vergessenen: Zur Rezeption der Philosophie des Nicolaus Cusanus vom 15. bis zum 18. Jahrhundert*, Aschendorff: Münster 1989.

Meijering, Eginhard Peter, "Zehn Jahre Forschung zum Thema Platonismus und Kirchenväter," *Theologische Rundschau* N.F. 36:4 (1971), 303–320.

Meillassoux-Le Cerf, M., *Dom Pernety et les Illuminés d'Avignon, suivi de la transcription de la Sainte Parole*, Archè: Milan 1992.

Meinel, Christoph, *Die Alchemie in der europäischen Kultur- und Wissenschaftsgeschichte*, Otto Harrassowitz: Wiesbaden 1986.

"Okkulte und exakte Wissenschaften," in: Buck, *Die okkulten Wissenschaften*, 21–43.

[Meiners, Christoph], *Revision der Philosophie*, vol. 1, Johann Christian Dieterich: Göttingen / Gotha 1772.

Meinhold, Peter, *Geschichte der kirchlichen Historiographie*, vol. 1, Karl Alber: Freiburg / Munich 1967.

Mendes-Flohr, Paul, "Introductory Essay: The Spiritual Quest of the Philologist," in: Mendes-Flohr (ed.), *Gershom Scholem: The Man and his Work*, State University of New York Press / The Israel Academy of Sciences and Humanities: Albany / Jerusalem 1994, 1–28.

Menocal, María Rosa, *The Ornament of the World: How Muslims, Jews, and Christians Created a Culture of Tolerance in Medieval Spain*, Little, Brown and Company: Boston / New York / London 2002.

Mercati, A., *Il Sommario del Processo di Giordano Bruno*, Biblioteca Apostolica Vaticana: Vatican City 1942.

Merkel, Ingrid and Allen G. Debus (eds.), *Hermeticism and the Renaissance: Intellectual History and the Occult in Early Modern Europe*, Folger Books: Washington / London / Toronto 1988.

Mertens, Michèle (ed. and trans.), *Zosime de Panopolis: Mémoires authentiques* (*Les alchimistes grecs* IV.1), Les Belles Lettres: Paris 1995.

[Mesmer, Franz Anton], *Kurze Geschichte des thierischen Magnetismus bis April 1781*, Michael Macklot: Karlsruhe 1783.

Mesnard, Pierre, "La démonomanie de Jean Bodin," in: *L'opera e il pensiero di Giovanni Pico della Mirandola nella storia dell'umanesimo*, vol. II, Florence 1965, 333–356.

Meumann, Markus, "Diskursive Formationen zwischen Esoterik, Pietismus und Aufklärung: Halle um 1700," in: Neugebauer-Wölk (ed.), *Aufklärung und Esoterik* (2008), 77–114.

Meyer, J. F. von, "Die Schutzgeister," *Magikon* 1 (1840), 152–161.

Micheli, Giuseppe, "The History of Philosophy in Germany in the Second Half of the Seventeenth Century," in: Bottin *et al.*, *Models of the History of Philosophy*, 371–473.

Michels, Karen, "Die Kulturwissenschaftliche Bibliothek Warburg," in: Faber and Holste, *Kreise, Gruppen, Bünde*, 225–238.

Millen, Ron, "The Manifestation of Occult Qualities in the Scientific Revolution," in: Margaret J. Osler and Paul Lawrence Farber (eds.), *Religion, Science, and Worldview: Essays in Honor of Richard S. Westfall*, Cambridge University Press 1985, 185–216.

Miller, Clyde Lee, *Reading Cusanus: Metaphor and Dialectic in a Conjectural Universe*, The Catholic University of America Press: Washington 2003.

Minns, Denis and Paul Parvis (ed. and comm.), *Justin, Philosopher and Martyr: Apologies*, Oxford University Press 2009.

Moellering, H. Armin, *Plutarch on Superstition: Plutarch's De Superstitione, its Place in the Changing Meaning of Deisidaimonia and in the context of his Theological Writings*, The Christopher Publishing House: Boston 1963.

Moldaenke, Günter, *Schriftverständnis und Schriftdeutung im Zeitalter der Reformation. Teil 1: Matthias Flacius Illyricus*, W. Kohlhammer: Stuttgart 1936.

Molland, Einar, *The Conception of the Gospel in the Alexandrian Theology*, Jacob Dybwad: Oslo 1938.

Möller, Helmut and Ellic Howe, *Merlin Peregrinus: Vom Untergrund des Abendlandes*, Königshausen & Neumann: Würzburg 1986.

Mollier, Pierre, "Des Franc-Maçons aux Templiers: Aperçus sur la constitution d'une légende au siècle des lumières," in: *Symboles et mythes dans les mouvements initiatiques et ésotériques (XVIIe–XXe siècles): Filiations et emprunts* (Special issue *ARIES*), Archè / La Table d'Émeraude: Paris 1999, 93–101.

"Neo-Templar Traditions," in: Hanegraaff *et al.*, *Dictionary*, 849–853.

Monfasani, John, *George of Trebizond: A Biography and Study of his Rhetoric and Logic*, Brill: Leiden 1976.

Review of Woodhouse, *Renaissance Quarterly* 41:1 (1988), 116–119.

"Platonic Paganism in the Fifteenth Century," in: Mario A. di Cesare (ed.), *Reconsidering the Renaissance: Papers from the Twenty-First Annual Conference*, Medieval & Renaissance Texts & Studies: Binghamton, New York 1992, 45–61.

"Marsilio Ficino and the Plato–Aristotle Controversy," in: Allen and Rees, *Marsilio Ficino*, 179–202.

"A Tale of Two Books: Bessarion's *In Calumniatorem Platonis* and George of Trebizond's *Comparatio Philosophorum Platonis et Aristotelis*," *Renaissance Studies* 22:1 (2007), 1–15.

Monfasani, John (ed.), *Collectanea Trapezuntiana: Texts, Documents, and Bibliographies of George of Trebizond*, Medieval & Renaissance Texts & Studies / Renaissance Society of America: Binghamton, NY 1984.

Mora, George (ed.), in collaboration with Benjamin Kohl (associate ed.), John Shea (trans.), John Weber, Erik Midelfort, and Helen Bacon, *Witches, Devils, and Doctors in the Renaissance: Johann Weyer, De praestigiis daemonum*, Medieval & Renaissance Texts & Studies: Tempe, Ariz. 1998.

Moran, Bruce, "Paracelsianism," in: Hanegraaff *et al.*, *Dictionary*, 915–922.

Moreau, J., "Eusebius von Caesarea," in: Theodor Klauser *et al.* (eds.), *Reallexikon für Antike und Christentum: Sachwörterbuch zur Auseinandersetzung des Christentums mit der antiken Welt*, vol. VI, Anton Hiersemann: Stuttgart 1966, 1052–1088.

Mosès, Stéphane, *L'ange de l'histoire: Rosenzweig, Benjamin, Scholem*, Les Éditions du Seuil: Paris 1992.

Mozzani, Eloïse, *Magie et superstitions de la fin de l'Ancien Régime à la Restauration*, Robert Laffont: Paris 1988.

Mras, Karl, *Die Praeparatio Evangelica*, vol. II, Akademie-Verlag: Berlin 1956.

Muccillo, Maria, *Platonismo, Ermetismo e "Prisca Theologia": Ricerche di storiografia filosofica rinascimentale*, Leo S. Olschki: Florence 1996.

"La 'prisca theologia' nel 'De perenni philosophia' di Agostino Steuco," *Rinascimento* 28 (1988), 41–111.

Mühlpfordt, Günter, "Ein kryptoradikaler Thomasianer: C. A. Heumann, der Thomasius von Göttingen," in: Schneiders, *Christian Thomasius*, 305–334.

Müller, Baal, *Kosmik: Prozeßontologie und temporale Poetik bei Ludwig Klages und Alfred Schuler. Zur Philosophie und Dichtung der Schwabinger Kosmischen Runde*, Telesma: n.p. 2007.

Müller-Jahncke, Wolf-Dieter, "Makrokosmos und Mikrokosmos bei Paracelsus," in: Volker Zimmermann (ed.), *Paracelsus: Das Werk – die Rezeption*, Franz Steiner: Stuttgart 1995, 59–66.

Mulsow, Martin, *Moderne aus dem Untergrund: Radikale Frühaufklärung in Deutschland 1680–1720*, Felix Meiner: Hamburg 2002.

"Reaktionärer Hermetismus vor 1600? Zum Kontext der venezianischen Debatte über die Datierung von Hermes Trismegistos," in: Mulsow, *Ende des Hermetismus*, 161–185.

"'Philosophia italica' als reduzierte prisca-sapientia-Ideologie: Antonio Persios und Francesco Patrizis Rekonstruktion der Elementenlehre," in: Mulsow, *Ende des Hermetismus*, 253–280.

"Epilog: Das schnelle und das langsame Ende des Hermetismus," in: Mulsow, *Ende des Hermetismus*, 305–310.

"Ambiguities of the *Prisca Sapientia* in Late Renaissance Humanism," *Journal of the History of Ideas* 65:1 (2004), 1–13.

Mulsow, Martin (ed.), *Das Ende des Hermetismus: Historische Kritik und neue Naturphilosophie in der Spätrenaissance. Dokumentation und Analyse der Debattte um die Datierung der hermetischen Schriften von Genebrard bis Casaubon (1567–1614)*, Mohr Siebeck: Tübingen 2002.

Munck, Johannes, *Untersuchungen über Klemens von Alexandrien*, W. Kohlhammer: Stuttgart 1933.

Mussies, Gerard, "The Interpretatio Judaica of Thot-Hermes," in: M. Heerma van Voss, D. J. Hoens, G. Mussies, D. van der Plas, and H. te Velde (eds.), *Studies in Egyptian Religion Dedicated to Professor Jan Zandee*, Brill: Leiden 1982, 89–120.

"Moses," in: Hanegraaff *et al.*, *Dictionary*, 804–806.

Nagel, Alexandra H. M., "Marriage with Elementals: From *Le Comte de Gabalis* to a Golden Dawn Ritual," unpubl. Master Thesis, University of Amsterdam 2007.

Napoli, Giovanni di, "Il concetto di 'philosophia perennis' di Agostino Steuco nel quadro della tematica rinascimentale," in: di Napoli, *Studi sul Rinascimento*, Giannini: Naples 1973, 245–277.

Nasr, Seyyed Hossein, "Shihāb al-Dīn Suhrawardi Maqtūl," in: M. M. Sharif (ed.), *A History of Muslim Philosophy, with Short Accounts of Other Disciplines and the Modern Renaissance in Muslim Lands*, vol. 1, Otto Harrassowitz: Wiesbaden 1963, 372–398.

"Henry Corbin, 'L'exil occidental': Une vie et une oeuvre en quête de l'Orient des Lumières," in: Nasr, *Mélanges*, 3–27.

Nasr, Seyyed Hossein (ed.), *Mélanges offerts à Henry Corbin*, McGill University, Montreal, Canada Institute of Islamic Studies, Teheran Branch: Teheran 1977.

Naudé, Gabriel, *Apologie pour tous les grands personnages qui ont esté faussement soupçonnez de magie*, François Targa: Paris 1625.

Nauert, Charles G., *Agrippa and the Crisis of Renaissance Thought*, University of Illinois Press: Urbana 1965.

Needham, Joseph, *Science and Civilization in China, vol. II: History of Scientific Thought*, Cambridge University Press 1956.

Nestle, W., "Die Haupteinwände des antiken Denkens gegen das Christentum," *Archiv für Religionswissenschaft* 37 (1941–1942), 51–100.

Neugebauer, Otto, "The Study of Wretched Subjects," *Isis* 42:2 (1951), 111.

Neugebauer-Wölk, Monika, "Esoterik im 18. Jahrhundert – Aufklärung und Esoterik: Eine Einleitung," in: Neugebauer-Wölk, *Aufklärung und Esoterik* (1999), 1–37.

"'Höhere Vernunft' und 'höheres Wissen' als Leitbegriffe in der esoterischen Gesellschaftsbewegung: Vom Nachleben eines Renaissancekonzepts im Jahrhundert der Aufklärung," in: Neugebauer-Wölk, *Aufklärung und Esoterik* (1999), 170–210.

"Esoterik in der frühen Neuzeit: Zum Paradigma der Religionsgeschichte zwischen Mittelalter und Moderne," *Zeitschrift für historische Forschung* 27:3 (2000), 321–364.

"Esoterik und Christentum vor 1800: Prolegomena zu einer Bestimmung ihrer Differenz," *Aries* 3:2 (2003), 127–165.

"Aufklärung – Esoterik – Wissen: Transformationen des Religiösen im Säkularisierungsprozess: Eine Einführung," in: Neugebauer-Wölk, *Aufklärung und Esoterik* (2008), 5–28.

"From Talk about Esotericism to Esotericism Research: Remarks on the Prehistory and Development of a Research Group," in: Hanegraaff and Pijnenburg, *Hermes in the Academy*, 135–141.

"Der Esoteriker und die Esoterik: Wie das Esoterische im 18. Jahrhundert zum Begriff wird und seinen Weg in die Moderne findet," *Aries* 10:2 (2010), 217–231.

Neugebauer-Wölk, Monika (ed.) with Andre Rudolph, *Aufklärung und Esoterik: Rezeption, Integration, Konfrontation*, Max Niemeyer: Tübingen 2008.

Neugebauer-Wölk, Monika (ed.) with Holger Zaunstöck, *Aufklärung und Esoterik* (Studien zum Achtzehnten Jahrhundert 24), Felix Meiner: Hamburg 1999.

Newman, William R., *Gehennical Fire: The Lives of George Starkey, an American Alchemist in the Scientific Revolution*, Harvard University Press: Cambridge Mass. / London 1994.

"The Occult and the Manifest among the Alchemists," in: F. Jamil Ragep and Sally P. Ragep (eds.), *Tradition, Transmission, Transformation: Proceedings of Two Conferences on Pre-Modern Science held at the University of Oklahoma*, Brill: Leiden / New York / Cologne 1996, 173–198.

"*Decknamen* or Pseudochemical Language? Eirenaeus Philalethes and Carl Jung," *Revue d'Histoire des Sciences* 49:2–3 (1996), 159–188.

Promethean Ambitions: Alchemy and the Quest to Perfect Nature, The University of Chicago Press: Chicago / London 2004.

"Brian Vickers on Alchemy and the Occult: A Response," *Perspectives on Science* 17:4 (2009), 482–506.

Newman, William R. and Anthony Grafton, "Introduction: The Problematic Status of Astrology and Alchemy in Premodern Europe," in: Newman and Grafton, *Secrets of Nature*, 1–37.

Newman, William R. and Anthony Grafton (eds.), *Secrets of Nature: Astrology and Alchemy in Early Modern Europe*, The MIT Press: Cambridge, Mass. / London 2001.

Newman, William R. and Lawrence M. Principe, "Alchemy vs. Chemistry: The Etymological Origins of a Historiographic Mistake," *Early Science and Medicine* 3 (1998), 32–65.

Newman, William R. and Lawrence M. Principe (eds.), *Alchemy Tried in the Fire: Starkey, Boyle, and the Fate of Helmontian Chymistry*, The University of Chicago Press: Chicago / London 2002.

Nicolet, Jean and Michel Tardieu, "Plethon Arabicus: Identification et contenu du manuscrit arabe d'Istanbul, Topkapi Serāi, Ahmet III 1896," *Journal Asiatique* 268 (1980), 35–57.

Nock, Arthur Darby, Review of Carl Andresen, *Journal of Theological Studies*, n.s. 7 (1956), 314–317.

"Préface," in: Nock and Festugière, *Corpus Hermeticum*, vol. I, i–x.

Nock, A. D. and A.-J. Festugière, *Corpus Hermeticum*, 4 vols., Les Belles Lettres: Paris 1991, 1992, 2002.

Noll, Richard, *The Jung Cult: Origins of a Charismatic Movement*, Princeton University Press 1994.

Nooijen, Annemarie, *"Unserm grossen Bekker ein Denkmal"? Balthasar Bekkers Betoverde Weereld in den deutschen Landen zwischen Orthodoxie und Aufklärung*, Waxmann: Münster / New York / Munich / Berlin 2009.

Norton, Robert E., *Secret Germany: Stefan George and his Circle*, Cornell University Press: Ithaca / London 2002.

Nowotny, Karl Anton, "The Construction of Certain Seals and Characters in the Work of Agrippa of Nettesheim," *Journal of the Warburg and Courtauld Institutes* 12 (1949), 46–57.

Obrist, Barbara, *Les débuts de l'imagerie alchimique (XIVe–XVe siècles)*, Le Sycomore: Paris 1982.

"Die Alchemie in der mittelalterlichen Gesellschaft," in: Meinel, *Die Alchemie*, 33–59.

"Les rapports d'analogie entre philosophie et alchimie médiévales," in: Margolin and Matton, *Alchimie et philosophie*, 43–64.

Oexle, Otto Gerhard, "Krise des Historismus – Krise der Wirklichkeit: Eine Problemgeschichte der Moderne," in: Otto Gerhard Oexle (ed.), *Krise des Historismus – Krise der Wirklichkeit: Wissenschaft, Kunst und Literatur 1880–1932*, Vandenhoeck & Ruprecht: Göttingen 2007, 11–116.

Olson, Carl, "Theology of Nostalgia: Reflections on the Theological Aspects of Eliade's Work," *Numen* 36:1 (1989), 98–112.

Oppenheim, Janet, *The Other World: Spiritualism and Psychical Research in England, 1850–1914*, Cambridge University Press 1985.

Origen, *Contra Celsum* (Henry Chadwick, ed. and trans.), Cambridge University Press 1953.

Owen, Alex, *The Place of Enchantment: British Occultism and the Culture of the Modern*, The University of Chicago Press: Chicago / London 2004.

Pagel, Walter, "Jung's Views on Alchemy," *Isis* 39:1–2 (1948), 44–48.

Paracelsus: An Introduction to Philosophical Medicine in the Era of the Renaissance, S. Karger: Basle / New York 1958.

Panaino, Antonio, "De Zoroastre à Georges Gémiste Pléthon: Phénomènes d'interactions culturelles entre monde iranien, islamique et byzantin autour du bassin méditerranéen," in: Josiane Boulad-Ayoub and Gian Mario Cazzaniga (eds.), *Traces de l'autre: Mythes de l'antiquité et Peuples du Livre dans la construction des nations mediterranéennes*, Ets / Vrin: Pisa / Paris 2004, 321–341.

Paracelsus, *Sämtliche Werke* (Karl Sudhoff and Wilhelm Matthiessen, eds.), Oldenbourg: Munich 1933.

Theologische Werke 1: Vita Beata – Vom Seligen Leben (Urs Leo Gantenbein, ed. and intro., in collaboration with Michael Baumann and Detlef Roth), Walter de Gruyter: Berlin / New York 2008.

Parry, G. J. R., "Puritanism, Science and Capitalism: William Harrison and the Rejection of Hermes Trismegistus," *History of Science* 22:3 (1984), 245–270.

Partee, Charles, *Calvin and Classical Philosophy*, Brill: Leiden 1977.

Partridge, Christopher, *The Re-Enchantment of the West*, 2 vols., T & T Clark: London / New York 2004.

Parvis, Sara, "Justin Martyr and the Apologetic Tradition," in: Parvis and Foster, *Justin Martyr*, 115–127.

Parvis, Sara and Paul Foster (eds.), *Justin Martyr and his Worlds*, Fortress Press: Minneapolis 2007.

Pasi, Marco, "La notion de magie dans le courant occultiste en angleterre (1875–1947)," unpubl. Ph.D. dissertation, École Pratique des Hautes Études (Sorbonne): Paris 2004.

"Occultism," in: von Stuckrad, *Brill Dictionary of Religion*, vol. III, 1364–1368.

"Il problema della definizione dell'esoterismo: analisi critica e proposte per la ricerca futura," in: Grossato, *Forme e correnti*, 205–228.

"Theses de magia," *Societas Magica Newsletter* 20 (2008), 1–8.

"The Modernity of Occultism: Reflections on Some Crucial Aspects," in: Hanegraaff and Pijnenburg, *Hermes in the Academy*, 59–74.

"Correnti esoteriche occidentali," in: Alberto Melloni (ed.), *Dizionario del sapere storico-religioso del Novecento*, Il Mulino: Bologna 2010, 585–601.

Pasqually, Martines de, *Traité sur la réintégration des êtres dans leur première propriété, vertu et puissance spirituelle divine* (Robert Amadou, ed.), Diffusion Rosicrucienne: Le Tremblay 1995.

Passavant, Johann Carl, *Untersuchungen über den Lebensmagnetismus und das Hellsehen*, H. L. Brönner: Frankfurt a.M. 1821.

Pattison, Mark, *Isaac Casaubon, 1559–1614*, 2nd edn, Clarendon Press: Oxford 1892.

Paulet, Jean-Jacques, *L'antimagnétisme, ou origine, progrès, décadence, renouvellement et réfutation du magnétisme animal*, London 1784.

Pereira, Michela, *The Alchemical Corpus Attributed to Raymond Lull*, The Warburg Institute: London 1989.

Pernety, Antoine-Joseph, *Les fables egyptiennes et grecques dévoilées & réduites au même principe, avec une explication des hiéroglyphes, et de la guerre de Troye*, vol. I, Bauche: Paris 1758.

Perrone Compagni, Vittoria, "Introduction," in: Agrippa, *De occulta philosophia libri tres*, 1–53.

Petrarch, *Lettres familières: Tome III: Livres VIII–XI* (André Longpré, trans.; Ugo Dotti, ed.), Les Belles Lettres: Paris 2003.

Petrus Bonus, *Pretiosa margarita novella de thesauro, ac pretiosissimo philosophorum lapide*, Venice 1557.

Peuckert, Will-Erich, *Das Leben Jacob Böhmes*, Eugen Diederichs: Jena 1924.

Die Rosenkreutzer: Zur Geschichte der Reformation, Eugen Diederichs: Jena 1928.

Pansophie: Ein Versuch zur Geschichte der weissen und schwarzen Magie (1936), 2nd edn, Erich Schmidt: Berlin 1956.

Theophrastus Paracelsus, Kohlhammer: Stuttgart / Berlin 1941, 1943, 1944.

Sebastian Franck: Ein Deutscher Sucher, R. Piper & Co.: Munich 1943.

Die grosse Wende: Das apokalyptische Saeculum und Luther (1948), 2 vols., Wissenschaftliche Buchgesellschaft: Darmstadt 1966.

Geheim-Kulte, C. Pfeffer: Heidelberg 1951, repr. Nikol: Hamburg 2005.

Astrologie: Geschichte der Geheimwissenschaften Band 1, W. Kohlhammer: Stuttgart 1960.

Gabalia: Ein Versuch zur Geschichte der magia naturalis im 16. bis 18. Jahrhundert, Erich Schmidt: Berlin 1967.

Das Rosenkreutz, 2nd rev. edn, Erich Schmidt: Berlin 1973.

Piaia, Gregorio, "Jacob Bruckers Wirkungsgeschichte in Frankreich und Italien," in: Schmidt-Biggemann and Stammen, *Jacob Brucker*, 218–237.

Piatigorsky, Alexander, *Freemasonry: The Study of a Phenomenon*, The Harvill Press: London 1997.

Pico della Mirandola, Gianfrancesco, *Examen Vanitatis doctrinae gentium*, in: Giovanni Pico della Mirandola and Gian Francesco Pico, *Opera Omnia*, vol. II, facs. repr. Georg Olms: Hildesheim 1969, 710–1264.

Pico della Mirandola, Giovanni, *De hominis dignitate / Heptaplus / De ente et uno* (Eugenio Garin, ed.), Vallecchi: Florence 1942.

On the Dignity of Man / On Being and the One / Heptaplus (Charles Glenn Wallis, Paul J. W. Miller, and Douglas Carmichael, ed. and trans.), Hackett Publishing Company: Indianapolis / Cambridge 1965.

Oeuvres philosophiques (Olivier Boulnois and Giuseppe Tognon, ed. and trans.), Presses Universitaires de France: Paris 1993.

Commento sopra una canzone d'amore (Paolo de Angelis, ed.), Novecento: Palermo 1994.

Pietikäinen, Petteri, *C. G. Jung and the Psychology of Symbolic Forms*, Annales Academiae Scientiarum Fennicae: Saarijärvi 1999.

Pike, Kenneth L., *Language in Relation to a Unified Theory of the Structure of Human Behaviour, Pt. 1: Preliminary Edition* (1954), 2nd edn Mouton: The Hague 1971.

Pingree, David, "The Diffusion of Arabic Magical Texts in Western Europe," in: Biancamaria Scarcia Amoretti (ed.), *La diffusione delle scienze islamiche nel medioevo europeo*, Accademia Nazionale dei Lincei: Rome 1987, 57–102.

"Hellenophilia versus the History of Science," *Isis* 83:4 (1992), 554–563.

Pisi, Paola, "I 'tradizionalisti' e la formazione del pensiero di Eliade," in: Arcella, Pisi, and Scagno, *Confronto con Mircea Eliade*, 43–133.

Places, Édouard des (ed. and trans.), *Oracles Chaldaïques, avec un choix de commentaires anciens*, Les Belles Lettres: Paris 1996.

Planis Campy, David de, *L'ouverture de l'escolle de philosophie transmutatoire metallique, ou, La plus saine et veritable explication & conciliation de tous les Stiles desquels les Philosophes anciens se sont servis en traictant de l'oeuvre Physique, sont amplement déclarées*, Charles Sevestre: Paris 1633.

Plethon, George Gemistos, *Traité des Lois*, in: Rémi Brague, *Une cité idéale au XVe siècle: L'utopie néo-païenne d'un Byzantin. Pléthon: Traité des Lois*, J. Vrin: Paris 1982.

Plumpe, Gerhard, "Alfred Schuler und die 'Kosmische Runde'," in: Manfred Frank, *Gott im Exil: Vorlesungen über die neue Mythologie, II. Teil*, Suhrkamp: Frankfurt a.M. 1988, 212–256.

Plutarch, *Isis et Osiris*, in: *Plutarch, Oeuvres morales* v.2 (Christian Froidefond, ed. and trans.), Les Belles Lettres: Paris 1988.

Poel, Marc van der, *Cornelius Agrippa, the Humanist Theologian and his Declamations*, Brill: Leiden / New York / Cologne 1997.

Polman, P., "Flacius Illyricus, historien de l'église," *Revue d'histoire ecclésiastique* 27 (1931), 27–73.

L'élément historique dans la controverse religieuse du XVIe siècle, Duculot: Gembloux 1932.

Pope, Alexander, *Poetical Works* (Herbert Davis, ed.), Oxford University Press 1967.

Porphyrius, *"Gegen die Christen,"* 15 *Bücher: Zeugnisse, Fragmente und Referate* (Adolf van Harnack, ed.), Verlag der Königl. Akademie der Wissenschaften: Berlin 1916.

Porreca, David, "Hermes Trismegistus: William of Auvergne's Mythical Authority," *Archives d'Histoire Doctrinale et Littéraire du Moyen Age* 67 (2000), 143–158.

Postel, Guillaume, *Des admirables secrets des nombres platoniciens* (Jean-Pierre Brach, ed. and trans.), J. Vrin: Paris 2001.

Pott, Martin, *Aufklärung und Aberglaube: Die deutsche Frühaufklärung im Spiegel ihrer Aberglaubenskritik*, Max Niemeyer: Tübingen 1992.

"Christian Thomasius und Gottfried Arnold," in: Blaufuß and Niewöhner, *Gottfried Arnold*, 247–265.

Preisendanz, Karl, *Papyri graecae magicae / Die griechischen Zauberpapyri*, Teubner: Leipzig 1828.

Principe, Lawrence M., *The Aspiring Adept: Robert Boyle and his Alchemical Quest*, Princeton University Press 1998.

"Reflections on Newton's Alchemy in Light of the New Historiography of Alchemy," in: James E. Force and Sarah Hutton (eds.), *Newton and Newtonianism: New Studies*, Kluwer: Dordrecht / Boston / London 2004, 205–219.

"Alchemy I: Introduction," in: Hanegraaff *et al.*, *Dictionary*, 12–16.

" Revealing Analogies: The Descriptive and Deceptive Roles of Sexuality and Gender in Latin Alchemy," in: Hanegraaff and Kripal, *Hidden Intercourse*, 209–229.

The Secrets of Alchemy, The University of Chicago Press: Chicago / London 2012.

Principe, Lawrence M. (ed.), *Chymists and Chymistry: Studies in the History of Alchemy and Early Modern Chemistry*, Watson Publishing International: Sagamore Beach 2007.

Principe, Lawrence M. and William R. Newman, "Some Problems with the Historiography of Alchemy," in: Newman and Grafton, *Secrets of Nature*, 385–431.

Puech, Henri-Charles, "Numénius d'Apamée et les théologies orientales," in: *Mélanges Bidez*, vol. ii, Institut de philologie et d'histoire orientales: Brussels 1934, 745–778.

Puliafito, Anna Laura, "Searching for a New Physics: Metaphysics of Light and Ancient Knowledge in Francesco Patrizi da Cherso," in: Gilly and van Heertum, *Magia, alchimia, scienza*, vol. ii, 255–266.

"Hermetische Texte in Francesco Patrizis *Nova de Universis Philosophia*," in: Mulsow, *Ende des Hermetismus*, 237–251.

Pullapilly, Cyriac K., *Caesar Baronius: Counter-Reformation Historian*, University of Notre Dame Press: Notre Dame / London 1975.

Purnell, Frederick, "Francesco Patrizi and the Critics of Hermes Trismegistus," *Journal of Medieval and Renaissance Studies* 6:2 (1976), 155–178; repr. in Mulsow, *Ende des Hermetismus*, 105–126.

"A Contribution to Renaissance Anti-Hermeticism: The Angelucci–Persio Exchange," in: Mulsow, *Ende des Hermetismus*, 127–160.

"The Theme of Philosophic Concord and the Sources of Ficino's Platonism," in: Garfagnini, *Marsilio Ficino*, 397–415.

Quantin, Jean-Louis, *Le catholicisme classique et les pères de l'église: Un retour aux sources (1669–1713)*, Institut d'Études Augustiniennes: Paris 1999.

Quétel, Claude, *Histoire de la folie, de l'antiquité à nos jours*, Tallandier: Paris 2009.

Quispel, Gilles, *Gnosis als Weltreligion: Die Bedeutung der Gnosis in der Antike*, 2nd edn, Origo: Zurich 1972.

"Hesse, Jung und die Gnosis: Die 'Septem sermones ad mortuos' und Basilides," in: Quispel, *Gnostic Studies*, vol. II, Nederlands Historisch-Archaeologisch Instituut in het Nabije Oosten: Istanbul 1974, 241–258.

Rachewiltz, Siegfried de (ed.), *Joseph Ennemoser: Leben und Werk des Freiheitskämpfers, Mediziners und Magnetiseurs (1787–1854)*, Haymon Verlag: Innsbruck / Vienna 2010.

Ragon [de Bettignies], Jean-Marie, *Orthodoxie maçonnique, suivie de la maçonnerie occulte et de l'initiation hermétique*, E. Dentu: Paris 1853.

Raith, Werner, *Die Macht des Bildes: Ein humanistisches Problem bei Gianfrancesco Pico della Mirandola*, Wilhelm Fink: Munich 1967.

Ramaswamy, Sumathi, *The Lost Land of Lemuria: Fabulous Geographies, Catastrophic Histories*, University of California Press: Berkeley / Los Angeles / London 2004.

Raphael, *The Familiar Astrologer: An Easy Guide to Fate, Destiny, and Foreknowledge, as well as to the Secret and Wonderful Properties of Nature*, William Bennett: London 1841.

Raschke, Carl A., *Painted Black*, HarperCollins: New York 1990.

Rattansi, P. M., "Some Evaluations of Reason in Sixteenth- and Seventeenth-Century Natural Philosophy," in: M. Teich and R. Young (eds.), *Changing Perspectives in the History of Science*, Heinemann Educational: London 1973, 148–166.

Review of Westman and McGuire, *Journal of the History of Philosophy* 19:3 (1981), 392–396.

Reibnitz, Barbara von, "Der Eranos-Kreis: Religionswissenschaft und Weltanschaaung oder der Gelehrte als Laien-Priester," in: Faber and Holste, *Kreise, Gruppen, Bünde*, 425–440.

Reil, Johann Christian, "Ueber die Eigenschaften des Ganglien-Systems und sein Verhältniss zum Cerebral-Systeme," *Archiv für die Physiologie* 17 (1807), 189–254.

Renard, Jean-Bruno, "Le mouvement *Planète*: Un épisode important de l'histoire culturelle française," *Politica Hermetica* 10 (1996), 152–167.

Reuchlin, Johannes, *De verbo mirifico / Das wundertätige Wort (1494)* (Widu-Wolfgang Ehlers, Lothar Mundt, Hans-Gert Roloff, and Peter Schäfer, eds;

Sämtliche Werke Bd. 1.1), frommann-holzboog: Stuttgart / Bad Cannstatt 1996.

On the Art of the Kabbalah / De Arte Cabalistica (Martin and Sarah Goodman, trans.), University of Nebraska Press: Lincoln / London 1983.

Riedweg, Christoph, *Ps.-Justin (Markell von Ankyra?) Ad Graecos de Vera Religione (bisher "Cohortatio ad Graecos"): Einleitung und Kommentar*, 2 vols., Friedrich Reinhardt: Basle 1994.

Riess, Ernst, Review of Lynn Thorndike, *The Classical Weekly* 20, no. 26 (1927), 209–211.

Riffard, Pierre A., *L'ésotérisme: Qu'est-ce que l'ésotérisme / Anthologie de l'ésotérisme occidental*, Robert Laffont: Paris 1990.

Ringer, F. K., *The Decline of the German Mandarins: The German Academic Community, 1890–1933*, Harvard University Press: Cambridge, Mass. 1969.

Roberts, J. M., *The Mythology of the Secret Societies* (1964), Watkins: London 2008.

Rocke, A. J., "Agricola, Paracelsus, and 'Chymia'," *Ambix* 32:1 (1985), 38–45.

Rogalla von Bieberstein, Johannes, "Die These von der freimaurerischen Verschwörung," in: Helmut Reinalter (ed.), *Freimaurer und Geheimbünde im 18. Jahrhundert in Mitteleuropa*, Suhrkamp: Frankfurt a.M. 1983, 85–111.

Röhr, Julius, *Der okkulte Kraftbegriff im Altertum* (Philologus Supplementband 17, Heft 1), Dieterich: Leipzig 1923.

Romano, A., "Crispo, Giovan Battista," in: Alberto M. Ghisalberti *et al.* (eds.), *Dizionario biografico degli Italiani*, Istituto della Enciclopedia Italiana: Rome 1960–.

Rossi, Paolo, "Hermeticism, Rationality and the Scientific Revolution," in: M. L. Righini Bonelli and William R. Shea (eds.), *Reason, Experiment, and Mysticism in the Scientific Revolution*, Science History Publications: New York 1975, 247–273.

Roszak, Theodore, *The Making of a Counter Culture: Reflections on the Technocratic Society and its Youthful Opposition*, Faber & Faber: London 1970.

Where the Wasteland Ends: Politics and Transcendence in Postindustrial Society, Anchor Books: Garden City 1973.

Rotondò, Antonio, "Cultura umanistica e difficoltà di censori: Censura ecclesiastica e discussioni cinquecentesche sul Platonismo," in: *Le pouvoir et la plume: Incitation, contrôle et répression dans l'Italie du XVIe siècle*, Université de la Sorbonne Nouvelle: Paris 1982, 15–50.

Ruderman, David B., *Kabbalah, Magic, and Science: The Cultural Universe of a Sixteenth-Century Jewish Physician*, Harvard University Press: Cambridge, Mass. / London 1988.

Rudolph, Kurt, "Intellektuelle, Intellektuellenreligion und ihre Repräsentation in Gnosis und Manichäismus," in: Antes and Pahnke, *Religion von Oberschichten*, 23–34.

"Mircea Eliade and the 'History' of Religions," *Religion* 19 (1989), 101–127.

Ruler, Han van, "Minds, Forms, and Spirits: The Nature of Cartesian Enchantment," *Journal of the History of Ideas* 61:3 (2000), 381–395.

Rupnow, Dirk, Veronika Lipphardt, Jens Thiel, and Christina Wessely (eds.), *Pseudowissenschaft: Konzeptionen von Nichtwissenschaftlichkeit in der Wissenschaftsgeschichte*, Suhrkamp: Frankfurt a.M. 2008.
Russell, Colin A., "The Conflict of Science and Religion," in: Gary B. Fengren (ed.), *Science and Religion: A Historical Introduction*, The Johns Hopkins University Press: Baltimore 2002, 3–12.
Rutkin, H. Darrel, "Astrology," in: Katherine Park and Lorraine Daston (eds.), *The Cambridge History of Science, vol. III: Early Modern Science*, Cambridge University Press 2006, 541–561.
Saffrey, H. D., "Les Néoplatoniciens et les Oracles Chaldaïques," in: Saffrey, *Recherches sur le Néoplatonisme après Plotin*, Vrin: Paris 1990, 63–79.
Saint-André, Mr. de, *Lettres de Mr. De St. André, conseiller-medecin ordinaire du Roy; A quelques-uns de ses Amis, au sujet de la Magie, des malefices et des sorciers, Où il rend raison des effets les plus surprenans qu'on attribue ordinairement aux Démons; & fait voir que ces Intelligences n'y ont souvent aucune part; & que tout ce qu'on leur impute, qui ne se trouve ni dans l'Ancient, ni dans le Nouveau-Testament, ni autorisé par l'Eglise, est naturel ou supposé*, Robert-Marc Despilly: Paris 1725.
Saint-Martin, Louis-Claude de, *Theosophic Correspondence 1792–1797*, Theosophical University Press: Pasadena 1982.
Salaman, Clement, *Asclepius: The Perfect Discourse of Hermes Trismegistus*, Duckworth: London 2007.
Saliba, John A., *Christian Responses to the New Age Movement: A Critical Assessment*, Geoffrey Chapman: London / New York 1999.
Salverte, Eusèbe, *Des sciences occultes, ou essai sur la magie, les prodiges et les miracles* (1829), J.-B. Baillière: Paris 1843.
Santamaria, Olivier, "Etude de l'ésotérisme: Aspects méthodologiques," in: E. Granjon, G. Balzano, B. Decharneux, and F. Nobilio (eds.), *Esotérisme et initiation: Etudes d'épistémologie et d'histoire des religions*, Éditions Modulaires Européennes: Brussels 2010, 7–20.
Santinello, Giovanni (ed.), *Storia delle storie generali della filosofia*, 5 vols., La Scuola: Rome etc. 1979 (vols. I–II); Antenore: Rome / Padua 1988, 1995, 2004 (vols. III–V).
Santucci, James A., "Forgotten Magi: George Henry Felt and Ezekiel Perkins," in: Jean-Baptiste Martin and François Laplantine (eds.), *Le défi magique: Esotérisme, occultisme, spiritisme*, vol. 1, Presses Universitaires de Lyon: Lyon 1994, 131–142.
Sarton, George, Review of Lynn Thorndike, *Isis* 6:1 (1924), 74–89.
Review of Lynn Thorndike, *Isis* 23:2 (1935), 471–475.
Introduction to the History of Science, vol. 1, Krieger: New York 1975.
Savonarola, Girolamo, *Scritti filosofici* (Giancarlo Garfagnini and Eugenio Garin, eds.), vol. 1, Belardetti: Rome 1982.
Sawicki, Diethard, *Leben mit den Toten: Geisterglauben und die Entstehung des Spiritismus in Deutschland 1770–1900*, Ferdinand Schöningh: Paderborn / Munich / Vienna / Zurich 2002.

Schäfer, Peter, "'Die Philologie der Kabbala ist nur eine Projektion auf eine Fläche': Gershom Scholem über die wahren Absichten seines Kabbalastudiums," *Jewish Studies Quarterly* 5 (1998), 1–25.

"Das jüdische Monopol," *Süddeutsche Zeitung*, September 11, 2004.

"'Adversus cabbalam' oder: Heinrich Graetz und die jüdische Mystik," in: Peter Schäfer and Irina Wandrey (eds.), *Reuchlin und seine Erben: Forscher, Denker, Ideologen und Spinner*, Jan Thorbecke: Ostfildern 2005, 189–210.

"Geschichte und Gedächtnisgeschichte: Jan Assmanns 'Mosaische Unterscheidung'," in: Birgit E. Klein and Christine E. Müller (eds.), *Memoria – Wege jüdischen Erinnerns: Festschrift für Michael Brocke zum 65. Geburtstag*, Metropol: Berlin 2005, 19–39.

Schaffer, Simon, "Occultism and Reason," in: A. J. Holland (ed.), *Philosophy, its History and Historiography*, D. Reidel: Dordrecht 1985, 117–143.

Scheible, Heinz, *Die Entstehung der Magdeburger Zenturien: Ein Beitrag zur Geschichte der historiographischen Methode*, Gerd Mohn: Gütersloh 1966.

Schiffmann, G. A., *Die Entstehung der Rittergrade in der Freimaurerei um die Mitte des XVIII. Jahrhunderts*, Bruno Zechel: Leipzig 1882.

Schilbrack, Kevin, "Religion, Models of, and Reality: Are We Through with Geertz?," *Journal of the American Academy of Religion* 73:2 (2005), 429–452.

Schimmel, Annemarie, "Einleitung," in: Henry Corbin, *Die smaragdene Vision: Der Licht-Mensch im persischen Sufismus*, Eugen Diederichs: Munich 1989, 7–17.

Schlögl, Rudolf, "Hermetismus als Sprache der 'unsichtbaren Kirche': Luther, Paracelsus und die Neutralisten in der Kirchen- und Ketzerhistorie Gottfried Arnolds," in: Trepp and Lehmann, *Antike Weisheit und kulturelle Praxis*, 165–188.

Schmidt-Biggemann, Wilhelm, *Theodizee und Tatsachen: Das philosophische Profil der deutschen Aufklärung*, Suhrkamp: Frankfurt a.M. 1988.

Philosophia perennis: Historische Umrisse abendländischer Spiritualität in Antike, Mittelalter und Früher Neuzeit, Suhrkamp: Frankfurt a.M. 1998.

"Einleitung: Johannes Reuchlin und die Anfänge der christlichen Kabbala," in: Schmidt-Biggemann, *Christliche Kabbala*, 9–48.

"History and Prehistory of the Cabala of JHSUH," in: Giulio Busi (ed.), *Hebrew to Latin, Latin to Hebrew: The Mirroring of Two Cultures in the Age of Humanism*, Institut für Judaistik, Freie Universität Berlin / Nino Aragno: Berlin / Turin 2006, 223–241.

Schmidt-Biggemann, Wilhelm (ed.), *Christliche Kabbala*, Jan Thorbecke: Ostfildern 2003.

Schmidt-Biggemann, Wilhelm and Theo Stammen (eds.), *Jacob Brucker (1696–1770): Philosoph und Historiker der europäischen Aufklärung*, Akademie Verlag: Berlin 1998.

Schmitt, Charles B., "Who Read Gianfrancesco Pico della Mirandola?," *Studies in the Renaissance* 11 (1964), 105–132.

"Gianfrancesco Pico's Attitude Toward his Uncle," in: *L'opera e il pensiero di Giovanni Pico della Mirandola nella storia dell'umanesimo*, vol. II, Istituto nazionale di studi sul Rinascimento: Florence 1965, 305–313.

"Perennial Philosophy: From Agostino Steuco to Leibniz," *Journal of the History of Ideas* 27 (1966), 505–532.

Gianfrancesco Pico della Mirandola (1469–1533) and his Critique of Aristotle, Martinus Nijhoff: The Hague 1967.

"*Prisca theologia* e *Philosophia Perennis*: Due temi del Rinascimento italiano e la loro fortuna," in: Giovannangiola Tarugi (ed.), *Il pensiero italiano del Rinascimento e il tempo nostro*, Leo S. Olschki: Florence 1970.

"Reappraisals in Renaissance Science," *History of Science* 16 (1978), 200–214.

"Gianfrancesco Pico: Leben und Werk," in: Gianfrancesco Pico della Mirandola, *Über die Vorstellung: De imaginatione* (Eckhard Kessler, ed.), Wilhelm Fink: Munich 1984, 8–20.

Schmitt, Jean-Claude, "Les 'superstitions'," in: Jacques le Goff and Rene Remond (eds.), *Histoire de la France religieuse*, Les Éditions du Seuil: Paris 1988, 417–551.

Schneider, Hans, "Das *Platonisch-Hermetische Christenthum*: Ehre Gott Daniel Colberg's Bild des frühneuzeitlichen Spiritualismus," in: Nicola Kaminski, Heinz J. Drügh, and Michael Herrmann (eds.), *Hermetik: Literarische Konfigurationen zwischen Babylon und Cyberspace*, Max Niemeyer: Tübingen 2002, 21–42.

Schneiders, Werner, *Aufklärung und Vorurteilskritik: Studien zur Geschichte der Vorurteilstheorie*, frommann-holzboog: Stuttgart / Bad Cannstatt 1983.

Schneiders, Werner (ed.), *Christian Thomasius 1655–1728: Interpretationen zu Werk und Wirkung, mit einer Bibliographie der neueren Thomasius-Literatur*, Felix Meiner: Hamburg 1989.

Scholarios (George Gennadios), *Oeuvres complètes de Gennade Scholarios* (L. Petit, M. Jugie, and X. A. Sidéridès, eds.), 8 vols., Maison de la Bonne Presse: Paris 1928–1936.

Scholem, Gershom G., "Zur Geschichte der Anfänge der Christlichen Kabbala," in: *Essays Presented to Leo Baeck on the Occasion of his Eightieth Birthday*, Horovitz: London 1954, 158–193.

Major Trends in Jewish Mysticism, Schocken: New York 1946.

"Zum Verständnis der messianischen Idee im Judentum," in: Scholem, *Judaica 1*, Suhrkamp: Frankfurt a.M. 1963, 7–74.

"Der Name Gottes und die Sprachtheorie der Kabbala," in: Scholem, *Judaica 3*, 7–70.

"Zehn unhistorische Sätze über Kabbala," in: Scholem, *Judaica 3*, 264–271.

Judaica 3: Studien zur jüdischen Mystik, Suhrkamp: Frankfurt a.M. 1970.

"Considérations sur l'histoire des débuts de la kabbale chrétienne," in: *Kabbalistes chrétiens*, 17–46.

"Identifizierung und Distanz: Ein Rückblick," in: Adolf Portmann and Rudolf Ritsema (eds.), *Denken und Mythische Bildwelt* (Eranos Jahrbuch 48), Insel Verlag: Frankfurt a.M. 1981, 463–467.

"Die Stellung der Kabbala in der europäischen Geistesgeschichte," in: Scholem, *Judaica 4*, Suhrkamp: Frankfurt a.M. 1984, 7–18.

Briefe I: 1914–1947 (Itta Shedletzky, ed.), C. H. Beck: Munich 1994.

Briefe II: 1948–1970 (Thomas Sparr, ed.), C. H. Beck: Munich 1995.

"The Beginnings of the Christian Kabbalah," in: Dan, *Christian Kabbalah*, 17–51.

"Reflections on Modern Jewish Studies," in: Scholem, *On the Possibility of Jewish Mysticism in Our Time & Other Essays* (Avraham Shapira and Jonathan Chipman, ed. and trans.), The Jewish Publication Society: Philadelphia / Jerusalem 1997.

Briefe III: 1971–1982 (Itta Shekletzky, ed.), C. H. Beck: Munich 1999.

Schott, Heinz and Ilana Zinguer (eds.), *Paracelsus und seine internationale Rezeption in der frühen Neuzeit: Beiträge zur Geschichte des Paracelsus*, Brill: Leiden / Boston / Cologne 1998.

Schröder, Winfried, "Einleitung," in: Wachter, *De primordiis Christianae religionis*, 7–32.

Schubert, Gotthilf Heinrich, *Ansichten von der Nachtseite der Naturwissenschaft*, Arnold: Dresden 1808.

Die Symbolik des Traumes, C. F. Kunz: Bamberg 1814; 2nd exp. edn 1821.

Schuhmann, K., "Francesco Patrizi en de Hermetische filosofie," in: Gilles Quispel (ed.), *De Hermetische Gnosis in de loop der eeuwen*, Tirion: Baarn 1992.

Schulte, Christoph, "'Die Buchstaben haben . . . ihre Wurzeln oben': Scholem und Molitor," in: Eveline Goodman-Thau, Gerd Mattenklott, and Christoph Schulte (eds.), *Kabbala und Romantik*, Max Niemeyer: Tübingen 1994, 143–164.

Schultze, Fritz, *Georgios Gemistos Plethon und seine reformatorischen Bestrebungen*, Mauke's Verlag: Jena 1874.

Schulze, Werner, *Zahl, Proportion, Analogie: Eine Untersuchung zur Metaphysik und Wissenschaftshaltung des Nikolaus von Kues*, Aschendorff: Münster 1978.

Schuré, Edouard, *Les grands initiés: Esquisse de l'histoire secrète des religions*, Perrin: Paris 1889.

Schuster, Georg, *Die geheimen Gesellschaften, Verbindungen und Orden*, 2 vols., Theodor Leibing: Leipzig 1906.

Schweizer, Stefan, *Anthropologie der Romantik: Körper, Seele und Geist. Anthropologische Gottes-, Welt- und Menschenbilder der wissenschaftlichen Romantik*, Ferdinand Schöningh: Paderborn / Munich / Vienna / Zurich 2008.

Sebastian, Mihail, *Journal 1935–1944*, William Heinemann: London 2001.

Sebti, Meryem, "Avicenna (Abū ʿAlī al-Husayn ibn ʿAbd Allāh ibn Sīnā)," in: Hanegraaff *et al.*, *Dictionary*, 143–147.

Secret, François, "Du 'De occulta philosophia' à l'occultisme du XIXe siècle," *Revue de l'histoire des religions* 186 (1974), 55–81; repr. in: *Charis: Archives de l'Unicorne* 1 (1988), 5–30.

Les Kabbalistes Chrétiens de la Renaissance (1964), new revised edn Arma Artis / Archè: Neuilly-sur-Seine / Milan 1985.

Hermétisme et Kabbale, Bibliopolis: Naples 1992.

Segal, Robert A., *The Gnostic Jung*, Princeton University Press 1992.

"Joseph Campbell on Jews and Judaism," *Religion* 22 (1992), 151–170.

Review of Noll, *Journal of Analytical Psychology* 40 (1995), 596–608.

"Joseph Campbell as Antisemite and as Theorist of Myth," *Journal of the American Academy of Religion* 67:2 (1999), 461–467.

Segal, Robert A. (ed.), *The Allure of Gnosticism: The Gnostic Experience in Jungian Psychology and Contemporary Culture*, Open Court: Chicago / La Salle, Ill. 1995.

Shamdasani, Sonu, "Encountering Hélène: Théodore Flournoy and the Genesis of Subliminal Psychology," in: Théodore Flournoy, *From India to the Planet Mars: A Case of Multiple Personality with Imaginary Languages* (Sonu Shamdasani, ed.), Princeton University Press 1994, xi–li.

"Memories, Dreams, Omissions," *Spring* 57 (1995), 111–132.

Cult Fictions: C. G. Jung and the Founding of Analytical Psychology, Routledge: London / New York 1998.

"Misunderstanding Jung: The Afterlife of Legends," *Journal of Analytical Psychology* 45 (2000), 459–472.

"Reply," *Journal of Analytical Psychology* 45 (2000), 615–620.

Jung and the Making of Modern Psychology: The Dream of a Science, Cambridge University Press 2003.

Jung Stripped Bare by his Biographers, even, Karnac: London 2005.

Shayegan, Daryoush, "L'homme à la lampe magique," in: Nasr, *Mélanges*, 29–31.

Sheridan, Geraldine, *Nicolas Lenglet Dufresnoy and the Literary Underworld of the Ancien Régime*, The Voltaire Foundation at the Taylor Institution: Oxford 1989.

Shorr, Philip, *Science and Superstition in the Eighteenth Century: A Study of the Treatment of Science in Two Encyclopedias of 1725–1750*, Columbia University Press: New York 1932.

Shumaker, Wayne, *The Occult Sciences in the Renaissance: A Study in Intellectual Patterns*, University of California Press: Berkeley / Los Angeles / London 1972.

Natural Magic and Modern Science: Four Treatises 1590–1657, Medieval & Renaissance Texts & Studies: Binghamton, NY 1989.

Sibly, Ebenezer, *A New and Complete Illustration of the Occult Sciences: or, the Art of Foretelling Future Events and Contingencies, by the Aspects, Positions, and Influences, of the Heavenly Bodies . . .* , 4 vols., London 1790.

A Key to Physic and the Occult Sciences: Opening to Mental View, the System and Order of the Interior and Exterior Heavens; the Analogy betwixt Angels and the Spirits of Men; and the Sympathy between Celestial and Terrestrial Bodies . . . The Whole Forming an Interesting Supplement to Culpeper's Family Physician, London n.d. (1794?), repr. 1800, 1802, 1806.

Silberer, Herbert, "Phantasie und Mythos (Vornehmlich vom Gesichtspunkte der 'funktionalen Kategorie' aus betrachtet)" (1910), repr. in: Bernd Nitzschke (ed.), *Zu Fuss durch den Kopf: Wanderungen im Gedankengebirge. Ausgewählte*

Schriften Herbert Silberers, Miszellen zu seinem Leben und Werk, Archiv der Edition Diskord: Tübingen 1988, 95–175.

Sincerus Renatus (Samuel Richter), *Die wahrhaffte und vollkommene Beschreibung des philosophischen Steins der Bruderschaft aus dem Orden des Gülden- und Rosenkreutzes denen Filiis Doctrinae zum Besten publiciret*, Breslau 1710.

Sloterdijk, Peter and Thomas H. Macho (eds.), *Weltrevolution der Seele: Ein Lese- und Arbeitsbuch der Gnosis von der Spätantike bis zur Gegenwart*, 2 vols., Artemis & Winkler: Gütersloh 1991.

Smith, Jonathan Z., *Imagining Religion: From Babylon to Jonestown*, The University of Chicago Press: Chicago / London 1982.

Drudgery Divine: On the Comparison of Early Christianities and the Religions of Late Antiquity, The University of Chicago Press: Chicago / London 1990.

Relating Religion: Essays in the Study of Religion, The University of Chicago Press: Chicago / London 2004.

Snoek, J. A. M., *Initiations: A Methodological Approach to the Application of Classification and Definition Theory in the Study of Rituals*, Dutch Efficiency Bureau: Pijnacker 1987.

"The Earliest Development of Masonic Degrees and Rituals: Hamill versus Stevenson," in: M. D. J. Scanlan (ed.), *The Social Impact of Freemasonry on the Modern Western World* (The Canonbury Papers 1), Canonbury Masonic Research Center: London 2002, 1–19.

"Illuminés d'Avignon," in: Hanegraaff *et al.*, *Dictionary*, 597–600.

"Researching Freemasonry: Where are We?," CRFF Working Paper Series No. 2, Centre for Research into Freemasonry and Fraternalism: Sheffield n.d.

"Freemasonry," in: Magee, *The Cambridge Companion to Western Mysticism and Esotericism.*

Soster, Maria, "Le développement de la pensée d'Henry Corbin pendant les années trente," Unpublished Mémoire de D.E.A. d'Histoire de la Philosophie, Université Paris I, Paris 2001/2002.

Sounes, Howard, *Seventies: The Sights, Sounds and Ideas of a Brilliant Decade*, Pocket Books: London / Sydney / New York / Toronto 2006.

[Souverain, Jacques], *Le Platonisme dévoilé, ou essai Touchant le Verbe Platonicien*, Pierre Marteau: Cologne 1700.

Spener, Philipp Jakob, "Erste Vorrede!," in: Balthasar Köpke, *Sapientia Dei*, unpaginated.

Spineto, Natale, "Mircea Eliade and Traditionalism," *Aries* 1:1 (2001), 62–87.

Spini, Giorgio, "Historiography: The Art of History in the Italian Counter-Reformation," in: Eric Cochrane (ed.), *The Late Italian Renaissance 1525–1630*, MacMillan: London 1970, 91–133.

Sprague de Camp, L., *Lost Continents: The Atlantis Theme in History, Science, and Literature*, Dover: New York 1954.

Stammen, Theo, "Jacob Brucker: 'Spuren' einer Biographie," in: Schmidt-Biggemann and Stammen, *Jacob Brucker*, 74–82.

Stäudlin, Carl Friedrich, *Geschichte der Sittenlehre Jesu*, vol. 1, Vandenhoeck-Ruprecht: Göttingen 1799.

Stauffer, Isabelle Gloria, "Undines Sehnsucht nach der Seele: Über Paracelsus' Konzeption der Beseelung von Elementargeistern im *Liber de nymphis, sylphis, pygmaeis et salamandris, et de caeteris spiritibus*," *Nova Acta Paracelsica: Beiträge zur Paracelsus-Forschung*, Neue Folge 13 (1999), 49–100.

Stausberg, Michael, *Faszination Zarathushtra: Zoroaster und die Europäische Religionsgeschichte der Frühen Neuzeit*, 2 vols., Walter de Gruyter: Berlin / New York 1998.

Stein, Ludwig, "Handschriftenfunde zur Philosophie der Renaissance," *Archiv für Geschichte der Philosophie* 1 (1888), 534–553.

Stephens, Walter, *Demon Lovers: Witchcraft, Sex, and the Crisis of Belief*, The University of Chicago Press: Chicago / London 2002.

Stetten, Paul von, "Jacob Brucker," in: *Hausleutners Schwäbisches Archiv*, Stuttgart 1788, 281–305.

Steuco, Agostino, *De perenni philosophia Libri* x (1540), Nicolaus Bryling & Sebastianus Francken: Basle 1542.

Stevenson, David, *The Origins of Freemasonry: Scotland's Century 1590–1710*, Cambridge University Press 1988.

The First Freemasons: Scotland's Early Lodges and their Members, Aberdeen University Press 1988.

"James Anderson (1679–1739): Man and Mason," in: R. William Weisberger, Wallace McLeod, and S. Brent Morris (eds.), *Freemasonry on Both Sides of the Atlantic: Essays Concerning the Craft in the British Isles, Europe, the United States, and Mexico*, East European Monographs / Columbia University Press: Boulder / New York 2002, 199–242.

Stöckelle, A., "Eugen Heinrich [Jenő Henrik] Schmitt," in: *Österreichisches Biographisches Lexikon 1815–1950*, vol. x, Verlag der Österreichische Akademie der Wissenschaften: Vienna 1994, 253–254.

Stratton, Kimberly B., *Naming the Witch: Magic, Ideology, and Stereotype in the Ancient World*, Columbia University Press: New York 2007.

Strebel, J., "Prolegomena zum paracelsischen Buch über die Elementargeister," *Nova Acta Paracelsica: II. Jahrbuch der Schweizerischen Paracelsus-Gesellschaft*, Birkhäuser: Basle 1945, 173–186.

Stronks, G. J., "The Significance of Balthasar Bekker's The Enchanted World," in: Marijke Gijswijt-Hofstra and Willem Frijhoff (eds.), *Witchcraft in the Netherlands*, Universitaire Pers: Rotterdam 1991, 149–156.

Stuckrad, Kocku von, "Entsprechungsdenken als Grundform esoterischer Wirklichkeitsdeutung: Das Beispiel Astrologie," *Spirita* 13:1 (1999), 12–17.

Das Ringen um die Astrologie: Jüdische und christliche Beiträge zum antiken Zeitverständnis, Walter de Gruyter: Berlin / New York 2000.

"Recent Studies on Western Esotericism: Some Reflections," *Numen* 49 (2002), 212–218.

Geschichte der Astrologie: Von den Anfängen bis zur Gegenwart, C. H. Beck: Munich 2003.

Schamanismus und Esoterik: Kultur- und wissenschaftsgeschichtliche Betrachtungen, Peeters: Louvain 2003.

"Discursive Study of Religion: From States of the Mind to Communication and Action," *Method & Theory in the Study of Religion* 15 (2003), 255–271.

"Relative, Contingent, Determined: The Category 'History' and its Methodological Dilemma," *Journal of the American Academy of Religion* 71:4 (2003), 905–912.

Was ist Esoterik? Kleine Geschichte des geheimen Wissens, C. H. Beck: Munich 2004.

Western Esotericism: A Brief History of Secret Knowledge, Equinox: London / Oakville 2005.

"Western Esotericism: Towards an Integrative Model of Interpretation," *Religion* 35 (2005), 78–97.

"Christian Kabbalah and Anti-Jewish Polemics: Pico in Context," in: Hammer and von Stuckrad, *Polemical Encounters*, 3–23.

"*Astrologia Hermetica*: Astrology, Western Culture, and the Academy," in: Hanegraaff and Pijnenburg, *Hermes in the Academy*, 51–58.

Locations of Knowledge in Medieval and Early Modern Europe, Brill: Leiden / Boston 2010.

"Reflections on the Limits of Reflection: An Invitation to the Discursive Study of Religion," *Method & Theory in the Study of Religion* 22 (2010), 156–169.

"Utopian Landscapes and Ecstatic Journeys: Friedrich Nietzsche, Hermann Hesse, and Mircea Eliade on the Terror of Modernity," *Numen* 57 (2010), 78–102.

Stuckrad, Kocku von (ed.), *The Brill Dictionary of Religion*, 4 vols., Brill: Leiden / Boston 2007.

Styers, Randall, *Making Magic: Religion, Magic, and Science in the Modern World*, Oxford University Press 2004.

Subtelny, Maria E., "History and Religion: The Fallacy of Metaphysical Questions (A Review Article)," *Iranian Studies* 36:1 (2003), 91–101.

Suhrawardī, *The Philosophy of Illumination: A New Critical Edition of the Text of Hikmat al-ishrāq with English Translation, Notes, Commentary, and Introduction* (John Walbridge and Hossein Ziai, eds., trans., and comm.), Brigham Young University Press: Provo, Utah 1999.

Sullivan, Lawrence E. (ed.), *Hidden Truths: Magic, Alchemy, and the Occult*, MacMillan: New York 1989.

Sul ritorno di Pletone (Un filosofo a Rimini), Raffaelli: Rimini 2003.

Szulakowska, Urszula, *The Alchemy of Light: Geometry and Optics in Late Renaissance Alchemical Illustration*, Brill: Leiden / Boston / Cologne 2000.

Tambiah, Stanley Jeyaraja, *Magic, Science, Religion, and the Scope of Rationality*, Cambridge University Press 1990.

Tambrun, Brigitte, "Marsile Ficin et le 'Commentaire' de Pléthon sur les 'Oracles Chaldaïques'," *Accademia* 1 (1999), 9–48.

"Plethon, Georgios Gemistos," in: Hanegraaff *et al.*, *Dictionary*, 960–963.

Pléthon: Le retour de Platon, Vrin: Paris 2006.

Tambrun-Krasker, Brigitte (ed., trans., and comm.), Μαγικά λογια των απο Ζωροαστρου μαγων. Γεωργίου Γεμιστου Πλήθωνος Έξηγησις είς τά αυτα λογια: Oracles Chaldaïques. Recension de Georges Gémiste Pléthon / La recension arabe des Μαγικά λογια (Michel Tardieu), The Academy of Athens / Vrin / Editions Ousia: Athens / Paris / Brussels 1995.

Tardieu, Michel, "Pléthon lecteur des oracles," *Mêtis* 2 (1987), 141–164.

Taylor, Marc C., *Critical Terms in Religious Studies*, The University of Chicago Press: Chicago / London 1998.

Telle, Joachim, *Parerga Paracelsica: Paracelsus in Vergangenheit und Gegenwart*, Franz Steiner: Stuttgart 1991.

"Astrologie und Alchemie im 16. Jahrhundert: Zu den astroalchemischen Lehrdichtungen von Christoph von Hirschenberg und Basilius Valentinus," in: Buck, *Die okkulten Wissenschaften*, 227–253.

Tertullian, *De praescriptione haereticorum / Vom prinzipiellen Einspruch gegen die Häretiker* (Dietrich Schleyer, trans. and comm.), Brepols: Turnhout 2002.

Tester, Jim, *A History of Western Astrology*, The Boydell Press: Rochester 1987.

Thalmann, Marianne, *Der Trivialroman des 18. Jahrhunderts und der romantische Roman: Ein Beitrag zur Entwicklungsgeschichte der Geheimbundmystik* (1923), repr. Kraus: Nendeln/Liechtenstein 1967.

Theophrast, *Characters* (James Diggle, ed., trans., and comm.), Cambridge University Press 2004.

Thiers, Jean Baptiste, *Traité des superstitions, selon l'écriture sainte, les decrets des conciles, et les sentimens des saints pères, et des théologiens*, 4 vols., 2nd edn, Antoine Dezallier: Paris 1787.

Thomas, Keith, *Religion and the Decline of Magic: Studies in Popular Beliefs in Sixteenth- and Seventeenth-Century England* (1971), Penguin: London 1973.

Thomasius, Christian, *Cautelae circa Praecognita Jurisprudentiae Ecclesiasticae*, Halle 1712.

Thomasius, Jacob, *Schediasma Historicum, Quo, Occasione Definitionis vetustae, qua Philosophia dicitur ΓΝѠ ΣΙΣ ΤѠ ʹΝ ʹΟΝΤѠΝ, varia discutiuntur Ad Historiam tum Philosophicam, tum Ecclesiasticam pertinentia: Imprimis autem inquiritur in ultimas Origenes Philosophiae Gentilis, & quatuor in ea Sectarum apud Graecos praecipuarum; Haereseos item Simonis, Magi, Gnosticorum, Massalianorum & Pelagianorum; Denique Theologiae Mysticae pariter ac Scholasticae*, Philippus Fuhrmann: Leipzig 1665.

Thorndike, Lynn, *The Place of Magic in the Intellectual History of Europe*, n.p.: New York 1905.

A History of Magic and Experimental Science, 8 vols., Columbia University Press: New York 1923–1958.

"*L'Encyclopédie* and the History of Science," *Isis* 6:3 (1923), 361–386.

Review of James Harvey Robinson, *The Journal of Modern History* 9 (1937), 367–369.

"Renaissance or Prenaissance?," *Journal of the History of Ideas* 4:1 (1943), 65–74.

"Whatever Was, *Was* Right," *The American Historical Review* 61:2 (1956), 265–283.

"Some Letters of George Sarton (1922–1955)," *Isis* 48:3 (1957), 323–334.

Thorndike, Lynn and Pearl Kibre, *A Catalogue of Incipits of Mediaeval Scientific Writings in Latin*, Mediaeval Academy of America: Cambridge, Mass. 1937.

Tigerstedt, E. N., "The Decline and Fall of the Neoplatonic Interpretation of Plato: An Outline and Some Observations," *Commentationes Humanarum Litterarum* 52 (1974), 1–108.

Interpreting Plato, Almqvist & Wiksell International: Uppsala 1977.

Tilton, Hereward, *The Quest for the Phoenix: Spiritual Alchemy and Rosicrucianism in the Work of Count Michael Maier (1569–1622)*, De Gruyter: Berlin / New York 2003.

"Rosicrucianism," in: Magee, *The Cambridge Companion to Western Mysticism and Esotericism*.

Tolomio, Ilario, "The 'Historia Philosophica' in the Sixteenth and Seventeenth Centuries," in: Bottin *et al.*, *Models of the History of Philosophy*, 66–160.

Toussaint, Stéphane, "Ficin, Pic de la Mirandole, Reuchlin et les pouvoirs des noms: A propos de Néoplatonisme et de Cabale chrétienne," in: Schmidt-Biggemann, *Christliche Kabbala*, 67–76.

Trang-Ni [Henry Corbin], "Regard vers l'Orient," *La Tribune indochinoise* 2:1 (1927), 4–5.

Trapp, J. B., "Introduction," in: Frances Yates, *Giordano Bruno and the Hermetic Tradition*, Routledge: London / New York 2002, xvii–xxvi.

Travaglia, Pinella, *Magic, Causality and Intentionality: The Doctrine of Rays in al-Kindi*, Sismel: Florence 1999.

Treitel, Corinna, *A Science for the Soul: Occultism and the Genesis of the German Modern*, The Johns Hopkins University Press: Baltimore / London 2004.

Trepp, Anne-Charlott, "Religion, Magie und Naturphilosophie: Alchemie im 16. und 17. Jahrhundert," in: Lehmann and Trepp, *Im Zeichen der Krise*, 473–493.

Trepp, Anne-Charlott and Harmut Lehmann (eds.), *Antike Weisheit und kulturelle Praxis: Hermetismus in der frühen Neuzeit*, Vandenhoeck & Ruprecht: Göttingen 2001.

Treske, Erika, *Der Rosenkreuzerroman "Le Comte de Gabalis" und die geistigen Strömungen des 17. und 18. Jahrhunderts*, Emil Ebering: Berlin 1933.

Trinkaus, Charles, *In Our Image and Likeness: Humanity and Divinity in Italian Humanist Thought*, vol. ii, The University of Chicago Press: Chicago / London 1970.

Trompf, Garry W., "Macrohistory," in: Hanegraaff *et al.*, *Dictionary*, 701–716.

Turcanu, Florin, *Mircea Eliade: Le prisonnier de l'histoire*, La Découverte: Paris 2003.

Tylor, Edward Burnett, *Primitive Culture: Researches into the Development of Mythology, Philosophy, Religion, Language, Art, and Custom* (1871), 2 vols., John Murray: London 1913.

Ullmann, Manfred, *Die Natur- und Geheimwissenschaften im Islam*, Brill: Leiden 1972.

Ullmann-Margalit, Edna (ed.), *The Scientific Enterprise: The Bar-Hillel Colloquium. Studies in History, Philosophy, and Sociology of Science*, vol. iv, Kluwer: Dordrecht / Boston / London 1992.

Urban, Hugh B., "Syndrome of the Secret: 'Esocentrism' and the Work of Steven M. Wasserstrom," *Journal of the American Academy of Religion* 69:2 (2001), 437–447.

Vallemont, M. L. L. de, *La physique occulte, ou traité de la baguette divinatoire, et de son utilité pour la découverte des sources d'eau, des minières, des tresors cachez, des voleurs & des meurtriers fugitifs, avec des Principes qui expliquent les phenomènes plus obscurs de la NATURE*, Jean Boudot: Paris 1709.

Vanloo, Robert, *L'utopie Rose-Croix du XVIIe siècle à nos jours*, Dervy: Paris 2001.

Var, Jean-François, "Martinism: First Period," in: Hanegraaff *et al.*, *Dictionary*, 770–779.

"Pasqually, Martines de," in: Hanegraaff *et al.*, *Dictionary*, 931–936.

Vasoli, Cesare, "Der Mythos der 'Prisci Theologi' als 'Ideologie' der 'Renovatio'," in: Mulsow, *Ende des Hermetismus*, 17–60.

Vernière, P., "Un aspect de l'irrationnel au XVIIIe siècle: La démonologie et son exploitation littéraire," in: Harold E. Pagliaro (ed.), *Irrationalism in the Eighteenth Century*, The Press of Case Western Reserve University: Cleveland / London 1972, 289–302.

Versluis, Arthur, *Wisdom's Children: A Christian Esoteric Tradition*, State University of New York Press: Albany 1999.

"What is Esoteric? Methods in the Study of Western Esotericism," *Esoterica* 4 (2002), 1–15.

"Novalis," in: Hanegraaff *et al.*, *Dictionary*, 869–871.

Magic and Mysticism: An Introduction to Western Esotericism, Rowman & Littlefield: Lanham 2007.

Versnel, H. S., "Some Reflections on the Relation Magic–Religion," *Numen* 38 (1991), 177–197.

Viatte, Auguste, *Les sources occultes du Romantisme: Illuminisme, Théosophie 1770–1820* (1927), 2 vols., Honoré Champion: Paris 1979.

Vickers, Brian, "Frances Yates and the Writing of History," *Journal of Modern History* 51 (1979), 287–316.

"Introduction," in: Vickers, *Occult and Scientific Mentalities*, 1–55.

"Analogy versus Identity: The Rejection of Occult Symbolism, 1580–1680," in: Vickers, *Occult and Scientific Mentalities*, 95–163.

"On the Function of Analogy in the Occult," in: Merkel and Debus, *Hermeticism and the Renaissance*, 265–292.

"Kritische Reaktionen auf die okkulten Wissenschaften in der Renaissance," in: Jean-François Bergier (ed.), *Zwischen Wahn, Glaube und Wissenschaft: Magie, Astrologie, Alchemie und Wissenschaftsgeschichte*, Verlag der Fachvereine: Zurich 1988, 167–239.

"Critical Reactions to the Occult Sciences during the Renaissance," in: Ullmann-Margalit, *Scientific Enterprise*, 43–92.

"The 'New Historiography' and the Limits of Alchemy," *Annals of Science* 65:1 (2008), 127–156.

Vickers, Brian (ed.), *Occult and Scientific Mentalities in the Renaissance*, Cambridge University Press 1984.

Vigenère, Blaise de, *Traicté des Chiffres, ou secretes manieres d'escrire*, Abel L'Angelier: Paris 1586.

Villars, Nicolas Pierre Henri Montfaucon de, *Comte de Gabalis, ou entretiens sur les sciences secrètes* (1670), Pierre de Coup: Amsterdam 1715 (critical edition by Didier Kahn, Champion: Paris 2010).

The Count of Gabalis: Or, The Extravagant Mysteries of the Cabalists, Exposed In Five Pleasant Discourses On The Secret Sciences, done in English, By P. A. Gent, Printed for B. M., Printer to the Cabalistical Society of the Sages, at the Sign of the Rosy-Crucians: London 1680.

Le Comte de Gabalis / La critique de Bérénice (Roger Laufer, intro. / comm.), A. G. Nizet: Paris 1963.

Vollhardt, Friedrich (ed.), *Christian Thomasius (1655–1728): Neue Forschungen im Kontext der Frühaufklärung*, Max Niemeyer: Tübingen 1997.

Voltaire, François de, *Oeuvres de Voltaire* (Louis Moland, ed.), 52 vols., Garnier: Paris 1883.

Dictionnaire philosophique, comprenant les 118 articles parus sous ce titre du vivant de Voltaire avec leurs suppléments parus dans les Questions sur l'Encyclopédie, Garnier: Paris 1967.

Treatise on Tolerance and Other Writings (Simon Harvey, ed.), Cambridge University Press 2000.

Wachter, Johann Georg, *De primordiis Christianae religionis / Elucidarius cabalisticus / Origines juris naturalis* (Winfried Schröder, ed.), frommann-holzboog: Stuttgart / Bad Cannstatt 1995.

Wagner, Siegfried, *Die Essener in der wissenschaftlichen Diskussion vom Ausgang des 18. bis zum Beginn des 20. Jahrhunderts: Eine wissenschaftsgeschichtliche Studie*, Alfred Töpelmann: Berlin 1960.

Waite, Arthur Edward, *The Mysteries of Magic: A Digest of the Writings of Eliphas Lévi, with Biographical and Critical Essay*, Kegan Paul, Trench, Trübner & Co.: London 1897.

The Hidden Church of the Holy Graal (1909), Cosimo: New York 2007, 546.

Shadows of Life and Thought: A Retrospective Review in the Form of Memoirs, Selwyn & Blount: London 1938.

Walbridge, John, *The Leaven of the Ancients: Suhrawardī and the Heritage of the Greeks*, State University of New York Press: Albany 2000.

The Wisdom of the Mystic East: Suhrawardī and Platonic Orientalism, State University of New York Press: Albany 2001.

"Suhrawardī and Illuminationism," in: Peter Adamson and Richard C. Taylor (eds.), *The Cambridge Companion to Arabic Philosophy*, Cambridge University Press 2005, 201–223.

Walker, D. P. "The *Prisca Theologia* in France," *Journal of the Warburg and Courtauld Institutes* 17 (1954), 204–259.

Spiritual and Demonic Magic from Ficino to Campanella (1958), Pennsylvania State University Press: University Park 2000.

The Ancient Theology: Studies in Christian Platonism from the Fifteenth to the Eighteenth Century, Cornell University Press: Ithaca 1972.

Walser, Ernst, *Gesammelte Studien zur Geistesgeschichte der Renaissance*, Benno Schwabe & Co.: Basle 1932.

Wasserstrom, Steven M., *Religion after Religion: Gershom Scholem, Mircea Eliade, and Henry Corbin at Eranos*, Princeton University Press 1999.

"Jewish–Muslim Relations in the Context of the Andalusian Emigration," in: Mark D. Meyerson and Edward D. English (eds.), *Christians, Muslims, and Jews in Medieval and Early Modern Spain: Interaction and Cultural Change*, University of Notre Dame Press 2000, 69–87.

"Response: Final Note to Significance Seekers," *Journal of the American Academy of Religion* 69:2 (2001), 459–463.

Waszink, J. H., "Some Observations on the Appreciation of 'The Philosophy of the Barbarians' in Early Christian Literature," in: *Mélanges offerts à mademoiselle Christine Mohrmann*, Spectrum: Utrecht / Antwerp 1963, 41–56.

Webb, James, *The Occult Underground*, Open Court: La Salle, Ill. 1974.

The Occult Establishment, Open Court: La Salle, Ill. 1976.

Webb, Ruth, "The *Nomoi* of Gemistos Plethon in the Light of Plato's *Laws*," *Journal of the Warburg and Courtauld Institutes* 52 (1989), 214–219.

Weber, Max, *Wissenschaft als Beruf 1917/1919, Politik als Beruf 1919* (Studienausgabe der Max Weber–Gesamtausgabe Band I/17; Wolfgang J. Mommsen and Wolfgang Schluchter, eds.), J. C. B. Mohr (Paul Siebeck): Tübingen 1994.

Webster, Charles, *Paracelsus: Medicine, Magic, and Mission at the End of Time*, Yale University Press: New Haven / London 2008.

Wedemeyer, Christian K. and Wendy Doniger (eds.), *Hermeneutics, Politics, and the History of Religions: The Contested Legacies of Joachim Wach and Mircea Eliade*, Oxford University Press 2010.

Weder, Katharine, "'das jenig das am subtilesten und am besten gewesen ist': Zur Makrokosmos-Mikrokosmosbeziehung bei Paracelsus," *Nova Acta Paracelsica: Beiträge zur Paracelsus-Forschung*, Neue Folge 13 (1999), 3–47.

Weill-Parot, Nicolas, *Les "images astrologiques" au moyen âge et à la Renaissance: Speculations intellectuelles et pratiques magiques (XIIe–XVe siècle)*, Honoré Champion: Paris 2002.

"Astral Magic and Intellectual Changes (Twelfth–Fifteenth Centuries): 'Astrological Images' and the Concept of 'Addressative' Magic," in: Bremmer and Veenstra, *Metamorphosis of Magic*, 167–187.

"Pénombre Ficinienne: Le renouveau de la théorie de la magie talismanique et ses ambiguités," in: Stéphane Toussaint (ed.), *Les cahiers de l'humanisme*, *vol. II: Marsile Ficin ou les mystères Platoniciens*, Les Belles Lettres: Paris 2002, 71–90.

Weiner, Herbert, *9¹/² Mystics: The Kabbala Today*, Collier Books: New York 1969.

Weldon, Stephen P., "Table of Contents & Introduction" to *Isis* Current Bibliography of the History of Science and its Cultural Influences, *Isis* 93 (2002), i–ix.

Westfall, Richard S., *Never at Rest: A Biography of Isaac Newton*, Cambridge University Press 1980.

Westman, Robert S., "Magic Reform and Astronomical Reform: The Yates Thesis Reconsidered," in: Robert S. Westman and J. E. McGuire, *Hermeticism and the Scientific Revolution*, William Andrews Clark Memorial Library, University of California: Los Angeles 1977, 1–91.

Weyer, Jost, "The Image of Alchemy in Nineteenth and Twentieth Century Histories of Alchemy," *Ambix* 23:2 (1976), 65–79.

Wiggershaus, Rolf, *The Frankfurt School: Its History, Theories and Political Significance*, Polity Press: Cambridge 1994.

Wilber, Ken, *Up from Eden: A Transpersonal View of Human Evolution*, Routledge & Kegan Paul: London / Henley / Melbourne 1981.

Wild, Ignaz, "Zur Geschichte der Qualitates Occultae," *Jahrbuch für Philosophie und spekulative Theologie* 20 (1906), 307–345.

Wilken, Robert Louis, *The Christians as the Romans Saw Them*, Yale University Press: New Haven / London 2003.

Willmann, Otto, *Geschichte des Idealismus, vol. III: Der Idealismus der Neuzeit*, orig. 1897, repr. Scientia Verlag: Aalen 1979.

Wilmhurst, Walter Leslie, "Introduction," in: Atwood, *Suggestive Inquiry*, (1)–(64).

Wilson, David B., "The Historiography of Science and Religion," in: Gary B. Fengren (ed.), *Science and Religion: A Historical Introduction*, The Johns Hopkins University Press: Baltimore 2002, 13–29.

Wind, Edgar, *Pagan Mysteries in the Renaissance*, W. W. Norton & Company: New York / London 1958.

Windschuttle, Keith, *The Killing of History: How Literary and Social Theorists are Murdering Our Past*, The Free Press: New York 1996.

Winter, Alison, *Mesmerized: Powers of Mind in Victorian Britain*, The University of Chicago Press: Chicago / London 1998.

Wirszubski, Chaim, *Pico della Mirandola's Encounter with Jewish Mysticism*, Harvard University Press: Cambridge, Mass. / London 1989.

Wolfson, Elliot R., *Through a Speculum That Shines: Vision and Imagination in Medieval Jewish Mysticism*, Princeton University Press 1994.

—— "Beyond the Spoken Word: Oral Tradition and Written Transmission in Medieval Jewish Mysticism," in: Yaakov Elman and Israel Gershoni (eds.), *Transmitting Jewish Traditions: Orality, Textuality, and Cultural Diffusion*, Yale University Press: New Haven / London 2000, 166–224.

—— *Language, Eros, Being: Kabbalistic Hermeneutics and Poetic Imagination*, Fordham University Press: New York 2005.

—— "*Imago Templi* and the Meeting of the Two Seas: Liturgical Time-Space and the Feminine Imaginary in Zoharic Kabbalah," *RES* 51 (2007), 121–135.

Woodhouse, C. M., *George Gemistos Plethon: The Last of the Hellenes*, Clarendon Press: Oxford 1986.

Yarker, John, *The Arcane Schools: A Review of their Origin and Antiquity, with a General History of Freemasonry and its Relation to the Theosophic, Scientific, and Philosophic Mysteries*, William Tait: Belfast 1909.

Yates, Frances A., *Giordano Bruno and the Hermetic Tradition*, Routledge and Kegan Paul / The University of Chicago Press: London / Chicago 1964.

The Art of Memory, The University of Chicago Press: Chicago / London 1966.

"The Hermetic Tradition in Renaissance Science," in: Charles S. Singleton (ed.), *Art, Science, and History in the Renaissance*, The Johns Hopkins Press: Baltimore / London 1967, 255–273.

The Rosicrucian Enlightenment, Routledge & Kegan Paul: London 1972.

The Occult Philosophy in the Elizabethan Age, Routledge & Kegan Paul: London 1979.

"Autobiographical Fragments," in: Yates, *Ideas and Ideals in the North European Renaissance: Collected Essays, Volume III*, Routledge & Kegan Paul: London / Boston / Melbourne / Henley 1984, 278–322.

Zambelli, Paola, *The Speculum Astronomiae and its Enigma: Astrology, Theology and Science in Albertus Magnus and his Contemporaries*, Kluwer: Dordrecht / Boston / London 1992.

L'ambigua natura della magia: Filosofi, streghe, riti nel Rinascimento, Marsilio: Venice 1996.

White Magic, Black Magic in the European Renaissance, Brill: Leiden / Boston 2007.

Zedler, Johann Heinrich, *Grosses vollständiges Universal-Lexikon aller Wissen-schaften und Künste, welche bisshero durch menschlichen Verstand und Witz erfunden und verbessert worden*, Zedler: Halle / Leipzig 1732–1754.

Zimmermann, Rolf Christian, *Das Weltbild des jungen Goethe: Studien zur Hermetischen Tradition des deutschen 18. Jahrhunderts*, 2 vols., Wilhelm Fink: Munich 1969/1979.

"'Ich gebe die Fackel weiter!': Zum Werk Will-Erich Peuckerts," in: Will-Erich Peuckert, *Das Rosenkreutz*, 2nd rev. edn, Erich Schmidt: Berlin 1973, VII–LI.

Person index

Person index

Subject index

Abraham, 18, 21, 27, 46, 89, 134, 144, 209, 246, 337
Adam, 62–63, 85, 87, 105, 110, 183, 204
Adam Kadmon, 113
Agathodaemon, 35
Aglaophemus, 8, 16, 45, 48, 89
Agnosticism, Methodological, 123, 150, 310, *357–358*
Alchemical versus Platonic Paradigm, 68, 73, *192–195*, 200–201, 258, 264, 353
Alchemy, 53, 110, 134, 146, 154, 156–157, 171, 181–184, 188–189, *191–207*, 194, 197–198, 207, 210–212, 216, 221–224, 226, 232, 237, 240–242, 248–250, 253, 275, 288–291, 293–295, 305–306, 314, 320, 325–327, 345, 348–349, 352, 377
Alterity. *See* Identity/alterity
Amateur scholars, 154, 218, 220–221, 239, 245, 249, 255
American Academy of Religion (AAR), 352, 358
Analogy, 164–165, 185–187, 189–191, 245, 294, 344–347, 353
Ancient theology. *See Prisca Theologia*
Ancient Wisdom discourse/narrative, 7–12
Animal magnetism. *See* Mesmerism
Animism, 163
Anti-apologeticism, 6, 11, 72–73, 78, 81, *102*, 103, 114–115, 117, 120–122, 125–128, 137, 146–148, *150–151*, 154, 164, 266, 313–314, 336–337, 369–370
Anti-eclectic historiography, *152*, 197, *377–378*
Anti-paganism, 78–93, 102, 148, 151, 212, 217, 372
Anti-patristic polemics, 93–100
Anti-platonism, 78, 89, 96–97, 99, 102, 148, 217
Anti-semitism, 282, 301, 303, 306
Apologeticism, 6–7, 11, 17, 19–20, 22, 54, 57, 61, 94, 173, 183, 313, 356, 360, 364–365, 367, 376
(*See also* Christian apologists)
Arabs, 53, 85, 119

Archaeus, 264, 289
Archetypes, 271, 284, 294, 305–306, 308–309, 344
Arianism, 92
Aristotelianism, 34, 51, 79, 104, 109, 171, 175, 179, 331, 344–347, 349
Armenians, 119
Asclepius, 173, 175, 192, 330, 332–333
Association for the Study of Esotericism (ASE), 359
Assyrians, 17, 85, 119
Astral light, 246
Astral magic, 83, 154, 173, 175, 332–333
Astrology, 15, 52–53, 81, 107, 131, 135, 146, 154, 156–157, 160, 163–164, 171–173, 176–177, 183–184, 186, 188–190, 220–221, 226, 229, 232, 236–238, 240, 275, 294–295, 314–315, 320, 326–327, 344–345, 362, 377
Atlantis, 76
Auguries, 135
Averroism, 347, 349
Azarias, 21

Babylon/Babylonians, 14–15, 17, 85
Barbarians, 14–15, 17, 21, 23–24, 34, 37, 59, 61–63, 101, 104, 110, 132–133, 135, 142
Biblicism, 82, 84, 107, 122, 141
Böhmians, 109
Brahmans, 14, 37, 62, 101, 132, 242
Brill academic publishers, 359

Calvinism, 194
Cambridge Platonists, 102
Cappadocians, 119
Carbonari, 242
Cardonians, 86
Carmelites, 213
Carpocratians, 109
Cartesianism, 155, 294, 345
Cathars, 242, 354
Causality. *See* Instrumental Causality
Celts, 17, 24, 119

462

Made in the USA
Monee, IL
26 April 2023